Religion in
Southeast Asia

Religion in Southeast Asia

An Encyclopedia of Faiths and Cultures

JESUDAS M. ATHYAL, EDITOR

ABC-CLIO

Santa Barbara, California • Denver, Colorado • Oxford, England

Copyright © 2015 by ABC-CLIO, LLC

Library of Congress Cataloging-in-Publication Data

Religion in Southeast Asia : an encyclopedia of faiths and cultures / Jesudas M. Athyal, editor.

pages cm

Includes bibliographical references and index.

ISBN 978–1–61069–249–6 (hardback) — ISBN 978–1–61069–250–2 (ebook)

1. Southeast Asia—Religion—Encyclopedias. I. Athyal, Jesudas, 1957– editor.

BL2050.R43   2015

200.959′03—dc23   2014038752

ISBN: 978–1–61069–249–6
EISBN: 978–1–61069–250–2

19 18 17 16 15   1 2 3 4 5

This book is also available on the World Wide Web as an eBook.
Visit www.abc-clio.com for details.

ABC-CLIO, LLC
130 Cremona Drive, P.O. Box 1911
Santa Barbara, California 93116-1911

This book is printed on acid-free paper ∞

Manufactured in the United States of America

Contents

Alphabetical List of Entries

Topical List of Entries

BIOGRAPHIES

Alatas, Syed Hussein
Attas, Syed Muhammad Naquib al-
Belo, Carlos Filipe Ximenes
Bhikkhu, Buddhadasa
Bhikkhuni, Dhammananda
Calungsod, Pedro
Duc, Thich Quang
Emerito, Nacpil
Ghosananda, Maha
Hanh, Thich Nhat
Ileto, Reynaldo C.
Koyama, Kosuke
Kyaw Than, U

Loh, I-to
Maarif, Ahmad Syafi'i
Oka, Gedong Bagus
Sayadaw, Mahasi
Siddique, Muhammad Abdul Aleem
Rais, Muhammad Amien
Ruiz, Lorenzo
Santo, Ignacia del Espiritu
Sayadaw, Thamanya
Simatupang, T. B.
Sin, Cardinal Jaime Lachica
Sivaraksa, Sulak
Wahid, Abdurrahman

BRUNEI DARUSSALAM

Buddhism
Christianity
Islam
Malaysia

Minorities
Religious Conversions
Religious Discrimination and Intolerance
Shari'a

BUDDHISM

Bhikkhu, Buddhadasa
Bhikkhuni, Dhammananda
Buddhism
Dharma/Dhamma
Duc, Thich Quang
Engaged Buddhism
Ghosananda, Maha
Hanh, Thich Nhat
Hòa Hảo Buddhism
Interreligious Relations and Dialogue
Khmer Buddhism

Liberation Theologies
Missionary Movements
Pilgrimage
Religious Conversions
Santi Asoke
Sayadaw, Mahasi
Sayadaw, Thamanya
Sivaraksa, Sulak
Thien Buddhism
Water Festivals

GENERAL RELIGIONS

HINDUISM

INDONESIA

ISLAM

LAOS

PAPUA NEW GUINEA

PHILIPPINES

SINGAPORE

THAILAND

Preface

Religion in Southeast Asia: An Encyclopedia of Faiths and Cultures provides a comprehensive introduction to the complex world of the faiths and practices of the Southeast Asians. Rapid changes in Asia and the West necessitated a publication such as this. Increased migration to the United States in recent decades has redrawn the societal and demographic map of this nation. Religions such as Buddhism, Islam, and Hinduism and their institutions, beliefs, and cultures are already a part of the landscape of the United States. The immigrants today play a high-profile role at various sectors in this country, pointing toward the need for a closer understanding of their faiths. While the immigrants have brought the faiths and cultures of Asia closer to the West, the forces of globalization have brought the traditions, cultures, and lifestyles of the West closer to Asia. The emergent pluralist societies in both the contexts, and the consequent challenges they raise, point toward the need for a publication such as this.

While this volume will be relevant to a wide cross-section of the society, more specifically, it is addressed to several target groups. The primary audience of the publication will be the high schools, colleges, and libraries of the United States. Following the decision of the National Council for the Social Studies (NCSS) to recognize the study of religion as an integral part in meeting its Curriculum Standards, the public schools and colleges in the country have started to focus more sharply on a study of world religion. Reference materials that provide accurate and sufficient information to support student research on world religions will become absolutely necessary in such a context. This volume, which provides comprehensive research material on the religions and cultures of Southeast Asia, will enormously benefit students and researchers in broadening their horizon.

The encyclopedia provides valuable and user-friendly reference material for several other sections as well. Southeast Asia has rapidly emerged as a major buyer and seller of goods for the American market. Understanding people and their religions and cultures is an essential part of sound business practices. Considering the enormous potential of U.S.-Asian (including ASEAN) business dealings, this volume will capture the interest of additional users such as business librarians, journalists, and policy makers. In the context of globalization, the publication has the further purpose of providing businesspersons and all those who deal with Southeast Asians at diverse levels as well as the general public with nontechnical information. As the American-Asian partnership in business grows, such resources would become valuable.

Recent geopolitical developments and the increased American involvement at the global level indicate that Southeast Asia will probably be a major arena for U.S.

international relations in the twenty-first century. In the overall highly complex context of the region where religions play a more prominent role in public life and daily life than in most other parts of the world, the encyclopedia will be a cross-cultural link, facilitating a more organic relationship with Southeast Asia.

In short, this volume serves to bring together various strands of movements and thoughts on religion and culture in Southeast Asia and to benefit a wide cross-section of the society. While the publication is not meant for the specialist in religion, it is geared toward both the academic and lay audience. As far as we are aware, this will be the first publication that contains all the essential information on the religions and cultures of Southeast Asia for the American student, researcher, businessperson, geopolitical analyst, and layperson who are interested in the emerging U.S. interface with Asia. The format of the volume is conducive for accurate as well as easy reading. The contributors of the articles were requested to write at a level and in a style that is accessible, accurate, and jargon free. Each article contains a list of references for further reading and cross-references for students interested in more detailed information. The volume also has over 50 sidebars, a comprehensive bibliography, a list of topical categories, and an index.

As the editor, I am indebted to many people who were a part of this publication project during the last few years. I am grateful to Mr. George Butler, ABC-CLIO editor for religion and history, who asked me to undertake this project. He and Ms. Barbara Patterson, ABC-CLIO project coordinator, provided the infrastructural support. The articles and sidebars in the volume were written by a team of distinguished scholars spread across North America, Europe, and Asia. We deeply regret that the renowned Thai scholar Pattana Kitiarsa, who was a part of this team, passed away during the course of this project. There were others who supported this project throughout, with their counsel, articles, and moral support. Some of their names need to be mentioned: Alimatul Qibtiyah (Indonesia), David Scott (USA), Ruchi Agarwal (Thailand), Alexandra Kent (Cambodia), Wesley Ariarajah (Switzerland) and Adrian Bird (USA). My wife Dinah Oommen and our son Jacob Athyal provided the needed support at home. I am indebted to all these dear ones.

Note

Since the target audience of this encyclopedia is high school students in the United States who will be writing term papers on Southeast Asia, we have followed the policy of alphabetization by last name for all the biographical articles in order to facilitate easy location of entries in the book. We recognize that some Asian names are alphabetized differently. However, we are following this pattern in this publication as our primary goal in it is for its contents to be easily accessible to our students.

Jesudas M. Athyal

Introduction

This encyclopedia covers the religious and cultural traditions of the Southeast Asian countries such as Brunei, Cambodia, Indonesia, Laos, Malaysia, Myanmar (Burma), Papua New Guinea, the Philippines, Thailand, Timor Leste (East Timor), and Vietnam. Southeast Asia is home to most of the world religions. While Buddhism and Islam are the major religions here, Christianity, Hinduism, and a host of primal, folk and other religions have a long history in different parts of the region. In our current period, characterized by increased globalization and traffic across borders, it is vital that we have a clear understanding of the various religions, cultures, and their traditions in this region. This volume discusses themes that are important in the overall highly complex context of Southeast Asia, where religions play a more prominent role in public life and daily life than in most other parts of the world. A few themes relevant in the context of religion in Southeast Asia, and discussed in this volume, are outlined below.

Southeast Asia: The Crucible of Pluralism

Southeast Asia presents a picture of marked contrast with regard to the presence of religions. Most of the countries in the region have a dominant majority religion, with several minority groups existing side by side. The entire state of Papua New Guinea is composed of minorities. While Indonesia as a country has the largest number of Muslims in the world, the Philippines is over 90 percent Christian. Buddhism is the majority religion of several countries including Thailand, Cambodia, Laos, and Burma. In each of these places, religious minorities account for a significant number of the population.

The region is also dotted with ethnic and linguistic groups, making it a crowded marketplace of faiths and cultures. Most Asian countries have laws that protect the faith, practice, and cultures of the minorities, but in practice, the minority groups tend to be viewed as second-class citizens. The majority faith and culture of a country is often portrayed as the norm, a yardstick the other citizens are expected to reach. There are even overt attempts, such as in Indonesia, to consciously implement policies of forced assimilation, also called, "Indonesianization." By overt or covert means, the majority communities often lay out the ground rules for the minorities.

Religious diversity in most countries in the region is often the result of historical developments, where the majority of the people accept a new religious tradition while some within the community choose to remain in the tradition they had belonged to. Thus, while many Southeast Asian nations adopted Buddhism, a number of tribal groups within these countries continued in their indigenous faiths and practices. While the Philippines embraced Roman Catholicism under Spanish rule, a significant minority remained Muslim. In Indonesia, the majority of the population adopted Islam, but it continued to have minority Buddhists, Hindus, Christians, Confucians, and peoples with their tribal religious heritages. Minority religious groups are also created by mission activities from the outside, or through the mobilization of population movements, as in the case of the many Buddhist-majority nations of Southeast Asia.

Most nations in the region have religious freedom written into their national constitutions, and several of them are also signatories to the international charters and conventions on religious freedom. A number of nations have taken steps to promote respect for religious plurality in the interest of nation-building. They are committed to the human and religious rights of individuals and groups to believe and practice their religion, which is protected by international conventions. However, discrimination and intolerance are real problems in the region, too, like in most other parts of the world. Religious intolerance and discrimination often lead to violent conflicts, resulting in social disruption, obstruction, and political turmoil.

Migration: Intranational and International

Large-scale intraregional migration in Southeast Asia (SEA) led to the interdependence of the various nations in the region. In the 1980s and 1990s, migration within the region was seen especially from less developed countries that had excessive labor supply to the more developed ones. There was a direct link between such mobility and rapid economic growth on the one hand, and declining fertility in the newly industrialized economies on the other. Some SEA nations, such as Singapore, Malaysia, and Thailand that are popular countries of destination for the immigrants, strive to preserve a balance within and among their ethnic groups and to resist any security risk. Countries from which most immigrants originate—such as the Philippines, Indonesia, Vietnam, Cambodia, Laos, and Burma—are more concerned with managing recruitment, protecting their workers, reducing homeland unemployment, and providing training and industrial experience. In both instances, the rapidly increasing mobility of people has been consistently regarded as both one of the reasons and one of the effects of unusual socioeconomic and political transformations within the region.

There was also significant international migration, leading to a closer understanding of the faiths and cultures of the immigrants and the high-profile role they play in their new locations. The Southeast Asian presence in the United States has been an important factor in redefining the religious and cultural landscape of this country, especially in recent decades. During the first two centuries of U.S. history, almost all its people came from Europe. The Immigration Act of 1965, however, had facilitated increased migration from Asia, including Southeast Asia. By the 1970s itself, there were as many Asians as Europeans coming to the United States to live and work on a permanent basis. The last few decades have seen an increased Asian immigrant presence in this country. Several places in the United States have become minority-majority regions—i.e., where ethnic and religious minorities constitute the majority of the population. Religions such as Buddhism, Islam, and Hinduism have become a part of the religious landscape of this country. By the 1990s, the United States" population growth was more than one-third driven by migration, as opposed to one-tenth before the Immigration Act. Ethnic and racial minorities, as defined by the Census Bureau, rose from 25 percent in 1990 to 30 percent in 2000. According to the 2000 census, roughly 11 percent of U.S. residents were foreign-born, a major increase from the low of 4.7 percent in 1970. Subsequent data indicates that the number of Asians increased from 19 percent in 2000 to 36 percent by 2010 among all the new immigrants.

"Little Traditions"

While religion is often discussed in terms of dominant faith traditions such as Islam, Buddhism, Christianity, Hinduism, and such, the "little traditions" in each of these and indigenous beliefs that fall outside the pale of "world religions" often tremendously influence the lives of ordinary people in a great way. This volume discusses a number of such "little traditions" and some of the leaders behind these. The role of Engaged Buddhism, one of the major Asian religious movements of the twentieth century, in redefining religion for the common people, for instance, is important. Engaged Buddhism has received inspiration from Mahatma Gandhi's nonviolent social activism, Christian charitable activities and modern, Western forms of social and political analysis. However, Engaged Buddhism is deeply Buddhist. It is a practical expression of the foundational Buddhist values of compassion and loving-kindness. Engaged Buddhism does not ask Buddhists to choose between traditional Buddhist spirituality, such as meditation, and social action; it sees them as two sides of the same coin. That is, a person practices meditation, generosity, moral self-discipline, etc., in order to become more selfless and compassionate and in order to develop inner strength and inner peace. One would then be in a better position to "make peace" and be helpful to society. Engaged Buddhism has played a positive role in resolving the major twentieth- and twenty-first-century conflicts in Southeast Asia. Thich Nhat Hanh, Sulak Sivaraksa, and several other leaders of Engaged Buddhism advocate an alternative reading of Buddhist scriptures aimed at empowering individuals with moral and ethical foundations to engage the world and bring changes for the better. In the ultimate analysis, Engaged Buddhism advocates human rights, environmental sustainability, social justice, rights for the poor and dispossessed, nonviolence, and fighting racism and discrimination, among many other worthy social causes.

There have also been other forms of little traditions. One of the haunting images from the Vietnam crisis of the 1960s was Malcolm Browne's photo of the self-immolation of the Buddhist monk, the Venerable Thich Quang Duc. While the monk's protest was primarily against the anti-Buddhist policies being pursued by the government, it also symbolized the unpopular involvement of the United States in Vietnam. In the years and decades that followed this tragic event, the memory and message of Thich Quang Duc has been etched in the history of

Vietnamese Buddhism. He continues to be an inspiration for people around the world who are struggling for freedom.

Islam in Southeast Asia also has had movements that redefine traditional interpretations of religion. Ahmadiyya, as an Islamic reformist and messianic movement based on the teachings of Mirza Ghulam Ahmad, strives toward building a world free of war, violence, hunger, and persecution. The movement aims at the revitalization of religion. Muhammadiyah, the largest Islamic movement in Southeast Asia and perhaps in the world, is another example of a modernist and reformist group that has the ability to combine theological purification and social reformation. Muhammadiyah employs pragmatic ways, including adopting the Western educational system, to achieve its goals.

The Sai Baba movement is a forum that has a great sway among the Hindus in the diaspora. In the 1970s, there was a growing interest in the Indian Hindu saint Sathya Sai Baba, and it was around this time that the Malaysian middle-class Indians and some Malaysian Chinese began to develop what was to become a renowned Sai Baba organization in that country. In Malaysia and Singapore, the movement grew strong under the leadership of middle-class, politically well-connected Indians. Many of these Indians had grown up under a strong British and Christian influence, and they aspired to rekindle their Hindu identity while cleansing it of any association with folk practices such as blood sacrifice, spirit possession, and fire-walking that were common among the Indian plantation laborers, who also arrived in Malaya under the British colonial rule.

Religion and Society

Scholars have described Southeast Asia as characterized by two realities: religiosity and poverty. The majority of people in the region adhere to, or are deeply influenced by, the great religious traditions of Asia, including Confucianism, Buddhism and Taoism, as well as a variety of diverse popular traditions. In short, the overwhelming majority of the poor lives in a rich religio-cultural context. Given the essence of diversity in Asia, it is clear that there will be no easy solution to the situation of injustice, poverty, indignity, or oppression. While common problems exist across the region, each context provides a different set of issues to be addressed. It is also the case that diverse religions understand the root cause of human oppression in different ways. Buddhism, in accordance with the teachings of the Buddha, names human suffering as the chief problem to be overcome through the path of enlightenment. For many Christians, the primary cause of human oppression is sin, both on a personal and a broader systematic level, which needs to be overcome through a process of action and theological reflection to bring about the holistic transformation of the individual and society. Islam, Hinduism, and the other faith traditions too have distinct approaches to solving the perennial problems of the society.

No discussion on religion in Southeast Asia is complete without identifying women's roles in and contributions to religion. While poverty and injustice exist across the society, the status of women needs to be of special significance. On the one hand, women are among the poorest in the society, and on the other, they are at the forefront in observing the various religious practices and rituals. While religious movements in Asia have traditionally been patriarchal, women are increasingly asserting their voices. The relevant question is, what are the common features and significant contributions of women to religion in the region.

The various dimensions of women's presence in religion and culture in Southeast Asia addressed in this volume demonstrate the complexity of the roles that women play as they embody their religious beliefs in every aspect of society. An important component of several renascent and reform movements in the various religions was the efforts of Asian women to claim their place under the sun. This publication discusses Aisyiyah and Nasyiatul Aisyiyah, two organizations in Indonesia that are committed to facilitating the dignity of women in accordance with Islamic teachings. Along with the other women's movements in the region, these organizations strive to represent women's interests not only through education, but also by struggles aimed at women's empowerment. Even while respecting the image of the traditional wife and mother in the society, Aisyiyah and Nasyiatul Aisyiyah could visualize an ideal of womanhood that aimed to realize the full potential and full scope of women's rights and duties.

Women's initiatives have not been confined to the social realm alone, but extend to their participation in the religious life as well. This volume also discusses Dhammananda Bhikkhuni, the first woman to openly practice her religion in Thailand as a fully ordained Theravada Buddhist monk who works within the Theravada Buddhist context of the country. Even though the official Thai Buddhist bodies are yet to formally recognize the legitimacy of her ordination and status as a Theravada bhikkhuni, female monks appear to be gaining a degree of acceptance. Women like Dhammananda Bhikkhuni ground their concern and work for justice within the framework of hierarchical religious structures.

Within the broader context of the interface between religion and society, liberation has become an urgent concern in Southeast Asia, especially in the latter part of the twentieth century. The influence of liberation theologies has been witnessed among the different religions in the region, each turning to its own sources and traditions in order to refocus attention on the emancipation of people from oppression. Diverse forms of liberation theologies in Southeast Asia, discussed in this publication, encourage mutually, enriching conversation and joint action initiatives across the religious spectrum. To be in solidarity with the people in their concrete historical contexts involves forging and nurturing relationships among the adherents of various religious faiths and identifying and challenging the causes of oppression without being destructively invasive to diverse religious identities.

The Challenges of Fundamentalism and Secularism

Religion in Southeast Asia has in general been defined by tolerance, moderation, and pluralism. The majority of Muslims, for instance, reject interpretations of religion that are sympathetic to violence or extremism, as in some other parts of the globe. Unlike in the Middle East, Islam in Southeast Asia facilitated the development of civil society and democracy. Even though Indonesia has the largest Muslim population in the world, it is not an Islamic state but provides formal space for the different religious traditions in the country. Muslims in the region generally support the secular state in the sense that the state's basis is not religion. Radical Islamist or extremist groups who may be labeled fundamentalist had traditionally not demonstrated any broad appeal among masses in Southeast Asia even as some segments in these societies have experienced a resurgence of religious belief. Secular and nationalist parties are generally preferred during elections in the region even as religion remains a core value of the people. The majority Muslim, Buddhist, Christian, and other populations of the region have officially shunned the fundamentalist and violent path.

Despite a tradition of tolerance and pluralism, however, across Southeast Asia there has been a resurgence of religion in recent times. While it is true that only a small minority may be called fundamentalist, it is equally important to note that groups that advocate extremism are active in most of the countries in the region and, to a certain extent, enjoy official patronage. Even though, for the most part, the grievances of radical Muslims in the region have been confined to limited geographical spaces, since the early 1990s, there has been a noticeable expansion of both radical Islamists and their transnational connections. Some Muslims would argue for the implementation of a strict Islamic law in the society but would not advocate the use of violence. However, some others—arguably, fringe groups—in the region indulge in terroristic activities in the name of religion. The resurgence of religion is in part inspired by links to the Middle East and elsewhere in the world. However, Islam is not the only religion that is affected by fundamentalism. The situation in Burma, where the minority Rohingya Muslims are being brutally and violently persecuted by chauvinistic Buddhists, has been described by human rights groups such as Amnesty International as "genocide." Fundamentalist upsurge in multiracial societies like Southeast Asia could tear apart their social fabric and generate political instabilities. As a region of great strategic importance, religious as well as political developments there will be watched carefully. It needs, however, to be reiterated that nonfundamentalist forms of religion is the hallmark of all religions.

Discussions on religious fundamentalism are closely linked to the concept of secularism. In the 1950s and 1960s, it was fashionable to speak about secularization as a process linked to the decline of religion. There were great expectations that under the impact of modernization—characterized by urbanization, market economy and the explosion of information—the influence of religion would gradually decline, especially in Eastern societies. As the sectarian and fundamentalist forces were on the rise around the world, such expectations were abandoned. Rather than an era of rampant secularization and the decline of religion, the current period is characterized by a revival of religion and, indeed, the return of the sacred. The resurgence of religious fundamentalism that accompanied the revival of religion in most traditional societies has considerable significance for pluralistic societies such as in Southeast Asia with their fragile intercommunal framework. While academic notions about the retreat of religion and the universalization of the secularization process were highly exaggerated, it is important to note that most traditional societies had a religious basis rooted largely in a secularist worldview. Such an approach does not imply that religion has little significance in public life or politics. Modern history has shown that reformed religion is often the best basis for building a secular society that recognizes the unity of humanity and that can transcend divisive spiritual, communal, and materialist forces in the society, and yet make space for authentic expressions of spirituality.

A

AHMADIYYA

Ahmadiyya refers to two Islamic reformist and messianic movements based on the teachings conveyed by Mirza Ghulam Ahmad in the Punjab region in the 1880s. The movements are amongst the most active and controversial movements in modern Islam. Their adherents are referred to as Ahmadis or Ahmadi Muslims. Most Ahmadis live in Pakistan, but there are also communities in other regions such as India, West Africa, Europe, and Indonesia. Their organizations are officially called Ahmadiyya Anjuman Ishaat-i Islam Lahore (AAIIL) and Jamaat-i Ahmadiyya or Ahmadiyya Muslim Jama'at (AMJ). The latter is sometimes referred to as Qadiani. The AAIIL today is significantly smaller than the AMJ. Mirza Ghulam Ahmad first announced his spiritual standing in 1882. In 1888–1889, the movement was formally established. After his death in 1908, the succession was handed to the first "Khalifat Al-Masih" (Successor of the Messiah). After "Khalifat Al-Masih's" death in 1914, the community split. The reasons were personal frictions, disagreement on the nature of Mirza Ghulam Ahmad's position, the future of the community's leadership, and the attitude toward non-Ahmadi Muslims. The AMJ emphasized Mirza Ghulam Ahmad's claim to prophethood. They also saw the religious authority of Mirza Ghulam Ahmad's successors as equivalent to that of the founder himself and considered all non-Ahmadi Muslims infidels. The followers of the AAIIL instead insisted that Mirza Ghulam Ahmad had only proclaimed himself as a Mujaddid (divine reformer). They proposed a group leadership in the form of a council and held that only those who would excommunicate Ahmadis were infidels.

The main controversy, both between the two branches and between them and the mainstream Sunni Islam, has been on the interpretations of Mirza Ghulam Ahmad's varying claims to being a Mujaddid, a Muhaddath (someone spoken to by God or an angel), the Mahdi (the redeemer who will rule before the Day of Judgment) and the promised Messiah. Mirza Ghulam Ahmad's claim of having been called a prophet is the most controversial aspect, as it is said to clash with the Islamic dogma of the finality of Muhammad's prophethood. For this reason, the AMJ is much more controversial than the AAIIL. Following anti-Ahmadi riots in the 1950s and in 1974, the National Assembly of Pakistan amended the constitution and declared the belief in the finality of Muhammad's prophethood as central to qualify as a Muslim. In 1974, the Muslim World League declared the Ahmadiyya community to be outside Islam. Additionally to the attitude toward prophethood, the Ahmadis were accused of originally being fostered by British imperialism because of their rejection of violent jihad. As a consequence of the tensions and the legal criminalization of Ahmadi religious activities in Pakistan, the AMJ moved their headquarters to London in the early 1980s. The fifth caliph in the succession of Mirza Ghulam Ahmad is Mirza Masroor Ahmad. He has been holding this position since 2003. From London, he runs the missionary activities of the organization and delivers a weekly Friday sermon that is transmitted via satellite and Internet. Additionally, through their text publications and the elaborate website, the AMJ runs a global television network.

Both factions have established themselves in Southeast Asia. The AMJ considered Sumatra and Java amongst their most successful missions. The first missionaries arrived in the 1920s. After initial bonding with the local Muhammadiyah organization, disagreement over theological questions led to mild tensions between the AMJ and the other Muslims. In the following decades, more centers were established. The AMJ is most active in West Java. The organization claims 400,000 Indonesian members. The government's figures are much lower, at 50,000–80,000. In 1980, the Indonesian National Ulama Council issued a fatwa (Islamic legal opinion) declaring the AMJ deviant and its members apostates. The fatwa was renewed in 2005. Similar fatwas were issued in Malaysia and Brunei. In 2008, after violent attacks against Ahmadis and their supporters, the government issued a Joint Ministerial Decree, limiting Ahmadi religious practice. A similar ban was enforced in Malaysia, withdrawing from the Ahmadiyya communities the right to hold Friday prayers at their mosques. Violence against Ahmadis by opposing groups has increased in Indonesia. An attack in West Java in 2011 left several Ahmadis dead and the perpetrators received sentences that many found too lenient. Subsequently, Ahmadi activities were banned in several districts.

Saskia Louise Schäfer

See also: Indonesia; Islam; Malaysia; Messianic Movements; Missionary Movements; Muhammadiyah; Reform Movements; Religious Discrimination/Intolerance.

Further Reading

Beck, Herman. "The Rupture between the Muhammadiyah and the Ahmadiyya." *Bijdragen tot de Taal-, Land- en Volkenkunde (BKI)* 161, no. 2–3 (2005): 210–46.

Friedmann, Yohanan. "Ahmadiyya." *Encyclopaedia of Islam*. Vol. 3. Brill Online, 2012.

International Crisis Group. "Indonesia: Implications of the Ahmadiyah Decree." *Asia Briefing No. 78, Jakarta/Brussels*, July 7, 2008.

Valentine, Simon Ross. *Islam and the Ahmadiyya Jama'at: History, Belief, Practice.* New York: Columbia University Press, 2008.

AISYIYAH AND NASYIATUL AISYIYAH

Founded in 1917 with the name Sapa Tresna and renamed in 1920 as "Aisyiyah" (the name inspired by Prophet Muhammad's wife Aisha), it is the first major Islamic feminist organization in Indonesia. One of the largest women's groups in the country, Aisyiyah is dedicated to the full engagement of women in religion, state, and society. Affiliated with the modernist Indonesian Islamic organization, Muhammadiyah, Aisyiyah works closely with its parent organization in the areas of social, educational, and health care programs throughout Indonesia. Aisyiyah's central offices are located in Yogyakarta and Jakarta.

According to the "Identity, Vision and Mission" of Aisyiyah, the organization is committed to facilitating the dignity of women in accordance with Islamic teachings. Along with the other women's movements in Indonesia, this organization too strives to represent women's interests not only through education, but also by struggles aimed at women's empowerment. Aisyiyah's identity has evolved in response to the challenges it faced within the mainstream patriarchal society of the country that was battered by democratization and waves of modernization during the twentieth century. A part of this process was the emergence of Nasyiatul Aisyiyah, the young women's organization that was originally a section of Aisyiyah but secured autonomous status in 1965. Siti Syamsiyatun's study describes how Nasyiatul Aisyiyah, even while respecting the image of traditional wife and mother in the society, could visualize an ideal of young womanhood that aimed to realize the full potential and full scope of women's rights and duties (Syamsiyatun). In seeking to implement this vision, both Nasyiatul Aisyiyah and its parent organization Aisyiyah encountered difficulties and resistance from the established social, cultural, and religious institutions of the country. Despite such challenges at the operational and ideological levels, they could contribute richly to the enlargement of women in particular, and human rights and social justice in general, in Indonesian society.

Jesudas M. Athyal

See also: Indonesia; Islam; Muhammadiyah; Muslimat NU; Nahadlatul Ulama; *Pesantren*; Women.

Further Reading

Aisyiyah website: http://www.aisyiyah.or.id/ (accessed March 20, 2014).

Robinson, Kathryn, and Sharon Bessell. *Women in Indonesia: Gender, Equity and Development*. Singapore: Institute of Southeast Asian Studies, 2002.

Syamsiyatun, Siti. "A Daughter in the Indonesian Muhammadiyah: Nasyiatul Aisyiyah Negotiates a New Status and Image." *Journal of Islamic Studies* 18, no. 1 (2007): 69–94. http://jis.oxfordjournals.org/content/18/1/69.abstract (accessed March 20, 2014)

ALATAS, SYED HUSSEIN

Syed Hussein Alatas was a Malaysian academician who contributed richly to the discourse on progressive religion, multiracialism, colonialism, and the postcolonial theory, especially in the Asian context. Born in Bogor in Indonesia in 1928, he also came to be known as a crusader against corruption. While doing postgraduate studies at the University of Amsterdam in the 1950s, he founded the journal *Progressive Islam*, in which many Islamic intellectuals wrote.

Syed Hussein's commitment to progressive religion prompted him to get involved in political activities, even though he was primarily an academician. Disillusioned with the established political parties, he, along with several other intellectuals founded, in 1968, Gerakan (the Malaysian People's Movement Party).

Gerakan was successful in the following year's general elections but Syed Hussein soon became disillusioned with this experiment and, along with others, formed Pekemas (the Social Justice Party of Malaysia) in 1972. Pekemas too was committed to the values of democracy, justice, and progressive religion, but in 1978, it collapsed as a political party.

Syed Hussein certainly made a deeper impact in the academic field than in party politics. His long association with the University of Malaya began in 1960 when he joined the institution as a part-time lecturer in philosophy. In the following years, he held several positions there and, in the 1980s, served as the vice chancellor of the university. He was also associated with the National University of Singapore and with several other institutions. Among his many books, *The Myth of the Lazy Native* made a valuable contribution to Malaysian historiography and postcolonial scholarship.

The journal *Progressive Islam* reflected the thinking of a young Syed Hussein as he sought, in the 1950s, a synthesis between religion and state for social transformation. In later life, however, he clarified that what he meant was a form of Islamic philosophy of the state and not the political instrumentalization of the Shari'a law. The devastating influence religious fundamentalism had in public life promoted the mature Syed Hussein to move closer toward a nationalist, secularist perspective. He died in 2007.

Jesudas M. Athyal

See also: Attas, Syed Muhammad Naquib al-; Colonialism, Fundamentalism; Islam; Nationalism; Orientalism; Postcolonial Theory; Shari'a; Study of Religion; Syncretism.

Further Reading

Alatas, Masturah. *The Life in the Writing: Syed Hussein Alatas*. Kuala Lumpur: Marshall Cavendish, 2010.

Alatas, Syed Hussein. *The Democracy of Islam: A Concise Exposition with Comparative References to Western Political Thought*. Bandung and The Hague: W. van Hoeve, 1956.

Alatas, Syed Hussein. *The Myth of the Lazy Native: A Study of the Image of the Malays, Filipinos and Javanese from the 16th to the 20th Century and Its Function in the Ideology of Colonial Capitalism*. London: Frank Cass & Company, 1977.

ANCESTOR WORSHIP

Ancestor worship is one of the oldest religious practices in Southeast Asia. It is based on the essential principles of family devotion and a sense of responsibility toward past, present, and future generations. Practices vary, but common beliefs include an understanding that spirits of deceased ancestors continue to affect the lives of their descendants, rewarding those who remember them with offerings and punishing those who fail to do so. On special days such as funerals and death anniversaries, paper money and other ritual offerings are burnt and special food is offered at the ancestral altar.

Doan Ngoc Tram, 80, places fruits on the family altar at her home in Hanoi. Above the altar are photographs of relatives who have passed away. (Hoang Dinh Nam/Getty Images)

Ancestor spirits take their place among different types of supernatural beings who are recognized but not actively included in ritual activities. At the same time, they may be the focus of organized cults of worship, such as for the Kachin of Upper Burma. The beliefs and practices related to an ancestor's spirits are evident among Vietnamese and the Chinese living in Southeast Asia.

Vietnam

The religions of Vietnam include Buddhism, Daoism, Confucianism, Catholicism, Cao Dai, and Hòa Hảo. Despite their diverse beliefs, almost every Vietnamese household also maintains a family altar and practices some form of ancestor worship. Although urbanization has led to the breakdown of many traditions, family altars remain critically important. Practitioners include Communist Party members, ethnic minorities, and members of the diaspora. The practice is carried out overseas and also figures in return visits to Vietnam during the *Tet* New Year holidays.

Tet, the Vietnamese New Year, is the most important celebration of the Vietnamese culture, and it includes family reunions, rituals for the ancestors, and the exchange of gifts. During this occasion, the Vietnamese return home to worship at the family altars and to visit the graves of their ancestors as a sign of respect.

Ruchi Agarwal

Essential elements of a family altar include a cloth, preferably in red and gold; an incense burner; and incense. Red is considered a color of happiness, and incense is believed to make the spirits feel welcome to return home. Lighting it is an invitation to the ancestors. The altar will usually include a photo of ancestors or a tablet with the name of the deceased relatives carved on it. Offerings are made to the altars on a regular basis. After the ancestors have had their fill, offerings are consumed by living family members.

Upon the death of a family member, the rest of the family must follow rituals of veneration, lighting incense and offering food and fake paper money at graveside and at the family altar. It is thought that a failure to carry out these rites will preclude the spirit from finding its way home, forcing it to wander around aimlessly. Homeless spirits are believed to be a source of bad luck for their families.

Thailand

In Thailand, ancestor worship entails offerings to house spirits. The practice is particularly widespread in the country's northern region. With the construction of a house, an offering is made to a house spirit ("phi ruan"), and when a family member dies, a procession takes place to lead the spirit of the dead back home after the funeral. In northeastern Thailand, ancestor spirits are remembered and commemorated on a regular basis. There are also rituals for placating spirits who are thought to have caused illness to a living descendant. Ancestral spirits become troublesome with a failure of the family to make merits or when quarrels over property inheritance exist.

Singapore

In Singapore, the names of deceased ancestors are inscribed upon pieces of red paper rather than wooden tablets. These *kong-ma-pai* are placed alongside the idols of family gods on a household altar. Offerings are made and incense sticks burned there on a regular basis. The practice is in decline in Singapore, in part because of the housing situation. Most families live in tiny apartments allotted by the Housing Development Board, and altars are not compatible with the designs of such buildings.

Ruchi Agarwal

See also: Buddhism; Cao Dai; Christianity; Communism; Confucianism; Daoism (Taoism); Diaspora; Hòa Hảo Buddhism; Myanmar (Burma); Popular Religion; Singapore; Spirit Mediumship; Study of Religion; Thailand; Vietnam.

Further Reading

Jellema, K. "Returning Home: Ancestor Veneration and the Nationalism of Doi Moi Vietnam." In *Modernity and Re-enchantment: Religion in Post-Revolutionary Vietnam*, edited by Philip Taylor, 57–89. Singapore: ISEAS Publishing, 2007.

Kuo, C. E. "Confucianism and the Chinese Family in Singapore: Continuities and Changes." In *Confucianism and the Family: A Study of Indo-Tibetan Scholasticism*, edited by Walter

H. Slote and George A. De Vos, 231–48. Albany: State University of New York Press, 1998.

Lauser, A. "Ancestor Worship and Pilgrimage in Late Socialist Vietnam." In *Religion, Identity, Postsocialism*, edited by Chris Hann, 123–26. Halle/Saale: MPI for Social Anthropology Halle, 2010.

Winzeler, L. Robert. *The Peoples of Southeast Asia Today: Ethnography, Ethnology, and Change in a Complex Region*, chap. 8, 143–71. New York: AltaMira Press, 2011.

ANIMISM

Despite the pressures of modernization, animism continues to be a factor in the religious scenario of Southeast Asia. The meaning of the term animism has changed in recent years. In its earlier use, animism means the belief that all beings, including animals, plants, objects, and heavenly bodies or weather phenomena, are endowed with souls and personalities. This also entails the possibility that soul and body may separate, or the existence of beings without permanent bodies, like spirits. In more recent understandings in anthropology, animism denotes the notion that the relations between human beings and nonhumans are essentially social. It contrasts with a naturalist stance in which these relations are essentially natural and thus can be described in terms of the natural sciences. Both understandings of animism more or less cover the same cultural phenomena, but their emphasis is different. While the earlier concept considers animism as a religious belief and thus

Danong, an indigenous Moken man, performs an animistic ritual in his village in the Ko Surin National Park, Thailand. Animistic rituals are performed with a variety of end results in mind, including increased fertility and personal protection from evil. (Taylor Weidman/Getty Images)

scientifically false, the current definition sees animism as practices and relationships that constitute an alternative to a natural scientific approach to the world.

Animism belongs to the oldest analytical terms in social anthropology, going back to Edward Burnett Tylor's "Primitive Religion." Tylor envisaged animism as a "primitive" philosophical concept that underlies all religion, distinguishing it from materialism. However, anthropologists used the term in the sense of a type of religion that is different from, say, monotheism or polytheism. Since the mid-twentieth century, anthropologists increasingly hesitated to employ the term, for two reasons. First, Tylor's concept was laden with evolutionist and colonialist notions of the superiority of modern science. Second, the term covered too many diverse phenomena. It thus suggested similarities between traits that are actually quite different, ranging from ancestor worship to the notion of animated rocks or thunder.

It is only since the mid-1990s that animism once again became subject of an inspiring and serious debate in scholarly inquiry, led by anthropologists such as Philippe Descola or Tim Ingold. It is now being seen as an alternative perspective on nonhumans and the environment, different from the mechanistic and objectifying approach of modern natural science. In this view, relations between humans and nonhumans are based on communication and the assumption that the nonhuman sphere consists of persons, not objects.

Animist practices are unlike most world religions, in that they are not based on doctrinal texts or established hierarchies of priests and experts. Rather, animist ideas allow engaging with natural species and spirits in ways that are partially tried and tested by tradition, but might just as well be contextual, experimental, and improvised. Animist forces and spirits are often not moral agents, but, like human beings, can be benevolent or dangerous according to context. Relations with them need to be negotiated. For the same reason, animism is not necessarily restricted to non-modern societies. Animist relations and practices might coexist with naturalist ones.

Animist relationships with nonhumans appear in two contexts in Southeast Asia: in peripheries and beside world religions. In particular, upland regions in between China, Vietnam, Thailand, Laos, and Myanmar, the interior of Borneo, and some areas in Indonesia and the Philippines are home to groups that do not identify with any world religion and are therefore often called animist. On the other hand, animist relations coexist with world religions, sometimes in stable and sometimes in tense relationships. In particular, Buddhism usually goes along with the veneration of ancestral, territorial, or other spirits. Similar observations were made in Muslim and Christian societies. However, dogmatic and rationalist movements within these religions attempt to curb animist relationships. Such attempts at reform and purification have recurred in various guises over many centuries, but overall had only limited success. As many animist relations are constitutive of places and communities in Southeast Asia, they have proven to be highly resilient.

A number of factors characterize Southeast Asian animisms, although neither of them is universal: ancestor veneration, territorial spirits, communication via offerings and sacrifice, and invisibility. There is also a characteristic contrast. On the one hand, there is a widespread notion of spirits with benevolent or malevolent intentions, some being former human beings, others being bodiless spirits of places. They are like persons; that is, they are able to communicate and act socially. On the other hand, there are concepts of impersonal life-forces that need to be channeled by ritual in order to promote the fertility of human beings, plants, and animals. In some cases, a single concept used in a particular society—like *semangat* among Malays until the mid-twentieth century—might cover a broad range of meanings, from personal beings to impersonal beings. Often, the degree of personhood ascribed to a particular being depends on context and the intensity of the relationship with it. The more intense the communication, the more personal the respective being might appear.

Many Southeast Asian societies, in particular those of farmers and city dwellers, have relations with ancestral spirits and those of territories. Ancestors are often seen as the dead members of society, caring for but sometimes also intimidating their living descendants. Elaborate mortuary rituals transform the dead into various components, some of whom remain close to the living and might endanger or protect them. Invisible aspects of the person, like "souls," might become part of the houses in which their descendants live. In such cases, the organization of kinship groups is a crucial factor in determining to whom such an ancestral spirit belongs.

In societies converted to Islam or Christianity, relationships with ancestors are a crucial point of debate. While Muslim or Christian doctrine often insists on the removal of the dead to a transcendent sphere like heaven or hell, local social structures are built on their continued presence among the living.

Spirits of territories are particularly important where communal spaces—like villages, cities, and rice fields—are conceptually separate from domains beyond human society, like forest and open sea. While settlements are associated with protective spirits, places beyond them are dangerous and ambiguous. In some cases, human beings are conceived as moving between these places in various phases of their existence. They are alive and embodied in settlements, but become disembodied, or embodied in animals, in the wilderness after death. Social spaces thus often define a difference between internal and external spiritual forces. Such external forces are sometimes seen as detrimental to internal forces, which need to be protected. But often enough, local communities need to appropriate external spirits and life-forces in order to reproduce themselves. In some areas, an important means to this end, now defunct, was headhunting, by which dead outsiders were turned into local protective spirits.

Many Southeast Asians communicate with the spirits, as with the living, by offering gifts and sacrifices. In many rural areas of Southeast Asia, domestic animals are hardly ever killed outside ritual contexts, and in predominantly animist societies, this often happens in order to regulate relations with spirits. Food is thus shared between humans and spirits, sometimes in smaller offerings of cooked food, drink, tobacco, or alcohol. This way, relationships with spirits are established in terms of human sociality, thus obliging the spirits to accord to the social rules of the living. The ritual hunt or the letting of human blood without killing are less common forms of such communication by exchange.

Spirits in Southeast Asia are only partially accessible to the senses, and this, once again, depends on communication. Many Southeast Asians distinguish humans and spirits by claiming that the latter are invisible. Yet, spirits continually make themselves known to the senses, sometimes in dreams or trances, but even in sight, touch, or hearing in everyday situations. These appearances are judged as—often unwanted—attempts of spirits to enter into closer relationships with human beings. People might respond to this by temporarily intensifying these relationships and giving them a sensual form in the controlled situation of rituals. In the latter, spirits receive gifts or are sometimes even given shape in figurines or animated objects. The sensual appearances of spirits are thereby subordinated to human sociality, rendering them more accessible to communication and control.

In present-day Southeast Asia, relationships with spirits and invisible life-forces are neither a matter of the past nor an indicator of backwardness. Reformist and modernist versions of world religions, and to a lesser degree naturalist modernities, challenge these relations and attempt to dismiss them as superstitious or irrational. Yet, for many people, including educated city dwellers, these relations remain of crucial importance for the social world they live in.

Guido Sprenger

See also: Christianity; Indonesia; Interreligious Relations and Dialogue; Islam; Laos; Myanmar (Burma); Philippines; Religious Conversions; Spirit Mediumship; Thailand; Vietnam.

Further Reading

Allerton, Catherine, ed. *Spiritual Landscapes of Southeast Asia. Anthropological Forum* 19, no. 3 (special issue, 2009).

Århem, Kaj, and Guido Sprenger, eds. *Animism in Southeast Asia.* London: Routledge, 2015.

Descola, Philippe. *Beyond Nature and Culture.* Translated by Janet Lloyd. Chicago: University of Chicago Press, 2013.

Endres, Kirsten, and Andrea Lauser, eds. *Engaging the Spirit World: Popular Beliefs and Practices in Modern Southeast Asia.* Oxford and New York: Berghahn, 2013.

Harvey, Graham, ed. *The Handbook of Contemporary Animism.* Durham, UK: Acumen, 2013.

Ingold, Tim. *The Perception of the Environment: Essays on Livelihood, Dwelling, and Skill.* London: Routledge, 2013 [2000].

Tylor, Edward B. *The Origins of Culture and Religion in Primitive Culture.* Volumes 1 and 2 of the 1873 edition of *Primitive Culture.* New York: Harper & Brothers, 1958 [1873, 1871].

ARMENIANS

Armenians, a predominantly Christian ethnic group native to the Armenian Highland in the Middle East, had a long association with Southeast Asia. Their skills as a mercantile community were widely acknowledged. While there are few authentic records available to prove the details with regard to the coming of the Armenians to the region, several historians have noted that as far back as the early sixteenth century, there were Armenians in Southeast Asia. There are also indications that the Armenian merchants from India traded with ports on the Malay peninsula, especially Malacca and Penang, from the early seventeenth century onward. There was a resident Armenian community in Malacca, and this was followed by resident communities in Penang, Kedah, Johare/Riau, and other places.

The Armenian presence in Indonesia too goes back several centuries. It is generally accepted that there was an Armenian community in Indonesia from as far back as the middle of the seventeenth century. The original Armenian immigrants to the country could have come from the Netherlands. It is also believed that from the beginning, there was large-scale Armenian migration from Iran to Indonesia as well. The Armenians also traded on the north coast of Bali, and it is possible that there was a small Armenian community there in the nineteenth century. The details are, again, not available. According to historian E. H. Ellis, the pioneer Armenian settlers in Indonesia were so seriously and deeply absorbed in their commercial pursuits that they did not leave any written records of either their commercial activities or the important events of the group's religious, social, or cultural life, which could have been of historical value.

The Armenians also played an important role in the trade and commerce of the Philippines. Murillo Velarde, a Jesuit historian, had noted that the Armenians, among the other Orthodox Christians, were present in the Philippine capital city of Manila as early as 1618. According to Ellis, during the first half of the eighteenth century, some Armenians reached Manila from Madras, where at that time there was a rich and flourishing Armenian community. They facilitated commercial links between the Philippines and India in the eighteenth century. These arrivals at different periods strengthened the Armenian community in the Philippines and enabled them to emerge as a key player, especially in the area of local trade.

The Armenians are believed to have been present in Myanmar (Burma) as well, from at least the middle of the sixteenth century, but in comparison to the rest of Southeast Asia, they played a unique role in that country. While the Armenians elsewhere in the region kept a low profile by confining themselves to the realm of trade, in Myanmar they were actively involved in the political process and functioned as middlemen between the Burmese court and the Europeans. The Armenians, who from the beginning were a small community, however, soon began to decline in their few pockets of influence in the region. By the nineteenth century, there was only one church in the whole of Myanmar, the Armenian Apostolic Church of St. John the Baptist in Yangon.

By the nineteenth century, the Armenians had spread to Singapore as well. They consolidated themselves in Singapore by establishing a church with a congregation and a resident priest. The architectural skills of the Armenians have added richly to the cultural landscape of that region. The Armenian Apostolic Church of St. Gregory the Illuminator is the oldest Christian church in that nation. George Drumgoole Coleman, the architect of many of Singapore's finest historical buildings, built that church, a building acclaimed as perhaps the finest landscape in the early architectural development of that nation, even though, from the beginning, the Armenians in Singapore too were a very small community.

A number of reasons can be cited for the enormous success of the Armenians as a trading community in Southeast Asia. As they came from a Christian nation that was surrounded by Muslims, they were experts at interacting with diverse religious groups. They were also skillful negotiators and served as middlemen, often between the Asians and the Europeans. Besides, as an itinerant community, the Armenians did not have a country to call their own, and therefore, they harbored no colonial interests. Family networks and kinship connections played an important role in their trade. As they did not pose any serious threat to others, they were acceptable to the wider public. All these factors contributed to the long and rich association of the Armenian community in Southeast Asia.

By the nineteenth century, however, the number of Armenians in Southeast Asia had dwindled to a tiny fraction of the total population. They were to be found primarily in Myanmar, the Malay peninsula (particularly Penang and Malacca), and Java in Indonesia alone. Soon their number declined substantially in those places as well. Despite their success in trade and commerce, for a number of reasons, the Armenians declined, as a community, in most of Asia. As largely an ethnic group, their socializing was confined to their own people, further restricting their mingling with the local people and limiting their chances of taking local roots. Also, in the predominantly non-Christian sociocultural climate of Southeast Asia, the Armenians as a Christian community were generally treated as outsiders, welcomed only as visitors and traders. Their own lack of interest outside trade and commerce, especially in recording and preserving their heritage and history, also contributed to the eventual decline of the Armenians as a distinct community in Southeast Asia.

Jesudas M. Athyal

See also: Christianity; Colonialism; Diaspora; Ethnicity; Indonesia; Islam; Jesuits; Malaysia; Myanmar (Burma); Philippines; Singapore.

Further Reading

Bakhchinian, Artsvi. "Armenians in Indonesia: An Unpublished Research about the Armenians in Indonesia." Beirut: *Haigazian Armenological Review* 23 (2003).

Galstaun, Arshak C. "About the Armenian Church of St. Gregory the Illuminator in Singapore." Typescript, 4 pp., May 1982. Singapore: Department of Oral History and Archives.

Sarkissian, Margaret. "Armenians in South-East Asia." *Crossroads: An Interdisciplinary Journal of Southeast Asian Studies* 3, no. 2–3 (1987): 1–33.

Wright, Nadia H. *Respected Citizens: The History of Armenians in Singapore and Malaysia.* Melbourne: Amassia Publishing, 2003.

ATHEISM/AGNOSTICISM

Since atheism in general rejects belief in the existence of God or deities and agnosticism is indifferent to any such belief, it would seem as if the Southeast Asian context that is steeped in religiosity is alien to atheistic and agnostic trends. Yet, for a number of reasons, these are not only present but also vibrant in the Asian societies. For historic, cultural, and ideological reasons, the Asian societies define religion, and consequently atheism, differently from the West, especially as belief in God is not the central aspect of several Asian worldviews. In particular, Buddhism, Hinduism, Confucianism, and Daoism are seen by many of their practitioners as cultures, traditions, and ways of life and not as religions in a technical sense. Since these worldviews do not adhere to any prescribed format of religion, atheism too is accommodated within their fold. This phenomenon is seen throughout Asia. In Vietnam, for instance, as many as 81 percent of the population call themselves atheists, agnostics, or nonbelievers even as many of them also consider themselves as followers of indigenous religions or Buddhism.

In modern times, there are growing atheistic or rationalist movements in Asia. Several countries in East Asia are among the most irreligious societies in the world. In Southeast Asia too, from the Muslim majority countries of Indonesia and Malaysia, to Buddhist-majority Thailand, secular Singapore, and Christian-majority Philippines, atheism is on the rise. A growing number of Singaporeans identify themselves as nonbelievers, and these are present in all ethnic traditions and religious backgrounds. The Humanist Society of Singapore serves as an umbrella organization for the atheists, agnostics, humanists, and freethinkers of the country. Functioning under the motto "offending religious feelings since 2009," the "Filipino Freethinkers" is the largest and most active organization for rational thought in the Philippines. Since religion and state are clearly and permanently separated in the Philippines, there is a fertile ground for the work of atheistic groups. The atheistic movement is also active in countries such as Indonesia and Malaysia.

While there is a great deal of accommodation for atheism within the worldviews of Southeast Asia, atheists also face discrimination and marginalization in some contexts. Thailand does not accord any legal status to atheists, and they are forced to declare themselves as belonging to one of the mainline religions. The generally negative attitude towards atheists leads to their stigmatization and ostracization in Thai society.

Jesudas M. Athyal

See also: Buddhism; Christianity; Confucianism; Daoism (Taoism); Hinduism; Humanism; Indonesia; Islam; Malaysia; Philippines; Religious Discrimination/ Intolerance; Secularism; Singapore; Syncretism; Thailand; Vietnam.

Further Reading

"Filipino Freethinkers Turns Four—Offending Religious Feelings since 2009." http:// filipinofreethinkers.org/2013/02/01/ff-turns-four-offending-religious-feelings-since-2009/ (accessed December 19, 2013).

Humanist Society (Singapore) website. http://humanist.org.sg/ (accessed December 19, 2013).

Marcel Thee. "Raising Kids without God: Atheist Parents in Indonesia." *Jakarta Globe*. http:// www.thejakartaglobe.com/features/raising-kids-without-god-atheist-parents-in -indonesia/ (accessed December 19, 2013).

Southeast Asian Atheists website. http://www.sea-atheists.org/ (accessed December 19, 2013).

ATTAS, SYED MUHAMMAD NAQUIB AL-

Syed Muhammad Naquib al-Attas is a Malaysian philosopher and litterateur who has made significant contributions in the areas of traditional Islamic studies, Malay language and literature, history, and philosophy. Born in 1931 in Bogor, Java, in a Muslim family with a long lineage of saints and scholars, his primary education in Johor, Malaysia, was interrupted by the Japanese occupation of Malaysia, during which he had to move to Java. In 1946, after the Second World War, he returned to Johor to complete his studies. As a keen student, he developed an interest in Islamic studies, Malay language, Western classics, and history. His thorough grounding in these and related areas soon elevated him to the status of a scholar firmly rooted in the Malay nationalist context and yet an internationalist.

While al-Attas contributed richly in several sectors, his pioneering work is considered to be in a revival of studies in Sufism and Malay literature. His PhD thesis on the mysticism of the seventeenth-century Sumatran Sufi scholar Hamzah Fansuri is considered the most comprehensive work in this area. As Malaysia emerged independent in 1957 from colonial rule and was poised to begin a process of nation building, al-Attas's contributions toward conceptualizing and consolidating Malay as the national and academic language was important. He played an important role in kindling a nonsectarian form of nationalism that focused on the renaissance of the indigenous language, literature, history, and identity.

Al-Attas's contributions also embraced the broad area of civilization in relation to contemporary realities. In his book *Islam and Secularism*, he discussed how Christianity fought in vain against the secular tide. Instead of converting the world to Christianity, he affirmed, it converted Christianity to the world. As a scholar, al-Attas acknowledged the contributions of modern science, rationalism, and secularism; but he warned, especially the youth, that the pursuit of knowledge without a firm spiritual basis will be catastrophic to humankind.

In 1987, with al-Attas as the founder and director, the International Institute of Islamic Thought and Civilization (ISTAC) was established in Kuala Lumpur for the study and promotion of Islamic and other civilizations, philosophy, and contemporary issues. He has authored 27 authoritative works on various aspects of Islamic thought and civilization, particularly in the areas of Sufism, the Malay language, and literature and philosophy. He has also lectured in universities and other academic centers around the globe. In recognition of his contributions, numerous awards and honors have been conferred on him. In 1994, King Hussein of Jordan honored him with membership at the Royal Academy of Jordan, and in 1995, the University of Khartoum conferred upon him the Degree of Honorary Doctorate of Arts.

Jesudas M. Athyal

See also: Alatas, Syed Hussein; Colonialism; Islam; Malaysia; Nationalism; Secularism; Study of Religion; Sufism.

Further Reading

Attas, Syed Muhammad Naquib al-. *Islam and Secularism*. Kuala Lumpur: Muslim Youth Movement of Malaysia (ABIM); reprint, Kuala Lumpur: ISTAC, 1993.

Attas, Syed Muhammad Naquib al-. *The Oldest Known Malay Manuscript: A 16th Century Malay Translation of the 'Aqa'id of al-Nasafi*. Kuala Lumpur: University of Malaya, 1988.

Attas, Syed Muhammad Naquib al-. *Prolegomena to the Metaphysics of Islam: An Exposition of the Fundamental Elements of the Worldview of Islam*. Kuala Lumpur: ISTAC, 1995.

Attas, Syed Muhammad Naquib al-. *Some Aspects of Sufism as Understood and Practised among the Malays*. Singapore: Malaysian Sociological Research Institute, 1963.

B

BAHÁ'Í FAITH

The Bahá'í Faith originated in the 1860s, emerging out of the earlier Babi movement. The Bahá'í prophet-founder was Baha'u'llah (1817–1892), a notable from northern Iran who spent much of his life in various parts of the Ottoman Empire as a religious exile. Baha'u'llah proclaimed that he was a new divine messenger who had come to unite the peoples of all religions and establish a divinely ordered global society of peace and justice.

Most of the earliest Bahá'ís were Persians from the Shi'i branch of Islam, but already during Baha'u'llah's lifetime, his Faith had begun to attract Persian Jews and Zoroastrians and Levantine Christians. It was also during this period that a Bahá'í missionary teacher named Jamal Effendi (d. 1898) began to establish the basis for a Bahá'í community in India and Southeast Asia. Initially, the only part of Southeast Asia to have Bahá'ís was Burma, Bahá'í communities being established in Rangoon and Mandalay from 1878 onward. A missionary journey to what were then the Dutch East Indies generated some interest, but apparently had no permanent result. The Burmese community grew significantly during the early 1900s with conversions of hundreds of villagers in the Daidenaw area of the Irrawaddy Delta. With the help and encouragement of the city Bahá'ís, the villagers established a school and other communal institutions. The Burmese Bahá'ís formed part of a larger joint community with the Bahá'ís of India, establishing one of the first "national" Bahá'í councils in 1923.

This situation remained almost unchanged until the 1950s and early 1960s, despite attempts to establish a Bahá'í community in the American Philippines during the interwar period. By the 1950s, Shoghi Effendi (1897–1957), the great-grandson of Baha'u'llah and the head of the Bahá'í Faith at the time, encouraged the Indian Bahá'ís to try to establish the Faith in other parts of Southeast Asia. The results were impressive, with particularly large and dynamic communities being established in South Vietnam, the Philippines, Sarawak, and Indonesia, but Bahá'í communities were established in all parts of Southeast Asia at this time, with the possible exception of Communist North Vietnam. By 1964, there were registered Bahá'ís living in 905 localities across the region with elected local Bahá'í councils ("spiritual assemblies") being established in 533 of these. Initially, a "regional spiritual assembly" was established embracing the entire area apart from Burma (1957), but individual national Bahá'í assemblies were soon elected in most of the component countries. Of note, the newly converted Bahá'ís comprised a mixture of peoples and religions, with former Christians, Buddhists, and Hindus being joined by large numbers of "tribal" peoples with their own indigenous beliefs in the Mentawai

The Bahá'í Gardens and Golden Dome in the Mount Caramel section of Haifa, Israel. In the Bahá'í faith, there are national, regional, and local administrative centers. These centers are meant to complement the houses of worship, and the buildings are generally located near each other. (telhami/iStockphoto.com)

Islands of Indonesia and amongst the Iban of Borneo. Although most of the earliest Burmese Bahá'ís had been of Muslim background, there were very few Muslims amongst the new Bahá'ís.

Since this period of growth, the various national Bahá'í communities have followed diverse trajectories, with the Bahá'ís of Indochina sharing the horrors of war along with the rest of the population and the Bahá'í Faith being restricted by official decree in both Indonesia and Vietnam for a while. Bahá'ís are now well established across the whole region, with a strong commitment to promoting education, social development, and women's rights as well as promulgating their religion. There is an extensive Bahá'í literature in all the major languages of the region. In 2012, Cambodia was chosen as the site for one of the first local Bahá'í temples (Houses of Worship) in the world.

Amongst the eminent Bahá'ís of the region, the following should be mentioned: First, Syed Mustafa Roumie (Rumi) (1852–1942), a Middle Eastern Muslim from what is now Chennai (Madras) in India, who accompanied Jamal Effendi to Burma and remained there after his departure, marrying into an Indo-Burman trading family and becoming a mainstay of the Burmese Bahá'í community. He was murdered by a nationalist mob during the chaotic conditions of World War II and was posthumously honored by Shoghi Effendi as one of the most preeminent Bahá'í teachers in the world.

Second, Shirin Fozdar (1905–1992), an Indian Bahá'í of Persian Zoroastrian background who achieved prominence both as a Bahá'í teacher and administrator and as an advocate of women's rights. She became a member of the executive committee of the All-Asian Women's Conference in the early 1930s and represented this body at the League of Nations to press for a Universal Declaration of Women's Rights. Together with her husband and several of her children, she settled in Singapore in 1950 as a Bahá'í pioneer, later being the major figure in the establishment of the Singapore Council of Women. She was also active in promoting the Bahá'í Faith in other parts of Southeast Asia, notably Thailand, where she lived from 1961 to 1971 and established a Bahá'í school.

Third, Dr. Rahmatu'llah Muhajir (1923–1979), an Iranian Bahá'í physician who pioneered to the Mentawai Islands in Indonesia together with his wife in 1954. Working tirelessly to promote the health and well-being of the islanders in a region that was then extremely poor, backward, and disease-ridden, he attracted several thousand of them to the Bahá'í Faith. The Muhajirs left Indonesia in 1958 after Rahmatu'llah was appointed as one of the principal international leaders and teachers of the Faith.

There is as yet no systematic study of the Bahá'ís of Southeast Asia; only a few local studies and academic papers.

Peter Smith

See also: Buddhism: Cambodia: Christianity; Education; Hinduism; Indonesia; Islam; Missionary Movements; Myanmar (Burma); Philippines; Reform Movements; Religion and Society; Women.

Further Reading

Manisegaran, A. *Jewel among Nations: An Account of the Early Days of the Baha'i Faith in West Malaysia.* Ampang, Selangor: Splendour Publications, 2003.

Muhajir, Iran Furutan. *Dr Muhajir: Hand of the Cause of God, Knight of Baha'u'llah.* London: Baha'i Publishing Trust, 1992.

Ong, Rose. *Vignettes from the Life of Shirin Fozdar: Asia's Foremost Feminist.* Singapore: n.p., 2000.

Smith, Peter. *A Concise Encyclopedia of the Baha'i Faith.* 2nd ed. Oxford: Oneworld, 2002.

Smith, Peter. *An Introduction to the Baha'i Faith.* Cambridge: Cambridge University Press, 2008.

BELO, CARLOS FILIPE XIMENES

Carlos Filipe Ximenes Belo is a Roman Catholic priest and bishop who played a crucial role in achieving a just and peaceful solution to the conflict that led to the formation of the nation of East Timor. Born in 1948 in Wailakama near Vemasse on the north coast of East Timor, Belo did his basic education in Baucau and Ossu and went to Dare Minor Seminary in Dili for Christian theological studies. He became a member of the Salesian Society in the Roman Catholic Church and was ordained a priest in 1980. In 1983, he was appointed by the pope as the apostolic administrator of the Dili diocese, and he became, in 1988, the head of the Catholic Church in East Timor.

As Indonesian forces invaded the nation in 1975 and started massacring its citizens, Belo shed his passive and submissive image and openly criticized the brutality. Since the Catholic Church was the only institution in East Timor that could communicate with the outside world then, he played a crucial role in bringing to the attention of the international community the plight of his fellow citizens. Belo risked his own life and sheltered a number of resistance leaders who were being hunted by the invading soldiers. With rare courage, he stood up to the aggressors and demanded independence and self-determination for the people of the nation. Due to the tireless efforts of Bishop Belo and several others, East Timor attained independence in 2002.

Belo's contributions for a just and peaceful solution to the conflict in East Timor were internationally recognized. Along with Jose Ramos-Horta, he was awarded, in 1996, the Nobel Peace Prize. Belo also received the John Humphrey Freedom Award from the Canadian human rights group Rights and Democracy; the Prize for Lusophonic Personality of the Year, given by *Movimento Internacional Lusófono* in the Lisbon Academy of Sciences; and an honorary doctorate from CEU Cardinal Herrera University in Valencia, Spain.

In independent East Timor, while there was great pressure on Bishop Belo to run for the office of president, he resisted it and affirmed that he would leave politics to the politicians. Since, during his 19 years of episcopal ministry (1983–2002) there, he had spoken about Christian mission and the need for missionaries, he felt the time had come for him to dedicate himself as a missionary. And, with the permission of the pope and the rector major of the Salesian Society, in 2004, Belo took up missionary work in Maputo, the capital of Mozambique. Whatever be the circumstances and the challenges, Belo was firmly convinced that his faith should be translated as a struggle for peace and justice in the society around him.

Jesudas M. Athyal

See also: Christianity; Federation of Asian Bishops' Conferences; Indonesia; Missionary Movements; Religion and Society, Timor Leste (East Timor).

Further Reading

Belo, Carlos Filipe Ximenes. "Nobel Lecture." December 10, 1996. http://www.nobelprize. org/nobel_prizes/peace/laureates/1996/belo-lecture.htm (accessed December 3, 2013).

Garulo, Carlos. "The Nobel Prize for Peace: Who Is Bishop Belo?" *ANS Mag: A Periodical for the Salesian Community* 3, no. 23 (November 1996): 6–8 (English language edition).

Kohen, Arnold. *From the Place of the Dead: The Epic Struggles of Bishop Belo of East Timor*. New York: St. Martin's Press, 1999.

Shenon, Philip. "Timorese Bishop Is Calling For a War Crimes Tribunal." *New York Times*, September 13, 1999. http://www.nytimes.com/1999/09/13/world/timorese-bishop-is -calling-for-a-war-crimes-tribunal.html (accessed December 3, 2013).

BHIKKHU, BUDDHADASA

Buddhadasa Bhikkhu was a Buddhist monk, intellectual, philosopher, and social and political activist. He is best known for his defiant stance toward those in authority whom he considered to be corrupted by power, money, and material trappings of modern society. Buddhadasa founded the now famous Suan Mokkh temple and meditation retreat in the Surat Thani province of Thailand (then Siam) in 1932. He was ordained as a Buddhist monk in 1926.

Buddhadasa Bhikkhu was born Nguam Panitch in 1906 in southern Thailand and ordained in the Mahanikai fraternity at Wat Nok Temple on July 29, 1926 (Mackenzie 2007, 24). He was raised in rural Thailand and received formal primary education at Wat Nau Temple School and secondary education at Sarapi Uthit private school (Payulpitack 1991, 79). After ordination, Buddhadasa spent a short time at a temple in urban Bangkok. He found urban Bangkok unsuitable for Dhammic practice and, in 1932, left Bangkok for an abandoned temple in his home province, eventually restoring and founding the renowned Suan Mokkh Temple. Buddhadasa was a monk of the forest tradition. Forest monks live more aesthetic lives and have stricter regimes such as eating once per day and not leaving temple grounds except for alms.

Buddhadasa was part of the Buddhist reform movement, which has been attempting to change Theravada Buddhism in Thailand of the Rama IV tradition and came to prominence in the 1980s (Puntarigvivat 2003, 189). He advocated a reading of Buddhism that demythologized Thai Buddhism and the Tipitaka (the original Buddhist Scripture) in order to center Buddhist practice and principles on and in the individual (Sirikanchana 2010, 17). Buddhadasa's intellectual and reformist Buddhism is centered on five understandings: the ultimate role of wisdom, rejection of supernatural beliefs and practices, rejection of consumerism and materialism, rejection of literal teachings of Buddha and faith in Buddhist monastic discipline, and the belief that Nibbana (enlightenment) can be found in this life, meaning a tacit rejection of karma. Buddhadasa is known for his criticism of Thai governments for hypocritical social laws and the Thai *sangha* for indulging in worldly security instead of teaching dhamma to younger monks (Payulpitack 1991, 123–24). Buddhadasa also rejected the Thai social tradition of Buddhist rituals and rights, thus advocating a focus on purely individual practice of Buddhism delinked from monks, temples, and traditional Thai social belief and practices (Bhikkhu 1996, 5–19). Buddhadasa taught that Buddhists should be active in addressing social, environmental, political, and cultural problems of the present and not waiting for the future or next life. Furthermore, rationalism and Buddhism could be combined to address issues such as poverty, oppression, social injustice, and environmental sustainability.

Buddhadasa was given honorary membership in the prestigious Siam Society and was also the first person to be granted an honorary doctorate degree in Buddhism from the Mahachulalongkorn Buddhist University as well as honorary doctorates at four other Thai universities. In 2005, Buddhadasa was honored by UNESCO by being named as one of the world's great personalities who promoted interreligious understanding via dialogue (UNESCO n.d.). He passed away in 1993.

William J. Jones

See also: Buddhism; Dharma/Dhamma; Myth/Mythology; Reform Movements; Religion and Society; Study of Religion; Thailand.

Further Reading

Bhikkhu, Buddhadasa. *Handbook of Mankind.* Translated by Ariyananda Bhikkhu. Thailand: Buddha Dharma Education Association, 1996.

Mackenzie, Rory. *New Buddhist Movements in Thailand: Towards an Understanding of Wat Phra Dhammakaya and Santi Asoke.* New York: Routledge. 2007.

Payulpitack, Suchira. "Buddhadasa's Movement: An Analysis of Its Origins, Development, and Social Impact." PhD diss., University Bielfield, 1991.

Puntarigvivat, Tavivat. "Buddhadasa Bhikkhu and Dhammic Socialism." Translated by Bruce Evans. *Chulalongkorn Journal of Buddhist Studies* 2, no. 2, (2003): 189–207.

Sirikanchana, Pataraporn. *In Search of Thai Buddhism.* Bangkok: Office of National Buddhism, 2010.

BHIKKHUNI, DHAMMANANDA

Born in 1945 as Chatsumarn Kabilsingh, Dhammananda Bhikkhuni is the first female to openly practice her religion in Thailand as a fully ordained Theravada Buddhist monk. She is the abbess of the kingdom's first—and for the moment, the only—temple for fully ordained nuns, Songdhammakalyani Temple in Nakorn Pathom (a southwestern suburb of Bangkok). Although traditional Buddhist canon distinguishes between and allows for both male (*bhikkhu*) and female (*bhikkhuni*) monks, the Thai *sangha* does not permit the local ordination of women, let alone the establishment of a female monastic order. Instead, women choosing to devote themselves to Buddhist practice in Thailand have done so as unordained nuns or *mai chii*, a category not found in old Theravada Buddhist texts.

Dhammananda Bhikkhuni's interest in Buddhism came from her mother and grandmother, Voramai Kabilsingh and Mae Che Somcheen. Voramai was ordained as a bhikkhuni in Taiwan in 1971. Mae Che Somcheen turned to Buddhism when her children had grown and eventually became the chief nun at Ganikaphala Temple in central Bangkok.

Dhammananda Bhikkhuni completed a master's degree at McMaster University in Canada before getting her doctorate in Buddhism from Magadh University in India. As a layperson, she spent more than 20 years of her life as a professor of religion and philosophy at Thammasat University in Bangkok, Thailand.

Married and with children, she decided to enter the monkhood in 2000, adhering to lay precepts and practicing meditation at Fo Guang Shan Temple in Taiwan. Her commitment to the spiritual path deepened, and in February 2001, she flew to Sri Lanka to become a female novice according to the Theravada tradition. Two years later, she was ordained as a female Buddhist monk (bhikkhuni). She received higher ordination in Sri Lanka along with three other women, one American and two Burmese. The ordination was conducted by twelve senior bhikkhus and 10 senior bhikkhunis.

Dhammananda Bhikkhuni is the first fully ordained bhikkhuni to begin practicing Theravada Buddhism in Thailand. The Thai *sangha* has yet to formally recognize the legitimacy of her ordination and her status as a Theravada bhikkhuni. Female monks appear to be gaining a degree of acceptance, however. There are now four Theravada Bhikkhunis and 20 female novices in the country, ordained either in Sri Lanka or in Thailand.

Dhammananda has published around 40 books and translations, many under her lay name, Dr. Chatsumarn Kabilsingh. The titles include *Thai Women in Buddhism* (1991); *Bhikkhuni: The Reflection of Gender in Thai Society* (2004); and *Happiness in the Making* (2004), among others. She also oversees the publication of *Yasodara*, a quarterly newsletter that focuses on the activities of Buddhist women and bhikkhunis around the world. A Nobel Peace Prize nominee, she has served as a councillor at the International Committee on Peace Council.

Known to her followers as Luang Mae (the Revered Mother), she currently serves at Wat Songdhammakalayani, a temple that was built in 1960 by her mother Bhikkhuni Ta Tao Fa Tzu (Voramai Kabilsingh). Wat Songdhammakalayani is the only temple in Thailand with fully ordained nuns.

Ruchi Agarwal

See also: Buddhism; Thailand; Women; Women's Monastic Communities.

Further Reading

Falk, L. M. *Making Fields of Merit: Buddhist Female Ascetics and Gendered Orders in Thailand.* Denmark: NIAS Press, 2007.

Kabilsingh, Chatsumarn. *Thai Women in Buddhism.* Berkeley, CA: Parallax Press, 1991.

Queen, Christopher S., and Sallie B. King. *Engaged Buddhism: Buddhist Liberation Movements in Asia.* Albany: State University of New York Press, 1996.

BRUNEI DARUSSALAM

Brunei Darussalam is a constitutional sultanate located in the Southeast Asian island of Borneo. It is bordered on the south, southwest, and southeast by Malaysia, with the country's 5,765-square-kilometer land area split in two by the Limbang Corridor. Possessing a tropical climate, the country is bordered on the north, northwest, and northeast by the South China Sea. The capital is Bandar Seri Begawan.

By July 2013, the population was expected to reach 415,717. According to 2004 figures, 66.3 percent of the population is comprised of Malay; Chinese make up 11.2 percent, indigenous 3.4 percent, and others 19.1 percent. Islam is the official religion, with 67 percent of the population identified as Muslim, 13 percent Buddhists, 10 percent Christians, and 10 percent others.

A British protectorate from 1888 until it gained independence on January 1, 1984, Brunei used to be a powerful maritime kingdom, governed by a sultanate with a society deeply rooted in Islam, which is also the state religion (Sunni branch). Muslim citizens are subject to the government's interpretation of Islamic or *shari'a* law. The various religions in the country coexist peacefully, according to reports, with no overt discrimination based on religious beliefs and practices.

A 2010 report by the U.S. State Department noted, however, that there are restrictions on non-Muslim religious groups, on areas that include proselytization and receiving of religious literature for use in houses of worships or schools. Non-Muslims were also required to conform to Islamic guidelines and generally have limited access to religious literature, places of worship, and public religious gatherings. The government also actively pursues its campaign to inculcate the Malay Islamic Monarchy ideology. The report added that non-Muslim religious leaders claimed undue influence and some faced threats of fines or imprisonment.

George Amurao

See also: Buddhism; Christianity; Islam; Malaysia; Minorities; Religious Conversions; Religious Discrimination/Intolerance; *Shari'a*.

Further Reading

U.S. Central Intelligence Agency. "Brunei." The World Factbook, https://www.cia.gov/library/publications/the-world-factbook/geos/bx.html (accessed September 7, 2014).

U.S. Department of State. "Brunei—International Religious Freedom Report 2010." http://www.state.gov/j/drl/rls/irf/2010/148858.htm (accessed September 7, 2014).

BUDDHISM

Buddhism is one of the major world religions. Its origins can be found in India in the sixth century BCE, in the teachings of Siddhartha Gautama. Buddhism later spread to most parts of Asia, through China, Korea, and Japan, and on to the West. Today, Buddhism has over 300 million followers worldwide. Buddhism teaches individuals to reach the state of nirvana by adhering to the path of Buddha. There is no personal god in Buddhism but rather, a belief in impermanence. Anyone can reach enlightenment through practice, wisdom, and mediation.

History of Buddhism

The word Buddhism implies the devotion to "the Buddha," which means the "Awakened One" or the "Enlightened One." From the earliest times, Buddhist tradition has suggested several former Buddhas who have lived on earth in the past or will in the future. However, in many contexts, "the Buddha" more commonly refers to the one known in history as Gautama to the Theravada Buddhists, and Sakyamuni to the Mahayana Buddhists. Born to a royal family that ruled over the land of the Sakyans at Kapilvastu in present-day Nepal around 490 BCE,

On Asaha Puja Day, the beginning of the Buddhist Lent, Buddhist monks walk with lighted candles around the temple at Wat Muang-Ang Thong, Thailand. (TuelekZa/iStockphoto.com)

Sangha is the order of fully ordained monks and nuns that sustain the continuity of the dharma among humankind. It represents the Third Gem in the Triple Gem (Buddha, dharma, sangha) in Buddhism and has survived for over 2,500 years. The *sangha* exists in close interaction with the laity where the two share interdependence. The laity provides the members of the *sangha* with material provisions such as food, robes, medicines, etc., and the *sangha* in return provides the lay community with the Buddhist teachings.

Ruchi Agarwal

Siddhartha did not lead a typical life. Legends say that in 623 BCE, on a full-moon day, Queen Mahamaya was traveling from Kapilvastu to Devadaha, to give birth to her child at her parental home. Halfway between the two cities, she gave birth to a son while standing in a grove of trees now known as Lumbini. King Ashoka erected a stone pillar over 300 years after the event to mark this sacred place, which is now a famous Buddhist pilgrimage site.

On the fifth day after the birth, his father, King Suddhodana invited eight wise men for the naming ceremony, and they were also asked to predict the baby's future. The prince was named Siddhartha. The invited Brahmins predicted that he would either become a great king or a great teacher when exposed to any sufferings. Queen Mahamaya passed away on the seventh day after the childbirth, and Siddhartha was raised by his aunt. He grew up in all the luxuries and was encouraged to excel in education by his father. At the age of 16, Siddhartha was married to his cousin, the beautiful princess Yashodhara. However, he was still not happy and longed to see the world beyond his palace.

At the age of 29, Siddhartha left the palace with his charioteer Channa to explore the world outside his palace. He was deeply touched by what he had never seen before, the "Four Passing Sights": an old man weakened with age; a sick man crying in pain; a dead man whose corpse was taken for cremation; and a wandering *sannyasin*. Siddhartha was saddened by seeing aging, sickness, and death for the first time. He was inspired by the *sannyasin* and decided to leave the palace, his wife, and his newborn son to understand life and sufferings, and to find a solution to sufferings in the world. His search for enlightenment began by practicing strict asceticism. With six years of hardship, Siddhartha realized that neither luxury nor starvation can provide him with a deeper understanding of life, and instead, followed the Middle Path. He gained enlightenment in a village, Bodh Gaya, under a Bodhi tree as he sat down in meditation. He saw his past lives, death, and rebirths and realized that he had eliminated all desires and ignorance within himself. By now, he had become the "Awakened One," a Buddha. With this awakening, Buddha gave his first sermon to a group of ascetics with whom he practiced earlier. These ascetics became the very first disciples of Buddha. Buddha continued to spread his teachings in India for the next 45 years gaining several followers until his death at the age of 80 in a small town called Kusinara.

Buddha lived his life in the time when an early form of Hinduism, "Brahmanism," was influential. His teachings shared some of the basic ideas of Brahmanism, such as karma and rebirth, moksha, existence of gods, yogic practices, and the value of spiritual insight. However, his ideas on these differed from Brahmanism, as he did not accept some of their key features. He rejected the authority of Vedas, sacrifices to gods, and the social system of caste. Buddhism was open to people of all social classes. The social order of monks and nuns known as the *sangha* was introduced by Buddha himself. Many followers became monks and nuns; others remained lay-people providing material support to the monks and nuns, who in return gave lay-people teachings and advice. This mutual relationship still lies at the heart of the different schools of Buddhism.

The Buddha was a wandering teacher attracting followers with his charisma. As more followers joined, a monastic community with rules and regulations formed over time. However, Buddha never regarded himself as the leader of the community and thus did not appoint a successor upon his death. He instead encouraged people to follow his teachings (dharma) and the monastic order. This soon led to disagreements on the issues of monastic practice and the doctrine. With the absence of a central authority, a number of different traditions developed. The most serious disagreement occurred a century after Buddha's death between the "Elders" (*Sthaviras*) and the "Universal Assembly" (*Mahasanghikas*). Different records provide contradictory accounts. Some see it as a doctrinal dispute on the status of Buddha as compared to an Arahant (seen as inferior to Buddha). However, the more likely cause of the division seems to be an attempt of the Elders to amend the monastic rules by introducing additional rules of conduct. The division occurred as Buddhism began to spread to other parts of India and came across new customs and ideas. This raised questions on whether to stick to the old traditions or accommodate new beliefs and practices. Eventually, the two groups separated—a "Great Division" that led to a number of further divisions and subschools. Most died out over time with the exception of Theravada (from the Elder tradition). The legacy from the earlier schools led to a revolutionary new movement known as the Mahayana.

Teachings of Buddhism

Since Buddha does not refer to a unique individual, Buddhism focuses less on a person as the founder, but rather on the teachings of Buddha. These teachings include ways to help individuals develop compassion and avoid illusions that cause attachments and bring suffering to an individual and to those the individual interacts with. The guide to this process is known as the dharma or dhamma, patterns of reality and cosmic order discovered by Buddha, Buddhist teachings, the path, and the ultimate goal of Buddhism, nirvana. Dhamma is thus the most important element of Buddhism.

Buddha's teachings are recorded in different collections of scripture known as "canons," deriving from the oral tradition at the time of Buddha and preserved through communal chanting. The most essential one is the Pali Canon, written in Pali in Sri Lanka around the middle of the first century BCE. The scripture consists of three baskets, or *Pitaka*: *Sutta* (Buddha's sermons), *Vinaya* (monastic rules), and the *Abhidhamma* (scholastic works). Since Buddhism lacked a central authority, several different schools emerged. Each school compiled their own canons in different languages. However, the Pali Canon remained authoritative for the Theravada school.

The Spread of Buddhism

Buddhism, Christianity, and Islam are the great missionary religions of the world, actively spreading their message and practice beyond their place of origin. The spread of Buddhism goes to the time when Buddha himself sent out enlightened disciples to spread teachings. This marked the beginning of the spread of Buddhism both within India and beyond, becoming the main form of Indian religion for export and spreading literate culture as well.

The spread of Buddhism gained a considerable boost in the third century with the great Mauryan ruler, King Ashoka, who extended his empire through conquest. During one of the battles on the east coast in Orissa, he experienced guilt and turned to Buddhism. Thereafter, Ashoka ruled according to Buddhist principles and Buddhism flourished under his reign, with missionaries sent to the courts of rulers to Southeast Asia and to the West.

Within India, great Buddhist universities were established such as Nalanda, which flourished between the seventh and the twelfth centuries. Important Buddhist centers were also set up both in the south and the northwest, which became an important gateway to central Asia and the Far East. Buddhism, however, was under attack with the Muslim Turks' invasion in India in the tenth century. Several works of art were destroyed and libraries were burned down. Only with the Moguls in the sixteenth century was stability and religious tolerance restored. However, by this time, Buddhism had virtually disappeared from the land of its birth.

Buddhism in Southeast Asia

Buddhism survived in the rest of Asia with Mahayana Buddhism in the north and Theravada in the south. The important Theravada countries in Southeast Asia are Myanmar (Burma) and Thailand. Theravada Buddhism might have been introduced here by one of the missionaries of Ashoka and has been present among the native Mons since the early centuries of the Christian era. Southeast Asia also received the influence of both Buddhism and Hinduism from South Asia, which was historically looked upon for cultural inspirations. Under the domination of the Khmer Empire from the fifth to the fifteenth centuries, several forms of Hinduism and Mahayana Buddhism were popular. According to the Burmese chronicles, different schools of Buddhism flourished under King Anawarhta (1044–1077). However, he promoted Theravada Buddhism, and as a result, almost 90 percent of the population in Burma is Theravada Buddhist.

Theravada has long been established in parts of the neighboring territory of present-day Thailand, in the Mon kingdom of Haripunjaya and the kingdom of Dvaravati. In the eleventh century, missionaries were sent to this region from Burma. The Theravada Buddhism received royal patronage, and today over 90 percent of the Thai population is Buddhist.

Cambodia, Laos, and Vietnam share a similar history. However, a much more syncretic religious system is found in these countries, with a mix of Theravada, Mahayana, and local indigenous religions. One of the reasons for the successful spread of Buddhism is that it tends to incorporate existing beliefs of local gods and spirits, with its own cosmology. Thus it is common to find Buddhists in villages who look to local gods to find solutions to everyday problems while turning to Buddhism for answers to the broader questions of human life.

Ruchi Agarwal

See also: Bhikkhu, Buddhadasa; Bhikkhuni, Dhammananda; Dharma/Dhamma; Duc, Thich Quang; Engaged Buddhism; Goshananda, Maha; Hanh, Thich Nhat; Hòa Hả;o Buddhism; Interreligious Relations and Dialogue; Khmer Buddhism; Liberation Theologies; Missionary Movements; Pilgrimage; Religious Conversions; Santi Asoke; Sayadaw, Mahasi; Sayadaw, Thamanya; Sivaraksa, Sulak; Thien Buddhism; Water Festivals.

Further Reading

Harvey, P., ed. *Buddhism*. London and New York: Continuum, 2001.

Harvey, P. *An Introduction to Buddhism: Teachings, History, and Practices*. Cambridge: Cambridge University Press, 1990.

Hazra, Kanai Lal. *History of Theravada Buddhism in South-East Asia with Special Reference to India and Ceylon*. New Delhi: Munshiram Manoharlal Publishers Pvt. Ltd., 1982.

Ingram, Daniel M. *Mastering the Core Teachings of the Buddha*. 3rd ed. The Independent Universe, 3rd ed. 2007.

Keown, D. *Buddhism: A Very Short Introduction*. Oxford: Oxford University Press, 2013.

Smith, Huston, and Philip Novak. *Buddhism: A Concise Introduction*. New York: HarperCollins Publishers, 2003.

Swearer, Donald K. *The Buddhist World of Southeast Asia*. Albany: State University of New York Press, 1995.

Thera, Piyadassi. *The Buddha, His Life and Teachings*. Kandy, Sri Lanka: Buddhist Publication Society, 1982.

C

CALUNGSOD, PEDRO

Pedro Calungsod is a Filipino saint, the second to be elevated by the Catholic Church to sainthood, and is the patron saint of the youth. He was believed to have been born in 1654. He was martyred on April 2, 1672, in Guam while working as a lay catechist and assistant to the Jesuit mission engaged in preaching and baptizing native Chamorros.

Calungsod was born sometime in 1654. Historians have speculated where he was born: whether in Cebu, southern Leyte, or Ilo-ilo, all of which were part of the Diocese of Cebu in central Philippines at that time. According to records, Calungsod was trained as a catechist in a Jesuit-run boarding school in the Visayas region. Along with several boys, he was sent to Antipolo to become part of Father Diego Luís de San Vitores' Mission to the Ladrones (present-day Guam).

On August 7, 1667, the group left the port of Cavite aboard the ship *San Diego*. They reached the island of Guam on June 15, 1668, after sailing first to Acapulco in Mexico to get provisions. The missionaries under Father de San Vitores established the first church and mission house in the town of Agana. The Jesuits and their young assistants labored hard due to the difficult terrain and the prevalence of typhoons in the island. The group also had to contend with native shamans/priests who opposed the Catholic missionaries. One of these was a Chinese named Choco who spread rumors that the baptismal water used by the missionaries was poisonous, implying that it was the cause of the recent rash of deaths of infants. Native shamans supported this allegation. As a result, many of the converts turned their backs on Christianity.

On April 2, 1672, Father de San Vitores and Calungsod, who was by then estimated to be 17 years old, were in the village of Tumhon looking for a runaway companion when they learned that the wife of the chieftain named Matapang had just given birth to a daughter. Matapang, who had been a Christian, was among those who believed the rumors circulated by Choco. The father refused vehemently to have his daughter baptized and shouted at Father de San Vitores and Calungsod. The two withdrew to the nearby beach where they gathered the village's children and led them in singing hymns.

Agitated by the incident, Matapang went out and sought a friend named Hirao. When he came back with his companion, he learned that Father de San Vitores and Calungsod had been able to convince his wife to let his daughter be baptized. This sent Matapang into a frenzy, and he and Hirao attacked the two unarmed Christian workers. The village chief hurled spears at Calungsod until he finally hit him in the chest. Hirao killed him with a slash from a machete. Father de San

Vitores was able to give Calungsod the last rites before he himself was killed by the two Chamorros. They carried the bodies to their boat, weighted them with large stones, and took them to the sea where they cast the bodies.

The members of the Jesuit mission started the process for the beatification of Father Diego on January 9, 1673. However, it was overtaken by major events like the expulsion of the Jesuits. In 1981, the documents of the Jesuit's beatification were discovered as Agana prepared for the celebration of its 20th year as a diocese. Father Diego was beatified on October 6, 1985.

Work on having Calungsod beatified began in the 1980s, and on March 5, 2000, Calungsod was beatified by Pope John Paul II and was canonized on October 21, 2012, by Pope Benedict XVI in Rome. His feast day is on April 2.

George Amurao

See also: Christianity; Jesuits; Missionary Movements; Philippines; Shamanism.

Further Reading

Agence France Press. "Filipino Catholics Celebrate Pedro Calungsod's Canonization." Rappler.com, October 21, 2012. http://www.rappler.com/nation/14586-filipino -catholics-celebrate-pedro-calungsod-s-canonization (accessed September 17, 2014).

Esmaquel, Paterno, II. "What History Says about Pedro Calungsod." Rappler.com, October 19, 2012. http://www.rappler.com/nation/14485-what-history-says-about- pedro-calungsod (accessed September 17, 2014).

Leyson, Ildebrando Jesus Aliño. "A Catechetical Primer on the Life, Martyrdom and Glorification of Blessed Pedro Calungsod—Part 1." http://www.pedrocalungsod.org/ index.php/life/76 (accessed September 17, 2014).

Uy, Jocelyn R. "Calungsod Seen to Spark Holiness, Faith Revival," *Philippine Daily Inquirer*, October 21, 2012. http://newsinfo.inquirer.net/293304/saint-pedro-calungsod-seen -to-spark-holiness-faith-revival (accessed September 17, 2014).

CAMBODIA

Cambodia is predominantly a Theravada Buddhist country similarly to its nearest neighbors Laos and Thailand in Southeast Asia. Buddhism was introduced gradually to the early kingdoms during the first centuries of Christian era. The rulers of king- doms known as Funan, Chenla, and Kambuja/Angkor based their right to rule on Hinduistic concepts of divine king *devaraja* and Buddhist notions of future Buddha *bodhisattva*. The French colonial era introduced Christianity, as Catholic Vietnamese colonial officials were posted to administer French Cambodia. Christianity remains a minority religion, although in recent years Christianity has been proselytized among the northeastern minority Mon-Khmer tribes by evangelical groups. The second-largest religion after Buddhism is Islam, which is practiced predominantly by the ethnic Chams, who now live in central parts of Cambodia, particularly in Kompong Cham.

Cambodia has experienced dramatic political changes during the last 100 years. From the French colonial era, Cambodia emerged independent relatively smoothly in November 1953, as King Norodom Sihanouk (1921–2012) managed to exploit the Cold War rivalries and pressure the Western powers to stop supporting the French colonial rule in Cambodia. Sihanouk himself turned out to be a *devaraja*-like authoritarian ruler and crushed the political opposition until the most radicalized sections of the opposition, later known as the Khmer Rouge, emerged in the capital city in April 1975 and started to violently dismantle state institutions, religion, and education. The Vietnamese invaded what was called "Democratic Kampuchea" in January 1979 and introduced their own rule for the next 10 years. The end of the Cold War witnessed the Vietnamese troops leaving Cambodia and some former Khmer Rouge and other pro-Vietnamese politicians trained by the Vietnamese took over Cambodia. Prince Sihanouk returned from his long exile and had himself enthroned yet again, reigning until 2004 when he abdicated and one of his sons Prince Norodom Sihamoni (b. 1953) was enthroned as the new king.

Novice monks worship at the giant Buddha statue at Angkor Wat, Siem Reap, Cambodia. Originally built as a Hindu temple in the early 12th century, the complex at Angkor Wat is the largest religious monument in the world. It became a Buddhist temple in the 13th century. (Anthony Brown/iStockphoto.com)

Presently, the Cambodian population is about 15 million, of whom 50 percent are under the age of 25. According to the semiofficial statistics, Buddhists dominate with over 96 percent, whereas Muslims make up 2 percent. Ethnically,

Cambodia's highland, forest-dwelling, animist minorities—collectively known as *Khmer Leou* (upper Khmer)—mainly inhabit the northeastern provinces, where they have practiced rotating agriculture for generations. The absorption of Cambodia's economy into today's global marketplace has exposed these peoples to the risk of alienation of land. Ignoring laws protecting indigenous rights, officials have been granting land concessions to large companies and silencing local protesters. As the highlanders' spirit forests, where their ancestors dwell, become gutted of precious hardwood trees and then cleared for various forms of exploitation, an entire cosmos is put under threat.

Alexandra Kent

the breakdown is given as 90 percent being ethnic Khmer, 5 percent Vietnamese, 1 percent Chinese, and the rest consisting, for instance, of ethnic Chams. Statistics in Southeast Asia tend to be notoriously unreliable, as religious and ethnic diversity are sensitive issues in most countries.

The early kingdoms that located approximately in the region now included in Cambodia left behind some impressive temples and temple ruins. The kingdom of Funan is assumed to have located somewhere in the Mekong Delta in present-day southern Vietnam and southeastern Cambodia. Archaeologists have found some ruins of temples, which seem to indicate that Hindu gods and goddesses were known in the kingdom. These findings were interpreted by the French colonial scholars such as George Coedes and Louis Finot that the region had already before the French intervention benefitted from "Western" cultural influences from India. At its extreme interpretation, the Indianization theory suggested that whole mainland Southeast Asia and Java in present Indonesia were conquered, occupied, and colonized by Indians. These excesses are now rejected, but the fact remains that Indian religions, architectural influences, and a writing system applied to the local languages prevail. Funan is assumed to have existed approximately from the fifth century CE for a few centuries and was followed by yet another "Indianized" kingdom mentioned in the Chinese Annals as Chenla (Zhenla). The French scholars of the French School of Far Eastern studies (Ecole Francaise d'Extreme Orient—EFEO) assumed that these kingdoms were predominantly ethnically Khmer.

Contemporary with Funan, Chenla, and the most well-known Kambuja or Angkor at the northern banks of Tonle Sap Lake, existed the kingdom of Champa. This kingdom is assumed to have been a network of related kingdoms ruled and dominated by the ethnic Chams. Also, the Chams were well versed in Sanskrit, Hindu gods and goddesses, architecture, and ideological concepts. The Chams are somewhat of an anomaly among the Mon-Khmer speaking peoples of present-day Cambodia and Vietnam, as their language is related to the Malay languages. It was in the interests of the French colonial scholars to reconstruct a glorious Khmer empire that the French then could claim to have restored. Hence, the role and history of the Chams in the region remained marginalized, and only recently has more research been carried out about these people and their role in Cambodian and Vietnamese history.

The great monuments of Angkor are predominantly Hindu, dedicated to Hindu gods and kings. The reliefs of Angkor depict the battles described in the Hindu epics of Ramayana and Mahabharata, presenting them together with the battles fought by the kings of Angkor, thus aligning them with the Hindu glories. The most important Buddhist monument in the Angkor area is Bayon, depicting the face of King Jayavarman VII 216 times in the towers of Bayon. His face is interpreted as representing the face of a *bodhisattva*. The *bodhisattva* myth indicated that the king has in his cycles of rebirths reached the highest level, where he could have entered in nirvana, but has remained in the world out of compassion for his fellow-beings. The myth is regarded as a Mahayana Buddhist myth, as the equivalent highest stage of the Theravada Buddhist is an *arahat*, who does not and cannot concretely help anyone, but is there as an example for others to follow. The *bodhisattva* myth is essential in Mahayana Buddhism as it encourages people to follow an assumed *bodhisattva*, who then can take along a large group of people on his "vehicle"—Mahayana is often translated as the Great Vehicle—and bring them to nirvana. The myth is so appealing that it is also followed by many Theravada Buddhists.

The French scholars who regarded themselves as saviors of the Khmer culture did not only restore the temples into their assumed earlier glory, but also started to teach the European version of Buddhism to the Cambodian people. Theravada Buddhism is known to be tolerant and inclusive, where people can, besides Buddha, pay respect to ancestors, spirits of nature, Hindu gods, and Mahayana *bodhisattvas*. The European Buddhist tradition, translated to European languages by scholars such as Max Müller and T. W. Rhys Davids, presented Buddhism as a philosophical, practically atheistic religion, where an individual should rely on his or her own reason and moral judgment.

The indigenous Buddhism appeared "unorthodox" if not heretic in the eyes of Western scholars; hence the French decided to send two young Cambodian monks, Chuon Nath (1883–1969) and Huot Tath (1891–1975) to study Sanskrit with the French Indologist Louis Finot in Hanoi. Both later became supreme patriarchs *sangharaja*. The monastic order *sangha* was under the French patronage. In the mid-nineteenth century, the Siamese prince Mongkut—later King Rama IV—started to reform the Siamese *sangha* by establishing a new royalist sect, Thammayutnikai; these influences spread to Cambodia, too. Siam was nominally politically independent, and the French perceived the Siamese influences to be destabilizing. French authorities started establishing Pali-language schools for monks in the region and established the Buddhist Institute in Phnom Penh in 1930, led by Suzanne Karpeles from EFEO.

The Buddhist *sangha* has played a crucial political role in Cambodia. One of the most famous Cambodian monks is Hem Chieu (1898–1943), who led demonstrations against the French-language policies in Cambodia. In 1942, he was arrested and died in prison. The Siamese-style division into Mahanikay and Thommayuth sects was adopted in Cambodia as well, and during Sihanouk's political rule (1955–1970), there were two supreme patriarchs *sangharaja* heading their respective sects. During the Khmer Rouge regime, the monks were regarded as "parasites" living on the expense of the ordinary hardworking people, and many of the monks were disrobed and even killed. During the Vietnamese occupation (1979–1989), the *sangha* was revived. One of the internationally most famous monks of the era was Preah Maha Ghosananda (1928–2007), who started reviving Buddhism in the refugee camps at the Thai-Cambodian border.

While allegedly purifying Khmer Buddhism from magico-animistic and Hinduistic elements, the French ended up also "purifying" the Khmer national identity, which extended to include the idea of the purity of the Khmer race, language, and culture. These ideas of "purity" led to Khmer racial chauvinism, which was promoted by the anticolonial nationalistic policies propagated by Sihanouk, Lon Nol, and Pol Pot alike. This Khmer chauvinism led to discrimination and outright massacres of Vietnamese and Chams particularly during the Khmer Rouge era.

The numbers of the Chams killed during Pol Pot's rule remain contested, but we are probably talking about hundreds of thousands. The Chams have gradually recovered from the dark period, partly with the generous assistance of fellow Muslims of both Malaysia and Thailand. New mosques have been constructed as well as *madrasas*, and the Cambodian Cham Muslims have been offered opportunities to study in the neighboring countries.

Marja-Leena Heikkilä-Horn

See also: Buddhism; Cao Dai; Christianity; Colonialism; Ethnicity; Ghosananda, Maha; Hinduism; Indonesia; Islam; Khmer Buddhism; Minorities; Vietnam.

Further Reading

Edwards, Penny. *Cambodge: The Cultivation of a Nation, 1860–1945*. Chiang Mai, Thailand: Silkworm Books, 2007.

Harris, Ian. *Cambodian Buddhism: History and Practice*. Chiang Mai, Thailand: Silkworm Books, 2005.

Harris, Ian. *Buddhism in a Dark Age: Cambodian Monks under Pol Pot*. Honolulu: University of Hawaii Press, 2013.

Taylor, Philip. *Cham Muslims of the Mekong Delta: Place and Mobility in the Cosmopolitan Periphery*. Copenhagen: NIAS, 2007.

CAO DAI

Cao Dai, or Caodaism, or *Cao Đài Đại Đạo Tam Kỳ Phổ Độ* (the "third great way of salvation"), is an indigenous religion of Vietnam that appeared in the 1920s under the French colonial presence. The founders are a group of both Vietnamese civil servants and Daoist masters. Encouraged by spirit-mediumship communication with deities, they rapidly constituted a canon, rituals, and a hierarchy translated literally from Catholicism (with a pope, cardinals, and other officials). Theologically, the divinity residing in the "high tower" (*Cao Đài*) is an *avatar* (incarnation) of the Chinese Jade Emperor. He undertakes a syncretistic unification into the pantheon of the Sino-Vietnamese Three Teachings (Buddhism, Confucianism, and Daoism), Jesus, and spiritualist figures (Victor Hugo and Joan of Arc). Before the impending end of the world, Caodaists have the responsibility to save humanity through conversion. Theology interferes clearly here with politics, and the Cao Dai texts encourage Vietnamese patriotism and the overthrow of the French colonial rule.

Caodaism emerged from distinctly Chinese-Vietnamese salvationist groups or "redemptive societies" (*minh* sects). This category refers to a wave of new Chinese religious movements that appeared in early twentieth-century China (including Xiantiandao, Daoyuan, and Yiguandao). Like these groups, Caodaism challenged the collapse of the imperial order and the irruption of modernity in Vietnam, by propagating millenarian expectations, the worship of the Golden Mother of the Jasper Pond, spirit-mediumship, and so forth. Compared to these Chinese groups, Caodaism drew its hierarchical inspiration from the Catholic Church and was thoroughly influenced by an Occultist colonial culture (as Western Spiritualism, Freemasonry, and Theosophical Society).

Jeremy Jammes

The members of Caodaism (highly educated and businesspeople, landowners, and peasant population) went over 500,000 in the 1930s and have sustained to rise even during the crackdown on Caodaists during the Catholic regime of Ngo Dinh Diem. The latter succeeded in dismantling the Cao Dai army, which was trained and equipped by the Japanese, French, and American states for struggling against Communism. Engaged in the country's decolonization, Caodaism maintained a competitive relationship with other nationalistic movements from the 1930s onward. In the years after 1976 (the independence of the Socialist Republic of Vietnam), a violent repression took place against Caodaist pro-American or pro-French leaders. But since the 1986 political and economic reform, Hanoi has been aspiring to connect its ideology with a more market-based economy and a certain social and religious peace. In exchange for transparency in all its religious activities, Caodaism was granted the status of "religion" in 1995 following which building renovation permits were delivered more freely, and the "Holy See" of Tây Ninh was opened to tourists.

Currently the community is constituted by a network of holy sees and meditation centers formed during the twentieth century in accordance with political or theological rivalries inside the leadership. Caodaist "profiles" vary from the politically consensual and regional Organ for Universalizing Cao Dai teachings (Co' quan Phổ thông Giáo lý) in Ho Chi Minh City, to the local but meditative branch of Chiếu Minh. Finally, there are between one million and four million Caodaists in Vietnam, and 15,000–30,000 living abroad, mainly in the countries where boat people found asylum (in the United States, Australia, France, and Cambodia). Although Caodaist temples are much more visible in the southern part of Vietnam, they have been planted throughout the country. The Cao Dai nationalistic canon is vivacious today through international and missionary networking activities (scouting, preaching, publishing and e-propaganda, and pilgrimages).

Jeremy Jammes

See also: Buddhism; Christianity; Colonialism; Communism; Confucianism; Daoism (Taoism); Diaspora; Globalization; Nationalism; Religious Conversions; Ritual Dynamics; Spirit Mediumship; Vietnam.

Further Reading

Jammes, J. *Les oracles du Cao Đài: étude d'un mouvement religieux vietnamien et de ses réseaux.* Paris: Les Indes savantes, 2014.

Werner, J. S. *Peasant Political and Religious Sectarianism: Peasant and Priest in the Cao Dai in Vietnam.* New Haven, CT: Yale University Southeast Asia Studies, 1981.

CHRISTIAN CONFERENCE OF ASIA

The Christian Conference of Asia (CCA) is a regional Christian ecumenical organization in which 17 National Councils and 100 denominations (churches), spread over 21 Asian countries, are members. In total, CCA represents 55 million Christians in Asia. Councils (national councils of churches and national Christian councils) are full members of the organization along with the churches. CCA is actively involved

On December 30, 1987, the Singapore government closed the head office of the Christian Conference of Asia (CCA), located in Singapore then, and deported the staff, accusing them of supporting "subversive movements" and indulging in political activities. The charges against CCA also included a "Marxist plot," which the government claimed to have discovered in 1987. It is, however, important to note that the crackdown on CCA happened at a time when the government of the country had swung to the right. The organization, eventually, moved its offices elsewhere.

Jesudas M. Athyal

in most of the Southeast Asian countries. The history of the organization goes back to 1957 when, at a meeting in Prapat, Indonesia, in March 1957, the East Asia Christian Conference (EACC) was constituted as a body of churches and national councils of churches in Asia. Two years later, in May 1959, the first Assembly of EACC met in Kuala Lumpur, Malaysia. In recognition of the reality that EACC represents the churches all over Asia, a decision was taken in 1973 at the assembly in Singapore to change the name of the organization to Christian Conference of Asia. The offices of CCA are located in Chiang Mai, Thailand.

All the members of CCA are required to confess Jesus Christ as God, believe in the Scriptures, and commit themselves to the values of freedom, equality, and justice for all in accordance with the basics of the Christian faith. The organization strives to bring about unity among the churches, foster interfaith dialogue, and address social and economic problems that plague Asian society. In all its programs, CCA seeks to be the voice of ecumenical Christianity in the pluralistic context of Asia.

Since its founding, CCA has made a deep impact on the religious life of Southeast Asia. Apart from the inaugural assembly held at Prapat, Indonesia, in 1957, the assemblies held in various places in the region include the meetings in Kuala Lumpur, Malaysia (in 1959); Bangkok, Thailand (1964 and 1968); Singapore (1973); Penang, Malaysia (1977); Manila, Philippines (1990); Tomohan, Indonesia (2000); Chiang Mai, Thailand (2005); and Kuala Lumpur, Malaysia (2010). In addition to periodic assemblies, CCA organizes a number of seminars, workshops, and consultations all over Asia, in accordance with the vision and purpose of the organization.

The Christian Conference of Asia has been actively involved in upholding interreligious dialogue and also championing peace and justice concerns in the various Southeast Asian countries. The general secretary of CCA attended the Mekong Mission Forum (MMF) held in Phnom Penh, Cambodia, in April 2013. She appreciated and honored the invitation received from the president of MMF, who is the secretary for Papua New Guinea, Pacific and East Asia Centre for "Mission OneWorld" of the Evangelical Lutheran Church in Bavaria. The CCA has also been involved in the democratization and developmental work of Myanmar, where there were growing religious tensions giving rise to a situation where the military had to intervene. In all its programs, CCA works together with the national and regional churches, other religious groups, and secular organizations in building a peaceful, just, and sustainable society in Asia.

Jesudas M. Athyal

See also: Cambodia; Christianity; Federation of Asian Bishops' Conferences; Indonesia; Interreligious Relations and Dialogue; Koyama, Kosuko; Kyaw Than, U.; Loh, I-to; Malaysia; Nacpil, Emerito; Papua New Guinea; Philippines; Religion and Society; Singapore; Thailand.

Further Reading

CCA, Hong Kong and WACC, United Kingdom. *Refugees and their Right to Communicate: Perspective from South East Asia.* Hong Kong and London: CCA and WACC, 2001.

Koshy, Ninan, ed. *A History of the Ecumenical Movement in Asia.* Volumes 1 and 2. Geneva, Switzerland: WSCF, YMCA, and CCA, 2004.

CHRISTIANITY

Christianity in Southeast Asia refers to the variegated forms of Christianity in the southeastern corner of the Asiatic continent. Since the emerging of newly independent churches and nations at the end of World War II, Southeast Asian Christianity has become a third main strand of Asian Christianity that has traditionally been articulated in Chinese and South Asian terms. It is marked by nuanced conversations between many ethnicities, languages, beliefs, and cultures amid

Christian faithful visit the Latin Rite Roman Catholic Redemptorist Church at Manila, in the Philippines. Catholicism is a significant religion in the Philippines. (ArtPhaneuf/iStockphoto.com)

Southeast Asian Christianity is marked by nuanced conversations between many ethnicities, languages, beliefs, and cultures amid contrasting nation-building experiences. Southeast Asian Christianity can be seen as a microcosm of world Christianity in the twenty-first century. It is an important indicator for the future of Christianity in a globalizing and post-Christendom age.

Michael Nai-Chiu Poon

contrasting nation-building experiences. More importantly, it emerges amid huge intellectual shifts in postmodern Western society, where secularism is replacing Christianity as the driving force of civilizational progress and social harmony. The plural condition of Southeast Asian Christianity, therefore, can be seen as a microcosm of world Christianity in the twenty-first century. It is an important indicator for the future of Christianity in a globalizing and post-Christendom age.

Southeast Asia has historically been a place of convergence and a crossroad where migrant communities have largely coexisted with and enriched one another. Unlike mainland America, Europe, or Africa, Southeast Asia does not consist of a continuous land mass. Instead, it is punctuated by intervening seas and barrier mountain ranges, which make subregions able to maintain distinctive social identities. For Christianity, Catholics are traditionally strong in the northern part of Southeast Asia: the Philippines, Vietnam, and Cambodia. Protestants in the Philippines and Indochinese countries have close historical ties with the United States. Malaysian and Singaporean churches keep strong intellectual and church links with Britain and America. Their Indonesian counterparts toward the south look to the Dutch. With the exception of the Catholic-dominant Philippines, present-day Christianity lives as a minority among other powerful spiritual traditions: Islam in Malaysia and Indonesia; Buddhism and Hinduism in Myanmar, Laos, Cambodia, and Thailand; Confucianism and Communism in Vietnam. Accuracy of statistics on religious adherents varies with the state policy and the political situation. Christians roughly constitute 12 percent of the population in Indonesia, Brunei, and Malaysia; less than 2 percent in Myanmar, Thailand, Laos, and Cambodia; 8 percent in Vietnam; 18 percent in Singapore; and over 90 percent in Timor Leste and the Philippines.

Christian demography and distinctiveness in different parts of Southeast Asia are shaped by intricate interplays between colonial policy, Western missionary strategy, and social ecology. Roman Catholics were the first to arrive in the region in the sixteenth century. The Jesuits and Dominicans came with the Portuguese to Ambon, Ternate, Morotai, and Solar in Indonesia. The Philippines became the Christendom in Asia under three and a half centuries of Spanish rule. Protestantism was introduced to the Philippines only after the Spanish defeat to the Americans in 1902. Catholicism entered Vietnam and Cambodia in the seventeenth and eighteenth centuries. The transfer of power from the Portuguese to the Dutch East India Company led to the absorption of many Catholics into the Protestant church. In the nineteenth century, Protestants used Malacca, Penang, and Singapore as staging ground for China missions. In the early twentieth century, the British collaborated with Methodist missionary societies to organize the mass migration of Fuh-chow Chinese Christians to Sibu and Sitiawan to work in rubber plantations.

Christian conversion is often an identity-certifying act for minority groups. There is a strong Christian presence among the non-Muslim Bataks in northern Sumatra, the Karens in Burmese- and Buddhist-dominated Myanmar, and the non-Thai ethnic groups in Thailand. Ethnic Chinese, as a significant minority in Southeast Asia, has played a major role in the cross-fertilization and dissemination of Christianity in the region. The Overseas Chinese Missionary Society, founded in 1929 in Shanghai, was the first Chinese-led missionary society formed with the aim to evangelize Southeast Asian peoples. The successful evangelistic campaigns of the revivalist John Sung (1901–1944) from 1935 to 1940 led to mass conversion and the strengthening of local Christian leadership. Such revivals galvanized local Christian communities to face the hasty departure of foreign missionaries and hard times during the Japanese military occupation of Southeast Asia from 1941 to 1945.

Cultural Legacy of Western Missions

The fertile and intricate cultural experiences in Southeast Asia produced some of the most outstanding linguists, culture interpreters, and ecumenical leaders. Adoniram Judson (1788–1850), Baptist missionary to the Karens, compiled the first Burmese-English dictionary. Hendrik Kraemer (1888–1965) in Java was an eminent Islamic scholar and leader in ecumenism. The Episcopalian bishop Charles Brent (1862–1929), who pioneered missionary work among the mountain people in the Philippines, organized the first World Conference on Faith and Order in 1927.

Bible translation provided an important occasion for sustained engagement, often for the first time, with canonical writings and ancient texts outside Western Christendom. Bible translation as well led to the Romanization of eastern Asian languages and the development of moveable types in printing presses, which contributed to the democratization of eastern Asia.

Systematic Bible translation began with Protestant mission initiatives. A. C. Ruyl's translation of Bible portions into high Malay accompanied the Dutch mission to Indonesia in 1629. The translation consisted of the Gospel of Matthew and selection of Bible portions meant for catechetical and liturgical use. Before the twentieth century, Bible translation focused on the two main cultural and linguistic worlds in the territory: the Confucian-Buddhist world to the northeast, and the Malay world to the southeast. The earliest translations were mainly in classical languages. Among the earliest Malay translations was D. Brouwerious's translation of the whole New Testament in 1668. The first Malay Bible in high Malay appeared in 1733; translation in Jawi script followed in 1758. Robert Morrison and William Milne's translation of the Chinese Bible appeared in 1823 in Malacca. Translations in other local languages appeared as missionaries became more aware of the variety of languages in the territory. H. C. Klinkert's translation of the Bible into "low Malay" appeared in 1863. The Bible also became available in different Indonesian (e.g., Javanese, Sundanese, Toba Batak) and Chinese languages (e.g., Cantonese, Hakka, Amoy, Fuh-chow).

The Bible, once translated into the local Asian languages, often assume a canonical status alongside other Asian classical texts. Its elevated status, however, makes further revisions difficult. This contributes to a conservative outlook among Southeast Asian Christians.

Developments from the Mid-Twentieth Century

Region-wide focused development of Christianity began only after the end of World War II, in response to two practical needs. First, the profound social, economic, and political revolutions that came with the departure of former colonial powers and the founding of independent nations; and secondly, the perceived Communist threat to the region that followed the Communist victory in China demanded concerted response. Air travel, for the first time, made intraregion exchanges viable. From the 1950s, the United States has played an important role in resourcing the infrastructural development of Southeast Asian Christianity. After all, the Asia Pacific has become increasingly important geopolitically and economically, and so the United States has huge interest in shaping Southeast Asian affairs, including the religious scene.

Southeast Asian churches held a series of region-wide conferences between the late 1940s and the early 1970s that have made a huge contribution to the modern ecumenical movement, and to regional collaboration. Region-wide Christian organizations played an important role in promoting worldwide Christian cooperation from the 1940s to the 1970s. The East Asia Christian Conference with the theme "The Christian Prospect in Eastern Asia" that met in Bangkok in 1949 was the first occasion at which newly established national councils of churches in Asia gathered together to consider their Christian task on a continental scale. In 1957, the Protestant church leaders from 11 Asian countries founded the East Asia Christian Conference (now called Christian Conference of Asia) in Indonesia. In 1963, "Situation Conferences" were held in Madras (India), Amagisanso (Japan), and Singapore to explore ways that geographically neighboring churches across different denominations can work together to strengthen local Christian witness.

Southeast Asia as well became a pioneer and experimental ground for developing regional-level theological education accreditation body and degree programs (up to the doctoral level) to meet the diverse needs of newly founded seminaries across Southeast Asia. The 1950s to the 1970s were a golden period in Southeast Asian Christian intellectual development. Shoki Coe (1914–1988) and Kosuke Koyama (1929–2009) provided pivotal leadership. Together, they helped the churches to conduct their life and witness more responsively to the urgent contextual issues of secularity, technology, and human justice in nation-building processes, while keeping faith in the Christian beliefs. Coe's contextualizing theology became a lasting contribution to world Christianity.

Southeast Asian state authorities mainly keep religion under close watch, for fear of interreligious unrest. Christianity especially comes under scrutiny because of its international networks. Southeast Asian churches therefore mostly stay clear of political matters. Nevertheless, there are notable examples where Christians, especially among Roman Catholics, make public stands against authoritarian governments. In the 1970s, the Catholic priest Edicio de la Torre and the Christians for National Liberation opposed President Ferdinand Marcos's martial law in the Philippines. Cardinal Jaime Sin's support for the People Power Revolution led to the end of Marcos's government in 1986. Several Catholic social activists were also arrested in Singapore in 1987 on the charge of subverting the country's political and social order.

Charismatic Christianity, missionary outreach, and revivals offer Southeast Asian Christians ways to express their faith in forms that are more acceptable to the public. Singapore, Indonesia, and Sarawak have been the scene of significant revivals from the late 1960s to the early 1970s. Christian practices among megachurches in the west coast of America exercise huge influence on Southeast Asian churches.

Southeast Asian Church Music

Southeast Asian Christianity can best be understood and sensed through what Christians compose, play, and sing. Hymn composition is, in fact, a profound spiritual undertaking, especially in the multicultural settings in Southeast Asia. Composers need to be sensitive to the grammar of cultures, decipher the syntax and penetrate the semantics. Shoki Coe's student I-to Loh is the most accomplished church music composer and liturgist in the closing decades of the twentieth century. Up to the 1960s, most Asian hymn writers and composers mainly adopted Western musical style in their compositions. Churches mainly used Western hymns translated into local languages. Compositions from the 1970s showed more sensitive integration between lyrics and music. Loh was the driving force in contextualizing Asian church music. His use of monophony, scale and melodic character, nonlexical syllables, and symbolic acts in worship set a new standard of Asian church music. His innovative pan-Asian attempts in setting texts from one ethnic group to musical languages of another Asian ethnicity are a particularly significant present-day development. Most of his hymns are collected in the hymnal *Sound the Bamboo* that he and his colleague Francisco Feliciano edited.

Peoples in Southeast Asia traditionally associate music and musical instruments with political and spiritual powers. Gongs and drums are often regarded as the spiritual center of the ensemble. Music is imbued with religious significance, connecting peoples to the spiritual world. For example, ritual chanting (known as *timang*) is widely practiced among Ibans in Sarawak and Western Kalimantan. This spiritual significance is carried through to hymn singing among Christianized peoples in Southeast Asia. Congregational singing, in the form of exchange between choir or soloist and the congregation, takes on this spiritual significance.

Christians in Southeast Asia, however, have largely ignored their own intellectual and spiritual tradition. Western hymns and musical style continue to be popular in

Southeast Asia, especially among the young people in urban centers like Singapore and Manila. This is not merely due to the missionary legacies, but also to the role Western Christian music assumes in the globalizing age. It allows Christians in isolated societies and politically restrictive nations to see themselves as belonging to a larger transnational community.

Michael Nai-Chiu Poon

See also: Buddhism; Cambodia; Christian Conference of Asia; Colonialism; Communism; Confucianism; Contextualization; Federation of Asian Bishops' Conferences; Globalization; Hinduism; Interreligious Relations and Dialogue; Islam; Jesuits; Koyama, Kosuke; Laos; Liberation Theologies; Loh, I-to; Malaysia; Minorities; Missionary Movements; Music; Myanmar (Burma); Philippines; Religious Conversions; Secularism; Sin, Cardinal Jaime Lechica; Singapore; Thailand; Vietnam.

Further Reading

England, John C. *Asian Christian Theologies: A Research Guide to Authors, Movements, Sources.* 3 vols. Maryknoll, NY: Orbis, 2002.

Ginsburg, N. S., and J. E. Brush. *The Pattern of Asia.* Englewood Cliffs, NJ: Prentice-Hall, 1958.

Koyama, Kosuke. *Waterbuffalo Theology: A Thailand Theological Notebook.* Singapore: SPCK, 1970.

Loh, I-to. *In Search for Asian Sounds and Symbols in Worship.* Edited by Michael Poon. Singapore: Trinity Theological College, 2012.

Neill, Stephen C., and M. R. Mullins. "Christianity: Christianity in Asia." In *Encyclopedia of Religion,* edited by L. Jones. Detroit, MI: Macmillan Reference USA, 2005.

Poon, Michael. "The History and Development of Theological Education in South East Asia." In *Handbook of Theological Education in World Christianity,* edited by D. Werner, 375–403. Oxford: Regnum, 2010.

CHRISTMAS ISLAND

Christmas Island is a territory of Australia in the Indian Ocean. The island has no known indigenous people, and the place was uninhabited until the late nineteenth century. The geographic isolation of the island served for long as a natural barrier against human settlement there. Christmas Island has undergone exploration and annexation, mainly led by the various European colonial nations. Britain annexed the island in 1888, but in 1958, it was handed over to Australia. The Cocos (Keeling) Islands are located about 560 miles to the west of Christmas Island, and these two places together are called the Australian Indian Ocean Territories.

The residents of Christmas Island are a mixed ethnic group. While the majority of the people are of Chinese origin, there are smaller groups of European-Malay origin. The rich diversity of the island has helped the people there to adapt and blend, in the process creating an eclectic culture that is a mix of Chinese, Malay, Australian, and European traditions. Jan Adams and Marg Neale, who taught on Christmas Island in the 1980s, wrote a book titled *Christmas Island: The Early Years, 1888 to 1958: Historic Photographs with Many Untold Tales from the Early Years of Christmas Island, an Isolated Island in the Indian Ocean* that provide valuable information on the rich history of this land.

Buddhism is the religion of the majority of the people on Christmas Island. There are also sizable numbers of Muslims, Christians, and others. A Christian church, a Muslim mosque, and a Bahá'í center exist alongside a number of Chinese temples as well as Buddhist, Daoist, and Confucian places of worship. Despite a vast diversity in religions, languages, and races, the people of Christmas Island work together in harmony, freely sharing and borrowing from each other's traditions. The early Chinese and Malay immigrants to the island introduced strong religious and cultural practices; the ethnic festivals rooted in these practices are celebrated throughout the year. Major religious and cultural festivals such as Christmas, Easter, Chinese New Year, and Hari Raya are also observed by the whole community. The island is known for its religious harmony and tolerance.

From the late 1980s, refugees and asylum seekers from various countries have landed on Christmas Island. These people are often unwelcome guests and have to face tremendous hardship. In 2010, around 50 asylum seekers died as their boat crashed into the rocks near the island. Christian missionaries have been working, since 2009, among the refugees and asylum seekers. Proselytization and advocacy are not encouraged by the authorities and the missionaries are primarily involved in educational activities such as teaching English.

Jesudas M. Athyal

See also: Bahá'í Faith; Buddhism; Christianity; Cocos (Keeling) Islands; Confucianism; Contextualization; Diaspora; Daoism (Taoism); Ethnicity; Islam; Missionary Movements.

Further Reading

Adams, Jan, and Marg Neale. *Christmas Island: The Early Years, 1888 to 1958: Historic Photographs with Many Untold Tales from the Early Years of Christmas Island, an Isolated Island in the Indian Ocean.* Canberra, Australia: Bruce Neale, 1993.

"Christmas Island." *New World Encyclopedia.* http://www.newworldencyclopedia.org/entry/Christmas_Island (accessed September 18, 2014).

Narushima, Yuko. "Missionaries providing lessons for Christmas Island detainees." *Sydney Morning Herald*, July 2, 2009. http://www.smh.com.au/national/missionaries-providing-lessons-for-christmas-island-detainees-20090701-d594.html (accessed September 18, 2014).

Stokes, Tony. *Whatever Will Be, I'll See: Growing Up in the 1940s, 50s and 60s in the Northern Territory, Christmas and the Cocos (Keeling) Islands, New South Wales and the Australian Capital Territory, Volume I.* Privately published, 2012.

Trussel, Stephen. "The History and People of Christmas Island." http://www.trussel.com/kir/xmasi.htm (accessed September 18, 2014).

COCOS (KEELING) ISLANDS

A territory of Australia in the Indian Ocean, the Cocos (Keeling) Islands is a cluster of 27 islands. Due to the geographic isolation of the islands, they had remained uninhabited until the nineteenth century. The first settlement in the island was in 1826 by an English merchant, but even in the following decades, the residents there had little contact with the outside world. The British Empire annexed the islands in

1857, and in 1955, they were handed over to Australia. Christmas Island is located about 560 miles to the east of the Cocos Islands and these two places together are called the Australian Indian Ocean Territories. The main languages of the Cocos Islands are a Cocos dialect of Malay and English.

The total population of the Cocos Islands is only 600 people, and they live on the two inhabited islands—West Island and Home Island. The majority of the residents are of Malay ethnic background, most of whom live on Home Island, while the ethnic Europeans—the minority group—live on West Island. Islam is the religion of the majority of the people, and most of them are of Malay origin. There is an Islamic Council of Cocos Keeling Islands that oversees the welfare of the Muslims. There are also a Cocos (Keeling) Islands Muslim Small Business Association and a few mosques. The Christians on the islands are largely Europeans and Australians with a few Chinese, and they are affiliated to a number of denominations. While the Anglicans are part of the Anglican Church of Australia, the Catholics are under the jurisdiction of the Archdiocese of Perth, Australia. Apart from Muslims and Christians, there are also small groups of Bahá'í and Chinese folk religionists.

The Cocos Islands were, for a long time, a private and commercial property, and religion there was rarely a matter of public concern. As a territory under Australia, the islands permit all residents the freedom to profess and practice the religion of their choice. While traditionally, the majority of the islanders were affiliated to Islam or mainline Christianity, younger religious groups such as the Pentecostals and Charismatics are gaining ground in the twenty-first century. The number of people who are not affiliated to any religious group is also on the rise. In general, the islanders are held together by a sense of solidarity rooted in shared cultural practices, religious beliefs, and close family ties.

Jesudas M. Athyal

See also: Bahá'í Faith; Christianity; Christmas Island; Diaspora; Ethnicity; Islam.

Further Reading

Bunce, Pauline. *The Cocos (Keeling) Islands: Australian Atolls in the Indian Ocean*. Victoria: John Wiley & Sons Australia Ltd, 1988.

"Cocos (Keeling) Islands." http://www.regional.gov.au/territories/Cocos_Keeling/ (accessed October 17, 2014).

Islamic Council of Cocos Keeling Islands. http://www.islamicfinder.org/getitWorld.php ?id=35222 (accessed September 18, 2014).

Mullen, Ken. *Cocos Keeling: The Islands Time Forgot*. Sydney: Angus & Robertson, 1974.

Stokes, Tony. *Whatever Will Be, I'll See: Growing Up in the 1940s, 50s and 60s in the Northern Territory, Christmas and the Cocos (Keeling) Islands, New South Wales and the Australian Capital Territory, Volume I*. Privately published, 2012.

COLONIALISM

Since prehistoric times, the region of Southeast Asia has been influenced by external forces. Most such contacts, at least in the early stages, were at the level of trade and commerce. China and India were key players in this process, influencing not only

Viet Minh troops celebrating after the transfer of power from the French in 1954. The Viet Minh, or League for the Independence of Vietnam, was formed on May 19, 1941, and sought to free Vietnam from the French. (Howard Sochurek/Getty Images)

trade but also the cultures and religions of the region. The history of colonialism in Southeast Asia in the modern times, however, is understood largely as starting with the intervention of the European nations in the region from the sixteenth century onward. The European contacts, initially for the purposes of trade and commerce, eventually led to colonization. Even as the Asian empires and kingdoms grew weaker, the Europeans consolidated their strength in the region. By the 1800s, the Europeans were in a position to exert their authority over much of Southeast Asia. The only country in the region that remained independent during the long period of colonization was Thailand.

Religion played a key role in the colonization of Southeast Asia. The "Christian" European countries provided the churches, both Catholic and Protestant, with a climate conducive to encourage the arrival of missionaries in the colonized lands. This alliance between colonialism and Christian mission, in most cases, led to the colonization of non-Christian peoples by Christian nations. In this sense, it can be argued that the modern Christian mission originated in the context of Western colonialism.

Primarily, six Western countries had colonies in Southeast Asia: France, Portugal, the Netherlands, Great Britain, Spain, and the United States. Portugal, the first European colonizing nation in the region, had only a minimal impact there. The Portuguese conquered Malacca in 1511 and held it till the Dutch captured it in 1641. Other than that, Portugal was in control of only a small portion of land on the island of Timor. The colonization of the Netherlands in Southeast Asia, on the other hand, fell into two periods: the first was the 1600s and 1700s when the

Dutch East India Company was active in the region. The Company's primary interest was in trade and commerce, not political control. After the Company collapsed, however, the Dutch government came into the scene and tried to bring the Indonesian archipelago under its control. That was the second phase that culminated in the Second World War, after which the Indonesians put up a stiff resistance against Dutch colonialism. In 1949, after four years of fighting, the people of Indonesia gained their independence.

Spain has a long history of colonization in Southeast Asia. The Spaniards gained control over the Philippines in the sixteenth century, but they were defeated in the Spanish-American War in 1898. Another European power in the region, Great Britain, which had conquered India, conquered also the neighboring Burma and controlled it as a province of India. The Burmese people, therefore, had two sets of rulers—the British, who were the ultimate authorities, and the Indians, who were the intermediate power. Soon after India became independent of the British, the Burmese too gained their independence in 1948. Apart from Burma, the other areas in Southeast Asia that were under British control were Penang, Singapore, and Malacca. All these places too eventually became independent. France, yet another European colonial power in Southeast Asia, captured Saigon in Vietnam in 1859. The French subsequently moved west and north and, by the early twentieth century, completed the conquest of Indochina. After the Second World War, as the decolonization process gained momentum in Southeast Asia, the Vietnamese rejected French rule and became independent in 1954.

The United States, among the last Western powers to have a colonial presence in Southeast Asia, moved into the Philippines toward the end of the nineteenth century, as a result of its peace accord with Spain. Following the Philippine-American War a few years later, however, the U.S. government gradually started withdrawing from the region, and the Philippines attained complete independence in 1946. Not only were European nations and the United States involved in the colonization of Southeast Asia; there were also Asian nations. In particular, the role played by Japan is important. During the Second World War, the Japanese Imperial Army invaded the region and reached Burma, Indonesia, Vietnam, and the Philippines. When Britain ended its protectorate of the Sultanate of Brunei in 1984, it marked the end of nearly five centuries of European colonization in Southeast Asia.

The long history of colonization in Southeast Asia eventually culminated in vibrant decolonization movements in most of the region. Nationalist movements, active in most countries in the region, imparted a considerable degree of self-respect and an urge for self-rule to the Asian nations. The Eastern spiritual ethos ensured that anticolonial struggles, while vibrant and violent at times, did not lead to excessively bloody consequences. The decolonization movements gained momentum during the Second World War, following which the United Nations was established, thus creating a platform for the erstwhile colonialists and the colonized to relate to each other as equal partners. The Commonwealth of Nations, a fellowship of Great Britain and her erstwhile colonies, is another such forum.

In the second half of the twentieth century, the process of decolonization in most of Southeast Asia was replaced by "neocolonialism," characterized by the geopolitical practice of using the globalization of capitalism and cultural hegemony— often by Western and wealthier nations—to control a poorer nation or society. Multinational corporations that exploit the labor and natural resources of erstwhile colonies, often with the backing of former colonizers, play a key role in the neocolonization process. Of recent, "outsourcing" that involves the offshoring and relocation of a business, often from a richer nation to a poorer one, has become an important part of neocolonization. While trade and commerce played a key role in the physical colonization of a nation in earlier centuries, it is paradoxical that trade and commerce is once again the primary component of neocolonization.

The colonial era, like all other phases in history, will be scrutinized closely and judged for its contributions and shortcomings. While colonization, in general, resulted in the exploitation and marginalization of the colonized people and nations, the account is more complex in nations that had peoples who were domestically oppressed. There were cases where the minority groups of a nation who were exploited for long by the elite and the dominant classes of the same nation found the colonization by an alien nation to be a welcome change that eased their burden of oppression. However, it can safely be argued that, by and large, colonization was among the most dehumanizing chapters in human history that exploited and oppressed the poorer nations and people of the world.

Jesudas M. Athyal

See also: Brunei Darussalam; Christianity; Globalization; Humanism; Indonesia; Liberation Theologies; Minorities; Missionary Movements; Myanmar (Burma); Nationalism; Orientalism; Philippines; Timor Leste (East Timor); Vietnam.

Further Reading

Dharmaraj, Jacob S. *Colonialism and Christian Mission: Postcolonial Reflections.* Delhi: ISPCK, 1993.

Emerson, R. (1937). *Malaysia: A Study in Direct and Indirect Rule.* New York: Macmillan Company, 1937.

Furnivall, J. S. *Colonial Policy and Practice: A Comparative Study of Burma and Netherlands India.* New York: New York University Press, 1956.

Kahin, George McTurnan. *Nationalism and Revolution in Indonesia.* Ithaca, NY: Cornell University Press, 1952.

Marr, David G. *Vietnamese Anti-Colonialism 1885–1925.* Berkeley: University of California Press, 1971.

Patti, Archimedes L. A. *Why Vietnam? Prelude to America's Albatross.* Berkeley: University of California Press, 1980.

COMMUNISM

Communism and religion have a long-standing antagonistic relationship with each other, and Southeast Asia has not been an exception to this global phenomenon. Yet, both also have factors of mutuality that are unique to the region. While religiosity is an everyday reality for most Asians, Communism offered, for the oppressed and marginalized sections of the society, relief and liberation, and a new social order that was rooted in equality and justice. Alongside religion, Communism too, therefore, took a strong foothold in several parts of the region. This entry will briefly examine the relationship between these two forces—Communism and religion—in the Southeast Asian context with a specific focus on the areas where they converge and diverge.

Religion, Nationalism, Communism

While Communism had minimal influence in Southeast Asia prior to 1940, in the following decades, the battle between Communism and anti-Communism is seen as central to the history of the region. Several reasons can be cited for this, the primary one being the Cold War during which the U.S.-led Western nations made a concerted attempt to "contain Communism" all over the world, Southeast Asia included. This move eventually led to the direct military intervention of the United States and to the prolonged and protracted conflict in Indochina—commonly called the "Vietnam War"—involving Vietnam, Laos, and Cambodia that lasted for almost two decades, until 1975.

Even before U.S. intervention in the region, the Communist movement was present in several parts of Southeast Asia. The Indonesian Communist Party (Indonesian: *Partai Komunis Indonesia*, PKI) was at one point the strongest Communist party outside the Soviet Union and China. President Sukarno's policy of "Guided Democracy" under the principle of NASAKOM (Religion, Nationalism, Communism) initially not only favored PKI, but also helped to foster a healthy relationship between the Communist Party and Islam, in the largest Muslim-majority nation in the world. However, PKI's growing popularity, with membership running to the millions, threatened the balancing act between the Communists, the military, and Islamic groups. The ascendancy of PKI was viewed with suspicion by not only the rulers of Indonesia, but also the United States and several other anti-Communist Western powers. In the massacre of 1965, PKI was crushed and hundreds of thousands of its members systematically murdered. General Suharto, who succeeded Sukarno as president, introduced the "New Order," which was predominantly marked by the depoliticization of Islam.

Hasan Raid, one of the members of PKI who survived the massacre, later published his autobiography, titled *The Struggles of a Muslim Communist*. Raid outlined the common features between Communism and Islam and affirmed that, in a social context characterized by inequality and injustice, the messages of both religion and Communism are the same—a call for radical social transformation. According to Raid, the goal of the Communist Party and the Muslims should be to fight for truth and justice on all fronts so that there is no further violence or injustice in the society.

Communism and Religion, Converge and Diverge

Myanmar (Burma) offers another context in which the forces of military, religion and Communism intertwined in the public sphere. Founded in 1939, the Communist Party of Burma (CPB) has the distinction of being the oldest existing political party in the country. The party has a long history of anti-imperialist struggles against the British Empire, and later against the indigenous military rulers of the country. The military banned CPB and also published a widely distributed pamphlet titled *Dhammantaraya* (Dhamma in Danger) that announced to the public that the Communists were enemies of Buddhism. The CPB met this offensive with another publication, *Rip off the Mask*, that reaffirmed the Communists' support for Buddhism and also for the individual's freedom to practice any religion.

No other country in Southeast Asia was as much in the frontline of the Cold War as Vietnam. The country had to go through a prolonged war during this volatile period. While the Americans steadfastly opposed the Vietnamese Communists, the Communist Party of Vietnam (CPV) and the nationalist anticolonial movement had a symbiotic relationship with each other, and therefore, during most of its history, the Communist movement was welcomed by the public as a legitimate voice of Vietnamese nationalism.

In the postwar period, the relationship between religion and Communism took diverse forms in Vietnam. The Buddhist Church of Vietnam (or, Buddhist *Sangha* of Vietnam) was formed in the North with the patronage of the government, but a Unified Buddhist Church that opposed the Communist government continued to operate in the South. In general, since the war, the government has granted greater freedom for the practice of religion. The "Pure Land Buddhism" formed in 2007 is officially recognized by the government and has wide support among the public. The world-renowned Buddhist leader Thich Nhat Hanh has been working, since 2005, to facilitate better relationship between the Communist government and Buddhism in his homeland of Vietnam. It is also important to note that unlike Burma and Tibet, where Buddhist monks took to the streets to protest authoritarian governments, Vietnam has not seen any such violent protests led by the clergy, partly due to the space that is available for communication and limited cooperation between the Communists and the Buddhists.

Social Transformation

In the Philippines, there is a long history of collaboration between the Communists and Christians. Long before the Roman Catholic Church under the leadership of Cardinal Sin got involved in the protest movement against President Marcos, in the 1970s itself, several radical priests were already working alongside the New People's Army (NPA), which was the armed wing of the Communist Party of the Philippines. Inspired by the spirit of the Second Vatican Council and the theology of liberation movement, these priests affirmed the need for the Christian Church to identify itself with the oppressed and marginalized sections of the society and to work alongside them for radical social transformation. NPA also worked closely with the Basic Christian Community (BCC) movement for awareness building, especially in the rural areas and Christian parishes of the Philippines. The programs of NPA, however, often resulted in violence and bloodshed, which were not endorsed by the church.

The post–Cold War period characterized by the decline of Communism in many places around the world had a profound impact in Southeast Asia as well. Among other factors, the traditional hostility of mainline Communism toward religion too contributed to the decline of the Communist movement. Consequently, several countries in the region banned Communist parties and in other places, Communism declined for a variety of reasons. Yet, in the latter part of the twentieth century, Neo-Communist movements that function beyond the traditional Marxist framework have emerged with a willingness to work with all progressive sections including religion. These leftist groups, along with the religious sections that affirm reformation and social justice, have been involved in struggles against common threats—the militarization of Southeast Asia, the forces of globalization and economic liberalization active in the region, religious fundamentalism, and sectarianism.

Jesudas M. Athyal

See also: Atheism/Agnosticism; Buddhism; Cambodia; Christianity; Fundamentalism; Hanh, Thich Nhat; Indonesia; Islam; Myanmar (Burma); Nationalism; Philippines; Secularism; Singapore; Vietnam.

Further Reading

Anderson, Benedict. *The Spectre of Comparisons: Nationalism, Southeast Asia and the World.* Brooklyn, New York: Verso, 1998.

Duiker, William J. *The Communist Road to Power in Vietnam.* Boulder, CO: Westview Press, 1996.

Johnson, Kay. "The Fighting Monks of Vietnam." *Time,* March 2, 2007. http://www.time.com/time/world/article/0,8599,1595721,00.html (accessed September 18, 2014).

Parsa, Misagh. *States, Ideologies, and Social Revolutions: A Comparative Analysis of Iran, Nicaragua and the Philippines.* Cambridge: Cambridge University Press, 2000.

Raid, Hasan. "The Struggles of a Muslim Communist." http://mrzine.monthlyreview.org/2011/raid090311.html (accessed September 18, 2014).

CONFUCIANISM

From within the spiritual and intellectual ferment of the sixth century BCE, which gave rise to the voices of the Buddha and Lao Tzu, emerged the teaching of "Kung-fu-tzu," more commonly known to us today as Confucius (551–479 BCE). This great teacher drew from ancient truths in order to make them relevant to the development of order and harmony in the midst of social chaos. During a particularly turbulent time in Chinese social and political history, this quest became primary, generating several strategies for the road ahead. The most prominent philosophical voice to emerge during this period was that of Confucius, and thus "Confucianism" was born, built upon the application of age-old truths in the context of the present and the future. The Confucian focus on developing a harmonious, just, and ordered society has been influential beyond the realm of China and has made a significant impact within Southeast Asia, particularly in those areas that have had historical encounters with China, including Vietnam and Singapore.

The "Analects," the name given to the collective teachings of Confucianism, have been one of the most influential texts in world history. The "Five Classics" of Confucius include the celebrated *Yiging,* or *I Ching,* a book that explores the ancient

A statue of Confucius at the Quan Cong temple in Hoi An, Vietnam. The temple was founded in 1653 and is dedicated to Quan Cong, a revered Chinese general who lived in the 3rd century CE. (Luca Tettoni/Passage/Corbis)

secrets of life and introduces the interaction of the *yin* (feminine, passive, Earth) and *yang* (masculine, aggressive, Heaven).

The most effective way to overcome the chaos generated during the early period of the Chou dynasty was to return to the stability of classical virtues. Eminently rooted in a "this-worldly" approach, Confucius was more concerned with life before death than after it, more concerned with the sacred in the midst of the world rather than beyond it. Social harmony is developed through generating an effective system geared toward individual character building, which in turn allows for society to flourish. The relationship between the person and community becomes intertwined, avoiding the extremes of narcissistic individualism or exclusive communalism.

A review of Chinese influence in the Southeast Asian region throughout history will naturally lead us to a study of the influence Confucianism had around the world. As one of China's "Three Teachings," alongside Buddhism and Daoism, Confucianism's considerable influence, in the realm of philosophical and religious thought, ethics, and rituals stretches across Southeast Asia, penetrating deep into the culture of the Chinese diaspora. Stephen Prothero may be correct in suggesting that it is impossible to understand present-day life in Singapore or Vietnam, for example, without recognizing the "long shadow" of Confucianism.

Adrian Bird

In order to develop wise leaders, wisdom must be crafted and nurtured appropriately, and this is most effectively done through education. The capacity of the human to be good and to avoid evil is dependent on effective education, establishing self-disciple set within the broader confines of social relationships. The centrality of education is not reduced to the process of knowledge acquisition, but is understood more broadly as a process of character development. It is a way humans are nurtured to become fully human. While ethics is central to the teaching within Confucianism, this is not intended as a fixed set of dos and don'ts, but rather as a way of encouraging wisdom and participation in the service of greater social harmony. Becoming fully human is to become wise to the virtues of life together, and to applying these virtues to day-to-day living.

Within Confucianism there are five essential relationships central to the development of personal and social ethics, between: father and son; subject and ruler; husband and wife; elder brother and younger brother; and friend and friend. These relationships (in theory if not always in practice), are based on mutuality in order to promote social harmony. Let the ruler be the ruler, and the elder brother the elder brother; but this role must be implemented without abusing power within the relationship. Disharmony occurs when these relationships do not allow for essential mutuality and accountability. Disharmony within a society also comes when either a person does not know his or her role within society or fails to effectively fulfil that role. Conformity to social etiquette is central to Confucianism in seeking to establish personal human flourishing and a flourishing society. It begins with filial piety, nurturing relationships within the family, expanding into all aspects of life and to all social relationships.

The influence of Confucianism in Southeast Asia comes as a result of the encounter with China, which quickly became established as one of China's "Three Teachings" alongside Buddhism and Daoism. During long periods of Chinese rule in Vietnam, one of the more welcome influences was that of Confucian teaching. Since independence in the latter part of the tenth century, Vietnam has maintained its interest in Confucian ideas, in particularly the rich Confucian emphasis on education, disciple, learning, and the respect of teachers. Though Vietnam has faced many challenges through conflict and a lack of natural resources, education is acknowledged as both a hope and source for human resource development within the country. While there have been many ideological and political influences within Vietnam, the "invisible hand" of Confucian principles remains a constant.

Confucianism has also had a significant presence in Singapore as a result of Chinese migration. Making up three-quarters of Singapore's resident population, Singaporean Chinese highlight the merging of religious identity between Buddhism and Daoism. Though Confucianism is not given the same "religious" status within general census polls, given its association with humanism, the influence of Confucianism remains significant. Yet to dismiss Confucianism as nonreligious is perhaps more a criticism of traditional understandings of religion, prompting us to reevaluate what it means to be religious. Indeed, Confucianism comprises a range of interrelated components, including philosophy, anthropology, ethics, politics, and theology, all of which become important in a broader understanding of social

order and harmony. While the impact of Confucianism in Singapore remains difficult to quantify, the role of Confucianism in providing important intellectual resources in the process of establishing Singapore as one of the four economic
"Asian Tigers" remains an interesting point of debate.

Adrian Bird

See also: Buddhism; Daoism (Taoism); Education; Humanism; Lao Tzu (Laozi);
Religion and Society; Singapore; Thien Buddhism; Vietnam.

Further Reading

Brock, Colin, and Lorrane Pe Symaco. *Education in South-East Asia*. Oxford Studies in
    Comparative Education. Oxford: Symposium Books, 2011.
Fisher, Mary Pat. *Living Religions: An Encyclopaedia of the World's Faiths*. London and
    New York: I. B. Tauris Publishers, 1997.
Gomes, Gabriel J. *Discovering World Religions: A Guide for the Inquiring Reader*. Bloomington,
    IN: iUniverse, 2012.
Leibo, Steven A. *East and Southeast Asia: The World Today Series*. 45th ed. Lanham, MD:
    Stryker-Post Publications, 2012.
Oxtoby, Willard G., and Alan F. Segal, eds. *A Concise Introduction to World Religions*. Oxford:
    Oxford University Press, 2007.
Prothero, Stephen. *God is Not One: The Eight Rival Religions that Run the World, and Why their
    Differences Matter*. New York: HarperOne Publishers, 2010.

CONTEXTUALIZATION

In religious studies, "contextualization" refers to the adaptation of sacred scriptures,
concepts, and practices within a distinct social and cultural environment by integrating nontheological aspects of such an environment into the thus contextualized
religion, and by assigning new meaning to formerly established religious ideas and
customs as a means to reinterpret them within the new theological framework. As
a distinct concept, contextualization is most developed in Christian missiology,
although as a practice it also exists in other proselytizing world religions, particularly Islam, but also Buddhism and Hinduism. In Christianity, the term usually
refers to the adaptation of church liturgy, art and music, preaching and theology
to the traditional practices and ethos of an indigenous community. Notably this is
not just a matter of translation, but rather one of reappropriation. It is believed that,

When Catholics were persecuted and killed in early nineteenth-century Vietnam under
Emperor Canh Tinh, an appearance of the Virgin Mary surprised them while hiding in
the jungle. Wearing traditional Vietnamese clothing and surrounded by angels, the
Holy Virgin appeared to teach them how to cure illness with herbal infusions. This localized miracle has, in turn, transformed some aspects of universal Catholic theology since
Pope John Paul II recognized the importance of the apparition. More than a dozen
churches outside of Vietnam now bear the name of Our Lady of La Vang.

Christian Oesterheld

in consequence, both the sociocultural context and the contextualized religion undergo a transformation.

The term "contextualization" is sometimes used interchangeably with other concepts, such as "inculturation," "localization" (and derived from this "local theology") or "indigenization," or simply "adaption" and "accommodation." Beyond the indigenization of Christian faith, contextualization in the broadest sense is presently also discussed in relation to the localization of world religions more generally; in Southeast Asia, this includes particularly Buddhism, Hinduism, and Islam. However, most studies on non-Christian world religions prefer to adopt the more neutral categories of indigenization or localization, since "contextualization" has become a firmly established concept of Christian (Protestant) missiology, with "inculturation" as its Catholic pendant. Nevertheless, the theological use of the two terms dates back to the 1970s only. The Taiwanese philosopher and theologian Shoki Coe is credited with having first introduced a distinct concept of contextualization during a 1972 World Council of Churches consultation (see Wheeler 2002). The exact origins of the catholic idea of inculturation remain unclear. Its first use in official Vatican documents is attributed to John Paul II in his "Apostolic Exhortation on Catechesis' (Catechesi Tradendae) of October 1979 (see Schineller 1990), prepared by discussions during the Second Vatican Council (1962–1965), particularly the influential encyclical 'Joy and Hope" (Gaudium et Spes). Since the 1980s, both terms have been commonly used in theology and missiology and generated a broad range of research, practical application, and conceptual discussions.

Although terminologically, "contextualization" and "inculturation" appear to be fairly novel inventions, the missiological practices they refer to are as old as the church itself. They date back to the earliest days of Christian missionary work in the apostolic age, when the church expanded from the Judaic to the Hellenistic world and beyond, encountering diverse cultural traditions. This holds to be true until the Middle Ages, with St. Patrick's mission in Ireland often evoked as a significant episode of contextualization. However, during the colonial expansion of European powers toward the Americas, Africa, and Asia, Christian missions seem to have become less adaptable to their newly encountered, exotic surroundings. As a result, more Eurocentric and dogmatic varieties of theological interpretation and liturgical life have dominated the missionary endeavor until around the mid-twentieth century. Notable exceptions to this are some of the early Jesuit missions in various parts of Asia, who engaged in a fruitful dialogue with local cultures and religions, often despite disapproval from the Vatican. Probably best known among them are Roberto de Nobili in India, Alessandro Valignano in Japan, and Matteo Ricci in China, who integrated local cultural concepts into Christian theology.

Histories of Contextualization in Southeast Asia

Historically, the region of Southeast Asia has been heavily influenced by Indian, Chinese, and Arabic cultures, and political realms in the region have, sometimes in turn, been Buddhist polities, Hindu kingships, or Islamic sultanates. All of these cultural and religious traditions have been strongly localized, leading to novel forms of "Javanese" Islam, "Balinese" Hinduism, or "Thai" and 'Khmer' Buddhism, among others. During the Islamization of Java, for example, animistic and Hindu-Buddhist cultural elements were often tolerated in various forms of folk Islam but have also been retained at some of the Javanese courts. This resulted in syncretic traditions like the *kebatinan* ("inwardness"), a localized amalgam of traditional religious ideas, mystic Hindu elements, and Islamic teachings with strong influences of Sufism. Localized Javanese Islam also recognizes a number of local saints, particularly the Wali Songa, whose graves have become destinations for local pilgrimages, historically acknowledged as a form of minor *hajj*.

Being the religion of colonial overlords, one would assume that Christianity, on the contrary, eluded such processes of localization and indigenization. However, belying the widespread assumption of the early Christian missions' complicity with colonial regimes, it seems that a great number of missionaries in Southeast Asia did not attempt to "Europeanize" their converts. Like in China and India, Jesuit missionaries were the most prominent proponents of contextual Christianity in the sixteenth and seventeenth centuries. St. Francis Xavier (1506–1552), for example, one of the earliest missionaries to Asia, urged for a dialogue with local traditions and the use of native languages in preaching—at a time when the church in Europe still insisted on the fully Latinized Mass. He is credited with having converted more people than anybody else since the apostle St. Paul, including thousands in Southeast Asia, and was able to establish Christianity as an alternative modernity for the indigenous population formerly subjected to their regional overlords at the Hindu and increasingly Islamized courts. In the late sixteenth and early seventeenth centuries, a similar strategy was pursued by Francisco Blancas de San Jose, a Dominican missionary to the Philippines. In his sermons, he discussed the institution of serfdom and peonage and offered the voluntary submission to Jesus Christ as an alternative. His *Sermones* were published in Tagalog, making them accessible to a growing Christian community in the Philippines. The still continuing use of the old Tagalog term for local rulers, *panginoon* (or *panginuan*), as a translation for the Lord Jesus, stems from this time. Similarly, in Indonesia, the term *Tuhan Yesus* is based on the old Malay term for court dignitaries, *tuan*.

Indeed, some of the most fundamental issues of theological contextualization during the early missionary period arose from matters of biblical and liturgical translation. Concepts such as that of an "almighty God," the "trinity" or "salvation" did not exist in Southeast Asian languages, and the most suitable correspondents needed to be figured out, often adapting Christian terminology to established religious ideas. This even included the reconceptualization of terms that had earlier been adopted from other world religions and had become part of "local" vernaculars by the time Christian missionary work began in the region. In the Philippines, early missionaries extended the denotation of the supreme god in the local pantheon, *Bathalang Maykapal* (from Sanskrit *Bhattara Guru*), to the Christian idea of God. Similarly, in Indonesia and the Malay world, *Allah* is (still) used in Bible translations and Christian prayers, although recently this has been outlawed for Malaysian Christians by religious state agencies. The issue of translation becomes inherently theological when considered a matter of conceptual appropriation. "Bread" in the

Christian prayer Our Father, for example, cannot easily be translated into "rice" due to the variety of terms in each local language used to refer to a particular sort, state, or preparation of "rice." Consequently, local versions of the Our Father may use more abstract terms indicating the desire for God's basic care beyond the provision of mere nutrition (e.g. *kanin* in Filipino, or *rejeki* in Indonesian).

Matters of translation during the early missionary encounters in Southeast Asia were not limited to the appropriation of Christian concepts. There were also attempts to indigenize style and form of biblical scriptures and liturgical texts. Amid the usually more puritan and pietistic agenda of the early nineteenth century, the Protestant missionary Coenrad L. Coolen restyled the Psalms in the form of traditional Javanese poetry (*macapat*), made use of the form of Muslim prayer in local versions of the Confession of Faith, or accommodated biblical stories in the recitative style (*suluk*) of the Javanese shadow play (*wayang*), linking Christ to the focal point of Javanese messianic expectations, the *Ratu Adil* or "Just King" (Poplawska 2011, 188–89).

It should be stressed that these early visions of contextual theology were personal strategies of some missionaries and do not represent a systematic ecclesiastic approach. Many were concentrated in certain areas of Hindu-Islamic maritime Southeast Asia. On the predominantly Buddhist mainland, for example in Thailand and Cambodia, the lack of success of Christian missionaries is often attributed to their disrespect for local culture and lifestyles. An exception to this is the French Jesuit missionary Alexandre de Rhodes (1591–1660), who successfully proselytized in Vietnam, adapting Christian theology to local concepts, and creating a Latinized version of the Vietnamese language that is still used as the official national language today (Phan 1998). In the early twentieth century, there were some missionaries, like Father Franz von Lith (1863–1926), who called for a "local, situational, or relevant theology" (cited in Poplawska 2011, 189). Yet only in 1974, in the wake of the Second Vatican Council, the Federation of Asian Bishops' Conferences (FABC) promulgated a "dialogue of life" as the most urgent task for the church in Asia, particularly including the dialogue with Asian culture(s) as well as with the "great religious traditions of Asia" (Lambino 1987, 72).

Local Theology in Contemporary Southeast Asia

The diversity of Southeast Asian cultural and socioreligious traditions poses a challenge to endeavors of contextualization, but at the same time, it provides many opportunities and diverse possible avenues. Southeast Asian theologies seek mutual enrichment of universal Christian values and concepts and local cultures by contextualizing the Gospels both vis-à-vis traditional practices and institutions (e.g., the prevalence of healers and "wise men," or communal rituals to celebrate spiritual differentiation), and in relation to scriptural and oral traditions of mythology (often localized forms of the Hindu epics *Ramayana* and *Mahabharata*, but also indigenous cosmologies). The conceptual richness of local theologies in the region is difficult to grasp in a brief review. However, some common themes can be identified as: first, interpretations of the role of Jesus Christ; second, localizations of the ecclesiastical community and its social responsibility; and third, the indigenization of liturgy and church architecture.

The outlook of contemporary Southeast Asian Christology has been discussed during a Special Asian Synod in the Vatican, resulting in the document "Church in Asia" (*Ecclesia in Asia*), officially promulgated by Pope John Paul II in 1999. In order to appeal to Asian cultural and religious sensibilities, this exhortation suggests "Jesus Christ as the Teacher of Wisdom, the Healer, the Liberator, the Spiritual Guide, the Enlightened One, the Compassionate Friend of the Poor, the Good Samaritan, the Good Shepherd, the Obedient One." These characterizations of Jesus Christ allude to themes, which had been developed locally since the 1970s. Jesus as a "Teacher of Wisdom," for example, corresponds to social values of respect for the experience and knowledge of the elders throughout many Southeast Asian cultures, or to the Hindu-Javanese idea of a *guru* more particularly. In 1977, the influential Jesuit priest J. B. Bannawiratma published his master's thesis on *Jesus the Guru*, discussing Christian theological encounters with Javanese cultural traditions and comparing depictions of Jesus as a teacher in the Gospel of St. John with Javanese shadow play (*wayang*) stories, e.g., those where the small spirit of Dewa Ruci wisely instructs the giant Bima (see Steenbrink 2000, 2–3). The concept of "Jesus as Healer" proves to be even more widely applicable. With a still incomplete medical infrastructure in rural Southeast Asia, people continue to seek treatment from ritual specialists, and ideas of magical and spiritual healing are widespread, readily accommodating the miraculous qualities of faith. Currently, charismatic movements, both Protestant and Catholic, tend to focus on this aspect. Probably the most contentious concept for a contemporary Southeast Asian Christology is the imagination of Jesus as a "Liberator" and "Compassionate Friend of the Poor," reflecting a quest for peace and justice in some regional (and temporal) schools of liberation theology, especially in the Philippines during the period of martial law, or in the context of West Papua's independence struggle.

Due to the minority status of Christianity in most of contemporary Southeast Asia, contemporary ecclesiology in the region emphasizes the significance of "family networks of evangelism and homes as places of hospitality" (Farhadian 2010, 109), thereby likening Southeast Asian Christian communities to (fictive) kinship systems bound by a shared faith. This might explain the recent expansion of evangelical Christianity in the region, as well as the long-standing tradition of alternative socio-religious movements and independent churches in regions where mainstream Christianity had long taken root, e.g., the Iglesia ni Cristo, or the Aglipayan Church in the Philippines.

The indigenization of church architecture, music, and liturgy, which gradually evolved since the late nineteenth and early twentieth centuries, has presently developed into a rich and complex artistic landscape, representing the cultural diversity of Southeast Asia. Hymnals include a variety of local tunes and traditional instruments have largely replaced guitars and keyboards during church services (see Poplawska 2011). Church buildings can be remindful of Hindu and Buddhist temples, or of traditional clan houses and communal halls, ornamented with indigenous designs and often integrating pre-Christian concepts in their spatial arrangements.

In Catholic churches, images and statues show Jesus and Mary with Asian faces, crowned by local regalia and dressed in traditional attire. The church liturgy often includes indigenous dances or other forms of traditional performances. A good example for this is the development of *wayang wahyu*, a Christian form of shadow theater using biblical characters as an alternative way of "reading" the Holy Scriptures.

As mentioned earlier, contextualization might be conceptually most pronounced in Christianity, but as practice, it can also be found in other world religions in contemporary Southeast Asia. Rural versions of folk Buddhism in mainland Southeast Asia, for example, continue to acknowledge the existence of local spirits (*phi* in Thai, *nat* in Burmese, or *neak ta* in Khmer), and ordained monks sometimes double as shamanistic healers. In contrast to Christianity, however, such processes of contextualization in Buddhism are less institutionalized and often lack formal authorization from national Buddhist organizations. Likewise, in Indonesia, localized versions of Islam, like the *kebatinan*, are still popular, although a tendency toward the purification of Islamic beliefs and practices can be noted, propagated by increasingly fundamentalist organizations like the Islamic Defenders' Front (*Front Pembela Islam*). With easier access to the holy sites of Islam in Mecca and Medina, due to cheaper airfares and offers of organized *hajj* travel packages, the significance of local sacred sites on the island of Java has been decreasing as well.

Christian Oesterheld

See also: Buddhism; Christianity; Colonialism; Federation of Asian Bishops' Conferences; Hinduism; Interreligious Relations and Dialogue; Islam; Jesuits; Khmer Buddhism; Loh, I-to; Localization of Hinduism in Indonesia; Messianic Movements; Minorities; Missionary Movements; Music; Study of Religion; Wali Sanga (Wali Songo).

Further Reading

Farhadian, Charles E. "A Missiological Reflection on Present-Day Christian Movements in Southeast Asia." In *Christian Movements in Southeast Asia: A Theological Exploration*, edited by Michael Nai-Chiu Poon, 101–20. Singapore: Trinity Theological College 2010.

Lambino, Antonio B. "Inculturation in Asia: Going beyond First Gear." *Landas* 1 (1987): 72–80.

Phan, Peter C. *Mission and Catechesis: Alexandre de Rhodes and Inculturation in Seventeenth-Century Vietnam.* Maryknoll, NY: Orbis Books, 1998.

Poplawska, Marzanna. "Christianity and Inculturated Music in Indonesia." *Southeast Review of Asian Studies* 33 (2011): 186–98.

Schineller, Peter. *A Handbook on Inculturation.* New York: Paulist Press, 1990.

Steenbrink, Karel. "Five Catholic Theologians of Indonesia in Search for an International or Local Identity." *Exchange* 29 (2000): 2–22.

Wheeler, Ray. "The Legacy of Shoki Coe." *International Bulletin of Missionary Research* 26 (2002): 77–80.

D

DANCE AND DRAMA (THEATER)

In Southeast Asian states, traditional performing arts are strongly intertwined with the expression of religious beliefs. Across the region, theater and dance constitute a way to perform another dimension of reality in which it is possible to interact with magic and supernatural domains. The religious significance of dance and drama spans social and cultural categories; performing arts are both a tool of royal elites to associate themselves with the sacred, and a fundamental component of rural spirituality around continuity and renewal. As a result of centuries of war, trade, and cultural influence, customs of dance, drama, and theater in multiple countries in the region share fundamental characteristics with particular adaptations to form and content.

The function of religious performing arts is to provide a medium through which a group of persons can communicate and interact with gods and deities, ancestors' spirits, or other supernatural entities that this group identifies as a source of protection. In such a context, dance and drama are primarily collective offerings. The performance is a response to the needs (health, power, fertility, maintenance of the cosmic order) of the community that anticipates or rewards some level of benefit in exchange for enactment. The content of the plot and the way it is staged through body and sound expressions subtly carry the very purpose of each performance.

The staged libretti in Southeast Asian countries are usually drawn from Indian epics such as the *Ramayana* and the *Mahabharata* as well as didactic Buddhist tales, the *jatakas*. Local heroic novels carrying religious moral ideas, such as the stories of Panji, are also widely performed while indigenous legends inspired from chthonian cults also support ritual representations. The theatrical retelling of these literary pieces gather distinctive features that differentiate religious expressions from ordinary daily life. Thus, dancers' verbal expressions are sung rather than spoken, and shadow puppets' characters show distortedly dramatic body shapes while gong-chime ensembles' music serves as the necessary and omnipresent support to the performance. Masks and costumes also contribute to dissimulate the artist, allowing him or her to fully impersonate a character.

Royal courts of Southeast Asia fostered the most spectacular performing arts to serve religious purposes as well as to be attributes of kings' dominance. Through warfare and trade over the last two millennia, kingdoms competing for wealth and influence regularly exchanged cultural, religious, and artistic items and practices. India has been the strongest foreign influence on art, literature, and religion in the region, with the exception of Vietnam, whose traditions were more heavily influenced by China. Ritual arts and artists who were conveying the knowledge linked to performance, along with literati and religious representatives, were considered

At the Preah Vihear temple in Cambodia, near the disputed border with Thailand, dancers perform during a traditional ceremony. (AP Images/Heng Sinith)

as symbols of the rulers' power and taken as war prisoners, offered to a vassal kingdom, or brought along trade routes with foreign merchants as they sought to strengthen a relationship with a local sovereign. In all cases, the adoption and adaptation of ritual knowledge from powerful neighbors, through performing arts as well as other media, was a way to reinforce the potency of a king. It is thus not surprising that some ritual performances bear strong similarities in the different courts of the region, contributing to a sense of the region's cultural unity.

There are three primary configurations of performance in Southeast Asia. Some involve the enactment of the story by only female dancers, such as the Khmer *lkhon kbach boran* and the Javanese *bedhaya* and *serimpi*.

Other performances are all-male drama, such as the Thai *khon*, Khmer *lkhon khol*, or Balinese *wayang wong*. The third form is shadow theater, particularly represented with the small, articulated puppets of the Indonesian and Malaysian *wayang kulit*, traditions implemented prior to the adoption of Islam. The use of large leather panels in the Thai *nang yai* and Khmer *sbaek thom* is also original to the area. Marionette theater can also be found in multiple places within the region, from Burmese *yokhte pwe* to Vietnamese water puppet theater. Some forms mix different media, such as the women and the string puppets dancing together in Burma (see Miettinen 1992).

Court traditions are distinct from village-level rituals. Nonetheless, these characterizations are not mutually exclusive; there are dynamic interactions between rural

---

The *Ramayana* story illustrates religious values and social morals as it depicts the quest of the prince Rama through exile and war, demonstrating human qualities and flaws as well as supernatural powers. His opposition to Ravana, who abducted Rama's wife Sita, is often seen as an allegory of the balance of cosmic order. The twists and turns of the epic are expressed in theater performances throughout the region and its main protagonists are considered godlike figures. Within the sacred space of the stage, dancers and puppeteers incarnating them are perceived as establishing a connection between people and supernatural entities.

Stéphanie Khoury

and court spheres as well as artistic influences. Most of the court theater forms can be found ritually performed in village Buddhist or Hindu temples throughout the region (see Khoury 2012; Spies and de Zoete 2002). In Cambodia, scholars believe that court ritual dance and theater were implemented on the basis of local fertility and spirit worship rites, a practice typically associated with rural dramatizations (see Cravath 1986). Rural forms, which bear similarities to court male and female theatrical performances, are particularly dedicated to communication with spirits through the possession of villagers.

Minority groups in the region are located in mountainous border areas between states and on remote islands of Indonesia. Even if often converted to Christianity within the past two centuries, they also have dances and theater-like performances that link to fertility, particularly rainmaking dances, and spirit worship rituals that are specific to each group. Popular religious performing arts are more particular to one place or ethnic group and are primarily based on local legends and indigenous beliefs and aesthetics.

In today's Southeast Asia, contemporary politics has had an impact on the practice of ritual performing arts in implementing their secularization via a process of institutionalization to promote an idea of national culture (see Mattani 1996; Osman 1974). In such cases, the ritual expressivity has been replaced with aesthetical concerns. Nonetheless, ritual arts remain in practice as people navigate the demands of current life and the lasting relevance of religious performance.

Stéphanie Khoury

See also: Buddhism; Cambodia; Christianity; Ethnicity; Hinduism; Islam; Minorities; Music; Popular Religion; Puppetry; Religious Conversions; Ritual Dynamics; Spirit Mediumship; Vietnam; Women.

Further Reading

Cravath, Paul. "The Ritual Origins of the Classical Dance Drama of Cambodia." *Asian Theatre Journal* 3, no. 2 (1986): 179–203.

Khoury, Stéphanie. "Ramayana et cultes populaires au Cambodge: l'exemple du *Lkhon Khol*." In *Théâtres d'Asie à l'œuvre: Circulation, expression, politique*, edited by G. Toffin and H. Bouvier, 107–24. Paris: PEFEO, 2012.

Mattani, Rutnin Mojdara. *Dance, Drama, and Theatre in Thailand: The Process of Development and Modernization*. Chiang Mai, Thailand: Silkworm Books, 1996.

Miettinen, Jukka O. *Classical Dance and Theatre in South-East Asia*. Singapore: Oxford University Press, 1992.

Osman, Mohd. Taib, ed. *Traditional Drama and Music of Southeast Asia*. Kuala Lumpur: Dewan Bahasa dan Pustaka, Kementarian Pelajaran Malaysia, 1974.

Spies, Walter, and Beryl de Zoete. *Dance and Drama in Bali*, Hong Kong: Periplus, 2002.

DAOISM (TAOISM)

The influence of philosophical and religious Daoism in Southeast Asia is notoriously difficult to capture with any precision. As one of the three historically prevalent religions of China, alongside Confucianism and Buddhism, the spread of Daoism into

With the hope of receiving divine blessings, a worshipper reads out queries to dangkee Tay Kim Huat, who is possessed by the Taoist god Fa Zhu Gong. Dangkees are mediums who allow deities to possess their bodies in order to perform rituals and give advice to Taoist believers. (Roslan Rahman/Getty Images)

Southeast Asia is typically found within Chinese diaspora communities, particularly in Singapore, and in Malaysia. Daoism is also present in multivarious and popular forms in Thailand, Taiwan, the United States, and Europe.

Daoism emerged in the seventh century BCE, in China through the teaching of Lao Tzu, and has developed over the course of time in significant ways, including the formation of revered texts such as the *Daodejing* and the *Zhuangzi*. Significantly, the natural disposition of fluidity within Daoist thought and practice has allowed it to be influenced by Confucianism, particularly the focus on filial piety and propriety. Since the second century, Daoism has also been influenced by Buddhism, developing religious rituals, meditation techniques, and community

> To wander is to be free, drifting marvelously wherever one pleases! Free from the social conventions, rituals and norms of society that prevent us from being true to ourselves. Those who resonate with these words, encouraged to journey on the wanderer's path, owe a debt of gratitude to the ancient philosophical wisdom that lies at the heart of Daoism. The influence of Daoist thought and practice in Southeast Asia will not be too readily observed in conventional analysis of religious structures and institutions, but rather, within the intrinsic, subjective depths of the human spirit and culture.
>
> *Adrian Bird*

gatherings in monastic settings. The absorption of wider religious influence is regarded as a useful means to attaining the goal of human flourishing in accordance with the Dao.

As a result of Chinese migration to Singapore, it is estimated that close to 11 percent of the population there adheres to Daoism, and in 1990, the Taoist Federation of Singapore was established in order to promote Daoist teaching both in Singapore and around the world. Given the complex blending of Buddhist and Daoist elements, however, many adherents of Daoism declare themselves to be Buddhist, which makes accurate statistics difficult to come by. This should not lead us to underestimate or undervalue the influence of Daoism in Singapore, and there are many temples devoted to Daoist deities. Perhaps the most influential school of Daoist thought in Singapore is the Zhen Yi school, popularly known as the "Way of Orthodox Unity," a Daoist movement that emerged in the seventh-century Chinese Tang dynasty.

Daoism arrived in Malaysia with Chinese settlers and has been influential largely through its syncretism with Buddhism. The Federation of Taoist Associations Malaysia was formed in 1994 with the goal of teaching Daoist philosophy and religious practices and connecting Daoist associations across the country into a network of relations in order to promote a pure Daoist way of life. Given the work of the federation, Daoism is now recognized as an official religion of Malaysia and works with the interreligious Malaysian Consultative Council to preserve and promote religious freedom within the country.

Given the roots of Daoist presence in Chinese religious thought and practice, the increasing migration of Chinese communities in Southeast Asia and beyond, and the climate of religious change in the postmodern world, Daoism continues to have an influence within present-day philosophical, secular, and religious discourse, as individuals and communities seek to flourish and live in harmony with one another.

Adrian Bird

See also: Buddhism; Confucianism; Diaspora; Interreligious Relations and Dialogue; Lao Tzu (Laozi); Malaysia; Secularism; Singapore.

Further Reading

Gomes, Gabriel J. *Discovering World Religions: A Guide for the Inquiring Reader.* Bloomington, IN: iUniverse, 2012.

Lao Tzu. *Tao Te Ching.* Translated with an Introduction by D. C. Lau, London: Penguin Books, 1963.

Leibo, Steven A. *The World Series Today, 2012: East and Southeast Asia.* 45th ed. Lanham, MD: Stryker-Post Publications, 2012.

Prothero, Stephen. *God Is Not One: The Eight Rival Religions that Run the World—and Why Their Differences Matter.* New York: HarperCollins Publishers, 2010.

DHAMMAKAYA

Dhammakaya (Thammakaay) is a new Buddhist group in Thailand. It has generated controversy due to its emphasis on concentration meditation, its preoccupation with geographically choreographed mass ceremonies, and its open soliciting of large cash donations. Dhammakaya emerged in the late 1960s when a young Kasetsart University student in Bangkok started to meditate under the instruction of a white-clad Buddhist nun (*mae chii*), Khun Yay (b. 1909). Khun Yay had been a student of a respected old monk, Luang Pho Sot (Mongonthepmuni, b. 1884) at Wat Paknam in Bangkok. Through his meditation, he had discovered the *dhammakaya* body—the most refined of inner bodies—which is eternal and free from defilement. Hence the result of the Dhammakaya meditation method is to reach the dhammakaya level, which is often regarded as a form of enlightenment or *nirvana*. The young university student Chaiboon Sutipol (b. 1944) was ordained as Dhammajayo and became the abbot of Dhammakaya temple. He was later joined by another Kasetsart University student, Phadet Pongswardi (b. 1941), who was ordained as Dattajivo and held the position of a deputy abbot for many years.

The first Dhammakaya temple was started north of Bangkok in Pathum Thani province. The foundation stone of the temple was laid by the popular princess Mahachakri Sirindhorn, and the state Buddhist authorities of the Council of Elders (*mahatherasamkhon*) led the opening ceremony in 1980. Many well-known military leaders, politicians, and prime ministers have been publicly attending meditation sessions in Dhammakaya.

The temple has expanded to become a "world centre of Buddhism," covering now up to one square kilometer of land. A stated aim is that one can see the temple compound from the moon. The present main chedi (stupa) is a huge golden temple constructed of 300,000 gold-plated bronze Buddha statues, donated by the lay followers. There is space for 600,000 people to gather around the chedi. The meditation hall, where the sermons are nowadays organized, is a giant hall that can accommodate 200,000 people. In the middle is a golden statue of Buddha, a golden statue of Luang Pho Sot, and a larger-than-life statue of the abbot Dhammajayo. There are also statues and pictures of Khun Yay, who passed away in 2002.

The Dhammakaya movement remains controversial due to its activities. The farmers in Pathum Thani initially resisted the expansion of the temple. Many Thai Buddhists are skeptical about the meditation techniques and consider them as equal to "fast food." The abbot has been hit with several criminal charges of embezzlement, but despite the scandals, the group has never faced threats to exclusion from the state Buddhist hierarchy. The group is assumed to be under the protection of the Council of Elders, partly due to its generous contributions to the council.

What attracts the people to Dhammakaya is its orderliness and cleanliness—there are no stray dogs or cats roaming around the impeccably neat Dhammakaya park compound. Dhammakaya monks are all university graduates and are expected to devote their entire lives to the monastery. Enthusiastic white-clad volunteers assist visitors. The temple attracts particularly middle-class Bangkokians of Sino-Thai origins. The more donations the laypeople give, the higher status they gain in the group and the fancier Buddha amulet to indicate their status. The Dhammakaya people preoccupy themselves with ceremonies, meditation courses, and in 2011 the Dhammakaya monks set out for a "*dhutanga*" pilgrimage on roses. The laypeople laid down millions of petals of red roses on the streets on which the Dhammakaya monks were walking.

The Dhammakaya temple frequently invites monks from the provinces to attend larger ceremonies and don them with the bright orange Dhammakaya robes. Dhammakaya has branches around Thailand and in 21 countries overseas. The group has its own Dhammakaya Channel (DMC), where the abbot is preaching seemingly nonstop.

Marja-Leena Heikkilä-Horn

See also: Buddhism; Diaspora; Religion and Society; Thailand.

Further Reading

Dhammakaya website, http://www.dhammakaya.net (accessed September 17, 2014).

Jackson, Peter A. *Buddhism, Legitimation, and Conflict: The Political Functions of Urban Thai Buddhism.* Singapore: ISEAS, 1989.

Scott, Rachel M. *Nirvana for Sale? Buddhism, Wealth, and the Dhammakaya Temple in Contemporary Thailand.* Albany: State University of New York Press, 2009.

DHARMA/DHAMMA

Dharma in Hinduism

Dharma is a central principle of the Hindu faith, a religion with more than a billion followers. Hindus believe that dharma was revealed in the Vedas. The term dharma comes from the Sanskrit word "*dhri*," meaning to uphold or to sustain, and may be translated as "religion," "law," "order," "duty," or "ethics." It stands for all the principles and purposes, influences, and institutions that shape the character of man both as an individual and as a member of the society. It is the law of right living, and its observance safeguards both happiness on earth and salvation. Dharma is a combination of ethics and religion, which regulates the life of a Hindu. The laws of dharma consider the fasts and feasts, social and family ties, personal habits and tastes.

The *Mahabharata*, the great epic, contains a discussion on the topic of dharma. When asked by Yudhistir to explain the meaning and scope of dharma, Bhishma, who has mastered the knowledge of dharma, replies: "It is most difficult to define Dharma. Dharma has been explained to be that which helps the uplifting of living beings. Therefore, that which ensures the welfare of living beings is

---

The *Mahabharata*, an ancient revered epic written in Sanskrit, is an important source of information on the development of Hinduism between 400 BCE and 200 CE and is regarded as a text of both dharma and history. The story revolves around the rivalry between two groups of cousins: the five sons of King Pandu and 100 sons of the blind King Dhrtarstra who fought a war to possess the ancestral kingdom, Bharata. Respected as a foundation text for Indian religions, thoughts, cultures and philosophy, it is well known to the people in Southeast Asia and greatly influenced the cultures of Java, Malaysia, Thailand, and Bali.

Ruchi Agarwal

surely Dharma. The learned rishis have declared that which sustains is Dharma" (*Mahabharata*, Shanti Parva 109: 9–11).

Others explain dharma as that which is indicated by the Vedas as conducive to the highest good. There are four aspects of human life: dharma (duty); artha (profit); kama (pleasure); and moksha (liberation). Dharma controls the pursuit of both kama and artha. For those in whom dharma predominates are of sattvik (virtuous) nature, while the wealth seekers are rajasik (passionate) and those of pleasure are tamasik (ignorant). Dharma therefore comprises of every type of righteous conduct covering every aspect of life that is essential to the welfare of an individual and the society. Those who observe the laws of dharma automatically attain moksha (eternal bliss). Therefore, dharma, artha, kama, and moksha shape the ends of life.

Dharma comprises ritual action. A proper performance of rituals is important to the ordering of individual lives and the community. The Dharmashastras (religious manuals, the earliest source of Hindu law) details the different types of rituals. It is part of the dharma to name and bless a child, to initiate their education, and to perform the last rites of parents. Rituals are acts that have a role in the ordering of the world, as it should be.

Different individuals have different obligations and duties according to their age, gender, and social position. Even though dharma is universal, it is also particular and functions within concrete circumstances. Each person has his or her own dharma, known as sva-dharma. Bhagwad Gita, a text set before the great battle of *Mahabharata*, illustrates the importance of sva-dharma. The epic depicts the warrior Arjuna, riding his chariot, questioning his charioteer Krishna as to why he should fight a battle against his own relatives and teachers. Krishna assures him that the battle is a righteous one and that Arjuna must fight, as it was his sva-dharma as a warrior to fight the battle. He must fight with detachment from the results of his actions and within the rules of the warrior's dharma. Therefore, not acting according to one's own dharma is wrong and called *adharma*. Krishna says in Bhagwad Gita that whenever *adharma* overshadows dharma, he will appear on earth to save the righteous and destroy the wicked.

Dharma is thus also the social order, one's duty as part of a division of the society, a varna (caste) or jati (birth group). The Rig Veda defines four varnas that emerge from parts of the body of the divine being that created the universe. These include the Brahmins (priests), Kshatriyas (warriors), Vaisyas (merchants), and the Sudras (servants). Each of the varnas serves God's creation in their own capacities—for example, priests by their spirituality, warriors by their heroism, merchants by their skills, and servants by their service. When the different varnas fulfill their respective duties, the society is considered to be just and in accordance with the dharma. Correct action in accordance to dharma is understood as a service to humanity as well as to God.

Dharma in Buddhism

In Buddhism, dharma is the doctrine that is the universal truth common to all individuals at all times. Buddhists believe that human beings can free themselves from suffering by practicing meditation and cultivating a lifestyle prescribed by the Buddha. The teachings of Buddha, delivered in India some 2,500 years ago, are also referred to as the *Dharma*. He often said that he gave so many teachings in distinctive ways that every human being could hear them in the way that benefit them the most. This suggests that there is no one right way of understanding Buddhist teachings. Buddha provided vehicles to help provide different approaches to experience and awaken through the dharma teachings. These vehicles are referred to as the Three Baskets that can be referred to as: the Hinaya teachings, including sutras; Buddha's stories; and teachings such as the Dhammapada and other Theravadin lineage teachings. Several of these practices are still alive in Southeast Asia. Mahayana teachings, including the Zen traditions, are still alive in Asia (Japan, Korea, China, and Southeast Asia); whereas Vajrayana teachings developed mostly in Tibet, Mongolia, parts of Nepal, and other central Asian countries.

There is no hierarchy or competition between traditions and paths in Buddhism. Each individual is on a journey together with others and called the *sangha*, having a goal of offering support to one another in order to liberate from suffering. The wheel is an important symbol in Buddhism, as it depicts the cycle of life and death. According to Buddhist thoughts, when one dies, he or she is reborn into a new form that could be of a deity, human, animal, some lower form, or an inhabitant of hell. All positive actions cause good karma and direct one into being reborn in a higher form. One's bad karma may result in rebirth in a lower form. As part of the Dharma, Buddha taught the Four Noble Truths that forms the basis of Buddhist thought.

1. Life is suffering
2. Suffering is caused by craving
3. Suffering can have an end
4. The Eight-Fold path leads to the end of suffering.

Buddhists believe that suffering is due to the impermanence of life, and the ultimate goal in Buddhism is to end the cycle of suffering. The achievement of this goal is called nirvana.

Buddha's ideas applied to people irrespective of their rank in life, and specified that individuals be in charge of their own destiny. These ideas were in contrast with the ideas of Brahmanism that dominated during Buddha's lifetime. Brahmanism encouraged the offering of gifts to priests for salvation. The society was divided into castes that determined one's duty or dharma. Buddhism differed as it did not believe in social distinctions between human beings, and so it was accessible to anyone. Buddha believed that compassion should be cultivated among all living beings.

With the spread of Buddhism to China by the second century CE, the new ideas of karma, reincarnation, hell, monks, and enlightenment were introduced. Later, Buddhism was brought from China to other countries in Asia, such as Korea, Japan, Thailand, Myanmar, Sri Lanka, Cambodia, Laos, and Vietnam. The Buddha Dharma was thus adopted and became an integral part of the society.

Ruchi Agarwal

See also: Buddhism; Cambodia; Hinduism; Laos; Myanmar (Burma); Study of Religion; Thailand; Vietnam.

Further Reading

Cox, A. *Dharma Friends*. Bloomington, IN: Xlibris Corporation, 2002.

Gavin, F. "Hindu Concepts." *Religions on BBC* online edition, 2009. http://www.bbc.co.uk/religion/religions/hinduism/concepts/concepts_1.shtml (accessed December 16, 2013).

Klostermaier, K. *A Concise Encyclopedia of Hinduism*. Oxford: Oneworld Publications, 1998.

Radhakrishnan, S. "The Hindu Dharma." *International Journal of Ethics* 33, no. 1 (October 1922): 1–22. Chicago: University of Chicago Press, 1922.

Smith, D. *Dharma Mind, Worldly Mind: A Buddhist Handbook on Complete Meditation*. Thailand: Aloka Publications, 2002.

DIASPORA

To understand diaspora, one has to look into the specific circumstances that have led the involved group to resort to migration. It also entails knowing its origin and how such a movement has eventually developed over time. Diaspora originally referred to the Jewish experience of being spread in various places caused by a tragic event that had traumatized the group as a whole. This set the historical knowledge and experience of victimhood at the hands of an oppressor. The use and understanding of the term has been a subject of debate, as some scholars say that for a movement to be considered a diaspora, it should include some characteristics that mostly express the Jewish experience. On the other hand, others are careful not to generalize any apparent diasporic movement, observing precautionary measures and interpreting any movement in the light of the many possible changes to the term. To gain a comprehensive understanding of diaspora as it happens in the twenty-first century, it is necessary to focus on its historical development, how it relates to migration, and the particular qualities that make every diasporic movement a unique experience altogether.

Between the 1980s and 1990s, a huge growth in migration within Southeast Asia (SEA) was seen especially from less developed countries that had excessive labor supply. This expansion was fueled by the rapid economic growth and declining fertility in the newly industrialized economies. Migration in SEA can be best understood in the light of immigration and emigration, a practice that has produced the culture of interdependence among SEA nations. *Immigration* refers to the movement of the people from one country to another country. *Emigration* refers to the act of leaving one country for another to live permanently. SEA governments of immigration, also known as countries of destination, such as Singapore, Malaysia, and Thailand, are primarily concerned with preserving a balance within and among their ethnic groups and fighting any security risk. On the other hand, SEA governments of emigration, also known as countries of origin, such as the Philippines, Indonesia, Vietnam, Cambodia, Laos, and Burma, are more concerned with managing recruitment, protecting their workers, reducing homeland unemployment, and providing training and industrial experience. In both cases, the fast-increasing mobility of people has been consistently regarded as both one of the reasons and one of the effects of unusual socioeconomic and political transformations within the region.

Lacking in resources, Singapore depends greatly on the importation of labor at various skill levels. Based on the 2007 census, Singapore had a total population of 4,588,600, with 3,583,100 Singapore residents and 1,005,500 nonresidents (NRs). In 2006, these NRs were classified as lower-skilled, coming from the Philippines, Malaysia, Thailand, Indonesia, Sri Lanka, India, and China.

Malaysia, a second-wave tiger economy, suffers as well from severe labor shortages, particularly in the plantation sector. In 2006, Malaysia was said to have had an estimated 2.6 million foreign laborers. What is worth noting about Malaysia's immigration practices relates to some of the controversies caused by the country's complicated ethnic composition.

Although Thailand is considered a country of immigration, at the same time it is also considered a country of emigration. The 1980s saw the government heavily exporting Thai workers to the Middle East. In the 1990s, the Thai labor export shifted to Taiwan, Malaysia, Japan, and Singapore. Although a good number of Thais still go abroad to work, due to decreasing fertility and rapid economic growth, many Thais have started refusing "3D jobs" (dirty, dangerous, and difficult). However, the problem of human trafficking that involves Thai women for the sex industry still remains. As a country of destination, Thailand's construction, agricultural, and manufacturing employment opportunities have attracted huge numbers of Burmese, Cambodian, Laotian, and Bangladeshi workers.

Among the countries of emigration in SEA, the Philippines is considered to have the strongest and best-established protection and reintegration programs for the estimated 2.2 million Overseas Filipino Workers (OFWs), as surveyed in 2011. With the 1973 Balikbayan Program, a labor-export policy adopted by then president Ferdinand E. Marcos, and two landmark bills passed and approved in 2002 reintegrating Filipino migrants, a culture of emigration has become second nature to many Filipinos.

While it is important to look at the role of the economy in migration, the role of religion and how it links to diaspora is crucial as well. In many cases, religion, migration, and diaspora can be viewed within the context of a migrant's religious faith in coping with the harsh realities migration brings and/or the context of how migration is propelled by religion.

For instance, religion is deep-seated in almost every Filipino as innate as the Spanish influence is, culturally. Having been colonized by Spain for 333 years, the mind-set of suffering, submission, and sacrifice has become well entrenched in almost every Filipino's consciousness. It is not surprising then that this awareness has been fundamentally structured and expressed in various migration-related movements. A closer look at the Philippine labor export strongly demonstrates the Filipino workers as those who sacrifice to provide the needs and address the interests of their families and the country, an act that painstakingly connects with the Filipinos' dominant religious faith, Catholicism. The other strand through which diaspora is interspersed with religion is called instrumental religion. Instrumental religion, a process through which migrants undergo as they use, take advantage of, and seek comfort from their faith and related observances, provides them some sense of security. In addition, it allows them to handle and survive the varied forms and degrees of difficulties they encounter in their overseas work, many times invoking the Bible to rationalize their difficulties.

Having observed in a country of destination an old Vietnamese Buddhist woman who maintains two altars in her house and everyday bows in prayer with her incense, an Asian scholar argues that religion remains to be a tradition never altered by migration. The Rohingya in Burma, on the contrary, are in an ongoing struggle and live a migratory life, propelled by a number of factors including religion. This xenophobia against the Rohingya in Burma has caused them to suffer from many forms of injustices, including brutal religious repression. Religion may have been used in various ways by migrants or may have been instrumental in a people's migration and engagement in diasporic activities, but such a situation leads to one general concept maintaining that religious faith allows them to carry on and endure the challenges within a diasporic environment.

Analiza Perez-Amurao

See also: Buddhism; Cambodia; Globalization; Indonesia; Judaism; Laos; Malaysia; Migration; Myanmar (Burma); Philippines; Singapore; Southeast Asian Religions in the USA; Thailand; Vietnam.

Further Reading

Ananta, A., and E. N. Arifin. *International Migration in Southeast Asia.* Singapore: ISEAS Publications, 2004.

Cohen, R. *Global Diasporas: An Introduction.* New York: Routledge, 2008.

Constable, N. *Made to Order in Hong Kong: Stories of Migrant Workers.* 2nd ed. Ithaca, NY: Cornell University Press, 2007.

Cruz-Tulud, G. "Faith on the Edge: Religion and Women in the Context of Migration." *Feminist Theology* 15, no. 9 (September 4, 2006): 9–25.

Llorente, S. R. R. "A Futuristic Look into the Filipino Diaspora: Trends, Issues, and Implications." *Asia Pacific: Perspectives* 7, no. 1 (2007): 33–38.

Safran, W. "Diasporas in Modern Societies: Myths of Homeland and Return." *Diaspora* 1, no. 1 (1991): 83–99.

Vasquez, M. *More Than Belief: A Materialist Theory of Religion.* Oxford: Oxford University Press, 2011.

DUC, THICH QUANG

One of the haunting images from the Vietnam crisis of the 1960s was Malcolm Browne's photo of the self-immolation of the Buddhist monk, the Venerable Thich Quang Duc. Born in the village of Hoi Khanh in Central Vietnam in 1897, Duc's birth name was Lam Van Tuc. At a young age, he left home to study Buddhism and, at the age of 20, was ordained as a monk with the name Thich Quang Duc. As a religious leader, he traveled all over the country, consolidating Buddhism and building temples. In 1953, he was appointed as the Head of Rituals Committee of the United Vietnamese Buddhist Congregation, a position that he held until his death.

As Ngo Dinh Diem, the president of Vietnam, began pursuing policies favoring Christians and discriminating against the Buddhists, the Buddhist monks took up the mantle of a nonviolent struggle against the Diem government. In a country that is predominantly Buddhist, the struggle symbolized the large-scale discontent of the people against an unpopular regime. In an ultimate act of protest, on June 11, 1963, Thich Quang Duc along with hundreds of monks took out a procession and, on the road outside the Cambodian embassy in Saigon, Duc committed self-immolation. A series of events followed this horrific act, and there was international pressure on Diem to resign. Later that year, the military captured power and he was assassinated.

Thich Quang Duc's death was a defining moment in the crisis that had gripped Vietnam during that period. While the monk's protest was primarily against the anti-Buddhist policies being pursued by the government, it also symbolized the unpopular involvement of the United States in Vietnam. In the years and decades that followed this tragic event, the memory and message of Thich Quang Duc has been etched in the history of Vietnamese Buddhism. He also continues to be an inspiration for people around the world who are struggling for freedom.

Jesudas M. Athyal

See also: Buddhism; Christianity; Engaged Buddhism; Hanh, Thich Nhat; Peace-Building; Religion and Society; Ritual Dynamics; Study of Religion; Vietnam.

Further Reading

Gettleman, Marvin E. *Vietnam: History, Documents and Opinions on a Major World Crisis.* New York: Penguin Books, 1966.
Thich Nhat Hanh. *Vietnam: Lotus in a Sea of Fire.* New York: Farrar, Straus & Giroux, 1967.
Tucker, Spencer C. *Encyclopedia of the Vietnam War.* Santa Barbara, CA: ABC-CLIO, 2000.

E

EDUCATION

Education in Southeast Asia is acknowledged as an issue of central developmental concern. The policy goals established are implemented with varying degrees of success, depending on the historical and contextual realities of a given region. The diversity that exists both across Southeast Asia and internally within a particular nation makes any broad-stroke understanding of education problematic. This diversity is manifest in many forms, including language, culture, religion, and history as well as political and economic stability, all of which have an impact on the educational landscape. Education has certainly been variously influenced by the legacy of colonial presence, including British presence in Myanmar, Malaysia, and Singapore; the Portuguese presence in Timor-Lester; the French in Cambodia, Laos, and Vietnam; and the Spanish and American presence in the Philippines. There is much validity in Vina Mazumdar's assertion that education in the region is a compromise between indigenous knowledge systems and Western-imposed systems. Religious, cultural, and ideological factors all serve to shape emerging movements, which develop in response to particular histories of imperialism. Thailand, which has no such Western colonial legacy, has a different historical narrative in which education is understood, though Thailand remains influenced by the globalizing forces that affect all countries in Southeast Asia.

Political and economic stability are essential components for developing an effective infrastructure for educational progress. The Republic of Indonesia is acknowledged as one of the few countries in Southeast Asia to have achieved close to universal basic education, a success attributable to a range of factors, including postindependence political consolidation, decentralized educational control, and economic development. The education system in Singapore has also received international acclaim, particularly in the area of mathematics and science.

The diverse subcontinent of Southeast Asia makes it difficult to form a coherent narrative of the region as a whole. Despite this reality, however, education stands tall, lying at the heart of each nation's vision for the future. Educational goals and initiatives are statements of intent and hope that cannot shy away from challenging questions about political and economic infrastructure, religion, national and minority group identity, urban and rural shifts, gender, employment, justice, and equality. Education in the region has, therefore, become one of the most important areas of twenty-first-century research and concern, finally beginning to receive the attention it deserves.

Adrian Bird

The government of Singapore has placed a high priority on education since coming to power in 1959, emphasizing the importance of education in terms of national economic development and social cohesion. A strong economy has allowed for the development of a strong educational infrastructure at primary, secondary, and tertiary levels. Where such stability is less established, foundations are being laid and educational goals remain largely future oriented. Timor-Leste achieved independence in 2002, following Portuguese colonial rule and Indonesian military occupation, and is currently in the process of developing an education system from the vantage point of freedom of self-determination. This development, under the broad concept of "decolonization," faces the added challenge of economic underdevelopment, which makes Timor-Leste one of the poorest nations in the region, despite optimistic projections for economic growth in the coming years. Leaders in Laos are working to overcome the effects of colonial history and civil revolution in order to rise above their externally identified status as "least developed country." Here, education is considered to be a critical component in attaining the broader goals of poverty reduction and economic growth.

While acknowledging the problematic nature of any broad-stroke themes due to contextual specific items, there are important issues that recur in dialogue on education in Southeast Asia. These include, but are not limited to, issues of gender, the use of language in the midst of multilinguistic plurality, and education for minority groups.

In terms of student enrollment, Southeast Asia is above the world average for female participation, and much progress has been made in overcoming the challenges of social-cultural constraints to female education, particularly in Indonesia and the Philippines. Certainly the issue of gender remains critical, as demonstrated by the seriousness of this issue in the policy goals of the Association of Southeast Asian Nations (ASEAN). The issue of gender is of course much more complex than assessing educational enrollment and participation figures, yet the fact that these complexities are being acknowledged is certainly a positive step.

Diversity not only exists across Southeast Asia, but it is also intrinsic to the fabric of each nation. The existence of ethnic and religious minorities in many Southeast Asian countries has an impact on both educational planning and implementation. While ethnic minority rights have been acknowledged as key issues within educational planning forums, this can at times be held in tension with the pursuit of a national identity. The promotion of the dominant Burman identity in Myanmar, for example, exists at the expense of minority ethnic and religious groups in the country, leading to continued interethnic tensions within the nation.

The selection of language within educational institutions is also a central issue of contention, particularly in the midst of ethnic and linguistic diversity. There are a variety of strategies adopted to deal with this tension. Indonesia, a nation of over 6,000 islands and 256 linguistic groups, applies a policy of transitional bilingualism in which the early education years are conducted in the mother tongue of the inhabitants, while the later years are conducted in the national language, Bahasa Indonesia. Until recently, the use of Thai dialect within the system of education of Thailand has failed to meet the needs of the Malay-speaking Muslims in the south of the country.

A further tension to be noted exists between traditional and modern, secular forms of education. This tension exists particularly where religious institutions have traditionally been responsible for education. Examples include the role of the Buddhist monk in the monastic setting of pre-Independence Burma, or the role of Islamic clerics in the *pesantren* (Islamic boarding leaning centers/mosques) of Indonesia. Secular models of education thus add to the complexity of the educational paradigm, posing questions about the goals and implemental strategies to be adopted within the educational process. The emergence of Muhammadiyah in Indonesia is a modernist and reformist Muslim movement that seeks to work within this tension. Considered the largest modernist movement in Southeast Asia, Muhammadiyah integrates "secular" subjects alongside traditional Islamic teachings taught previously in the *pesantren*. Across Southeast Asia, public schools exist alongside private schools, offering a breadth of diversity to meet the needs of majority and minority religious groups.

Other factors worthy of note include the continued disparity between the urban-rural educational contexts, the establishment and development of educational institutions from primary to tertiary levels, and the adequate supply and training of teachers at all levels. A further consideration exists as countries across Southeast Asia seek to decentralize the education structure and increase the capacity of educational efforts across the nation. Financial investment, the acquisition of economic support to finance such efforts, is both enormous and open to corruption at various levels, providing another source of challenge to the effective implementation of educational development.

Adrian Bird

See also: Buddhism; Cambodia; Colonialism; Ethnicity; Islam; Laos, Malaysia; Minorities; Muhammadiyah; *Pesantren*; Singapore; Thailand; Timor Leste (East Timor); Vietnam; Women.

Further Reading

Brock, Colin, and Lorrane Pe Symaco. *Education in South-East Asia*. Oxford Studies in Comparative Education. Oxford: Symposium Books, 2011.

Leibo, Steven A. *The World Today Series 2012: East and Southeast Asia*. 45th ed. Lanham, MD: Styker-Post Publications, 2012.

Mazumdar, Vina. *Gender Issues and Educational Development: An Overview from Asia*. http://www.cwds.ac.in/OCPaper/GenderIssuesVM.pdf (accessed May 30, 2013).

ENGAGED BUDDHISM

Engaged Buddhism, also known as Socially Engaged Buddhism, is a movement of nonviolent social, political, economic, and environmental activism that developed in the Buddhist world in the twentieth century and continues in the twenty-first. Engaged Buddhism is found throughout Buddhist Asia as well as the West. It did not begin from a single founder or single national struggle, but arose again and again in separate responses to the crises and dilemmas facing the Buddhist world in the

Part of a group of nearly 10,000 South Vietnamese march across a bridge over the Perfume River in Hue during a non-violent demonstration against the policies of the Saigon government and President Nguyen Cao Ky, on March 3, 1966. (AP Images/Eddie Adams)

twentieth century—the war in Vietnam, the Chinese occupation of Tibet, the Cambodian Holocaust, deep poverty in Sri Lanka, the caste system in India, the military dictatorship in Burma/Myanmar, colonialism and its aftermath, the suppression of women, and the challenges of modernization and Westernization. This article will focus on the movement in Southeast Asian countries.

The first to use the term "Engaged Buddhism" was Vietnamese Zen master and Engaged Buddhist leader Thich Nhat Hanh, who during the Vietnam War advocated that Buddhism be "*engagé*," French for pledged or involved, having a sense of responsibility to society. Nhat Hanh himself was influenced by the Chinese monk Venerable Yin Shun, an advocate of "Humanistic Buddhism," a this-worldly Buddhism that encourages compassionate *bodhisattva* action in daily life. Engaged Buddhism has received inspiration from Mahatma Gandhi's pioneering of nonviolent social activism, along with Christian charitable activities and modern, Western forms of social and political analysis. However, Engaged Buddhism is fundamentally Buddhist. At its base, it is a practical expression of the foundational Buddhist values of compassion and loving-kindness. Engaged Buddhism does not ask Buddhists to make a choice between traditional Buddhist spirituality, such as meditation, and social action; it sees them as two sides of a single coin. For example, Thich Nhat Hanh says that one needs to "be peace" in order to make peace (Hanh 1987). That is, one practices meditation, generosity, moral self-discipline, etc., in order to become more selfless and compassionate and in order to develop inner strength and inner peace. One should then be in a better condition to "make peace" and be helpful to society.

Engaged Buddhism has played a central role in major twentieth- and twenty-first-century conflicts.

Vietnam

During the war in Vietnam, Buddhist monks, nuns, and laypersons engaged in a "Struggle Movement" to try to end the war, being especially effective from 1963 to 1966. Striving to maintain their compassion for all persons on both sides of the war, they created a "Third Way" alternative to the warring sides of the (Communist) North and (U.S. allied) South; this Third Way practiced principled nonviolence and pledged to be against no one but only on the side of life. One of their major leaders and their spokesperson in the West was Thich Nhat Hanh.

The dilemma of the Vietnamese Struggle Movement was to find ways powerful enough to bring the war to an end without themselves engaging in violence. They staged street protests, strikes, and boycotts with massive public support and succeeded in bringing down successive South Vietnamese governments that they perceived as being too intent on prosecuting the war. Some individuals immolated themselves in order to try to move others so deeply that they would want to stop supporting the war, though this action was never endorsed by the movement's leadership. The movement also worked to alleviate what suffering they could, evacuating villages caught in the cross-fire of battle, reconstructing destroyed villages, arranging care for war orphans, aiding military deserters and draft resisters, and bringing medicine to remote areas. In the end, the movement did not succeed in ending the war; however, it remains one of the great examples of courageous and principled nonviolent struggle in the midst of war.

Myanmar (Burma)

In 1962, the Burmese military took control of Burma. They instituted a brutal police state government documented by Human Rights Watch and Amnesty International as grossly violating the human rights of the Burmese people with summary executions, condoned rape of women and children, the destruction of the villages of ethnic minorities, forced labor, forced portage, and torture. In 1988, large demonstrations led by students and Buddhist monks broke out across Burma, demanding democracy and human rights. In 1990, national elections were held; Aung San Suu Kyi, a self-described lay Engaged Buddhist, won the election with some 80 percent of the vote. The military government refused to accept this outcome, and Suu Kyi was arrested. In 2007, monks (and nuns) again filled the streets calling for democracy and human rights; this came to be known as the "Saffron Revolution," after the color of the monks' robes. These protests were violently put down by the government. Many monks were killed, imprisoned, and tortured, or they fled into exile. In 2010, Aung San Suu Kyi was released from house arrest, having spent 15 of the previous 21 years in detention. In 2012, after the government instituted some reforms, Suu Kyi won a seat in the Burmese Parliament, formally becoming the leader of the opposition.

Cambodia

During the Khmer Rouge era in Cambodia (1975–1979), between one million and two million out of a total of seven million Cambodians were killed, and the Buddhist monastic *sangha* was almost entirely wiped out. In 1978, the monk Maha Ghosananda, who had been out of the country, returned to lead a movement of healing and reconciliation. He urged Cambodian refugees to cultivate loving-kindness for all people and to heal their wounds by forgiving those who had killed their families (His own entire family had been killed by the Khmer Rouge). He also strove to bring full pacification to the dangerously divided country, where battles still were occurring in the countryside, by working for reconciliation among the leadership of the mutually hostile factions.

In 1992, Maha Ghosananda, who was called the "Gandhi of Cambodia," led the first Dhammayietra (or Dhammayatra, loosely, peace walk or pilgrimage of Truth) to accompany refugees returning for the first time to their homes. The Dhammayietra was widely credited with helping the repatriation to be successful. A year later, he led a second Dhammayietra immediately before the first national elections. This Dhammayietra was credited with helping to make the elections successful by easing the atmosphere of fear and eliciting heavy participation. The Dhammayietras became annual events, focusing on such issues as land mines, domestic violence, deforestation, and basic morality, though participation fell off drastically after Maha Ghosananda's death in 2007. Maha Ghosananda and the Dhammayietra movement have been criticized as being too focused on forgiveness and reconciliation and insufficiently concerned with justice and accountability. However, it is the case that despite the genocide, there has been no blood bath of revenge in Cambodia.

Other major efforts and contributions of Engaged Buddhism in Southeast Asia include environmental protection and restoration work, the effort to restore the Theravada Buddhist bhikkhuni (nuns) order, and work to combat rural poverty.

Sallie B. King

See also: Buddhism; Cambodia; Colonialism; Hanh, Thich Nhat; Humanism; Maha Ghosananda; Myanmar (Burma); Reform Movements, Religion and Society; Sivaraksa, Sulak; Vietnam.

Further Reading

Ghosananda, Maha. *Step By Step: Meditations on Wisdom and Compassion*. Berkeley, CA: Parallax Press, 1992.

Hanh, Thich Nhat. *Being Peace*. Berkeley, CA: Parallax Press, 1987.

Queen, Christopher S., and Sallie B. King, eds. *Engaged Buddhism: Buddhist Liberation Movements in Asia*. Albany: State University of New York Press, 1996.

Suu Kyi, Aung San. *Freedom from Fear and Other Writings*. London: Penguin Books, 1991.

ETHNICITY

Southeast Asia has a long history of diverse and sometimes competing religious belief-systems and syncretism. At the same time, the region is home to various ethnic groups who have to deal with their respective states. The very symbolically charged term "ethnicity" can best be understood if attention is turned to this region between China and India. This article will concentrate on Laos—the land between Myanmar (Burma), Thailand, Cambodia, Vietnam, and China—to exemplify the state of affairs in Southeast Asia, and which can be used as an example for wider comparison. The argument here is twofold: firstly, to point out how ethnicity has shaped the interaction between ethnic groups and the state; and secondly, to show how its meaning has changed in the scientific discourse over time.

In order to obtain a working definition, the first glimpse is into how the term is contemporarily applied in Laos, where the concept of ethnic group/ethnicity can be translated as *sonpao* (ຊາວະຫນາຕິ). The term *sonpao* is embedded in the discourse of everyday life in the villages as well as in the more municipal areas. For instance, "ethnic travel eco-guide service" is only one of the innumerable advertisements that can be found in travel agencies concerning visits to see ethnic groups. In this discourse, ethnicity depicts something ancient, traditional, and foreign and is defined by the unchanging traits of a group.

This is the opposite of how the term "ethnicity" is defined in the scientific discourse of today. Following the contemporary scientific consensus, social relations exhibit ethnic features when cultural differences are articulated and stressed. And, just as important, the social identity of a person or group is negotiable and changeable, depending on the context, and not fixed throughout space and time. A group or person may choose between several identities through self-attribution as well as by the attribution of others. Thus, Thomas Eriksen, who did fieldwork among multiethnic Mauritius suggests the use of the term "social identity" instead of ethnicity, which can be applied in a wider sense (Eriksen 1993, 157). This seems to be wise, especially as the term ethnicity connotes problematic concepts such as tribe, race, nation-building, and globalization. With regard to globalization, for instance, on the one hand arguments state that the ongoing modernization has a homogenizing effect on society—i.e., ethnic groups—in trying to adapt to the state lose their identity. On the other hand, it became clear that ethnic groups are stressing their borders and identity even more. But it is beyond the scope of this article to deal with these concepts as well; what is important here is the religious component of ethnicity.

Ethnicity can indeed scarcely be written about without considering religion, especially if one goes back to precolonial Southeast Asia. At that time, Southeast Asia was a ragbag of conjoined territories, also entitled a "mandala-structure." In this mandala, power was at the center and radiated to the peripheries, where it became weaker and weaker. Politics and religion were intertwined: at the core of each mandala stood a king, legitimating his power by being a Buddhist king. Thus, religion linked territories and people, and borders were not strongly marked. But at the same time, religion distinguished people from one another: the Buddhist state-elite were at the center, cultivating wet rice, and the "animist minorities" were at the periphery in the high mountains, growing slash-and-burn fields, with no supra-village political order. Still, it is important to note that this dichotomy never was exclusive, as there also were combining elements. For instance, both sides were economically linked through trade.

The French colonialists, arriving in the seventeenth century, did not care for the fluid borders they found. They applied Western concepts of territorial borders and nationalism and they divided the region they called "Indo-Chine" into arbitrary and artificial political and administrative units (Pholsena 2006, 22–24, 28, 29, 35). The political heteronomy of today's Southeast Asia resulting from Western forces not only changed the profile of Southeast Asia, but it also generated conflicts. In Laos, for instance, the French colonial rulers, by their politics of taxation and classifying the population in order to create easy-to-govern units that did not depict reality, fueled national pride and caused revolts among some highland groups, which otherwise would not have occurred (Pholsena 2006, 19, 32ff.). But even in academic writing, the oversimplified view of the majority and some easily defined and well-demarcated ethnic groups persisted; for instance, *the* Shan and *the* Kachin or *the* Thai and *the* Karen. Each ethnic group was described by applying culturally defined labels, such as languages, clothes, or religion, and was very often invented by the colonial rulers, missionaries, and the state, or even by scholars.

In the 1960s, the scientific discourse started to do away with this oversimplified picture. After Edmund Leach (1970 [1954]), who had already stressed social organization more heavily than the harder-to-define term "culture," it was Fredrik Barth (1969) who changed the emphasis from the cultural traits of a group to the border, distinguishing groups or people. Barth showed how ethnic identity is ascribed, both through one's own group and through other groups. Thus ethnicity is more an aspect of a relationship than a set of criteria in its own right. Each group applies identity markers in relation to other groups or to the state. The identity marker itself is not important, but how it is valued in relation to other groups. For instance, the Samtao, a small Mon-Khmer-speaking group of—following the state census—about 3,533 people living in the north of Laos use religion as a major identity marker. They define themselves as Buddhists, while the Khmu with whom they live are practicing *saatsanaa phi* (ສາດສະໜາຜີ literally translated: religion spirits, thus believe in spirits). In their case, clothes and language are not identity markers anymore. Other Samtao groups in Laos, China, Burma, or Thailand may choose clothes or language as an identity marker. Thus *the* Samtao do not exist. This line of argument comes from Michael Moerman (1965) and Frederic Lehman (1967), writing in the tradition of Edmund Leach.

Still, far from accepting their heterogeneousness and distinctness, many Southeast Asian states are trying to equalize and homogenize ethnic groups. Their differentness is, in another way, too well stressed, used, and promoted. An example of this phenomenon is mentioned above; many Southeast Asian states market their ethnic groups for tourists. In this instance, the "majority" often defines itself with regard to the "minority." In the first place, it can be seen that the terms "minority" and "majority" are highly relational. Secondly, many majorities are minorities at the same time, such as the Lao Lum, who are the majority in Laos but a minority in the northeast of Thailand. Thirdly, if ethnicity comes into play, the general opinion that minority equals ethnic is misleading. For example, the Lao Lum valley-dwellers predominantly define themselves as Buddhists, as distinct from the people living in the highlands (especially the Khmu) who are associated with "animism."

Thus, the Lao Lum in this sense are as ethnic as any minorities in the country; but still, in Laos there is no travel agency declaring "visit ethnic Vientiane" (the capital of Laos), and the term ethnic is reserved for the groups living in the hills. Thus, in the scientific discourse, the term "ethnicity" has to be applied carefully. It may be difficult to throw this term completely overboard, as the people who are being investigated use it in this way, and this has to be taken into account; but still it is important to thoroughly define the term or, where possible, use "social identity" instead.

Yet there is another level at which ethnicity can be observed, namely the state level. Laos, for instance, has created and still creates its self-identity by providing demarcation from Thailand. Thailand is identified with the modern West, and the state tries to promote a picture of the "traditional" Lao family, with the mother wearing the *sin* (the long skirt for women) and of the families of ethnic groups living in stilt-houses, the opposite of new houses made of stone. But if one observes the youth of today, it also can be seen that Thailand is very much copied (Pholsena 2006, 52ff.). Nevertheless, both countries have in common that their identity is first and foremost preserved and created by Theravada Buddhism. When the communist regime came into power in Laos in 1975, they tried to get rid of Buddhism (and the spirit cults) at first, but noticing that this policy was not working well, they installed and promoted Buddhism again. In Thailand, Buddhism, with the king as its guardian, is the state religion. In addition, Myanmar and Cambodia in mainland Southeast Asia are also Theravada Buddhist. Religion, especially in Southeast Asia, is one of the major ways of creating, defining, and expressing identity.

Eva Sevenig

See also: Cambodia; Colonialism; Laos; Minorities; Myanmar (Burma); Thailand; Vietnam; Women.

Further Reading

Barth, Fredrik. "Introduction." In *Ethnic Groups and Boundaries: The Social Organization of Culture Difference*, 9–38. Bergen/Oslo: Universitets Forlaget, 1969.

Eriksen, Thomas H. *Ethnicity and Nationalism: Anthropology, Culture and Society*. London: Pluto Press, 1993.

Leach, Edmund R. *Political Systems of Highland Burma: A Study of Kachin Social Structure*. London School of Economics Monographs on Social Anthropology 44. London: University of London and the Athlone Press, 1970 [1954].

Lehman, Frederic K. "Ethnic Categories in Burma and the Theory of Social Systems." In *Southeast Asian Tribes, Minorities and Nations 1*, edited by Peter Kunstadter, 93–124. Princeton, NJ: Princeton University Press, 1967.

Moerman, Michael. "Who Are the Lue? Ethnic Identification in a Complex Civilization." *American Anthropologist* 67 (1965): 1215–29.

Pholsena, Vatthana. *Post-War Laos: The Politics of Culture, History and Identity*. Singapore: Institute of Southeast Asian Studies, 2006.

Sprenger, Guido. "Differentiated Origins: Trajectories of Transcultural Knowledge in Laos and Beyond." *Sojourn: Journal of Social Issues in Southeast Asia* 26, no. 2 (2011): 224–47.

Wijeyewardene, Gehan, ed. *Ethnic Groups across National Boundaries in Mainland Southeast Asia*. Singapore: Institute of Southeast Asian Studies, 1990.

F

FEDERATION OF ASIAN BISHOPS' CONFERENCES

The Federation of Asian Bishops' Conferences (FABC) is a voluntary association of the Roman Catholic Church in Asia. The purpose of the organization is to foster among its members solidarity and co-responsibility for the welfare of church and society in Asia, and to promote and defend whatever is for the greater good. There are 19 Bishops' Conferences and nine associate members under the FABC, and the organization is active in most of the Southeast Asian nations.

The function of FABC is to study ways and means of promoting the Christian fellowship, especially in the light of the deliberations and resolutions of the Second Vatican Council and postconciliar official documents. The organization seeks to respond to the needs of Asia, and strives to intensify the dynamic presence of the church in the total development of the peoples of the region. The FABC also helps in the study of problems of common interest to the church in Asia, and investigates possibilities of solutions and coordinated action. A main concern of the organization is to promote intercommunication and cooperation among local churches and bishops of Asia and to render service to episcopal conferences of Asia in order to help them to meet better the needs of the people of God. Through all these programs, the FABC facilitates an ordered development of organizations and movements in the church at the international level and fosters ecumenical and interreligious communication and collaboration.

The FABC functions through a hierarchy of structures consisting of the Plenary Assembly, the Central Committee, the Standing Committee, and the Central Secretariat. The Plenary Assembly is the supreme body of FABC and is composed of all presidents of member-conferences or their officially designated persons, Bishop-delegates are elected by the member-conferences, associate members, and members of the Standing Committee. The Plenary Assembly meets in ordinary session every four years. The Central Committee of FABC is composed of the presidents of member-conferences or their officially designated episcopal alternates and oversees the implementation of the resolutions and instructions of the Plenary Assembly. This committee meets every two years. The Standing Committee, composed of five bishops elected from different parts of Asia, implements the resolutions and instructions of the Central Committee. It provides direct guidance and support to the Central Secretariat and other organs of FABC.

The Central Secretariat is the principal service agency and an instrument of co-ordination within the FABC and with outside offices and agencies. Various offices assist the Central Secretariat, each handling specialized ministries and areas of concern. These offices are the Office of Human Development, the Office of Social

Communication, the Office of Laity, the Office of Theological Concerns, the Office of Education and Student Chaplaincy, the Office of Ecumenical and Interreligious Affairs, the Office of Evangelization, the Office of Clergy, and the Office of Consecrated Life.

The Central Secretariat of FABC is located in Hong Kong and the Documentation Centre in Bangkok. The Documentation Centre plans to house and preserve all books published by the FABC as well as dissertations and other publications referring one way or the other to the Federation. The FABC Documentation Centre includes a conference room that can seat about 40 persons, a library and several small offices.

The FABC has a rich history of action and reflection in Southeast Asia. During the last four decades, the organization has produced a wealth of pastoral documents that stresses the importance of the local churches, enculturation and dialogue. The FABC documents repeatedly stressed "the triple dialogue"—with the poor, with local cultures, and with local religions. According to Stephen Bevan, the organization has yielded an impressive body of documents that are incredibly rich, amazingly visionary, and truly worth careful reading and study. As best they could and as often as possible, the Asian bishops wrote that successful evangelization requires building local churches upon local cultures, languages, and practices. In Southeast Asia, the FABC is involved in the difficult task of being a Christian organization that is also sensitive to the challenges of the pluralist context and yet seeking to meaningfully participate in the efforts to build a just and participatory society.

Jesudas M. Athyal

See also: Calungsod, Pedro; Christian Conference of Asia; Christianity; Contextualization; Ileto, Reynaldo C.; Interreligious Relations and Dialogue; Jesuits; Religion and Society; Ruiz, Lorenzo; Sin, Cardinal Jaime Lachica.

Further Reading

Eilers, Franz-Josef, ed. *Church and Social Communication in Asia: Documents, Analysis, Experiences (2nd Edition):* FABC-OSC Books, Volume 1. Manila: Logos Publications, 2008.

Eilers, Franz-Josef, ed. *Interreligious Dialogue as Communication: FABC-OSC Books, Volume 6.* Manila: Logos Publications, 2005.

Eilers, Franz-Josef, ed. *Social Communication in Religious Traditions in Asia, Volume 7.* Manila: Logos Publications, 2006.

Quatra, Miguel Marcelo. *At the Side of the Multitudes: The Kingdom of God and the Mission of the Church in the FABC Documents (1970–1995).* Manila: Claretian Publications, 2000.

Roman, Anthony, ed. *Social Communication Directory Asia: FABC Edition,* FABC-OSC Books, Volume 3. Manila: Logos Publications, 2004.

FEMINISM AND ISLAMIC TRADITIONS

In the midst of the emergence of a democratic society and the growing influence of Middle Eastern Islam in Southeast Asia, the Southeast Asian Islamic feminists are proposing a new paradigm and concepts about gender equality in Islam.

Indonesian Muslim students take part in a rally in Semarang, Central Java, on September 4, 2014, to mark World Hijab Day. During World Hijab Day, Muslim women foster religious tolerance and understanding concerning why Muslim women wear hijab. (WF Sihardian/NurPhoto/Corbis)

Indeed, they criticize the gender ideology that was promoted by the New Order as well as Islamists or *Salafi* revivalist groups. In addition, they argue that Islam could be a source of gender equality if Muslims interpret religious texts properly and contextually. If not, it might be possible that Muslims' understanding of the Islamic texts will create further gender problems in Southeast Asia.

The contemporary notion of Islamic feminism emerged in the early 1990s in various locations around the world, including in Indonesia, contemporaneous with the growth of Western literature on women in Islam (Badran 2005). There are various definitions of Islamic feminism. In the Indonesian context, Sinta Nuriyah Abdurrahman (as cited in Doorn-Harder 2006) posits herself as a feminist who considers *Pancasila*—the official ideology of the Indonesian state, which means "five principles": monotheism, humanitarianism, unity, democracy, and justice—and Islamic belief to be the foundations of her actions. She states that: "I am a feminist according to Indonesia's state ideology of *Pancasila*. That means that I base my action on my belief as a Muslim . . . My goal is equality between men and women, because it says in the Qur'an that men and women are each other's helpers" (Doorn-Harder 2006, 37).

One research finding reveals that Indonesian Islamic feminists encourage women not only to be active members in the public sphere, but also to keep harmonious and happy families. Imbuing a family with blessing, democracy, and love for each other is among the goals of Indonesian Islamic feminists (Jamhari and Ropi 2003).

Furthermore, this research showcases Indonesian Islamic feminists' struggle for equality in public life and equipollence in domestic life (Jamhari and Ropi 2003).

When discussing feminism and religious traditions in Islam, the terms "Islamic feminist" or "Muslim feminist" should be called into question. According to Cooke (2001), "Islamic" is more relevant than Muslim, because "Islamic feminist" suggests an Islamic tradition being considered by feminists, whereas "Muslim feminist" may simply refer to feminists who embrace Islam but do not necessarily practice its tenets. Cooke further describes an "Islamic feminism" as "a particular kind of self positioning that will then inform the speech, the action, the writing, or the way of life adopted by someone who is committed to questioning Islamic epistemology as an expansion of their faith position and not a rejection of it" (Cooke 2001, 59–61).

Muslim feminists debate the terms "Islam" and "feminism"; that is, whether or not the heritage of Islam is compatible with feminism, or whether a person can combine the Islamic belief with feminist conviction at one and the same time. The debate connects with the historical polemic between the Islamic world and the West, which sees some people perceiving that feminism is West-based and that Islam has its own values. Debate focusing on the compatibility between "Islam" and "feminism" shapes the formation of self-identity among gender activists in Southeast Asia, for example, referring to themselves as "feminists." According to Doorn-Harder (2006), young Indonesians who may have worked with nongovernmental organizations and have been influenced by Western feminists are more comfortable being called "feminists" than members of the older generation: "Younger women who are active in NGOs call themselves 'feminists.' What exactly the term 'feminist' means is not always clear. Many Indonesians and women . . . [of the] older generation are not comfortable being called feminists—it calls up images of western supremacy, individualism, and selfishness" (Doorn-Harder 2006, 36–37).

Saparinah Sadli, one of the older-generation activists, said: "I am reluctant to use [the term] Indonesian feminism because I am not sure that we have developed an Indonesian theory of feminism" (Sadli 2002). However, she refers to Musdah Mulia, who is younger than Sadli, as an "Indonesian Islamic feminist" (Mulia 2005). In the Indonesian context, reluctance to be called a feminist derives from the stigma attached to the feminist label. Feminists manifesting leftist (Communist) or liberal tendencies are seen as promoting individualism, selfishness, and immoral behavior such as free sex (Doorn-Harder 2006): they are thought to be anti-men and sympathetic toward lesbianism (Sadli 2002) .

Whatever their identity—feminist or nonfeminist—people assume that Muslims who are feminists should consider the religious texts, the Qur'an and Hadiths, as resources in their discussions. Since Islam has a fundamental role in Muslim society, its proponents might fail to promote gender equality if feminists fail to first consider the Islamic paradigm, norms, and values in their struggle or works. Non-Muslim scholars such as John Esposito and Miriam Cooke too maintain that discussion about women and gender in Islam has to be situated within an Islamic paradigm (Cooke 2001; Esposito and Mogahed 2007).

As a matter of strategy, Muslim feminists employ historical and hermeneutical approaches to justify their understanding of gender equality. The historical approach establishes a social, intellectual, and religious space wherein it is possible to deconstruct gender inequality interpretation. The hermeneutical approach allows Islamic feminists to find the true message in Islamic texts focusing on the context in which the text was written, the grammatical composition of the text, and the world-view of the text (Wadud 1999).

Muslim feminists believe that Islamic texts respect both men and women equally and that they are the source of gender equality. They argue that many Muslims understand gender equality in the texts inappropriately, because they have inter-preted them exclusively from a male perspective for centuries. The Muslim feminist scholar Asghar Ali Engineer (1992), in his book *The Rights of Women in Islam*, asserts that the Islamic feminist movement is an action of putting back justice between the sexes as respected in the era of the holy Prophet Muhammad. For this reason, employing hermeneutical and historical approaches, Muslim feminists tend to reread the texts emphasizing notions of equality and justice in men's and women's roles in the society, seeing them as "complementary and egalitarian rather than hier-archical and unequal" (Afsaruddin 1999, 23).

Prominent gender activist and Islamic scholar Nasaruddin Umar, in his work *Qur'an untuk Perempuan* (the Qur'an for Women), argues that when people read the Qur'anic verses addressing gender issues such as polygamy, inheritance, wit-nesses, reproductive rights, women's right to divorce and the public role of women, they will gain the impression that these verses are misogynistic. However, if people scrutinize them more closely, using "the analytic methods of semantics, semiotics and hermeneutics, and paying attention to the theory of *asbab nuzul*" (the reason why the verses were revealed), they will see that these gender verses are part of the process of creating justice and that the texts do not discriminate against women (as cited in White 2006).

In the Malaysian context, women activists from late 1945 joined with men against the British government's proposal for future colonization. They had moved from "the relative seclusion of their families and their home to involvement in national life" (Manderson 1980, 1). As a result, several women were appointed to the State Council in Johor, Selangor, Negeri Sembilan, and Perak in the 1950s (Manderson 1980). However, this achievement was rejected by some sections of the Muslim community by saying that women and girls were forbidden to be active in public events. Radical demands made by women for reformulation of *shari'a* (Islamic laws) were swiftly set aside. Religious feminists, including Sisters in Islam, took part in the establishment of the National Women Coalition (NWC) in 1992 (Ng, Mohamad, and Tan 2006). In 1999, *Reformasi Era* women's groups, including an Islamic organization through WAC (Women's Agenda for Change), launched 11 demands (women's charter) ranging from land to sexual rights (Ng, Mohamad, and Tan 2006).

Alimatul Qibtiyah

See also: Aisyiyah and Nasyiatul Aisyiyah; Bhikkhuni, Dhammananda; Indonesia; Malaysia; Oka, Gedong Bagus; Santo, Ignacia del Espiritu; Sexuality; *Shari'a*; Sisters in Islam; Women; Women's Monastic Communities.

Further Reading

Afsaruddin, A. *Hermeneutic and Honor: Negotiating Female "Public" Space in Islamic Societies.* Cambridge, MA: Center for Middle Eastern Studies of Harvard University, 1999.

Badran, M. "Between Secular and Islamic Feminism/s: Reflections on the Middle East and Beyond." *JMEWS: Journal of Middle East Women's Studies* 1, no. 1 (2005): 6–28.

Cooke, Miriam. *Women Claim Islam: Creating Islamic Feminism through Literature.* New York: Routledge, 2001.

Doorn-Harder, P. V. *Women Shaping Islam: Indonesian Women Reading the Qur'an.* Urbana: University of Illinois Press, 2006.

Engineer, Asghar Ali. *The Rights of Women in Islam.* New Delhi: Sterling Publishers, 1992.

Esposito, John L., and D. Mogahed. *Who Speaks for Islam? What a Billion Muslims Really Think.* New York: Gallup Press, 2007.

Jamhari and I. Ropi, eds. *Citra Perempuan dalam Islam: Pandangan Ormas Keagamaan.* Jakarta: Gramedia Pustaka Utama, PPIM-UIN Jakarta and Ford Foundation, 2003.

Manderson, L. *Women, Politics and Change: The Kaum Ibu UMNO Malaysia, 1945–1972.* Kuala Lumpur: Oxford University Press, 1980.

Mulia, Musdah. *Muslimah Reformis: Perempuan Pembaru Keagamaan* Bandung, Indonesia: Mizan, 2005.

Ng, Cecilia, Maznah Mohamad, and Beng Hui Tan. *Feminism and the Women's Movement in Malaysia: An Unsung (R)evolution.* London: Routledge, 2006.

Sadli, S. *Berbeda tetapi Setara.* Jakarta: Kompas, 2010.

Wadud, M. A. *Qur'an and Woman: Rereading the Sacred Text from a Woman's Perspective.* New York: Oxford University Press, 1999.

White, S. "Gender and the Family." In *Voices of Islam in Southeast Asia: A Contemporary Sourcebook*, edited by G. Fealy and V. Hooker. Singapore: Institute of Southeast Asian Studies, 2006.

FREEDOM OF RELIGION

Freedom of religion is a concept that supports the freedom of an individual or group to practice, worship, and believe in public and private. Today, the concept is strongly associated with human rights. Throughout history, the idea of religious coexistence has been institutionalized and practiced in different ways. Related concepts, mostly stemming from religious backgrounds and condemning deviance, are apostasy, blasphemy, and heresy. In its human rights–based conceptualization, religious freedom includes the right to determine one's own religion and the right to leave a religious group. Many consider it a fundamental right. In contemporary Southeast Asian countries, controversial political debates evolve around different interpretations of this right, often regarding the situation of religious minorities but also members of religious communities who are considered deviant either by the state or by politically powerful groups.

Ideas of religious coexistence have a long history. Well-known examples are the Achaemenid Persian Empire around 550 BCE, in which Cyrus the Great encouraged the practice of local customs and religious freedom and the Edicts of Asoka. Asoka the Great protected freedom of religious worship in the Maurya Empire in the third century BCE. Muslim tradition evokes the Covenant of the second Caliph Umar, the Constitution of Medina, and tolerates non-Muslims through the concept of *dhimmis*, literally "protected individuals." In various parts of the world, pockets of religiously tolerant rule existed. In the modern period, freedom of religion is strongly connected to the concept of human rights and traced back to the French Revolution. It is part of the Universal Declaration of Human Rights (1948) and the International Covenant on Civil and Political Rights (1966/1976). Today, the concept functions as a political instrument, mostly for activist causes and in the realm of foreign policy. There are several methods of measuring and evaluating the state of religious freedom in a given place, and the extracted data are used by human rights activists, minority interest groups, and foreign governments with military and/or economic interests. The concept is also used in measuring the grade of democratization of a political system and is imposed on countries as a condition for development schemes or economic cooperation.

Southeast Asia has a long history of religious interaction, long parts of it marked by exchange, acceptance, and tolerance. Situated at the crossroads of some of the world's major trading routes, cosmopolitan centers developed in which different religions influenced each other and peacefully coexisted. Hindu and Buddhist thought deeply influenced the area and blended with local belief and practice in the first century CE. By 1400, Islam thrived in the region, especially in insular Southeast Asia. The coexistence of beliefs and practices lets many scholars refer to Southeast Asian Islam as syncretistic. The period of imperialism and colonization eventually led to the formation of modern nation-states. In some countries, local religious practices were formally institutionalized and integrated into the colonial administrative systems. Some of these colonial politico-religious structures remain influential until today. Southeast Asia comprises a large variety of political systems, each with different degrees of state regulation.

In Brunei, the constitution states that the official religion is Islam according to the teachings of the Islamic Shafi'i school of law. This is supported through laws and policies, especially through education. Religious freedom is enshrined in the constitution. The various religious groups generally coexist in a tolerant milieu, although any non-Islamic religious materials being distributed are subject to confiscation and some members of minorities report discrimination on religious grounds. The government observes the following religious holidays as national holidays: Christmas Day, Eid ul-Fitr, Eid ad-Adha, First Day of Ramadan, First Day of the Islamic Calendar, Isra Me'raj, Prophet Muhammad's Birthday, and Revelation of Al-Quran.

In Cambodia, the constitution and other laws and policies protect religious freedom. Buddhism is the state religion. The government provides Buddhist training and education to monks and others in pagodas and permits Buddhist religious instruction in public schools. Foreign missionary groups largely operate freely. There are some tensions with minority religious groups, but their right to freedom of religion and worship is generally respected. The government observes the following religious holidays as national holidays: Khmer New Year; Pchum Ben; Visakha Bochea, honoring the Buddha's birth and death; and Meak Bochea, honoring the Buddha's enlightenment.

In Indonesia, the constitution protects religious freedom, but some restricting laws and regulations exist, and there is a lack of enforcement. The government officially recognizes six religions. Members of other religions and nonbelievers sometimes face administrative difficulties. Some groups express their opposition to religious pluralism through violent activity against individuals and groups they deem contradictory to their values—for instance, Christians, followers of traditional religious practice, and the Ahmadiyya community. The government observes the following religious holidays as national holidays: the Ascension of the Prophet, Eid al-Fitr, Eid al-Adha, the Muslim New Year, Good Friday, the Ascension of Christ, the Birth of the Prophet Muhammad, Christmas, the Buddhist holiday Vesak, and the Hindu holiday Nyepi. Additional Hindu holy days are recognized as regional holidays in Bali.

In Laos, the constitutional right to religious freedom exists but is restricted in practice. Authorities are suspicious of major supporters of religious communities other than Buddhism, especially Protestant groups. The potential of religions to create social divisions is stressed to impose restrictions. The government observes two religious holidays, the That Luang Festival and the Buddhist New Year.

Malaysia's constitution guarantees religious freedom. Restrictions are imposed through laws and policies. Islam is the religion of the state. The government and its connected institutions control most Islamic institutions. Non-Muslims are permitted to practice their religions openly but reports of discrimination exist. It is not allowed to teach Muslims about other religions. Islamic practices considered "deviant" are banned. The potential of religions to create social divisions is stressed to impose restrictions. The government observes the following religious holidays as national holidays: Eid al-Fitr, Eid al-Adha, the Birth of the Prophet Muhammad, Awal Muharram, Vesak Day, Deepavali, Thaipusam, and Christmas. Good Friday is officially observed only in East Malaysia.

In Myanmar, the authoritarian regime is strongly associated with Buddhism, even though it is not the official state religion. The government is accused of actively promoting Theravada Buddhism, which is practiced by 90 percent of the population. Buddhist doctrine is taught in public schools. There have been reports of violence against ethnic and religious minorities. The government observes the following religious holidays as national holidays: the Full Moon Day of Tabaung, Thingyan, Buddhist New Year's Day, the Full Moon Day of Kason, the Full Moon Day of Waso, the Full Moon Day of Thadinkyut, the Full Moon Day of Tazaungmone, Christmas, and Deepavali.

In the Philippines, the government ensures religious freedom through the constitution, laws, and policies. Muslims fall under the Code of Muslim Personal Laws and are subject to *shari'a*-inspired law. Some members of the Muslim minority hold that they suffer from economic discrimination. There are reports of religiously framed violence, particularly in the South. It observes the following religious holidays as national holidays: Maundy Thursday, Good Friday, Easter, All Saints' Day, Christmas Day, Eid al-Fitr, and Eid al-Adha

In Singapore, there is no state religion. Religious freedom is constitutionally guaranteed but restricted to some extent. The government restricts the right in banning some groups. There are also restrictions on speech or actions that are considered harmful for religious harmony. Muslims are governed through the Islamic Religious Council of Singapore which drafts the weekly sermons and regulates several religious matters. The school system offers classes for the major religions. There are official holidays for each major religion in the country: Eid al-Fitr, Eid al-Adha, Christmas, Good Friday, Deepavali, and Vesak Day.

In Thailand, the constitution and other laws and policies protect religious freedom. There is no state religion, but Theravada Buddhism receives significant government support. The government restricts the activity of some groups. There are reports of discrimination and violence in the mainly Muslim south. The government observes the following religious holidays as national holidays: Maka Bucha Day, Visakha Bucha Day, Asalaha Bucha Day, and Khao Phan Sa Day.

In Timor Leste, the government protects religious freedom through the constitution, laws, and policies. There are reports of societal abuses and discrimination based on religious affiliation, belief, or practice. The following religious holidays are national holidays: Good Friday, Assumption Day, All Saints' Day, the Feast of the Immaculate Conception, Christmas, Eid al-Fitr, and Eid al-Adha.

The Vietnamese constitution, legal code, and several resolutions provide for freedom of belief and worship, but restrictions exist. The government controls and oversees religious organizations under the Ordinance on Religion and Belief. The government limits the activities of religious groups and of individuals who are regarded as threatening the authority of the Communist Party of Vietnam. There are severe restrictions on foreign missionaries. Human rights organizations report abuses of religious freedom in the country. The government does not observe any religious holidays as national holidays.

Saskia Louise Schäfer

See also: Ahmadiyya; Brunei Darussalam; Buddhism; Cambodia; Christianity; Fundamentalism; Hinduism; Humanism; Indonesia; Islam; Laos; Malaysia; Minorities; Myanmar (Burma); Philippines; Reform Movements, Religious Discrimination/Intolerance; *Shari'a*; Singapore; Syncretism; Thailand; Timor Leste (East Timor); Vietnam.

Further Reading

Ahmed, Ishtiaq, ed. *The Politics of Religion in South and Southeast Asia.* New York: Routledge, 2011.

Bouma, Gary D., Douglas Pratt, and Rod Ling, eds. *Religious Diversity in Southeast Asia and the Pacific: National Case Studies.* New York: Springer, 2010.

Saeed, Abdullah, and Hassan Saeed. *Freedom of Religion, Apostasy and Islam.* Farnham, Surrey: Ashgate Publishing, 2004.

U.S. Commission on International Religious Freedom, Annual Reports. http://www.uscirf.gov (accessed May 8, 2013).

Zagorin, Perez. *How the Idea of Religious Toleration Came to the West.* Princeton, NJ: Princeton University Press, 2003.

FUNDAMENTALISM

Fundamentalism is a much-discussed and much-misunderstood term, especially in the context of Southeast Asia. There is a serious problem of definition of the term as it is used in a variety of meanings. Fundamentalism is essentially a Western

Christian construct. The term is too much loaded with Christian presuppositions and Western stereotypes and has serious limitations when applied to other religions and across cultures. Currently the word is most often associated with Islam. What is termed Islamic fundamentalism hits headlines in the media, usually relating it to terrorist acts. Fundamentalism has emerged as a major issue in the national politics of several countries and in international relations.

Fundamentalism refers to a belief in a strict adherence to a set of basic principles (often religious in nature), sometimes as a reaction to a perceived doctrinal compromise with modern social and political life under secularization. It is the perceived response of traditionally religious people to the rapid changes in society that downgrades and constrains the role of religion in the public sphere. It is a discernible pattern of religious militancy by which "true believers" assert religious identity and search for viable alternatives to secular institutions, strictly maintaining ancient or fundamental doctrines of the religion they profess. Every single fundamentalist movement in Judaism, Christianity and Islam has a profound fear of "annihilation," convinced that modern secularization forces want to wipe out religion.

Fundamentalism stems from the attempt of a group of conservative Protestants in the United States early in the twentieth century to define what they called to be the fundamentals of Christianity. They defended conservative Christianity against liberal views in addressing such topics as scriptural authority, Christology, and evangelism. By the late 1930s, theological conservatives rallying around the "fundamentals" came to be known as "fundamentalists." Fundamentalism in its origin was a domestic Christian issue and was apolitical.

In the 1950s and 1960s, it was fashionable to speak about secularization and the decline of religion. Western theologians joined sociologists in arguing that modernization would weaken or even destroy religion's grip over traditional cultures, reduce the political significance of religion, and diminish individual attachment to religious values. Harvey Cox eloquently described what happened to these theories. In 1965, he had written a book entitled *The Secular City* about the world of declining religion. In his book *Religion in the Secular City* in the early 1980s, he admitted that rather than an era of rampant secularization and religious decline, it appeared to be more of an era of religious revival and the return of the sacred. The resurgence of religion was largely political—or, rather than the revival of religion, what we witnessed was a political revival in the name of religion. In theory the distinction may not apply so much to Islam, the political dimension of which occupies center stage in the current debate.

In an interview with Karen Armstrong, Bill Moyers asked: "You said once that you felt the fundamentalists were trying to restore God to the world?" Armstrong replied, "Yes, all fundamentalists feel that in a secular society God has been relegated to the margins, to the periphery and they are all in different ways seeking to drag him out of that peripheral position, back to center stage. They drag God back into the political world by denying democratic aspirations."

Ninan Koshy

Islamic political movements are called fundamentalist, and fundamentalism is equated with militancy and militancy with terrorism. It is highly misleading to lump all Islamists, ranging from the Justice and Democratic Party of Turkey to Al Qaeda, together in a single category as fundamentalists. What has become the term for all Islamic movements is not based on a clear understanding of either the nature of the Islamic faith and the radical movements it has given rise to, or of the social and economic conditions in the countries concerned.

The term Islamic fundamentalism is ambiguous. It falls far too short of capturing the reality of the complex social movements. It has mainly been used to delineate the position of two distinct types of forces within the Muslim world: those who have used Islam mainly as a cover for violent anti-Western action that cannot find justification within the bounds of Islamic dictates; and those who have used Islam as an active ideology both of resistance and assertion, repudiating foreign ideologies as unacceptable and unworkable.

Islamic fundamentalism has appeared in several countries, and its Wahabi version is promoted and financed worldwide by Saudi Arabia. The Iran hostage crisis of 1979–1980 marked a turning point in the use of the term "fundamentalism." The media, in an attempt to explain the ideology of Ayatollah Khomeini and the Iranian revolution to a Western audience, described it as a "fundamentalist version of Islam" by way of analogy to the Christian fundamentalist movement in the United States. The term gradually gained academic respectability. Thus was born the term "Islamic fundamentalism," which would become one of the most common usages of the term.

From the time of the Iran revolution and continuing to the present, Islamic fundamentalism has become an issue of international concern. It represents a variety of broad-based religious movements that have swept over much of the Muslim world from North Africa to Southeast Asia. The clash of civilization thesis propounded by Samuel Huntington and others has strengthened fundamentalist forces, as it is argued that future conflicts will be between civilizational regimes, equating civilization with culture and culture with religion. It is a recipe for conflicts between religions.

For the vast majority of Muslims, the resurgence of Islam is a reassertion of cultural identity, formal religious observance, family values, and morality. The establishment of an Islamic society is seen as requiring a personal and social transformation that is prerequisite for the Islamic government. Effective change is to come from below through a gradual social transformation brought about by implementation of Islamic law.

Western policies, especially those of the United States in the Middle East, have to take much of the blame for the promotion of that particular brand of fundamentalism that is seen in the area today and spreading to other parts of the world. The Cold War period from 1949 fueled anti-Western sentiment, as Muslims saw Western powers, especially America, supporting dictatorial regimes in the region to suit Western interests. When references are made to jihad, it is good to remember that Ronald Reagan presented the Cold War as a "Holy War," and that George Bush described, at least in the beginning, the War on Terror as a "Crusade." In the U.S. list of enemies in the War on Terror, only Islamic nations find a place.

There is a tendency to link fundamentalism automatically with violence. This has no justification. Only a tiny proportion of fundamentalists worldwide take part in violent activities, including terrorism. The vast majority are simply struggling to live what they regard as a good religious life in a world that seems to be increasingly inimical to faith. There are fundamentalists in all religions challenging the secular hegemony of the modern world, but they do not resort to violence. Most of the fundamentalists are not violent.

All religiously based violence is not perpetrated by fundamentalists. Religion is sometimes used as a justification for violence by people and groups not specifically religious or having faith in God. The prevailing association between fundamentalism and violence, particularly terrorism, is often an exercise in labeling for the purpose of condemnation with little regard for the nature of the movement, its motivations, and context. Fundamentalism is a construct whose relationship to violence is highly problematic.

Islam in Southeast Asia has always been defined by tolerance, moderation, and pluralism. Indonesia has the largest Muslim population in the world. Muslims in the region generally support the secular state in the sense that the state's basis is not religion. They eschew the interpretations of Islam that tend to violence or extremism, as in the Middle East or South Asia. The majority of them shun the radical variants of Islam found in the Middle East. Unlike in the Middle East, Islam in Southeast Asia facilitated the development of civil society and democracy. Only a small minority may be called fundamentalist, advocating the establishment of Islamic regimes governed by *shari'a*, the law based on the Qur'an.

But across the region, an Islamic resurgence has taken place in recent times. For the most part, the grievances of radical Muslims across Southeast Asia have been local. However, since the early 1990s, there has been a noticeable expansion of both radical Islamists and their transnational connections. The resurgence is in part inspired by links to the Middle East, Afghanistan, and Pakistan. Many Southeast Asians returning from Islamic religious schools in the Middle East and Pakistan have brought with them a new radical, militant, and extremist form of Islam.

Radical Islamist or extremist parties who may be labeled fundamentalist have not demonstrated broad appeal among masses in Malaysia and Indonesia during elections, even as some segments of these societies have experienced a resurgence of Islamic belief. Secular and nationalist parties are generally preferred by voters in Indonesia and Malaysia, even as Islam remains a core value of the people. In these countries, however, there is a noticeable advance in fundamentalist interpretations of Islam among the Muslim communities. There are several militant groups in Southeast Asia who have indulged in terrorist activities in the name of Islam. There are also fundamentalists in Southeast Asia who would argue for strict Islamic law but would not advocate the use of violence. Islamic fundamentalist upsurge in multiracial societies such as Indonesia and Malaysia could tear apart their social fabric and generate political instabilities. As a region of great strategic importance, religious as well as political developments in the region will be watched carefully.

Ninan Koshy

See also: Christianity; Freedom of Religion; Indonesia; Islam; Malaysia; Religion and Society; Secularism; *Shari'a.*

Further Reading

Armstrong, Karen. *The Battle for God: Fundamentalism in Judaism, Christianity and Islam.* New York: Ballantine Books, 2001.

Emerson, Michael O., and David Hartman. *The Rise of Religious Fundamentalism.* Notre Dame, IN: University of Notre Dame, 2006.

Juergensmeyer, Mark. *Terror in the Mind of God: The Global Rise of Religious Violence.* Berkeley: University of California Press, 1998.

Tibi, Bassam. *The Challenge of Fundamentalism, Political Islam and the New World Order.* Berkeley: University of California Press, 1998.

G

GHOSANANDA, MAHA

Maha Ghosananda (full title, Samdech Preah Maha Ghosananda) was, perhaps, the most significant Buddhist leader of the Theravada tradition in Cambodia in the second half of the twentieth century. As the Khmer Rouge (the Communist Party of Cambodia) seized control of the country in the 1970s and systematically targeted and assassinated Buddhist monks, the future of religion in that country itself was in serious jeopardy. In the face of continued violence, Maha Ghosananda and his followers preached the Buddhist values of reconciliation and compassion and urged the people to "remove the land mines of hatred" from their hearts. In the post-Communist transition period, he contributed tremendously to revive Cambodian Buddhism and to bring peace and normalcy in the society.

Born in the Takéo Province of Cambodia in 1929 in a farming community, from a young age Ghosananda showed a keen interest in religious matters. At the age of eight, he began his formal association with Buddhism as a temple boy. At 14, he was ordained as a novice, and he studied Pali, the liturgical language of Theravada Buddhism, at a local school. He did his higher studies in Phnom Penh and Battambang and went on to do a doctorate in Pali at the Nalanda University in India.

Thefour years' rule of Khmer Rouge in the country that led to the loss of approximately two million lives (due to political executions as well as starvation and diseases) led Maha Ghosananda to the realization that religion needed to be actively engaged in the real-life situations of the people. In order to bring peace and hope to a people ravaged by war and social injustice, he started "Dhammayietra," an annual peace walk that crossed Cambodia from the Thai border and traveled all the way to Vietnam. In the last decade of his life, Maha Ghosananda turned his attention to the environmental devastation that was caused primarily by illegal logging in Cambodia. During this period, the theme of Dhammayietra turned to deforestation and illegal logging and the links between these and militarism and the ongoing civil war in the country. Trees were planted throughout the pilgrimage, and he reminded the villagers that protecting ourselves and protecting our environment is the "Dhamma of the Buddha."

In recognition of his services, Maha Ghosananda was nominated by several organizations for the Nobel Peace Prize. He was the recipient of the Rafto Prize (1992), which is a human rights award; the Niwano Prize (1998) for interreligious cooperation; and the Courage of Conscience Award (1998) that was instituted to promote the causes of peace, justice, nonviolence, and love. Maha Ghosananda died in Northampton, Massachusetts, on March 12, 2007.

Jesudas M. Athyal

See also: Buddhism; Cambodia; Communism; Dharma/Dhamma; Engaged Buddhism; Interreligious Relations and Dialogue; Khmer Buddhism; Religion and Society; Sivaraksha, Sulak; Thailand; Vietnam.

Further Reading
Bhikkhu, Santidhammo. *Maha Ghosananda: The Buddha of the Battlefield.* Thailand: S. R. Printing, 2009.
Ghosananda, Maha. *Step by Step: Meditations on Wisdom and Compassion.* Berkeley, CA: Parallax Press, 1991.
Kraft, Kenneth, Maha Ghosananda, Tenzin Gyatso, and Sulak Sivaraksa. *The Path of Compassion: Writing on Socially Engaged Buddhism.* Berkeley, CA: Parallax Press, 1988.

GLOBALIZATION

Globalization, in the context of Southeast Asia, is a multidimensional phenomenon. It has economic, political, religious, and cultural dimensions. In its sweep, it affects all nations and peoples. Its direct impact is felt all over the world. Since the first appearance of the term in 1962, globalization has gone from jargon to cliché. The *Economist* has called it "the most abused word in the twentieth century." Certainly no word in recent memory has meant so many different things to different people.

The Copenhagen Seminar for Social Progress (1997) in dealing with "globalization as a trend and as a political project," distinguishes between globalization as a stage in the historical evolution of humanity, and globalization as a political project guiding the world in a particular direction. The "project" is global capitalism, or the application of the theory and practice of market economy to the world as a whole. It is actively pursued by a number of governments and by the economic and financial elites of the world.

From the perspective of Southeast Asia, the central element of globalization as a project is to focus on the promotion of liberal economic policies and the transformation of state-motivated national development efforts into neoliberal policies. The globalization project is linked in particular to the growing concentration of control over the global economy by a relatively small number of large, oligopolistic, transnational corporations that have emerged from merger-driven and technology-facilitated changes to the global political economy of the last few decades. The project is legitimized in the name of a free-enterprise and free-trade vision of the global economy.

There is a lot of evidence to show that economic globalization has produced injustice, inequality, poverty, and a spiritual crisis. Even leading proponents of

In an interview, John Kenneth Galbraith said: "I am a consultant to *The American Heritage Dictionary of the English Language* and I won't allow the word globalization. It is an ugly word." He preferred the term internationalism. Global, however, is not international, as it has no reference to nations or people.

Ninan Koshy

globalization concede that in the failure to deliver a more just global economic order, globalization may hold within it the seeds of its own demise. The concern is not only about the unjust consequences of globalization, but the fact that the concept of justice is alien to globalization. We have an analytical deficit occasioned by the failure of economic globalization to assess the threat to its legitimacy emanating from its theoretical and practical myopia toward justice issues. The paradigm of development under globalization is only about growth. It does not include two important components in the ecumenical understanding of development: justice, and people's participation.

An institution that has been profoundly transformed under globalization is the state. The language of globalization, especially in its neoliberalist guise, is about the managerialist capacity of the modern state. But it has failed to recognize the manner in which the internationalization of finance can exacerbate the "democratic deficit." The Asian Development Bank, a key player in Southeast Asia, identifies as a major function of the state the provision of an appropriate enabling environment for private enterprise. The intervention in the market is in favor of capital; not labor, not people. The crisis of the welfare state consequent to globalization has caused misery to millions of people.

The globalization of recent decades has seldom been a democratic choice by the peoples of Southeast Asia—the process has been business-driven, by business strategies and tactics for business ends. Governments have helped, by incremental policy actions and by major actions that were often taken in secret, without national debate and discussion of where the entire project was leading. The undemocratic process, carried out within a democratic façade, is consistent with the distribution of benefits and costs of globalization, and the fact that globalization has been a tool serving elite interests.

Though the role of force in globalization was evident much before the terrorist attacks of September 11, 2001, and the response of the United States of the declaration of the "War on Terror," scholars of globalization had not explained the issue adequately. Globalization emerges out of earlier forms of global political changes, often brought about by military means and associated with Western imperialism and the internationalization of capital. *The National Security Strategy of the USA* (2001) made it clear that the opportunity of the War on Terror would be utilized to promote globalization. Globalization and militarism should be seen as the two sides of the same coin.

The *Human Development Report* (1999, 4–5) makes some important observations on globalization and culture under the heading "Cultural Insecurity": "Globalization opens people's lives to culture and all its creativity and to the flows of ideas and knowledge. But the new culture carried by expanding global markets is disquieting ... Today's flow of culture is unbalanced, heavily weighted in one direction, from rich countries to poor. ... Such onslaught of foreign culture can put cultural diversity at risk and make people fear for their cultural identity." With regard to regions like Southeast Asia, as a result of globalization, there is the emergence of an increasingly Western-dominated international culture, a trend that has sparked concerns about the erosion of national identities and traditional values.

Southeast Asia has been one of the main beneficiaries of globalization in the sense of open markets, trade, and capital flows. Almost all countries of the region have registered impressive growth. But since the paradigm of neoliberalism does not include distributive justice, the benefits have disproportionally gone to the rich. While new social welfare measures have not been initiated, traditional safety nets have been dissolved. The result has been increasing inequality and, for several sections of people, intensified poverty. This is the case even in China, where growth has been remarkable as a result of the Communist state embracing capitalist globalization.

The Asian financial crisis of 1997 was a turning point for the globalization project not only in Asia but throughout the world. Before the financial crisis, the East Asian economy was considered to be an exemplary model from which Western countries should learn. The stringent conditions imposed by the International Monetary Fund drove countries of the region into economic depression. The Asian financial crisis highlighted the inevitability of crisis under globalization in the midst of global over-production and the speculative excesses of financial liberalization. The perils of globalization became evident.

The impact of globalization on Asia's security is complex. In some ways the impact has been positive: economic integration has reduced the potential for conflict, particularly in Southeast Asia. Nevertheless, globalization may give rise to new security concerns and aggravate existing tensions. There are new transnational threats, and regional institutions have weakened.

Ninan Koshy

See also: Engaged Buddhism; Freedom of Religion; Fundamentalism; Secularism.

Further Reading

Berger, Mark T. *The Battle for Asia, From Decolonization to Globalization*. Oxford: Routledge Curzon, 2004.

Held, David, Anthony G. McGrew, David Goldblatt, and Jonathan Perraton. *Global Transformations: Politics, Economics and Culture*. Stanford, CA: Stanford University Press, 1999.

Human Development Report 1999. Published for the United Nations Development Programme (UNDP). New York and Oxford: Oxford University Press, 1999. http://hdr.undp.org/sites/default/files/reports/260/hdr_1999_en_nostats.pdf (accessed October 22, 2014).

Nissanke, Machiko, and Erik Thorbecke, eds. *The Poor under Globalization in Asia, Latin America and Africa*. Oxford: Oxford University Press, 2010.

Stiglitz, Joseph E. *Globalization and Its Discontents*. New York: W. W. Norton & Company, 2003.

GODDESS TRADITIONS

The scope and antiquity of goddess traditions are remarkable. Female sacred images are associated with some of the oldest archaeological evidence of religious expression and yet still have efficacy in the contemporary world. Goddess images are depicted in a wide range of forms, from symbolic or suggestive representations, such as abstract reproductive organs, to fully elaborated icons decorated with the finery of royalty. They are linked to all major aspects of life, including birth, initiation, marriage, reproduction, and death. They display the elaborate variegation of religious experiences in different cultural contexts. Indeed, theories about goddess worship have been advanced ever since the emergence of the social science disciplines in the nineteenth century. Religion specialists in the fields of anthropology, sociology, folklore, psychology, and comparative mythology have contributed numerous theories to explain the phenomenon of goddess worship.

While there are no universal characteristics of goddess traditions, certain common themes, such as nurturing or punishing mothers, protectors of community, images of national identity, symbols of virginity and purity,

A Statue of Quan Am, Goddess of Mercy, inside Quan Am Pagoda in Ho Chi Minh City, Vietnam. While goddess worshiping traditions vary by location, all are deeply linked to the human experience and include all major stages of life: birth, initiation, marriage, reproduction, and death. (Anders Blomqvist/ Getty Images)

the origins of the fertility of crops and human beings, demonstrate how deeply rooted goddess veneration is within human experience.

In Southeast Asia, Vietnam, where the goddess tradition, *Đạo Mẫu* is the oldest religious tradition in the region, predating even the Chinese occupation, offers a good example. Veneration of goddesses, once dismissed as superstition by the

---

The scope and antiquity of goddess traditions are remarkable. Female sacred images are associated with some of the oldest archaeological evidence of religious expression and yet still have efficacy in the contemporary world. In Vietnam, the Lady of the Realm, *Bà Chúa Xứ*, provides a useful and interesting case study of Southeast Asian goddess veneration. Another, quite different goddess tradition is to be observed in the Thai Goddess of Rice, *Mae Phosop*.

David C. Scott

Communist government, has recently grown in popularity and is now accepted and widely practiced in Vietnam and in Vietnamese communities overseas.

Goddesses are considered to control everything that happens on earth, and their veneration addresses concerns of daily life and desires for good health. Goddesses protect and support, and they bring good fortune and strength to overcome misfortune. They are generally approached for help with issues considered to be connected with femininity, such as fertility, marriage, or female sickness.

In most temples and other places of worship, in northern Vietnam particularly, a trinity of goddesses are represented: the Goddesses of Heaven (white), Water (red), and Mountains and Forests (green). However, in many texts, four goddesses will be represented, including the Goddess of Earth (yellow). The colors for Water and Heaven are often the other way around.

As in many goddess traditions the world over, Vietnamese goddesses are embodied on earth to perform good deeds or miracles, in a different guise each time to avoid recognition. Faithful devotees will know all the incarnations of the different goddesses and believe that they coexist in spirit.

If a devotee desires to call on the goddess for help—particularly if their goals in life are not being met—they will often visit a shaman, a spirit medium. The problem will be explained to the medium, and they will know which incarnation, or incarnations, to call upon. The medium and entourage will be paid and a ceremony arranged at a temple—more likely a small local temple rather than a grand major one—for everyone involved.

In fact, the tradition draws together fairly disparate beliefs and practices. These include the veneration of goddesses such as the Lady of the Realm, the Lady of the Storehouse, and Princess Liễu Hạnh. Legendary figures such as the Trung Sisters and Lady Trieu, as well as the cult of the Four Palaces, also have their devotees. Further, as was mentioned above, the goddess tradition is commonly associated with spirit medium rituals, much as practiced in other parts of Asia such as Taiwan, Singapore, and Hong Kong.

Of these, the Lady of the Realm, *Bà Chúa Xứ*, provides a useful and interesting case study. Popular folklore regarding the discovery of the goddess begins with the appearance of a stone image on the peak of an island as the water level in the Mekong Delta receded. Local lore is divided about the explanation. Either her image was placed there in some primeval time, or she emerged extraordinarily from the rock. Another account has the Lady of the Realm possessing a young village girl and revealing herself to the villagers who reside on the summit of Sam Mountain. In order to be more conveniently located so her devotees could readily venerate her, 40 sturdy young men tried but failed to transport her down the mountain. Finally, the Lady of the Realm reappeared to inform the people that nine virgins were sufficient to bring her down the mountain, where her temple is located to this day, at the base of Sam Mountain in the Mekong Delta village of Vĩnh Tế.

The Lady of the Realm is among the goddesses who have attained popularity in southern Vietnam. Portrayed as a statue made of stone and cement, she presides over a massive shrine decorated with offerings made to her by devotees. Her annual festival takes placed at the commencement of the monsoon season, when she is bathed and vested with a new robe by postmenopausal women of the village. Pivotal is a succession of sacrifices, including a large pig for roasting. Following an invocation of the goddess for peace and prosperity, a program of operatic performances is provided. All this takes place in a festive atmosphere around the shrine, the most popular religious site in southern Vietnam, where visitors can expect to witness such things as beauty queen contests, a house of horrors, karate competitions, magicians plying their art, gambling, and numerous places to feast

Responding to the pleas of her devotees, the goddess assists them in such matters as success in commerce, health, fecundity, domestic harmony, studies, and even foretelling the future. In return, the devotee is obligated to keep the promises he or she has made to the goddess. Having sought the gracious assistance of the goddess, the devotee is required to keep promises made and to express gratitude for her aid. Indeed, she is well known for her retaliation against those who recompense her. Pilgrimage is a significant means of repaying the Lady of the Realm for her favors. Indeed, the often onerous act of making a pilgrimage to the shrine in Vĩnh Tế is regarded as an act of thankful recompense. Significantly, by far the largest number of pilgrims are women, of all ages.

Having gone into some detail in considering the case study of the Lady of the Realm, it is important to remember that, as we have previously noted, there is in Southeast Asia a vast array of types of goddess veneration linked to all major aspects of life, including birth, initiation, marriage, reproduction, and death.

Space permits only a brief concluding description of an example of another, quite different goddess tradition, the Thai Rice Goddess. In most rice-growing countries in Asia, rice is not merely a crop; it is the very essence of life, the spirit of rice residing in the Rice Mother, or the Rice Goddess. Nurturing Thailand's cultural roots as well as its people's bodies, rice is believed to be a female deity, named *Mae Phosop.* Since time immemorial, Thai folk have considered rice to be indispensable to their well-being; indeed, to their very survival. Cultivators perform a variety of rites throughout the growing season to express their profound respect for and gratitude to the Rice Goddess for the prosperity and wealth they believe she will bring. Failure in this, it is believed, will result in hunger, sickness, and poverty.

So it is that the range, antiquity, and array of goddess traditions in Southeast Asia, as in the world over, constitute a remarkably continuous phenomenon in the history of the human race.

David C. Scott

See also: Ancestor Worship; Pilgrimage; Ritual Dynamics; Shamanism, Spirit Mediumship; Thailand; Vietnam; Women.

Further Reading

Bachofen, J. J. *Myth, Religion and Mother Right.* Translated by Ralph Manheim. Princeton, NJ: Princeton University Press, 1967.

Eliade, Mircea. *Patterns in Comparative Religion.* Translated by Mary Sheed. Lincoln: University of Nebraska Press, 1996 (originally published 1958).

Encyclopedia Britannica. 1985 ed. S.v. "God and Goddess."

Neumann, Erich. *The Great Mother: An Analysis of the Archetype*. 2nd ed. Princeton, NJ: Princeton University Press, 1963.

Paul, Diana. "Kuan-Yin: Savior and Savioress in Pure Land Buddhism." In *The Book of the Goddess Past and Present*, edited by Carl Olson, 161–75. New York: Crossroad Publishing Company, 1983.

Preston, James J., ed. *Mother Worship, Theme and Variations*. Chapel Hill: University of North Carolina Press, 1982.

HANH, THICH NHAT

One of the best known and most respected Zen masters in the world today, poet, scholar, and peace and human rights activist Thich Nhat Hanh has led an extraordinary life. Born in central Vietnam in 1926, he entered a monastery at the age of 16, where he received training in Zen and the Mahayana school of Buddhism. He was ordained a monk in 1949. The Vietnam War confronted the monks with the question: adhere to the contemplative life and remain meditating in the monasteries, or help villagers suffering under bombings and other devastation of the war. Nhat Hanh was one of those who chose to do both, helping to found the "Engaged Buddhism" movement. His life has since been dedicated to the work of inner transformation for the benefit of individuals and society.

In Saigon in the early 1960s, Thich Nhat Hanh (fondly known as *Thay* or "Teacher" by his students) founded the School of Youth Social Service (SYSS), a grassroots relief organization that rebuilt bombed villages, set up schools and medical centers, resettled homeless families, and organized agricultural cooperatives. Rallying some 10,000 student volunteers, the SYSS based its work on the Buddhist principles of nonviolence and compassionate action. Despite government denunciation of his activity, Nhat Hanh went on to found a Buddhist university, a publishing house, and a powerful peace activist magazine in Vietnam.

After visiting the United States and Europe in 1966 on a peace mission, Nhat Hanh was banned from returning to Vietnam. On subsequent travels to the United States, he made the case for peace to federal and Pentagon officials. Indeed, he may have changed the course of U.S. history when he persuaded Martin Luther King Jr. to oppose the Vietnam War publicly, and so helped to galvanize the peace movement in the United States. The following year, Dr. King nominated him for the Nobel Peace Prize. Subsequently, Nhat Hanh led the Buddhist delegation to

Thich Nhat Hanh is one of the best known and most respected Zen masters in the world. Poet, scholar and human rights activist, he has led an extraordinary life. The Vietnam War confronted him and fellow monks with the question: adhere to the contemplative life and remain meditating in the monasteries, or help villagers suffering under bombings and other devastation of the war? Nhat Hanh was one of those who chose to do both, helping to found the "Engaged Buddhism" movement. His life has since been dedicated to the work of inner transformation for the benefit of individuals and society.

David C. Scott

the Paris Peace Talks. In September 2001, just a few days after the terrorist attacks on the World Trade Center, he addressed the issues of nonviolence and forgiveness in a memorable speech at Riverside Church in New York City.

Nhat Hanh has also received recognition for his prolific writings on meditation, mindfulness, and peace. He has published some 100 titles of poetry, prose, and prayers, with more than 40 in English, including the best-selling titles *Call Me by My True Names*, *Peace Is Every Step*, *Being Peace*, *Touching Peace*, *Living Buddha Living Christ*, *Teachings on Love*, *The Path of Emancipation*, and *Anger*.

In addition to the several monastic communities he established in Vietnam, in 1982, Nhat Hanh founded Plum Village, a Buddhist community and meditation center in France, where he continues his work of teaching meditation and alleviating the suffering of refugees, boat people, political prisoners, and hungry families in Vietnam and throughout the Third World. Plum Village has remained the primary locus where Nhat Hanh teaches, writes, and gardens. He also leads retreats worldwide on "the art of mindful living," whose key teaching is that, through mindfulness, we can learn to live in the present moment instead of in the past and in the future. Dwelling in the present moment is, according to Nhat Hanh, the only way to truly develop peace, both in one's self and in the world.

David C. Scott

See also: Buddhism; Communism; Education; Engaged Buddhism; Peace-building, Reform Movements; Religion and Society; Religious Discrimination and Intolerance; Sivaraksa, Sulak; Southeast Asian Religious in the USA; Study of Religion; Thien Buddhism; Vietnam.

Further Reading

McLeod, Melvin, ed. *The Pocket Thich Nhat Hanh*. Boston: Shambhala Publications, 2012.

Warren, Mobi, trans. *Fragrant Palm Leaves: Journals 1962–1966*. New York: Riverhead Books, 1998.

Willis, Jennifer Schwamm, ed. *A Lifetime of Peace: Essential Writings by and about Thich Nhat Hanh*. New York: Marlowe & Co., 2003.

HINDUISM

Hinduism is a major religion of India with a long and complex history. It is also a way of life that embraces many aspects of South Asian culture. Its origins date back to the Indus valley civilization of 2500 BCE. The word "Hindu" was initially a Persian toponym used for people living beyond the Indus River. The term was later employed by the British to refer to all of the peoples of Hindustan (northwest India), irrespective of their religious practices. Subsequently, it came to denote the culture and religion of high caste priests and was eventually appropriated by Indians to construct a national identity opposing British colonial rule.

Hinduism does not have a single historical founder. It also lacks a unified system of belief, a centralized authority, and a bureaucratic structure. A combination of traditions, it is difficult to define. Most Hindu traditions are linked to a body of sacred

Hindus praying at the Pura Ulun Danu Batur temple in Bali. (WEKWEK/iStockphoto.com)

texts called the Vedas. Others are based upon rituals deemed important for salvation. Common components include a belief in reincarnation (samsara) determined by the law of cause and effect (karma), and an understanding of salvation as the transcendence of this cycle. It is a polytheistic religion that allows for multiple forms of divinity. This is usually centered upon the "Trimurthi," a triad of Brahma, Visnu, and Siva, the deities deemed responsible for the creation, preservation, and destruction of the universe.

Hinduism in Southeast Asia

Hinduism spread into Southeast Asia over many centuries along with South Asian practitioners. India has long had relations with the region, links dating back over 2,000 years. Indian settlement in Southeast Asia is documented from as early as the sixth century BCE. The great epic *Ramayana* refers to Suvaranbhumi and Yavadvipa. Another epic, *Purana*, mentions Malaya-dvipa and Yavadvipa. Although the exact

Mount Meru, the sacred mountain that is considered to be the center of the physical and metaphysical universes, is believed to be at the center of a huge continent known as *Bhu-mandala* and expands two billion miles in each direction. *Bhu-mandala* is divided into several islands called *dvipas*, including *Jambudvipa* (Rose-Apple Tree Island) that is believed to be closest to Meru and thus to earth and has about two dozen celestial mountains. The ancient Hindu diviners described this extra cosmographical feature to the earth and visited it often.

Ruchi Agarwal

locations of these places are not known, they are all thought to be located in Southeast Asia. The *Niddesa*, a Pali canon dating back to the first centuries of Christian era, also has several Sanskrit toponyms associated with places in "Farther India."

Coedès notes a variety of factors that contributed to the development of Indian settlements in Southeast Asia. One was the invasion of the Kushans into India around the first century CE, which put pressure on the local population. Another pertained to the opportunities open for the high caste Indians to pursue their fortunes in places outside of India. A number of other scholars also suggest that Indian contact with Southeast Asia was largely commercial in origin. The interaction between the Mediterranean and the East started with the campaign of Alexander, the establishment of the Asoka Empire, the Seleucid Empire, and the Roman Empire. These led to an increase in the trade of luxury goods by the first century. Van Leur (1955, 55) points out that the Indian trade was based more on the handicraft industry and was carried out by small traders who carried the goods, exchanged them, and established foreign enclaves on the Southeast Asian ports. Indian settlements in the region eventually resulted in the formation of Indic kingdoms on the Indochinese Peninsula and pre-modern Indonesia.

Migrants brought with them traditional arts, religious beliefs, and customs as well as Sanskrit, which was used as a sacral language. They also left behind a significant cultural legacy. From the end of the nineteenth century, European scholars studying Southeast Asia's antiquities realized the extent of the influence of Sanskrit culture on the region's religion, art, and architecture. As noted by Coedès, other influences include conceptions of royalty characterized by Hindu or Buddhist cults, local literary expression through Sanskrit, local use of mythological elements from the *Ramayana* and *Mahabharata, the Puranas* and other Sanskrit texts, and the local observance of laws such as the *Dharmasastras* (sacred law of Hinduism) and the *Manava Dharmasastra* (Laws of Manu). In many instances, cultural transmission involved the retention of Brahmin priests as court functionaries, a practice that had earlier emerged in South Asia.

Buddhism, of course, constituted another contribution. Buddhist monks arrived in the region sometime during the first century CE. Buddha images from the second and third centuries have been discovered in Siam (Thailand), Champa (Cambodia), Sumatra, Java, and Celebes (Indonesia). Several sculptures belonging to the Amaravati school have been found at the site of Phra Pathom (Nakorn Pathom) and the site of Phong Tuk (located in northwest of Nakorn Pathom). These date back to the third or fourth centuries.

Hindu Gods in Southeast Asia

Over time, forms of Hinduism and Buddhism developed that incorporated aspects of local cultures in Southeast Asia. Elites continued to draw upon and make use of South Asian religious practices in their daily lives, however. Numerous inscriptions indicate the central role of Brahmins in the religious lives of Southeast Asian peoples. Popular local forms of Hinduism included Saivism, with Siva being the supreme deity, and Vaishnavism, where Visnu is the supreme deity. Several temples dedicated to Siva and Visnu were built in the ancient Khmer empire. One such example is Angkor Wat, the largest Hindu temple in the world at the time of its construction in the twelfth century. It was initially dedicated to Visnu but was later transformed into a Buddhist temple.

Throughout the region, Siva is worshipped both in human form and as a lingam carved in different styles. In his human form, he is widely known as the *Natraja*, Lord of the Dance, and also as the great yogi. The discovery of Natraja statue in Mi-son style in Cambodia is an evidence of that. Siva's worship in the form of lingam is still common today among Cham Brahmins in Binh Thuan and Ninh Thuan provinces. Saivism became popular among the Cambodian rulers in the seventh century acting as way of measuring and explaining their expertise. In fact the names of the rulers ended with a Sanskrit name, Varman. Saivite cults thereafter became popular in Southeast Asia, especially during warfare. Yet another cult of Saivism, showing a goddess as the Siva's sakti, became a strong feature of Tantric Buddhism found in many parts of Southeast Asia by the eighth century, and came to play an important role in thirteenth- and fourteenth-century Indonesia.

As for Visnu, his 10 avatars are known by many different names in the region. He was famous as Rama and Krishna in local myths and legends. The *Ramayana* and *Mahabharata* served as inspiration for Southeast Asian art and literature, as well as providing themes for its drama and ballet. Several images of Visnu are found in different parts of Southeast Asia. Among these is one found in Champa in Ananthasayam posture, with Brahma rising on a lotus from Visnu's naval. In Burma as well, images of Visnu, Durga, Surya, and others have been discovered. An example would be the temple of Na-hluang Kyaung, where the main deity is Visnu.

The third of the Hindu *trimurti*, Brahma, plays a less prominent role in Southeast Asian Hinduism. Instead, other Gods gained popularity and appeared in Southeast Asian mythology. Among them were Yama, the lord of the underworld who judges humankind, as well as Surya, Indra, and the serpent gods.

The Hindu concept of the universe as a central continent, Jambudvipa, with its central cosmic mountain, Mount Meru, made its way into Southeast Asian thought through the vehicle of Buddhism. So did the belief that all life was subject to periodic creation and destruction and the idea that world history, from creation to annihilation, was divided into four yugas (periods of immense length), which together formed a kalpa, a day in the life of Brahma.

With the spread of Buddhism and Islam, Hinduism was eclipsed in several parts of Southeast Asia and now seems to play a secondary role in the religious life of the region. Significant Hindu enclaves remain, however. If Islam now predominates in Indonesia, some 20,000 Hindu temples can be found in Java and Bali alone. Moreover, Balinese Hinduism, known as Agama Hindu Dharma, retains a theological foundation derived from Indian philosophy and indigenous beliefs. These include ancestors and spirit worship in shrines where agricultural goods are offered on a regular basis.

In Thailand as well, a Buddhist majority continues to draw upon and make use of earlier Hindu practices long patronized by local elites. Garuda, the eagle-like creature that serves as Visnu's steed, functions as the country's national emblem. Thai understandings of kingship are informed by the concept of Devraja (God-King), and monarchs of the current dynastic line make use of the prefix Rama, an incarnation of Visnu, in their reign names. Hindu priests officiate at royal rites, state ceremonies, and national festivals. Many of the country's festivals are also of South Asian origin. These include Songkran, the water festival; Triyampawai, or Tripawai, festival of Swing; the Ploughing ceremony, festival to bring good harvest; and Loy Krathong, the festival of lights. Temples and shrines dedicated to Brahma, Siva, and Visnu can also be found around the country. Indeed, virtually every market in the capital city of Bangkok has its own Hindu shrine to guarantee the prosperity and well-being of local merchants.

Throughout Southeast Asia, large numbers of Hindus continue to practice their faith. In Indonesia, as many as 20 million believers can be found, with numbers particularly concentrated in Bali, Central Java, East Java, and Lampung provinces. In Malaysia and Singapore, Hinduism remains the principal religion of ethnic Indian minorities, which constitute 6.3 percent and 4 percent of the total local populations, respectively. In Thailand, the number of believers is estimated to be in the hundreds of thousands. An equally large or perhaps larger number can also be found in Myanmar, with official estimates at around 900,000. Indeed, small but significant Hindu communities are tallied in every country in the region: Vietnam has some 50,000, the Philippines 175,000, Timor 5,000, and Brunei some 272.

Ruchi Agarwal

See also: Buddhism; Dharma/Dhamma; Diaspora; Indonesia; Interreligious Relations and Dialogue; Localization of Hinduism in Indonesia; Missionary Movements, Myanmar (Burma), Oka, Gedong Bagus; Pilgrimage; Sathya Sai Baba Movement, Thailand; Thaipusam; Water Festivals.

Further Reading

Bentley, G. Carter. "Indigenous States of Southeast Asia." *Annual Review of Anthropology* 15 (1986): 275–305.

Coedès, George. *The Indianized States of Southeast Asia*. Edited by Walter F. Vella. Translated by Susan Brown Cowing. Honolulu, HI: East-West Center Press, 1968.

Desai, Santosh N. *Hinduism in Thai Life*. Mumbai: Popular Prakashan, 1980.

Flood, Gavin D. *An Introduction to Hinduism*. Cambridge: Cambridge University Press, 1996.

Hall, D. G. E. "South-East Asian Proto-History." Chap. 2 in *A History of South-East Asia*, 4th ed. London: Macmillan Asian Histories Series, 1981.

Heine-Geldern. Robert. "Conceptions of State and Kingship in Southeast Asia." In *The Journal of Asia Studies*, vol. 2. Cambridge: Cambridge University Press, 1942.

Kumar, Bacchan. "Religious Positivity." Chap. 12 in *Hindu Positivism in Southeast Asia*, edited by S. M. Tripathi and Nagendra Kr. Singh. New Delhi: Global Vision Publishing House, 2001.

Tarling, Nicholas, ed. *The Cambridge History of Southeast Asia*. Vol. 1. Cambridge: Cambridge University Press, 1992.

HÒA HẢO BUDDHISM

Hòa Hảo, which can be translated as "Supreme Harmony," refers to a local Buddhist movement from the Mekong Delta in southwestern Vietnam that arose at the end of the colonial period and grew during the revolutionary context of the so-called Indochina War, then the Vietnam War. The definition of the 1986 "Đổi Mới" policy of renovation began to change favorably the state-religion relations. The community has been officially estimated at over one million followers in southern Vietnam and several dozens of thousands of followers overseas.

During the summer of 1939, Huỳnh Phú Sổ, a young man from a middle-class farming family, publicly predicted terrible disasters in his village (Hòa Hảo). He reinterpreted the basic tenets of Buddhism under a messianic form that would provide redemption and show a path toward salvation. To do so, he reshaped the mid-nineteenth-century local millenarian beliefs (*Bửu Sơn Kỳ Hương*) and reactivated the messianic figure of the "Buddha Master of Western Peace" (*Phật Thầy Tây An*). His eloquence, his poetry, and his published moral prophecies (*sấm giảng*) reinforced his charisma. The "Pontiff Huỳnh" strove to unify and purify the practice of Mahayana Buddhism, rendering it respectful with the Four Debts of Gratitude and compatible with ancestor worship, a social-humanist commitment and a simple peasant life.

The French colonial authorities and then the Japanese were quickly concerned by this new case of mysticism. From August 1945, by institutionalizing Hòa Hảo Buddhism, Huỳnh Phú Sổ tried to demonstrate the harmonious compatibility of patriotic engagement, democratic values, and Buddhist precepts. But his "disappearance" in April 18, 1947, sealed a political rivalry between Hòa Hảo believers and Communist partisans, reactivating at the same time the belief of a second coming of their messiah.

An autonomous religious organization tried to emerge, and the founder's family did maintain religious authority by becoming the guardian of the sanctuary and of the doctrine. But the religious community fatally splintered into politico-military sects or feudal organizations. Under the Diệm regime (1955–1963), all of Hòa Hảo's civil organizations were dismantled. In 1964, a new religious policy recognized the legal status of Hòa Hảo Buddhism, but after April 1975, Hòa Hảo's religious life once again faced severe upheaval as its organizations were dismantled. While central authorities tried to reduce the Hòa Hảo cult to a local practice, certain

---

Hòa Hảo Buddhism can be considered as a renovated form of *Millenarianism*. The former expression of this millenarian belief, the Bửu Sơn Kỳ Hương, appeared in the Mekong delta in the middle of the nineteenth century and was concomitant with the beginning of the French military conquest of the southern provinces of Vietnam. These popular beliefs became a strong link to unite under charismatic leaders some local movements of resistance as far as the middle of the twentieth century. In this way, it can be understood at the same time as the matrix of regional religious communities and of anticolonialist movements.

Pascal Bourdeaux

networks of the original church were structured within the Vietnamese diaspora groups. The recognition of religious sentiments and the social utility of religions in 1991 ushered in a new era. In May 1999, the government recognized Hòa Hảo Buddhism as a religion. Institutionalization is now progressing with reduced tension, and the community is currently allowed to expand its charitable and social activities and diffuse its religious teachings.

Hòa Hảo Buddhism has very few ritualized and intellectualized practices. Private ceremonies and worship do not need pagodas, statues, or monks' mediation. Its precepts are essentially practiced within domestic circles. Followers must assume social responsibilities and accept the supervision of the doctrine's secular committees and lay experts. This religion, in the ultimate analysis, is based on compassion and the sincerity of individual action.

Pascal Bourdeaux

See also: Ancestor Worship; Buddhism; Colonialism; Communism; Diaspora; Humanism; Messianic Movements; Morality; Religion and Society; Vietnam.

Further Reading

Biography and Teaching of Prophet Huynh Phu Sô. Saigon: Central Committee for the Diffusion of Hoa Hao Buddhism, 1966 (translation of: Giáo hội Phật Giáo Hòa Hảo, *Sấm giảng thi văn - toàn bộ* của Huỳnh Phú Sổ, ban phổ thông giáo lý trung ương ấn hành).

Bourdeaux, Pascal. "Réflexions sur l'institutionnalisation du bouddhisme Hòa Hảo. Remise en perspective historique de la reconnaissance de 1999." *Social Compass* 57, no. 3 (2010): 372–85.

Nguyễn, Long Thành Nam. *Hòa Hảo Buddhism in the Course of Việtnam's History*. New York: Nova Science Publishing, 2004. (First ed., *Phật Giáo Hòa Hảo trong dòng lịch sử dân tộc*, edited by Đuộc Tú Bi. Santa Fe, CA: 1991).

Nguyễn, Văn Hầu. *Nhân thúc Phật Giáo Hòa Hảo* [Conceive Hòa Hảo Buddhism]. Long Xuyên: Hương Sen xuất bản, 1968.

Tai, Hue-Tâm Ho. *Millenarianism and Peasant Politics in Vietnam*. Cambridge, MA: Harvard University Press, 1983.

HUMANISM

This entry briefly addresses the issue of humanism in Southeast Asia, identifying key factors that help to navigate an inexhaustible area of study, and providing distinct examples to help elaborate on points highlighted.

Humanism and Contextualization

The substance of humanist action and discourse is born within the lived reality of individuals, communities, and nations as they seek to overcome human suffering in the quest for a just society. While there are points of common concern across the nations of Southeast Asia, such as the provision of education or poverty alleviation, these are framed within particular locations and contexts. The concerns of those caught in the web of the sex trade in Thailand differ from the concerns of rural Indonesian farmers pressured by economic forces to become re-skilled and relocate to the vastly growing urban centers. The struggles of the Islamic Rohingya minority community, persecuted for their religious and ethnic identity, differ from the struggles of the Chin, Kachin, and Shan Christian minority groups, even though these struggles occur in the same nation. The struggles of people living in the aftermath of devastating war and civil conflict, such as in Vietnam and Cambodia, will differ from the struggles of women in Timor Leste seeking educational advancement. The struggles of those living with the continued threat of undetonated bombs in the aftermath of war, including the people of Laos, differ from the struggle of the poorest communities in the Philippines; or of those who live in communities destroyed by natural disaster, such as the 2004 tsunami that devastated parts of Southeast Asia, including Indonesia and Thailand, or the earthquake and volcanic devastation in the Philippines during the 1990s.

The study of humanism in Southeast Asia must therefore take cognizance of the vast diversity that exists across the subcontinent; each nation has its own historical narrative, or rather *narratives*, which serve to make up the content for humanistic discourse and action. This diversity is manifest in multiple forms, including culture, language, and religion as well as social, political, and economic stability. Across the subcontinent, there are also competing political, ideological, and religious solutions offered to address nationalist concerns, which in turn influence the rise of humanist concerns.

Though the contextualization of humanism remains essential, however, it is vital that attempts are made to identify national, transnational, and global influencing forces that shape contextual concerns. Economic development, for example, cannot be assessed purely on a national level, but must take into consideration broader globalizing forces that continue to play such an important role in regional and national capacity building.

Nonreligious Foundations

Each nation within Southeast Asia is not simply a static entity, but is historically dynamic and complex. Milton Osborne provides a useful case in point here, observing that current political developments in Myanmar (Burma), including the reintroduction of the exiled Aung San Suu Kyi into the political arena after 15 years of house arrest under the country's military regime, mark a striking point of departure from the traditional forms of political authority in recent decades. Such a shift brings new and widespread hope in political and social transformation and marks a sharp contrast to the authoritarian military regime which led to the Saffron Revolution in 2007.

The term humanism transcends any simplistic reductionism to any particular subject field and is relevant to many research areas, including the political, economic, social, psychological, ethical, and religious realm. The twentieth century witnessed the rise of significant secular and humanist groups such as the International Humanist and Ethical Union, a network that includes the Humanist Society of Singapore, the Philippine Atheists and Agnostics Society, and significant advocacy work in Indonesia. Without direct recourse to the religious or the supernatural, secular humanism advocates the building of a just, compassionate, and humane society in which individuals and communities can work together to shape and give meaning to their lives. While the International Humanist and Ethical Union does acknowledge and recognize the right of the individual to religious belief and practice, the network is essentially nonreligious, building its foundation on belief in the power of human agency and collaborative efforts to bring about social harmony in a given context.

Religious Foundations

Yet, the proliferation of the nonreligious voice to the humanistic narrative cannot discount the contribution of diverse religious voices, which remain essential to the broader narrative. Indeed, we must caution against the tendency to polarize religion and humanism, as though they are mutually exclusive categories. While religion, generally speaking, is concerned with the transcendental or "other worldly," it is also essentially concerned with the human struggle in the midst of the world. Given the majority allegiance to some form of religious identity, however this may be interpreted, it is clear that religion remains an important component of discourse concerning humanism in Southeast Asia.

The religions of Southeast Asia, including Islam, Buddhism, Christianity, Daoism, and Confucianism, all seek to effectively contribute to the conversation on humanism, each drawing upon critical sources central to their particular beliefs, traditions, and practices in order to establish praxis-oriented strategies to help overcome the struggles of the people. For example, in Thailand, leaders such as Bhikkhu Buddhadasa sought to interpret traditional Theravada Buddhism from a social and political perspective. This he considered essential to the context of rapid change experienced in Thailand in the twentieth century. The rise of "Humanistic Buddhism," aimed at nurturing compassion for others in a bid to create a more harmonious society, has the potential to make a significant impact in a context such as Thailand, where Buddhism is the majority religion.

Capacity to Address Humanist Concerns

Assessing the causes of human struggle in order to formulate effective plans to overcome those struggles is in itself complex, and within Southeast Asia there are competing political, ideological, and religious solutions offered to address particular concerns. Humanism is concerned with multifaceted and interrelated factors, including justice, peace, education and skills training, health, and economic stability. The effectiveness of any short- or long-term action or goals are further affected by incidences of political or economic corruption. It will also depend on the capacity to implement effective strategies to overcome particular issues in particular locations across a given nation. Where there is a strong infrastructure in place, such as in Singapore or Indonesia, there are greater opportunities for education, economic stability and development, and political stability. In nations working to develop a more resilient and effective infrastructure to address some of the basic needs of the people, humanistic discourse takes on a different level of urgency. Tensions are naturally exacerbated in a context of economic and political corruption, for example the scandals currently affecting political rule in the Philippines, as well as in the context of ethnic and cultural diversity within a given region, such as in Myanmar. One of the major difficulties experienced in Southeast Asia arises from the tension in the quest for national unity amidst cultural, ethnic, linguistic, and religious diversity. This tension is manifest in many ways, and the question of power and access to power to implement humanist goals remains central. These challenges have historically led to ongoing tensions and clashes in the region as minority ethnic or religious groups struggle for independence, religious freedom, stability, and justice.

Again, we must mention the broader global context in which local and national economic development takes place, which continue to be central to building the infrastructure and capacity to address humanistic concerns.

Humanism in Southeast Asia remains a central component of the secular, political, social, economic, and religious discourse of the region. The quest for justice, peace, and economic stability and growth can be understood only in the context in which this search takes place, amidst the complexity of ethnic, ideological, linguistic, historic, religious, and economic diversity.

Adrian Bird

See also: Atheism/Agnosticism; Bhikkhu, Buddhadasa; Christianity; Contextualization; Education; Engaged Buddhism; Globalization; Islam; Liberation Theologies; Secularism.

Further Reading

Brock, Colin, and Lorraine Pe Symaco. *Education in South-East Asia.* Oxford Studies in Comparative Education. Oxford: Symposium Books, 2011.

Dayley, Robert, and Clark D. Neher. *Southeast Asia in the New International Arena.* 6th ed. Boulder, CO: Westview Press, 2013.

International Humanist and Ethical Union. http://iheu.org/category/location/asia/south -eastern-asia/ (accessed April 28, 2014).

Leibo, Steven A. *The World Today Series 2012: East and Southeast Asia.* 45th ed. Lanham, MD: Styker-Post Publications, 2012.

Osborne, Milton. *Southeast Asia: An Introductory History.* 11th ed. New South Wales, Australia: Allen & Unwin, 2013.

Palatino, Mong. "Southeast Asia: Home to the World's Longest Ongoing Civil Wars." http:// globalvoicesonline.org/ (accessed April 28, 2014).

Torre, Miguel A de la, ed. *The Hope of Liberation in World Religions.* Waco, TX: Baylor University Press, 2008.

ILETO, REYNALDO C.

A leading scholar on religion and anticolonial movements in Southeast Asia, Reynaldo C. Ileto was born in 1946. He has incorporated historiography with literature, discourse analysis and critical theory in analyzing the Philippine revolution, the first anticolonial and pro-independence conflict of the region. His particular focus has been on the revolution from the end of the nineteenth to the beginning of the twentieth centuries. His groundbreaking work, *Pasyon and Revolution: Popular Movements in the Philippines, 1840–1910*, was cited in 2009 as among the 10 "Most Influential Books on Southeast Asia" by an international body commissioned by the Institute of Southeast Asian Studies.

Born and raised in Manila, he earned a bachelor's degree at the Ateneo de Manila University before pursuing an MA and PhD in history at the Southeast Asia Program of Cornell University in the United States. Ileto held teaching positions at the University of the Philippines, James Cook University, and the Australian National University before taking up a professorship at the Southeast Asian Studies Program at the National University of Singapore (NUS) in 2002. Ileto has also held a number of distinguished positions including the Tañada Chair at De La Salle University (Manila), the Burns Chair in History at the University of Hawaii at Manoa, and senior fellowships at Kyoto University and Tokyo University of Foreign Studies. Following his retirement from the NUS in 2012, Ileto continued to hold an adjunct appointment at the Australian National University.

Ileto analyzes the Spanish and American colonization of the Philippines from a critical, postcolonial perspective. In *Pasyon and Revolution* (1979), Ileto discussed how Tagalog peasantry engaged with Friar-imposed vernacular Passion epics, and argued that this provided the sentimental and ideological framework on which emancipatory projects of postcolonial nationalism formed "from below" in the nineteenth century. Ileto's path-breaking contribution was to examine how the trope of Christ's suffering and sacrifice was seen in terms of local moral-philosophical notions of debt of interiority (*utang na loob*), empathy (*damay*), power (*kapangyarihan*), and light (*liwanag*). Rising above the narrow-minded exclusionary nationalist historiography of his period, Ileto shifted the focus of emancipatory postcolonial nationalism from the elites to the religious masses.

In the latter part of his career, Ileto is also known for his polemical critique of American orientalist scholarship about the Philippines. Throughout his teaching career, he took seriously his task as a mentor and encouraged the younger generation to pursue serious research on the imperialist discourses that continued to pervade much of postwar scholarship on Philippine history and society.

In recognition of his distinguished contributions, he was awarded a number of honors, among which are the Harry Benda Prize, the Ohira Prize, the Philippine National Book Award, and the Fukuoka Asian Culture Prize. In 2012, the Ateneo de Manila University conferred the prestigious *Gawad Tanghal ng Lahi* award on Ileto in recognition of his contributions to the study of Filipino cultural and social life.

Julius Bautista

See also: Christianity; Colonialism; Education; Morality; Nationalism; Orientalism; Philippines; Postcolonial Theory; Singapore; Study of Religion.

Further Reading

"Forum on Orientalism and Philippine Politics." *Philippine Political Science Journal* 23, no. 46 (2002): 119–74.

Hui, Yew Foong. "The Ten Most Influential Books on Southeast Asia" *SOJOURN: Journal of Social Issues in Southeast Asia* 24(1): 2009.

Ileto, Reynaldo C. *Diorama Experience: A Visual History of the Philippines*. Makati City: Ayala Foundation, 2004.

Ileto, Reynaldo C. *Filipinos and Their Revolution: Event, Discourse, and Historiography*. Quezon City, Philippines: Ateneo de Manila University Press, 1998.

Ileto, Reynaldo C. "Orientalism and the Study of Philippine Politics." In *Knowing America's Colony: A Hundred Years from the Philippine War*, Philippine Studies Occasional Paper Series no. 13, 41–65. Honolulu: University of Hawai'i at Manoa, 1999.

Ileto, Reynaldo C. *Pasyon and Revolution: Popular Movements in the Philippines, 1840–1910*. Quezon City, Philippines: Ateneo University Press, 1979.

INDONESIA

The Republic of Indonesia (*Republik Indonesia*) is a country in Southeast Asia, straddling the equator whose capital city, Jakarta, is the most populous city in Southeast Asia. Its neighbor to the north is Malaysia, and to the east is Papua New Guinea. The country has approximately 17,000 islands, of which 6,000 are inhabited; 1,000 of these are permanently inhabited, according to the U.S. Department of State. The country has 33 provinces with over 206 million people in 2000; this increased to 238 million in 2010, of which 51.17 percent are male and 49.83 percent female. Indonesia is the world's fourth-most populous country after China, India, and the United States. The population distribution of the larger islands are: the island of Sumatra, which covers 25.2 percent of the entire Indonesian territory and is inhabited by 21.3 percent of the population; Java, which covers 6.8 percent of the territory and is inhabited by 57.5 percent of the population; and Papua which covers 21.8 percent of the territory and is inhabited by 1.5 percent of the population.

Indonesia is the country with the largest Muslim population in the world—203 million adherents. Indonesia is followed by Pakistan (174 million), India (161 million), and Bangladesh (145 million). During the last three decades of 1971–2000, Muslims have increased in population. The percentage of Muslims

Muslims bowed in prayer at the Istiqlal Mosque in Jakarta. Over the last several decades, the Muslim population has steadily increased in Indonesia. (hasim/iStockphoto.com)

increased from 87.51 percent in 1971 to 88.22 percent in 2000. The percentage of Christians has also increased, from 7.39 percent in 1971 to 8.92 percent in 2000 (Suryadinata et al. 2003). The other religious groups, according to the 2000 census, are Hindus, 1.81 percent; Buddhists, 0.84 percent; and others, 0.20 percent (Suryadinata et al. 2003). Indonesia is a multiethnic society with more than 1,000 ethnic/subethnic groups, but only 15 of these groups reach more than 1 million. The two largest ethnic groups, based on the 2000 census, are Javanese, 41.71 percent; and Sundanese, 15.41 percent. These are followed by Malay, 3.45 percent of the total population; Madurase 3.37 percent; Batak, slightly more than 3 percent; and Minangkabau, 2.7 percent (Suryadinata et al. 2003). Indonesia's national motto, "*Bhinneka Tunggal Ika*" ("Unity in Diversity"; literally, "many, but one"), articulates the diversity of ethnicity and cultures, and the understanding of religion that shapes the country.

Pribumisasi Islam (Indigenization of Islam) is an attempt to de-ideologize Islam and locate it within the framework of the pluralistic Indonesian society. With *pancasila* as the national ideology, every socioreligious group has equal right to contribute to the Indonesian state and society with their own values. In this connection, Islam should be one of the complementary components of the state, and Muslims should develop a national consciousness. *Pribumisasi* encourages the understanding of Islam in accordance with the local context. It affirms that religion that meets the contemporary demands will not be uprooted from the Indonesian culture and tradition.

Bambang Budiwiranto

The popular belief systems in Indonesia before the arrival of Hinduism, Buddhism, Islam, and Christianity were animism and dynamism, which believe that all creatures such as mountains, sea, stone, trees, and human beings have soul and power. Such power sometimes is useful and sometimes is dangerous. Hinduism was introduced to Indonesian at around the second century by Indian traders. Sri Agastya is one of the known leaders who introduced Hindu to the community. The Kingdom of Kutai in East Kalimantan is proof that the influence of Hinduism had existed in Indonesia since the fourth century. Since the eighth century, Hinduism developed in Bali, and until today, Bali is known as the island of gods. The Prambanan temple is one of the known Hindu temples in Yogyakarta. The golden age of the Hindu-Javanese civilization was during the Majapahit Kingdom in the fourteenth century.

Buddhism was brought to Indonesia around the fourth century when Indian traders arrived on the islands of Sumatra, Java, and Sulawesi. Around 423 CE, Monk Gunawarman came to Java to spread Buddhism. One of the known kingdoms that embraced Buddhism was Kaling or Ho Ling which had a woman queen, Ratu Sima. The world's largest Buddhist monument, Borobudur, was built by the Kingdom of Sailendra, and around the same time, the Borobudur temple also was built. The temple is considered one of the "Seven Wonders of the World." Many tourists, not only Buddhists or Hindus but also other religious adherents, come to visit these temples every year.

There are several theories about when Islam was introduced to Indonesia. One of them is that Islam came to Indonesia in the seventh century, and it gives the evidence that there is a trader community from the Arab region in Baros village at the coast of North Sumatra. Further, the first kingdom run by Muslims, at around the ninth century, was in Perlak (Hasymy 1993). Another theory explains that Islam came to Indonesia from Gujarat in India, and yet another states that the religion spread through the west coast of Sumatra and then developed to the east in Java in the thirteenth century. This period saw kingdoms being established with Muslim influence, namely Demak, Pajang, Mataram, and Banten. By the end of the fifteenth century, 20 Islam-based kingdoms had been established, reflecting the domination of Islam in Indonesia until the present time, although some of these kingdoms do not have any power. Today, the majority of Muslims live in Java and Sumatra, which comprise almost two-thirds of the total Indonesian population. Around 98 percent of Muslims in Indonesia are Sunni followers. There are other sects such as Syiah and Ahmadiyya.

Woodward (2001) argues that the current phenomena of Indonesian Islamic thought can be classified into five variants: (1) indigenized Islam, in which a group formally identifies itself as Muslim, but in practice, tends to syncretize religion with local cultural systems; (2) the traditional Sunni Islam of Nahdlatul Ulama (NU), which highlights the classical, legal, theological and mystical texts, and whose adherents usually come from *pesantren* (Islamic boarding houses) and rural areas and accept a local culture as long as Islamic values are not contested; (3) the Islamic modernism of Muhammadiyah, which concentrates on modern education and social agendas and rejects mysticism, and whose adherents are mostly from the urban areas; (4) Islamist groups, which promote a highly politicized and anti-Western interpretation of Islam, whose discourse centers on *jihad* and *shari'a* law, and who are most commonly found on university campuses and in large urban areas; and, (5) Neo-modernism, which tries to discover an Islamic foundation for many types of modernity including tolerance, democracy, gender equity, and pluralism, and whose adherents are concerned more with Muslim values and ethics than with the law. NU was established in Surabaya in 1926 to strengthen traditional Islam. This organization is seen as traditionalist due to its being supported by people in the rural areas. *Pesantren* in this classification refers to NU-affiliated *pesantren*. It has a membership of approximately 40 million (Saeed 2005). Muhammadiyah is an Indonesian Islamic organization representing a reformist socioreligious movement and advocating *ijtihad* (creative interpretation of the Qur'an and Hadith). The movement, founded in 1912 by Ahmad Dahlan in the city of Yogyakarta, is one of the two largest Islamic organizations in Indonesia and has 30 million members (Saeed 2005). Although the leaders and members of Muhammadiyah are often actively involved in shaping the politics in Indonesia, it is not a political party

In terms of the way Indonesian Muslims understand religious texts, there are three categories: literalist, moderate, and progressive/contextualist. The literalist category usually tends to have literal and conservative ideas and to represent Islamist groups. The last category, the progressive/contextualist, refers to the "liberal" orientation, of which the majority of followers are neo-modernist. The moderate category spans the position between the other two. The term "progressive/contextualist" refers to the neo-modernist orientation that usually employs a contextual approach and has a liberal progressive orientation. According to Abdullah Saeed, neo-modernists espouse three dominant ideas:

> First, neo-modernists assert that the Qur'an was a text revealed at a certain time and in a certain context and circumstances, which it reflected and responded to. This idea de-emphasises the total "otherness" of the Qur'an that the classical tradition stressed so strongly. Second, they argue that the Qur'an is not exclusively a book of law but an ethical-moral guide, with both particular and universal dimensions. The particular dimension is limited in scope and is essentially a reflection of the context in which the Qur'an was revealed: the cultural, historical and legal aspects directly related to the situation in Arabia at the time. The universal dimensions are related to areas that are not bound by [the] specific context of seventh-century Arabia. The third idea relates to [the] emphasis that classical Muslim scholars placed on certain aspect of the Qur'an, and which neo-modernists argue should be re-thought. (Saeed 2005, 9)

The Neo-modernists, who are committed to the idea that the worth of a human being is measured by the person's character (Safi 2003), argue that Muslims need to learn and adopt Western advances in education, science, and politics to strengthen and modernize the Muslim community. Neo-modernism combines knowledge and respect for classical learning with receptivity to modern ideas, including Western influences (Barton 1995). Progressive Muslims have produced a growing body of literature that reexamines Islamic tradition and addresses pluralism issues on both theoretical and practical levels (Esposito 1998).They argue that a fresh interpretation of Islamic sources and a reformulation of Islam is urgently needed (Esposito 1998). Based on their philosophies and strategies, it may be suggested that *pembaharuan* (the movement toward the renewal of Islamic education, doctrine, and practice in order to make them more participatory and inclusive for Muslims in the contemporary society) is closely allied to the philosophy and strategies proposed by activists in the gender equality movement in Indonesia. It is important to note that in this context, the affiliation to various organizations and the orientation of people's thought do not always coincide. For example, not all people from NU or the Muhammadiyah organization have moderate orientation.

Like other religions, Christianity, both Catholicism and Protestant, was also brought by immigrants, specifically the Portuguese, Dutch, and English, starting from the sixth century. The main areas of mission were in eastern Indonesia, such as in Maluku, North Sulawesi, Nusa Tenggara, Papua, and Kalimantan. Later, Christianity spread from the coastal ports of Borneo, and missionaries arrived among the Torajans on Sulawesi. Parts of Sumatra were also targeted, most notably the Batak people, who are predominantly Protestant today (Aritonang 2004). Three provinces in which Protestants make up more than 90 percent of the population are Papua, Ambon, and North.

In terms of the country's basic religious condition, *pancasila*, belief in the one and only God, is the first principle of Indonesia's philosophical foundation. According to the law, the Indonesian constitution guarantees freedom of religion as stated in Article 29: "(1) The State shall be based upon the belief in the One and Only God, (2) The State guarantees all persons the freedom of worship, each according to his/her own religion or belief." However, the government recognizes only six official religions (Islam, Protestantism, Catholicism, Hinduism, Buddhism, and Confucianism). The law requires that every Indonesian citizen hold an identity card that identifies that person with one of these six religions. Indonesia does not recognize agnosticism or atheism, and blasphemy is illegal. Because of that, religious values and the interpretation of religious texts are quite influential aspects on the country's political, economic, and cultural life. In 1965, there was a conflict between the Indonesian government and the Indonesia Communist Party in which thousands of people were killed. One of the results of this tragedy was that President Suharto issued the New Order law, according to which every citizen has to have an ID card that mentions their religion. This policy impacted on the increasing number of people who converted to one of the six official religions.

Since independence, Indonesia has had the Ministry of Religious Affairs (MORA), which has the responsibility for tolerance among religious adherents as well as their practices. Many of the state religious schools and universities are under MORA management. At the nongovernmental level, the country has *Majelis Ulama Indonesia* (MUI) or Indonesian Ulema Council. MUI's members consist of representatives from religious organizations such as NU, Muhammadiyah, Syarikat Islam, Perti, Al Washliyah, Math'laul Anwar, GUPPI, PTDI, and DMI dan Al Ittihadiyyah. Lately, MUI issued a fatwa about "deviant sects" such as Ahmadiyya and syiah, creating discrimination in the society against these organizations. Another tragedy happened on August 2012, when the local community attacked and burned the residence of a Syiah's follower. Two people were killed and hundreds lost their houses in that event. Yet another tragedy was the terrorist bombing on October 12, 2002, at a nightclub in Bali that killed more than 200 people, mostly tourists.

Alimatul Qibtiyah

See also: Ahmadiyya; Animism; Atheism/Agnosticism; Buddhism; Christianity; Communism; Hinduism; Islam; Localization of Hinduism in Indonesia; Muhammadiyah; Nahdlatul Ulama; Oka, Gedong Bagus; *Pesantren*; *Shari'a*.

Further Reading

Aritonang, S. J. *Sejarah Kristen dan Islam di Indonesia*. Jakarta: Gunung Mulia, 2004.

Barton, G. " 'Neo-Modernism': A Vital Synthesis of Traditionalism and Modernism in Indonesia Islam." *Studi Islamika* 2, no. 3 (1995): 1–75.

Esposito, J. L. *Islam and Politics*. 4th ed. Syracuse, NY: Syracuse University Press, 1998.

Hasymy, A., ed. *Sejarah Masuk dan Berkembangnya Islam di Indonesia*. Medan: PT Almaarif. 1993.

Saeed, Abdullah. *Approaches to the Qur'an in Contemporary Indonesia*, 107–34. London: Oxford University Press, 2005.

Safi, O. *Progressive Muslims: On Justice, Gender and Pluralism*. Oxford: Oneworld, 2003.

Suryadinata, L., A. Ananta, E. Arifin, and Nurvidya. *Indonesia's Population: Ethnicity and Religion in a Changing Political Landscape*: Institute of Southeast Asian Studies; IG Publishing, 2003.

U.S. Department of State. "U.S. Relations with Indonesia." http://www.state.gov/r/pa/ei/bgn/2748.htm (accessed November 14, 2013).

Woodward, M. "Indonesia, Islam and the Prospect of Democracy." *SAIS Review* 21, no. 2 (2001): 29–37.

INTERRELIGIOUS RELATIONS AND DIALOGUE

Most of the Southeast Asian nations have one religion as a significant majority with a scattering of other religious traditions. Indonesia, Malaysia, and Brunei, for instance, are dominated by a large Muslim majority, whereas Thailand and Indochina are predominantly Buddhist in character. The Philippines is mostly Roman Catholic, with a significant minority of Muslims in the island of Mindanao. Further, in all these countries, there are a number of tribes that follow their tribal religious heritages that have not received the national recognition they deserve. In most of these countries, religious and ethnic identities are closely related so that interreligious issues also become interethnic issues.

By and large, Southeast Asia has had interreligious harmony for much of its post-colonial history. More recently, however, the use of religious or ethnic identities for political purposes has resulted in tensions and conflicts. In response, governments

There were periods of time in Southeast Asian history when religious traditions living side by side in mutual respect and tolerance was taken for granted. But the advent of religions with exclusive claims and evangelistic zeal, and the increased use of religious sentiments for political ends have radically changed the situation, calling for conscious efforts to promote interfaith relations and dialogue.

S. Wesley Ariarajah

and interested groups in many of the Southeast Asian countries have been making attempts to promote interreligious harmony and dialogue through interfaith forums and conferences.

Malaysia and Singapore are good examples of countries where religious and ethnic identities are closely interrelated such that interethnic issues also become interreligious issues. In Singapore, most of the people of Chinese origin are Confucians, Buddhists, Daoists, or those who had converted to Christianity from these traditions. Those of Indian origin are predominantly Hindus, and those of Malaysian extraction are mainly Muslim. While religious freedom is ensured to all, the government of Singapore has instituted programs to hold these communities together. They serve to promote interreligious, interethnic, or interracial harmony. They are also described as attempts to promote multiculturalism.

Malaysia has had a long period of multicultural and multireligious harmony among its predominantly Muslim population with significant-minority Christian, Buddhist, and Hindu populations. However, in the 1960s and 1970s, some of the political elements in Malaysia began to emphasize the Malay ethnicity and the Islamic character of Malaysia, creating fears and uncertainties among the other ethnic and religious minorities. An example of this tension is the controversy over the Arabic term for God, Allah. Since the name is not a proper name of a God but simply denotes a Higher Being in the Arabic language, it was used by both Christians and Muslims to denote the reality that they called "God." A faction of the Muslim community began to insist that the term Allah is the word for the God whom Muslims worshipped, and Christians should be barred from using that word. Soon it became a major controversy that had to be dealt with in the courts of law. The notion that Malaysia is a Muslim country that belongs to the Malays was used as a political tool and had some currency for a while. But recognizing the social chaos this can bring in a multireligious nation, the government created a ministerial department to bring about dialogue and understanding between the various ethnic/ religious communities so that peace and stability of the country might be preserved. There are also other Christian and Islamic initiatives to promote interfaith relations and dialogue in Malaysia.

At the time when Indonesia became independent from Dutch rule, it had over 85 percent Muslims but with significant Christian, Buddhist, and Hindu populations on its different islands. There was also an attempted Communist revolution that threatened the stability of the nation. The major actors in the postindependence movement, however, were more interested in building a united nation than in building a nation based on an ethnic or religious identity. This was a priority because Indonesia comprises over 17,500 islands of a number of tribes speaking a great variety of languages. The new nation was built by developing a common language, Bahasa Indonesia, and five commonly agreed norms or principles, called *pancasila*. The five principles, variously translated, comprised of belief in one God, commitment to justice and humanity, nationalism or loyalty to the nation, democracy, and social justice. Under these five principles, Islam, Roman Catholic and Protestant forms of Christianity, Buddhism, and Hinduism were officially accepted as the religious traditions of Indonesia. Even though many other tribal and ethnic religious practices persist, accepting these four religions officially resulted in interreligious harmony in the nation. Recently, some political elements made an attempt to radicalize the Islamic community with the call to declare Islam as the official religion of Indonesia. The attempt to radicalize the Muslim community resulted in periodic conflicts where some Christians and churches came under attack. But the program of the radical elements did not receive wide support. The principles of *pancasila* and the continued government recognition of the multireligious reality of Indonesia have helped the nation to hold together. There are also a number of institutions that seek to promote Christian-Muslim dialogue in Indonesia. The Institute for Interfaith Dialogue in Indonesia (INTERFIDEI), established in 1991, has regular programs of education, research, and publications that focus on interfaith relations.

Thailand, which is among the few Asian countries that did not come under Western colonization, remains 97 percent Theravada Buddhist but with minority presence of all other religious traditions such as Christianity, Islam, Mahayana Buddhism, and a number of tribal religions. Historically, there had been periodic tension between successive kings of Thailand and Roman Catholic missions. The country was sometimes closed and other times open to Christian missionary work from outside. Buddhism is the official religion of Thailand today, even though there is religious freedom for the other minority religions. Christian missionary activity continues to raise tension from time to time. At one point, there was organized Buddhist opposition to attempts at indigenization by Christian churches. They were seen as ploys toward evangelization and were opposed on the ground that it would lead to confusion and deception.

When the borders of Thailand as a state were defined, it included a significant number of Muslims with a Malay Islamic heritage in its southern region. Despite many attempts to integrate them, the Muslim community in the south has maintained their identity. In the 1960s, this group was radicalized and began to advocate for a separate state for the Muslim minority, leading to conflict with government forces. More recently, there have been clashes between Buddhists and Muslim groups in the south of the country, leading to the call to pay greater attention to interfaith relations and the political issues behind them. Some of the Thai Buddhist leaders have been in the forefront in the international scene in Buddhist-Christian dialogues and in conversations on "engaged Buddhism" that call Buddhism to be more engaged on questions of social justice and human rights.

Human and political rights are also the main issues in neighboring Myanmar (Burma), which had a prolonged civil war since its independence in 1948 resulting in military dictatorship since 1962. Nearly 90 percent of Myanmar's population are Theravada Buddhists. However, 4 percent of the population are Christians, and another 4 percent, perhaps 6 percent, are Muslims. The military dictatorship recognizes Buddhism as the religion of the nation but keeps it under its strict surveillance. Muslims and Christians, whose identities are closely identified with tribal identities, and the other tribal religions see themselves as suppressed minorities. Opportunities for interfaith relations are limited.

Buddhism is also the dominant religion in the Indochina nations of Laos, Cambodia, and Vietnam. Historically, from about the first century BCE, Hinduism from India had spread into most of Southeast Asia, leaving its cultural heritage in

Thailand, Myanmar, all of Indochina, and Indonesia. Even today, the island of Bali in Indonesia remains Hindu in character, and there are large ruins of ancient Hindu temples in Laos, Cambodia, and Vietnam. The Theravada school of Buddhism eventually established itself in Laos and Cambodia as the majority religious tradition. Vietnam, with the influx of Chinese from mainland China, has a mixture of Mahayana Buddhism, Confucianism, and Daoism; although after its Communist history, most Vietnamese today may claim that they have no religious affiliation. With the arrival of the French in Indochina, Roman Catholicism also found significant expression. Today one can encounter most forms of Christianity as small minorities. Cambodia hosts a number of interfaith events and has an active interfaith group that seeks to promote understanding and harmony among the religious communities. Interreligious relations, however, has not been a major priority in Indochina, which has until recently been experiencing great turmoil at the political front.

The religious situation of the Philippines, also a nation made up of islands, was dominated by tribal religions in its early history. From the thirteenth century, however, Islam began to exert its influence from Malaysia and Indonesia. The arrival of the Spanish from the sixteenth century resulted in the Philippines gradually becoming the only Christian-majority country in Asia, with nearly 80–85 percent of the population embracing the Roman Catholic faith. Eventually many other forms of Christianity also found expression, and there is freedom of practice for all religions. The second-largest island of the Philippines, Mindanao, in the eastern part of the country, however, remained predominantly Islamic and refused to accept its incorporation into the modern state of the Philippines. The armed struggle for the independence of Mindanao from the Philippines has also taken the form of conflict between Christians and Muslims. A number of Christians and Muslims seek to separate the political struggle from its religious dimensions and work toward promoting Christian-Muslim relations. Both in the capital, Manila, and inside Mindanao, organizations set up by Christians and Muslims seek to promote interfaith relations and solidarity across the political divide.

It is important to recognize that in all these Southeast Asian countries, there is an ongoing "Dialogue of Life" in which people relate to each other easily across the religious divides. Further, since Buddhism, which is the majority religion in a number of countries, is nonexclusive and is practiced more as a way of life and a cultural home rather than a religion with clearly defined doctrines, interfaith relations in these countries has not been a problem.

It is significant that unlike in other parts of Asia and the world, in a number of the Southeast Asian countries such as Indonesia, Malaysia, Singapore, and Cambodia, the governments themselves take initiatives or even set up government departments to promote interfaith relations. This has mainly to do with the fact that, as stated earlier, religious and ethnic or racial identities are closely related and interreligious conflicts can easily turn into interethnic conflicts that would have wider implications for the nation and in the region. Further, in most of these countries, some of the religious minorities are economically more powerful than their numerical strength suggests. Holding the diverse religions in harmony, therefore, is a priority national interest to the governments concerned.

Even though there are no robust interfaith movements in the Southeast Asian countries, they are fully involved in the regional and global interfaith movements such as the Asian and the World Conference on Religion and Peace, the Parliament of World's Religions, and the dialogue initiatives taken by the regional Buddhist organizations, the Christian Conference of Asia, and the Roman Catholic Federation of Asian Bishops Conference. Thai, Cambodian, and Vietnamese leaders often represent the Buddhist religious tradition in international dialogue forums because they represent the earliest forms of Buddhism, unlike the North and North Eastern Mahayana traditions. Indonesian Muslims are increasingly recognized in international interfaith conferences as representatives of the largest Islamic nation in the world that also presents a face of Islam as distinct from the Islam in the Middle East. A number of universities in the United States and Europe have interfaith initiatives and exchange programs in which Southeast Asian religious traditions actively participate.

Despite the periodic tensions and conflicts incited by radical elements and the low intensity wars for independence in some parts of its nations, Southeast Asia, on the whole, has a record of good relations among its peoples of different religious traditions.

S. Wesley Ariarajah

See also: Buddhism; Cambodia; Christian Conference of Asia; Christianity; Colonialism; Communism; Confucianism; Daoism (Taoism); Engaged Buddhism; Ethnicity; Federation of Asian Bishops' Conferences; Hinduism; Human Rights; Indonesia; Islam; Koyama, Kosuke; Laos; Malaysia; Minorities; Myanmar (Burma); Nationalism; Oka, Gedong Bagus; Philippines; Religion and Society; Religious Discrimination/Intolerance; Singapore; Vietnam.

Further Reading

"Engaged Practice" (resources). http://www.dharmanet.org/lcengaged.htm (accessed September 20, 2014).

Islam, Syed Serajul. *The Politics of Islamic Identity in Southeast Asia.* Singapore: Cengage Learning Publications, 2004.

Leinmeyer, Cindy. "Religion Southeast Asia." http://www.niu.edu/cseas/outreach/pdfs/origins_religion.pdf (accessed September 20, 2014).

Ong, Aiwah. "The Politics of Multiculturalism: Pluralism and Citizenship in Malaysia, Singapore and Indonesia." *Journal of Social Issues in Southeast Asia*, July 30, 2005.

ISLAM

Islamization of Southeast Asia

Islam is a religion revealed to the Prophet Muhammad and its teachings are rendered to the Qur'an. About 250 million people in Southeast Asia embraced Islam and live in the "Muslim archipelago" of Indonesia, Malaysia, South Thailand, and the southern Philippines.

Muslims offer prayers as they gather against violence carried our by suspected separatist militants in Narathiwat on February 7, 2014. More than 5,900 people, mainly civilians, have been killed in the conflict waged by insurgents seeking greater autonomy from Buddhist-majority Thailand, which annexed the region a century ago. (Madaree Tohlala/Getty Images)

Islam was brought to Southeast Asia by Muslim traders from the Arabian world and India in the seventh century. The Sufi teachers intensified the Islamization process after the twelfth century. They introduced Islam to rulers, married with their families and achieved political power. Pasai became the first Muslim kingdom in Sumatra in 1300, followed by Malacca in the 1400s. These kingdoms accelerated Islamization in inland areas.

Compared to Africa and the Arab Peninsula, Islam in Southeast Asia has distinctive characteristics. First, Islam was spread by using the method of *penetration pacifique* toward the people and there was almost no conquest that was common in the Arab Peninsula. Second, Islam in Southeast Asia is the least Arabicized version of the religion. The Muslim priests presented Islam to the people by stressing the

During the 1970s and 1980s, the Indonesian New Order attempted to restrict political Islam due to its insistence on establishing an Islamic state. The programs of the New Order included the introduction of a "Marriage Law" to remove Islamic law from the domain of Muslim marriage and divorce. The military was summoned to suppress religious extremists. The government affirmed that *pancasila*, and not Islam, would be the sole basis for political parties and mass organizations.

Bambang Budiwiranto

suitability of Islam for local cultures and by avoiding any radical changes in belief and religious practices. It was Islamic mysticism that facilitated the mixture of Islam with pre-Islamic cultural forms.

The Portuguese occupation of Malacca in 1511 caused an interruption in the Islamization process. The Muslims had to spread their faith in the other parts of the archipelago. In Java, the spread of Islam was associated with Wali Sanga, such as Sunan Kalijaga of the Demak kingdom that replaced the Majapahit kingdom in 1527. The Mataram Sultanate of Yogyakarta encroached upon Java, and its ruler, Sultan Agung, sought religious legitimation from the authorities in Mecca. In the fourteenth century, some sultanates established themselves in the southern Philippines. In 1500, the Islamic societies in Sumatra, Java, Sulawesi, and Moluccas were established, and ethnic groups such as the Cham in Cambodia and Arakanese in Myanmar were converted to Islam.

When Sufi teachers came to the archipelago in the seventeenth century, they stressed the importance of the Islamic legal aspect. They became religious advisers for sultans such as Nurruddin Al-Raniri and Sultan Iskandar Muda of Aceh. They urged the sultans to implement the Islamic law. They also wrote books on *aqa'id*, *fiqh*, and *tasawwuf*, influencing the development of Islam.

The Era of Colonialism

With the exception of the southern Philippines and South Thailand, Islam was, by and large, co-opted and controlled by colonialism. In Malaya, the British applied the noninterference policy in religious affairs. The British left the control of religion and customs to sultans and regional chiefs. However, the British broke its policy and the British law was enacted as the law for the Malay states after the establishment of Straits Settlements (Penang, Singapore, and Malacca) in 1826. The Malay sultan continued in the office, but his power was controlled by the British Residents who acted through legislative councils, and the sultan had to adhere to their "advice." The Residents regulated Islam only related to public affairs. The effect was to secularize the state and to divorce religion from state functions.

Pan-Islamism and local revolts waged under the banner of Islam caused the Dutch to apply a special policy on Indonesian Islam. The Dutch distinguished between Islam as religion and Islam as politics. The former dealt with rituals such as prayers, fasting, and pilgrimage to Mecca. This "Islam" was tolerated because it would not endanger Dutch colonialism. However, "political Islam" was repressed.

The Dutch also implemented "the reception theory," in which Islam was allowed legal consequence only to the extent permitted by *adat* (local custom). Islam was subordinated to local culture. In 1882, the Dutch issued "priest-court regulation," administering family law such as marriage in Java and Madura. The policy on performing *hajj*, however, had a positive impact on Islam. Muslims absorbed Islamic modernism and spread it to Indonesia. Muhammadiyah, established in 1912, was inspired by Islamic modernism. It focused on social and religious renewal.

In 1565, Spain interrupted the expansion of Islam in the Philippines and transformed it into a Christian nation. For about 300 years, the Spaniards failed to impose their rule over the southern Philippine Muslims (Moro) except to demand the acceptance of Spanish sovereignty by Sultan Sulu in Jolo and some *datus* (heads of clans) of the southern Mindanao. The United States replaced Spain as the colonial power in the Philippines in 1898, and, as the armed struggle of the Moro people diminished, they gradually recognized the American power. The American colonialism tried to integrate Muslims under the Philippines government. The Moro people refused the plan and asked the United States not to include Mindanao and Sulu in the Philippines. Although America allowed Muslims to observe their religion, it promoted the de-Islamization of the Moro people's way of life.

The Era of Postcolonialism

Islam became Malaysia's official religion, and the rulers of the state are the guardians of Islam and of Malay customs. Although Muslims constitute only half of the population, Malaysia is a Muslim country. The Malays are identified as Muslims. Those from non-Malay ethnic background, whenever they become Muslims, are said to become Malay (*masok Melayu*).

Unlike Partai Islam se-Malaysia (PAS), which strives for the implementation of the *shari'a* law, UMNO, the ruling party, is concerned with Malay nationalism. After the 1969 riot in which rural people demanded equal position in economy, UMNO's concern shifted. It implemented the New Economic Policy (NEP) to increase the opportunity of Malays and *bumiputera* for them to participate in economic activities. This policy also emphasized the promotion of Malay culture and Islam.

The demands from PAS, ABIM, and a new generation have encouraged the government to promote Islamization in Malaysia. The government uses Islamic symbols and rhetoric and relates them to its political programs. The government has equated Islam with modern values, established Islamic institutions, and increased its involvement in Islamic international forums. The government co-opted young leaders of ABIM by incorporating them into the government body. It also co-opted the opposition (PAS) by implementing Islamization programs in economic and social aspects.

By defending its pluralistic society, Malaysia is still able to become a Muslim state. It maintains Chinese and Indian ethnic cohesion and, at the same time, supports Islamization and Malay identity. Compared to other Muslim countries in the Middle East, Malaysia recognizes and tolerates with ease the rights of the minority groups.

Indonesia

Islam is not the state ideology of Indonesia, although Muslims constitute a majority in the country. This sparked a debate among the Muslim leaders who led the war against the government. Darul Islam proclaimed an Islamic state in West Java, Aceh, and South Sulawesi in the 1940s. During the period of parliamentary democracy in the 1950s, the religion-based political parties brought back the idea of an Islamic state. However, this effort failed and caused antagonistic relation between Islam and the state.

During his regime (1968–1998), Suharto contained "political Islam" and forced Islamic political parties to fuse into one party (PPP) and to adopt *pancasila* as their ideology. This caused the marginalization of Islam from national politics. In the 1970s, young intellectual Muslims promoted cultural Islam that revitalized the religion through nonpolitical activities such as intellectual, educational, and social transformation. This movement was easily accepted by Muslims and the state. In the 1990s, the government began to accommodate Islam by sponsoring activities such as the establishment of the Muslims Intelligentsia Association and Islamic banks. The government also recruited Muslim leaders as state officials. This was the honeymoon period between Indonesian Islam and the state.

Islamic political parties flourished after the fall of Suharto in 1998. Although they participated in the 1999, 2004, and 2009 general elections, they never won. The nationalist parties such as PDIP and Demokrat, who supported non-Islamic issues, won the elections. Although Islam played an important role in social life, Muslims channeled their political preference to non-Islamic parties. This showed that Islamic issues were not attractive to Muslim voters. Islamic political parties formed a coalition with Demokrat both in parliament and the government.

The Southern Philippines

The Philippine government tried to integrate the Moro people into the educational and legal system but neglected the reality that Islam had an important place in the Moros' way of life. It also induced the migration of Christian people to the South. As a result, the Moros became a minority and are marginalized.

In the 1950s, Muslims from the Middle East came to the region to teach Islam. They also sent young Moros to pursue university studies in Egypt. This raised the Moro people's awareness about their local situation. The Moros' refusal to the integration programs caused the government to intensify its discrimination and repression programs. In 1968, the army massacred young Moro recruits in Corregidor Island. This was followed by the killing of Muslims in Cotabato, Lanao, and Zamboanga. Such repression triggered the emergence of secession among the Moro people as the best way to maintain their cultural and religious identity. Under the leadership of Nur Misuari, the Moros established the Moro National Liberation Front (MNLF) and conducted an open war after President Marcos declared martial law in 1972. The Tripoli agreement that recommended autonomy for the Moros was signed by MNLF and the government. Instead of implementing the autonomy, the government conducted a plebiscite referendum.

The government appeased the Muslims by allowing them to hold positions in the bureaucracy, formulating an educational system that accommodated Islamic identity, enacting family law and building centers of Islamic studies in Mindanao State University and University of the Philippines. In the 1980s, the government improved the *madrasah* (Islamic school) system and recognized Islamic holidays. The government also granted autonomy to 10 provinces in the framework of national unity. The Moderate Muslims who were satisfied with the solutions joined the government, including Salipada Pendatum, who then formed the Muslim Association of the Philippines (MUSAPHIL).

Nur Misuari, the Moro leader, prepared Moro graduates from Arab universities as the new MNLF generation. They were exposed to radical movements in the Arab world during their study. Other secessionist organizations emerged such as MILF (the Moro Islamic Liberation Front) and its Abu Sayyaf faction. These groups aim at establishing an Islamic state by means of armed struggle. The government cracked down on MILF in 2000, and a peace talk between the government and MILF was held in 2001.

South Thailand

The Muslims in Patani, Narathiwat, Yala, and Saiburi of Thailand have struggled for long to maintain their Islamic and cultural identity. Since the beginning of the twentieth century, the Thai government has launched an assimilation policy requiring Muslims to adopt the Thai way of life. In 1938, the Phibun Songkhram regime compelled the Muslims to use the Thai language and adopt Thai names and customs, and it banned the Islamic family law and traditional dress. The Muslims were also restrained from holding bureaucratic positions.

The Muslims opposed the policy and signed a petition in 1947 to demand autonomy for their provinces. This petition proposed that Muslims should have their leader, Malay should be recognized as a formal language and used in *pondok* (Islamic boarding schools), the Islamic law should be implemented, and all revenues should be allocated to the local people. In response, the government detained Haji Sulong, an Islamic Religious Council president, and repressed Muslims, forcing them to become refugees in Malaysia. This move stimulated protest from Malaysia and Singapore. Haji Sulong finally was sentenced to seven years in jail, but served only three and a half years. In 1954, Haji Sulong mysteriously disappeared together with his oldest son and other three followers.

The Phibun regime changed the policy, recognized religious freedom, permitted the use of Malay in schools, and appointed a Muslim as an adviser to the government on Islamic affairs. However, in the 1960s, the government gave land to the Thai people who were migrating to the south. This was to marginalize the Muslims and to increase the presence of Thai immigrants in the region.

The Muslim community was dissatisfied with the government that treated them violently. This caused the rise of separatist organizations such as Pattani United Liberation Organization (PULO) that aim at establishing an Islamic state. Led by young intellectuals, PULO has networks in Saudi Arabia, Malaysia, and West Asia and a guerilla training center in the Middle East. It conducted military operations in Yala, Pattani, and Narathiwat. Although PULO has support from the Islamic conference organization, many view the Pattani problem as a Thai domestic affair.

The Radicalism Issue

The 2002 Bali bombing that happened in the Muslim archipelago, which was dominated by tolerant Muslims, shocked the world. The event caused concern that

Southeast Asia would be the emergent hotbed of the international terrorism network. In relation to its global war on terror, Malaysia, Singapore, the Philippines, and Cambodia cooperated with the United States and allowed their troops to battle with terrorist suspects. Indonesia and Thailand, however, would not cooperate with the United States in combating terrorist suspects.

Initially, Indonesia did not believe that terrorist suspects existed in the country. However, after members of the Malaysia Militant Group and Jamaah Islamiyyah (JI) were detained by Malaysia and Singapore, Indonesia arrested Abu Bakar Ba'asyir. He was accused of having connections with the Bali Bombing suspects who had links with Al-Qaeda. Ba'asyir was also accused of leading the Indonesian JI. Currently, Indonesia has an antiterror special force that has raided terrorist suspects in Java, Sulawesi, and Sumatra.

Radical movements, however, do not represent Islam in Southeast Asia. They are led by the Afghan war veterans and linked to the international terrorism network that uses Islamic fundamentalism as an ideology.

Bambang Budiwiranto

See also: Ahmadiyya; Aisyiyah and Nasyiatul Aisyiyah; Alatas, Syed Hussein; Attas, Syed Muhammad Naquib al-; Colonialism; Feminism and Islamic Traditions; Fundamentalism; Indonesia; Maarif, Ahmad Syafi'i; Malaysia; Minorities; Muhammadiyah; Muslimat NU; Nahdlatul Ulama; *Pesantren*; Philippines; Pilgrimage; Rais, Muhammad Amien; *Shari'a*; Siddique, Muhammad Abdul Aleem; Sisters in Islam; Sufism; Thailand; Wahid, Abdurrahman; Wali Sanga (Wali Songo).

Further Reading

Azra, A. *The Origins of Islamic Reformism in Southeast Asia: Network of Malay-Indonesian and Middle Eastern Ulama in the Seventeenth and Eighteenth centuries.* Crow Nests, NSW, Australia: Allen & Unwin, 2004.

Drewes, G. J. W. "New Light on the Coming of Islam to Indonesia?" In *Readings on Islam in Southeast Asia*, edited by A. Ibrahim, S. Siddique, Y. Hussein, et al., 7–19. Singapore: ISEAS, 1985.

Esposito, J. L., and J. O. Voll. *Islam and Democracy.* New York: Oxford University Press, 1996.

Hefner, R. W. "South-East Asia from 1910." In *The New Cambridge History of Islam*, edited by F. Robinson, vol. 5, *The Islamic World in the Age of Western Dominance*, 591–622. Cambridge: Cambridge University Press, 2010.

Hooker, M. B., ed. *Islam in South-East Asia.* Leiden and New York: Brill, 1988.

Houben, V. J. H. "Southeast Asia and Islam." *ANNALS of the American Academy of Political and Social Science* 588 (2003): 149–70.

Majul, C. A. *The Contemporary Muslim Movement in the Philippines.* Berkeley, CA: Mizan Press, 1985.

Noer, D. "Contemporary Political Dimension of Islam." In *Islam in South-East Asia*, edited by M. B. Hooker, 183–215. Leiden and New York: Brill, 1988.

Ricklefs, M. C. "Islamization in Java: Fourteenth to Eighteenth Centuries." In *Readings on Islam in Southeast Asia*, edited by A. Ibrahim, S. Siddique, and Y. Hussein, et al., 36–43. Singapore: ISEAS, 1985.

J

JAINISM

Jainism is a religion of Indian origin that advocates the path of nonviolence toward all living beings. The origin of Jainism can be traced back to the ascetic Mahavir, who was a contemporary of Buddha as both lived in India around 2,600 years ago. Mahavir preached abstention from hurting living beings not just by physical acts, but also through mind and speech. Jainism, therefore, advocates spiritual independence and the equality of all forms of life. The religion is divided into two major sects: Digambara and Śvētāmbara. Monks of the Digambara order do not generally wear clothes, whereas the Śvētāmbara monastics have no such restrictions and they wear white seamless clothes. There are also differences between the two in their understanding of women monastics, with the Śvētāmbara order being more open to women's equal participation.

The practitioners of Jainism—known as Jains—believe that nonviolence and self-control are the ways for salvation and liberation from the cycle of reincarnations. In fact, the Jains are accepted as some of the most peace-loving people in the world. They are so passionately wedded to the principle of nonviolence that besides being strict vegetarians, several senior monks cover their mouths with a towel, especially when they travel, so as to prevent any tiny life-forms (like insects and germs) from entering their mouths. Fasting is also an essential part of the routine of Jains, and they abstain from food, often for several days and even months, as an act of penitence, cleansing, and devotion.

While most Jains reside in India, the religion traveled to different places, primarily with the Indian merchants and traders who went all over the world. Today, there are Jain communities in Belgium, the United States, Canada, Japan, Hong Kong, and several other places. There are Jain communities also in several places in Southeast Asia. There is a small but historically significant Jain presence in Malaysia. Some members of this ancient community arrived in the fifteenth and sixteenth centuries in Malacca, which today has a moderately active Jain community. The only Jain temple in Southeast Asia is also located in Malaysia, at Ipoh. Apart from serving the small Jain congregation in Ipoh, the temple functions also as a cultural center that benefits the wider community. It is a small but beautiful symbol of Malaysia's diverse and vibrant pluralist heritage.

For over 100 years, there has been an active Jain community in Singapore. While there are few historical documents available on the arrival of the first Jains in Singapore, it is believed that they reached there in the early years of the twentieth century. In the initial years, the programs of the community were conducted sporadically, but after the Second World War, the Jains of Singapore were organized. In 1972, the Singapore Jain Religious Society was formed and registered as a religious society. Having felt the need to have a physical structure that can serve as the meeting point for the community, in 1978, land measuring about 1,000 square meters was purchased and a two-story building built there. A hall in the building is used for religious functions. There is also an office, library, kitchen, store, parking lots, and open spaces.

The Singapore Jain Religious Society plays a key role in upholding the values and traditions of the faith in that nation. According to the rules of the society, any Jain, whether belonging to the Śvētāmbara or Digambar sect, and speaking any language, can become a member and carry out Jain religious activities. They need only adhere to the fundamental principles of the religion. While the Singapore Jains hail originally from the Gujarat region of India, there are also small communities of Marwadi, Punjabi, and Tamil Jains. The Tamil Jains of Singapore are organized under the banner of the Singapore Tamil Jains Forum.

Indonesia too has a historically significant Jain presence, as the accounts of ancient trade and commerce indicate. The Jain merchants from India are believed to have traveled to Java-dvipa, Maha dvipa, and many other such islands and places in the country. Archeologists have successfully unearthed Jain idols and temples in some of the other Southeast Asian countries too, such as Cambodia and Myanmar. Further study is required to prove their historical origins.

While Jainism is an ancient religion that made an especially deep impact in the areas of art, architecture, and literature, today it is a small group confined to a few centers. The Jains in the diaspora, particularly in Southeast Asia, add to the rich pluralistic tradition of the region. Wherever they go, the Jains represent the values of peace, nonviolence, unity, and integrity.

Jesudas M. Athyal

See also: Cambodia; Indonesia; Malaysia; Myanmar (Burma); Singapore; Women.

Further Reading

Charpentier, Jarl. "The History of the Jains." *The Cambridge History of India*. Vol. 1. Cambridge: Cambridge University Press, 1922.

Singapore Jain Religious Society. http://www.sjrs.org.sg/ (accessed September 17, 2014).

"The Only Jain Temple in Southeast Asia" (courtesy: emedia.com.my and New Straits Times). http://www.jainheritagecentres.com/abroad/malaysia.htm (accessed September 17, 2014).

Vyas, R. T., and P. S. Umakant. *Studies in Jaina Art and Iconography and Allied Subjects in Honour of Dr. U. P. Shah*. New Delhi: Abhinav Publications, 1995.

Wiley, Kristi L. *The A to Z of Jainism*. New York: Scarecrow Press, 2009.

JESUITS

History

The presence of the Society of Jesus (the Jesuits, founded in 1540) in Southeast Asia has a very long history, dating back to the earliest missionary movement of the order. Francis Xavier, one of the founding members of the Jesuits and the most renowned Jesuit missionary, stayed in Malacca (now Malaysia) for some period in his Asian missionary journey. Arriving there in 1545, he even studied Malay language, while his companions founded a school shortly after. This mission was short-lived due to the arrival of the Dutch, who took over Malacca in 1641. During his stay in Asia, Xavier also passed through the Moluccas (now part of Indonesia) and baptized some natives upon his arrival in 1546. In the same journey, he also briefly visited the islands of Moro in the Philippines.

Then, in the Philippines, the first Jesuits from Mexico arrived in 1581, while the French Jesuit missionary, Alexandre de Rhodes, settled in Indochina (Vietnam) in 1619. In Southeast Asian countries, however, the significant growth of the Jesuit mission came as a fruit of missionary work during modern European colonialism. The Philippines became a Jesuit province in 1605 but was suppressed in 1768, so the current Province of Philippine Jesuits was actually founded in 1958. In the Dutch East Indies (Indonesia), the Jesuit missionaries started to work among the natives only in the late nineteenth century. The great Jesuit missionary in Java, Father Franciscus van Lith (d. 1926) founded a vibrant Catholic community in Java, and the growth of the Indonesian Jesuits has been very closely related to this missionary work under Dutch colonialism.

Work and Ministries

At present, there are around 1,400 Jesuits in Southeast Asia, a very tiny presence compared to the whole population. The contemporary Jesuit works in this region are colored by the complexity of the Southeast Asian reality. In response to the diversity and plurality of religions in this area, the Jesuits emphasize the ministry of interreligious and intercultural dialogue as one of the most distinctive pillars of their presence in this area. The Jesuits have also been working in the area of development and social works, responding to the growing problem of poverty and social crises such as wars and conflicts that result in internally displaced people and refugees. In this respect, it should be noted that the Jesuit Refugee Service, the Jesuit NGO specializing in the long-term service, advocacy, and accompaniment of the refugees, was founded in 1980 in response to the crisis of the Vietnamese boat people. In general, throughout their history, the Jesuits in this area have been aware of their call to be involved with the poor and marginalized, such as: the lepers in the island of Culion, the Philippines; landmine victims in Cambodia; or rural parishes in south central Java, West Papua, Thailand, and East Timor. Recently, some Jesuits have died for the cause of the poor in this region; for example, Richie Fernando in Cambodia (d. 1996) and Albrecht Karim Arbie and Tarcicius Dewanto in East Timor (1999).

The postcolonial condition has also led the Jesuits in this area to address the question of indigenous people as they are being left behind by the rapid growth of some modern nation-states in this area. Furthermore, the era of globalization has also been affecting Southeast Asian societies and creating some problems such as migration. Asia is the biggest source of migrant workers in the world. It has very large intraregional flows of migrant workers as well. The Philippines, Indonesia, and Vietnam have been top suppliers of migrant workers to China, Korea, Singapore, and Japan as well as Europe, the Middle East, and North America. The Jesuits have been trying to respond to the plight of these workers through networking for changing the policies and practices that affect these vulnerable people. In the same spirit, the Jesuits in Southeast Asia have started in recent years to pay more attention to environmental issues, among others, by creating a program called "Flights for Forest," asking all Jesuits and partners in this area to contribute US$5 for every flight taken. These contributions go into a fund to be used for forest renewal activities in Cambodia, Indonesia, and the Philippines.

In the field of education, the Jesuits in the Philippines and Indonesia run some very prestigious high schools and colleges. In this area, the need for an integral and humanistic education characteristic of the Jesuits is high due to the youthful population in the region. In Indonesia, it is through education that the Jesuits have found acceptance among large non-Christian segments of the society. Internally for the local church, Jesuits in Southeast Asia are also involved traditionally in the education of local clergy, such as San Jose Seminary (since the early seventeenth century) and Loyola School of Theology on the campus of the Ateneo de Manila University, as well as the Sanata Dharma University School of Theology and St. Paul Major Seminary in Yogyakarta. Jesuits in Vietnam, before being expelled in 1975, were running the Pontifical College in Dalat to educate local priests. Everywhere in this region, even when their number is small such as in Malaysia and Singapore, Jesuits are actively engaged in the formation of the spiritual life of religious, clergy, and laypeople as well.

In the area of culture and public life, some notable Jesuits, such as Horacio de la Costa (d. 1977) in the Philippines and Franz Magnis-Suseno (b. 1936) in Indonesia, are recognized in their own countries and in the region as influential public intellectuals. In the area of culture, the Jesuits are running different enterprises such as printing press and communication media; for instance, Kanisius Publishing House and SAV Puskat in Indonesia, Jesuit Communications Foundation in the Philippines, and Casa de Produção Audiovisual (CPA) in East Timor.

In some sense, the contemporary Jesuit work in Southeast Asia continues the earlier spirit of the great Jesuit missionaries to this area, such as Xavier, Rhodes, van Lith, and others. These were towering missionary figures whose legacy, such as the principle of adaptation to the local contexts (enculturation), not forcing Western forms and concepts of Christianity, has been a source of inspiration for the ways in which the contemporary Jesuits engage the reality of Southeast Asia.

The Future

In recent years, the number of Jesuits has grown rather significantly in Vietnam and East Timor, while tending to be steadier in Indonesia and the Philippines. In present-day Indonesia, the largest Muslim country in the world, has the largest concentration of Jesuits in the whole region, numbering over 350 members. In Vietnam, the order is flourishing despite some restrictions by the Communist government. This is a surprising development given the struggle of the Catholic

Church and the Jesuit Order in that country in the past few decades under Communism. They lost the support of foreign missionaries, mostly French Canadians who fled to different countries in the area as a result. However, the persecution and corresponding struggle, in fact, opened up a different course of the order's development in this country. In East Timor, the increasing number of native Jesuits has also been a feature after the independence of the country from Indonesia in early 2000s. In Myanmar, the vocation to the Jesuits seems to be doing well, although still in a very initial stage. While in other parts, such as Thailand, Malaysia, and Singapore, the number of the Jesuits will continue to be small but steady. It is very likely that the overall number of Jesuits in Southeast Asia will be stable in the near future.

In contrast to their European missionary beginning, the future of the Jesuits in this region will be marked by more intensive collaboration between different countries in this area as well as East Asia, such as Korea, China, and Japan. Jesuits from the Philippines and Indonesia, for example, have been working in Cambodia, Myanmar, Thailand, and East Timor; while young Jesuits from Myanmar, Thailand, and East Timor undergo their studies and obtain some work experience in other countries in the region as well. Regional cooperation is a new feature that will continue to be decisive in the future development of the Jesuit order in Southeast Asia.

Albertus Bagus Laksana, S.J.

See also: Christianity; Colonialism; Communism; Contextualization; Education; Federation of Asian Bishops' Conferences; Globalization; Indonesia; Interreligious Relations and Dialogue; Malaysia; Missionary Movements; Myanmar (Burma); Philippines; Postcolonial Theory; Religion and Society; Thailand; Timor Leste (East Timor); Vietnam.

Further Reading

Aritonang, Jan Sihar, and Karel Steenbrink, eds. *A History of Christianity in Indonesia.* Leiden and Boston: Brill, 2008.

Camps, Arnulf. *Studies in Asian Mission History, 1956–1998.* Leiden: Brill, 2000.

Kolvenbach, Peter-Hans, S.J. "Francis Xavier and the Asian Jesuits," *Vidyajyoti Journal of Theological Reflection* (VJTR) 66 (2002): 716–24.

Jesuit Conference of Asia Pacific (official website): http://www.sjapc.net/ (accessed November 15, 2013).

Phan, Peter C. *Mission and Catechesis: Alexandre de Rhodes and Inculturation in Seventeenth-Century Vietnam.* Maryknoll, NY: Orbis Books, 1998.

Schurhammer, Georg, S.J. *Francis Xavier: His Life, His Times.* Vol. 3. Translated by M. Joseph Costelloe S.J. Rome: Jesuit Historical Institute, 1980.

JUDAISM

While there are accounts of Jewish presence in Southeast Asia that go back over 1,000 years, the history of Judaism in the region in the modern times is traced back to the arrival of the early European explorers and settlers. Most countries in the region had small but significant numbers of Jews till the 1940s, but in the twenty-first century, there is only a minuscule presence of Jews in Southeast Asia. However, the rich Jewish heritage in the region, in the form of synagogues and cemeteries and other markers, enrich the cultural and architectural landscape of the region.

Malaysia has a long Jewish heritage that goes back to the ninth century CE though historical records of this are scarce. Much later, in the nineteenth century, there was an influx of Jewish trading families from Baghdad to Malaya. That community was concentrated mainly in the state of Penang and also in Negri Sembilan and Malacca, and they contributed richly to the development of trade and commerce in the region. In the late 1970s, however, there was a large-scale exodus of Jews from the country, resulting largely from the anti-Semitic sentiments sweeping the country then. The Malaysian Jewish community left behind a lasting legacy, in the form of heritage and traditions. These include the Penang Jewish Cemetery, established in 1805 and believed to be the oldest single Jewish cemetery in the country.

The Jewish presence in the Philippines can be traced back to the sixteenth century, when Spain was in control of the country. During the Spanish Inquisition, many Jews fled Spain, with some of them reaching the Philippines. Among them, there were also the Sephardi Jews, some of whom settled down in Northern Samar of the country. While a small Jewish community survived in the Philippines in the following centuries, the Christianized laws of the Spanish colonial rulers did not permit them to be formally organized. Following the Spanish-American War of 1898, however, Jews in the Philippines were officially recognized and given the freedom to openly practice their religion. During the Holocaust in Europe in the 1930s, Manila emerged as a safe haven for Jews, and a large number of them migration to the country. At the beginning of the twenty-first century, there were a few hundred Jews in the country, which also included some recent converts.

In Indonesia, Judaism is not one of the official six religions, but there is a heritage of over 400 years of Jewish presence in that country. The first Jews are believed to have reached Indonesia in the seventeenth century, along with the Dutch East India Company. Even after the Company was liquidated in 1800, a small number of Jews remained in the archipelago. In his report on the Indonesian Jews, Jacob Halevy Saphir (1822–1886) had noted that this was a tiny community with an uncertain future. The early decades of the twentieth century, however, saw a growth in the Indonesian Jewish community with their number reaching several thousand, a change mainly due to the influx of Jewish refugees from Nazi Europe. With the end of the Second World War and the founding of the nation of Israel, however, most Jews left the country, leaving behind only a tiny community.

Some of the other countries in the region have younger histories of Jewish presence. The original Jews in Singapore were immigrants from Baghdad in the nineteenth century. The arrival of a large number of Ashkenazi Jews and others in recent years has strengthened the Jewish population of the city-state. In Vietnam, the arrival of the Jews followed the French colonization in the nineteenth century. As the French withdrew from the country in the 1950s, however, most of the Jews too left Vietnam. While there are practically no native Jews in Vietnam now, since the country established diplomatic relations with Israel in 1993, there has been a steady increase in the number of the Jews coming from outside. The Jewish heritage of Myanmar (Burma) too goes back to the nineteenth century, when a sizable number of Jews reached Burma from India. They prospered as trading communities, though following the Japanese invasion of the country in the early 1940s, most of them fled to India, leaving behind only a handful of Jews.

While many countries in Southeast Asia had fairly active Jewish communities—some with several centuries of history—by the beginning of the twenty-first century, the Jews of the region had dwindled drastically. Several reasons can be cited for this. The Jews were active traders and businesspersons but did not take adequate steps to preserve their own faith, culture, and practices in their new locations. Intermarriage with the local people further eroded the distinctiveness of this community. Also, in the Muslim-majority countries of the region, there were, at times, strong anti-Semitic sentiments, even with the support of the rulers, prompting Jews in large numbers to leave the countries. The founding of Israel in 1948 and the welcome the new nation extended to Jews worldwide provided a further incentive for the Jews in Southeast Asia to leave the region. In the following decades, most Southeast Asian Jews migrated to Israel or to one of the Western nations. Thus, while the original Jewish communities have virtually disappeared from the region, their legacy remains in many places and has recently been rekindled, in some countries, following the arrival of new teams of expatriate Jews, mainly for diplomatic and business purposes.

Jesudas M. Athyal

See also: Christianity; Colonialism; Diaspora; Freedom of Religion; Indonesia; Malaysia; Myanmar (Burma); Philippines; Singapore; Vietnam.

Further Reading

Fishchel, Walter. "New Sources for the History of the Jewish Diaspora in Asia in the 16th Century." *Jewish Quarterly Review* 40, no. 4 (April 1950): 380.

Jewish Center of Cambodia website. http://www.jewishcambodia.com/ (accessed September 17, 2014).

Nathan, Eze. *The History of Jews in Singapore, 1830–1945.* Singapore: HERBILU Editorial & Marketing Services, 1986.

"Philippines Jewish Community." *Jewish Times Asia.* http://www.jewishtimesasia.org/manila/269-manila-communities/576-philippines-jewish-community (accessed September 17, 2014).

"Synagogues of Indonesia." *Jewish Virtual Library.* http://www.jewishvirtuallibrary.org/jsource/vjw/indonesia.html (accessed September 17, 2014).

Tugend, Tom. "Vietnamese Boat People Become Israeli." *Jerusalem Post.* http://www.jpost.com/Arts-and-Culture/Entertainment/Vietnamese-boat-people-become-Israeli (accessed September 17, 2014).

KHMER BUDDHISM

Today, some 90 percent of ethnic Khmers declare themselves to be Theravada Buddhists. Islam is practiced by the Cham minority and animist customs are followed by minority groups in the hills. However, prior to the advent of Theravada Buddhism, the Khmer kingdom operated as a Hinduized state. During the Angkorean era (classically said to fall between 802 and 1431 CE), inscriptions tell us that the king's power was absolute; he was regarded as having unique access to divine power, which he was to channel into the world to ensure the prosperity and power of an extensive militarized empire.

It was during the thirteenth century that Theravada Buddhism took root in Cambodia. Angkorean inscriptions reveal that the Khmer king Jayavarman VII (r. 1181–1218) had been a devout Mahayana Buddhist. During his reign, around 1180, Shin Tamalinda, believed to be a son of Jayavarman VII, joined a Burmese-led mission to Ceylon to study the Pali canon. At this time, Sinhala Theravada Buddhism was gaining influence throughout the region, and by the end of the 1200s, it had spread throughout much of Cambodia.

Unlike Hinduism, which seems to have had little resonance with rural daily life and to have functioned largely as a means to legitimate domination by the nobility, Theravada Buddhism became grafted onto local traditions of ancestor and spirit worship. The new religion was preached rather than imposed upon the people. The previous monopoly on moral authority enjoyed by the king was now moderated by the fact that young village men began to ordain and thereby also to gain religious credentials. With higher ranks of the brotherhood of monks (*sangha*) connected to the royal court, the king's power also became subjected to moral imperatives of the 10 Buddhist principles of right governance (Pali *dasarajad-hamma*), that he should embody: generosity, morality, liberality, uprightness, gentleness, self-restraint, non-anger, non-hurtfulness, forbearance, and non-opposition. These new norms of non-egocentrism and considerateness applied to rulers as well as those they ruled. The security of the kingdom was now envisaged as depending upon the protection provided by a monarch who conducted himself in accordance with the teachings of the Buddha. The arrival of this humble, inclusive form of religion coincided with the cessation of the monumental building projects of the Angkorean Empire and the decline of Brahmanic and Mahayana Buddhist religious traditions.

Most of the Theravada Buddhist monks were based in the villages, and this meant that the ecclesiastical structures were decentralized into quasi-egalitarian monastic communities. The village monastery offered a field of merit for villagers, but it also

On February 6, 2003, the Venerable Sam Bunthoeun was shot dead by two men as he was entering the grounds of a temple in central Phnom Penh. He had established a highly successful insight (vipassanā) Meditation Center at Oudong, not far from Phnom Penh. The center offered monks, nuns, and laypeople instruction in this meditation technique. It is believed that he was killed because he encouraged the monks to vote in the elections of 2003. His body was not cremated but instead embalmed and kept in refrigeration at the Oudong center for visitors to witness.

Alexandra Kent

constituted a center for the redistribution of wealth, a library and source of Buddhist knowledge. The pagodas provided primary schooling for boys, care for orphan boys, and a refuge for the elderly, particularly women who could be ordained as lay-nuns (*don chee*) by vowing to follow 8 or 10 Buddhist precepts. The pagodas were the foci of social and cultural activities, and although the *sangha* adapted and reformed over the years, the monks remained strong protectors of local culture and tradition. In the nineteenth and twentieth centuries, the Khmer *sangha* was a major moral and institutional force that offered steadfast resistance to foreign cultural influences. For instance, the monks resisted the French efforts to supplant Buddhist-based education and Khmer as the language of instruction with the French system and reacted vigorously against French efforts to Romanize the Khmer alphabet. From the villagers' point of view, the pagoda and the *sangha* represented an important buffer to imposters or the excesses of their own rulers and provided a source of comfort and moral order until 1975.

The pivotal cultural position occupied for so long by Buddhism means it has long been an object of concern for Cambodian leaders. Earning moral legitimacy from the monkhood was important for reaching the hearts of the people—as exemplified by Sihanouk's strategy in the 1960s. This also helps explain why Buddhism was so rapidly dismantled by the Khmer Rouge when they took power in April 1975 and began establishing their new utopian Communist order.

The Khmer Rouge era was unique in breaking apart the religious fundament of Cambodian rural life. Accounts by survivors and historians detail the ways in which the cadres broke down kinship bonds in favor of loyalty to "*Angkar*" (the party) and tried to erase families' spiritual traditions. By 1978, Buddhism had been declared dead by Yun Yat, the minister of culture, information, and propaganda of the Democratic Kampuchea regime.

Prior to the Khmer Rouge era of 1975–1979, there were an estimated 88,000 Buddhist monks in the country and around 3,500 monasteries for a population of just over seven million. In general, some three-quarters of men over the age of 17 would likely have spent one or two years in the *sangha* as novices or monks. The Buddhist *sangha* was still the major transmitter of Khmer literacy and civility, and indeed, the first Khmer-language newspaper was founded by the Buddhist Institute in 1936, which later became a hotbed of Khmer nationalism.

It is believed that over one-third of monks were executed or forced to disrobe and break their vows by the Khmer Rouge, and many died of starvation and disease.

Pagodas were abandoned, razed, damaged, or desecrated. The complete destruction of Buddhism (as well as the spirit realm) meant that the most important traditional resources for managing suffering and grief were no longer available. For many Khmer people, their identity, so tightly bound to Buddhism, was shaken by the inadequacy of their culture both in preventing the horror they experienced and in providing an explanation. Some older Cambodians identify this era as having extinguished the world as they knew it.

After the Vietnamese invaded in 1979 and succeeded in ousting the Khmer Rouge, they set about restarting Buddhism in a bid to earn legitimacy among the Khmers. They selected seven former Khmer monks for re-ordination but thereafter maintained strict control of the *sangha*. Only men over the age of 50 were permitted to ordain, and monks were forbidden from performing alms rounds. Despite government prohibition, young novitiates were observed in rural areas throughout the 1980s. This betrays something of the importance Buddhism held for rural Cambodians. After only two years, over 700 pagodas had been restored. While there was and still is a heavy investment from local people of labor, time, and resources, much reconstruction was and continues to be heavily sponsored by overseas Khmer or by powerful people from Phnom Penh.

After the Vietnamese withdrawal in 1989, the new government relaxed restrictions on Buddhism and the number of monks increased rapidly, reaching more than 60,000 by the late 2000s. However, in the absence of knowledgeable, experienced older monks, the establishment of legitimacy for novitiates was problematic, and there have been numerous scandals associated with young monks in recent years. Pagoda reconstruction also began in earnest in the early 1990s, though today's pagodas differ widely. Some perform community services and provide a variety of facilities to their constituency, while others focus on offering "magical" services or meditation, and still others are more or less dormant.

Where lay pagoda committees are lacking, monks themselves may handle money and in so doing break their vows and hazard their reputations. Some monks cultivate their links to politicians as a means of securing donations for their pagodas instead of prioritizing the will of their constituents and pagodas that work together with international Nongovernmental organizations risk being viewed as servants of the international community.

Two factors have also deeply politicized the Cambodian *sangha* since the fall of the Khmer Rouge. Firstly, the youngest of the monks who were re-ordained in 1979, the Venerable Tep Vong (born in 1930) was subsequently appointed by the Vietnamese as head of a unified Cambodian *sangha* but was also made a high-ranking official in the People's Republic of Kampuchea government. Vong is now the supreme patriarch of the larger of the two Cambodian Buddhist orders, but his former connection to the Vietnamese and his close ties to the ruling Cambodian People's Party undermine his Buddhist credentials for many, who view him as a mouthpiece for the current, Vietnamese-spawned government.

Secondly, when a new constitution was drawn up for Cambodia in 1993, following the withdrawal of the Vietnamese, it included the right of universal adult suffrage, and this included monks. This meant that the Cambodian monastics, instead of representing the Buddhist ideals of equanimity and detachment, now became embroiled in partisan politics. Many pagodas came to bear party colors. However, in 2002, the supreme patriarch, Vong, prohibited monks from voting, ostensibly because this would contravene their religious vows though many understood that it was to contain monastic support for the opposition. In 2006, the patriarch lifted the prohibition but warned monks against participating in any mass movements critical of the government. All these factors undermine the monks' independence as moral overseers of those with worldly power.

Nevertheless, many restored pagodas have once again become important centers of cultural activity for festivals, death rituals, and merit-making activities. Both the annual festival of the dead (Khmer *pchum ben*) and the ceremony held at the end of the rainy season retreat (*kathin*), when parishioners make merit by donating new robes to the monks, are popular. Similarly, the water festival, when the pagodas release their pirogues for racing on the river, is a major annual event. And inside some pagodas, there are extraordinary efforts being made to spiritually heal the disorders that have so brutally disrupted Khmer culture. Although many Cambodians lament the vacuum left by the tragic destruction of Khmer Buddhism, many of those who remember how things used to be still see Buddhism as the storehouse of power to recreate civility and order in their splintered, shared world. Whether the growing ranks of young Cambodians, who were born into a post–Khmer Rouge world of consumerist values will, as they mature, come to accredit Buddhism with this power remains to be seen.

Alexandra Kent

See also: Ancestor Worship; Animism; Buddhism; Cambodia; Hinduism; Islam; Nationalism; Spirit Mediumship; Vietnam; Water Festivals; Women's Monastic Communities.

Further Reading

Coedès, George. *The Indianized States of Southeast Asia.* Honolulu: University of Hawaii Press, 1996.

Harris, Ian. *Cambodian Buddhism: History and Practice.* Honolulu: University of Hawaii Press, 2008.

Kent, Alexandra, and David Chandler, eds. *People of Virtue: Reconfiguring Religion, Power and Moral Order in Cambodia Today.* Copenhagen: NIAS Press, 2008.

Keyes, Charles F. "Communist Revolution and the Buddhist Past in Cambodia." In *Asian Visions of Authority: Religion and the Modern States of East and Southeast Asia*, edited by Charles F. Keyes, Laurel Kendall, and Helen Hardacre, 43–74. Honolulu: University of Hawaii Press, 1994.

Marston, John, and Elizabeth Guthrie. *History, Buddhism, and New Religious Movements in Cambodia.* Honolulu: University of Hawaii Press, 2004.

KOYAMA, KOSUKE

The Rev. Dr. Kosuke Koyama was a leading Asian Christian theologian during the twentieth century who is specially remembered for his sensitivity to other religions and for his conviction that Christianity should be compatible with the various

As a non-Western theologian, Kosuke Koyama outlined an Asian interpretation to world religions. He famously remarked that Buddhism and Christianity do not communicate, but Buddhists and Christians do. Accordingly, he discarded the abstract ideas of world religions and instead freely used Asian terms of ordinary folk, such as rice, banana, cockfighting, and rainy season to convey his message. About Jesus washing the feet of his disciples, Kosuke interpreted: "Looking at us, Jesus would say: you must be tired; let me wash your feet; the food is ready."

Jesudas M. Athyal

Asian traditions. Born on December 10, 1929, in Tokyo, Japan, he was baptized as a Christian at the age of 15. Having graduated from Tokyo Union Theological Seminary in 1952, he came to the United States for advanced studies. He earned a bachelor's degree from Drew University in 1954 and a doctorate from the Princeton Theological Seminary in 1959. Koyama was subsequently sent by the United Church of Christ in Japan to be a missionary in Thailand. His tenure in Thailand shaped him as a path-breaking Asian Christian thinker and practitioner who theologized in the context of the local realities.

In 1968, Koyama moved to Singapore to become dean of the South East Asia Graduate School of Theology. In Singapore, he was also the editor of the *South East Asia Journal of Theology*. From 1974 to 1978, he served as the senior lecturer in religious studies at the University of Otago in New Zealand. In 1980, he joined the Union Theological Seminary in New York, where he was the first holder of the John D. Rockefeller Jr. Chair in Ecumenics and World Christianity, a position in which he continued until his retirement in 1996. He died on March 25, 2009, in Springfield, Massachusetts, of pneumonia complicated by esophageal cancer.

Koyama represented a paradigm shift in Christian theology that affirmed that the starting point of theology must be people's own experience. He wrote 13 books, which outline his conviction that the Christian Gospel must communicate with the cultures and religions of each context. His most well-known book, *Water Buffalo Theology*, emerged out of his efforts to communicate the Christian message to the farmers in northern Thailand—who cultivate fields with water buffalo—as he served as a missionary and teacher there from 1960 to 1968. He made the book's case in poetic, not academic, language and placed the challenge of the Gospel squarely in the middle of the plurality of Asian religions. In a climate where interfaith dialogue was becoming fashionable in intellectual circles, he noted that dialogue is *not* between Christianity and Buddhism, but rather between Christians and Buddhists. Beyond the Aristotelian roots of Western theology and epistemology, he discerned the everyday challenges faced by a Thai farmer as the location of theology. The "frog croaking" and "mosquito humming" in the paddy fields of northern Thailand became, for him, the context of theology. It was an intensely contextualized and particular way of seeking the meaning of faith.

Koyama's book *No Handle on the Cross* is a meditation from Southeast Asia in which he argues that Asians—Christians as well as Buddhists, Muslims, and Hindus—are beginning to realize that Western Christianity has preached a gospel without the cross. Jesus did not carry his cross as a businessman carries his briefcase, he noted. While we would like to domesticate and control the cross, in actuality, it is awkward and clumsy to carry. The meaning and the message of the cross, therefore, is that the broken Christ is trying to heal a broken world. This reality should be realized, Koyama concluded, in the midst of the awkward and harsh realities of Asia. His other books include *Fifty Meditations and Theology in Contact* (1975), *Mount Fuji and Mount Sinai* (1984), *Pilgrim or Tourist* (1974), and *Three-Mile-an-Hour God* (1978).

Despite his focus on the "particular" in contextual theology, Koyama acknowledged that theology's particularity can flourish only if it maintains a dialectical linkage with the wider theological and ecumenical world. Accordingly, he became an influential voice for ecumenism, speaking at conferences around the world and teaching classes on Buddhism, Confucianism, Hinduism, Islam, and Judaism. He believed that he had a mission to teach about different religious traditions because it was the Christian thing to do.

Koyama's lasting contribution in the Southeast Asian context can be described as helping to bridge the boundaries between East and West, between the various religious traditions. About his own faith, he had noted that while Christianity came to Asia in the garb of Western culture and philosophy, to appeal to the Asian people, the Gospel must take indigenous roots. Koyama will be remembered as an important figure in the development of a contextual Asian theology.

Jesudas M. Athyal

See also: Buddhism; Christianity; Christian Conference of Asia; Contextualization; Hinduism; Interreligious Relations and Dialogue; Islam; Singapore; Thailand.

Further Reading

Irvin, Dale T., and A. E. Akinade, eds. *The Agitated Mind: The Theology of Kosuke Koyama.* Maryknoll, NY: Orbis Books, 1996.

Koyama, Kosuke. "I Desire Mercy and Not Sacrifice: An Ecumenical Interpretation." Lecture delivered in Halifax, Nova Scotia, November 4, 1996. http://homepage.accesscable.net/~dpoirier/hfx96txt.htm (accessed September 19, 2014).

Koyama, Kosuke. *No Handle on the Cross: An Asian Meditation on the Crucified Mind.* London, Bloomsbury: SCM Press, 1976.

Koyama, Kosuke. *Water Buffalo Theology.* 2nd ed. Maryknoll, NY: Orbis Books, 1999.

Martin, Douglas. "Kosuke Koyama, 79, an Ecumenical Theologian, Dies." *New York Times,* March 31, 2009. http://www.nytimes.com/2009/04/01/world/asia/01koyama.html?_r=0 (accessed September 19, 2014).

Morse, M. *Kosuke Koyama: A Model for Intercultural Theology.* Frankfurt: Peter Lang, 1991.

KYAW THAN, U

U Kyaw Than, popularly addressed as Kyaw Than, is perhaps the best-known Christian from Myanmar (Burma) in the ecumenical and Christian circles in many parts of the world. He represented his country and the churches in Myanmar for well over 60 years at Asian and global ecumenical and church gatherings. His books

When one thinks of ecumenism in Southeast Asia, Myanmar, as a country, does not immediately come to one's mind. But the country has good reasons to be proud of its true son, Kyaw Than, who has made ecumenical contribution and given ecumenical leadership in Asia spanning over many decades, putting Myanmar firmly on the ecumenical map.

S. Wesley Ariarajah

and articles, and his lectures in many parts of the world, cover the subjects of ecumenism, mission, church unity and the role of Christians in the university.

Kyaw Than was born on December 17, 1923, in Pakokku, Myanmar. After graduating with honors from the University of Yangon, he served on its faculty while earning his master's degree. In 1981, in recognition of the contributions he had made as professor and lay ecumenical leader, the Senate of the South East Asia Graduate School of Theology (SEAGST) conferred on him the doctor of divinity degree in church history.

Kyaw Than's ecumenical career began when he was appointed the associate general secretary of the World Student Christian Federation (WSCF) in 1950, a position he held with distinction until 1956. In this capacity he traveled to universities in Europe, United Kingdom, North America, Australia, and New Zealand. He also engaged actively in ecumenical leadership training of undergraduate students in Asia.

His involvement in the Asian ecumenical scene began when he was invited to succeed the late bishop R. E. Manikam as the joint East Asia secretary of the International Missionary Council (IMC) and the World Council of Churches (WCC). He was an active participant in the organization of the first meeting, in Prapat, Indonesia, of the East Asia Christian Conference (EACC), which later became the Christian Conference of Asia (CCA). At the EACC's first assembly in Kuala Lumpur, Malaysia (1959), he was elected associate general secretary, and in 1968 he succeeded D. T. Niles as general secretary and served in this position until after the fifth Assembly of the EACC in Singapore in 1973.

His global ecumenical involvement was enhanced when he was elected to the Central Committee of the WCC at the fifth WCC Assembly in Nairobi, Kenya, in 1975. He was later elected to the Executive Committee of the Central Committee and served the council until 1992. He was also invited to chair the History Working Group of the WSCF to produce a centenary publication edited by Philip Potter.

Kyaw Than served as visiting professor of mission at the Yale Divinity School in the United States and at the Vancouver School of Theology in Canada (1974–1976). Following this, he became the William Paton Fellow at Selly Oak Colleges in Birmingham, United Kingdom. In 1978, he returned to Myanmar to teach at the theological schools on Seminary Hill, Insein, until 1984. He was also appointed as director of the Training Institute for Christian Participation in National Development (TICPIND) by the National Council of Churches in Myanmar with special responsibility for the development of the Chins, an ethnic minority in the northwestern border region.

Since 1984, Kyaw Than has been serving at the Mahidol University, Thailand, the University of Oregon, and the Lutheran School of Theology in Chicago, Illinois. He is also active in Buddhist-Christian relations and dialogue. Very few if any of the Christians in the Southeast Asian region, have served the church and the ecumenical community for so long and so well.

S. Wesley Ariarajah

See also: Buddhism; Christianity; Christian Conference of Asia; Indonesia; Interreligious Relations and Dialogue; Malaysia; Myanmar (Burma); Singapore; Thailand.

Further Reading

Selected Academic Works by U Kyaw Than:

"Building Communities of Peace for All." In *Christian Conference of Asia Consultation Report*, edited by Hope Antone. Hong Kong: Clearcut Publishing, 2003.

"Days of Discovery and Days of Change." In *Living in Oikoumene*, edited by Hope Antone. Hong Kong: Clearcut Publishing, 2003.

"Revisiting Jesus' Pedagogy as Teacher." In *Commission on Theological Concerns Bulletin*, edited by Hope Antone. Hong Kong: Clearcut Publishing, 2004.

"Towards a Common Future." In *Asia-Africa Spirit and Struggle amidst Globalization*, edited by Josef Wityatmadja. Hong Kong: Clearcut Publishing, 2005.

"Towards a Culture of Religious Diversity and Communal Harmony." *Currents* (LSTC Journal). Chicago: Lutheran School of Theology at Chicago, 1992.

L

LAO TZU (LAOZI)

Lao Tzu, or Laozi, is the founder of Daoism, one of the primary philosophical and religious teachings originating in China. The influence of Lao Tzu's teaching through Daoism can be observed today across Southeast Asia, including Taiwan, Hong Kong, Japan, Vietnam, Korea, and Singapore. The classic work in the Daoist tradition is variously called the *Daodejing*, the *Tao Te Ching*, or simply by the name of its alleged author, *Lao Tzu*. The *Daodejing* is believed to have been written in the third or fourth centuries BCE, though the ideas within the work are considered to be much older. The *Daodejing* has inspired many, both within and beyond Asia, and is the most widely translated book after the Christian Bible.

Despite the popularity of the *Daodejing* throughout history, little is known about its reputed author, Lao Tzu. The earliest and subsequent classical biography of Lao Tzu is recorded in the Shih chi history of China, written in the first century BCE by Ssu-ma Ch'ien (145–86 BCE) This version of the story recounts how Lao Tzu, whose name was Li Erh, was a native of the state of Ch'u and worked as the historian in charge of the archives in the Chinese imperial city of Luoyang. Witnessing the disintegration of Chinese society, Lao Tzu retired from his position and traveled west. Upon reaching the border, Lao Tzu encountered the Keeper of the Pass, who requested from Lao Tzu that he write down the wisdom of his philosophical learning. Lao Tzu obliged the request of the Keeper, writing in around 5,000 characters the meaning of the "way," otherwise known as the *dao*, or "path," in which one is taught how to appropriately behave and to assist in leading others. This is considered to be the "Classic of the Way and Its Power." After writing his enigmatic work, Lao Tzu departed into the distant mountains, not to be heard from again. Speculation over what eventually happened to Lao Tzu has become the source of many a legend.

Another feature of Ch'ien's biography is his description of a meeting between Lao Tzu and Confucius in which the wisdom of Lao Tzu dominates over that of his inquirer. Indeed, there are plenty of stories of alleged debates between the two great philosophers, usually depicting Lao Tzu as the victor, though it is likely that these stories emerged during a time of anti-Confucian polemical writing by Daoist members during the fourth century BCE.

The stories surrounding the life of Lao Tzu have long been debated, to the point of questioning whether or not he was a historical figure. Even the historical narrative presented by Ch'ien suggests several possible identities for Lao Tzu, including a man named Tan, a historian of Chou, who lived 129 years after the death of Confucius. Ch'ien admits that the world is unable to know where the truth in the story is to

> Man or myth, there is no disputing the impact and influence of Lao Tzu throughout history. The written words that form part of the Daoist sacred inheritance, attributed to the legendary figure Lao Tzu in the midst of his wandering journey to freedom from chaos and conformity, continue to resonate prominently in the context of Southeast Asia.
>
> *Adrian Bird*

be found. The name "Lao Tzu" means "old man," reflecting the essence of mature wisdom in the source of Daoist teaching. Indeed, to emphasize the wisdom of Lao Tzu, one legend suggests he was in his mother's womb for 82 years prior to his birth, emerging as an aged man with white hair and fully able to communicate to those around him.

One thing that is certain is the influence of Lao Tzu's teaching within Daoism over the centuries. To roam in the company of the Dao, the source from which everything is created and sustained, and to which all things return, is to live free to the self and free from the entrapment of all forms of conformity that would restrain us. The power of such a message, in a world that stresses conformity to social, political, and cultural norms, continues to resonate deeply with individuals and communities across Asia, Southeast Asia, and the rest of the world.

Adrian Bird

See also: Confucianism; Daoism (Taoism); Freedom of Religion; Religion and Society.

Further Reading

Gomes, Gabriel J. *Discovering World Religions: A Guide for the Inquiring Reader.* Bloomington, IN: iUniverse, 2012.

"Lao Tzu Biography." *Encyclopedia of World Biography.* http://www.notablebiographies.com/Ki-Lo/Lao-Tzu.html (accessed November 16, 2013).

Lao Tzu. *Tao Te Ching.* Translated with an Introduction by D. C. Lau. London: Penguin Books, 1963.

Oxtoby, Willard G., and Alan F. Segal, eds. *A Concise Introduction to World Religions.* Oxford: Oxford University Press, 2007.

Prothero, Stephen. *God Is Not One; The Eight Rival Religions that Run the World—and Why Their Differences Matter.* New York: HarperCollins Publishers, 2010.

"Taoism." *Patheos Library.* http://www.patheos.com/Library/Taoism.html (accessed November 16, 2013).

LAOS

Laos is a landlocked country in mainland Southeast Asia. It borders China and Myanmar to the north, Thailand to the west, Vietnam to the east, and Cambodia to the south. The climate is tropical. The population is 6.5 million, living on an area of 85,000 square miles. A single-party state, Lao government is dominated by the Leninist Lao People's Revolutionary Party. The capital is Vientiane; the official

Two women from Laos pray in front of a local Buddhist temple at the banks of the Mekong River in Southern Laos. They are holding burning incense sticks between their folded hands. (guenterguni/iStockphoto.com)

language is Lao. The 49 official ethnicities are divided into lowland Lao, Lao of the mountain slopes, and Lao of the hilltops. The ethnic dimension bears strong religious and political connotations.

Religion in General

The constitution of 1991 declares "the right and freedom to believe or not to believe in religions." Decree 92 (2002) defines the rules for religious practice. While it legitimizes a broad range of activities (printing of materials, proselytization by Lao citizens, contact to overseas groups, etc.), each is contingent on a tedious process of approval by the Department of Religious Affairs of the National Front for

The history of Christianity in Laos is integrally linked to the missionary movements led by the various (and often warring) mission bodies and denominations. The Christian faith reached the region in 1642 with the Jesuit Giovanni-Maria Leria. Five years later, he was pressured out of the kingdom by religious fanatics. The first Protestant missionary in Laos was the Presbyterian Daniel McGilvary. In the early decades of the twentieth century, the Swiss Anabaptists and the Christian and Missionary Alliance too were active in the country. In 1975, all the missionaries had to leave the country.

Michael Kleinod

Construction. Both the constitution and Decree 92 simultaneously proclaim religious freedom and stress the potential threat religion poses to national stability. The state is the final arbiter regarding whether religious practice is "beneficial" or not. Officially recognized religions include Buddhism, Christianity, Islam, and Bahá'í. The National Census (2005) counts 67 percent Buddhists, 1.5 percent Christians, less than 1 percent Muslims and Bahá'í, and 31 percent "others" (mainly animists). The census does not regard animism as a religion for its lack of written doctrines.

Buddhism

Theravada Buddhism is the religion of the dominant ethnic group, the lowland Lao, and other Tai-Kadai speaking groups. In precolonial times, Buddhism occupied a rather clear place in the political space of the Lan Sang kingdom and its successor states: Theravada was the central legitimizing source of kingship. From French colonialist rule onward, the Buddhist Order (sangha) gradually lost its traditional social functions: education and health care were taken over by state institutions, the Order relegated to the religious sphere in the narrow sense (rituals, meditation, Buddhist education). Parts of the sangha were instrumental for the independence movement (1945–1975) in gaining popular support. After 1975, it lost its traditional relative autonomy, and the Lao United Buddhist Organization united the opposing Thammayut and Mahanikay sects, and Buddhism was brought under direct party control. Instead of eradicating religion, the state reduced the sangha to a means for building socialism by streamlining Buddhist doctrines and practices, excluding "superstitions" such as ideas of heaven and hell, karma, and religious merit. Many left the sangha or the country. This restrictive attitude through the 1970s undermined the government's legitimacy rather than Theravada's popularity being diminished among the broader population. After the introduction of market economy in the 1980s, the sangha found itself in a state of ideological uncertainty but kept conforming to the party line. Today, Theravada is being (re)established as central to Laos's national identity. Experts observe a re-Buddhification: Buddhist symbols and rituals are integrated into state functions (e.g., the That Luang Festival, or the "new City Pillar" in Vientiane). Buddhist practice is largely exempt from the regulations set down in Decree 92, and Buddhism is financially supported and promoted by the government (even though it is not an official state religion).

At the same time, Buddhism's central role in constituting national identity is problematic, not least because roughly half of the population are ethnic minorities who, for the most part, do not adhere to Buddhism at all. Additionally, even lowland Lao are increasingly less likely to become monks for a longer period in life. The average is three to four years, and most enter for education reasons. There is high fluctuation within the sangha, a very low average age, and rank-and-file monks constitute only a minority. Although the amount of time monks devote to Buddhist study has increased recently and the sangha's organization has been strengthened, the devaluation of monastic education for a life considered desirable, especially among younger generations, cannot be concealed. In rural areas, the vat

(Buddhist monastery) is still the center of the village, also providing traditional services such as education. This, however, is due to either traditionalism among the elders or poor infrastructure of government services in peripheral regions. The *vat* is often the only institution to provide *at least some* education, a chance to escape rural poverty. Many young monks and novices leave for monasteries in urban areas and quit at the next available occasion. Moreover, about half of Buddhists are estimated to practice out of habit instead of belief. Sociologically, the current process of social differentiation splits Buddhist practice into performance, knowledge, and belief, and distributes these aspects differently among emerging groups and milieus.

Animism

Although the National Census distinguishes animism, or belief in spirits (*phii*), from religions (*sadsana*) such as Buddhism, *sadsana phii* is commonly used to denote spirit worship. This shows that animism and Buddhism are no distinct categories in everyday life, including among "Buddhist" lowland Lao. Animist-magical ideas are widespread and often frame the way "proper" religions are seen and practiced. The *baci*-ritual (wrist tying), based on the belief in *khwan* ("souls"), has become an icon of Lao-ness, as has the *haw phii* (spirit house) in front of every urban Lao home. Even in Vientiane, the capital, there is a sacred forest inhabited by *phii* and taken care of by the nearby *vat*. The existence of spirits is generally taken for granted, also by modern urban Lao. Animism is thus not an archaic remnant, but vital for mediating Laos's social transformation. However, modernity—a value accepted also by "animistic" minority groups—is equated with lowland Lao Buddhism and contrasted with animism, which implies backwardness. The logic that ethnic minorities are poor because they are animists is common and has its effects on national development programs and on the way "target groups" relate to their "traditions." There are instances where sacred forests are turned into "productive" land by villagers themselves, claiming that spirits are a thing of the past.

Christianity

The legal situation is more restrictive for Christian Lao than for Buddhists. For congregations to be recognized, they must be members either of the Roman Catholic Church, the Lao Evangelical Church, or the Seventh-day Adventist Church. Due to Laos's colonial history, Christianity is seen as a foreign religion that presents a potential national security threat. Most Catholic Lao belong to Hmong and Khmu minorities. Especially the Hmong, some clans of which were and still are involved in antigovernment activities, raise strong stability concerns for the government. Since the 1990s, evangelicalism in Laos has one of the highest growth rates worldwide, due to very low absolute numbers, the relative novelty of this phenomenon, and the effort put into missionary work. Hundreds of Protestant groups, largely backed by U.S. organizations, are active especially among ethnic minorities. Established by NGOs with religious affiliations providing humanitarian aid, many of these new groups are not registered with the aforementioned associations.

The religious fervor of some evangelical groups often goes hand in hand with a political opposition toward the "communist" government.

The law is reported to be applied rather arbitrarily among Christian groups. Protestants, especially, complain that legal regulations are used to restrict religious activities. Moreover, the decentralized structure of Lao administration enables independent action on the part of local officials that is not in line with the central government's agenda. Outright crackdowns on Christians, such as the closing of churches or the forced renunciation of faith, typically happen in the provinces, while freedom of religious practice is, for the most part, a reality in urban centers. Repression is generally legitimized with the law, but "Lao" identity can justify it as well—e.g., the intention not to lose the title of a heritage site, as reported from Luang Namtha Province. However, also, "religious freedom" is instrumentalized by those hoping to cash in on the weakening of the Lao state.

Bahá'í and Islam

Bahá'í, a rather young Iranian religion propagating unity of all religions and of humankind, has roughly 10,000 adherents in the urban centers of Vientiane and Pakse. Around 400 Muslims are split in two groups: permanent residents from the Indian subcontinent, and ethnic Cham people who fled the Pol Pot regime. The latter constitute the Lao Muslim Society, which counts Lao nationals as well as foreign diplomats among its members. Each group runs a mosque in Vientiane. Since 2001, the Muslim community is under closer scrutiny by the government but practice has not been restricted. Additionally, a small number of Muslims from Yunnan Province, China, live in the far north of the country.

Overall, the traditional predominance of Buddhism is likely to continue given its privileged position for the legitimization of the modern Lao state. However, it has lost its monopoly for interpreting social existence, and with further international integration, the trend toward religious diversification will likely continue. Since colonial times, Buddhism has been integrated into the firm structures of the nation-state and has become one political actor among others. Animist-magical ideas are widespread and have blended with Buddhist or Christian doctrine. It will largely depend on Laos's socioeconomic development whether these continue to be salient for making sense of Lao society in the future.

Michael Kleinod

See also: Animism; Bahá'í Faith; Buddhism; Christianity; Colonialism; Communism; Ethnicity; Freedom of Religion; Islam; Minorities; Missionary Movements; Religion and Society; Secularism; Spirit Mediumship; Thailand; Uplanders.

Further Reading

Compass Direct News. "Lao Police Arrests Pastor for Spreading Faith." *Christian Post*, June 11, 2012. http://www.christianpost.com/news/lao-police-arrest-pastor-for -spreading-faith-76464/ (accessed September 19, 2014).

Holt, John. *Spirits of the Place: Buddhism and Lao Religious Culture*. Chiang Mai, Thailand: Silkworm Books, 2011.

Ladwig, Patrice. "The Genesis and Demarcation of the Religious Field: Monasteries, State Schools, and the Secular Sphere in Lao Buddhism (1893–1975)." *SOJOURN: Journal of Social Issues in Southeast Asia* 26, no. 2 (2011): 196–223.

McDaniel, Justin. *Gathering Leaves and Lifting Words: Histories of Buddhist Monastic Education in Laos and Thailand.* Seattle: University of Washington Press, 2008.

Rehbein, Boike. "Differentiation of Sociocultures, Classification, and the Good Life in Laos." *SOJOURN: Journal of Social Issues in Southeast Asia* 26, no. 2 (2011): 277–303.

Sprenger, Guido. "Political Periphery, Cosmological Center: The Reproduction of Rmeet Sociocosmic Order and the Laos-Thailand Border." In *Centering the Margin: Agency and Narrative in Southwest Asia Borderlands*, edited by Alexander Horstmann and Reed L. Wadley, 67–84. New York and Oxford: Berghahn Books, 2006.

Stuart-Fox, Martin. *Buddhist Kingdom, Marxist State: The Making of Modern Laos.* Bangkok: White Lotus Press, 2002.

U.S. Department of State. "July–December, 2010 International Religious Freedom Report." http://www.state.gov/documents/organization/171656.pdf (accessed May 22, 2013).

LIBERATION THEOLOGIES

Liberation theology emerged as a new social and theological movement in Latin America in the 1960s, wrestling afresh with questions about God's relationship with the poor and the oppressed in a context of poverty and injustice. Liberation voices sought to understand and interpret the Christian Gospel in light of the lived reality of suffering, struggle, and hope of the poor. Challenging theologies that seemed removed from the concrete historical contexts of so many people's lives, liberation theologians such as Gustavo Gutiérrez argued that the church must be actively involved in the struggle for liberation from any kind of oppression, including economic, social, racial, or religious oppression. Liberation theology can thus be considered a theology "from below," or as a "theology of struggle," which understands the Cross of Christ as a symbol of challenge, struggle, and hope essentially rooted in the critical contextual realities of the people. Justice, as an essential component of humanization, is considered an issue of utmost theological importance.

Given the reality of poverty, oppression, and injustice around the world, it is of little surprise that the influence of liberation theology has extended far beyond the continent of Latin America, in the course of the last several decades. The question of liberation has become an urgent one in Southeast Asia in the latter part of the twentieth century.

Despite the increasing attention given to contextual liberation theologies emerging around the world, particularly across Asia and Africa, building on the initial momentum generated in Latin and North America, Southeast Asia receives only scant notice. Perhaps this is due to the association of liberation theology to its Christian roots, which seem far removed from the religiously diverse context of Southeast Asia. Understood as a concept essential to *religious* discourse and action, Southeast Asia becomes a valuable resource for further investigation, adding intriguing and stimulating voices to the broader liberation theological narrative.

Adrian Bird

The influence of liberation theology has been witnessed among the different religions in Southeast Asia, each turning to its own sources and traditions in order to refocus attention on the liberation of the people from oppression. While acknowledging that the term "liberation theology," which was essentially developed and articulated within the context of a Christian worldview, is problematic in the context of other religions, Irfan A. Omar also acknowledges that the search for the revival of liberating principles that places the human at the center of religious discourse exists within all religious movements.

Certainly liberation theology in Southeast Asia has its own distinctive realities, questions, stories, and voices to be heard. Bastiaan Wielenga observes that in contrast to Latin America, the distinctive reality of Asia is the religio-cultural context, where the overwhelming majority of the oppressed and the poor are non-Christian. Indeed, despite the shifting centers of Christianity around the world, the majority of people in Southeast Asia adhere to, or are deeply influenced by, the great religious traditions of Asia, including Confucianism, Buddhism, and Taoism, as well as a variety of diverse popular traditions. The significant presence of Islam serves to add further diversity to the Southeast Asian religious landscape. This means that liberation theology in Southeast Asia takes on many forms and encourages mutually enriching conversation and joint action initiatives across the religious spectrum. To be in solidarity with the people in their own concrete historical contexts means forging and nurturing relationships between people of different religious faiths, identifying and challenging the causes of oppression without being destructively invasive to diverse religious identities.

Given the essence of diversity in Southeast Asia, it is clear that there will be no easy solution to the problems of injustice, poverty, indignity, or oppression. Though common points exist across the region, each context provides a different set of issues to be addressed. It is also the case that different religions understand the root causes of human oppression in different ways. Stephen Prothero reminds us that different religions offer different analysis of the human "problem," and consequently offer different solutions to overcoming the problem. Buddhists, following the teachings of the Buddha, name human suffering as the chief problem to be overcome through the path of enlightenment. For many Christian liberation theologians, the primary cause of human oppression is sin, both on a personal and on a broader systematic level, which needs to be overcome through a process of action and theological reflection to bring about holistic transformation of the individual and society. Despite such differences, Choan Seng Song acknowledges that there are points of commonality to the experience of suffering, a realism that calls for the creative encounter of the Cross of Christianity with the Lotus of Buddhism, building bridges across the religious divide in order to name and challenge shared contextual struggles.

While interreligious relations become critical to the quest for liberation, this task is made more complex by the rawness of historical memory. There are cases in which the very human struggles identified are caused by interreligious tension, manifest through one religion's support of oppressive or destructive ideologies, or hegemonic theological dogmas. In this sense, religion in Southeast Asia plays a double role, with the potential to abuse power to justify oppression as well as to join in the struggle against injustice and discrimination. Bastiaan Wielenga names patriarchy, prevalent among many religions, and caste discrimination (in contexts such as Myanmar and Bali), to highlight the potentially oppressive role of religious legitimization of human suffering. In order to build bridges across religious boundaries, relationships require a commitment to transformation on a holistic level in order to work toward justice, freedom, peace, and security for all, drawing on diverse religious sources to attain prescribed goals. This is no easy task, particularly as interpretations of "justice" and "freedom" are often done in such a way as to suit individual or collective interests, reinforcing oppressive norms through the power of religious interpretation. The challenges are many, yet the need is great.

Unlike the Philippines, whose population is predominantly Christian, most Christian groups in Southeast Asia exist as marginalized minority communities, a fact that affects the impact that can be made in the struggle of the poor. Given this reality, Christian theological responses to social, economic, and political concerns have been essentially stimulated through ecumenical gatherings and networks such as the Ecumenical Association of Third World Theologians (EATWOT) and the Christian Conference of Asia (CCA). These networks provide important avenues for solidarity, study, and action in the struggles of the people. EATWOT, for example, has focused on a variety of significant themes in the region, holding important think-tank conferences on the themes "Towards a Methodology of Doing Theology in the midst of Human Struggles" and "Indigenous Peoples' Struggles for Justice and Liberation in Asia." The minority status of Christian communities in Southeast Asia means that involvement in protest and advocacy movements has also come through alliances made with secular movements, where people are empowered to struggle against oppression and towards justice.

It has been noted that different religions in Southeast Asia have also sought to respond to the cry for liberation, though context again determines the analysis and response in a particular location. The experience of minority Rohingya Muslims in Myanmar, who face ongoing persecution and discrimination at the hands of Buddhist and government groups, will be very different to the Muslims of Indonesia or Malaysia, where they form the majority religious group in the region. Once again, particular contexts determine particular human realities, influencing the impact of liberation theology for a given people.

Responding to the influence of liberation theology, Islamic revivalism in the latter part of the twentieth century can be seen to operate on the principles of liberation theology, challenging political conditions that seek to determine the destiny of people in the midst of their particular socioeconomic and cultural contexts. Justice is intrinsically embedded within the Qur'an, and inspires a passion for resistance against all forms of injustice. While liberation theologians assert that Jesus came to liberate humanity from all forms of bondage including material poverty and social injustice, it needs to be noted that Muslim revivalist movements also began as a struggle for social, political, and economic liberation.

Liberation theology has also had an influence on Buddhist thinkers in Thailand seeking to develop a Buddhist social ethic that will create liberation for the oppressed and disenfranchised people of Thailand. Even though Buddhism is often criticized as a religion concerned mainly with personal enlightenment and an individual turning from greed, Tavivat Puntarigvivat urges that greed be understood in sociopolitical terms as a built-in mechanism for oppressive social structures. Puntarigvivat describes the plight of Thai farmers unable to sustain their families through agriculture as a result of structural systems of poverty, and the increasing number of young girls who are forced to turn to prostitution as part of the illegal sex trade industry. While acknowledging that prostitution is against the teaching of the Buddha, Puntarigvivat is critical that the Thai *sangha* (community of monks) has historically remained silent about this issue. The reality of prostitution, as a by-product of unjust economic and social structures as well as a form of gender oppression, is one that Buddhist thinkers are seeking to address through the influence of liberation theology, using Buddhist sources to create a social ethic toward liberative transformation. Buddhist activists such as Buddhadasa Bhikkhu (1906–1993) sought to reinterpret Buddhism to incorporate sociopolitical concerns, encouraging social and political praxis in line with the Buddha's teaching. Challenging personal and corporate greed, Buddhadasa discouraged the hoarding of surplus goods for profit, encouraging distribution for the well-being of all. Many Buddhist-based grassroots movements have emerged, including the bhikkhuni movement, to address concrete issues in Thailand, which seek to empower men and women to become actively involved in the struggle to overcome very real oppression and discrimination, both at the local level and at the broader structural level of the country. In neighboring Myanmar, the Buddhist monks were central to the "Saffron Revolution," the antigovernment protests of 2007, which began as a people's protest against the economic policies of the ruling junta.

With an emphasis on praxis, which stresses both theological reflection and action, liberation theology has been a radical movement that has significantly influenced the various religions of Southeast Asia, a region in which the question of liberation remains critical. Liberation theology, emerging with varied religious expressions and drawing on a diverse array of theological sources and traditions, seeks the liberation of the people from their particular contexts of oppression, working toward the transformation of both the individual and, essentially, the society, so as to remove the obstacles for human freedom and justice. Within this process, it is vital that religious groups come together for mutual enrichment and support, ensuring that all minority groups within a given region are afforded due recognition, dignity, and rights, and encourage mutual accountability in order to prevent liberation movements from becoming sources of oppression for future generations.

Adrian Bird

See also: Aisyiyah and Nasyiatul Aisyiyah; Bhikkhu, Buddhadasa; Bhikkhuni, Dhammananda; Buddhism; Christianity; Christian Conference of Asia; Communism; Confucianism; Daoism (Taoism); Engaged Buddhism; Federation of Asian Bishops' Conferences; Freedom of Religion; Humanism; Interreligious Relations and Dialogue; Islam; Minorities; Reform Movements; Religion and Society; Women.

Further Reading

De La Torre, Miguel A., ed. *The Hope of Liberation in World Religions*. Waco, TX: Baylor University Press, 2008.

England, John C., Jose Kuttianimattathil, John Mansford Prior, Lily Quintos, David Suh Kwang-sun, and Janice Wickeri, eds. *Asian Christian Theologies: A Research Guide to Authors, Movements, Sources: Volume 2, Southeast Asia*. Delhi: Indian Society for Promoting Christian Knowledge (ISPCK); and Maryknoll, NY: Orbis Books, 2003.

Leibo, Steven A. *The World Today Series 2012: East and Southeast Asia*. 45th ed. Lanham, MD: Styker-Post Publications, 2012.

Prothero, Stephen. *God Is Not One; The Eight Rival Religions that Run the World, and Why Their Differences Matter*. New York: HarperOne Publishers, 2010.

Rowland, Christopher, ed. *The Cambridge Companion to Liberation Theology*, 2nd ed. Cambridge: Cambridge University Press, 2007.

LOCALIZATION OF HINDUISM IN INDONESIA

Although being the world's largest Islamic country, much of contemporary Indonesian culture is still strongly influenced by Hindu traditions. The national motto, *Bhineka Tunggal Ika*, usually translated as "unity in diversity," is of Hindu-Javanese heritage, as is the national emblem featuring the *garuda*, originally Lord Vishnu's vehicle, which also gave name to the Indonesian national airline, Garuda Indonesia. At the same time, the portion of Indonesia's population professing Hinduism as their religion is vanishingly low and mainly concentrated on the island of Bali, with some pockets in Java and central Borneo.

Historically, Hinduism came to Indonesia as a religion of kingly courts, and only certain aspects of its mythology and cosmology penetrated the fringes of the traditionally concentric polities on the islands of Java, Sumatra, and Borneo (see van der Kroef 1951). In many indigenous societies of the archipelago, particular aspects of Hinduism have been localized and continue to influence the widely adaptive local religions, integrating Hindu symbolism, aspects of ritual practice, and cosmology into indigenous religious frameworks. After Indonesian independence, none of the local belief systems—dubbed *kepercayaan*—was officially recognized as *agama* ("religion") in the context of Islamic monotheist conceptualizations, and in order to sustain their faith, strongly Hinduized local religions had to readopt universalized forms of an Indian Hindu Dharma framework in order to gain official state recognition. In consequence, some odd recontextualized versions of "Hinduism" exist in contemporary Indonesia, most prominently the *Agama Hindu Kaharingan* in Central Kalimantan on the island of Borneo, and the *Agama Hindu Bali*.

Hinduism(s) in Bali and Borneo

Evidence of Hindu influence on the island of Bali dates back to the first millennium of common estimation but became more pronounced after the defeat of the influential Hindu-Javanese kingdom of Majapahit in the fifteenth century, when the court sought refuge on the island of Bali and was able to reestablish a new dynasty here. A distinctly localized form of Hinduism developed during this time, with the

Balinese identifying the mythical Mount Meru of Indic cosmology with their own sacred mountain Gunung Agung in the center of the island and incorporating indigenous spirits and divinities into the Hindu pantheon. In many local traditions of Balinese Hinduism, the ancient buffoon Twalen is still seen as an older brother to the Indian Hindu god Siva.

The syncretic Balinese religion was traditionally known as *Agama Tirtha*, the "religion of the Holy Water," and recognized a diversity of local forms of *adat*, or "custom," instead of a universally standardized version of faith and ritual practice. A mixture of Hindu-Buddhist scriptures, orally related mythologies, and localized rituals became the basis for religious life. However, constitutionally being a "monotheist" state, the Indonesian Ministry of Religious Affairs stipulates that every officially acknowledged religion has to acknowledge one highest divinity, must have a holy book (likening the Qur'an or the Bible), fixed places of worship and regular liturgical services, and observe annual religious holidays. In consequence, the highly syncretic *Agama Tirtha* in Bali had to be purified and altered to adhere to these requirements in the 1950s, and was acknowledged as an official version of Hinduism (*Agama Hindu Bali*) in 1958. Many of the local divinities had to be downgraded to become demons or saints, and the diverse local traditions (*adat*) found on the island were standardized (Picard 2004).

Three decades later, adherents of the Central Borneo tradition of *Kaharingan*, a set of diverse but not dissimilar local religions, sought Indonesian state recognition in comparable ways, reassigning new roles to former spirit beings and divinities, devising a standardized version of the myth of creation in form of a holy book, and institutionalizing regular religious ceremonies (Baier 2007). However, in contrast to the Balinese case, it can be argued that the basic tenants of *Agama Kaharingan* display as much Christian and Islamic influences as they are rooted in Hindu traditions. It seems that "Hinduism" here is used as a vehicle to receive authorization from state agencies for the continuation of indigenous religious life, even at the expense of compromising the magical prowess of traditional *adat*. In reaction to this, some communities in central Kalimantan have opted to formally convert to Christianity instead and, at the same time, to safeguard local traditions in "customary," semireligious ways (Schiller 1997).

Christian Oesterheld

See also: Buddhism; Christianity; Contextualization; Hinduism; Indonesia; Islam; Minorities; Myth/Mythology; Religious Conversions; Spirit Mediumship; Syncretism.

Further Reading

Baier, Martin. "The Development of the Hindu Kaharingan Religion: A New Dayak Religion in Central Kalimantan." *Anthropos* 102 (2007): 566–70.

Picard, Michel. "What's in a Name? Agama Hindu Bali in the Making." In *Hinduism in Modern Indonesia: A Minority Religion between Local, National, and Global Interests*, edited by Martin Ramstedt, 56–75. London and New York: RoutledgeCurzon, 2004.

Schiller, Anne. *Small Sacrifices: Religious Change and Cultural Identity among the Ngaju of Indonesia*. New York and Oxford: Oxford University Press, 1997.

van der Kroef, Justus M. "The Hinduization of Indonesia Reconsidered." *Far Eastern Quarterly* 11 (1951): 17–30.

LOH, I-TO

I-to Loh is a leading Asian church musician and ethno-musicologist in the second half of the twentieth century. More than any other contemporary Asian Christian theologian, he advances the work of theological contextualization that Shoki Coe began in the post–Pacific War period. His life and work explores the intrinsic connection of theology to spirituality, liturgy to music, faith to culture, and local to universal. His legacy is embodied both in the hymnals he produced and in his imprint on his students, many of whom hold key position in churches and seminaries in Asia and in the West.

Loh was born in 1936 at Tamsui, Formosa (Taiwan). His father Loh Sian-chhun was a pioneering evangelist and itinerary preacher among the Amis, Pinuyumayan, Paiwan, Rukai, and Tao tribes, at a time when Taiwan was successively occupied by two Asian powers—Japan and then by the autocratic Kuomintang regime that led to the island in 1949. His life and work would be marked by sensitive alertness to suppressed voices, mental strength, and cathartic discipline. Loh entered Tainan Theological College in 1955, at which time it was the trailblazing theological college in Asia under the helm of Ng Chiong-hui (C. H. Hwang, or more commonly known in the West as Shoki Coe). Missionaries Isabel Taylor, Kathleen Moody, and George Todd awoke in him the search in contextualization in church music. After graduating from Tainan Theological College in 1963, he pursued further studies at Union Seminary in New York and Columbia University. In 1982, he received his doctorate at the University of California (Los Angeles) for his studies on the tribal music of Taiwan, focusing particularly on the Ami and Puyuma styles.

Loh served as academic dean of the newly established Asian Institute of Liturgy and Music, based in Manila, from 1982 to 1994. From 1995 to 2003, he taught at Tainan Theological College and Seminary, which he served as president from 1995 to 2002. Loh composed over 100 original hymns and anthems, and edited over 20 hymnals. The editing of hymnals in fact became the occasions in which he probed new horizons, embraced new colleagues, and made new conceptual connections, from *New Songs of Asian Cities* (1972), to *Hymns from the Four Winds* (1983), *Sound the Bamboo* (1990, 2000), and *Sèng-si* (2009). *In Search for Asian Sounds and Symbols in Worship* (Loh 2012), the accessible collection of his literary work in English, also contains a full bibliography of his works.

More than any other contemporary Asian theologian, I-to Loh advanced the work of theological contextualization that Shoki Coe began in the post–Pacific War period. His life and work explored the intrinsic connection of theology to spirituality, liturgy to music, faith to culture, and local to universal.

Michael Nai-Chiu Poon

Loh is a theologian as well as a musician and composer who gives expression to the spiritual traditions of Pacific Rim Christianity from Southeast Asia to the American West Coast. His life and work represent the challenges and new horizons of Asian theology. Ironically, he finds a more receptive audience in the United States than in Asia. He was the first non-Caucasian to be awarded Fellow of the Hymn Society of North America and Canada in 1995, and was the recipient of the Global Consultation on Music in Mission's 2006 Award. He is a visiting professor of worship, Asian, and global church music at seminaries in Hong Kong, Singapore, Malaysia, and Taiwan.

Michael Nai-Chiu Poon

See also: Christian Conference of Asia; Christianity; Colonialism; Contextualization; Malaysia; Missionary Movements; Music; Philippines; Singapore.

Further Reading

Lim, S. H. *Giving Voice to Asian Christians: An Appraisal of the Pioneering Work of I-To Loh in the Area of Congregational Song.* Saarbrucken: VDM Verlag, 2008.

Loh, I-to. *Hymnal Companion to Sound the Bamboo. Asian Hymns in Their Cultural and Liturgical Contexts.* Chicago: GIA, 2011.

Loh, I-to. *In Search for Asian Sounds and Symbols in Worship.* Edited by Michael Nai-Chu Poon. Singapore: Trinity Theological College, 2012.

MAARIF, AHMAD SYAFI'I

Ahmad Syafi'i Maarif is a leading Indonesian thinker who had served as the chairman of Muhammadiyah, one of the largest organizations in the country. Born in 1935 in West Sumatra, Indonesia, through his family and schooling, he had become acquainted with the teachings of reformed Islam. Even as a devout Muslim deeply rooted in his religious tradition, he became convinced that the peaceful coexistence of humankind was the aim of true religion. While conferring on him, in 2008, the Ramon Magsaysay Award for Peace and International Understanding, the Magsaysay Committee commended Syafi'i's role in guiding Muslims to embrace tolerance and pluralism as the basis for justice and harmony in Indonesia and in the world at large.

As an idealistic young man growing in the young nation of Indonesia, Syafi'i worked initially with the Islamic party of Masyumi. During this period, he was committed to the radical view of establishing an Islamic state, and he wrote a number of articles espousing these views. As democratic forces receded in that country, Masyumi was dismantled and Sukarno ascended to almost absolute power; the space for freedom and democracy, however, was severely restricted. Syafi'i went to the United States for higher studies where he met the Pakistani reformist thinker Fazlur Rahman who was then a lecturer at the University of Chicago. Rahman, perhaps more than any other person, influenced his subsequent political and religious thinking. Enamored by the depth of Rahman's knowledge and his deep commitment, Shafi'i discarded his fundamentalist views and became convinced that Islam can be the path of peaceful coexistence with fellow human beings.

Syafi'i returned to Indonesia a transformed man. He became an advocate of Islamic pluralism that affirmed that his country's model of *pancasila*—in which both believers in all religions and nonbelievers as well could participate—alone is viable to guide the society forward in the path of peace and justice. As a keen student, he was also determined to probe the spiritual and philosophical roots of the backwardness of his people. He realized that poverty bred radicalism and therefore, a commitment to social justice—and not any vague notion of the establishment of a religious state—should be the concern of faith communities. He was particularly critical of the way religious symbols were exploited for material benefits. In this context, he saw young people as the greatest hope to foster tolerance and in combatting the forces of bigotry.

While Syafi'i had his critics, he soon rose to be one of the leading religious and social thinkers of Indonesia. As the three-decade-long dictatorship ended and the country was posed on a process of democratization in the 1980s, he assumed the leadership of Muhammadiyah with around thirty millions members and supporters. As the chairman of Muhammadiyah during the tumultuous 1990s, he led the civil society in the path of moderation, tolerance and pluralism.

Despite his immense popularity in Indonesia, Maarif stayed away from political office. He founded the Maarif Institute for Culture and Humanity as an organization that is rooted in Islamic values and promotes interreligious dialogue and co-operation. He is also a Senior Lecturer at the Yogyakarta State University in Yogyakarta, Indonesia.

Jesudas M. Athyal

See also: Fundamentalism; Indonesia; Interreligious Relations and Dialogue; Islam; Muhammadiyah; Rais, Muhammad Amien; Secularism.

Further Reading

Hermawan, Ary. "Ahmad Syafii Maarif: The Odyssey of an Indonesian Muslim Pluralist." *Jakarta Post*, September 18, 2008. http://muhammadiyahstudies.blogspot.com/2010/03/ahmad-syafii-maarif-odyssey-of.html (accessed March 31, 2014).

Maarif, Ahmad Syafi'i. *Islam, Mengapa Tidak? (Islam, Why Not?)*. Yogyakarta, Indonesia: Shalahuddin Press, 1984.

Ramon Magsaysay Award Foundation. "Maarif, Ahmad Syafii: Magsaysay Award Citation." http://www.rmaf.org.ph/newrmaf/main/awardees/awardee/profile/154 (accessed March 31, 2014).

MALAYSIA

Malaysia was formed in 1963 when peninsular Malaya, which gained independence from Britain in 1957, was joined with Sabah, Sarawak, and Singapore in 1963 (with Singapore departing the federation in 1965). Sabah and Sarawak are commonly referred to as East Malaysia, whereas peninsular Malaysia is referred to as West Malaysia. The capital city of Malaysia is Kuala Lumpur.

A census in 2010 found that Malaysia had a population of 28.3 million, of which 71 percent live in urban areas. According to that census, the majority ethnic group was Bumiputera, at 67.4 percent. Translated, Bumiputera means "sons of the soil," and this category is in turn composed of Malays, who constitute 63.1 percent of the total population; and an array of aboriginal groups, among the largest of which are Ibans, who constitute 30.3 percent of Sarawak, and Kadazan/Dusun, who make up 24.5 percent of Sabah. Malaysians with Chinese ancestry make up 24.6 percent of the population, and those with Indian ancestry 7.3 percent of the population.

The largest religious group in Malaysia is Muslims, at 61.3 percent of the population. Other religious groups include Buddhists (19.8 percent), Christians (9.2 percent), and Hindus (6.3 percent). Also present is what is sometimes referred to as Daoism or Confucianism, or "Chinese traditional belief." While there is a high degree of correlation between ethnic and religious affiliations so that it is a common assumption that Malays practice Islam, most Indians practice Hinduism, and the Chinese practice Christianity or Buddhism, it is also the case that the ethnic and religious identities overlap. There are, for example, large numbers of Malaysians with

Bangladeshi Muslims living in Malaysia offer a prayer during the first day of Eid al-Fitr, which marks the end of the fasting month of Ramadan in Kuala Lumpur, Malaysia. (AP Images/Lai Seng Sin)

Chinese and Indian ancestry who are Muslim, which is the religion associated with the Malay ethnic group. Islam is also the official religion of Malaysia; however, other religions including Buddhism, Christianity, Hinduism, and Sikhism have vibrant communities as well as religious festivals officially recognized as holidays.

There has been a strong tradition of interreligious camaraderie, such as when the end of Ramadan (known as Hari Raya) coincides with Deepavali or Chinese New Year, which constitute the portmanteau celebrations of Kongsi Raya and Deepa-Raya, respectively. Malaysia is also host to one of the largest celebrations of the Hindu festival of Thaipusam, which draws to the Batu Caves temple in Selangor thousands of participants, many from overseas.

Islam in Malaysia

Politically, Islam is the most salient religion. According to historians, Islam was introduced to the Malay Peninsula in the fifteenth century as a result of Muslim

---

While in Islam, a fatwa may be regarded as a legal opinion or declaration, in Malaysia, fatwas have the force of law. According to the Federal Territories Syariah Criminal Offences Act of 1997, any Muslim who gives, propagates, or disseminates any opinion concerning Islamic teachings, Islamic law, or any issue, contrary to any fatwa shall be guilty of an offense. Punishments include fines, jail, or both. However, because *shari'a* law is a state matter and not a federal matter, a fatwa in one state may not be in effect elsewhere. Malaysians can find out about fatwas in effect in different states through the official online government "e-Fatwa portal."

Julian CH Lee and Caryn Lim

traders from India, Persia, and South Arabia who conducted their business in trading ports in Southeast Asia including Malacca. Conventionally, Malacca is said to have been settled by inhabitants of present-day Singapore, who fled to what became Malacca around 1400. The leader, Paramesvara, was likely to have been of the Hindu faith but converted to Islam upon his marriage to the daughter of a ruler from Sumatra, who had himself converted to Islam.

Because Islam is embedded in the settlement myth at the root of Malaysia, and because it is so closely associated with the majority ethnic group of the country, in contemporary Malaysia, Islam has played significant roles in the social, political, and legal realms. Legitimacy of this presence is founded, according to some, in the mention of it in the constitution of Malaysia. Article 3 of Malaysia's constitution states that "Islam is the religion of Federation." It goes on to state that "other religions may be practiced in peace and harmony in any part of the Federation." Furthermore, the constitutional definition of a Malay person is someone who, in addition to being a person who speaks the Malay language and who "conforms to Malay custom," also "professes the religion of Islam."

Other Religions

Whereas on the whole, Muslims constitute the majority in population, in the East Malaysian states of Sarawak and Sabah, Christianity is significantly represented, with about 38 percent and 33 percent of the populations identifying as Christian, respectively. The dominance of Islam in terms of both presence and political power is thus much less pronounced. In comparison with peninsular Malaysia, the different religious milieu in Sabah and Sarawak may be attributed to the divergent histories of migration and the significant indigenous population in this region. Christian missionaries who arrived with European colonialists from the sixteenth century onward successfully proselytized many indigenous groups in Sabah and Sarawak, whose traditional beliefs are often described by Christianity as animistic. According to the 2010 census, less than 2 percent of the population today fit into the category of religion that combines what are labeled "folk" or "tribal" religions with Chinese religions such as Daoism and Confucianism.

In the context of the significant political and legal impacts of Islam in Malaysia (described in further detail below), a number of organizations have sought to protect the interests of non-Muslim Malaysians and have called for greater interfaith dialogue and cooperation. Of particular significance is an umbrella body that seeks to represent their interests in the social and political arenas—the Malaysian Consultative Council for Buddhism, Christianity, Hinduism, Sikhism and Taoism (MCCBCHST). This council has been vocal in advocating for improved recognition of the rights of non-Muslims in Malaysia and arguing against an array of circumscriptions placed on non-Muslims including restrictions on the construction of places of worship, the translation of religious texts into the Malay language, and on the above-mentioned ability for Malaysians to officially convert from Islam to another religion.

Religion and Politics

Religion and politics are increasingly intertwined in Malaysia, owing in part to the above-noted correlations between ethnic and religious identities and to the often sectarian nature of political groups. Regularly contested are a number of issues that appear related to the bearing of Islam on state and society. These include the position of Islam as provided for in the constitution, the secular organization of the state, and the application of *shari'a* law and its effects on non-Muslims.

The meaning of the constitutional mention of Islam is contested. Some Malaysians espouse a greater formal role for Islam in society and argue that these and other constitutional mentions mean that the tenets and values of Islam should guide and inform Malaysian society, government, and law. Proponents of this view would include an array of Islamic civil society groups, Parti Islam SeMalaysia (the Islamic Party of Malaysia), and, increasingly, the United Malays National Organisation (UMNO), from which Malaysia's prime ministers have all come. Among their arguments is that Article 3 of the constitution is not a meaningless article and that Islam must be central to Malaysian society and government.

However, there are Malaysians who contest this point of view and argue that the country is, in effect, a secular nation. Evidence assembled in support of this position includes the argument that, as recognized in a judicial precedent (in the case of *Che Omar bin Che Soh*), the reference to Islam in Article 3 does not suggest that Malaysia is an Islamic state, but that for the purposes of ceremonies of state, Islam should be the religion used. Other support is drawn from comments made in the 1980s by Malaysia's first prime minister, Tunku Abdul Rahman, who oversaw the transition to independence and who denounced attempts to emphasize the prominence of Islam in the constitution in a manner not intended by those who drafted it.

A further contestation in Malaysia relates to the ability of Malaysians to officially convert from Islam to another religion. Whereas non-Muslim Malaysians may legally convert to Islam, the reverse is increasingly not the case, with judicial precedents in recent years, such as in the case of *Lina Joy v. Majlis Agam Islam Wilayah & Anor*, finding that those officially registered as Muslims could not freely convert from Islam without the express permission of the Shari'a Courts in Malaysia. Those who disagree with this finding argue that Article 11 of Malaysia's constitution protects freedom of religion, and that having to apply to the Shari'a Court is an undue impediment to this freedom.

Arguments in defense of this finding are sometimes founded in a conservative orthodox view that conversion from Islam is not permissible. Other arguments are founded in Article 160 of the constitution. As noted above, it notes that a Malay person is by legal definition a Muslim. Therefore, with respect to Malay persons, conversion is by definition impossible. Dissenters from this view argue that the definition in Article 160 exists only for interpreting the law when it refers to Malay persons and that it is not prescriptive.

The official recognition of a Malaysian's religion as Islam has a number of legal consequences. These include being subject to *shari'a* law. *Shari'a* law applies only to Muslims and in addition to enabling an array of benefits, such as access to some charitable funds, also subjects Muslim Malaysians to laws that seek to regulate the conduct of marriage, divorce, moral behavior, and issues of testate, among other things. These laws, for example, enable polygamy and proscribe *khalwat* (close proximity between unmarried and unrelated men and women). The legal and religious interpretations of Islam in Malaysia largely follow the Shafi'i *madhab* (school of law).

The salience of Islam in Malaysia has also led to the pursuit of Islamically orientated businesses. Malaysian businesses and research institutions have made significant investments in developing Islamic banking products and developing the commercial production of goods that are *Halal* (permissible for consumption). The local, regional, and global market for these products is considerable and growing, and Malaysia has sought to become a leader in the development of Islamic financial services and global hub for the production of *Halal* goods.

Julian CH Lee and Caryn Lim

See also: Buddhism; Christianity; Colonialism; Confucianism; Daoism (Taoism); Ethnicity; Freedom of Religion; Globalization; Hinduism; Interreligious Relations and Dialogue; Islam; Religious Conversions; Religious Discrimination and Intolerance; Secularism; *Shari'a*, Singapore; Thaipusam.

Further Reading

Ackerman, Susan E., and Raymond L. M. Lee. *Heaven in Transition: Non-Muslim Religious Innovation and Ethnic Identity in Malaysia.* Honolulu: University of Hawaii Press, 1988.

Fernando, Joseph M. "The Position of Islam in the Constitution of Malaysia." *Journal of Southeast Asian Studies* 37, no. 2 (2006): 249–66.

Fischer, Johan. *Proper Islamic Consumption: Shopping among the Malays in Modern Malaysia.* Copenhagen: NIAS Press, 2008.

Goh, Robbie B. H. *Christianity in Southeast Asia.* Singapore: ISEAS, 2005.

Houben, Vincent J. H. "Southeast Asia and Islam." *Annals of the American Academy of Political and Social Science* 588 (2001): 149–70.

Kamarulnizam Abdullah. *The Politics of Islam in Contemporary Malaysia.* Bangi: Penerbit Universiti Kebangsaan Malaysia, 2003.

Lee, Julian C. H. *Islamization and Activism in Malaysia.* Singapore: ISEAS, 2010.

MELANESIAN RELIGION

Melanesia is a region of islands and states east of Indonesia and north of Australia; it includes East Timor, West Papua (under Indonesian control), Papua New Guinea (PNG), Bougainville, the Solomon Islands, Vanuatu, Fiji, New Caledonia, and Torres Strait in northern Australia. Broadly speaking, this is where Muslim Asia meets the Christian and *kastom*-influenced Pacific, where there are profound differences in culture and belief.

The term *kastom* is a Tok Pisin/Bislama word derived from our understanding of the English word "custom," which is defined by the *Pocket Oxford Dictionary* as a practice that has become habitual, established usage. In using the term *kastom*, the most important of all terms relating to Melanesian religion, what is referred to is

Group of women during church service, Mindre, Papua New Guinea, Melanesia. (Heiner Heine imageBROKER/Newscom)

a full range of indigenous philosophy and spiritual movements whose principles may not have changed for millennia, or may have reached back to the old beliefs and reconstituted themselves after an unhappy period of contact with rival theologies such as Christianity. They are not necessarily traditional, often fusing a mix of ideas with a modern organization or Christian syncretism.

In a Melanesian (and Pacific generally) context, *kastom* refers to a wide range of traditional and cultural practices that cover daily life, religious and chiefly duties, community obligations, material culture, trade, warfare, sexuality, and all the other traditions that make this region distinct. But unlike our more secular notion of "custom," *kastom* is imbued with a spiritual undercurrent, as if the ancestors are always watching. It is their gaze, hovering within the system of tribal law, which gives *kastom lo* (traditional law) its power. Around the world, where Christianity has taken hold, it is usually the end of ancestral spirits, officially at least. In Melanesia, this is not so—both remain powerful currents in society.

Melanesia is, like Africa, host to literally thousands of tribes and languages. New Guinea Island alone has one-quarter of the world's languages, and Vanuatu in particular is the most linguistically diverse country, per capita, on earth, with more than 120 languages for just 270,000 people. With such cultural diversity, it is no surprise that there is also great religious and spiritual diversity. Professor Gary Trompf has declared that Melanesia is "home to the most complex religious panorama on earth."

Melanesia is a dynamic religious region where belief systems ebb and flow and experimentation is widely practiced. Today it is a region with strong foundations of *kastom*, cult, cargo cult, and new religious movements, together with a long-running current of Christianity and syncretic Christian movements. Islam is also on the rise with thousands of highlanders in Papua New Guinea having converted in recent years and a growing *umma* in every Melanesian country.

Since its introduction more than 100 years ago in most places (and less than 40 years ago in others), Christianity was quickly adopted and has had more impact on Pacific communities than any other global faith. The vast majority of Melanesians (and other Pacific islanders) identify themselves as Christian. They draw from a range of Christian traditions including Catholicism, Anglicanism, and Seventh-day Adventism but recent decades has seen a steep rise in Pentecostal and evangelical groups with a more distinctly Pacific flavor, such as the South Seas Evangelical Church. Yet it appears that Christianity has reached its high-tide mark in the Pacific now, and a range of other faiths, including Buddhism, Bahá'í, and Islam, are putting down roots.

Islam is the fastest growing of these new faiths, reflecting a global pattern, and is likely to increase its membership due to its offer of new pathways to wealth and services as well as some cultural similarities such as polygamy. Importantly, Islam and traditional Melanesian *kastom* share the same notion that belief is a total way of life, a 24/7 practice, where daily life cannot be separated from belief. This contrasts with secular governments and a "Church on Sunday" approach for much of Christianity in the region.

In parts of Melanesia, Islam has deeper roots—such as in western coastal communities of West Papua that have been in contact with Indonesian and Arabic traders for centuries. In Fiji, the British brought Indians to work on sugar cane plantations more than 100 years ago, thus establishing both strong Hindu and Islamic communities in Fiji that remain. However, one of the challenges for Islam is that pigs are revered across Melanesia, symbolic of wealth and status for *Big Men*. They are used in trade, gifted for *kastom* ceremonies and reconciliation, and pig tusks even appear on the Vanuatu flag.

What makes Melanesia unique, beyond its adoption of global monotheistic faiths, is its wealth of *kastom* beliefs and practices. This is rooted primarily in rituals related to ancestral worship and appeasement and management of *tabus* and environment. Melanesia is also famous in anthropology and theology for its curious range of "cargo cults," millenarian movements that sought to win "whitemen's goods" by claiming it was delivered by their ancestors and white people were intercepting the "cargo" destined for the indigenes. Although churches and colonial administrations dismissed many such nativistic movements as "cargo cults," in fact many of these movements became the seed for nationalist movements that would win independence for their nations. Many cults remain active today, such as the John Frum movement in Tanna, Vanuatu. *Kastom* and cult movements continue to play an important role in both triggering conflict and ending conflict through *kastom* reconciliation movements. Many contemporary conflicts in Melanesia, such as the struggle for independence in West Papua and Bougainville, protection of *kastom* land on Guadalcanal in the Solomons, and indigenous rights in Fiji, have the spiritual backing of important *kastom* and cult movements.

It is also worth noting the role of women since Melanesia is perhaps the only place left on earth that is largely matrilineal—it is women who own the land, not men. This influences the important role women play in *kastom* and religious movements in order to preserve land rights.

Since Melanesian philosophy is usually dynamic and constantly evolving rather than, say, the timeless, all-encompassing, all-time consciousness of the (Australian) Aboriginal Dreamtime, it can even be said that what we see today as *kastom* movements are sometimes in fact anti-*kastom*. That is, they are a new form, different to both traditional ancestor worship and Christian theology, but often blending their traditional spirit world with some of the organizational elements of Christianity.

Underlying this inherent religious dynamism, the Papua New Guinean statesman and philosopher Bernard Narakobi pointed out that Melanesians are not and have never been slaves to their cultural practices, if they believed these were obstructing them. He added that the Melanesians liberate themselves by establishing new communities with new hopes and future. The most popular conception of Melanesian philosophy is the *Melanesian Way*, a term of uncertain origin and hazy meaning, but one that is widely used to describe Melanesian responses to life. It was popularized by Narakobi in his book of the same name. It is hard to say if it is much different from the *Pacific Way*, which seems grounded in similar values. If it can be boiled down to a simple idea, it is perhaps a deep belief in building consensus and tolerance. To allow everyone to have their say on a matter and build consensus towards a community decision is the Melanesian Way. To show pride in *kastom* during a ceremony is the Melanesian Way. To be inclusive and tolerant of differences is the Melanesian Way.

Narakobi wrote eloquently on the fundamental philosophical foundations of his culture but understood the limitations of definitions. According to him, Melanesians are a spiritual people. Even before Christians came onto those shores, the people there felt and knew the forces of a source greater than themselves. Further, Narakobi affirmed that this was their divine power, the Melanesian Way. This vision sees the human person in his or her totality with the spirit world as well as the animal and the plant world. Such a human person is not the absolute master of the universe but an important component in an interdependent world of the person with the animal, the plant, and the spiritual. However he came to be, the Melanesian is.

Ben Bohane

See also: Ancestor Worship; Bahá'í Faith; Christianity; Colonialism; Ethnicity; Globalization; Hinduism; Islam; Papua New Guinea; Sexuality; Spirit Mediumship; Women.

Further Reading

Bohane, B. *Song of the Islands*. Port Vila, Vanuatu: Waka Press, 2013.
Lindstrom, L. *Cargo Cult*. Honolulu: University of Hawaii Press, 1993.
Narakobi, B. *The Melanesian Way*. Port Moresby: Institute of PNG Studies, 1983.

Trompf, G., and C. Loeliger. *New Religious Movements in Melanesia*. Port Moresby: University of Papua New Guinea Press, 1985.

Worsley, P. *The Trumpet Shall Sound*. London: Palladin Press, 1970.

MESSIANIC MOVEMENTS

The term "messianic" has transcended its original Judaic origins to encompass anything that involves redemption by a Davidic kingly figure. Hence, messianic movements are popular movements propelled by reverence and obedience to a divinely inspired leader who is seen as a liberator by the movement's adherents. It may be emancipation from foreign domination or alleviation from socioeconomic hardships.

In Southeast Asia's recent history, several messianic movements rose more often in reaction to the region's colonial experience. As the various peoples in the region grappled with the new order, some of them turned to their own past and spiritual legacy and longed for a savior from their pantheon of demigods, heroes, and kings. Still, there were some who melded these ancient beliefs with the Christian religion brought by their colonial masters and mined them for symbols that resonated with their own milieu.

The Philippines

During the 300-year Spanish colonial period in the Philippines, countless local messianic movements sprouted, led by charismatic leaders who promised that their groups, usually with indigenous religious influences, offered better living conditions in the near future. Only a few of these movements sought independence from Spanish rule. Among these was Tamblot, a *babaylan* or spiritualist from the island of Bohol, who led a revolt in 1622 in response to the Jesuits' growing influence in his area. There was Tapar from the neighboring island of Panay, who declared himself "God Almighty" in 1663 and appointed two of his aides as "Christ" and the "Holy Spirit" and later led his followers in attacking the town centers.

One notable messianic movement during the Spanish period was the Confradia de San Jose, a religious group open only to Filipinos that was formed in 1840 in Tayabas province by Apolinario dela Cruz, also known as Hermano Puli, who assumed a religious persona as he led his followers in challenging the local authorities. After a bloody battle with the Spanish authorities, Dela Cruz was betrayed by his followers. He was later executed by the government.

During the American period, messianic and nativistic movements broke out in several places in the archipelago. They were generally referred to as "colorum" from the Latin phrase *et saecula saecolorum* ("world without end"). Just like their predecessors in the Spanish era, these groups were characterized by religious devotion, hero worship, superstitious belief, and followers who believed that a messiah will come to deliver them from their current hardships.

The Guardia de Honor started as a lay group organized by the Dominicans. The Dominicans, however, lost control of this group in northern Luzon as a local *anitero* or animist Julian Baltazar (Apo Laqai), took over, assumed religious powers and prophesied that Judgment Day was coming soon. Even as the Dominicans cut off links with the Guardia de Honor by 1882, the group became stronger as it continued to attract followers. It refused to fight alongside the revolutionary forces during the Philippine Revolution, instead waging its own battles against the Spanish authorities, with Apo Laqai being venerated as "God Almighty," his successor, Antonio Valdez as "Christ" and another associate as the "Holy Spirit." Supported by the peasants in northern and central Luzon, it also resisted American authorities until the U.S. Army surrounded the group's stronghold in Central Luzon on March 1901, defeated them, and captured the leaders, who were later executed.

Tracing its roots to another religious group, the Santa Iglesia was reorganized by Felipe Salvador in Luzon and fought alongside Aguinaldo's forces. His exploits led to claims of mystical prowess and paved the way for more recruits among the different and warring ethnic groups of Luzon and who fervently believed that their amulets would protect them from the enemy's bullets. The Santa Iglesia remained resistant even to the American civil government, getting involved in clashes with the constabulary even as Salvador strengthened his mass base, until his capture and eventual execution in 1912.

A peasant-religious movement called Dios-Dios sprouted in the islands of Leyte, Samar, and Bohol in the 1800s. By the time of the Americans, members of this group, especially in Leyte and Samar, became recognizable with the red trousers that they wore, hence becoming more popularly known as the *Pulajanes* or "Reds." Groups of *Pulajanes* in these islands were led by so-called "popes" (i.e., Papa Pablo, Papa Dagohob, etc.) who organized attacks against constabulary forces and even regular army troops, massing their machete-wielding men in a frenzy-filled melee. They were also involved in kidnappings and arson attacks. A long war of attrition between U.S. Army regular troops and local constables against the *Pulajanes* ended only in 1911 when Papa Otoy, the last of the "popes," was killed in battle.

In 1925, a shopkeeper on the island of Panay, Florencio Entrencherado, claimed semidivine powers and proclaimed himself as Florencio I, emperor of the Philippines. Two years later, he led his 10,000 followers on an abortive insurrection.

Lao PDR

The Hmong is an ethnic minority group that settled not only in Laos, but also in Vietnam and parts of Thailand. In the past hundreds of years, messianic movements arose out of the local population in response to the control of French colonial masters and of ruling ethnic groups. One scholar described the Hmong worldview as seeing a close connection between deities and legendary Hmong kings. Majority of the masses eagerly awaited the coming of a chosen one, usually marked by supernatural abilities, who would lead them out from subjugation and reestablish a Hmong kingdom.

One such example was Paj Cai Vwj, born in a Hmong settlement in northern Vietnam. As a young man, he claimed a connection to Huab Tais, a legendary

Hmong messianic hero. Soon, thousands of Hmongs joined his call for rebellion in 1918, also known as the Paj Cai Revolt or "Madman's War," against French colonial officials and Lao and Tai opium tax collectors.

The coming of Christian missionaries to Southeast Asia also resulted in the majority of Hmongs being converted to Christianity. Messianic leaders soon rose, especially in the middle of the twentieth century, combining elements of the Christian faith and animist beliefs. Some of the shamans claimed the imminent return of a Hmong messiah. Several claimed to be incarnations of Jesus Christ. There was even a trio that branded themselves as the "Father, Son and Holy Spirit." There were countermovements, too, as seen in one self-proclaimed "Hmong King" who proclaimed a war against Christian missionaries.

The Cold War also served as a backdrop to several messianic movements. As the Vietnam War gripped Indochina, a prophecy that a messiah garbed in American military uniform distributing rifles would come circulated among the Hmongs.

A Hmong farmer who claimed he experienced divine revelation, Shong Lue Yang, developed the Pahawh script in 1959, enabling the Hmong language to be written down. With his divine claims, he announced that whoever uses this writing script would be saved from the hardship of the war. Taking on the title of "Savior of the Common People," Shong Lue Yang later on found himself caught between the two sides in the Laotian Civil War.

Myanmar

Among Myanmar's Karens, messianic movements have also played a major part in their long history of struggle against the government. The Karen National Union and its military arm, the Christian-led Karen National Liberation Army (KNLA), have been waging an insurgency for more than half a century. One of the groups it supports is a semi-independent unit composed of around 200 child warriors known as "God's Army," led by young twins named Luther and Johnny Htoo in the 1990s and the early part of the twenty-first century. The then 12-year-old twins were revered by their followers for their supposed supernatural abilities and immunity to bullets and mines.

One of KNLA's breakaway factions composed mostly of Buddhists formed the Democratic Karen Buddhist Army (DKBA), one of the hallmarks of which is its "militant nationalism,' heavily influenced by messianic elements. The majority of its members look forward to the arrival of a powerful Buddha-like political figure, who is believed to prepare the advent of Maitreya, the future Buddha.

George Amurao

See also: Ahmadiyya; Colonialism; Ethnicity; Laos; Minorities; Missionary Movements; Myanmar (Burma); Nationalism; Philippines; Spirit Mediumship; Vietnam.

Further Reading

Dimayuga, Paul. "Messianic Leaders of the Revolution." Philippine History Group of Los Angeles. http://www.bibingka.com/phg/religious/ (accessed May 9, 2014).

GlobalSecurity.org. "God's Army." http://www.globalsecurity.org/military/world/para/gods
    _army.htm (accessed May 9, 2014).

Ooi, Keat Gin, ed. *Southeast Asia: A Historical Encyclopedia from Angkor Wat to Timor*. Santa
    Barbara, CA: ABC-CLIO, 2004.

Smalley, William A., Chia Koua Vang, and Gnia Yee Yang. *Mother of Writing: The Origin and
    Development of a Hmong Messianic Script*. Chicago: University of Chicago Press, 1990.

Tan Samuel K. *A History of the Philippines*. Quezon City: University of the Philippines Press,
    1987.

Vincet, Marc, and Birgitte Refslund Sorenson, eds. *Caught between Borders: Response
    Strategies of the Internally Displaced*. London: Pluto Press, 2001.

MINORITIES

While no generally agreed-upon definition of "minorities" exists, the United Nations Subcommission on Prevention of Discrimination and Protection of Minorities had defined the term as a group numerically inferior to the rest of the population of a state, is in a nondominant position, and whose members possess ethnic, religious, or linguistic characteristics differing from those of the rest of the population. Minorities exist in almost all countries and are often subjected to discrimination and marginalization. There have been attempts in modern times to codify laws that would protect minorities. During the period between the First and Second World Wars, when minority rights were being universally acknowledged, the fear was expressed that including the minorities also in any official statement of rights might jeopardize the fragile state structures, especially of the emerging nations. Consequently, the clause on "minority rights" was not initially included within the Universal Declaration of Human Rights. However, at a later stage, a limited clause ensuring the rights of minorities were included as Article 27 of the International Covenant on Civil and Political Rights. Apart from such formal international covenants, it is also assumed that the modern liberal democratic setup is an antidote against any threats to minorities. This has been proven to be a mirage, as the "tyranny of the majority" often leads to the marginalization and suppression of minority voices, pointing toward the need for special provisions to protect the minorities. Minority rights, in the ultimate analysis, needs to be seen as civil rights and human rights that are not determined by a majority vote but considered as inalienable.

Southeast Asia presents a picture of marked contrasts with regard to the minorities. Entire states, such as Papua New Guinea, are composed of minorities. The wider region is not only the meeting point of diverse Eastern civilizations such as Indian and Chinese, but also the scene of religions and cultures that evolved and consolidated themselves during the period of colonialism. While Indonesia as a country has the largest number of Muslims in the world, the Philippines is over 90 percent Christian, and Buddhism is the majority religion of several countries including Thailand, Cambodia, Laos, and Burma. In all these places, religious minorities account for a significant number of the population. The region is also dotted with ethnic and linguistic minorities, making Southeast Asia the crowded marketplace of various minorities. Most Asian countries have laws that protect the faith, practice, and cultures of the minorities, but in practice, the minority groups tend to be viewed as second-class citizens. The majority faith and culture of a country is often portrayed as the norm, a yardstick the other citizens are expected to reach. There are even overt attempts, such as in Indonesia, which is consciously implementing policies of forced assimilation, also called "Indonesianiza-tion." By overt or covert means, the majority communities often lay out the ground rules for the minorities.

Religious Minorities

The office of the UN High Commissioner for Human Rights describes religious minorities as people who are victims of systematic discrimination and exclusion from key sectors of society, who experience publicly fueled prejudices and vilification based on national myths, who are often the subjects of acts of vandalism and desecration, and who experience prohibition or disruption of religious ceremonies, threats, and acts of violence. The term "religious minority" is broadly construed to cover all relevant groups of persons, including traditional and nontraditional communities or large and small communities. In modern times, the term "religious minorities" has also been extended to cover atheistic and nontheistic believers, too, along with racial, ethnic, and religious minorities.

In the Southeast Asian context, violations against religious minorities are often perpetrated by states or by nonstate actors, often in a climate of impunity, and they may originate from different political, religious, ideological, or personal motives. Even as Myanmar (Burma) emerges from decades of military rule and suppression of human rights into an era of democracy and freedom, the subjugation of the minority communities continue as a lingering reality. In this Buddhist-majority country, it has been alleged that the security forces often collaborate with Buddhist monks in attacking Muslim, Christian, and other minority groups. Unfounded fears that Muslims would force their religion on Buddhists and try to "steal" Buddhist women and that the Christians are agents of the United States are often expressed to justify such violence. The state machinery either is silent about these attacks on the minorities or tacitly supports it. Indonesia presents a different picture. While the country has made great strides in consolidating a stable and democratic government after five decades of authoritarian rule, Indonesia is not yet a bastion of tolerance. The authorities often fail to crack down on the extremists that target the minorities. Even though freedom of religion is guaranteed by Indonesia's constitution, blasphemy laws and regulations against proselytizing are routinely used to prosecute the minorities who include not only mainline groups such as Christians and Buddhists, but also atheists, Bahá'ís, and members of the Ahmadiyya faith, an Islamist reformist movement. The country has over 150 religiously motivated regulations restricting the rights of the minorities, and these are used routinely to trample upon the rights of religious and ethnic minorities.

Ethnic Minorities

Southeast Asia is home to a large diversity of ethnic groups that are highly heterogeneous and distinct from each other. Ethnic "majorities" and "minorities" are relational terms, as groups that are majorities in one context and during a particular period tend to be minorities in a different time and place. Yet, one of the casualties of modernization and globalization is a tendency to homogenize ethnic groups and to present them before the visiting tourists as museum pieces, frozen in time. With regard to tourism and several other areas, economy plays a major role in the insecurity experienced by the ethnic minority groups in Southeast Asia. The Chinese minorities becoming the target of riots in different parts of the region since the 1960s points toward the social and political backlash economic success could bring. The relative economic success of the large-scale Chinese and Indian immigrant groups in countries such as Malaysia too has given rise to local resentment and discrimination. Elsewhere, there are also sociopolitical factors. In Indonesia, ethnic and religious minority groups have long protested the Javanese-dominated central government, which was well known for its corruption during the three-decade rule of General Suharto. The country's military also had exploited sectarian and ethnic rivalries to maintain control and prevent any close scrutiny of its human rights abuses in the past. Burma is yet another state where the authoritarian regime exploited ethnic conflicts for its own advantage. The renewed effort of several Southeast Asian governments to counter radical and "terrorist" forces too ends up targeting the minorities in the region. In the name of fighting the Islamist militants, the authorities in the Philippines often also turn against the opposition activists. Indonesia is also a case where, following the terrorist bombing of Bali in 2002, the government labeled several critics as "terrorists." The rights of not only religious but also ethnic minorities are routinely trampled in large parts of Southeast Asia.

Ecological and environmental concerns too play a key role in the lives of minorities. According to the 2012 annual report of the Minority Rights Group International, the growing demand for natural resources across Southeast Asia threatens to endanger the lives of various minority groups. In the long-running armed conflicts in various parts of the region over the control of land and natural resources, the minority groups often end up being displaced from their habitat so as to make room for developmental projects. The minorities and the indigenous communities often lack the political clout and the financial and legal resources to counter these onslaughts.

New Religious Movements

New Religious Movements (NRMs) are defined as ethical, spiritual, or philosophical communities of modern origin that are often located in the midst of religious groups that are both dominant and traditional. NRMs usually emerge as an expression of protest or frustration at established religions and cultures, and they espouse approaches based on a novel way of perceiving spirituality, religion, or philosophy. Of the tens of thousands of NRMs worldwide, most are located in Asia and Africa. The Sathya Sai Baba movement in Singapore can be considered as an NRM that offers a novel path to spirituality in the multicultural environment of the city-state. In the urban pluralist context of Singapore, the Sai Baba movement transcends the traditional boundaries of Hinduism and appeals to a cross-section of people, cutting across the religio-cultural and linguistic divide. Another case, in a Christian setting, is the NRMs of the Philippines, which include Neo-Pentecostal groups. During the last few decades, Pentecostalism has moved from the margins to the mainstream, making deep inroads in the country, especially among the ethnic minority groups, and in the process redefining the religiosity of the masses. Pentecostalism has a pan-regional appeal, as it includes roughly 43 percent of Asian Christians. How the traditional and mainline churches would deal with this challenge, especially as the Pentecostal sweep appeals most to the minority groups, becomes a significant question.

The European and American colonization of most parts of Southeast Asia left an indelible imprint on the situation of the minorities in the region. In several cases, the colonizers reduced the status of the indigenous people to minorities, resulting in the widespread destruction of their religions, cultures, and languages. Despite the diverse ways in which colonialism alienated the minorities, however, the presence of the colonizers also ensured a certain protection for the minority groups, especially against the onslaught of the local and national dominant groups. The collapse of colonialism following the Second World War and the ascendancy of the dominant nationalist groups to power in the various Southeast Asian nations, in that sense, also resulted in a deeper level of alienation for the minorities. In the Burmese context, the postcolonial period coincided with a history of systematic persecution of the minorities. The direct and indirect role played by the various dominant Buddhist monastic groups in the riots against the Muslims and the Christians point towards the systemic manner in which the minority groups are internally victimized.

Jesudas M. Athyal

See also: Buddhism; Cambodia; Christianity; Colonialism; Ethnicity; Hinduism; Indonesia; Islam; Laos; Myanmar (Burma); Philippines; Religion and Society; Religious Discrimination and Intolerance; Sathya Sai Baba Movement; Singapore; Thailand.

Further Reading

Burke, Farkhunda. "Muslim Minorities and Majorities of Southeast Asia: Focus on Realities." *Pakistan Horizon* 57, no. 2 (April 2004): 37–49. http://www.jstor.org/discover/10.2307/41394045?uid=3739696&uid=2&uid=4&uid=3739256&sid=21102247449271 (accessed May 9, 2014).

Ghosh, Lipi, ed. *Political Governance and Minority Rights: The South and South-East Asian Scenario*. New Delhi: Routledge India, 2009.

Harsono, Andreas. "No Model for Muslim Democracy." *New York Times*, May 21, 2012. http://www.nytimes.com/2012/05/22/opinion/no-model-for-muslim-democracy.html?_r=1& (accessed May 9, 2014).

Heller, Monica. *Linguistic Minorities and Modernity: A Sociolinguistic Ethnography*. 2nd ed. London: Continuum International Publishing Group, 2006.

Hussain, Bonojit. "Burma: Lest We Don't See: A Genocide Is in the Making." *Countercurrents.org*. http://www.countercurrents.org/hussain140513.htm (accessed May 9, 2014).

Mallory, Walter H. "Chinese Minorities in Southeast Asia." *Foreign Affairs* 34, no. 2 (January 1956). http://www.foreignaffairs.com/articles/71236/walter-h-mallory/chinese-minorities-in-southeast-asia (accessed May 9, 2014).

Minority Rights Group International. "Key Issues for Religious Minority Rights in Asia." March 2005. http://www.refworld.org/cgi-bin/texis/vtx/rwmain?docid=469cbfa90 (accessed May 9, 2014).

Thio, Li-ann. "Constitutional Accommodation of the Rights of Ethnic and Religious Minorities in Plural Democracies: Lessons and Cautionary Tales from South-East Asia." *Pace International Law Review* 22, no. 1 (Winter 2010). http://digitalcommons.pace.edu/cgi/viewcontent.cgi?article=1025&context=pilr (accessed May 16, 2014).

United Nations Human Rights, Office of the High Commissioner for Human Rights. "Freedom of Religion: UN Rights Expert Reports on the Plight of Religious Minorities in the World." http://www.ohchr.org/en/NewsEvents/Pages/DisplayNews.aspx?NewsID=13083&LangID=E (accessed May 9, 2014).

MISSIONARY MOVEMENTS

Missionaries—people who travel from their home base to other places and propagate their faith, by word or deed—have been a historical reality in all societies, including Southeast Asia. While there is a general impression that the missionaries were primarily Christians, that is not the case, and certainly not in Southeast Asia. There were also Buddhist, Hindu, and Muslim missionaries that worked in various countries. During the Common Era, Buddhism, which had originated in the

The Phnong montagnard people in northeastern Cambodia celebrate a Catholic mass in a bamboo church. The mass is led by French missionary Gerald Vogin. (Yvan Cohen/Getty Images)

It has frequently been pointed out that the missionaries often colluded with the colonial powers to have dominion over the local people. Jacob S. Dharmaraj noted that colonizers and missionaries sailed on the same boat and that gun and gospel were carried on the same ship. This may be an extreme view, but there is a fair amount of consensus among historians, especially in Southeast Asia, that the missionaries in general supported the process of the colonization of the non-Western world.

Jesudas M. Athyal

Indian subcontinent, spread by sea to the north of Southeast Asia and from there to the east coast of China. Buddhism contributed significantly to cultural change in Asia, in the form of new social identities, new languages, and new institutions. The great Buddhist scholastic traditions built up monasteries and other places that emerged as key centers of learning. The itinerant Buddhist monks and other scholars contributed also to the growth of languages, especially by their work of translation. Even as Buddhism weakened in India, it flourished in Southeast Asia, and the region emerged as the center of the Theravada Buddhist tradition. The faith also developed distinct national and regional identities. As Buddhism reached Thailand, Vietnam, Cambodia, and other places in Southeast Asia, it developed its own particular form, indigenous to those places.

Trade played a key role in the spread of Islam in Southeast Asia. As early as the eleventh century, the Islamic faith is believed to have reached Indonesia. During the next two centuries, Islam was consolidated in that country. The religion reached Malaya and parts of Philippines by the fourteenth century. Today, Islam is the most widely practiced religion in Southeast Asia. Hinduism is not a proselytizing religion, and there was little overt missionary activity in Southeast Asia. The religion spread largely as merchants and traders from India traveled to other places. Hinduism took roots in some places in Indonesia, notably Bali, Central Java, East Java, and Lampung provinces. In Malaysia and Singapore, Hinduism is the principal religion of the Indian immigrants. There are sizable Hindu populations in Myanmar, Thailand, and a few other places as well.

The Christian missionary work in Southeast Asia went parallel to the Western colonization of the region, lending support to the theory that the process of colonization was the colonization of non-Christian peoples by Christian nations. Historians and other scholars acknowledge the role of individual missionaries who worked selflessly in serving the people. There were also missionaries who tried to work out the meaning of their faith in a specific culture. However, the criticism has been raised that the Christian missionary enterprise in Southeast Asia, in general, undermined the local cultures and religions. One of the characteristics of the new self-confidence of the emergent Christian leadership in Asia, therefore, was the rejection of the missionary pattern. Bishop Emerito Nacpil of the Philippines called on the mission societies to leave the churches in Asia alone for some time so that they could discover themselves and their ministry to the people and cultures of Asia.

While many of these criticisms are valid, a subaltern perspective would insist that the complexities of the Southeast Asian situation need to be sufficiently appreciated. A careful look at the history of the missionary movement in the region will reveal that the relationship of the missionaries with the colonial powers was often far from being cordial. Some scholars have pointed out that the commercial interests of the Western political powers in the region often clashed with the inclination of the missionaries to serve the local people. In particular, the translation of religious and secular literature to the local languages by the missionaries is important. Translation and vernacular renewal not only had a profound impact on the cultural and social renaissance of the indigenous people, but also played a role in empowering the people in their anticolonial struggles.

While traditionally, the Christian missionary work in Southeast Asia was carried out by mainline churches, such as the Roman Catholics and Anglicans, in the modern times, the Pentecostals and the other independent groups are playing a leading role. Pentecostalism has, in particular, appealed to the racial and ethnic minorities and social classes of Asia who lack political or ideological power. According to John Mansford Prior, a missionary priest in Indonesia since 1973, Pentecostalism is an urban phenomenon and is likely to be a growing one with the urbanization of the Asian societies. The people who have been uprooted from their villages and cultures, and who are somewhat insecure in the cities as migrants, join the new charismatic and Pentecostal communities because there they find warm fellowship.

While reviewing the missionary movements in Southeast Asia, the primary question is what impact it had on the wider society. Any generalization of the work of the missionaries would be too simplistic and inaccurate. The rich contributions many of them made, especially in the areas of health care, education, and social uplift, has been widely acknowledged not only within their own religious communities, but also by the wider society and the state. But there are also valid questions about how at least some of the Western missionaries played a role in the alienation of the Asian people from their cultures, values, and moorings. While rejecting the doctored history that undermines the role of the missionaries in the cultural rejuvenation and the awakening of the indigenous people, there is the need to critically review that period. Like all other phases in human history, the missionary movement too will be scrutinized closely and judged for its contributions and shortcomings.

Jesudas M. Athyal

See also: Buddhism; Christianity; Colonialism; Diaspora; Ethnicity; Hinduism; Indonesia; Islam; Nacpil, Emerito; Nationalism; Papua New Guinea; Philippines; Siddique, Muhammad Abdul Aleem.

Further Reading

Ariarajah, S. Wesley. *Gospel and Culture: An Ongoing Discussion within the Ecumenical Movement.* Geneva: WCC, 1994.

Ariarajah, S. Wesley. *Not Without My Neighbour: Issues in Inter-Faith Relations.* Geneva: WCC, 1999.

Dharmaraj, Jacob S. *Colonialism and Christian Mission: Postcolonial Reflections.* Delhi: ISPCK, 1993.

Kumar, Bacchan. "Religious Positivity." Chap. 12 in *Hindu Positivism in Southeast Asia,* edited by S. M. Tripathi and Nagendra Kr. Singh. New Delhi: Global Vision Publishing House, 2001.

Mohd, Taib Osman. "Islamisation of the Malays: A Transformation of Culture." In *Bunga Rampai: Some Aspects of Malay Culture.* Kuala Lumpur: DBP, 1988.

Prior, John Mansford. "In Asia, the Pentecostals Are on the March." Indian Christian Access Network, April 17, 2013. http://persecutedchurch.info/2013/04/17/in-asia-the-pentecostals-are-on-the-march/ (accessed May 9, 2014).

Williams, Paul. *Buddhism: Buddhist Origins and the Early History of Buddhism in South and Southeast Asia.* Oxford: Taylor & Francis, 2005.

MORALITY

The term morality is used to refer to the system of notions concerning the rightness or goodness of human behavior as assessed according to accepted norms. The issue of morality has been a central concern of social scientists since the time of Karl Marx, Emile Durkheim, and Max Weber. At the turn of the nineteenth century, Durkheim put forward his understanding of morality as the totality of shared rules according to which individuals, by adhering to them, recognize themselves as belonging to a society. He viewed religion as one means of instilling morality into society's members. Weber's renowned work, *The Protestant Ethic and the Spirit of Capitalism,* examined the moral impetus that Protestant religious ethics gave to profit-seeking labor and postulated that religion altogether would ultimately become redundant as societies modernized. Secular rationality, he believed, would inevitably come to replace religion as the dominant source of meaning and moral guidance.

Colonialism and its corollary, the discipline of anthropology, brought a growing awareness in nineteenth- and twentieth-century Europe of the diversity of cultural formulations of good and evil, right and wrong, and the plurality and historical specificity of moral systems. It became evident that moral and religious systems are not always forces of cohesion, but can also give rise to divisiveness and internal contestation. Furthermore, in many parts of the so-called developing world, modernity, far from replacing religion with rationality, has been attended by the intensification of religious fervor and of spirit propitiation.

The great religious diversity of Southeast Asia, where Buddhism, Hinduism, Christianity, Islam, and numerous highland animistic traditions have coexisted for

A high-ranking Hmong leader, Vang Pao, welcomed American weapons, wealth, and expertise and gathered thousands of Hmong fighters to tackle the common enemy, the Communists. The Hmong suffered heavy casualties. However, their efforts were kept from the American public for many years and this therefore became known as the "Secret War." Hmong insurgencies continue, in some measure to this day, often provoking harsh responses from the Lao government.

Alexandra Kent

centuries, makes this region a particularly rich ground for observing the relationship between religion, morality, and power. Throughout the region, religious schemes of moral order have always been interlaced with concerns about power: strength and protection, individual potency, and the powers of nature. The classical state in Southeast Asia did not arise spontaneously out of local notions of righteous leadership but was a cultural import that made ritual claims to moral supremacy. James Scott (2009) has argued that the Hinduized idea of the universal monarch provided the ideological apparatus for defining "civilized" life—sedentary wet-rice cultivation in lowland villages, acknowledgment of a social hierarchy and kingship, and profession of a major salvation religion (Buddhism, Hinduism, or, in the Philippines, Christianity). The monarch was often credited with access to cosmic power, which he could channel into the world to ensure prosperity and order. The proper behavior of the king governed therefore not only the human, but also the natural world. Moral order, legitimized by religious discourse and ritual, would thus have emanated from the powerful center through the valleys of the kingdom. From the lowland, state-centric perspective, recalcitrant nomadic highlanders who refused to submit to state control represented the opposite of civilized and morally ordered life; they were considered wild, savage, and sometimes even subhuman.

However, where colonial powers became established, they tended to undermine the divine status and religious legitimation of Southeast Asian monarchs. (The notable exception was Thailand, which was never colonized.) In their efforts to introduce their own secular moral order, with measures such as judicial and educational reforms arising from enlightenment philosophy in Europe, the colonial officials became the new, self-appointed custodians of morality. Although regional conflicts meant that the monarchs themselves may have deemed it politic to submit to the ambiguous protection of a colonial power, peasants often felt more threatened than protected by their foreign overlords and religious figures such as Buddhist monks, with their moral credibility and plentiful numbers, figured among those who led popular anticolonial uprisings.

After the Second World War and the wane of colonial influence, a new moral order was imposed upon many Southeast Asians with the advent of Communism. Once again, morality was enforced from above in ways that now departed radically from or even inverted long-held norms. The individual's primary moral responsibilities were to be shifted from family to the state and from religion to productivity. In 1960, the government of North Vietnam proclaimed that its policy of the Marxist-Leninist ideology must absolutely dominate the moral life of the people of the country, becoming their ideology and the basis on which a new morality can be built. In Vietnam, Laos, and Cambodia, the people found themselves subjected to a more or less brutally enforced moral system that was grounded in radically secular ideology and was largely intolerant of religious alternatives as well as monarchical authority. Once again, the highlands became areas of refuge and resistance.

In the late 1980s, as the Cold War was drawing to a close and command economies were yielding to global pressures for liberalization, the collectivist morality of the Communist era began to shift. Throughout the region, the dawn of a capitalist ethos in Southeast Asia gave rise to new moral uncertainties. While religion was recovering in countries such as Cambodia, it was also being subjected to a wave of new consumerist values. These values have affected not only formal religion, but also the numerous spirits that populate Southeast Asia.

Among other things, the transition to a market economy brought droves of young Southeast Asian women into the labor market to work in the factories that began mushrooming in urban areas. The anthropologist Aihwa Ong has famously argued that in Malaysia, this release of large numbers of women from their traditional moral spheres and their exposure to the gaze of male supervisors made them both vulnerable to and potential causes of moral disorder and that this found expression in mass spirit possession. One way to redeem the moral credentials of these women was to reinforce their Muslim identity by holding Islamic classes on factory grounds. Another was for women to veil themselves. However, the moral appropriateness of the use of veils by Muslim women in Southeast Asia has been a source of contention, with some arguing that the veil protects women's increasingly commodified bodies from the objectifying male gaze, while opponents, including the Malaysian and Indonesian governments, formerly rejected it as a Middle Eastern tradition and that had no basis in either Islamic or local mores.

The degree to which religion should be subordinated to the powers of secular government or, conversely, government should defer to the moral authority of clerics continues to rankle in the region. In Thailand, although monks continue to legitimate the state with their performance of rituals, particularly for the monarch, who remains a powerful symbol of moral order and continuity, many of these monks are internally conflicted about their sympathies in the ongoing friction between working-class "red shirts" and elite, traditionalist "yellow shirts."

Elsewhere, the cooptation or intimidation of religious figureheads by powerful elites, such as has taken place in Cambodia, can make it difficult for them to act as mouthpieces for ordinary people or to put a moral brake on power holders. The resulting tensions occasionally erupt, for instance in 2007, when Buddhist monks led massive demonstrations against military rule in Myanmar and the government responded with violent crackdowns.

When the clergy seems impotent to help people deal with the rapidly changing present and precarious future, the powers of sorcerers, spirit mediums, shamans, and astrologers may fill the moral vacuum. This seems particularly evident in countries undergoing a transition from a command economy to a free-market system. For example, the 1980s' Đổi Mới ("renovation") reforms in Vietnam sparked such an explosion of popular religious activity that it obliged the post-Communist state to recognize and frame this as part of the nation's cultural identity. This revival of spirit powers is echoed in other parts of Southeast Asia and has been seen by scholars as providing arenas for people to make moral negotiations about the rapid social, political, and economic changes taking place around them.

The absorption of Asian (as well as other) countries into the global market has created tensions between moral and economic values throughout the region. Governments find themselves caught between the demands of human rights defenders and those of businessmen and investors. On the one hand, the Universal Declaration of Human Rights (1948) and the United Nations' 2005 declaration of its "responsibility to protect" citizens from states that disregard the rights of their citizens have positioned the leaders of developing nations under the moral scrutiny of the international community. On the other hand, however, the so-called developing nations are pressured to open up their natural and human resources to foreign markets while at the same time ensuring the political stability that investors want. This means that although the new system of competition over resources excludes many groups from benefits and leaves them feeling vulnerable and unprotected by their governments, international as well as national elite interests in stability often outweigh moral considerations. The suppression by Asian governments of protests over inequality has therefore tended to be accepted as necessary for the greater good of stability.

Indeed, in the 1990s, some Asian leaders, particularly Prime Minister Lee Kuan Yew of Singapore and Prime Minister Mahathir Mohammad of Malaysia, reconciled their desire to bring about economic progress while silencing opponents by appealing to culture and morality. They argued against the universality of human rights and claimed there were specifically "Asian Values" that differed fundamentally from Western values. Among other things, these values supposedly included the foregoing of individual freedoms for the benefit of the collectivity: family or nation.

The Asian Values debate lost momentum after the financial crisis of the late 1990s, but moral anxieties continue to surface in other ways, and frequently through the medium of religion. Identity politics have been played out in bloody intercommunal strife between Buddhists and Muslims in both Myanmar and southern Thailand in the first decade of the twenty-first century. Strict interpretations of Islamic codes of conduct have also been gaining both political and popular support. In 2010, three women were caned in Malaysia for having committed adultery, and in 2013, the sultan of Brunei introduced tough *shari'a* laws for various moral transgressions: punishments were to include stoning to death for adultery, severing of limbs for theft, and flogging for violations ranging from abortion to alcohol consumption.

Despite the introduction of democratic election procedures in most Southeast Asian countries, it would seem that religion is set to continue playing an important role in the moral legitimacy of the region's leaders.

Alexandra Kent

See also: Brunei Darussalam; Buddhism; Cambodia; Christianity; Colonialism; Communism; Globalization; Hinduism; Humanism; Islam; Laos; Malaysia; Myanmar (Burma); Philippines; Religion and Society; Sexuality; Shamanism; *Shari'a*; Singapore; Spirit Mediumship; Uplanders; Vietnam; Women.

Further Reading

Bullock, Katherine. *Rethinking Muslim Women and the Veil: Challenging Historical and Modern Stereotypes.* London: International Institute of Islamic Thought, 2002.

Durkheim, Emile. *Moral Education: A Study in the Theory and Application of the Sociology of Education.* Translated by E. K. Wilson and H. Schnurer. New York: Free Press, 1961.

Heinz, Monica, ed. *The Anthropology of Moralities.* New York: Berghahn Books, 2009.

Hochel, Sandra. "To Veil or Not to Veil: Voices of Malaysian Muslim Women." *Intercultural Communication Studies* 22, no. 2 (2013): 40–57.

McCargo, Duncan. "The Changing Politics of Thailand's Buddhist Order." *Critical Asian Studies* 44, no. 4 (2012): 627–42.

Scott, James C. *The Art of Not Being Governed: An Anarchist History of Upland Southeast Asia.* New Haven, CT: Yale University Press, 2009.

Syed Mohammed Ad'ha Aljunied. "Colonial Powers, Nation-States and Kerajaan in Maritime Southeast Asia: Structures, Legalities and Perceptions." *New Zealand Journal of Asian Studies* 12, no. 2 (2010): 94–107.

MUHAMMADIYAH

Muhammadiyah is a Muslim organization that was established on November 18, 1912, by Ahmad Dahlan in Yogyakarta, Indonesia, about 33 years before Indonesia gained independence from Dutch colonialism. *Muhammadiyah* is an Arabic term that means "the followers of Prophet Muhammad." The long-term vision of Muhammadiyah is to uphold and uplift the teaching of Islam to establish the true Islamic society.

Many scholars categorize Muhammadiyah as a modernist and reformist Muslim movement because of its ability to combine theological purification and social reformation. Muhammadiyah practices an Islamic teaching based on the two main sources of Islam: *Al-Qur'an* (Qur'an) and *As-Sunnah* (Prophet Traditions). Muhammadiyah's mission of *da'wah* (Islamic propagation), therefore, strives to purify Islam from the practices of *takhayyul* (fancy), *bid'ah* (innovation) and *khurafah* (superstition). These practices, according to Muhammadiyah, are not only theologically "un-Islamic," but also sociologically irrational and contributing to the backwardness of Muslim societies. Therefore, Muhammadiyah theological reformation, from its formative years, has been accompanied by concrete and transformative social actions on the ground. In other words, Muhammadiyah aims to develop both personal and social pieties.

Muhammadiyah uses pragmatic ways to achieve its goals, including adopting the Western educational system. The first Muhammadiyah school sparked controversy among conservative *ulama* (Muslim scholars) because it integrated "secular" subjects such as mathematics, geography, foreign languages, and biology with "Islamic" subjects, which were the only subjects taught in traditional Islamic schools (*pesantrens*). Muhammadiyah also built other social services such as orphanages, clinics, and micro-credit institutions for the poor, all of which were organized using modern, rational-type bureaucratic principles. To expand its *da'wah*, Muhammadiyah created autonomous organizations, namely *Aisyiyah* (a women's organization), *Nashiatul Aisyiyah* (a young women's organization), *Pemuda Muhammadiyah* (Muhammadiyah Youth), *Ikatan Pelajar Muhammadiyah* (Muhammadiyah Student Association), *Ikatan Mahasiswa Muhammadiyah* (Muhammadiyah University Student Association), and *Tapak Suci Putra Muhammadiyah* (Muhammadiyah Martial Arts).

In 1978, James L. Peacock published a seminal book on Muhammadiyah that placed the organization as the largest modernist Muslim movement in Southeast Asia, perhaps in the world. This conclusion is, most likely, still valid given the fact that Muhammadiyah grew even faster since the publication of the book. In 2010, Muhammadiyah claimed to have 25 million members with branches all over Indonesia. It had 16,860 schools (from nursery/kindergarten to high school), 186 tertiary education institutions (universities and technical colleges), 284 health service units (hospitals and clinics), 509 orphanages, 868 micro-credit/finance institutions and 11,959 mosques and *mushalla* (small places for worship). Although Muhammadiyah is not a political party, with its large membership and extended social services network, the organization has been a very strong political force in Indonesia and Southeast Asia at large.

Raja Antoni

See also: Ahmadiyya; Aisyiyah and Nasyiatul Aisyiyah; Education; Indonesia; Islam; Maarif, Ahmad Syafi'i; Nahdlatul Ulama; *Pesantren*; Rais, Muhammad Amien; Reform Movements; Religion and Society; Women.

Further Reading

Jainuri, Achmad. "The Formation of the Muhammadiyah's Ideology, 1912–1942." PhD diss., McGill University, 1997. http://digitool.library.mcgill.ca/R/?func=dbin-jump -full&object_id=34523&local_base=GEN01-MCG02 (accessed May 9, 2014).

Noer, Deliar. *The Modernist Muslim Movement in Indonesia 1900–1942*. Kuala Lumpur: Oxford University Press, 1973.

Peacock, James L. *Purifying the Faith: The Muhammadijah Movement in Indonesian Islam*. Tempe: Arizona State University, 1992.

MUSIC

In Southeast Asia, music has always been a traditional medium for humans to establish a connection with nonhuman world(s). The practices of ancestor worship and offerings to various entities (spirits, deities, the deceased) are still performed through vocal and/or instrumental music. The musical aspect of these rituals, though often neglected, remains coessential to the religious rite.

In rural Southeast Asia, music may be part of rituals that aim to heal the community, prevent illness, sing for the rice and other crops, propitiate and praise the gods, ensure ancestorhood, and restore the balance between different worlds. Most of the time, it is combined with other artistic practices (dance, theater, narrative). Music may support various kinds of speeches. It is also considered to have its own efficacy. In the Toraja highlands of Sulawesi (Indonesia), ritual trances depend upon the songs that call the divinities to descend to the earth; at funerals, the deceased becomes an ancestor only if the hagiographic song that tells the story of his or her transformation is sung in a round dance (Rappoport 2011). Music for shamanism, magic, and curing implies a journey to other worlds. Whether it involves drumming, singing, or striking the gongs, music is performed to guide or accompany the traveler (shaman or patient) on his or her journey.

Musical forms vary from the most intimate chanted prayer to large gong-chime ensembles, differing according to place, from rural to urban settings. All Southeast

Indonesian dancers perform traditional Bali music during a parade as part of a week-long independence celebration in Jakarta, Indonesia, in 2005. (AP Images/Irwin Ferdiansyah)

Asian religions use speech in their liturgy. Ritual speech is usually transmitted through the vocalization that joins words, music, and acts. Words in rhythm, whether spoken, chanted, or sung (in narrative or lyric singing), are a form of address, a bringing into relation of humans, spirits, and gods.

Musical instruments also take part in most rituals, whether from local or world religions. The importance of bronze instruments is known through the diffusion of the bronze drum of the Dong Son period (late fourth century BCE) from northern Vietnam throughout Southeast Asia (Miller and Williams 1998, 58). The snails, frogs, and geometrical designs of heavenly bodies, carved on the surface of some of them, suggest that they may have been played during rain-making ceremonies (Kunst 1949, 105). From Cambodia to eastern Indonesia, knobbed gongs and drums are the most widespread instruments used in various kinds of rituals. Invested with a magic power, their fabrication and preservation are treated sacredly. Considered as intercessors between humans and gods, musical instruments are held by many peoples of Southeast Asia to be the vehicles carrying the singer's voice toward the spirits of the higher world. Thus, ritual specialists sometimes carry sonorous attributes, such as pellet bells, pellet drums, and clapper bells. Gongs are frequently arranged in sets (gong-chimes), in different kinds of ensembles, ranging from a few instruments to the large gamelan ensembles of Java and Bali, PĪ PHĀT ensembles of Thailand, and similar ensembles in Laos, Cambodia, and Burma.

The arrival of foreign religions (Hinduism, Buddhism, Islam, Christianity) has influenced local musical idioms to various degrees. Excavated bronze, terra-cotta images, and a fairly extensive number of metallic as well as wooden and bamboo instruments depicted in the stone reliefs of Southeast Asian temples offer a picture of music and dance during the Hindu-Buddhist religious ceremonies. The oldest depictions of musical instruments on Hindu-Buddhist temples date back to the seventh century CE. In addition, Indian epics, such the *Ramayana*, *Mahabharata*, and *Purana*, have been adopted in many parts of Southeast Asian, from Cambodia to Indonesia, since the third century CE; they are still performed through dance, shadow puppetry, and masked theater, in syncretic rituals combining local cults with Buddhism. Performing music and theater is first and foremost an offering to the spirits (Giuriati 1999). But it can also be performed for religious and political matters. In Java, gamelan orchestras belonging to *kraton* palaces were used for religious purposes. Courtly music was used to promote Hindu-Buddhist teachings, but once rulers embraced Islam, two processes led to the hybridity of their music.

On the islands of Southeast Asia, the Muslim music complex is nowadays prominent. Islam brought its own instrumentation and musical modes, from the Middle East, from the thirteenth century CE. The most widespread instrument used for devotional songs are types of frame drum, the short-necked, pear-shaped lute *gambus*, and the double-reed aerophone *serunai*. Devotional genres with clear links to Sufism (*qasidah*, *dikir, dabus*) have developed in many places (Yampolsky 2001). The relation between Islam and music has attracted the attention of many scholars, as court and rural forms of music are waning due to competition from Western popular musical idioms mixed with local languages. Popular culture has become a major force in the dissemination of contemporary Islam (Harnish and Rasmussen 2011). Christianity, as well, has brought new musical idioms from the West, such as tuning, modes, harmony, melodic form, and syntax, through vocal music (hymns) or instrumental music (wind band instruments), to be performed not only inside the churches but also within local rituals, together with traditional music. In Indonesia, it has also led to new forms of Christian popular music, such as the Indonesian *pop rohani* ("Christian pop" music) that can be heard on the radio in buses and shops. Despite religious changes, however, many small Southeast Asian societies continue to perform their own ritual music at various religious occasions.

Dana Rappoport

See also: Ancestor Worship; Buddhism; Christianity; Dance and Drama (Theater); Hinduism; Indonesia; Islam; Laos; Popular Religion; Puppetry; Ritual Dynamics; Shamanism; Spirit Mediumship; Sufism; Uplanders.

Further Reading

Giuriati, Giovanni. "Bidhi Sambah Gru Dham, Music as Ordering Factor of Khmer Religious Syncretism." In *Shamanic Cosmos: From India to the North Pole Star*, edited by E. Mastromattei and E. Rigopoulos, 89–106. New Delhi: D. K. Printworld, 1999.

Harnish, David, and Anne Rasmussen, eds. *Divine Inspirations: Music and Islam in Indonesia.* Oxford: Oxford University Press, 2011.

Kunst, Jaap. *Hindu-Javanese Musical Instruments.* La Hague: Njihoff, 1968 (1927).

Kunst, Jaap. *The Cultural Background of Indonesian Music.* Amsterdam: Koninklijke Vereeniging Indisch Instituut (Royal Institute for the Indies), 1949.

Miller, Terry, and Sean Williams. "Waves of Cultural Influences." In *The Garland Encyclopedia of World Music*, edited by Terry Miller and Sean Williams, Vol. 4, *Southeast Asia*. New York and London: Garland, 1998.

Rappoport, Dana. *Songs from the Thrice-Blooded Land: Ritual Music of the Toraja (Sulawesi, Indonesia)*. Paris: Editions de la Maison des sciences de l'homme, 2011.

Yampolsky, Philip. "Indonesia/General/Musical Overview/Genres and Ensembles." *Grove Music Online*, 2001.

MUSLIMAT NU

Muslimat Nahdlatul Ulama (Muslimat NU) was established on June 15, 1938, as part of the women's wing of Nahdlatul Ulama, but officially Muslimat NU was validated by Muktamar NU (National Congress of NU) in 1946. Muslimat NU became autonomous from the NU organization in 1952. Its vision is the existence of a society that is committed to the welfare of all in Indonesia, that is inspired by Islamic teaching and that also has Allah's blessing. The goals of Muslimat NU are to increase Indonesian women's awareness as Muslims and as Indonesian citizens; to improve the quality, independence, and devotion of women; to increase women's awareness of their duties and rights according to Islam; and to support NU's goals. The adherents of this organization mostly come from the *pesantren* (Islamic boarding schools) in Indonesia, and geographically, the majority are grounded in rural areas (Jamhari and Ropi 2003). One of the important achievements of Muslimat NU after gaining autonomy in the 20th National Congress in Surabaya was that the organization challenged the *pengadilan agama* (religious court) that had discriminated against women in cases of polygamy, divorce, and inheritance. In 1959, Muslimat NU succeeded in removing the *tabir* (physical partition) between men and women in the National Congress (Jamhari and Ropi 2003). In the first election in 1955, 10 percent of the NU members in the Parliament were women from Muslimat NU. Another contribution was that in 1969, Pimpinan Besar Syuriah NU (the supreme religious leadership in NU) decided the main principles of family planning in Indonesia as recommend by Muslimat NU.

One of the well-known activists of Muslimat NU, Khofifah Indar Parawansa, was the minister of Women's Empowerment of Indonesia during the presidency of Abdurrahman Wahid. In response to the United Nations' declaration of the Decade for Women and because of the demands of the local feminist nongovernmental organizations, she changed the name of the ministry from "Mentri Peranan Wanita" (Ministry for the Roles of Women) to "Mentri Pemberdayaan Perempuan" (Ministry of Women's Empowerment). This meant that she shifted the paradigm from women as objects of national development to women as subjects of national development. The most significant contribution of Parawansa as minister was the Presidential Instruction on gender mainstreaming in national development. Gender mainstreaming is a major strategy to ensure that women and men gain equal access to, and participate equally in development (Surbakti 2012). This instruction, which applies to all ministries, armed forces, police forces, high courts, heads of local governments, and heads of all government agencies, aims to mainstream gender in the planning, formulating, implementing, monitoring, and evaluating of all national development programs. Together with other NU affiliate organizations such as Fatayat NU, Rahima, and FK3 (Forum Kajian Kitab Kuning), the Muslimat NU is deeply committed to the gender issue.

Alimatul Qibtiyah

See also: Aisyiyah and Nasyiatul Aisyiyah; Education; Feminism and Islamic Traditions; Indonesia; Islam; Muhammadiyah; Nahdlatul Ulama; *Pesantren*; Reform Movements; Religion and Society; *Shari'a*; Women.

Further Reading

Doorn-Harder, P. V. *Women Shaping Islam: Indonesian Women Reading the Qur'an.* Urbana: University of Illinois Press, 2006.

Jamhari, and I. Ropi, eds. *Citra perempuan dalam Islam: Pandangan ormas keagamaan.* Jakarta: GramediaPustakaUtama, PPIM-UIN Jakarta & Ford Foundation, 2003.

MYANMAR (BURMA)

Myanmar (Burma) is a Southeast Asian country that borders India, Bangladesh, Laos, Thailand, and China, a country Rudyard Kipling described as a land quite unlike any other. The land Marco Polo referred to as "The Golden land," a land of legend, golden pagodas, and glorious temples, has recently drawn global media attention resulting from the people's response to authoritative military rule,

Burmese monks pray together at Kha Khat Wain Kyaung monastery, which is one of the three largest in the country, on December 13, 2011 in Bago, Myanmar. Approximately 90 percent of the Burmese population practices Buddhism and the monks number well over 500,000. (Paula Bronstein/Getty Images)

> Any study of Burma will be lacking if it fails to take into consideration the history of religion, in particular the deep roots of the Theravada Buddhist tradition, within the nation. Questions of political and cultural authority, education, and identity, must to some degree be observed through the lens of religion to be understood with any depth of meaning. The reality of religious, ethnic, and cultural diversity across the nation continues to be a cause of deep divide and tension in a land that has, until recently, sought to maintain national unity through the combined nexus of authoritarian, military, and traditional religious forces.
>
> *Adrian Bird*

including the emergence of minority ethnic liberation struggles and the "Saffron Revolution" of 2007, a protest struggle led by Buddhist monks. The country has also received attention as a consequence of the destruction caused by Cyclone Nargis in 2008. Media attention is also drawn to the figure of Aung San Suu Kyi, daughter of the founder of Burmese independence in 1948, a Nobel Peace Prize winner, and prominent opposition political leader who spent 15 years under house arrest prior to her release in 2010. If identity is in part captured in a name, then we immediately sense a tension when discussing this ancient land. In 1989, the military junta renamed Burma "Myanmar," an act that remains contentious and indicates the complexity of national identity in the midst of ethnic and religious diversity. The population of Myanmar is estimated at over 60 million, including multiple ethnic and linguistic groups of which Burman is the majority. The capital of Myanmar changed from Yangon/Rangoon to Nypyidaw in 2009. Speculation regarding this change in location is widespread, though the building of a spectacular new Buddhist pagoda to legitimize the change highlights the significance of the deep-rooted historical association of Buddhism within Myanmar.

Although religious diversity exists within Myanmar and continues to shape contemporary tensions, it would be difficult to overstate the significance of Buddhism within both the history and present context of the land. The presence of Buddhism in Myanmar can be traced to the fifth century CE, and by the eleventh century CE, Theravada Buddhism had struck deep roots into the social-political, cultural, and religious fabric of Burma. In present-day Myanmar, Buddhism continues to play a critical role, to the point that political authorities seek essential legitimacy not primarily through "performance criteria," such as their success in issues of human rights, economic development, and effective democracy, but rather in its capacity to fulfill the role of traditional Burmese kingship, including their role as protectors of the Buddhist faith. Political leaders therefore seek to emphasize their legitimacy and increase their credibility through establishing links with leading Buddhist figures. Although there have been various political strategies employed in postindependence Myanmar, none can ignore the significance of Buddhism, which lies at the heart of nationalist Burmese culture and identity. Melford E. Spiro argues that to be Burman is to be Buddhist. Without Buddhism, there could be no Burma, and those not Buddhist are for the most part considered as non-Burmese.

A national identity defined in religious terms becomes problematic for minority communities such as Christians, Muslims, or Hindus who are not part of the dominant ethnic Burman majority. Following independence, during Prime Minister U Nu's political campaign to make Buddhism the state religion, reassurance was offered to religious minorities that this act would not diminish their citizenship or their freedom of religion. Despite this assertion, the act was vehemently opposed by many minority religious groups, highlighting an ongoing suspicion against the hegemony of Buddhist and political forces. From 1954 to 1956, the sixth Great Buddhist Council was held in Rangoon, affirming the fundamental status of Buddhism in Myanmar. Commentator Eugene Smith notes that hosting such a prestigious event undoubtedly highlights the government's willingness and determination to promote Theravada Buddhism in Myanmar and in the world.

The cultural influence of Buddhism is witnessed in multiple ways, including art, literature, and architecture. While religion can be a significant component of culture, this does not necessarily imply that the people place great importance to it within their lives. Yet in Myanmar, the importance of Buddhism in people's lives is evident in many ways, including the percentage of family income devoted to Buddhism, the high number of males who enter the Buddhist monastic *sangha* (community of monks), and the deep reverence afforded those within the *sangha*.

Within Myanmar, no single institution is more important than Buddhism. Buddhist monks are highly revered and have traditionally played a vital role within society, upholding the Buddha dhamma (the truth proclaimed by the Buddha), and essentially providing an avenue for the attainment of karmic merit among the laity. Education in Burma has historically been the responsibility of the *sangha*, though the influence of the *sangha* was undermined with the introduction of secular education and mission schools during British rule (1886–1948). Yet the influence of the *sangha* and of Buddhism remains central to postcolonial Myanmar. Indeed, Myanmar is considered by much of Theravadan Buddhist Southeast Asia as having been the "protector of the faith" during the era of British colonial imperialism.

Perhaps one of the most intriguing developments within Buddhism in modern times has been the rise of the vipassanā (insight) meditation under the leadership of Mahasi Sayadaw, which had a profound impact on lay Buddhists. Traditionally, the role of redressing moral decline within the country had been the responsibility of the Kings and the *sangha*. Yet the emergence of the vipassanā movement caused a shift in the dynamics of traditional roles, with greater responsibility now on the people themselves toward self-purification in order to stem the reality of moral decline in this World Age. This development remains significant and is a source of tension in modern Myanmar, in which the traditional kingship role of protecting the Buddhist faith has been adopted by a military leadership.

Although the status of Buddhism as the basis of the nation's traditional culture remains unquestioned, minority religions continue to exist within the country. While Buddhism makes up 89 percent of the population, there are significant Christian (6 percent), Muslim (2.5 percent), and Hindu (> 1 percent) groups within the nation, which have a significant influence on the society as a whole. It is estimated that up to 90 percent of the Chin and Kachin in the western and northern part of the country, respectively, are Christian. Significant numbers of Christians are present also among the Karen, following the American Baptist Missionary presence in Burma during the nineteenth century. Foreign missionaries are no longer present in Myanmar, though long-term church ties to the outside world remain strong. Testimonies of widespread persecution against Christians, including the burning of churches and the use of labor to build pagodas on former Christian worship sites, exist in many Christian areas. Employment opportunities may also be restricted based on the double discrimination of ethnicity and religious affiliation. Lal Chhuangi argues that as long as the ethnic groups are denied religious freedom, ethnic equality, greater autonomy, innate rights, a federal system, and self-determination, there will be no peace, stability, or prosperity in Myanmar.

Muslims in Myanmar, including the Rohingya and the Panthay, face ongoing persecution and discrimination, often resulting in clashes with Buddhist and government groups. The Rohingyas, Sunni Muslims living along the border with Bangladesh, have been described by the United Nations as one of the most persecuted minorities, facing issues of forced migration and human rights abuses. These Muslims are considered by the nationalistic government to be Bengali, remnants of early-twentieth-century immigration movements under British rule, thus illegal immigrants of Myanmar with no legitimate claim to citizenship. This significantly impacts the lives of the Muslims in their day-to-day lives, restricting basic rights such as the right to travel and to own land, and is the cause of continuous tension and hostility between nationalist and Muslim groups.

Present-day Myanmar is at a political crossroads. Although a nominally civilian government replaced the military junta in 2011, the constitution established by the junta in 2008 entrenches the power and primacy of the military. President Thein Sein is a former military general and served as the prime minister of the state under the junta. The economy is one of the least developed in the world, suffering from the effects of decades of stagnation and ineffective management. Religious and ethnic conflicts remain a source of great tension, despite continued attempts to generate peace initiatives across ethnic and religious lines. The future of Myanmar depends largely on its ability to plot a course within the tension between modernity and deeply entrenched traditional modes of living, of which Buddhism plays a pivotal role.

Adrian Bird

See also: Buddhism; Christianity; Colonialism; Dharma/Dhamma; Ethnicity; Hinduism; Islam; Kyaw Than, U; Laos; Minorities; Missionary Movements; Nationalism; Religious Discrimination and Intolerance; Sayadaw, Mahasi; Thailand.

Further Reading

Jordt, Ingrid. *Burma's Mass Lay Meditation Movement: Buddhism and the Cultural Construction of Power.* Athens: Ohio University Research in International Studies, Southeast Asia Series, No. 115, 2007.

Lowenstein, Tom. *The Glories of Sacred Asia: Treasures of the Buddha.* New York: Metro Books, 2006.

Myint-U, Thant. *The Making of Modern Burma*. Cambridge: Cambridge University Press, 2001.

Purser, W. C. B. *Christian Missions in Burma*. Original publication by the Society for the Propagation of the Gospel in Foreign Parts, 1911.

Smith, Donald Eugene. *Religion and Politics in Burma*. Princeton, NJ: Princeton University Press, 1965.

Spiro, Melford E. *Buddhism and Society: A Great Tradition and Its Burmese Vicissitudes*. 2nd ed. Berkeley: University of California Press, 1970.

Steinberg, David I. *Burma: The State of Myanmar*. Washington, DC: Georgetown University Press, 2001.

Steinberg, David I. *Burma/Myanmar: What Everyone Needs to Know*. Oxford: Oxford University Press, 2010.

MYTH/MYTHOLOGY

The English word myth comes from the Greek *muthos* ("word" or "speech"), which owes its significance precisely to its contrast with the Greek word *logos*; the latter can also be translated as "word," but only in the sense of a word that elicits discussion, an "argument." *Muthos* in its meaning as "myth" is the word for a story concerning gods and superhuman beings. A myth is an expression of the sacred in words; it reports realities and events from the origin of the world that remain valid for the basis and purpose of all there is. Consequently, a myth functions as a model for human activity, society, wisdom, and knowledge. The word mythology is used for the entire body of myths found in a given tradition. It is also used as a term for the study of myths.

Reference to the sacred may prove problematic for some as defining the subject, "myth," in terms of something that lacks clarity more than the term itself. However, the distinction between "the sacred" and "the profane" emphasized by the philosophically inclined French sociologist Emile Durkheim is based on a sober observation: all human traditions and societies heed the sacred and mark it in one way or another. Its ultimate or metaphysical reality is not the issue. The most general characteristic of the sacred is not that it is exalted, but that it is distinct from ordinary, profane, this-worldly everyday things. In communicating the sacred, a myth makes available in words what by no other means is available. Its words are different from other words; most generally they have an extraordinary authority and are in that perceivable manner distinct from common speech. The language of myth does not invite discussion; it does not argue, but presents.

> A myth is an expression of the sacred in words; it reports realities and events from the origin of the world that remains valid for the basis and purpose of all there is. Consequently, a myth functions as a model for human activity, society, wisdom, and knowledge. The word mythology is used for the entire body of myths found in a given tradition. It is also used as a term for the study of myths.
>
> *David C. Scott*

In a number of instances, the myth is recited in a special archaic language, different from the vernacular. One such instance is a creation myth in the Ngaju-Dayak tradition (South Kalimantan, Borneo, Indonesia) featuring the water serpent, *tambon*, and the hornbill, *bungai*. Its unusual language is not meant to keep it secret, but rather serves to underline its significance, preserved by experts in the community. The narrative itself establishes not only the world at large, but at once, and within it, the land, orienting the villages and also their mirror-image counterparts in the heavenly realms; it creates the social divisions and their functions, as well as the principles of the legal system. As to the externals of its style, the myth is couched in lyrical poetry, as are many myths, including those expressed in vernaculars, in Southeast Asia.

A myth, whether its subject is the acts of deities or other extraordinary events, always takes us back to "beginnings of all things"; hence the cosmogony, the birth of the world, is a principal theme. The Ngaju-Dayak creation myth begins with the words: "It happened long ago, when everything was still in the jaws of the *tambon*; it was primeval time." In each case, the world to which the myth transports us is very different from our own; it is in fact a time beyond any human being's knowledge, and hence the events and realities dealt with are literally altogether different from facts humans are concerned with in their everyday lives.

Myth is one of the three forms of religious expression: that is sacred speech, sacred acts, and sacred places. As such, it occurs side by side in most traditions with sacred places or objects (or, in short, symbols) and sacred acts (that is, cult rituals). They can be expected to elucidate the entire religious life of a community, shedding light especially on the ritual acts and sacred objects that by themselves do not speak at all, or certainly not often or as clearly. For instance, a central temple or sacred grove may be of paramount significance in the life of a community, yet it is a chronicled myth that is most likely to explain this significance, its origin, its basis, and the reason for its pivotal role in the community's life.

At first sight, myths have much in common with many other forms of folk tradition. They deal with "supernatural" events, as fairy tales do; they deal with extraordinary figures comparable to those in legends and sagas, and so on. The authority of myths, already referred to, is, however, clearly distinguishable from features in other narratives. Typically, the myth presents itself as telling its listeners of a time altogether different from the time of our experience ("In the beginning . . ." or "Before heaven and earth were created . . ."), whereas the typical fairy tale, no matter how wonderful its events, begins "Once upon a time . . ."—that is to say, a time like ours. The saga's hero and the legend's saintly protagonist are no doubt superior to all ordinary human beings, yet their time is shown just like the historical time of our experience.

Epics present a special case, for they are often a prime source of our knowledge of myths: the *Mahabharata* and *Ramayana* are famous instances in Southeast Asian history. Nevertheless, epics do not have the authority of myths. The myths they narrate in the body of their texts and the mythological references they make can be seen as part of an educational pattern: in this manner, people should understand the basic, authoritative models in the religious tradition.

As to their purpose, myths are not, contrary to traditional assumption, essentially etiological, understood in the sense of explaining origins or causes. Until recently, many scholars saw in myths prescientific endeavors to establish causes for the universe, natural phenomena, and everything else that occupies modern scientists, thereby overlooking the fact that this preoccupation with causality is a very precisely determined feature of modern history. Myths are not attempts at causality preshadowing nineteenth-century scientific discussion. A myth does something else, and something more encompassing than presenting a reasonable, or even prereasonable, explanation of things. This is the reason why the Romanian historian of religion, Mircea Eliade has rightly emphasized the cosmogony as the fundamental myth. In whatever cultural or religious tradition a creation myth is recited, it is paradigmatic in a special manner because of the many things to which its sheer force as a model is able to give birth.

David C. Scott

See also: Animism; Christianity; Ethnicity; Hinduism; Indonesia; Orientalism; Popular Religion; Postcolonial Theory; Ritual Dynamics; Study of Religion; Water Festivals.

Further Reading

Campbell, Joseph, and Bill Moyers. *The Power of Myth*. New York: Anchor Books, 1988.
Cohen, P. "Theories of Myth." *Man* 4 (1969).
Durkheim, Emile. *The Elementary Forms of Religious Life*. Translated by Joseph W. Swain. Mineola, NY: Dover Publications, 2008. (Originally published 1915.)
Eliade, Mircea. *Myths, Rites, Symbols: A Mircea Eliade Reader*. Edited by Wendell C. Beane and William G. Doty. New York: Harper & Row, 1976.
Eliade, Mircea, and Willard R. Trask. *The Sacred and the Profane: The Nature of Religion*. New York: Harcourt, 1961.
Levi-Strauss, Claude. *Myth and Meaning*. Toronto: University of Toronto Press, 1978.
Murray, Henry A., ed. *Myth and Mythmaking*. New York: G. Braziller, 1960.

N

NACPIL, EMERITO

Emerito P. Nacpil, retired bishop of the United Methodist Church in the Philippines, is one of the prominent Christian theologians in Southeast Asia. He had also been deeply involved in the ecumenical movement at the local, regional, and global levels. He made significant contributions to Christianity in Asia as an Asian theologian, teacher, and administrator in the field of theological education and through his leadership as a bishop of the United Methodist Church.

Nacpil was born in February 18, 1932, in Tarlac in the Philippines. After his bachelor of arts degree, he received a bachelor of theology degree from the Union Theological Seminary in the Philippines and proceeded to the Drew University in Madison, New Jersey, to secure his PhD in systematic theology and philosophy of religion. Returning home, Nacpil took up responsibilities at Union Theological Seminary, first as professor, then as the academic dean, and later as president. During this time, he also chaired the Board of Ordained Ministry of the Middle Philippines Annual Conference.

In 1974, Nacpil was invited to become the executive director of the Association of Theological Schools in Southeast Asia and dean of the Southeast Asia Graduate School of Theology. In these positions, he did much to strengthen theological education in the region. During this time, the Philippines Central Conference of the Methodist Church elected him as bishop in 1980. He was reelected in 1984 and 1988 and served as bishop until his retirement in 2000. By then he had served as bishop in all three Episcopal areas in the Philippines—Baguio, Manila, and Davao areas. Later he was elected as the president of the Council of Bishops of the General Conference, where he was able to make significant contributions to the discussions on contemporary issues faced by the Methodist Church as a whole.

Bishop Nacpil was also involved in regional and global ecumenism, serving on the Faith and Order Commission and the Central Committee of the World Council of Churches. From the perspective of Southeast Asia, what stands out most are the cutting-edge theological contributions he made at the conferences and consultations held in the Asian region. As the executive director of the association of theological schools in the region, he developed the concept of "Asian Critical Principle," which advocated that one should seek to identify what is distinctively Asian and use this distinctiveness as the critical principle of judgment on matters dealing with the life and mission of the Christian community, its theology, and theological education. When globalization became a reality, he called for an "Expanded Asian Critical Principle" that can be applied to issues affecting the whole of Asia and the world.

> Not everyone in the Southeast Asian region who has had a thorough orientation in the Western theological tradition has been able to break out of the Western theological mode of thinking to articulate theology from an Asian perspective. When one mentions the pioneers in this respect, Emerito Nacpil will be among the top of the list.
>
> S. Wesley Ariarajah

Nacpil will also be remembered as one of the first among the "third world" theologians to call for a "moratorium" of Western missionary activity in Asia. He made this call in February 1971 at a consultation of Methodist missionaries and churches in Asia in Kuala Lumpur, Malaysia. In the presence of many of the missionary colleagues, he argued that the present structure of missionary engagement in Asia had to end and that the most missionary service that they can do under the present system was to "go home." He was convinced that while the Western missionaries must go home, the churches in Asia should discover their mission and become fully engaged in it. These ideas are spelled out in Nacpil's 1971 book, *Mission but Not Missionaries.* Among the many books he wrote and edited and the numerous articles he wrote, his volumes on *Mission and Change* (1968), *The Human and the Holy: Asian Perspectives in Christian Theology* (ed. 1978), and *Jesus' Strategy for Social Transformation* (1998 and 1999) are very widely used.

S. Wesley Ariarajah

See also: Christianity; Christian Conference of Asia; Globalization; Kyaw Than, U; Liberation Theologies; Missionary Movements; Philippines; Simatupang, T. B.; Study of Religion.

Further Reading

Nacpil, Emerito P. "The Critical Asian Principle." In *What Asian Christians Are Thinking,* edited by Douglas J. Elwood. Quezon City, Philippines: New Day Publishers, 1976.

Nacpil, Emerito P. *Mission and Change.* Manila: East Asia Christian Conference, 1968.

Nacpil, Emerito P., and Douglas J. Elwood, eds. *The Human and the Holy: Asian Perspectives in Christian Theology.* Maryknoll, NY: Orbis Books, 1980.

Tangunan, Wilfredo H. *Social Transformation in the Philippines: Three Methodist Contributions.* Ann Arbor, MI: ProQuest, 2007.

NAHDLATUL ULAMA

Nahdlatul Ulama (also, Nahdatul Ulama), commonly shortened to NU, is the biggest Islamic organization in Indonesia. This organization represents most traditional Muslim communities, which claim themselves as *Ahl al-Sunnah wa al-Jama'ah* ("The people of the tradition of Muhammad and the community"). Although most members of NU live in remote areas where most *pesantren* institutions (traditional Islamic educational institutions) are located, one of the leaders of the organization, K. H. Abdurrahman Wahid (Gus Dur) became the third president of Indonesia. NU, along with the reformist and modernist organization, Muhammadiyah, has been regarded as the mainstream Islam in the country. The basic principles of NU, which are represented in three concepts—*tawasuth* (moderate), *tasamuh* (tolerant), and *tawazzun* (equal)—became the characteristics of Islam in the country. With the estimate of its membership as high as 30 million, NU will continue to play a significant role in shaping the image of Islam in the country and become a role model for moderate Islam around the globe.

Nahdlatul Ulama, which literally means "the Awakening of Islamic scholars," was established by a number of *ulemas* (clerics) in Surabaya, East Java, on January 31, 1926. The establishment of the NU, led by Hadratussyaikh Hasyim Asy'ari and others, was triggered by the emergence of revivalist and modernist movements, which threatened the existence of traditional *ulema*

Muslims offer prayer for world peace during a rally held by Nahdlatul Ulama (NU), Indonesia's largest Muslim organization, in Surabaya, East Java, on March 9, 2003. Reading from the Qur'an and chanting for peace, tens of thousands of people gathered in Indonesia's second largest city for one of the country's largest rallies against a U.S.-led attack on Iraq. (AP Images/Dita Alangkara)

with a variety of religious traditions that the revivalists and modernists viewed as containing elements of TBC, which stands for *Tahayyul* (myth), *Bid'ah* (heresy), and *Churafat* (superstition). The direct tension between the traditionalist and the modernist Muslims in Indonesia has appeared since 1912, when K. H. Achmad Dahlan, along with other modernist Muslims, proclaimed the first modern Islamic organization called Muhammadiyah. As a reaction to this organization, along with the spread of *Wahhabism* (the religious movement known for its strict observance of the Qur'an) that conquered Hejaz, or Mecca and Madinah, in 1924, Nahdlatul Ulama set as its main goal to preserve the existence of the traditional *ulema* and their *pesantren* institutions, as well as the teachings of orthodox Sunni and Sufism.

Although NU is representing traditional Islam in Indonesia, this does not mean that the organization is run traditionally without a modern structure. Indeed, as in other modern organizations, NU also has a sophisticated structure. The highest body of NU is the Supreme Council, known as *Dewan Syuriah*. It is followed by the Executive Council, called *Dewan Tanfidziyah*. Leaders of both councils are chosen every five years through *Muktamar* (Conference), in which all NU branches at provincial and district levels have equal vote. Under the Executive Council, there are provincial and district boards, as well as some autonomous bodies, institutes, and committees, with the structure extending down to sub-branch representative council boards in villages, called *pengurus ranting*.

The role of NU in the establishment of the Republic of Indonesia is undeniable. A well-known fatwa (religious edict) of the NU to defend the independence of the country, which is known as "*Resolusi Jihad*" (Jihad Resolution), whipped up the spirit of fighting and resulted in the huge battle of Surabaya in 10 November 1945. NU is also known as the first Islamic organization that accepted the state ideology of *pancasila* as its basis. The significant role of NU becomes most evident in education. Currently, NU has around 17,000 *pesantren*, more than 4,000 schools (from elementary to high school levels), and 44 universities. Through its *pesantren* networks, NU also plays an active role in improving the living standards of rural communities.

Achmad Zainal Arifin

See also: Ahmadiyya; Aisyiyah and Nasyiatul Aisyiyah; Education; Indonesia; Interreligious Relations and Dialogue; Islam; Maarif, Ahmad Syafi'i; Muhammadiyah; Myth/Mythology; *Pesantren*; Rais, Muhammad Amien; Reform Movements; Religion and Society; Sufism; Wahid, Abdurrahman; Women.

Further Reading

Bush, Robin. *Nahdlatul Ulama and the Struggle for Power within Islam and Politics in Indonesia.* Singapore: Institute of Southeast Asian Studies, 2009.

Fealy, G., and G. Barton. *Nahdlatul Ulama, Traditional Islam and Modernity in Indonesia.* Clayton, Victoria, Australia: Monash Asia Institute, Monash University, 1996.

Pringle, R. *Understanding Islam in Indonesia: Politics and Diversity.* Honolulu: University of Hawaii Press, 2010.

Ricklefs, M. C. *A History of Modern Indonesia since c.1200.* 4th ed. New York: Palgrave Macmillan, 2008.

NATIONALISM

Nationalism can be defined as an ideological movement for the attainment and maintenance of autonomy, unity, and identity on behalf of a population some of whom have decided to form a "nation" (Smith 2000, 1). It is directly connected to the formation of nation-states in eighteenth-century Europe founded on the Treaty of Westphalia in 1648. The "nation" is a group or groups of people that have a common culture, communication system, traditions, history, beliefs, and ideas (Gellner 1983, 7). The "state" is an institution or set of institutions concerned with the enforcement of order, such as police, government, etc., that consists of a "nation" or "nations" (Gellner 1983, 4). As such, nationalism is the ability of a "nation" to articulate their wish, goals, needs to support itself, and the "state" that it is in. Nationalism is not only connected to the building of modern states, but critical to forming and supporting identities of people to the nation-state they belong to.

Early studies of nationalism can generally be categorized into two main strains, which were highly influential up to the emergence of revisionist historiography and postmodernism in the 1980s–1990s that are relevant to Southeast Asia:

Nationalism may be considered as a method for the expression of ideas, interests, values, and identity/identities of large collectives of people. Generally, this expression takes place against the backdrop of calls for independence or self-determination. More specifically, nationalism need not always express a view of independence from, but also inclusion within the policy of states. Regardless of the nature, sources, or purposes, nationalism provides an avenue for human collectives to express their wishes, desires, fears, needs, and histories (real or imagined) in ways that seek to empower the group.

William J. Jones

civic and ethic. Civic nationalism stresses secularism; upholds law and equality of all citizens; and holds that anyone that conforms to the rules, traditions, and laws of the state can be a part of it. Ethnic nationalism stresses the centrality of blood relations and common culture, history, language, religion, and traditions of a particular ethnic group or *ethnie* that dominates the state. Ethnic nationalism is considered to be exclusive in that only members of the particular ethnic group can truly belong (Smith 1998, 125–26). Later studies in nationalism with regard to Southeast Asia hold that the region's nations were a product of modernism and more similar to "imagined communities" than truly factual entities predating the modernity of the eighteenth century. Benedict Anderson stresses that modern nation-states are *socially constructed* (generally by elites) with the stated purpose of building modern political bodies able to compete and centralize resources to further construct identities of a similar nature. A nation of people draws on particular histories, myths, myths of origins, primordial states that transgress time and space, heroes, leaders, patriotism, and symbols (such as flags, songs and anthems, tombs of soldiers/unknown, etc.) in order to come together under a banner of singleness (Anderson 1983). Third-wave studies of nationalism with reference to Southeast Asia are drawn from cultural studies and stress how states of the region are particular and do not follow or fall into simple categories of definition as prior studies would indicate. This strain of thought puts forth the various forces involved in nation-building in postcolonial states such as the geopolitics of the Cold War, ideological struggles, struggles for control of economies and resources, ethnic tensions and identifications, maps and cartography, and control of state resources such as media, education, and economy, which in some cases consolidated states and in some cases created large-scale violence and suffering. The political use of nationalist symbols, be it monarchy, ancient kingdoms, ethnic diasporas, language, or religious communities, has a common thread in that when they are put into use, they become mediums for political mobilization for political structures, elites, leaders, and the masses of people (Brubaker 1996).

Southeast Asian nationalism is suggested by Sidel to be separated into a Mainland version and an Island version. The Mainland version (Cambodia, Burma, Laos, Thailand, Vietnam) stresses an exclusive conceptualization of dominant core of ethnicity and its history and symbols to internally colonize minority groups; whereas Island Southeast Asia (Indonesia, Malaysia, Philippines, Singapore) stresses a more inclusive fragmented and less stringent version of nationalism (Sidel 2012). Nationalism in Southeast Asia must take into consideration that all Southeast Asian states (with the exception of Siam/Thailand) were created in the twentieth century with the downfall of colonialism. Southeast Asian states are relatively new, and nationalism is especially strong in the region due to colonial histories of oppression, exploitation, and independence struggle. Some major factors heavily affecting the region are a high degree of diversity in language, ethnicity, and religion. The following are two cases of mainland and island nationalism and the role of religion in modern nation-building in Southeast Asia.

Indonesian nationalism is considered to be of the civic variety in order to account for the diversity of the Indonesian archipelago and the building of the state. Only for a short period of time during the presidency of Sukarno during his "Guided Democracy" period (1957–1965) did "NASAKOM"—the political concept based on Army, Islamic groups, and Communist—become the basis for nationalism (Leifer 2000, 156). This nonsecular nationalism has its roots in the "Jakarta Charter" of 1944 under Japanese rule, where Sukarno stated that every Indonesian should believe in his or her own particular God (Tarling 2004, 133). The Indonesian archipelago accommodates a huge diversity of peoples, and as such, under the corporatist rule of Suharto (1967–1998), religion was sidelined as a nationalist force, only gaining major expression in the race riots (Chinese pogroms) during the fallout of the Asian economic crisis of 1997–1998 (Sidel 2012).

Thai nationalism, while enduring periods of extremism during the Plaek Phibunsongkram premierships (1938–1944, 1948–1957), has its roots in the Rama VI (1910–1925) period of the current Chakri dynasty, which professed the current triad of Thai nationalism as Nation, Religion, King (Tarling 2004, 193). Buddhism as the official state religion and part of state ideology puts forth ethical and moral codes for people to follow, such as upholding their duty, industriousness, and upholding social hierarchy (Connors 2003, 238). The social hierarchy is connected by the Buddhist story of *The Three Worlds Cosmology of Phra Ruang* that links the hierarchy of gods and deities to karma according to which humans on earth are also subject to karmatic order of the Three Worlds and official state ideology (Jackson 1993). It is seen that Buddhist religious virtues, when upheld, legitimize the Thai/Siamese king and his right to rule, thus giving the Thai state a focus of national expression or embodiment via its virtuous Buddhist monarch.

William J. Jones

See also: Buddhism; Colonialism; Communism; Ethnicity; Freedom of Religion; Indonesia; Islam; Minorities; Myth/Mythology; Orientalism; Postcolonial Theory; Religion and Society; Secularism; Thailand.

Further Reading

Anderson, Benedict. *Imagined Communities: Reflections on the Origins and Spread of Nationalism*. London: Verso, 1983.

Brubaker, Rogers. *Nationalism Reframed: Nationhood and the National Question in the New Europe*. Cambridge: Cambridge University Press, 1996.

Connors, Michael Kelly. *Democracy and National Identity in Thailand*. New York: Routledge, 2003.

Gellner, Ernest *Nations and Nationalism*. Ithaca, NY: Cornell University Press, 1983.

Jackson, Peter. "Thai Buddhist Identity: Debates on the *Traiphuum Phra Ruang*." In *National Identity and its Defenders: Thailand 1939–1989,* edited by Craig Reynolds. Chiang Mai, Thailand: Silkworm Books, 1993.

Leifer, Michael. 2000. "The Changing Temper of Indonesian Nationalism." In *Asian Nationalism*, edited by Michael Leifer. London: Routledge.

Sidel, John T. "The Fate of Nationalism in the New States: Southeast Asia in Comparative Historical Perspective." *Comparative Studies in Society and History* 54, no. 1 (2012): 114–44.

Smith, Anthony D. *Nationalism and Modernism: A Critical Survey of Recent Theories of Nations and Nationalism*. London: Routledge, 1998.

Smith, Anthony D. "Theories of Nationalism: Alternative Models of Nation Formation." In *Asian Nationalism*, edited by Michael Leifer. London: Routledge, 2000.

Tarling, Nicholas. *Nationalism in Southeast Asia: "If the People Are with Us."* New York: Routledge, 2004.

OKA, GEDONG BAGUS

Born in 1921, Gedong Bagus Oka was a prominent Indonesian intellectual and a Hindu known for her contributions to the establishment of the Ashram Gandhi Canti Dasa in 1976. She was one of the first Balinese women to receive a liberal Western education under the Dutch colonial rulers of Indonesia. Exposed early on to Christian teachings and Western philosophy, she was able to reconcile Hindu-Balinese traditions by discovering the teachings of Mahatma Gandhi and, to a lesser extent, those of Swami Vivekananda. She dedicated a major part of her life to social work in Bali and Java, where she founded three centers for worship and community living ("Ashrams").

Oka grew up in Karangseam, East Bali, Indonesia. She was one of four Balinese girls sent to Hollandsch-Inlandsch School (Dutch School of Natives) in Yogyakarta during the prewar period. While studying, she stayed with the family of Professor Johanes Herman Bavinck, a professor at the College of Christian Theology in Yogyakarta, and there she was highly influenced by Christianity. Its spiritual, ethical, and democratic values challenged her and forced her to rethink her own Balinese Hindu traditions. She came to believe that Hindu religion in Bali was highly influenced by Balinese local culture and that many of its rituals were lacking in spiritual intensity. As a consequence, much of her remaining life was spent trying to promote a more spiritual approach in the local Balinese Hinduism. During Indonesia's independence struggle and formative years of the new Indonesian nation-state, she sought to promote a strong role of religion in society. Later, in the 1960s and early 1970s, her activities became more spiritually oriented with the foundation of the Yayasan Bali Santi Sena (the Balinese Peace Front).

She continued her studies at Christelijke Paedagogische Algemene Academy (Christian College) in Jakarta and thereafter taught at a higher secondary school in Singaraja. She returned to school to earn a bachelor's degree in English from the Udayana University in Bali in 1963 and remained there, teaching English at the Faculty of Letters between 1965 and 1972.

In order to promote the teachings of Gandhi, Gedong translated her English biography into Indonesian, which was published in 1975. In 1976 she founded the Ashram Gandhi Santi Dasa situated in the village of Candidasa, Bali. She spent most of her time managing the activities of the Ashram, which were geared toward practicing "svadeshi" (local self-sufficiency). Projects were designed to improve the local agriculture based on Balinese traditional knowledge. The Ashram also provided school education to orphans and the children from poor families in the community. Daily religious practices at the Ashram included prayers, chanting, yoga, meditation, and a simplified form of Vedic fire ritual. Students could also listen to spiritual lectures and study sacred literature available in the ashram library.

In 1996, she established the Ashram Bali Gandhi Vidhyapith in Denpasar, which educated students about Gandhi's thoughts at the local universities. Yet another Ashram was established in Yogyakarta, which now has followers from local Hindu community as well as Muslims and Christian Javanese. In 1999, she even served as a member of the Indonesian Parliament representing Bali.

Gedong's spiritual philosophy and her modern interpretation of Gandhian thoughts in the Hindu dharma brought her public prominence, praise from some quarters, and criticism from others. She died in Jakarta at the age of 82 in November 2002, following a period of prolonged illness. She is remembered for her immense contribution to interreligious harmony and education.

Ruchi Agarwal

See also: Christianity; Colonialism; Hinduism; Indonesia; Interreligious Relations and Dialogue; Women.

Further Reading

Bakker, F. L. *The Struggle of the Hindu Balinese Intellectuals: Developments in Modern Hindu Thinking in Independent Indonesia.* Amsterdam: VY University Press, 1993.
Ramstedt, Martin. "Two Balinese Hindu Intellectuals—Ibu Gedong Bagoes Oka and Prof. I Gusti Nguarah Bagun." *IIAS Newsletter* 23 (October 2000): 12–13.

ORIENTALISM

Orientalism is the title of a book by Edward Wadie Said (1935–2003), a Palestine-born, former professor of English and comparative literature at Columbia University. *Orientalism* appeared in 1978 and almost immediately became a milestone in Anglo-American literary theory as well as a foundational text of postcolonial theory. Taking "the Orient" as example, Said discloses the connections between Western culture, Eurocentrism, and colonialism in the scholarly and imaginative "construction" of non-European cultures.

From the eighteenth century onward, knowledge about "the Orient" was not only produced by professional Orientalists such as philologists, historians, archaeologists, anthropologists, geographers, etc., who studied the "Near" and "Middle East" as academics. Knowledge and imaginations about "the Orient" were ideologically infused by colonial power as well as economic and political interests. Through textual analysis and by appropriating Michel Foucault's notions of discourse and representation, Said examines "Orientalism" as a specific discourse, as "a style of thought based upon an ontological and epistemological distinction made between 'the Orient' and . . . 'the Occident'" and as a "Western style for dominating, restructuring, and having authority over the Orient" (Said 1978, 2, 3). Knowledge about the colonial "other" is never "pure" or "objective," Said argues, but intrinsically informed by the Occident-Orient relationship of power and domination. Orientalist discourses are implicitly driven to demonstrate the inferior cultural achievements of the colonized. The Orient is not an inert fact of nature, but a phenomenon constructed by naturalizing Orientalist assumptions and stereotypes (Ashcroft, Griffiths, and Tiffin 1998, 168).

Said initiated a new kind of study of colonialism by arguing that the creation of authoritative knowledge about non-European "others" cannot be detached from the process of maintaining power over them. The discursive formation of Orientalism directed awareness of the Oriental "other" in academic institutions, museums, colonial offices, the fine arts, literature, and politics. In that way, Orientalism became an exemplary model for analyzing politics of representation under the perspective of postcolonial critique. In the global intellectual arena, the accusation of being an Orientalist became a universal weapon of postcolonial scholarship directed against anything written by Westerners. Besides its significant influence, Said's book also aroused fierce criticism, even among intellectuals of the global South. One recurrent critique points to Said's tendency of fixing the West-East binary as a static feature. The hegemonic West as well as the misrepresented East are portrayed as homogenized entities without any realm for negotiation, change, and internal multivoicedness. Such a pilloried binarism is countered by the concept of hybridization and the deconstruction of binaries such as center/periphery, colonizer/colonized, Western/non-Western, etc.

Orientalism as a mode of "othering," based on the dichotomy of West versus the rest, is not restricted to the colonial past or exclusively Western. The threat scenario of a "clash of civilizations" as drawn by the influential U.S. political scientist Samuel Huntington sets the "human rights imperialism" of the West against the values systems of "the" Islamic and Confucian civilizations of the East. In the realm of Southeast Asian politics, this scenario was answered by a "reverse Orientalism" as the "Asian values" debate of the Singaporean school illustrates (Hill 2000). Proposed is a homogenous unit called Asia that has peculiar values (community, order, hierarchy, discipline) at its disposal, which are morally superior and far better suited to cope with modernity than Western values with their emphasis on fateful individual liberties (which lead to moral decline, breakup of the family, drug abuse, etc.). Despite the critique—that it is obviously neo-Confucian values defined as pan-Asian values with the intention to justify authoritarian rule and Confucian paternalism, to legitimate nation-building politics as well as to reinforce "Protestant" work ethic—the promotion of "Asian values" has been widely discussed in Southeast Asia, at least in the 1990s.

In the realm of consumer culture, to take another example, the recent branding of an "Indochine chic" functions partly as internal Orientalism. Strangely, it is the French colonial past, otherwise blamed for so many miseries of the present, that serves as a source of a sentimental, tasteful, desirable, and authentic culture, at least for the aspiring middle class in some Southeast Asian metropolises.

Within Southeast Asian studies, critique of Eurocentric distortions and colonial biases were addressed by historians and social scientists long before the publication of Said's *Orientalism*. Scholars such as Jacob C. van Leur and John R. W. Smail called for an autonomous Southeast Asian history beyond European narratives, chronologies, categories of analysis, and colonial arrogance. Syed Alatas's study

The Myth of the Lazy Native (1977) is a thorough analysis of the colonial construction of the image of the "backward native" and the use of this image as a moral pretext for the justification of the colonizer's civilizing mission.

Although frequently cited, Orientalism as a one-to-one model for historical analysis inspired not too many studies on Southeast Asia directly. It is mostly scholars in the field of Islamic studies, especially Malay studies, who make direct recourse on Said's text in their efforts to deconstruct Orientalist misrepresentations (e.g., Aljunied 2004). Generally speaking, Said's book took effect rather indirectly as an exemplary exercise in applied deconstruction. Deconstruction, a literary theory and method originally drafted by French philosopher Jacques Derrida, had significant impact on the social sciences and humanities since the 1970s. As one consequence thereof, the assumption of a primordial, inherent, or fixed cultural identity has been called into question since. Adrian Vickers's *Bali: A Paradise Created* (1989) as well as the work of Michel Picard (1996) demonstrate clearly that what is understood today as the essence of Hindu Balinese culture is a "coproduction" of the Dutch colonial administration, the Indonesian Ministry of Culture and Education, Western bourgeois desires, the tourism industry, and the Balinese people. In a similar vein, John Pemberton (1994) studied the molding of Javanese identity during the Dutch colonial period and its influence on Suharto's concept of nationalism, and Joel Kahn (1993) delineated the "constitution" of Minangkabau identity in the context of Dutch colonialism.

Another, far more spectacular case is the discovery of the "gentle Tasaday" in the Southern Philippine rainforest in 1971 (Nance 1975). Instantaneously, and in the midst of the gruesome Vietnamese war, these peaceful "stone-age" people represented the pristine state of humankind, the hope of humanity. A decade later, the Tasaday tribe turned out to be a hoax staged by the Philippine politician Manuel Elizalde. In 1988, the manufacturing of this "Invented Eden" (Hemley 2003) was deconstructed by linguists and anthropologists in an international conference. Due to the deconstructivist impact of Said's work, the notion that collective identities are discursively created, governed by unequal desires and political interests, is widely accepted within the academe.

In the long run, it has been the "postcolonial turn," decisively initiated by Said's work, that had more effective repercussions on Southeast Asian scholars than Orientalism as a text. Along these lines, Adrian Vickers calls for a "post-Saidian analysis" that "requires complex forms of cultural history and anthropology" and "needs to incorporate Southeast Asian modernities as Southeast Asian epistemologies" (Vickers 2009, 68).

Peter J. Braeunlein

See also: Colonialism; Confucianism; Ethnicity; Globalization; Humanism; Indonesia; Islam; Nationalism; Philippines; Postcolonial Theory; Study of Religion; Tourism.

Further Reading

Alatas, Syed Hussein. *The Myth of the Lazy Native: A Study of the Image of the Malays, Filipinos and Javanese from the 16th to the 20th Century and Its Function in the Ideology of Colonial Capitalism*. London: Frank Cass & Co., 1977.

Aljunied, Syed Muhd Khairudin. "Edward Said and Southeast Asian Islam: Western Representations of Meccan Pilgrims (Hajjis) in the Dutch East Indies, 1800–1900." *Journal of Commonwealth and Postcolonial Studies* 11, no. 1 (2004): 159–75.

Ashcroft, Bill, Gareth Griffiths, and Helen Tiffin, eds. *Key Concepts in Post-Colonial Studies.* London: Routledge, 1998.

Hemley, Robin. *Invented Eden: The Elusive, Disputed History of the Tasaday.* New York: Farrar, Straus and Giroux, 2003.

Hill, Michael. " 'Asian Values' as Reverse Orientalism: Singapore." *Asia Pacific Viewpoint* 41, no. 2 (2000): 177–90.

Kahn, Joel. *Constituting the Minangkabau: Peasants, Culture, and Modernity in Colonial Indonesia.* Oxford: Berg Publishers, 1993.

Nance, John. *The Gentle Tasaday: A Stone Age People in the Philippine Rain Forest.* New York: Harcourt Brace Jovanovich, 1975.

Pemberton, John. *On the Subject of "Java."* Ithaca, NY: Cornell University Press, 1994.

Picard, Michel. *Bali: Cultural Tourism and Touristic Culture.* Singapore: Archipelago Press, 1996.

Vickers, Adrian. "Southeast Asian Studies after Said." *Arts: The proceedings of the Sydney University Arts Association* 31 (2009): 58–72.

P

PAPUA NEW GUINEA

Papua New Guinea (PNG) is the largest country in the Pacific, occupying the eastern half of New Guinea Island, the world's largest tropical island. The western half (West Papua) was annexed by Indonesia in 1963 and endorsed by a controversial United Nations vote in 1969; but a long-running guerilla army campaign continues fighting for independence there, where its mainly Christian and animist Melanesian people see themselves as part of the Pacific rather than Asia. PNG has seven million inhabitants, making it the largest populated country in the Pacific—in fact, 88 percent of all Pacific islanders are from PNG. It has close to 1,000 languages and has such diversity of language and culture that it has often been called literally a "parliament of 1,000 tribes."

During the colonial period of the late nineteenth century, the northern half of PNG was German and the southern half British. However, after the First World War, the League of Nations (later continued by the UN) gave British Papua and German New Guinea to Australia to administer, together, on its behalf until its independence in 1975. Today, it remains an independent nation with a parliamentary democracy, and where most people identify as Christian.

Christianity arrived in PNG in the mid-nineteenth century with the arrival of the London Missionary Society, who brought with them a number of Christian converts from Tonga, Samoa, and Tahiti to help spread the Gospel. Soon Catholic, Anglican, Protestant, and other denominations began to spread across the vast jungles and mountains of New Guinea like wildfire; within 50 to 100 years, most Papua New Guineans had converted.

Previous to the arrival of Christianity, Papua New Guineans lived within small tribal boundaries and lived in a state that could be termed polytheistic and theocratic. That is, they were surrounded by a pantheon of spirits relating to land and sea, human and animal. The most powerful were ancestor spirits, their own ancestors who continued to exist and guide the tribe and individuals; ancestors who could be invoked to provide protection when needed or at times had to be appeased if they were considered malevolent and destructive. Chiefs and *Sangumas* (medicine men and women, shamans and assassins) exercised strong influence and control. There was no separation between tribal law and spiritual belief; people's entire lives were governed by the 24/7 spirit world they inhabited and their *kastom* (traditional beliefs and community responsibilities) obligations.

Kastom remains an important aspect of Papua New Guinean's lives today, as it is for most Melanesians. Although most Papua New Guineans would today consider themselves Christian, they continue to have great respect for the role of *kastom*, as well as a continuing belief in the existence of both ancestral spirits and the power of sorcery. Although Christianity is deemed a monotheistic faith, many Papua New Guineans, like their fellow Melanesians across the region, still see no issue with maintaining Christian values alongside their deep acknowledgement of ancestral spirits.

In many communities, male and female children still undergo elaborate initiation, seclusion, and circumcision rituals that have changed little in thousands of years. Some areas, such as in the Sepik River region, continue to use scarification to demonstrate manliness—one ritual involves young men having their backs cut and filled with ash so that their back looks like a crocodile skin. In the coastal Motu areas and elsewhere, women still tattoo themselves. In many villages, a *haus man* (men's house) and *haus meri* (women's house), which is the repository of important ritual objects, continue to exist, and it is *tabu* (forbidden) for a member of the opposite sex to enter, traditionally, on pain of death.

Sorcery continues to be believed in and used, to the extent that PNG today is considered to be facing a national crisis over sorcery-related deaths, often involving "witches" and some Christian fundamentalists. Although many cases are never prosecuted, police and NGOs claim hundreds of people are killed every year in PNG due to sorcery and witch-killings, something routinely condemned by PNG authorities who are seeking changes to the constitution and law to help counter these brutal deaths.

In its early period of Christian conversion, PNG followed mainly the established churches such as Anglicans and Catholics, especially as they had been first to arrive and become established. Since then, however, the mainstream churches have lost influence and a wider range of denominations, particularly Seventh-day Adventists, Jehovah's Witnesses, and a number of Pentecostal-type churches, have grown in numbers. The South Seas Evangelical Church and Assemblies of God are two such Pentecostal churches that have a distinctly Pacific identity, while dozens of other smaller, evangelical groups continue to emerge.

Just as in the rest of Melanesia, Papua New Guinea is a religiously dynamic nation whose people have a tendency towards experimentation. There are numerous Christian syncretic movements blending Christian values with local beliefs, while others have embraced more recently introduced faiths such as Islam and Bahá'í. In the past 20 years, several thousand have converted to Islam with a particular focus on the Chimbu area of the highlands, where an estimated 3,000 alone have converted. Islamic missionaries operate in remote highland villages and also the poor squatter settlements of major towns such as the capital, Port Moresby. Islam in PNG is on the rise and likely to take root as its missionaries suggest that what they offer is a *reversion* to *kastom*, rather than *conversion* to a new faith. The predominant Islamic tradition practiced is Sunni, while PNG's first imam is a Wahhabist from Nigeria. There are also hundreds of Ahmadiyya followers who have fled persecution in neighboring Indonesia and found sanctuary in PNG.

Also in common with the rest of Melanesia, PNG has a rich tradition of cult, cargo cult, and *kastom* movements. Some of these are movements of people who have turned their back on Christianity to return to traditional ways, others are a mix of *kastom* beliefs and Christian values, and still others still put primacy on the ability of ancestors to deliver modern goods to them if they are invoked ritually.

Ben Bohane

See also: Ahmadiyya; Ancestor Worship; Animism; Bahá'í Faith; Christianity; Colonialism; Fundamentalism; Indonesia; Islam; Melanesian Religion; Missionary Movements; Morality; Shamanism; Spirit Mediumship; Syncretism; Women.

Further Reading

Narakobi, B. *The Melanesian Way*. Port Moresby: Institute of PNG Studies, 1983.
Somare, M. *Sana: An Autobiography of Michael Somare*. Port Moresby, PNG: Niugini Press, 1975.
Souter, G. *New Guinea: The Last Unknown*. Sydney, Australia: Angus and Robertson, 1963.

PEACE-BUILDING

Southeast Asia is a laboratory of religion and peace-building. Peace-building is one of the most contested concepts in International Relations (IR) and Conflict Resolution Studies (CRS). Scholars and practitioners have never agreed on a single definition for peace-building; disagreeing on the issues such as its scope, who are the legitimate actors, and when the process is initiated and terminated. The "formal" definition of peace-building by the United Nations in *Agenda for Peace* only partly explains the term.

Relating religion and peace-building, especially in the context of Southeast Asia, provokes more contested debate. The concept and practice of peace-building is largely determined by IR, which has a very strong tradition of ignoring religion in its analysis. This is due to the prevailing influence of the "secular paradigm" or "theory of secularism" in IR as a key assumption of the rationalist-modernist way of thinking. According to the secular paradigm, knowing by believing is irrational, metaphysical, or even superstitious. Therefore, the mainstream IR discourse focuses more on power capability, economics, and strategic

Cardinal Jaime Sin delivers his homily during a mass-rally to oppose any moves to change the country's constitution on September 21, 1997, at Manila's Rizal Park. Sin was formally an influential leader of the Roman Catholic Church. (AP Images/Bullit Marquez)

interactions between formal state actors, leaving no room for religion as an organizing power for peace and security. However, the core theory of the secular paradigm has been proven untrue. Predictions that, through development and modernization, religion would be fully privatized and removed from the public sphere are false. "Public religion" has emerged over the last several decades, providing a pivotal role for religion in the social and political arenas.

In the meantime, after the fall of the Berlin Wall, there has been a dramatic change in the pattern of war and conflict in the world from interstate wars to intrastate wars. There has been a sharp increase in the number of intrastate conflicts including ethno-religious violent conflicts in the post–Cold War era. The reality in many parts of the world is that religion is not only used for mobilizing conflict, but it also involves organizing dialogue and bridging communication in divided societies, providing food and shelter for the victims of conflict, and conducting trauma healing and reconsolidation efforts. Religion becomes an inseparable part of the idea and practice of "peace-building from below."

In this context, there has been serious intellectual work and political advocacy to show that traditional approaches to conflict by IR and CRS cannot cope with this new reality. IR and CRS should take religion into account in their analysis and work. There has been a realization that there is a need to broaden the meaning of peace-building that is not limited to the post-conflict peace-building phase that is usually carried out by formal state actors. Peace-building includes all activities that ensure the absence of direct and cultural violence and the presence of peace, justice, and prosperity for all when these activities are promoted by both formal state and informal actors.

Throughout Southeast Asian countries, a series of developments have shown religions as not limited to private spiritual matters. Religion "went public" and contributed significantly to political and structural transformations. In 1992, a Buddhist monk, Samdech Preah Maha Ghosananda, initiated the "pilgrimage of truth" or Dhammayietra, to promote peace and reconciliation in Cambodia. The Dhammayietra was an annual pilgrimage of truth that took different themes in response to specific issues faced by Cambodians. In 1993, Maha Ghosananda led hundreds of Buddhist monks, nuns, and laity for Dhammayietra II, walking from Siam Reap to Phnom Penh. This monthlong journey took participants through conflict zones with land mines and cross fire. In this Dhammayietra, Maha Ghosananda aimed to develop popular support for free, fair, and democratic elections and build public confidence to overcome the intimidation and terror posed by the Khmer Rouge.

In 1986, Cardinal Jaime Sin, the Catholic archbishop of Manila, became an important part of the wave of protest against the dictatorship under President Ferdinand Marcos. He encouraged millions of Filipinos to take part in peaceful demonstration. This led to what would later be known as the "People Power Revolution," which forced Marcos to resign. In 2001, Cardinal Sin again acted as spiritual leader to call for mass rally to topple the corrupt government under Joseph Estrada.

In 1998, Muhammad Amien Rais, the chairman of Muhammadiyah in Indonesia (the largest modernist Muslim mass organization with about 25 million members), successfully led the "*reformasi*" (reformation) movement to topple President Suharto, who had ruled Indonesia for 32 years. In 1992, Rais started to call for regime change (*suksesi*) during the Muhammadiyah meeting called *Tanwir* in Surabaya. Since then, with support from pro-democracy organizations and student movements, the call for *suksesi* and *reformasi* became popular and received greater support from the public. Finally, on May 20, 1998, Suharto announced his resignation from the presidency.

Carlos Filipe Ximenes Belo, the Catholic bishop in Dili (1983–2002) who received the 1996 Nobel Peace Prize, strove for peace and justice for the East Timorese, who suffered from brutal military operations. Even in the context of internal political impasse and the ineffective pressure of the international community, Buddhist monks were among the most well-organized groups that frequently stood up against the military junta in Burma.

Southeast Asia is also a home of ethno-religious conflicts; at the same time, it is a base camp of "religious peace-builders." Intractable secessionist conflicts in southern Thailand and southern Philippines (Mindanao) have lasted for decades. Ethno-religious conflicts that occurred in Maluku and Poso (Indonesia) have divided people along religious lines. History has noted, however, that, although acting in a very notorious and complicated situation that involved a deep process of instrumentalization of religion, religious leaders and institutions in Southeast Asia were able to come up with genuine and creative initiatives for peace.

The *Lembaga Antar Iman Maluku-LAIM* (Maluku Interfaith Dialogue Foundation) led by Abidin Wakano and Jacky Manuputty, for example, initiated a series of activities that encouraged people from divided communities (Christians and Muslims) from various sectors of professions (youths, teachers, journalists, academicians, NGO activists, etc.) to "meet" and establish a foundation for reconciliation. LAIM has also worked with the Indonesian Council of Ulama in Maluku (MUI; *Majelis Ulama Indonesia di Maluku*) and the Synod of Protestant Church in Maluku (*Sinode Gereja Protestan Maluku-GPM*) in organizing "peace sermons," to ensure that imams and priests understand the concept of peace-building and their own practical ability to instill in religious adherents the importance of peace and reconciliation. The imams and priests came up with "guidelines" and "materials" on how to preach peace-oriented messages in churches and mosques.

In Nalapaan, a small village (*barangay*) in the municipality of Pikit in the Philippines, the local Catholic priest, Father Robert Layson, OMI, together with Muslim and *Lumad* (indigenous religion) leaders, declared the village a Space for Peace on February 1, 2001. The initiative to establish the Nalapaan Space for Peace was a response to the fact that Nalapaan is one of the worst conflict affected *barangay* in Mindanao. Since the declaration, the people of Nalapaan have lived in relative peace. Both the Armed Forces of the Philippines (AFP) and the Moro Islamic Liberation Front (MILF) respect the Space for Peace as part of the bottom-up process of peace-building.

Violent conflicts have devastated physical and social infrastructures. Peace can only be achieved through a coalition of people from different sectors including religious leaders and institutions. It is worth noting that many successful stories of "religious peace-builders" in Southeast Asia cannot be separated from the good partnership and communication with other peace constituencies such as local, national, and international nongovernmental organizations.

Raja Antoni

See also: Belo, Carlos Filipe Ximenes; Dhammakaya; Ghosananda, Maha; Indonesia; Interreligious Relations and Dialogue; Khmer Buddhism; Muhammadiyah; Rais, Muhammad Amien; Religion and Society; Sin, Cardinal Jaime Lachica.

Further Reading

Appleby, R. Scott. *The Ambivalence of the Sacred: Religion, Violence and Reconciliation*. Boston: Rowman & Littlefield Publishers, 2000.

Casanova, Jose. *Public Religions in the Modern World*. Chicago: University of Chicago Press, 1994.

Devetak, Richard, Anthony Burke, Jim George, eds. *An Introduction to International Relations*. 2nd ed. Cambridge: Cambridge University Press, 2012.

Pettman, Ralph. "In Pursuit of World Peace: Modernism, Sacralism, and Cosmopiety." *Global Change, Peace and Security* 22, no. 2 (June 2010): 197–212.

Ramsbotham, Oliver, Tom Woodhouse, and Hugh Miall. *Contemporary Conflict Resolution*. Cambridge: Polity, 2005.

Thomas, Scott M. *The Global Resurgence of Religion and the Transformation of International Relations: The Struggle for the Soul of the Twenty-First Century*. New York: Palgrave Macmillan, 2005.

PESANTREN

As the oldest Islamic educational institution in Indonesia, the role of *pesantren* (also called "*pondok*" or "*pondok pesantren*")—the Islamic boarding schools in Indonesia—is obvious. The ability of *pesantren* in providing low-cost or even free education for Muslims, especially in the remote areas of the country, has been widely acknowledged. Unlike similar Islamic educational institutions outside Indonesia, usually known as madrasah, the role of *pesantren* is not only limited to teaching Islamic knowledge, but also training in most aspects of human life. Many *pesantren* have actively participated in community development programs by providing vocational training for peasants or farmers in rural areas. Currently, according to the statistical data released by the Ministry of Religious Affairs, there are 27,218 *pesantren* across the country with 3,642,738 *santri* (students). This is an increase of more than three times from the data released in 1998, which only recorded 7,536 *pesantren*. Based on this development, it seems that *pesantren*, though still considered as traditional institutions, will continue to play their significant role not only in transmitting Islamic knowledge, but also in community development across the country.

There are at least two theories explaining the origin of *pesantren*. First, some scholars such as Geertz, Berg, Ziemek, and Kuntowijoyo claim that *pesantren* is an adaptation of the Hindu-Buddhist educational system that existed prior to the coming of Islam. This can be seen from the word "*pesantren*," which literally means a place for "*santri*." The word "*santri*" is derived from the Indian word "*shastri*,"

School children listen to speeches and pray before their lessons at Pesantren Walisongo Madrasah in Indonesia. (Thierry Tronnel/Corbis)

which means a person who understands the sacred book. The second theory claims that *pesantren* is influenced by the madrasah system in the Middle East that has developed since the twelfth century, especially under the Abbasid dynasty. Apart from this historical debate, most Javanese Muslims believe that Maulana Malik Ibrahim, also known as Syaikh Maghribi (d. 1419), is the initiator of *pesantren* in its simplest form. This tradition was continued by his son, Sunan Ampel, who built *Pesantren* Kembang Kuning in Surabaya, East Java. Later on, other *pesantren* were built by the other members of Wali Songa (the nine saints) throughout Java.

There are at least five basic elements for a *pesantren*: *pondok* (dormitory), mosque, *santri* (students), the teaching of *kitab kuning* ("yellow books"—the classical Islamic texts), and *kyai* (the leader, as well as the owner of *pesantren*). Currently, many *pesantren* add some new features, such as *madrasah*, public school, and some vocational programs operated within the *pesantren*. The use of *kitab kuning*, especially the works of scholars from Shafi'i *madhhab* (legal school), becomes the main characteristic that distinguishes *pesantren* from the other Islamic educational institutions. The ability of the *kyai* in mastering Islamic knowledge usually becomes the specialty of each *pesantren*. For example, if the *kyai* is an expert in Qur'anic studies, that leader's *pesantren* will be known as *pesantren* Qur'an, though this does not mean that the *santri* will learn only Qur'anic studies because most *pesantren* now have the madrasah system that offers other different branches of knowledge in Islam. Some examples of well-known *pesantren* include *Pesantren* Tebuireng in Jombang, *Pesantren*

Lirboyo in Kediri, *Pesantren* al-Munawwir in Yogyakarta, *Pesantren* Tegal Rejo in Magelang, and *Pesantren* Modern Gontor in Ponorogo.

Achmad Zainal Arifin

See also: Ahmadiyya; Aisyiyah and Nasyiatul Aisyiyah; Education; Indonesia; Islam; Maarif, Ahmad Syafi'i; Muhammadiyah; Nahdlatul Ulama; Rais, Muhammad Amien; Reform Movements; Religion and Society.

Further Reading

Dhofier, Z. *The Pesantren Tradition: The Role of the Kyai in the Maintenance of Traditional Islam in Java.* Tempe: Monograph Series Press, Program for Southeast Asian Studies, Arizona State University, 1999.

Hefner, R. W., and M. Q. Zaman. *Schooling Islam: The Culture and Politics of Modern Muslim Education.* Princeton, NJ: Princeton University Press, 2007.

Lukens-Bull, R. A. "Two Sides of the Same Coin: Modernity and Tradition in Islamic Education in Indonesia." *Anthropology and Education Quarterly* 32, no. 3 (2001): 350–72.

Pohl, F. "Islamic Education and Civil Society: Reflection on the Pesantren Tradition in Contemporary Indonesia." *Comparative Education Review* 50, no. 3 (2006).

PHILIPPINES

The Republic of the Philippines is an archipelagic nation of 7,107 islands located in the Southeast Asian region in the Western Pacific. The 2010 census cites its population as 92.34 million people (NSO 2012). Its capital, Manila, is one of the 16 cities and municipalities that comprise the Metropolitan Manila region. The Philippines is a nation of great ethnic diversity. The largest of its ethnic-linguistic groups are the Tagalogs, who make up 30 percent of the population, followed by Cebuanos/ Bisayans at around 17 percent and Ilocanos at close to 8 percent. A further 25 percent are classified as "others," including nontribal groups such as the Kapampangans, Moros, and Ivatans, each of whom maintain their distinct and rich religious and cultural traditions.

The Philippines leads the world in surveys about religion and belief, such as the 2012 survey taken by the National Opinion Research (NOR) Center at the University of Chicago, which involved over 30 countries in Europe, the United States, and Asia. The NOR survey found that 93.5 percent of Filipinos professed

---

The Sheik Karimul Makdum mosque, located in the island town of Simunul in Tawi-tawi, is the site of the first mosque in the Philippines. The original mosque was established by Karimul Makdum in 1380 and became a focal point for the spread of Islam throughout the region. Karimul Makdum's remains are buried in the vicinity of the mosque. It is an important site for Muslims in the region, who pay their respects to Karimul Makdum, and gather and consult with each other to promote peace and development. In 2013, Republic Act 10573 recognized the holy sites of Simunul as a national treasure.

Julius Bautista

that "I believe in God now and I always have," while 91.9 percent declared a belief in a personal God. In all, 60.2 percent of those surveyed are certain God exists, always believed in God, and strongly agree that there is a personal God. This is the highest among the surveyed countries, the next ones being Israel with 38 percent and the United States with 35 percent. Correspondingly, the Philippines is at the bottom of the list of patterns of nonbelief. Only 0.1 percent of Filipinos does not believe in God, never believed in God, and strongly disagree that there is a personal God (Smith 2012, 8–11).

In spite of great ethnic and linguistic diversity, the vast majority of Filipinos (over 90 percent) profess adherence to one faith, Christianity. In fact, the Philippines is the largest predominantly Christian nation in Asia and, along with Timor Leste, is one of two predominantly Roman Catholic countries in the region. The religious profile can be broken down further as such: Roman Catholic, 81 percent; Protestant, 7.3 percent; Iglesia ni Kristo (Church of Christ), 2.3 percent; Philippine Independence Church, 2.0 percent; Muslim, 5.1 percent; and Buddhist, 0.1 percent (Pangalangan 2010, 559).

Precolonial Religion

In precolonial times, the respect and worship accorded to deities corresponded to the physical features of the natural environment and with the human engagement in it. There was, thus, *Sipada*, the god of the rainbow; *Mandarangan*, the fire god; and *Magwaye*, the goddess of harvest. Filipinos believed in a spiritual realm, an otherworld, which indicated a belief in an afterlife. There were, as such, deities that reigned in these realms—*Agni*, the god of the netherworld; *Lalahon*, the god of Hell; and *Idiyanale*, the god of death (Agoncillo and Guerrero 1970, 44–45). There is a rich tradition of religious materiality in the form of the veneration of soul-spirits through material object. Idolatry, in the form of *anitos* in Tagalog or *diwata* in Bisayan, to whom offerings of food and prayer are made, was believed to bring good fortune. Ritual specialists and shamans, called *babaylanes*, conducted sacrifice and performed acts of healing by channeling their special connection to the divine spirits.

Filipino "folk Catholicism" is a term used to describe the way in which the faithful in the Philippines, then as now, have integrated precolonial beliefs into Catholic rites and rituals. Slippages in translation into native vernaculars, as well as associations made with preexisting indigenous notions of spirits and deities, contributed to the idiosyncratic nature of Filipino Catholicism. The use of amulets, the persistent belief in pre-Hispanic deities, and the practice of faith-healing and spirit-mediums signified that Catholicism was often accepted and interpreted in ways that Spanish friars did not intend. Yet, while "folk Catholicism" may be seen as a pejorative term, implying a lack of a sophisticated appreciation of doctrine, many Filipinos do not see their faith as diminished or corrupted. Rather, elements of both belief systems are integrated into the very fabric of life—such as in praying to both *Bathala* animist spirits and Roman Catholic patron saints in harvest time—without a sense of duality or theological friction.

Consolidation of Islam from the Fourteenth Century

There is some evidence, mainly philological, that the Hindu-Buddhist religious system that we find in other parts of Southeast Asia prevailed in the Philippines before the consolidation. In Luzon, for example, the region south of Maynila (modern-day Manila) was the homeland of nominally Islamic domains under Rajahs Sulaiman and Matanda; while the Buddhist-Hindu polities, such as that of Raja Lakandula, prevailed in a district called Tondo to the north (Agoncillo and Guerrero 1970, 22–23). However, this is not manifested in the contemporary landscape of the Philippines, at least not as prominently as the other major faith traditions observed by Antonio Pigafetta, an Italian who arrived in Cebu as the chronicler of the first Spanish expedition in 1521. He did single out a single "Moor" in Cebu who, he claimed, had been renamed Christopher upon his baptism into the Christian faith. Indeed, Arab merchants and traders came to the region in the ninth century, though it is not until the fourteenth century that the concerted efforts to spread the faith are recorded. Karim ul' Makhdum was an Arab missionary and scholar who was responsible for the Islamization of Malacca. From there, he traveled east to Sulu around 1380 and facilitated the conversion of the natives there. Following Mahdum's death, his missionary efforts were continued by the Sumatran prince Rajah Baguinda, who, with a force of invaders, settled in the capital of Sulu. There he would lay the foundations of a faith that would spread north to the Visayas.

Later, in 1450, a leader from Palembang married Rajah Baguinda's daughter and, having thus established himself among the local aristocracy, founded the sultanate of Sulu with himself as its sultan. Meanwhile, in a similar fashion, Sharif Kabungsuan from Johor arrived in Cotabato in 1475, intermarried with a native princess, Tunina, and proclaimed himself as the first sultan of Mindanao. From these two regions, Islam would begin a process in which other belief systems gradually became displaced, both by conquest and by the benefits of trading privilege (Hisona 2010).

Today, Philippine Muslim communities are largely concentrated in the southern island group of Mindanao, comprising 13 ethno-linguistic Muslim groups, where they practice the faith in accordance with a cultural legacy that predates the colonial regimes or the modern Philippine state. This includes rituals of courtship and marriage, child rearing, initiation, and laws governing family relations. Islamic culture and the arts, such as traditional wear, dance, and music, literature and decorative craft likewise flourish in Mindanao as they have since Islam's establishment. This cultural and religious distinctiveness has been the basis for attempts to carve an independent Islamic nation state, initially through the Moro National Liberation Front (MNLF). Under the Tripoli agreement signed in 1976, the MNLF accepted to establish autonomy within the framework of the Philippine legal system, even as the Moro Islamic Liberation Front (MILF), a faction of the MNLF, decided upon continuing an armed struggle for a separate state. Nevertheless, the Autonomous Region of Muslim Mindanao (ARMM) was created under the 1987 Philippine constitution, spanning two geographical areas covering a total of 12,288 square kilometers. As of this writing, it remained to be seen whether the new Peace Accords signed in 2012, which promises the creation of a new political entity called "Bangsamoro," will achieve full consummation.

Christianity from the Sixteenth Century

Compared to Islam, Roman Catholicism has a shorter history in the Philippines, though this historical legacy is much more widely commemorated and revered given its widespread adoption among the vast majority of Filipinos. The roots of Roman Catholicism go back to 1521, when the Portuguese explorer Ferdinand Magellan arrived in the archipelago to expand the religious and economic interests of Imperial Spain. Although the Philippines was not Magellan's principal destination, the sheer difficulty of the expedition's pioneering trans-Pacific voyage invested their landing with the perception of divine providence. This laid the foundations not only for subsequent expeditions to the islands, but the establishment of a colonial regime that was to last over 300 years—one of the longest in Southeast Asia. By 1570, a majority of those who came in contact with the Spanish had converted to Catholicism, mainly in the lowlands of the northern island of Luzon. For centuries, the cross and the sword came to symbolize the nature of Spanish dominion such that conversion to Roman Catholicism meant receiving the temporal protection of Spanish colonial forces as well as the privilege to engage in trade and economic activity. It became advantageous, therefore, to adopt the new faith, at least outwardly. By the end of the nineteenth century, the vast majority of Filipinos lived their lives according to the Faith and the temporal authority of the Spanish crown.

The American colonial presence began in the Philippines toward the beginning of the twentieth century after the Philippine-American war from 1899 to 1902. The American "Manifest Destiny" in the islands carried with it a proselytizing agenda, as President William McKinley famously declared the need to "Christianize" the Philippines in spite of the legacy of three centuries of Roman Catholicism in the islands. Thus, in the early part of the American colonial period, there were significant instances of anti-Catholic and anti-Spanish vitriol, which conceived of Spanish Catholicism as a decadent variant of the faith defined by clerical abuse, flamboyant worship, and idolatry. While some American Protestant missions achieved successful conversions, particularly in the highlands of northern Luzon, by the first half of the twentieth century, only a small fraction of Filipinos had turned away from their Catholicism.

In spite of the limited success of the American missionary endeavor, the 1890s to the 1930s could be described as a time in which Filipinos became exposed to new and alternative ways of believing in Christ. The nationalist movement that had gained momentum during the elite-led Propaganda Movement from the mid-1800s had encouraged the development of schismatic movements within the Catholic Church. Filipinos themselves were active in offering alternatives to the Roman Catholic Church and enjoyed some initial success in attracting disillusioned Catholics to their fold. In the early 1900s, Felix Y. Manalo formally established the *Iglesia ni Cristo* (INC), a Restorationist Unitarian Christian church which proclaimed Manalo as the last messenger of God, and that the Roman Catholic doctrines of the Trinity, the divinity of Jesus, and of the Holy Spirit have no biblical or theological basis. The INC is now the largest indigenous Christian church in the world, with an estimated membership of two to four million members (NSO 2012). Similarly, Gregorio Aglipay had broken away from the Roman Catholic Church to form the *Iglesia Filipino Independiente* (Philippine Independent Church), fueled largely by deep resentment at the Spanish clergy's reluctance to ensure the full participation of Filipino clergy in the sacraments.

Religion and Politics

In spite of the determined efforts of American Protestantism and indigenous Filipino Christian churches to gain converts, the Roman Catholic Church was able to maintain a foothold on their membership, particularly in rural areas. From its roots as Catholic welfare organizations in the aftermath of the Second World War, Roman Catholic clerics sought the endorsement of the pope in establishing the formal institutional foundations of the faith in the country. In 1968, the Holy See approved the establishment of the Catholic Bishops Conference of the Philippines (CBCP) as the official organization of the Catholic episcopacy in the country. Today, the CBCP comprises of over 90 active cardinals, archbishops, and bishops who oversee 16 archdioceses, 51 dioceses, seven apostolic vicariates, five territorial prelatures, and a military ordinate. Its functions, however, extend beyond that of ensuring the pastoral care of its flock. The CBCP's commitment to spiritual and doctrinal guidance has meant that it has played an active and significant role in influencing the course of Philippine politics.

Since its establishment, bishops and clergy have often been vocal about matters regarding the moral legitimacy of governmental policies, as well as of the moral fitness of the country's top officials. Two examples are particularly indicative. In 1986 and 2001, church leaders had been instrumental in galvanizing a number of members of its flock to the "People Power" revolutions that drove Presidents Marcos and Estrada from office. These revolutions were significant in the Philippine Church's position as arbiters of social and political morality. This position has been put to the test, even within operations of the legislative process. More recently, the church has faced its greatest challenge with regard to the push for reproductive health bills in the Philippine congress. As such bills are seen by clerics as a veiled attempt to legalize contraception and even abortion, CBCP clerics have evoked Vatican doctrines such as *Humane Vitae* in organizing sustained criticism and protest against their passage.

Julius Bautista

See also: Buddhism; Calungsod, Pedro; Christianity; Colonialism; Contextualization; Ethnicity; Hinduism; Interreligious Relations and Dialogue; Islam; Liberation Theologies; Missionary Movements; Nacpil, Emerito; Religion and Society; Religious Conversions; Ruiz, Lorenzo; Santo, Ignacia del Espiritu; Secularism; Sin, Cardinal Jaime Lachica; Spirit Mediumship.

Further Reading

Agoncillo, Teodoro A., and Milagros Guerrero. *History of the Filipino People*. Quezon City, Philippines: Malaya Books, 1970.

Hisona, Harold. "The Introduction of Islam to the Philippines and Filipinos | Philippine Almanac." *Philippine Almanac*, July 14, 2010. http://www.philippinealmanac.com/history/the-introduction-of-islam-to-the-philippines-and-filipinos-530.html (accessed October 25, 2014).

Pangalangan, Raul. "Religion and the Secular State: National Report for the Philippines." *Religion and the Secular State: Interim National Reports Issued for the Occasion of the XVIIIth International Congress of Comparative Law*, edited by Javier Martínez-Torrón, W. Cole Durham, and Brigham Young University, International Center for Law and Religion Studies, 559–71. Provo, UT: International Center for Law and Religion Studies, Brigham Young University, 2010.

Philippine Statistics Authority, National Statistics Office (NSO). *2010 Census of Population and Housing*, April 4, 2012. http://web0.psa.gov.ph/content/2010-census-population-and-housing-reveals-philippine-population-9234-million (accessed October 24, 2014).

Smith, Tom. "Beliefs about God across Time and Countries." National Opinion Research Center at the University of Chicago, April 18, 2012.

PILGRIMAGE

None of the major world religions were founded in Southeast Asia, and consequently, the region does not enjoy the presence of any primary religious pilgrimage centers. Yet, there is a long history of pilgrimage in Southeast Asia as diverse religions established themselves and became contextualized in different countries. The ninth-century Mahayana Buddhist Temple in Magelang of Central Java attracts pilgrims from all over the region. Bagan in Myanmar, where exist the remains of over 2,000 temples and pagodas, and Luang Prabang in Laos, with its numerous Buddhist temples and monasteries, too are well-known pilgrim centers. For Muslims, while the most sacred pilgrimage is considered to be the *hajj*, there is also a long tradition of non-*hajj* pilgrimage. Malaysia is important in this regard, not only for its locational importance in generating the largest number of *hajj* pilgrims but also as a center for "Islamic tourism" that is aimed at various countries and, particularly, the Arab nations.

Hinduism too has centers of pilgrim importance in Southeast Asia. The Balinese Sacred Mandala Pilgrimage covers nine *kahyangan jagat*, or "directional" Hindu temples in Bali, Indonesia. Out of these, six are considered as world sanctuaries. Pilgrimage to the "directional" temples is considered to cleanse spiritual obstacles and impurities from the visitors. There are also other temples that are centers of pilgrimage in Bali.

As one of the two Southeast Asian countries where Christianity is a majority religion, the Philippines is a key pilgrim center. Our Lady of Manaoag is a widely visited Roman Catholic pilgrimage site that is believed to possess healing powers. Sendangsono in Central Java of Indonesia too is historically important as the place where Rev. Van Lith, SJ, baptized 171 people in 1904, as this event heralded the birth of the church among the Javanese people. The location of the baptism is now a pilgrimage center.

Buddhist Pilgrims in the Shwedagon Pagoda at dusk on February 26, 2010. This pagoda is considered to be one of the most sacred to Burmese in Myanmar. (Nikada/iStockphoto.com)

Pilgrimage is central to popular religiosity. Since Asia does not have a tradition of tourism for pleasure and sightseeing alone like in the West, pilgrimage serves the purpose of both tourism and spiritual nurture. While opportunities for international pilgrimage are limited to the privileged few, travel to local and regional pilgrim centers is an essential part of the religious and social lives of the people.

Jesudas M. Athyal

See also: Buddhism; Christianity; Contextualization; Hinduism; Indonesia; Islam; Localization of Hinduism in Indonesia; Malaysia; Philippines; Popular Religion; Siddique, Muhammad Abdul Aleem; Tourism.

Further Reading

Albanese, Marilia. *The Treasures of Angkor* (paperback). Vercelli: White Star Publishers, 2006.

Bhardwaj, Surinder M. "Non-Hajj Pilgrimage in Islam: A Neglected Dimension of Religious Circulation." *Journal of Cultural Geography* 17, no. 2 (1998).

Jessup, Helen Ibbitson, and Barry Brukoff. *Temples of Cambodia: The Heart of Angkor.* Bangkok: River Books, 2011.

Snodgrass, Adrian. *The Symbolism of the Stupa.* Ithaca, NY: Cornell University, Southeast Asia Program Publications, 1985.

POPULAR RELIGION

The whole of Asia is home to world religions. Southeast Asia is home to the Theravada form of world Buddhism. The coming of Buddhism to Southeast Asia began with the sending of Buddhist missionaries by King Asoka of India during the third century BCE. He sent his Buddhist missionaries not only to all parts of India, but also southward to Sri Lanka (formerly Ceylon) and eastward to Myanmar (Burma), Laos, Thailand, and Cambodia around the period between the fifth and seventh centuries.

Buddhism, particularly the Hinayana school of Buddhism, is a major popular religion in Southeast Asian countries such as Myanmar, Thailand, Sri Lanka, and Cambodia. There are two schools of Buddhism in Southeast Asia. They are namely Mahayana, and Hinayana or Theravada schools. The Mahayana school spread first in northern India and then in China, Tibet, Korea and Japan. The Hinayana or Theravada school of Buddhism, which is also called Pali Buddhism or Southern Buddhism, with its scriptural emphasis in Pali canon, claimed that they were stuck to the original teaching of the Buddha; while the Mahayana school or Greater school of Buddhism which is also called Northern Buddhism, claimed that their vehicle was for all humankind to achieve universal salvation. Historically speaking, Buddhism originated in India with Gautama the Buddha as its founder. It then split itself into two main camps as mentioned above by the beginning of the Common Era. The term "Yana" means a "vehicle," and "Maha" means "great." "Hina" means small or lesser, so that "Hinayana" means "lesser vehicle" and Mahayana means "great vehicle." Buddhism as popular religion in Southeast Asia is seen to have existed alongside other local and indigenous beliefs such as spirit ("Nat") worship.

Buddhism was introduced to Sri Lanka around 250 BCE and became the national religion of the Sinhalese from that time. Since then, Buddhism and Buddhist culture, which had a long and dominant history and tradition, became the fundamental basis for the Sri Lankan national identity and religious heritage. Other religions alongside Buddhism include the influence of Indian Hinduism and other various local religious beliefs and traditions. Most Buddhist temples in Sri Lanka would have a room with an image of a Hindu god, Vishnu, and images of many other local gods which are being worshipped.

Myanmar (Burma)

Myanmar is predominantly a Theravada Buddhist country in Southeast Asia which is sandwiched between Thailand and India. The country is described as the land of golden pagodas in the abode of the Southeast Asia peninsula. Buddhism is believed to be practiced by 89.3 percent of the population, whereas Christianity is practiced by 5.6 percent, Islam by 3.8 percent, Hinduism by 0.5 percent, and primal religions (animism) by 0.2 percent, respectively. Burmese Buddhism represents the Theravada Buddhist tradition, which implies "the way of elders." This way is believed to be the classical, conservative, scriptural, and orthodox type of Buddhism, which can also be found in other Southeast Asian countries such as Sri Lanka, Thailand, Cambodia, and Laos. According to an Asokan tradition of India, Emperor Asoka (272–232 BCE) sent, after the third Buddhist Synod held in 273 BCE at Pataliputtara, India, his missionaries, namely, Maha Theras Sona and Uttara, to Thaton (Suvannabhumi, Burma) around 247 BCE. Since then, Theravada Buddhist tradition took its root deeply in the Burmese culture as well as in the lives of the Burmese people for many centuries. Buddhism in Myanmar has become not merely the majority religion of the state, but also the particular foundation of the life of the Burmese people, which helps preserve their worldviews, their conception of the meaning of human existence and destiny, and their idea of God. Buddhism has also served as the primal source of Burmese nationalism, arts, language, social life, politics, philosophy, religion, and culture. The Burmese Buddhists cannot think of nationality apart from their religion, for it is Buddhism that has wielded the Burmese people together, and the idea of nationhood owes its inception to Buddhism. For them, Buddhism not only has spiritual significance, but also the political significance of uniting the people. As Buddhism reached down into local communities to become a popular religion, compromises were made with the existing folk religion and the Buddhism lived and practiced in local, rural communities came to contain many elements of folk religion. This folk aspect of Buddhism, with its incorporation of local deities (*Nats*) and the cults associated with them, is much different from the pure literary Buddhism of the *Pitakas*. The commentaries and subcommentaries helped to make Buddhism a popular religion woven into the fabric of the Myanmar society.

Nat (Spirit) Worship in Myanmar

The original faith of the Burmese was a primitive animism, centered on the worship of the 36 Nats (spirits). The term "Nat" comes from the Pali word, "Natha" meaning Lord. *Nats* in Myanmar were of two categories: native spirits of the sky, trees, water, and other natural phenomena, and the wraiths of heroes and ancestors who had met a violent death. The most celebrated brother and sister Nats were the Mahagiri Nats, believed to be residing on Mount Popa, which is the seat of Nats. Around 1000 CE, Nat worship and Naga (Dragon) worship were still more prevalent than Buddhism. Historically, Shin Arahan brought Buddhism to Thaton in 1049. King Anawratha attempted to abolish the Nat worship from Buddhism, but it was not successful. Finally, he added one Nat, *Tha-gya-min* (the king of Nats), regarded as the guardian god of Buddhism, replacing the former guardian Nat, *Maha-giri,* to make him a guard to all other 36 Nats and then declared the total number of Nats as 37. King Anawratha allowed peoples to worship Nats as subordinated gods to the Buddha on the platform inside Shwezigone Pagoda, which he built. According to Maung Htin Aung, a Burmese historian, Nat worship is part of the Buddhist faith and the Burmese want to worship "Nats" without ceasing to be good Buddhists. In Myanmar, Nat (spirit) worship is a common religion practiced by majority Buddhists as part and parcel of Buddhism. Nat worship is especially associated with mountains, rivers, trees, houses, heroes, and many other figures. Nat worship is the most effective form of popular religion in Myanmar, while other observers commented that the true religion is Buddhism and that Nat worship is a superstition with less influence over the lives of the people than the Buddha.

Thailand

Thailand is also a Theravada Buddhist country where the Buddhist tradition and ways of life and practice are similar in many ways to those of the Buddhist faith and practice in Myanmar. Historically, Hinduism had influenced Thai Buddhism very strongly in the past so that the Thai (also called Siam) Buddhist temples today have similar features of the Hindu gods in India. Hindu elements can also be found in the Thai Buddhist festivals and offerings being made to the statues of the Buddha. For example, the flowers being offered to the images of the Buddha also need to be bathed as in Hindu cults. Hindu Brahmin priests are still consulted in Thai Buddhist society for various purposes. Priests go around the city walls to scare away evil spirits, and guns are fired in the night for the same reason. Indian mythology such as the *Ramayana* also appears in art in the Buddhist temples. Finally, like other countries, the Thai people still practice Buddhism combined or along with the worship of spirits (*Phis* in Thai) like the worship of spirits (Nats) in Myanmar.

Cambodia and Laos

The Theravada form of Buddhism can be found in Cambodia and Laos. There are numerous Buddhist temples, monasteries, and fine images of the Buddha and other figures. Cambodia and Myanmar had, along their histories, great pyramid temples such as famous ruined temples at Angkor, and thousands of ruins of Buddhist pagodas in Bagan, Myanmar.

Islam in Indonesia

Indonesians were originally animists, Hindus, and Buddhists. Islam spread to Indonesia about the end of the thirteenth century through Arab Muslim traders who had already entered the country as early as the eighth century. Indonesia, whose dominant religion today is Islam, is the most populous Muslim country in Southeast Asia; it has a larger Muslim population than any other country in the world, with approximately 202.9 million identified as Muslim, that is, 88.2 percent of the country's total population of 237 million. The majority of Indonesian Muslims adheres to the Sunni Muslim tradition mainly of the *Shafi madhhad*. Around one million are Shi'as who are concentrated around Jakarta.

Religions in the Philippines

The Philippines was first colonized by Spain in the late sixteenth century and later by the United States. During the colonial rules, the Catholic Christian missionaries arrived in the Philippines, making the country a predominantly Christian nation in East Asia, with approximately 92.5 percent of the population belonging to the Christian faith. Roman Catholicism is the predominant religion and the largest Christian denomination, with estimates of approximately 80 percent of the population belonging to this faith in the Philippines. The country has a significant Spanish Catholic tradition, and Spanish-style Catholicism is embedded in the culture, which was acquired from priests or friars. Islam reached the Philippines in the fourteenth century with the arrival of Muslim traders from the Persian Gulf, southern India, and their followers from several sultanate governments in maritime Southeast Asia. The Muslim population of the Philippines is estimated to be 5–9 percent, the majority of whom belong to Sunnites and other Muslims belong to a Shiite minority. Islam is the oldest recorded monotheistic religion in the Philippines. Islam's predominance reached all the way to the shores of Manila Bay, home to several Muslim kingdoms. During the Spanish conquest, Islam declined rapidly as the predominant monotheistic faith in the Philippines as a result of the introduction of Roman Catholicism by Spanish missionaries. Only the southern Filipino tribes resisted Spanish rule and conversions to Roman Catholicism.

Samuel Ngun Ling

See also: Animism; Buddhism; Cambodia; Christianity; Colonialism; Contextualization; Hinduism; Indonesia; Interreligious Relations and Dialogue; Islam; Laos; Missionary Movements; Myanmar (Burma); Myth/Mythology; Philippines; Religious Conversions; Spirit Mediumship; Syncretism; Thailand.

Further Reading

Aung, Maung Htin. *Folk Elements in Burmese Buddhism.* Rangoon: Buddha Sasana Council, 1959.

Luce, Gordon H. *Old Burma: Early Pagan.* New York: J. J. Augustin Publisher, 1969.

Nigosian, S. A. *World Faiths.* 2nd ed. New York: St. Martin's Press, 1994.

Parrinder, Geoffrey. *Introduction to Asian Religions.* New York: Oxford University Press, 1976.

Spiro, Melford E. *Buddhism and Society: A Great Tradition and Its Burmese Vicissitudes* 2nd expanded ed. Berkeley: University of California Press, 1982.

Tun, Than. "Religion in Burma, AD 1000–1300." *Journal of Burma Research Society* 42 (1959): 47.

POSTCOLONIAL THEORY

Postcolonial theory examines the implications and consequences of colonization on cultures and societies up to the present day. It endeavors to critically investigate claims to hegemonic knowledge and opposes the universalizing discursive power of Western rationality. As a committed intellectual project, postcolonial theory or postcolonialism dismantles the discursive construction of "the other" and strives for the recovery of subjugated and occluded ways of knowledge by focusing on the agency of marginalized societies, ethnic minorities, and subaltern subjects. Along with "class," "race," and "gender," the term "postcolonial" has become a quintessentially political concept, most effectively theorized in literary studies, history, and political science. Postcolonial theory has evolved in two stages.

The first stage was the period of decolonization after the Second World War. Many intellectuals and radical anticolonial activists were deeply influenced by Marxist political theory and the notion of cultural revolution as a means of fighting the subjective effects of colonialism and neocolonialism. In this first stage of postcolonialism, the most prominent thinkers were Aimé Césaire (1913–2008), Léopold Sédar Senghor (1906–2001), Albert Memmi (1920), and Frantz Fanon (1925–1961). The latter, who was born in Martinique and worked as a psychiatrist in Algeria, combined Marxism and psychoanalysis in his influential book *The Wretched of the Earth* (1961).

The second stage of postcolonial theory started in 1978 with the seminal text *Orientalism* by the literary theorist Edward W. Said (1935–2003). In this work,

Said scrutinizes the process by which the "Orient" was "invented" in European thinking. The Orient as such does not exist, Said argues, but was rather created by scholars, artists, writers, and politicians who naturalized various Orientalist stereotypes and conjectures. The underlying power relationship between the West and the oriental East is governed by interests (scholarly, geopolitical, aesthetic, etc.) and the will to understand, but also to manipulate and control. The colonial gaze on the exotic other, the downgrading of the other's culture, and the assertion of its backwardness are both conditions—and effects—of colonial practices. Said demonstrated impressively the applicability of Michel Foucault's discourse analysis and Jacques Derrida's concept of deconstruction. As a result, Said's Orientalism initiated a "postcolonial turn," characterized by an orientation toward representation, culture and identity, textual criticism, discourse, and deconstruction.

Together with Said, Gayatri Chakaravorty Spivak (1942 in Calcutta) and Homi K. Bhabha (1949 in Mumbai) form the "Holy Trinity of colonial-discourse analysis," as Robert Young coined it (Young 1995, 163). Gayatri Spivak is best known for her text, "Can the subaltern speak?" (Spivak 1985). Spivak focuses on nonelite groups in India who are less visible to colonial and Third World national-bourgeois historiography (such as subsistence farmers, unorganized peasant-labor, or tribals). In particular, she directs her analytical attention to the subject-position of the female subaltern, who is doubly vulnerable: economically exploited by the imperialist economy, and forcibly suppressed by the patriarchal system.

The colonial impact on individual and collective identities is a central concern for postcolonial theory and led to the development of key concepts such as hybridity, creolisation, mestizaje, in-betweeness, diasporas, and liminality. Of these concepts, Homi Bhabha's "hybridity" has been the most influential and controversial (e.g., Bhabha 1994). Referring to Fanon and post-Freudian psychoanalytical theory, Bhabha insists that hybridity and liminality are necessary attributes of colonialism. Thus, colonial identities are always unstable and in constant flux. Practices of creolization and syncretism are reevaluated in Bhabha's work. Hybridity offers a countermodel to every dominant culture. Migrants, artists, and intellectuals are not passive (post)colonial subjects; rather, these subjects who move between cultures are able to use their multiple belongings in creative and productive ways. It is within the "Third Space of enunciation," a contradictory and ambivalent in-between, where cultural identity always and everywhere emerges (Bhabha 1994, 3, 37).

From the beginning, postcolonial studies and its side branch, subaltern studies, were largely shaped by South Asian intellectuals. Later, Latin American and African academics as well as British scholars with a migrant background contributed significantly to postcolonial theory.

Southeast Asia, although a region deeply affected by colonialism, is lesser known for an academic milieu or outstanding academics with a distinct postcolonial theoretical profile. A striking exception is the Malaysian politician, public intellectual, and sociologist Syed Hussein Alatas (1928–2007). In his *Myth of the Lazy Native*, published in 1977 prior to Said's *Orientalism*, he analyzes the colonial construction of the image of the indolent, backward, and treacherous native and the use of this image as a moral pretext for the justification of the colonizer's civilizing mission.

Syed Farid Alatas, son of Syed Hussein Alatas, offers a stimulating contribution to postcolonial critique of hegemonic knowledge production in his book *Alternative Discourses in Asian Social Sciences* (2006).

Despite such contributions to postcolonial theory by native scholars in the region, Southeast Asia is largely absent in introductory textbooks and anthologies of postcolonial studies. This observation led the editors of the influential journal *Postcolonial Studies* to publish a volume on "Southeast Asia's Absence in Postcolonial Studies." Chua Beng Huat identifies the main reasons for this negligence as the "hot" Cold War in Southeast Asia and the dominance of the English language in postcolonial studies (Chua Beng Huat 2008). A telling example for a rather unknown Southeast Asian postcolonial approach is the Filipino intellectual movement Pantayong Pananaw (PP). The "for-us-from-us" approach is motivated by the ambition of "indigenizing" the historiography of the nation. It is assumed that there is a unique holistic Filipino culture enshrouded and expressed in a language, yet made invisible by the hegemonic knowledge production of the colonizers. Therefore, the use of Filipino language in the narration of Filipino history is indispensable, even though it risks intellectual isolation.

In Southeast Asian studies, postcolonial approaches influenced by continental philosophy (e.g. Foucault, Derrida) and referring to concepts such as mimicry, hybridity, agency, marginality, the subaltern, and the like became increasingly known in the 1990s. The Thai scholar Thongchai Winichakul outlines how notions of national identity were discursively constructed in the nineteenth century when the kingdom of Siam developed its internal colonialism. The "geo-body" of Siam was shaped by the adoption of modern mapping techniques imported by the Europeans. These techniques involved new conceptions of geography and boundary demarcations and were at once adopted by the Siamese rulers who imposed them on previously borderless, uncategorized, or differently categorized regions, peoples, and spaces (Winichakul 1994). Further studies exploring traces of the colonial in Thailand—the "never colonized" nation in Southeast Asia—are compiled in a volume edited by Rachel V. Harrison and Peter A. Jackson (2010). In the book, postcolonial theory is explicitly used to reflect on Thailand as a semicolonial nation. The relationship to power is as ambiguous (Jackson, in Harrison and Jackson 2010) as the relation toward foreigners, a phenomenon Pattana Kitiarsa labeled Siamese Occidentalism (Kitiarsa, in Harrison and Jackson 2010). Michael Herzfeld identifies Thai crypto-colonialism and its dilemmas (Herzfeld, in Harrison and Jackson 2010), while Rachel V. Harrison (in Harrison and/Jackson 2010) analyzes the making of Thai Identities by (en)countering the West in films, and Thanes Wongyamnva outlines the Thai appropriation of Foucault's "Discourse" (Wongyamnva, in Harrison and Jackson 2010).

Studies in which postcolonial theory is empirically tested, written mostly by U.S. scholars, are also noteworthy. In her multiple-award-winning book *In the Realm of the Diamond Queen* (1993), anthropologist Anna Tsing discusses the cultural and political construction of marginality and the protest against marginalizing discourses amongst the Meratus Dayak of Indonesia. Laurie Sears (1996) and Suzanne Brenner (1998) research issues of modernity, desire, and the feminine in

Indonesia through postcolonial theory. Sears shows how indigenous patriarchal fantasies of feminine behavior and Dutch colonial notions of proper wives are merged in the attempts to maintain control over images and actions of women. In her study on a merchant enclave in Solo (Java), Brenner portrays women and their power in the marketplace and the home. Her thorough analysis of mostly elite/colonial co-constructed discourses of status and hierarchy, "tradition" and "progressive modernity", and the role of gender within such discourses contributes to and confounds modernization theory.

Religion, in comparison with gender, race, power, or identity, never took center stage in postcolonial theory and remains a "blind spot." Accordingly, studies on religion in Southeast Asia from a decidedly postcolonial perspective are rare. The works of Reynaldo C. Ileto (1979) and Vicente Rafael (1988) are noteworthy exceptions. Both focus on Iberian Catholicism and the historical processes of its appropriation and reconfiguration in the Philippines. In his *Pasyon and Revolution*, Ileto shows how the "colonizer's gift," namely the Christian passion story, became the "grammar of dissent" during the nineteenth century's anticolonial upheavals. The passion narrative effectively functioned both as a colonial tool and, in special circumstances, as a language of liberation. By decoding the unfamiliar worldview behind the peasant unrest, he reveals various dynamics of popular Christianity, especially its revolutionary potential in the realm of politics, and furthermore, recalls a century's long tradition of anticolonial resistance of essentially religiously motivated revolts across Southeast Asia. In his work, Rafael scrutinizes the missionaries' attempts to convert Manila's populace to Christianity during the sixteenth and seventeenth centuries and the converts' reactions. Central to his attempt to reconstruct the conversion process as power negotiations are the analytical categories "localization" and "translation." Under such a perspective, conversion can be regarded as a debt transaction with the Spaniards and their God. He argues that while the natives did submit, they concomitantly hollowed out the colonizers' call to submission. It was the cultural and linguistic operation of translation that enabled the converts to evade the totalizing grip of the Christian religion "by repeatedly marking the differences between their language and interests and those of the Spaniards" (Rafael 1988, 211). In Thailand, it has primarily been Pattana Kitiarsa (1968–2013) who took inspiration and analytical strength from postcolonial theory. Kitiarsa (2005, 2012) applies Mikhail Bakhtin's and Homi Bhabha's versions of hybridity to frame and understand Thai popular religion (e.g., spirit-medium cults, millennial Buddhism, magic monks, Indian gods, and Chinese deities). In his work, Kitiarsa demonstrates that "hybridity" is a powerful conceptual tool far more suited to the analysis of contemporary religious transformation in Thailand than "syncretism."

Peter J. Braeunlein

See also: Alatas, Syed Hussein; Buddhism; Christianity; Colonialism; Communism; Contextualization; Ethnicity; Ileto, Reynaldo C.; Indonesia; Minorities; Missionary movements; Orientalism; Philippines; Popular Religion; Religious conversions; Sexuality; Study of Religion; Thailand; Women.

Further Reading

Alatas, Syed Hussein. *The Myth of the Lazy Native: A Study of the Image of the Malays, Filipinos and Javanese from the 16th to the 20th Century and Its Function in the Ideology of Colonial Capitalism.* London: Frank Cass & Co., 1977.

Bhabha, Homi K. *The Location of Culture.* London: Routledge, 1994.

Brenner, Suzanne. *The Domestication of Desire: Women, Wealth, and Modernity in Java.* Princeton, NJ: Princeton University Press, 1998.

Chua Beng Huat. "Southeast Asia in Postcolonial Studies: An Introduction." *Postcolonial Studies* 11, no. 3 (2008): 231–40.

Harrison, Rachel V., and Peter A. Jackson, eds. *The Ambiguous Allure of the West: Traces of the Colonial in Thailand.* Hong Kong: Hong Kong University Press, 2010.

Ileto, Reynaldo C. *Pasyon and Revolution: Popular Movements in the Philippines, 1840–1910.* Manila: Ateneo de Manila University Press, 1979.

Kitiarsa, Pattana. "Beyond Syncretism: Hybridization of Popular Religion in Contemporary Thailand." *Journal of Southeast Asian Studies* 36, no. 3 (2005): 461–87.

Kitiarsa, Pattana. *Mediums, Monks, and Amulets: Thai Popular Buddhism Today.* Chiang Mai, Thailand: Silkworm Press, 2012.

Rafael, Vicente. *Contracting Colonialism: Translation and Christian Conversion in Tagalog Society under Early Spanish Rule.* Manila: Ateneo de Manila Univ. Press, 1988.

Sears, Laurie. *Fantasizing the Feminine in Indonesia.* Durham, NC: Duke University Press; 1996.

Spivak, Gayatri Chakaravorty. "Can the Subaltern Speak? Speculations on Widow Sacrifice." *Wedge* 7/8 (Winter–Spring 1985): 120–30.

Tsing, Anna Lowenhaupt. *In the Realm of the Diamond Queen: Marginality in an Out-of-Way Place.* Princeton, NJ: Princeton University Press, 1993.

Winichakul, Thongchai. *Siam Mapped: A History of the Geobody of the Nation.* Honolulu: University of Hawaii Press, 1994.

Young, Robert J. C. *Colonial Desire: Hybridity in Theory, Culture and Race.* London: Routledge, 1995.

PUPPETRY

Perhaps there is no area of the world with the possible exception of South Asia that compares with Southeast Asia in the variety of dance and theatrical forms, as well as the number of performing troupes. Not only in the traditional royal court cities are to be found the conventional arts of dance, music, drama, and puppetry that have been cultivated for a thousand or more years, but also in the newer urban centers and in innumerable provincial towns and cities, to say nothing of the peripatetic troupes of actors, dancers, puppeteers, and singers who move from village to village in the rural areas.

In much of the world, dance, drama, and music are typically discrete arts, whereas throughout Southeast Asia, dance, drama, mime, music, song, and narrative are amalgamated into composite forms, frequently using masks or puppets. The viewer's senses, emotions, and intellect are assaulted concurrently with color, movement, and sound, giving rise to a marvelous fullness and intensity that is absent in much of the performing arts in the West.

While Thailand, Cambodia, Laos, and other Southeast Asian countries have their own puppets, the best known of the Southeast Asian puppet traditions is the shadow puppetry known as *wayang*, or the Indonesian and Malay traditions. *Wayang* is a generic Javanese term denoting traditional "theater" and/or "puppet."

Using opaque, often articulated forms in front of bright backdrop to create an illusion of shifting, "shadow puppetry" is an antique form of storytelling and amusement. Employing a stencil figure held between a source of illumination and a luminous backdrop, a variety of effects can be created by moving both the puppet and the light source, which enables a talented puppeteer to make figures walk, dance, struggle, and laugh.

A man controlling a Nang Yai puppet during a shadow theater performance in Thailand. (Luca Tettoni/Corbis)

The origins of shadow puppetry are unclear, whether native to Java or imported from India. However, the *wayang kulit* system of a sacred puppeteer, or *dalang*, who is accompanied by the percussive yet fluid music of a *gamelan* orchestra while he moves intricately constructed leather figures before an oil lamp casting trembling silhouettes on a luminous screen as he intones mythic narrative in ancient sanskritized indigenous languages, seems to have been invented in Indonesian tradition. Unlike the royal court art traditions, *wayang kulit* is a centuries-old folk tradition and is today Southeast Asia's most durable traditional theater configuration.

Performing arts, including several puppetry traditions, are a normal part of life throughout Southeast Asia. While Thailand, Cambodia, Laos, and other Southeast Asian countries have their own puppets, the best known of the region's puppet traditions is the shadow puppetry known as *wayang*, a generic Javanese term denoting traditional "theater" and or "puppet." Shadow puppetry is an ancient form of storytelling and entertainment using opaque, often articulated figures in front of an illuminated backdrop to create the illusion of moving images.

David C. Scott

As much a rite as a drama, the action is set in mythical time, some performed at animistic events invoking local spirits, others staging events from the Hindu epics, the *Ramayana* and *Mahabharata*, while the preponderance are basically creations of Java in which the five *Pandawa* brothers from the *Mahabharata* are situated in a variety of situations. Stories from Arab and other indigenous traditions also provide dramatic material. The presence of god-clown-servant figures and a gang of ogres insinuate popular mythical traditions significantly separated from more classical traditions Performances are also commissioned, such as offertory plays for the harvest, or animistic exorcisms to protect children from being harmed by *Kala*, the guardian deity of the underworld.

For the spectator to experience the symbolism of a *wayang* play is vicariously to struggle through the life cycle and to undergo mystical exercises. To this end, meditations and treatises on the plays have been composed that explicate their meaning in relation to local philosophies and theologies, as well as those of the world's religions.

The puppetry traditions of Southeast Asia have been an integral part of Southeast Asian experience for perhaps a thousand years, and they continue to be so, influencing the political and secular as well as the religious life of the region. Performances abound, not only in palaces and schools, but also in community life—at wedding and village festivals, amid the laughter of children and the gossip and meditative conversation of their elders.

David C. Scott

See also: Cambodia; Contextualization; Dance and Drama (Theatre); Hinduism; Indonesia; Laos; Malaysia; Music; Myth/Mythology; Religion and Society; Ritual Dynamics; Thailand.

Further Reading

Osnes, Beth. *The Shadow Puppet Theatre of Malaysia*. Jefferson, NC: McFarland & Co., 2010.

"Puppetry in Asian Cultures." The Roman World, September 11, 2007. http://www.ancientworlds.net/aw/Article/974780 (accessed May 12, 2014).

Van Ness, Edward C., and Prawirohardjo. *Javanese Wayang Kulit: An Introduction*. London: Oxford University Press, 1984.

Walujo, K. W. *Wayang Kulit as a Medium of Communication*. Surabaya, Indonesia: Department of Communication, Dr. Soetomo University, 1995.

Wolters, O. W. *History, Culture, and Region in Southeast Asian Perspectives*, Rev. ed. Ithaca, NY: Cornell Southeast Asia Program in collaboration with the Institute of Southeast Asian Studies, Singapore, 1999.

R

RAIS, MUHAMMAD AMIEN

Muhammad Amien Rais, born in Solo, Central Java, on April 26, 1944, is inevitably one of the key persons and leaders of the *reformasi* (reformation) movement that led the 1998 democratic transition in Indonesia. Since the 1990s, he actively pushed the importance of the political and regime change for a better Indonesia. As the chairman of Muhammadiyah (the largest Muslim modernist organization in Indonesia), he together with other civil society groups criticized the Suharto regime, which handcuffed political freedom, press freedom, and freedom of expression for the people. When he became one of the leaders of ICMI (*Ikatan cendekiawan Muslim Indonesia*, the Indonesian Association of Muslim Intellectuals), he raised the sensitive issues of the Suharto regime such as corruption, collusion, and nepotism into public concerns. Before Suharto ended his power in May 1998 as the result of this reformation movement, he was the one who advanced "succession" of political leadership to overthrow Suharto constitutionally.

Rais did his elementary and high school studies in Muhammadiyah educational institutions in Solo. He learned religious studies from his parents and at Islamic school *Khususiyah Al-Islam* in Solo. The young Rais was also involved in *Hizbul Wathan*, a scouting organization of Muhammadiyah. He pursued higher education at Gadjah Mada University, majoring in international relations. While he was a university student, Amien joined the Muhammadiyah Student Association (IMM) for which he produced many articles in mass media. Rais began his career as assistant lecturer soon after he graduated from the university in 1968. He gained his master's degree from the University of Notre Dame, Indiana, in 1974 and earned his PhD degree from the University of Chicago in 1981. His dissertation was entitled "The Moslem Brotherhood in Egypt: Its Rise, Demise, and Resurgence."

After returning from the United States, Rais was involved in the Muhammadiyah Central Board, and he gave speeches in many universities, joined many organizations such as the Indonesian Association of Muslim Intellectuals (ICMI), and wrote books and articles. In 1990, he was elected as the vice chairman of Muhammadiyah and in the 1995 congress in Aceh, he was elected as the chairman of Muhammadiyah. As chairman, Rais gave political and civic education for Indonesian people about the importance of religious power to fight against corruption, despotism, and authoritarianism. He also strove to encourage the Indonesian people to practice democracy, human rights, and to campaign against the corrupt and authoritarian regime. During the transition era, Muhammadiyah together with Nahdlatul Ulama were noted as the social organizations based on religious values that led and strongly supported the democratization of Indonesia.

After the fall of Suharto, Rais and the other reformist proponents established the National Mandate Party (*Partai Amanat Nasional*) on August 6, 1998. This party aimed to institutionalize and support the reform agenda in the political system. Instead of a religious basis, the party employed the pluralist ideology that corresponded with the Indonesian reality, which is comprised of many religions and groups. In 1999, Rais was appointed as the speaker of the People Consultative Assembly (*Majelis Permusyawaratan Rakyat*) of the Republic of Indonesia. During that period, the People Consultative Assembly was the highest political institution in the country's political system. As the speaker of the People Consultative Assembly (1999–2004), Rais was the champion of the Indonesian constitution's amendment process. The 1945 constitution was alleged as the source of authoritarianism in Indonesian political system. The amendment process led to political changes and the creation of institutions that are very important in supporting democratization.

Rais's religious viewpoints are moderate and he does not agree to the idea of the creation of an Islamic state in Indonesia, since there are no certain verses in the Qur'an and Hadist that support this notion. He is typically a Muhammadiyah activist who places his faith in action paradigm in thought and expressions. He values actions as more important than speculative and abstract thinking. After losing the presidential election in 2004, he set apart his life as the chairman of the National Mandate Party's Advisory Board, as Muhammadiyah's prominent preacher and figure, and as a continuing and influential professor at the Gadjah Mada University in Yogyakarta, Indonesia.

Ahmad Fuad Fanani

See also: Education; Indonesia; Islam; Morality; Muhammadiyah; Nahdlatul Ulama; Reform Movements; Study of Religion.

Further Reading

Hefner, Robert W. *Civil Islam, Muslim and Democratization in Indonesia*. Princeton, NJ: Princeton University Press, 2000.

Omar, Irwan. *Mohammad Amien Rais Putra Nusantara*. Singapore: Stamford Press, 2003.

Stepan, Alfred, and Mirjam Künkler. "An Interview with Amien Rais." *Journal of International Affairs* 61, no. 1 (Fall 2007): 205–16.

Uchrowy, Zaim. *Mohammad Amien Rais Memimpin Dengan Nurani: An Authorized Biography*. Jakarta: The Amien Rais Center, 2004.

REFORM MOVEMENTS

Southeast Asia is home to most of the world's religions, but with the accumulation of tradition, power, and wealth over the centuries, they have, in several places, become unable or unwilling to respond adequately to the changing context. Reform movements that challenge these tendencies and reaffirm the need for religions to be sensitive to their vision have emerged in all the religions. Reform movements in the religions of Southeast Asia have in particular defended democracy and human rights, resisted fundamentalist and theocratic tendencies, and upheld the right of religious and ethnic minorities, women, and the other marginalized sections to live and function freely. This entry will briefly examine such reform movements in the religions of the region.

Islam

As the most widely practiced religion in Southeast Asia, Islam has a rich tradition of religious reform that goes back several centuries. While reform movements in the earlier centuries were focused primarily on theological debates on orthodoxy and heresy, in more recent times, they have been concerned with the potential of religion for social transformation and the liberation of the marginalized sections of the society. As the world's most populous Muslim-majority country, Indonesia presents a picture to gauge the reformist and progressive role religion plays in public life. Even though the country is 87 percent Muslim, Islam is not the state religion of Indonesia, and there is a long tradition of Muslim reform movements in the country. Muhammadiyah, the reformist and modernist organization founded in 1912, combines theological purification and social reform. Muhammadiyah emphasizes the moral responsibility of people and the need to purify the people's faith in line with the Islam doctrines. Along with Nahdlatul Ulama, Muhammadiyah has been regarded as mainstream Islam in the country. Both the organizations have been particularly active at the level of education by running a number of institutions and also by supporting *pesantrens*, the Islamic boarding schools that have been providing low-cost and free education for Muslims, especially in the remote areas of the country.

Under the leadership of General Suharto, who was the president of Indonesia from 1967 to 1998, the state ideology of *pancasila* (five principles)—which affirms the supremacy of God but also upholds the "secular" values of democracy and social justice—was strengthened. A systematic attempt at depoliticization happened in the country, in the process creating a climate conductive for religious reform. In the post-Suharto era, there has been a revival of some of the radical Islamist organizations, leading to ethno-religious and interreligious conflicts that threatened the very foundation of the secular democracy. The reformist organizations and movements affirm that they are alert to these challenges and are committed to upholding the spirit of freedom of thought and expression in the midst of fundamentalist tendencies.

In Malaysia, too, reform movements within the context of Islam have been actively present for several years. In particular, the role played by Sisters in Islam (SIS), an organization that campaigns for gender equality and women's rights, is important. The original focus of the group was to challenge Islamic laws, policies, and traditions that were considered to be discriminative against women. Later, the group's areas of work expanded to include the larger issues of social justice, democracy, human rights, and legal reform. SIS also networks with other women's and reformist organizations in the country and abroad.

By and large, mainstream Islam in Southeast Asia has largely stayed away from extremist and fundamentalist forces that have reared their heads, time and again, in several other parts of the world. Progressive Muslim leaders affirm that the core values of Islam are compatible with democracy, pluralism, and human rights. Even though some interpretations of *shari'a* are discriminatory toward women,

Islam emphasizes women's right to practice their religion as equal believers. Women should also have the right to education, employment, and political participation. Reformist Islamic organizations and movements play a vital role in affirming these positive and liberative values of religion.

Buddhism

Engaged Buddhism, a movement of social, political, economic, and environmental activism that developed in the twentieth century, perhaps best represents the reformist face of Buddhism in Southeast Asia. The movement arose out of the grave social and political challenges—such as wars, famine, ethnic violence, and the oppression and marginalization of women—faced not only by the Buddhists, but also the wider world, in the twentieth century. Religion that should be providing answers for these problems that perplex humanity was found to be woefully inadequate and unwilling to take up these challenges. At the height of the Vietnam War, Thich Nhat Hanh—the highly respected Zen master who was born in Vietnam—and others were confronted with the question, whether to continue their contemplative life of meditation in the monasteries, or help villagers suffering under the war. They chose both: to be true to the essence of the Buddhist monastic life and yet be sensitive to the plight of the common people. Engaged Buddhism, born out of such a commitment, has been inspired by the nonviolent and pacifist principles of several religions and ideologies, but is fundamentally Buddhist.

Engaged Buddhism has taken contextual and regional forms in different countries. The Santi Asoke movement in Thailand rejects many of the traditional rituals in Buddhism by preaching and practicing a faith that is nonhierarchical and laity-oriented. The group also represents an alternative lifestyle that is simple, rural, and self-sufficient in food production. In Thailand also arose individual leaders like Buddhadasa Bhikkhu, who attempted to reform Theravada Buddhism. In particular, he demythologized Thai Buddhism and the *Tipitaka* (the original Buddhist Scripture) by focusing on the role of the individual in religious practice and principles. In politics, Buddhadasa questioned people in authority whom he considered to be corrupted by power, money, and prestige.

The Buddhist women's movements too have been an expression of reform in religion. They focus on the status and experiences of women in Buddhist societies and, in particular, on women's struggle for religious and social equality. They are also engaged in feminist reinterpretations of Buddhist tenets and in affirming Buddhist feminist identity in Asian Buddhist cultures and across national and ethnic boundaries. The women's movements have also been concerned about actively redefining the relationship of women to religious institutions and other dimensions of cross-cultural movements. The Buddhist women's movements have contributed greatly to bringing women's issues from the margins to the mainstream and in including the feminine, women, sexuality, and gender as a subfield in Buddhist studies.

Christianity

Christianity is often perceived as a foreign religion in Asia, primarily because its theology and practice have been closely identified with the history of Western missionary movement and even of colonialism. As the colonized nations became independent one by one under a strong impulse of nationalism and self-rule, the Asian Christians too realized that Western theology that had been passed on them as *the* theology was no more than a European theory that had evolved in contexts far removed from their own. Accordingly, the Asian Christians felt compelled to raise questions about the faith, practices, and liturgies that they had received. During the postcolonial period, the liberation theology movement played a major role in posing appropriate questions by placing ordinary people, and not the leaders, at the center of religion. Taking the *context* as the starting point, the Southeast Asian Christians at the grassroots level too set in motion a process of change that redefined theology and ecclesiology from the people's perspective.

The reforms in Asian Christianity took diverse forms in the various countries. In the Philippines in the 1970s and 1980s, the Christians played a key role in mobilizing the public against the authoritarian rule of President Marcos. Even before the Roman Catholic Church, under the leadership of Cardinal Jaime Lachica Sin, got involved in the anti-Marcos movement, lay Christian groups such as the Young Christian Socialist Movement and the International Fellowship of Reconciliation were actively present in the scene, by conducting seminars and other programs for leaders among the political parties, other community organizers, and students. These programs had a ripple effect in galvanizing the church hierarchy and the public to effectively counter the authoritarian forces in the country.

The awakening of women from traditional patriarchal structures too has been an integral part of the reform in Christianity. The Indonesia-based Asian Women's Resource Centre for Culture and Theology (AWRC) as an organization of women and women's organizations in Asia has been involved in seeking alternative patterns both in theology and praxis. Conceived at the Asian Women Theologians' Conference in Singapore in November 1987 by some women theologians who recognized the need to form a community of Asian women engaged in theology and ministry, AWRC has been leading the way in promoting Asian women's theology.

Reforms in Christianity had experienced ups and downs in the Asian context. While liberation theology had provided the theological foundation that had challenged the oppressive structures of state and other institutions, in the postcolonial period, Pentecostalism has emerged as a strong alternative. Especially in Singapore, Pentecostalism has, by and large, replaced liberal Christianity as the dominant form of Christianity, becoming popular *after* the state had consolidated its rule in the 1980s and suppressed liberal Christian movements, especially by expelling, in 1987, the Christian Conference of Asia from the country. Caught between the urge for social change that will liberate the marginalized people on the one hand, and a "prosperity gospel" that supports the ruling class and is individualistic and conservative in orientation on the other, reforms in Asian Christianity are indeed at a crossroads.

Hinduism and Bahá'í Faith

Arya Samaj is one of the Hindu reformist movements that is actively present in Southeast Asia. The founder of Arya Samaj, Swami Dayanand Saraswati (1824–1883), created the Samaj's 10 principles based on the Vedas, which are considered the earliest literary record of Indo-Aryan civilization and also are the sacred books of the Hindus. These principles aimed at reforming the individual and society through the physical, social, and spiritual betterment of humanity. Saraswati's aim was not to found a new religion, but the true development of humankind by the acceptance of the Supreme truth and rejection of falsehood through analytical thinking. Arya Samaj is actively present in many Southeast Asian countries. Arya Samaj Singapore, founded in 1927, organizes Vedic Satsang, where the members gather together and listen to religious and moral discourses by prominent preachers and leaders from India and neighboring countries. The Samaj has also been involved in educational and social reform activities that benefit not only the Hindus, but also the wider community. Arya Samaj is actively present in Malaysia, Indonesia, and Thailand as well.

The Bahá'í Faith, which emerged out of the earlier Babi movement in the nineteenth century, identifies its mission as uniting the peoples of all religions in order to establish a divinely ordered global society of peace and justice. Initially, the only part of Southeast Asia to have Bahá'ís was Burma, but in a religious revival in the middle of the twentieth century, the movement spread to South Vietnam, the Philippines, Sarawak, Indonesia, and several other locations in the region. Bahá'ís are now well established across the whole region, with a strong commitment to social development, the promotion of education, and women's rights. There is also an extensive Bahá'í literature in all the major languages of the region.

Jesudas M. Athyal

See also: Bhikkhu, Buddhadasa; Buddhism; Christianity; Colonialism; Contextualization; Education; Engaged Buddhism; Ethnicity; Fundamentalism; Globalization; Hanh, Thich Nhat; Hinduism; Indonesia; Islam; Liberation theologies; Malaysia; Messianic movements; Minorities; Muhammadiyah; Nahdlatul Ulama; *Pesantren*; Philippines; Santi Asoke; Secularism; Sexuality; *Shari'a*; Sin, Cardinal Jaime Lachica; Singapore; Sisters in Islam; Thailand; Vietnam; Women.

Further Reading

Ali, Muhamad. "The Rise of the Liberal Islam Network (JIL) in Contemporary Indonesia." *American Journal of Islamic Social Sciences* 22, no. 1 (2005). http://i-epistemology.net/attachments/877_ajiss22-1-stripped%20-%20Ali%20-%20The%20Rise%20of%20the%20Liberal%20Islam%20Network.pdf (accessed May 12, 2014).

Azyumardi, Azra. *The Origins of Islamic Reformism in Southeast Asia: Networks of Malay-Indonesian and Middle Eastern Ulama in the Seventeenth and Eighteenth Centuries.* Honolulu: Allen & Unwin and University of Hawaii Press, 2004.

Engineer, Asghar Ali. "The Hindu-Muslim Problem." In *Islam and Liberation Theology.* New Delhi: Sterling Publishers, 1990.

England, John C., Jose Kuttianimattathil, John Mansford Prior, Lily Quintos, David Suh Kwang-sun, and Janice Wickeri, eds. *Asian Christian Theologies: A Research Guide to Authors, Movements, Sources*, Vol. 2, *Southeast Asia.* Delhi: Indian Society for

Promoting Christian Knowledge (ISPCK), in association with Maryknoll, NY: Orbis Books, 2003.

Esack, Farid. *Qur'an, Liberation, and Pluralism*. Oxford: Oneworld, 1997.

Goh, Daniel, P. S. "State and Social Christianity in Post-Colonial Singapore." *Sojourn: Journal of Social Issues in Southeast Asia* 25, no. 1 (April 2010): 54–89. http://muse.jhu.edu/journals/soj/summary/v025/25.1.goh.html (accessed May 12, 2014).

Hanh, Thich Nhat. *Being Peace*. Berkeley, CA: Parallax Press, 1987.

Heikkilä-Horn, Marja-Leena. *Santi Asoke Buddhism and Thai State Response*. Turku, Finland: Åbo Akademi University Press, 1996.

Kurzman, Charles. "Liberal Islam: Prospects and Challenges." *The Liberal Institute*. http://www.liberalinstitute.com/LiberalIslam.html (accessed May 12, 2014).

Noor, Farish A. *Islam on the Move: The Tablighi Jama'at in Southeast Asia*. Amsterdam: Amsterdam University Press, 2012.

Queen, Christopher S., and Sallie B. King, eds. *Engaged Buddhism: Buddhist Liberation Movements in Asia*. Albany: State University of New York Press, 1996.

Tsomo, Karma Lekshe, ed. *Buddhist Women across Cultures: Realizations*. Albany: State University of New York Press, 1999.

Wahid, Abdurrahman. "Religious Tolerance in a Plural Society." In *Difference and Tolerance: Human Rights Issues in Southeast Asia*, edited by Damien Kingsbury and Greg Barton. Geelong, Australia: Deakin University Press, 1994.

Wertheim, W. F. "Religious Reform Movements in South and Southeast Asia." http://www.jstor.org/discover/10.2307/30123249?uid=3739696&uid=377567133&uid=2&uid=3&uid=3739256&uid=60&sid=21102043006493 (accessed May 12, 2014).

RELIGION AND SOCIETY

Religion guides the everyday lives of most Asians. While the modern, Western culture often draws a boundary between religion and society including the separation of church and state, religion for the Asians has a totalizing effect. Not only the spiritual realm, but also the social, political, economic, and ecological lives of Asians are often guided by religious traditions and values. Even as theocratically oriented monarchies gave way to democratic structures, religion continued to have a lingering effect on public life, shaping and reorienting the political narrative. The influence of religious structures on the social and economic scene of Southeast Asia is also important, especially as the region accounts for a large proportion of the world's poor. The role religions play in responding to the challenges to the ecology and environment is another significant area. This entry will briefly review the impact of Asian religions in public life, within the broader context of the interface between religion and society.

Buddhist Context

In many Southeast Asian nations, religions have played an important role in determining the course of political developments. While political as well as religious legitimacy imparted to the monarchy was a characteristic of several Southeast Asian societies, today monarchical forms survive, to some extent, only in Thailand and Cambodia. The constitution of Thailand ensures the protection of all religious groups, but the country has a long tradition of imparting primacy for Buddhism, which also involves interference in the political process of the country. While Thailand is now a constitutional monarchy, it is perhaps the only country in the world where the king is stipulated to be a Buddhist and the upholder of the Faith. Even though Buddhist monks have long demanded the inclusion of Buddhism as the official religion of the country, the government has not yet yielded to such demands. The monks, however, continue to enjoy several perks and benefits in public life. While the Thai king interferes only rarely in political affairs, he maintains the right to do so and has intervened occasionally, including during the riots of 1992. In several respects, Thailand is unique because it is the only country in the region that has maintained an unbroken monarchy that still draws its political legitimacy from the Buddhist worldview of the Thais, who are 90 percent Buddhist. Since Thailand is a functioning democracy with a free press, there is also the space for religious activism in the public sphere, including for Buddhist reformist movements such as Santi Asoke.

The concept of god-king is also a factor to be considered while discussing religion and society in a Buddhist context. In Cambodia, the tradition of god-king goes back to the *devaraja* of Angkor, but its legitimacy was seriously undermined following the overthrow of the head of state, Sihanouk, in 1970. While the institution of god-king within a Buddhist framework continues to play a prominent role in Thailand, it plays an ambiguous role in the legitimization of political power in Cambodia. Another context with a tradition of god-king is Burma, but the British colonial rule there dispensed with the Burmese royalty. However, the Buddhist leadership of the country continues to exert an influence in public life. Even though the "Saffron Revolution" of Burma in 2007 posed a serious threat to the military rule of the country, the movement was quickly suppressed. Religious programs that are deemed critical of the government have been strictly regulated or banned, but patronage is given to the monks who are willing to cooperate with the military.

Buddhism plays an important role in public life in Southeast Asia by its contributions to reviving the spirit of self-dignity and nationalism. For a great majority, to be Burmese or Lao was to be Buddhist. The Buddhist monks who became involved in the political sphere did so for a number of reasons. One was a religious response to rapid changes, especially as traditional values and lifestyle were increasingly being threatened by the forces of modernization and globalization. Another factor was a faith response to tyranny. Activist religious leaders like Sulak Sivaraksa were genuinely uncomfortable with the growth of authoritarian and military rulers even as democracy and freedom were suppressed in the region. In the Burmese context, on the other hand, young monks played an important role in the movement in countering the power of the military and in promoting the democratization of the country.

Christian Context

The Philippines in the 1980s was the arena of radical political action in which the Christian Church played a significant role. In a country where close to 85 percent of citizens are Catholic, the position the church took on public matters carried considerable weight with a large segment of the population. Initially, the poorer sections of the population, often assisted by clergy and laity who were committed to radical social action, took the initiative in countering the authoritarian regime of Ferdinand Marcos. After the assassination of the opposition leader Benigno Aquino in 1983, however, the hierarchy of the Catholic Church under the leadership of Cardinal Jaime Lachica Sin got involved in the struggle for freedom. The church also effectively used the media in the protests, with Radio Veritas run by the Catholic Church emerging as the only radio station that broadcasted programs that were critical of President Marcos. The involvement of the church ensured that the antigovernment protests did not become too violent but remained at the level of nonviolent protest. The founding of the Action for Peace and Justice (AKKAPKA) for the training and organization of the people was a major milestone in the promotion of nonviolent public action. Due to all these factors, the religious character of the Philippines revolution made the events there unique. At the core of the revolution against Marcos and the democratization of the country was the essence and values of religion.

The involvement of the Christian Conference of Asia (CCA) in the social and political scene of Asia that led to the closure of the CCA office and the expulsion of the organization from Singapore presented a related but different way in which Christianity played a role in Asian public life. The programs of CCA included its work at the grassroots level in conscientizing and mobilizing the masses to oppose the forces of injustice and violence. These were considered, by the authorities of Singapore, as radical steps for a religious organization and on December 30, 1987, the government closed the head office of CCA and deported the staff. The question remains: Why would a government take such a drastic action against a reputable religious organization? There are also valid questions about the implications of such draconian steps for the freedom of religions to protest systemic injustice and oppression. The action of the Singapore authorities was in tune with an increasing tendency of governments to monitor the activities of those religious organizations that were deemed independent and, especially, critical of the political powers.

Islamic Context

As the largest Muslim-majority country and the third-largest democracy in the world, Indonesia presents an interesting case study in gauging the interface between religion and society in Southeast Asia. The ease with which democracy is flourishing in the country is usually ascribed to the moderate forms of Islam Indonesians have adopted. Despite the country being 85 percent Muslim, it was never formally declared an Islamic state. The vast majority of Muslims in Indonesia is against fundamentalism and the interference of religion in politics. There is wide spread support for the governing principle of *pancasila*, a secular doctrine that has five principles of peaceful coexistence. Several factors—the fragmentation of Islamic authority in civil society, reforms in political institutions, and a deinstitutionalized political party system—have contributed to Islam reshaping the relationship between religion and politics. The diversity and decentralization of Islam in Indonesia too is an important factor that ensured that religion did not dictate the everyday lives of its citizens. The absence of a monopoly over Islamic authority in the country has led to the emergence of a plethora of leaders, thereby further weakening their importance and influence in public life. The diffused presence of Islam in the society also meant that various kinds of influences, including pre-Islamic beliefs and practices, contributed to shaping a largely secular-based religious response to social and political realities. While religion-based political parties are present in Indonesia, they could not take deep roots in the eclectic and democratic climate of the country. Recent years have seen the political influence of these parties and their mass organizations constantly diminished.

Social reform has also played a positive role with regard to the public face of religion in Indonesia. The status women enjoy in public life is an important factor in this regard. Thousands of students graduate every year from *pesantrens* (religious schools that impart both religious and secular education), and these are open to women also, thereby creating a space for them to formally acquire theological as well as general education. This openness has enabled the Indonesian society to be more receptive than most other Muslim-majority nations to matters of gender justice and equality. Many young people that come out of *pesantrens* are liberal and secular in their attitude, and they have become agents of change. They are also prepared to take on religious fundamentalists. The broad dynamics within civil society, state institutions, and reforms in political parties—all these factors have contributed to the emergence of moderate forms of Islam in the public life of the archipelago. The Indonesian society is a complex one ridden with problems of religious diversity, inequality, and the unemployment of youth. Yet, the country has demonstrated that Islam, democracy, modernity, and women's rights can all exist side by side.

Economic and Ecological Context

Religion is a key factor not only in the political process of Southeast Asia, but also in influencing the economic and ecological context of the region. Asian religions such as Buddhism and Hinduism find considerable value in suffering and renunciation, even in the face of extreme difficulties. There are also sections of Islam and Christianity that tend to gloss over the life of misery and suffering here on earth for the glories of a heavenly abode. In such a religious climate, it is possible for religiosity and poverty to exist side by side, without one influencing the other. The situation is further complicated because in the Southeast Asian context, institutionalized religion is often endowed with enormous wealth even as large sections of the society live in poverty. Yet, the spirit of reformation in religions has given rise to movements that identify the struggles for a just socioeconomic order as an integral part of the spiritual realm. The forces of globalization in modern times have led to situations where poverty and inequality are not only realities at the local and regional levels, but also are systemic problems at the larger level. Religious reform movements such as liberation theologies, in all the religions, focus on the need to address economic challenges at the local and global levels.

A religious response to the ecological challenges of Southeast Asia too is important. Most countries in the region are extremely vulnerable to global climate change. All are also densely populated and prone to floods, droughts, and groundwater depletion. Some, such as the Philippines and Papua New Guinea, would be devastated by a significant rise in the ocean level. Reduction in global climate change by reducing the extent of human-induced climate change, coupled with adequate domestic policies to promote climate resilience, becomes vital in such a context. The influence religions have on the Asian people needs to be a factor in ensuring the very survival of life in the region.

All across Southeast Asia, established religious hierarchies are in crisis. The demystification of the spiritual realm and a large-scale secularization process have led to a situation where the monopoly of the religious hegemonies are under threat. In most parts of the region, there are, indeed, tectonic shifts leading to the democratization of all religions. Despite all these changes, religions in Southeast Asia continue to influence the public domain, probably at a level unparalleled in the rest of the world. The role religion can play in positively influencing the political process, in ensuring a just economic order and sustainable ecology for all, therefore, becomes both a challenge and an opportunity.

Jesudas M. Athyal

See also: Buddhism; Cambodia; Christian Conference of Asia; Christianity; Colonialism; Education; Federation of Asian Bishops' Conferences; Fundamentalism; Globalization; Indonesia; Islam; Nationalism; *Pesantren*; Philippines; Reform Movements; Santi Asoke; Secularism; Sin, Cardinal Jaime Lachica; Sivaraksa, Sulak; Thailand; Women.

Further Reading

Boyd, Jeff. "The Role of the Church in the Philippines' Nonviolent People Power Revolution." Nonviolence and Christian Faith in the 20th Century. June 29, 2010. http://pacificador99.files.wordpress.com/2012/01/philippines-jeff-boyd.pdf (accessed May 12, 2014).

Buehler, Michael. "Islam and Democracy in Indonesia." *Insight Turkey* 11, no. 4 (2009): 51–63. http://www.columbia.edu/cu/weai/pdf/Insight_Turkey_2009_4_Michael_Buehler.pdf (accessed May 12, 2014).

Engineer, Asghar Ali. "Religion and Politics in Indonesia." http://andromeda.rutgers.edu/~rtavakol/engineer/indonesia.htm (accessed May 12, 2014).

Essen, Juliana M. "Santi Asoke Buddhist Reform Movement: Building Individuals, Community, and (Thai) Society." *Journal of Buddhist Ethics.* http://blogs.dickinson.edu/buddhistethics/files/2010/04/essen01.pdf (accessed May 12, 2014).

Kusalasaya, Karuna. "Buddhism in Thailand: Its Past and Its Present" http://www.accesstoinsight.org/lib/authors/kusalasaya/wheel085.html (accessed May 12, 2014).

Mydans, S. "Thailand Set to Make Buddhism the State Religion." *International Herald Tribune*, May 24, 2007.

O'Grady, Ron. *Banished: The Expulsion of the Christian Conference of Asia from Singapore and Its Implications.* Kowloon, Hong Kong: Christian Conference of Asia International Affairs Committee, 1990.

Stuart-Fox, Martin. "Buddhism and Politics in Laos, Cambodia, Myanmar and Thailand." Presented at the Cambodia, Laos, Myanmar and Thailand Summer School, Asia Pacific Week 2006, January 30, 2006. http://thaionline.anu.edu.au/_documents/ BUDDHISM_AND_POLITICS_IN_SOUTHEAST_ASIA.pdf (accessed May 12, 2014).

UST Social Research Center. *The Philippine Revolution and the Involvement of the Church.* Manila, Philippines: Social Research Center, University of Santo Tomas, 1986.

RELIGIOUS CONVERSIONS

The word "conversion" is used in almost all natural and human sciences to indicate some form of change that happens to alter an existent form into something new or different. The change can be natural or induced; it can be sudden or gradual; and it may retain or radically alter the qualities of that which undergoes change. The ambiguities that attend both the concept and the process of conversion in other areas can also be observed in religious conversions.

In the religious sphere, it is not unusual for a person to be awakened to a new understanding of the meaning of life, or to be introduced to a new set of beliefs about the nature and purpose of life, that leads him or her to move from a state of nonbelief or from a set of already accepted beliefs to a new one. In the case of Lord Buddha, for instance, while living within the Hindu ethos of his royal palace, he was awakened to a new understanding of the nature of existence and of the human predicament, which impelled him to move away from his Hindu heritage to begin a new movement, which became Buddhism. In a similar fashion, Confucius, deeply troubled by the social chaos in China at his time, decided to embark on a search for some principles to reorganize human relationships at all levels of society. His teaching eventually became Confucianism.

The teachings of both Buddha and Confucius attracted disciples, who also moved away from the beliefs that they previously held to embrace the new teachings, but in the Southeast Asian context, as also within the Hindu tradition in India, such moves to embrace new teachings are not considered conversions. In the Southeast Asian religious ethos, plurality of beliefs is not considered a problem. Someone embracing a new set of teachings or following a new teacher was not considered a "convert." Those who teach and attract new followers also do not require that their followers reject or break away from the religious traditions to which they had belonged. This meant that double or even multiple religious belonging is common in Southeast Asia. While a person follows the teachings of the Buddha, he or she might also be observing the rights and rituals of the tribal religion in their daily life.

The actual conversion experience is so internal to a person's life and experience that no one from the outside can decide whether a person converted out of his or her free will or because of subtle coercion or inducements. It is this reality that plagues the debate over conversion and religious freedom, which, despite all the arguments made from both sides, is likely to remain inconclusive.

S. Wesley Ariarajah

While having accepted the Buddhist teachings, one might continue to worship Hindu deities and be deeply influenced by the Confucian cultural ethos.

Historically there had been some skirmishes between the old and the new expressions of religious beliefs, but on the whole, conversion was not a major issue in Southeast Asia until the coming of Islam and Christianity. In the case of Buddhism and Confucianism, there are no initiation ceremonies, like baptism in Christianity, by which one "becomes" a Buddhist. There is an organized *sangha* for those who wish to join the Buddhist monastic order with ceremonies and vows attached to mark the entry into the order. But the laity is not organized into a Buddhist "church." In fact, the transformation of most of Southeast Asia to Buddhism took place gradually; the Buddhist monks were organized to spread the Buddha dhamma (dharma) among the people, but the people themselves were not separated into Buddhists and non-Buddhists.

It would appear that the strategy adopted by the Buddhist monks was not to launch a "missionary outreach" into a nation from the outside. In most cases, the monks first approached the kings of Southeast Asian countries with Buddhist teachings, highlighting the values of compassion, nonviolence, and peace. Once the rulers were convinced, they were able to spread the Buddhist teachings under royal patronage. For instance, in the eleventh century, King Anoratha of Burma (Myanmar) was convinced by the Buddhist missionaries, and he helped them to spread the teachings among his people. Similarly, at the end of the twelfth century, King Jayavarma VII of Cambodia enabled the spread of Buddhism in his land.

Even with royal patronage, Buddhism was not forced on the people. Rather, the Buddhist teachings were released into the whole nation to gradually transform the culture and the spiritual ethos of the nation to Buddhism. This transformation was not considered or named "conversions"; rather, it was considered a religious awakening by which people "embraced the teachings of the Lord Buddha." Further, Buddhism adapted itself to the culture of each of the Southeast Asian nations into which it was taken. Thus, Thai Buddhism has its own distinctive character even as Buddhisms in Myanmar, Cambodia, Vietnam, and Laos.

All this was to change radically with the advent of Islam and Christianity into Southeast Asia. Both these religions claimed to have received special revelations that were valid for all humankind. They also believed that the special revelations they have had would not "fit into" the religious traditions that were already present in Southeast Asia. Further, both traditions believed in building a closely knit community that would profess their faith to the exclusion of all other faith perspectives. In this context, conversion meant not only an inner spiritual transformation or a decision to follow a set of new beliefs; it also involved a decision to give up the beliefs that a person has had until then and to move into a new community. Since religion and culture are inseparable in Southeast Asia, those who embraced Islam or Christianity also had, to a large extent, to abandon the cultural heritage of the nation and enter a new cultural ethos of those who brought the message to them. Thus, with the coming of Islam and Christianity, the word "conversion" had new dimensions, like breaking away from the past, belonging to a new community, and developing a negative approach to the religion and culture from which one had moved. This understanding of religious conversion is alien to the Hindu and Buddhist approach to religion and may be the primary reason why missions failed in their attempt to convert India and the Buddhist-dominated parts of Southeast Asia.

This exclusive approach to what it means to belong to a religious tradition, especially the attempt to create an alternate community, met with considerable resistance in Southeast Asia. In the beginning successive kings of Siam (Thailand) barred Roman Catholic and Protestant missions from coming into Thailand to do mission work. However, the Southeast nations, including Thailand, were also interested in trade, education, and modern health care institutions, which the Western missionaries would bring into the country. Therefore, from time to time, some of the rulers relaxed the ban on mission activities. Eventually these institutions of education, health care, and economic development became the chief instruments in the hands of the missionaries to gain converts to Christianity.

Although colonization played a significant role in later years, initially both Islam and Christianity came into Southeast Asia through spice traders who brought their religion with them and propagated it. However, when the spice trade became lucrative, Western nations began to undertake political colonization of many parts of Asia. The Portuguese, Dutch, French, Spanish, and British colonized different parts of Southeast Asia, which provided new opportunity for missions to convert people to their particular brands of Christian faith, but with limited success. Eventually, much of Indonesia became Islamic, and the Philippines became Roman Catholic. But the bulk of Southeast Asia resisted the missionary efforts primarily because the Christian and Islamic understanding of conversion involved the creation of an alternate community that was discontinuous with the traditions and cultures of Southeast Asia.

Controversy over Christian and Islamic conversions continues to this day. Many continue to accuse Christians of the unethical practice of using humanitarian work in the areas of education, health care, and development as tools for conversion. In Thailand, Buddhist monks have challenged Christian attempts to indigenize the church by adopting the local music, symbols, and architecture as a ploy for conversion. In Malaysia, Muslims have an ongoing legal battle to ban Christians from using the Arabic word for God, Allah, partly for the fear that conversion to Christianity might be made easier by the belief that Christians and Muslims worshiped the same God. There is increasing pressure in some of the countries to legislate anti-conversions laws (as done in number of states in India), provoking debates on religious freedom and its abuse.

Much of the controversy over conversion today relates to the relationship between conversion and religious freedom. All nations in Southeast Asia are signatories to the United Nations Universal Declaration of Human Rights, which defines religious conversion as a human right: "Everyone has the right to freedom of thought, conscience and religion; this right includes freedom to change his religion or belief" (Article 18). Based on this declaration, the United Nations Commission on Human Rights (UNCHR) drafted the International Covenant on Civil and Political Rights, which is a legally binding treaty. It states that "Everyone shall have the right to freedom of thought, conscience and religion. This right shall include freedom to have or to adopt a religion or belief of his choice" (Article 18.1). This right is qualified to address the problem of forced or unethical conversions with the article: "No one shall be subject to coercion which would impair his freedom to have or to adopt a religion or belief of his choice" (Article 18.2).

There are, of course, many genuine conversions in Southeast Asia, where a person chooses voluntarily to move from Buddhism, Confucianism, or a tribal religion to Christianity or Islam. Christianity and Islam have some teachings, like belief in God, dignity and equality of all human beings, and an emphasis on community that are absent in Buddhist teachings, thus providing a genuinely alternate vision of religious life; and some are attracted to it. But it is also the case that services provided for humanitarian reasons become the vehicles of conversion. Therefore, even though Islam in Indonesia and Christianity in the Philippines were not forced on people in the way it was done in some other parts of the world, issues of "forced conversion," where political power is used to convert, "marital conversion," where marriage is used as a way to gain converts, and "economic conversion," where economic benefits serve as inducement to convert, are subjects that are very much alive in the conversion debates in Southeast Asia. In the scholarly world in Southeast Asia, there are discussions on the abuse of the rights given in the human rights declarations and conventions. Some have argued that by placing the emphasis on individual's right to change one's religion, the legitimate rights of communities to cohere as religious traditions have been compromised.

The aggravation against conversion to Christianity has increased mainly because of the activities of some of the Protestant evangelical groups that come from the United States and Korea and groups like the Seventh-day Adventists and Mormons who do door-to-door for evangelism. In 2007, Cambodia brought laws against going from door to door to for evangelical work and against doing anything that would serve as an inducement to convert. Vietnam deals with this problem by requiring all religious organizations and missions to register themselves with authorities responsible for religious affairs so that their activities are monitored. In Malaysia, even though the constitution provides freedom of religion to practice and propagate one's religion, it is illegal to convert a Muslim to another religious tradition. In Myanmar and Thailand, serious clashes have occurred between Christians and Buddhists and between Muslims and Buddhists over the issue of conversion. At the international level, there are attempts to develop codes of conduct for evangelism and to spell out unethical methods that should be avoided in one's attempt to propagate one's faith. These, however, have not been able to address adequately the social and cultural issues on conversion in Southeast Asia.

S. Wesley Ariarajah

See also: Buddhism; Cambodia; Christianity; Colonialism; Confucianism; Contextualization; Dharma/Dhamma; Hinduism; Interreligious Relations and Dialogue; Indonesia; Islam; Laos; Missionary Movements; Myanmar; Peace-Building; Philippines; Religious Discrimination and Intolerance; Thailand; Vietnam.

Further Reading

Camilleri, Joseph, and Sven Schottmann. *Culture, Religion and Conflict in Muslim Southeast Asia: Negotiating Tense Pluralisms.* New York: Routledge, 2012.

Finucane, Juliana, and R. Michael Feener, eds. *Proselytizing and the Limits of Religious Pluralism in Contemporary Asia.* Singapore: Springer, 2014.

Rafael, Vincent L. *Contracting Colonialism: Translation and Christian Conversion in Tagalog Society under Early Spanish Rule.* Durham, NC: Duke University Press, 2012.

Rambo, Lewis R. *Understanding Religious Conversion.* New Haven, CT: Yale University Press, 1993.

SarDesai, D. R. *Southeast Asia: Past and Present.* Boulder, CO: Westview Press, 2012.

RELIGIOUS DISCRIMINATION AND INTOLERANCE

Religious discrimination refers to unequal treatment of a person or a group based on what they do or do not believe, and religious intolerance happens when a religious or nonreligious group or a state specifically refuses to tolerate the presence of or the belief and practices of another group because of their religious identity. Discrimination can be overt or covert, informal or legalized. Discrimination and intolerance at the religious level happens mostly when a religion, which is in the majority, deals with one or many minority religious groups within the nation. Since almost all nations in Southeast Asia are multireligious to varying degrees, the question of how different religious traditions can coexist in a nation has become an important issue.

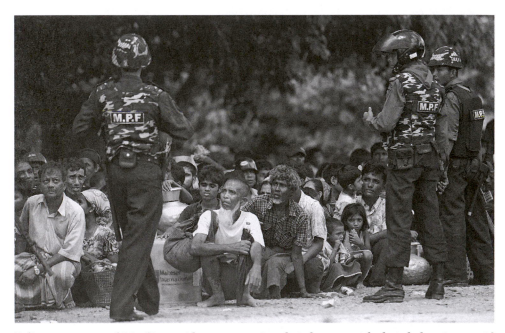

Policemen surround Muslim residents evacuating their houses with their belongings amid ongoing violence in Sittwe, the capital of Myanmar's western state of Rakhine, on June 12, 2012. Dozens of people were killed in a surge in sectarian violence in Myanmar, spurred by political and religious differences. (STR/Getty Images)

> When one sows the seeds of discrimination, it is only a matter of time before one reaps the harvest of discontent and strife. And if one practices intolerance, one is paving the way for a society that would never become a community. It is surprising that these simple truths seldom occur to those that have the responsibility to hold the community together.
>
> S. Wesley Ariarajah

Most of the countries in Southeast Asia have a dominant majority religious group with several minority religious groups among them. Most of the countries, such as Thailand, Myanmar, Cambodia, Laos, and Vietnam, have predominant Buddhist majorities with Hindu, Christian, Muslim, Sikh and Tribal minorities. Indonesia and Malaysia have Muslim majorities and the Philippines have a Christian majority, but in both there are significant numbers of other minority religious groups.

Discrimination and intolerance present two distinct problems to the Southeast Asian nations. The first is the question of the human and religious rights of individuals and groups to believe and practice their religion, which is protected by international conventions. The second relates to nation-building; religious intolerance and discrimination often leads to violent conflicts, resulting in social disruption obstructing attempts at nation-building.

Religious diversity in most Southeast Asian countries is often the result of historical developments, where the majority of the people accept a new religious tradition while some within the community choose to remain in the tradition they had belonged to. Thus, while many Southeast Asian nations adopted Buddhism, a number of tribal groups within these nations remained in their tribal religions; while the Philippines embraced Roman Catholicism under Spanish rule, a significant minority remained Muslim; in Indonesia, the majority of the population adopted Islam, but it continued to have minority Buddhists, Hindus, Christians, Confucians, and peoples with their tribal religious heritages. Minority religious groups are also created by mission activities from the outside or through population movements as in the case of Thailand, Myanmar, and other Buddhist-majority nations of Southeast Asia.

Most of the Southeast Asian nations have religious freedom written into their national constitutions and are signatories to the international charters and conventions on religious freedom. A number of them also have taken steps to promote respect for religious plurality in the interest of nation-building. The outstanding example of this is Indonesia. In 1945, President Sukarno, the first president of the postcolonial government, developed a political philosophy for the emerging new state based on the fusion of socialism, nationalism, democracy, and monotheism, called *pancasila* (five principles or values). Since the nation was made up of numerous islands, tribes, languages, and religious concentrations, Sukarno felt that a comprehensive and inclusive political ideology was needed, which should also respect the religious rights of the people. Even though there was considerable pressure from some Muslim leaders to name Islam as the religion of the state, Sukarno felt that such a move would lead to demands from some parts of Indonesia to break away.

However, in order to satisfy the Muslim majority, the *pancasila* ideology included monotheism as one of the basic principles. Under this arrangement, Indonesia named six religions as those recognized by the state—Islam, Roman Catholicism, Protestantism, Hinduism, Buddhism, and Confucianism. This was a very significant move in the largest Islamic country in the world, where about 68 percent of the population claim to profess Islam. The official recognition given to the minority religions had enabled Indonesia to hold together as a multireligious nation. However, there are complaints of discrimination against religious groups and the tribal religions that are outside the recognized six religions. More recently, especially from 1985, some Islamic groups have again begun to question the adequacy of the *pancasila* with the call for the Islamization of the country. But other Muslim groups and the powerful military continue to support a government that is based on monotheism but protects all the recognized religions.

However, both the United Nations and Amnesty International have pointed to the increasing number of violent incidents against religious minorities. In Sunni-dominated Indonesia, the Shi'a and Ahmadiyya sects of Islam also experience discrimination and violence. As political power of the extremist Islamic groups rise in Indonesia, the successive governments are walking a tightrope of not offending the Muslim majority and yet protecting the rights of other religious traditions.

Religion and ethnicity-based nationalism is another factor that leads to intolerance and discrimination in Southeast Asia, as illustrated in Myanmar. Here discrimination and violence is directed mainly against the Rohingya Islamic community and the Christians in the tribal areas. During the colonial rule, the British adopted an immigration policy that resulted in a large number of Bengali Muslims from neighboring India moving into Myanmar in search of labor. This group has been denied citizenship from the beginning, but their numbers have been on the increase, resulting in Islam, along with other Islamic groups in the country, reaching a little over 4 percent of the population. Frustrated with the continued denial of citizenship, a militant group of the Rohingya Muslims began a violent struggle for a separate state for the Muslims or for the Islamic region to be incorporated into Bangladesh, aggravating the Buddhist majority.

Christian missions, when permitted to do their mission work, strategically avoided working among the Burmese Buddhists and concentrated their work mainly among the Kachin, Chin, and Kayin tribal groups and among the Chinese migrants in Myanmar. The Christians today are also about 4 percent of the population.

Already in the 1930s, a Burman-Buddhist nationalist movement called "Doh Bama" (we Burma) arose with anti-Indian sentiments that eventually turned into an anti-Muslim campaign. In recent years, radical Buddhist movements have risen again with the view to advocate and promote the ethnic-religious identity of Myanmar and to suppress other religious minorities. A section of the Buddhist *sangha*, led by a senior abbot of the Mandalay Buddhist Monastery, Bikkhu Wirathu, founded the 969 economic-nationalist campaign, which encouraged Buddhists to shop only in Buddhist stores. The number, signifying the nine attributes of the Buddha, six of the dharma, and nine of the *sangha*, was intended to preserve the

Buddhist identity and heritage of Myanmar against what is considered "Islamic encroachment." The movement eventually led to violent clashes in which hundreds of Muslims were killed and mosques and homes destroyed, leading to international condemnation. The Christian minorities also reported sustained harassment and violence against them, resulting in loss of life and property.

Buddhist-Muslim tension is also on the rise in Thailand, where Buddhism is the established religion; about 95 percent of the population is Buddhist. However, in the deep south of Thailand, there is a large Muslim minority group that has been in conflict with the rulers in Bangkok for centuries. Even though only 4.6 percent of the Thai population is Islamic, in the southern provinces of Patani, Narathiwat, Satun, and Songkha, Muslims constitute about 75–85 percent of the population. Further, the Muslims in the south are culturally different from the Thai Buddhists and speak the language of the neighboring Malays. Historically, the successive Thai governments have tried to assimilate and integrate this Islamic region, but the Muslims have been struggling to get political recognition and even a possible separate state for themselves through political insurgency. The conflicts that ensured have led to brutal violent acts and death of thousands of citizens from both sides. Today some serious steps are underway to find a political compromise, but isolated conflicts continue.

Malaysia is also a multireligious state, but with about 65 percent of the population following the Islamic faith. Even though the Malaysian constitution stipulates Islam as the "Religion of the Federation," it also guarantees freedom of religion to minorities. The nearly 40 percent of communities of other faiths belonging to Buddhism, Christianity, Hinduism, Sikhism, and Daoism until recent years have had considerable religious freedom. The government has also been taking several steps to promote multiculturalism and tolerance.

However, with the rise of militant Islam in many parts of the world and pressures from the outside on the Malayan Muslims to assert their national identity, there is increasing deterioration of religious freedom. Successive governments are caught between preserving their electoral majority by pleasing the increasingly militant Muslim groups, and their commitment to ensure religious freedom to all religions. Under militant Islamic pressure, the government of Malaysia has now issued new restrictions on visas to foreign clergy, limiting their entry to six months. The foreign clergy already in the country have also been given an extension of six months to their visas, with the requirement that they leave the country when the visas expire. The hard-line Pan-Malaysian Islamic Party, now in the opposition, has been putting pressure to introduce the Islamic *shari'a* law as the common law, even though Malaysia already allows for religion-based laws for family, marriage, and inheritance.

There has also been a long dispute between Christians and Muslims over the use of the Arabic word "Allah" for God. Christians from the beginning have been referring to God as Allah, and translations of the Bible into Malay also refer to God as Allah. The sustained campaign by Muslim groups to ban Christians from using the word has resulted recently in the court ruling that the word can be used only by Muslims. Mutual animosity over the issue has resulted in a number of violent acts against Christians and their property.

It should be noted that successive governments of Malaysia and neighboring Singapore see the importance of interreligious harmony and the protection of the religious rights of all communities as the cornerstone of national stability and economic prosperity. In fact, social stability has truly been an important factor in their economic advancement. Therefore, both countries have government departments that undertake programs to promote interfaith dialogue and multiculturalism. In Malaysia, however, political pressure from radical Islamic groups is on the increase, with unknown consequences for the future.

It should be noted that majority of the people in Southeast Asia are at home with religious plurality; Buddhism, which is the prominent religion in Southeast Asia, places enormous emphasis on nonviolence, tolerance, and respect for all forms of life. However, ethnicity-based nationalisms, economic pressures, and political maneuvers contribute to rising cases of religious discrimination and intolerance. Excessive enthusiasm for mission among some Christian and Muslim groups also gives room to the feeling of being "encroached" in some of the majority-Buddhist nations. The revival of Islam in many parts of the world, especially in its militant forms, also plays an important role. On the one hand, it radicalizes the Islamic community with the call to assert themselves where they are in majority. On the other hand, this new self-assertion creates a fear of Islam even in nations where Islam is only a small minority.

Happily, in almost all the countries of Southeast Asia, the respective governments realize that discrimination and intolerance would destabilize the nations and are therefore establishing institutions to promote relationships between religious communities. Sectors within the various religious traditions also take initiatives for interfaith relations and dialogue. Hope for peace and harmony in many Southeast Asian nations depends on intensifying and strengthening these initiatives.

S. Wesley Ariarajah

See also: Ahmadiyya; Buddhism; Cambodia; Christianity; Colonialism; Confucianism; Ethnicity; Freedom of Religion; Fundamentalism; Hinduism; Indonesia; Interreligious Relations and Dialogue; Islam; Laos; Minorities; Missionary movements; Morality; Nationalism; Philippines; Religious Conversions; Singapore; Thailand; Vietnam.

Further Reading

Friend, Theodore, ed. *Religion and Religiosity in the Philippines and Indonesia: Essays on State, Society, and Public Creeds.* Baltimore: Johns Hopkins University Press, 2006.

Hefner, Robert W. *Politics of Multiculturalism: Pluralism and Citizenship in Malaysia, Singapore, and Indonesia.* Honolulu: University of Hawaii Press, 2001.

Liow, Joseph Chinyong. *Muslim Resistance in Southern Thailand and Southern Philippines: Religion, Ideology, and Politics.* Washington, DC: East-West Center, 2006.

Liow, Joseph Chinyong. *Piety and Politics: Islamism in Contemporary Malaysia.* New York: Oxford University Press, 2009.

Ramage, Douglas E. *Politics in Indonesia: Democracy, Islam and the Ideology of Tolerance.* London: Routledge, 1995.

Reid, Anthony. *Imperial Alchemy: Nationalism and Political Identity in Southeast Asia.* Cambridge: Cambridge University Press, 2009.

RITUAL DYNAMICS

In order to understand political, historical, cultural, social, or religious processes and how certain societies function, it is crucial to deal with ritual, because ritual reproduces relationships that are fundamental for society to work. This is particularly true for socio-cosmic societies in which social and cosmological relations intervene (Barraud and Platenkamp 1990; Sprenger 2006).

Guido Sprenger (2006, 52, 68, 69) defines ritual as actions a society accepts as being operative in creating and maintaining relationships between people themselves and people and the cosmos. Rituals are used as "instruments" to communicate, be it within a given society, with another society, or with spirits, gods, and ancestors. Ritual consequently is vital for the reproduction of society. Additionally, it is important to note that if one wants to analyze ritual, dimensions such as religion, social morphology, or ethnicity usually also will come into play. At the same time, ritual systems are not static, but flexible to adjust to changing circumstances; repetition may be one important feature of ritual actions, but just as important is the changing over time. Thus, "dynamics" in its generally understood meaning—connoting movement, transformation, or change—is often seen as a quality of ritual. Bruce Kapferer describes the connection between ritual and dynamics as being so strong that he does not define "dynamics" as the opposite of "statics," but as processes which are inherent to ritual (Kapferer 2006, 507).

This entry will look at the inner dynamics of ritual, in forms such as changes in ritual action, in terms of its connection with the second dimension of ritual dynamics: the interaction of ritual with other systems. Anthropological theories of history will also be utilized here, although in a somewhat sketchy and loose manner. Originally, the role of ritual in society was seen as rather static. Emile Durkheim (1858–1917) dealt with Aboriginal totemic rituals in Australia and explained how individuals are integrated into groups by conducting rituals on a regular basis and how this kind of ritual is intended to establish ties between the sacred and the profane worlds. Marcel Mauss (1873–1950) and Henri Hubert then closely analyzed how sacrifices were carried out. They understood rituals as collective systems, as *total social facts*, and therefore concluded that ritual does not necessarily have to be religious, but that it is likely to have political, economic, social, and cultural dimensions. Bronislaw Malinowski (1884–1942) focused more on the psychological dimension of ritual; i.e., that magic rituals reduce social tensions. The function of ritual was examined closely, and ritual obviously helps to create and maintain social coherence and harmony (see Bell 1997, 23–26, 28).

In contrast, Max Gluckman (1911–1975) investigated "rituals of rebellion" and demonstrated that ritual also expresses social tensions. He stated that ritual not only depicts social relationships, but actually forms them. Gluckman wrote in the tradition of Arnold van Gennep (1873–1957) who with his analysis of "rites de passage" heralded the contemplation of the dependence of social change and ritual. Victor Turner (1920–1983) developed these approaches further by examining the symbolism of rituals as a motor for changes in the socio-cosmic order. He paved the way for portraying ritual as a performance (see Bell 1997, 35–39, 42; Kapferer 2006, 511). Edmund Leach (1910–1989) used a linguistic model to present ritual as a mechanism for sociocultural change. He argued that ritual not only integrates people, but can also exclude them and that it often depicts ideal structures of society (see Bell 1997, 65, 68; Leach 1970 [1954], 278). Clifford Geertz (1926–2006), sharing this approach in his description of the cockfight in Bali, pointed out that ritual display can make experiences understandable. Furthermore, it forms the way the world is perceived. Ritual in all these theories communicates and molds ideas and values (see Bell 1997, 66, 67, 69). Likewise, it negotiates social, ethnic, and cultural identity. As Leach (1970 [1954]) stressed, it articulates and forms social hierarchies and power relations. One example is the Lao state, which uses Buddhist rituals to maintain and gain influence over the people. After the abolition of the monarchy in 1975, the new regime first tried to forbid religious activities, but since the 1980s, the ruling party has been slowly reestablishing religious rituals. Other examples include rituals conducted by ethnic groups in which a village is closed and nobody is allowed to enter or leave. Often, traditional dress is worn and sacrifices are made. On the inside, the coherence of society is articulated and enhanced. On the outside, the importance of borders is stressed (as an instance for Karen in Myanmar or Thailand; see Hayami 2004).

Power relations between state and ethnic groups also are visible when one considers the interaction between different religious systems. In Southeast Asia, the most fascinating ritual dynamics can be examined in relation to the communication between local belief systems and "world religions." In the case of Sri Lanka, Myanmar, Thailand, Laos, and Cambodia, the "world religion" is Theravada Buddhism. This includes the *su:khuan* ritual, which restores a balance of the body by tying the "soul" (Thai and Lao *khuan*) with cotton threads. This ritual mixes elements of Buddhism with those of local cosmologies. The dynamics of ritual systems can also be analyzed in multireligious rituals. An example is the interaction of Buddhism, Islam, and ancestor worship in South Thailand (see Horstmann 2011). Besides revitalizing processes, conversion processes in Southeast Asia can be traced. In the context of conversion, Josephus Platenkamp (1992) demonstrates how the Tobelo in eastern Indonesia, who officially converted to Christianity, conduct church rituals with recourse to pre-Christian ideas and values.

Thus, whether one deals with the dynamics of different religious systems or the interplay between ritual and kinship, social system, myth, identity, ethnicity, or changing ritual performances, "dynamics" always need to be taken into account when studying "ritual," in both socio-cosmic or "modern" societies.

Eva Sevenig

See also: Ancestor Worship; Buddhism; Christianity; Ethnicity; Myth/Mythology; Popular Religion; Spirit Mediumship.

Further Reading

Barraud, Cécile, and Josephus D. M. Platenkamp. "Rituals and the Comparison of Societies." *Bijdragen tot de Taal-, Land- en Volkenkunde* 146 (1990): 103–23.

Bell, Catherine. *Ritual: Perspectives and Dimensions.* Oxford: Oxford University Press, 1997.

Hayami, Yoko. *Between Hills and Plains. Power and Practice in Socio-Religious Dynamics among Karen.* Kyoto Area Studies on Asia: Center for Southeast Asian Studies, Kyoto University 7. Melbourne: Kyoto University Press, 2004.

Holt, John Clifford. *Spirits of the Place: Buddhism and Lao Religious Culture*. Honolulu: University of Hawaii Press, 2009.

Horstmann, Alexander. "Performing Multi-Religious Ritual in Southern Thailand." MMG working paper 11-05. Max Planck Institute for the Study of Religious and Ethnic Diversity, 2011. http://www.mmg.mpg.de/fileadmin/user_upload/documents/wp/WP _11-05_Horstmann_Performing-Multi-Religious-Ritual-in-Southern-Thailand.pdf (accessed September 23, 2014).

Kapferer, Bruce. "Ritual Dynamics." In *Theorizing Rituals: Issues, Topics, Approaches, Concepts*. Edited by Jens Kreinath, Jan Snoek, and Michael Stausberg. Leiden/Bristol: Brill, 2006.

Leach, Edmund R. *Political Systems of Highland Burma: A Study of Kachin Social Structure*. London School of Economics Monographs on Social Anthropology No 44. London: University of London and the Athlone Press, 1970 [1954].

Platenkamp, Josephus D. M. "Transforming Tobelo Ritual." In *Understanding Rituals*, edited by Daniel de Coppet, 74–96. London: Routledge, 1992.

Prager, Michael. "Structure, Process, and Performance in Eastern Indonesia Rituals: A Review Article." *Anthropos* 87 (1992): 548–55.

Sprenger, Guido. "The End of Rituals. A Dialogue between Theory and Ethnography in Laos." *Paideuma* 52 (2006): 51–72.

Swearer, Donald K. *The Buddhist World of Southeast Asia*. 2nd ed. Chiang Mai, Thailand: Silkworm Books, 2009.

RUIZ, LORENZO

St. Lorenzo Ruiz is the first Filipino saint, also considered as patron saint of Filipinos and the Philippines, having been martyred in Japan after refusing to renounce his Christian faith under pain of severe torture and execution by the authorities.

Ruiz was born in Binondo, Manila, around 1600 to a Chinese father and a Filipina mother. He received his education from the Dominicans in his parish and served as an altar boy. Later, he became a helper and clerk-sacristan in the church of Binondo and was also a member of the Confraternity of the Rosary. As a grown man, sources claimed that he worked as an "escriba" or calligrapher, transcribing birth, baptismal, and marriage certificates in beautiful penmanship. In 1636, he was implicated in a murder case. Already in his 30s, with a wife and three children, Ruiz must have known he stood no chance to obtain justice in the Spanish colony's courts. He asked for help from his Dominican patrons, who then included him among the group of Fray Domingo Ibanez, who at the time was going on a missionary mission. Ruiz at first thought that they were going to Taiwan, but the group was actually headed for Nagasaki, Japan, where Christians were being persecuted under the Tokugawa Shogunate.

Upon their arrival in Japan in 1636, Ruiz and his companions were arrested almost immediately. For more than a year, their Japanese captors subjected them to torture. They were tied upside down by their feet and dropped in a dry well, which had sharp stakes lining the bottom. Before they could be impaled, their torturers would stop the fall and demand that they renounce their faith. They were subjected to water torture. Bamboo needles were inserted in their fingernails.

Instead of giving in to the pain of prolonged torture, Ruiz was quoted as saying that he would never do it. He added that he was a Catholic and happy to die for God and that, even if he had a thousand lives to offer, he would offer them to God. He said this even if the Japanese authorities promised him release from prison and repatriation to the Philippines. Ruiz remained staunch in his faith.

On September 22, 1637, the Japanese authorities brought Ruiz and his 15 companions to a hill overlooking the bay of Nagasaki. Head wounds were inflicted on each of the missionaries, and they were hung upside down with their heads inside the well. In the next seven days, they died one by one, either from loss of blood or asphyxiation. Ruiz died on September 29, 1637. Pope John Paul II beatified Ruiz on February 18, 1981, in Manila, the first beatification to be held outside of the Vatican. On October 18, 1987, Ruiz was elevated to sainthood in Rome.

George Amurao

See also: Christianity; Education; Freedom of Religion; Philippines; Religious Discrimination and Intolerance.

Further Reading

"About San Lorenzo." Chapel of San Lorenzo Ruiz. http://www.chapelofsanlorenzoruiz.org/life.html (accessed May 12, 2014).

"St. Lorenzo Ruiz and Companions." American Catholic. http://www.americancatholic.org/Features/Saints/saint.aspx?id=1146 (accessed May 12, 2014).

"St. Lorenzo Ruiz." Catholic Online. http://www.catholic.org/saints/saint.php?saint_id=231 (accessed May 12, 2014).

S

SANTI ASOKE

Santi Asoke is a Buddhist sect in Thailand. It was established in the early 1970s by a group of followers to a monk called Bodhiraksa (b. 1934). Bodhiraksa's lay name was Mongkol "Rak" Rakpong, and he was a famous TV entertainer. Santi Asoke is controversial due to its strict adherence to vegetarian (vegan) and ascetic practices. The Asoke group differs from Thai Buddhism by rejecting magico-animistic rituals; the monks do not distribute Buddha amulets, sprinkle "holy water," or engage in fortune-telling. In the beginning, the group had no Buddha images in the temples. These practices led to the accusation that the group was "heretic." Bodhiraksa was also accused of deviating from the interpretations of Buddhist Pali concepts, and in 1975, the highest Buddhist state authority in Thailand, the Council of Elders (*mahatherasamakhom*), forced Bodhiraksa to disrobe. Bodhiraksa refused and started to ordain his own followers; the entire group hence became nominally outlawed by the state.

One of the major controversies has remained vegetarianism. The mainstream Buddhists argue that Buddha never declared that his monks must be vegetarians. Asoke monks argue that the first Buddhist Precept (*sila*) encourages practitioners to refrain from destroying life.

The name Santi Asoke refers to their urban temple and community in Bangkok. Asoke group runs about 10 villages around the country, Pathom Asoke in Nakhon Pathom, Sisa Asoke in Sisaket, Sima Asoke in Nakhon Ratchasima, Sali Asoke in Nakhon Sawan, Racthathani Asoke in Ubon Ratchathani, and Lanna Asoke in Chiang Mai are among the largest ones. About 50–100 lay people live in each Asoke village, grow organic vegetables and rice, and prepare herbal shampoos, detergents, and medicines. All the villages have public schools with about 50 to 100 students who study ordinary primary school, secondary school, or high school subjects as well as more practical vocational skills such as agriculture and herbal products, skills that they can support themselves with in the future.

The Asoke group consists of approximately 100 monks and 25 nuns known as *sikkhamats*. These numbers have remained stable for the last 20 years. The monks are called *samana*, as the Pali word *bhikkhu* and Thai word *phra* are reserved for the state Buddhist monks. The nuns are Ten-Precept nuns, which means that they follow Ten Buddhist Precepts and rely financially on the community support for their survival, as they—like the Asoke monks—are not allowed to use money. The monks and the nuns eat only one vegetarian meal a day before noon; no breakfast, and nothing else but pure water in the afternoon, contrary to many mainstream monks who eat a breakfast and a lunch, and in the afternoon drink yoghurt and other milk products. The monks and the nuns walk barefoot the whole day—not only on the alms round—and they live in very modest wooden huts (*kutis*). Hundreds of lay people live permanently in the Asoke villages and communities, and additionally there are many regular supporters of the Asoke group, people who may have attended one or two of the annual weeklong retreats in the villages. There are no membership cards; hence it is impossible to give any precise numbers. The Asoke people are often recognizable with their blue peasant pajamas, which symbolize their modesty and search for simplicity.

In the late 1980s, the Asoke group was involved in a court case when their most prominent lay supporter, Major General Chamlong Srimuang (b. 1935), while governor of Bangkok, established his own political party, *Palang Dharma* (The Power of Righteousness) and was planning to be a candidate for the Parliament. The state Buddhist *sangha* criticized the Asoke group's practices for years, and in 1989, the Asoke monks and nuns were detained. The nuns were released, but the monks were accused of being bogus monks, and they were forced to wear white robes symbolizing their lay status. They were not allowed to go for their alms rounds as they were not legally "monks." The court case lasted until the end of 1995, and the court sentenced the Asoke monks to a suspended sentence of two years. After two years, the Asoke monks changed back to their brown robes and continued their activities.

The sect has grown its own vegetables and rice since the 1970s and is practically self-sufficient in terms of food production. Asoke people refer to E. F. Schumacher's book, *Small Is Beautiful: Economics as if People Mattered* (1973), and particularly to the chapter "Buddhist Economics," where Schumacher argues that Buddhist

Anti-government demonstrators and members of the Santi Asoke sect, carrying blue flags, march in the Thai capital of Bangkok on March 14, 2006. Over 100,000 people turned out to protest against the government of former Prime Minister Thaksin Shinawatra. (Yvan Cohen/Getty Images)

economics must, due to Buddhist teachings, be based on the modest use of natural resources, minimum consumption, and self-sufficiency. After the Thai currency collapsed in 1997, "sufficiency economy" became a catchword in Thailand, promoted by the state. Santi Asoke's lifestyle became suddenly popular, and thousands of Thais and foreigners visited Asoke villages to learn about organic farming and "sufficiency economy." The Asoke version of "sufficiency economy" is called "meritism" (*bunniyom*), placing spiritual merit (*bun*) before profits.

When the telecom tycoon Thaksin Shinawatra was elected as prime minister in 2001, the Asoke people warmly supported him, mainly because he was regarded as a protégée of Chamlong. One of Thaksin's poverty-alleviating policies was to grant farmers a debt moratorium for three years and to require that the indebted farmers attended a training course, for instance, in an Asoke village. From 2001 to 2008, hundreds of thousands of Thai farmers were trained in organic farming in Asoke villages. The trainees received simultaneously daily preaching on vegetarianism, modesty, and self-sacrifice. New villages were established to accommodate all the training courses. The courses started to wind down when Chamlong broke up with Thaksin and the Asoke people joined the anti-Thaksin demonstrations in 2006 under the name Dhamma Army (*Kongthub Dharm*), which is an Asoke foundation responsible for the maintenance of vehicles. By turning against Thaksin, the Asoke group alienated itself from the pro-Thaksin rural population whom they had tried to help with their teachings.

Despite the political turmoil in Thailand, the Asoke group continues its work in organic farming, selling the surplus in their cooperatives in Bangkok and other cities. They run vegetarian restaurants, of which particularly the one in Chiang Mai is hugely popular. The Asoke group runs schools in several centers and the Asoke people are busy in publishing their weekly and monthly magazines and journals and in running their own TV channel called "For Mankind TV" (FMTV).

Marja-Leena Heikkilä-Horn

See also: Bhikkhu, Buddhadasa; Buddhism; Education; Reform Movements; Religion and Society; Thailand.

Further Reading

Heikkilä-Horn, Marja-Leena. *Santi Asoke Buddhism and Thai State Response*. Turku, Finland: Åbo Akademi University Press, 1996.

Heikkilä-Horn, Marja-Leena. "Santi Asoke Buddhism and the Occupation of Bangkok International Airport." *ASEAS: Austrian Journal of Southeast Asian Studies* 3, no. 1 (2010): 31–47.

Heikkilä-Horn, Marja-Leena, and Rassamee Krisanamis, eds. *Insight into Santi Asoke*. Bangkok: Fah Aphai Publishing Company, 2002.

SANTO, IGNACIA DEL ESPIRITU

The Venerable Ignacia del Espiritu Santo, also known as Mother Ignacia, was a Filipino Catholic Religious Sister who founded the Congregation of the Sisters of the Religious of the Virgin Mary (now known as the Religious of the Virgin Mary), considered as the first Filipino female congregation recognized by the Vatican. Mother Ignacia was declared venerable by Pope Benedict XVI in 2007.

Ignacia was born to a Chinese father from Amoy and a Filipina mother in Binondo, Manila, on February 1, 1663, and was baptized in the Church of the Holy Kings of Parian. Growing up as the eldest of four children, she had shown the traditional qualities of a daughter obedient to her parents' wishes. However, when told that she was expected to get married at the age of 21, Venerable Ignacia asked the Jesuit priest Father Paul Klein, who was a family friend and her spiritual adviser, for guidance. He gave her the Spiritual Exercises of St. Ignatius of Loyola. After spending time meditating during a retreat, Ignacia decided to enter the religious life and left her parents' home with only a needle and a pair of scissors.

During her time, the Spanish Catholic authorities prohibited Filipinos from becoming priests or nuns. Ignacia lived alone in a house near the Colegio Jesuita de Manila, headquarters of the Jesuits in the Philippines. Her self-imposed monastic life, marked by spiritual devotion and labor, attracted many followers among Filipinas. She accepted them, leading them in prayer and penance, performing many acts of public devotions, and receiving the sacraments at the church of St. Ignatius in the walled city of Manila. They also taught street children and less fortunate Filipinas. Though they have not yet received official recognition, their group became known as the *Beatas dela Compania de Jesus* (Blesseds of the Friends of Jesus). The "beatas," as the members came to be called, performed labor such as sewing and even begged for alms and for their food. Venerable Ignacia drew inspiration from the life of St. Mary and set an example before her congregation.

To gain recognition for her congregation, Venerable Ignacia wrote a history of her congregation and composed a constitution, and submitted them for approval in 1726. By 1732, the Archdiocese of Manila proclaimed official recognition of the *Beatas dela Compania de Jesus*. Soon after, Venerable Ignacia stepped down as mother superior and lived as an ordinary nun. In 1748, the archbishop of Manila recommended her group to the Spanish king for royal patronage. Two months later, she died at the age of 85 on September 10, 1748.

With the approval of Pope Benedict XVI on July 6, 2007, Manila archbishop Cardinal Gaudencio Rosales presided over the promulgation that officially accorded to Mother Ignacia the title "Venerable" at the Minor Basilica of San Lorenzo Ruiz in Binondo, Manila.

George Amurao

See also: Christianity; Philippines; Women; Women's Monastic Communities.

Further Reading

Darang, Josephine. " 'Venerable' Mother Ignacia del Espiritu Santo." *Philippine Daily Inquirer*, July 15, 2007. http://showbizandstyle.inquirer.net/lifestyle/lifestyle/view/20070715 -76678/Venerable-Mother-Ignacia-del-Espiritu-Santo (accessed May 12, 2014).

"Mother Ignacia del Espiritu Santo." Chapel of San Lorenzo Ruiz. http://www .chapelofsanlorenzoruiz.org/f/About_Mother_Ignacia.pdf (accessed May 12, 2014).

SATHYA SAI BABA MOVEMENT

The Indian miracle-working guru, Sathya Sai Baba, was one of the spiritual figures who had an influence on the religious scenario of Southeast Asia. Born on November 25, 1926, Sathya Sai Baba was among modern India's most renowned religious figures. During his lifetime, he attracted a following both in India and overseas. In Southeast Asia, interest in Sai Baba grew rapidly during the 1970s and became particularly intense among the Indian minority in Malaysia and also in Singapore, Thailand, Vietnam, and the Philippines.

Sai Baba was born into a non-Brahmin family of the *kshatriya* caste in the village of Puttaparthi, Andhra Pradesh, India, and was called Sathya Narayana Raju at birth. At 34 years of age, he claimed he would live another 59 years (until he was 94 years old) but he died aged 84 in March 2011, though some have explained the discrepancy as due to his reckoning according to lunar rather than solar years.

According to his biographers, Sai Baba's birth and early childhood were marked by miracles and mysterious events. Then, as a young teenager, he had a seizure but recovered quickly and afterward called his family and neighbors to his bedside and declared himself to be Sathya Sai Baba (Sai Baba of truth). With this, he was claiming to be the reincarnation of the Maharashtran ascetic saint Sai Baba of Shirdi, who died in 1918. He later explained that eight years after his death, there would be a third Sai Baba incarnation, Prema Sai Baba (Sai Baba of love).

Devotees have published various accounts of his miraculous cures and materializations of gold rings and trinkets, but his most common feat was to manifest sacred ash known as *vibhuti* by means of a circular movement of his right hand. This ash would be given to devotees, often for medicinal use. Belief in Sai Baba's paranormal powers became the hallmark of a devotee. Although he only once left India to visit his Gujarati devotees in Africa, many traveled to his ashram in Puttaparthi in order to experience one of his twice-daily appearances known as *darshan*, at which devotees could participate in the Divine by meeting the gaze of their Lord.

Sai Baba developed an ambiguous appearance that combined erotic and ascetic symbolism. He wore long robes, usually of the ascetic color orange or occasionally white, and the fabric could be glistening silk; but his lifestyle was modeled on that of the ascetic. He never married and spent his time in meditation or by giving blessings. His hair had an "Afro" appearance—neither long and matted like Hindu renunciants, nor neat and oiled like ordinary Indian men.

This ambiguous symbolism evidently appealed to the predicament of cosmopolitan overseas Indians who sought to reaffirm their Hindu identity without foregoing

---

The cofounder of the Hard Rock Café and the House of Blues, Isaac Tigrett, is one of Sai Baba's better-known devotees. He donated a large sum of money to enable the construction of the multispecialist hospital in Puttaparthi. At the age of 60, he moved into an apartment in Puttaparthi. Since Sai Baba's death in 2011, the economy of Puttaparthi has suffered a major decline but Tigrett is devising ways aimed at the overall development of the region.

Alexandra Kent

the comforts of modern life. The fact that Hinduism is seen by devotees as the original source of universal truth and of a modern, omnipotent God incarnate re-ennobles Indian culture and offers a readily accessible avenue to divine power. However, the public presentation of the movement as an interfaith organization promoting national unity and charity makes it politically palatable in the predominantly Muslim countries of Southeast Asia.

Sai Baba began to attract a following in India as a young man, but the number of devotees increased significantly, both in India and overseas, from the 1960s onward. During the 1970s, the movement was starting to become formalized. The movement has attracted influential devotees from politics, business, the sciences, and the professions. According to the International Sai Organisation website (http://www.sathyasai.org/default.htm), there are now 1,200 registered Sai Baba centers in 126 countries. Some 35 centers and 13 so-called devotional groups have been noted in Malaysia (see Kent 2005) and 17 in Singapore (see http://sathyasai. org.sg/sssos/singapore-sai-centres/). However, it is difficult to know how many devotees there are since many people worship Sai Baba privately, without registering as members or attending the centers. This is particularly pertinent to the question of Muslim devotees, for whom overt participation in non-Muslim worship is attended by considerable risk.

The organization, with its headquarters in Puttaparthi, is pyramidally structured with regional, national, and local chairpersons. In order to become registered, a center is required to have a chairperson, secretary, and treasurer and to provide worship, spiritual education, and charity activities. Support is through anonymous donations, and there are no membership fees. In Puttaparthi, the organization has sponsored the construction of a school, a college, and a large hospital. The movement has prompted some controversy. At least one organization in India has gone to some lengths to discredit Sai Baba by releasing films showing the guru performing "faked" materializations and books that contradict some of the devotees' miracle claims. Rumors have also circulated about Sai Baba sexually abusing devotees. In general, however, the movement has weathered the storms well.

The growing interest in Sai Baba in the 1970s coincided with the heightening of Islamic consciousness in Malaysia, and it was around this time that Malaysian middle-class Indians and some Malaysian Chinese began to develop what was to become a renowned Sai Baba organization in their country. Here, the movement grew strong under the leadership of middle-class, politically well-connected Indians, and some Chinese. Many of these Indians grew up under a strong British and Christian influence and now aspire to rekindle their Hindu identity while also cleansing it of association with the folk practices such as blood sacrifice, spirit possession, and firewalking that have been common among the Indian plantation laborers, who also arrived in Malaya under British colonial rule.

It is illegal in Malaysia both for Malay/Muslims to engage in any non-Muslim religious activity and for non-Muslims to proselytize among Malays. Attempts to influence the ruling Malays should therefore avoid phrasing themselves in terms of religion, ethnicity, and politics. It is against this background that the equivocality of the Sai Baba movement creates room for maneuver. The Malaysian Organization proclaimed itself to be an ecumenical body that aspired to assist the government in nurturing national unity and it developed an "ABC programme" (Action for Betterment of the Community) and a Friendship Group, ostensibly to promote interracial and interreligious harmony. This format also enabled Chinese and Indians to establish a politically unproblematic forum for solidarity. In theory, this public presentation allowed Malay Muslims to participate alongside their Indian and Chinese compatriots in performing community service. In reality, however, although some Malays are said to have experienced Sai Baba's miracles, their participation in the movement has been minimal and largely clandestine.

While it outwardly stresses universal values, the movement privately elevates Hinduism over other religions. For example, Sai Baba education programs set up by devotees usually promote a set of "universal human values"—*prema, shanti, ahimsa, sathya,* and dharma (love, peace, nonviolence, truth, and duty)—which, although they are said to underlie all religions, are ultimately seen to derive from Hinduism. Similarly, Sai Baba altars in Malaysia, as elsewhere, tend to display images and symbols from several of the world religions, including Islam, and include a picture of Sai Baba or his feet. However, the fact that *vibhuti* ash is said to appear miraculously on some of these altars and the fact that worship at the Sai Baba centers tends to follow the format of Hindu *puja* ritual again gives Hinduism primacy. Prayers include offerings of flowers to the image of Sai Baba, the chanting of Sanskrit mantras, the singing of devotional songs (*bhajans*) in Sanskrit and other languages, the recitation of prayers and the offering of burning camphor to the altar, and the distribution of *vibhuti* ash to the congregation. Overall, Sai Baba's own personhood and this way of using symbolism and ritual has enabled many Indians in Muslim Southeast Asia to reassert their Hindu identity to the Muslim majority in a politically and ethnically convivial format. During his lifetime, Sai Baba's claim to be a universal godhead thus helped redignify Indian culture for Indians in Southeast Asia and elsewhere, allowing them to claim that "God lives in India."

Alexandra Kent

See also: Contextualization; Diaspora; Ethnicity; Hinduism; Interreligious Relations and Dialogue; Popular Religion.

Further Reading

Babb, L. "Sathya Sai Baba's Magic." *Anthropological Quarterly* 56, no. 3 (1983): 116–24.

Bowen, D. *The Sathya Sai Baba Community in Bradford: Its Origin and Development, Religious Beliefs and Practices.* Monograph Series, Community Religions Project, Leeds: Department of Theology and Religious Studies, University of Leeds, 1988.

Kasturi, N. *Sathyam, Sivan, Sundaram: The Life Story of Bhagavan Sri Sathya Sai Baba.* 3 vols. Prasanthi Nilayam, A.P.: Sri Sathya Sai Books and Publications Trust, 1973–1975.

Kent, A. *Divinity and Diversity: A Hindu Revitalization Movement in Malaysia.* Copenhagen: NIAS Press, 2005.

Klass, M. *Singing with Sai Baba: The Politics of Revitalisation in Trinidad.* Boulder, CO: Westview Press, 1991. Reprint, Prospect Heights, IL: Waveland Press, 1996.

Pereira, Shane N. "A New Religious Movement in Singapore: Syncretism and Variation in the Sathya Sai Baba Movement." *Asian Journal of Social Science* 36 (2008) 250–70.

http://www.academia.edu/232635/A_New_Religious_Movement_in_Singapore_Syncretism
_and_Variation_in_the_Sathya_Sai_Baba_Movement (accessed May 12, 2014).
Swallow, D. A. "Ashes and Powers: Myth, Rite and Miracle in an Indian God-man's Cult."
Modern Asian Studies 16 (1982): 123–58.

SAYADAW, MAHASI

Born in Seikkam, Upper Burma, in 1904, the Venerable Mahasi Sayadaw (1904–1982) is highly revered as one of the great Theravada Buddhist meditation monks of his age, whose influence stretched well beyond the borders of Myanmar (Burma) into Asia and the Western world. Emphasizing the practical element of insight meditation, Sayadaw's teaching provided techniques for everyday practitioners to use in their pursuit of enlightenment. Following his death in 1982, Sayadaw's teaching continues to inspire generations of Buddhist practitioners.

Sayadaw was enrolled at the local monastery at the age of six and was initiated as a young novice at the age of 12, at which stage he was given the name Shin Sobana. At age 19, he elected to become ordained within the priestly Order, devoting himself to the study of Theravada texts, passing the rigorous government examinations required of all Buddhist monks. Excelling in the study of scriptures, he became known in 1941 as Mahasi Sayadaw, teaching vipassanā (insight) meditation at the Monastery in Seikkham, concentrating his efforts on combining scriptural knowledge with the teaching of meditation practice. In accordance with the teaching of the Buddha, Sayadaw believed that for any teaching to be effective, it must be put into practice. If a teaching proved to be beneficial, then it should be accepted, and if not, it should be discarded. The Mahasi wrote a comprehensive and widely circulated manual that dynamically combined both doctrinal and practical aspects of meditation.

Following the Independence of Myanmar in 1948, Sayadaw was invited to Rangoon to become the guardian of Myanmar's largest lay meditation center, the Mahasi Thathana Yeithka. This center was established to help revitalize the wisdom of the Buddha's teaching in order to help purify the state and society from moral decline. Within the center, monks serve as teachers and guides to the laity, who come to actively practice insight meditation techniques. The impact of the Mahasi Thathana Yeithka was such that within a few years, similar meditation centers were opened across Burma, and subsequently in other Theravada Buddhist countries including Thailand and Sri Lanka. Centers have now been established around the

---

Every once in a while someone comes along who makes a significant impact within the realms of a particular religion. One such figure, the Venerable Mahasi Sayadaw, is highly revered as one of the great Theravada Buddhist meditation monks of his age. His influence, from humble beginnings, is quite remarkable, not only for the impact he made within Buddhism in Myanmar (Burma), but within the international realm of Buddhism and in the world of meditation practice.

Adrian Bird

world, including India, Cambodia, Indonesia, and the United States. In recognition of his considerable spiritual attainments, distinguished scholarship and teaching, Sayadaw was awarded the prestigious title of "Exalted Wise One."

The Sixth World Buddhist Council, held in Burma between 1954 and 1956, was organized to promote the Buddha's teachings and practices according to the Theravada tradition, and had the goal of harmonizing the Scriptures and erasing discrepancies that had appeared within Buddhist texts over time. Within the council, Sayadaw played a preeminent role and served as the final editor in the process of interpreting and revising key passages of scripture.

The teaching of Sayadaw can be found within the extensive range of written publications in Burmese, as well as publications in English, including 'Practical Meditation Insight' and 'The Process of Insight.' The legacy of Sayadaw's contribution to Buddhism, and in particular to the teaching of practical meditation techniques, continues to have an impact around the world. Insight meditation, a technique in which the participant concentrates on the rising and falling of the abdomen during the breathing cycle while acknowledging the changes taking place within the mind and body, allows the participant to journey through the steps towards enlightenment.

That such a path could be taken not only by monks but everyday persons had a dramatic influence within the realm of Theravada Buddhism, generating waves of interest in the practice of insight meditation at the Mahasi Thathana Yeithka center. A prominent image at the center is that of a painting depicting the Buddha surrounded by laypeople listening to his teaching. The Buddha appears to be conditioning those gathered for enlightenment. Inspired by this approach, Sayadaw devoted himself to making the wisdom of Buddha accessible, through the application of simple meditation techniques, for those seeking a meaningful path of transformation and enlightenment.

Adrian Bird

See also: Buddhism; Dharma/Dhamma; Diaspora; Education; Myanmar (Burma); Religion and Society; Southeast Asian Religions in the USA; Thailand.

Further Reading

Jordt, Ingrid. *Burma's Mass Lay Meditation Movement; Buddhism and the Cultural Construction of Power.* Athens: Ohio University Research in International Studies, Southeast Asia Series, No. 115, 2007.

Kornfield, Jack. *Living Dharma: Teachings and Meditation Instructions from Theravada Masters.* Boston and London: Shambhala Publications, 2010.

Nyi, U Nyi. "Venerable Mahasi Sayadaw: A Biographical Sketch." Insight Meditation Online. http://www.buddhanet.net/mahabio.htm (accessed May 9, 2014).

Sayadaw, Mahasi. *The Progress of Insight: A Treatise on Buddhist Satipatthāna Meditation*, Translated by Nyānaponika Thera. Kandy, Sri Lanka: Buddhist Publication Society. 1985.

Silānandābhivumsa, Ashin. *The Venerable Mahasi Sayadaw: Biography.* Translated by U Min Swe. Rangoon, Republic of the Union of Burma: Buddha Sāsanā Nuggaha Organization, 1982.

SAYADAW, THAMANYA

Thamanya Sayadaw was an influential and charismatic Burmese Buddhist monk who passed away in 2003. His hagiographies give as his birth year either 1910 or 1912. He was born in the Karen state and educated in monasteries in Moulmein but he himself was an ethnic Pao. He was ordained as a novice monk at the age of 13. His monastic name was U Winaya, but after he established himself in Hpa-an in the Karen state on Thamanya Hill, he became known as Thamanya Sayadaw. He was one of the most venerated monks in Myanmar (Burma) throughout the 1990s and early 2000s. Some scholars have attempted to politicize him as the opposition leader Aung San Suu Kyi visited his temple. He was hence regarded as an opponent to the military rule that had restarted in 1988. He had allegedly refused the government patronage, which further enhanced his reputation as an antimilitary monk.

He was donated land by wealthy supporters, and he redistributed the land to the people in the area. In the 1990s, there were around 400 monks and 200–300 female ascetics in the temple. He had 4,000 to 5,000 households residing in the vicinity of his temple. These people were ethnic Pao, Mon, and Pwo Karen. Many Karen villagers had escaped the ongoing fighting between the Burmese military and the Karen armies. One basic rule for people to enter his compound was that they were not allowed to carry arms. Thus he managed to keep the army and the militias out of the temple, and the compound formed a "peace zone" in a war-torn region.

Sayadaw himself was a vegetarian—which is rare in Theravada Buddhism—and only vegetarian food was served in the temple compound. Sayadaw was also seen as radiating *metta* (compassion) and was visited by many educated middle-class people who granted him generous donations, thus enabling him to financially support the temple community and provide all pilgrims with vegetarian food. The temple ran schools for local children. Sayadaw also built roads. As is common in Burmese Buddhism, Sayadaw was also believed to have supernatural powers as a result of his ascetic practices, and hence his pictures became valued amulets to protect lay people against any mishaps in life. In 1991, the Ministry of Religious Affairs granted him a hierarchical title, Abhidhaja Agga Maha Sadhamma Jotika.

After his death, his body was preserved in the monastery in a glass mausoleum and was assumed to have magic power. His corpse was mysteriously removed from the mausoleum in April 2008 and was allegedly burnt. There is no reliable information about the events. The monks that time suggested that his body was snatched by one of the several armies fighting in the area. Thamanya's temple was a popular site of pilgrimage until 2008 but has somewhat declined after the disappearance of the body.

Marja-Leena Heikkila-Horn

See also: Buddhism; Education; Myanmar (Burma); Peace-Building; Religion and Society; Sayadaw, Mahasi; Study of Religion; Women's Monastic Communities.

Further Reading

Aung San Suu Kyi. *Letters from Burma*. New York: Penguin Books, 1997.

Tosa, Keiko. "The Cult of Thamanya Sayadaw: Social Dynamism of a Formulating Pilgrimage Site." *Asian Anthropology* 68, no. 2 (2009): 239–64.

SECULARISM

Any discussion on secularism in Southeast Asia today should take place in the context of the new debate about religion and politics, with the impression gaining ground that religion is playing an increasingly visible role in politics including international affairs. It may also be important to note that secularism is the separation between religious institutions and the state rather than that between religion and politics.

The term secularism was first used by the British writer George Jacob Holyoake in 1851. He invented the term to describe his view of promoting a social order separate from religion without actively dismissing or criticizing religious belief. An agnostic himself, Holyoake argued that "Secularism is not an argument against Christianity; it is one independent of it."

A distinction may be drawn between secularism and secularization. The meaning of secularism is generally political. In this sense, secularism refers to political arrangements that make separation between religious institutions and the state. Secularization refers to a widespread decline of religious practice and among ordinary people.

Secularism aims at avoiding the medieval pattern of state, which was theocratic. All states and societies in the medieval period have been theocracies. State and society were integrated with the authority of one "established religion" whose sanction determined the law of citizenship and social structure. A theocracy gives first-class citizenship only to the adherents of the established religion; the others are legally restricted in their religious practices and discriminated adversely in social life and the provision of social opportunities.

The secular state is antitheocratic in the sense that the state has no special relation to any one particular religion. Therefore, the adherents of all religions and no religion have the same status and rights of citizenship, including freedom of religion/belief and freedom from discrimination in civic life on the basis of religious belief. A secular state is one that guarantees individual and corporate freedom of religion, is not constitutionally connected to a particular religion, and does not seek either to promote or interfere with religion.

In the relation between religion and state, five aspects of religion are important. First, the view of history taken by a religion—whether human history is regarded as real and important. Second, the attitude of a religion to other religions. Third, the capacity a given religion has demonstrated for effective ecclesiastical organization.

"Well . . . secularism in Asia is not at all like the Western version. Here it is so connected to how we are and who we are. For me secularism in this part of the world means tolerance. When you go to a Catholic church in Sindh, in my hometown Larkana, there are no pews. They sit on the ground with their legs crossed. And they don't have candles but *diyas*. And they put rose petals on the picture of the Virgin Mary. We come from a region where we mix all these ideas and have done so for centuries beautifully" (Fatima Bhutto, Pakistani writer).

Ninan Koshy

Fourth, historical traditions of separation or fusion of political and religious functions. Fifth, the extent to which religion has tended to regulate social life.

Rajeev Bhargava points out that secularism is a complex, evolving idea. It is not a doctrine with a fixed content. It has no single meaning. Of course, not all meanings are equally valid for every society. Secularism has multiple interpretations that change over time. Different societies must work out their own distinctive conceptions of secularism and see which one of them is good for them.

Secularism is a principle that involves two basic questions. The first is the strict separation of the state from religious institutions. The second is that people of different religions and beliefs are equal before the law. Bhargava is of the view that there are two types of political separation. The first identifies separation with exclusion. For the second, to separate is to mark the distance or boundaries. In the first type, politics must keep off religion. The standoffishness may be robust or mild, interventionist or noninterventionist. The second does not demand total exclusion. Some contacts are possible, but some distance has to be kept. It can mean some form of political neutrality, or the respect of the boundaries between religion and politics.

Any theory of secularism must be able to offer a sketch of how the two must relate after separation. M. M. Thomas makes a distinction between "closed secularism" and "open secularism." Some would call it "negative secularism" and "positive secularism." "Closed secularism" is a form of narrow sectarian secularism, which refuses to be sensitive to tradition and faith. An "open secularism," while it puts questions to religion as any secularism should, listens to religious questions both from within and without. A secularism that takes religion and faith seriously will conform to democratic ideals, especially in a highly religious society.

The question may be raised whether it is possible to separate religion from politics. In Asian cultures, especially, it is difficult to disentangle the religious from the nonreligious and therefore practically impossible to separate strictly every religious from every nonreligious practice. The distancing of religion from state becomes necessary to protect individual citizens from their own oppressive, religiously sanctioned social customs. Thus secularism is related to individual liberty and equality. Secular states aim to end religious hegemony, oppression, and domination and to do so by separating them from religious structures.

There are two distinct values of secularism; one is the guarantee of religious liberty, and the other is the independence of citizenship from religious considerations. Religious liberty, when understood broadly, is one significant value of a secular state. It is important to note that religious freedom is not possible in the absence of other freedoms such as freedom of expression, and therefore the championing of religious liberty can be done only by championing all human rights. It also follows that full religious liberty ensures democratic freedoms. In multireligious societies, religious freedom can be guaranteed only in a secular polity.

A democratic framework is the most conducive climate for secularism. Democracy requires that there be no concentration of power in any one institution or any other group. If people who exercise authority in religious institutions begin to exercise power in political matters, then the democratic framework is undermined. Equally important is social justice. Without equality, democracy, and social justice, secularism cannot exist as a positive value in society.

The secular state faces challenges, especially after the end of the Cold War. One of the challenges is about the basis of nationalism. In many countries that struggled for independence, nationalism represented the aspirations of all the people in the territory. It is this nationalism that was called secularism in the postindependence period. But when the basis of a nation-state is interpreted in religious terms rather than in political terms, the secular state is threatened. A number of countries in the context of the collapse of the Soviet Union began to claim that a particular religion is the basis of their nationalism. This is especially true of situations where ethnicity and religion are coterminous. One of the features of the new world order—or rather, disorder—is the resurgence of identities based on ethnic and parochial religious allegiance. While the term "Christian states" is rather nebulous, the term Islamic in relation to a state clearly indicates that the basis is Islam.

In a way, secularism was offered to the non-Western world after the end of the Second World War as part of a package that also included modernization and development. Modernization was equated with Westernization and was rejected, and development failed to attain its promised objectives. This considerably weakened secularism.

The opposition to the secular state in many countries is that it is Western and Christian. That it is Western in its origin is not denied. But it has been conveniently adapted to particular situations and clearly accepted as an expression of indigenous sentiments. One prominent Christian theologian suggested long ago that the idea of secular state is not only culturally European, but specifically Christian. In *Christianity and World History*, Arend Theodor van Leeuwen argued that the separation of religion and temporal spheres for the political organization of the state was "Christianity's gift to the world."

In general, states in Southeast Asia can claim to be constitutionally secular in the sense that they do not ground the state's legitimacy on beliefs that transcend the world. But their ethos is religious, as the secular framework often masks a religious spirit. The ruling elites in Japan, Thailand, and Indonesia, for example, follow practices that may be called religious. In situations where the nonreligious cannot be differentiated from the religious, it may be correct to say that traditional practices have religious content, even when they are presented in nonreligious terms. This is distinct from secularization, which is a marked decline in religious belief. Modernization in the Western sense has not affected these societies. There is a continuing interplay between the secular form and religious substance within these states.

A related issue is the influence or role of the dominant or majority religion in constitutionally secular states. The majority religion tends to insist that its traditional religious practices—at least some of them—are national. Often the dominant religion defines what nationalism is, and it is within that definition that the secular has to function. This can lead to tensions, as is the case in many Asian countries. People who belong to minority religions are the greatest beneficiaries of secularism. They should be vigilant about secularism and should do whatever they can to protect and promote them. Sectarian approaches by minority religious groups can only weaken the secular fabric.

Ninan Koshy

See also: Atheism/Agnosticism; Christianity; Ethnicity; Freedom of Religion; Fundamentalism; Globalization; Indonesia; Islam; Minorities; Nationalism; Religion and Society; Thailand.

Further Reading

Bhargava, Rajeev. *Secularism and its Critics*. New Delhi: Oxford University Press, 1998.
Juergensmeyer, Mark. *Global Rebellion: Religious Challenge to the Secular State*. Berkeley: University of California Press, 2007.
Kosmin, Barry A., and Ariela Keysar. *Secularism and Secularity: Contemporary International Perspectives*. Hartford, CT: Institute for the Study of Secularism in Society and Culture, 2007.
Thomas, M. M. *The Church's Mission and Post-Modern Humanism*. Tiruvalla, Kerala: CSS, and Delhi: ISPCK, 1996.

SEXUALITY

Sexuality is an integral part of human culture and life. Sexuality is not only related to reproduction, but it has also been influenced by human customs, religions, arts, moralities, and laws. Sexuality is a fundamental aspect of human life, encompassing the physical, psychological, social, emotional, spiritual, cultural, and ethical dimensions of the human experience (Bruess and Greenberg 1994). Sexuality may include sexual development, human creation, sexual differences between males and females, desire, love, sexual expression, masturbation, sexual intimacy, premarital and extramarital sex, sexual orientation, abortion, contraception, circumcision, polygamy, contemporary marriage, and so forth.

In societies such as Indonesia, the texts of the Qur'an (the book of revelation that is believed by Muslims to be the Word of God) and Hadith (the practices and sayings ascribed to Muhammad, the last prophet of Islam) play a major role in understanding sexuality. These become sources of moral and practical guidance in Muslims' daily lives. However, although the sources or texts are the same, Islam does not have a static or monolithic tradition, because like other religions, Islam has interacted with many sociopolitical, economic, and geographic conditions at particular times (Ilkkaracan 2002). Based on this history, Islam also offers diverse interpretations of the texts.

In general, Islamic culture recognizes the power of sexual needs and desires. The subjects of sexuality are discussed in the Qur'an and in the Hadith. The discussion about sexual behaviors and sexual intimacy in Islam always relates to morality and marital and family life. Some texts regarding sexuality indicate that men and women have to be treated equally and have equal rights. For example, some verses in the Qur'an mention that a man's wife can be his garment and that he can be garment to her (Taqiyuddin and Khan 1995, 68). There are also verses that exhort the believers to live with their wives honorably (Taqiyuddin and Khan 1995, 168) and that a man's wife has a right over him (Hadith). Prophet Muhammad himself described legitimate sex as a good deed even though sex with a "forbidden woman" is an act of sin (Athar 1995, 14).

Based on these texts, Muslim couples are encouraged to enjoy sex equally. It means that sexual satisfaction in the Islamic view is necessary for both partners because the "garment" in this text is a symbol of comfort and also equality, a symbol in which the wife is a "garment" for the husband and the husband is a "garment" for the wife. In the Qur'an, it is mentioned that both the husband and wife have the same rights to enjoy and express their sexual desires, but with some limitations. The Prophet Muhammad asserted that spouses should not divulge the secrets of their sex lives to another person nor describe the wife's physical appearance to anyone. The Islamic faith also prohibits premarital and extramarital sex because sex in Islam always relates to marriage, and extramarital sex is perceived as hurtful. It means that Muslims cannot have sex with others when it will hurt the marriage partner. Therefore, faithfulness and loyalty in marriage are very important.

Similar to Muslims' beliefs, Christians and Buddhists also believe that the acceptable sexual relationship is only within marriage. However, unlike the Muslims and Christians who perceive sex outside marriage as sinful, Buddhism sees sexuality in moderate ways, neither too conservative nor too liberal (Wijaya 2007). In Thailand, for example, where more than 90 percent of the people practice Theravada Buddhism, it is believed that people who enter monkhood have to leave their sexual desires, whereas women have no such option. Women in the Buddhist tradition are allowed to shave their heads, but they have no official place, and their action is seen only as an individual expression of cutting off from sexual emotion (Silverman 2004). After the Vietnam War, Thailand has become known as a sex tourism destination. Although prostitution is illegal there, it is a practice protected, and women may choose to believe that suffering as prostitutes is the result of their karma. Ninety percent of Thai prostitutes are from poor families (Silverman 2004). Research has found that 75 percent of the advertising of products in the media in Thailand is sex driven and that the companies benefit from that (Wijaya 2007).

The Islamic tradition sees sex and sexuality positively, which is part of the Islamic teaching. Sex and sexuality are not against spirituality, but they are signs of God's mercy and blessings to humanity (Hassan 1991). In the Qur'an Arroom 30:21, it is mentioned that one of Allah's signs is that Allah created mates for each of us and that we should find rest in them. Allah also put between us love and compassion (Shakir 2005). For the Catholics, on the other hand, sex and sexuality is good for peasants, but it should be avoided by priests (Sipe 1995). Although a sexual relationship is acceptable only within marriage, premarital sex in the Philippines has become more common.

The Javanese see men's and women's sexuality positively and affirm that both of them have the right to enjoy sexual pleasure. In the kakawin world, both men and women have the right to enjoy pleasure in a sexual relationship (Creese 2004). However, the sexual attraction of a woman is based more on certain types and sizes of the parts of her body than a man's. In Serat Panitisastra, for example, it is described that a woman's sexual drive and attraction derive from her slender body, full breasts, a pretty face, big eyes, pointy nose, and light skin (Munir 2002; Sukri and Sofwan 2001). A good smell from perfume is also part of women's sexual attraction (Miharja 1960). A woman's body is significantly linked to her degree of sexual attraction.

Sexual relationships have been symbolized in a hierarchal way. In the *Serat Centhini*, for instance, the ideal woman is the one who is always there when her husband needs her, always smiles even though she is upset, and is still loyal to her husband even though he may have as many as 40 wives (Hadijaya and Kamajaya 1978). In the Javanese wedding ceremony, there is a ritual called *mijidadi* in which the bride washes the groom's foot after breaking an egg as a symbol of fertility. This ritual symbolizes the unequal sexual relationship between the wife and the husband (Munir 2002) because the Javanese epistemology of sexual intercourse, *manuggaling kawulagusti*—the union of servant and lord (Beatty 1999, 173)—also indicates inequality in the sexual relationship because the wife is a servant and the husband is the lord.

In terms of the contribution to conception, traditionally Javanese people see men and women equally. The creation and development of human beings, according to Riffat Hassan (1999), becomes a fundamental issue because it relates to the existence of women in the world. According to an old Javanese philosophical treatise, *Teaching of Wrahaspati*, men and women eat and drink the six tastes and then become life and body. A boy is born if there is more male essence than female essence. Conversely, if there is more female essence than male, then a girl is born. The male essence forms the bones, blood vessels, and marrow, and the female essence becomes the flesh, blood, and skin. Three come from the male and the other three come from the female (Creese 2004).

Alimatul Qibtiyah

See also: Buddhism; Christianity; Humanism; Indonesia; Islam; Philippines; Thailand; Vietnam; Women.

Further Reading

Athar, S. *Sex Education: An Islamic Perspective*. Chicago: KAZI, 1995.

Beatty, A. *Varieties of Javanese Religion: An Anthropological Account*. Cambridge: Cambridge University Press, 1999.

Brewer, C. *Holy Confrontation: Religion, Gender and Sexuality in the Philippines, 1521–1685*. Manila: Institute of Women's Studies, 2001.

Bruess, C. E., and J. Greenberg. *Sexuality Education, Theory and Practice*. Dubuque, IA: Brown & Benchmark, 1994.

Creese, H. *Women of the Kakawin World: Marriage and Sexuality in the Indic Courts of Java and Bali*. New York: An East Gate Book, 2004.

Hadijaya, T., and Kamajaya. *Serat centhini dituturkan dalam bahasa Indonesia*. Yogyakarta: U. P. Indonesia, 1978.

Hassan, R. "Women, Religion and Sexuality: Studies on the Impact of Religious Teaching on Women." In *An Islamic Perspective*, edited by J. Becher, 93–128. Philadelphia: Trinity Press International, 1991.

Hassan, R. "The Issue of Woman-Man Equality in the Islamic Tradition." In *Eve and Adam: Jewish, Christian, and Muslim Readings on Genesis and Gender*, edited by K. E. Kvam, L. S. Schearing, and V. H. Ziegler, 464–76). Bloomington: Indiana University Press, 1999.

Ilkkaracan, P. "Good Sex: Feminist Perspectives from the World's Religion." In *Islam and Women's Sexuality: A Research Report from Turkey*, edited by P. B. Jung, M. E. Hunt, and R. Balakrishnan, 61–77. New Jersey: Rutgers University, 2002.

Miharja, A. K. *Atheis: Nobel*. Melaka: TokoBuku Abbas Bandong, 1960.

Munir, L. Z. "He Is Your Garment and You Are His . . .": Religious Precepts, Interpretations, and Power Relations in Marital Sexuality among Javanese Muslim Women." *SOJOURN: Journal of Social Issues in Southeast Asia* 17, no. 2 (October 2002): 191(130).

Shakir, H. M. *English Translation of the Holy Qur'an*. http://www.searchtruth.com (accessed February 8, 2013).

Silverman, H. J., ed. *Talk about Sexuality in Thailand: Notion, Identity, Gender Bias, Women, Gay, Sex Education, and Lust*. Yogyakarta: Southeast Asia Consortium on Gender, Sexuality and Health, 2004.

Sipe, A. W. R. *Sex, Priests, and Power: Anatomy of a Crisis*. New York: Brunner/Mazel Publishers, 1995.

Sukri, Sri Suhandjati, and Ridin Sofwan. *Perempuan dan seksualitas dalam tradisi Jawa*. Yogyakarta, Indonesia: Kerja sama Pusat Studi Wanita (PSW), IAIN Walisongo dengan Gama Media, 2001.

Taqiyuddin, A. M., and M. M. Khan. *Interpretation of the Meaning of the Noble Qur'an in the English Language*. Saudi Arabia: Darussalam, 1995.

Wijaya, Y. W. *Seksualitas dalam Buddhism* [*Buddhism and Sex*]. Yogyakarta: Insight, 2007.

SHAMANISM

"Shamanism" emerged as a new concept in 1895, when Mihajlovski postulated the universality of the characters (*shaman*) described since the seventeenth century as ritual specialists in Siberian hunting societies (Hamayon 2010). With the growth of rationalizing observations and psychoanalysis, shamans have then been seen mainly as endowed with a pathological personality, giving them special skills in therapy. Mircea Eliade is the major author who contributed to reestablish these figures in the field of religion. He characterized shamans as mastering the techniques of ecstasy and made their practices known in Western societies through the American translation of his book in 1968. Insisting on the specific dimension of the communication established by shamans with spirits, as during their séances they are believed to leave for a journey into the spiritual world, Eliade also opposed it to practices of spirit possession, rather involving the coming down of spirits into their mediums. In this way, he contributed to the unawareness of practices of contact with the spirits in parts of the world where this reversed type of communication with the spiritual world was more present, including mainland Southeast Asia.

This could partly explain why mainland Southeast Asia was hardly noticed for its shamanic cultures until the 1990s—except for Hmong shamanism—although practices of establishing a direct contact with the spiritual world either through shamanic journeys or spirit possession were reported throughout the region. But there is another explanation for this undeserved neglect. Until the 1960s, knowledge of the region was dominated by an orientalist bias preventing scholars from looking at practices actually embedded in Buddhist and Confucian societies. At that time, very few specialists of religion would take seriously practices apparently so alien to the doctrinal content of the mainstream religion.

In the 1970s, the French anthropologist Condominas set up a research program on the distribution of shamanism and spirit possession in mainland Southeast Asia. The formulation of this program was the result of both new anthropological approaches of lowland societies pertaining to "great traditions" and of the formulation by de Heusch, in the African context, of the hypothesis that contrary to shamanism, spirit possession was more prone to be found in association with a world religion. While the findings of scholars published in 1973 and 1974 in the Journal *ASEMI* did not support the hypothesis that the distribution of shamanism and spirit possession was correlated to the expansion of Buddhism in mainland Southeast Asia, Condominas (1976) was able to draw the first general picture of the forms of spirit possession in the region. There, spirit possession tends to occur from a plurality of entities belonging to a particular pantheon, coming down successively in their mediums in a culturally determined order.

Other studies of rural lowland societies followed, paving the way to further characterization of the religious configurations in which spirit possession practices are present. In mainland Southeast Asia, the embodiment of spirits allows various kinds of transactions with the community involved, according to different functionalities: from a therapeutic purpose to the quest for a general prosperity of the people. In many cases, the spirits can be attributed to an ancestral origin, combined or not with a linear definition of the cult group. In other cases, the territorial dimension of the cults has prevailed, evolving into institutionalization at the level of the polity in the case of Burma and Vietnam. Burmese Nat, Thai *phiban*, or Viet *than* are all tutelary spirits having command on a territorial division, settled in sanctuaries imagined as palaces in which they are served by mediums (*natkadaw*, *nang thien*, or *ba dong*) and embodied at regular collective rituals occasions.

The Cold War obstructed this type of anthropological studies on rural societies and affected practices linked to the spiritual world. In revolutionary Laos, *phi* were reported to have been sent in re-education camps; in Cambodia, the displacement of local communities caused the *neak ta* to disappear; in Vietnam, the cult to the Four Palaces recessed into clandestine practice; while in North Thailand, matrifocal cults shrank, due to the evolving social position of the women. This decline of traditional spirit cults was apparently supporting the then dominant Weberian view that

---

Since Mircea Eliade characterized shamans as mastering the techniques of ecstasy and made their practices known in Western societies, mainland Southeast Asia was hardly noticed for its shamanic cultures, except for Hmong shamanism, although practices of establishing a direct contact with the spiritual world either through shamanic journey or spirit possession are pervasive in the whole region. More recently, the highly transactional nature of spirit possession made it possible for renewed forms of cult to flourish in modern and urban contexts.

Bénédicte Brac de la Perrière

A family at the Wat Tham Krabok refugee camp in Tham Krabok, Thailand, goes through a ritual as a shaman hands them strings to tie on their wrists during a "good luck" ceremony before leaving for the United States on August 5, 2004. (Paula Bronstein/Getty Images)

modernity would develop parallel to a *disenchanted world.* But the end of the Cold War produced a reversal of the situation. The neoliberal globalization that ensued went on a par with a significant revival of spirit mediumship in modern urban contexts across mainland Southeast Asia, regardless of the countries' political institutions (Jackson 2012). This resurgence of spirit cults had already been signaled by Comaroff in 1994 as a *re-enchantment* of the postmodern world.

Since this turnaround, an ever growing number of scholarly studies have drawn attention to the renewed importance of mainland Southeast Asia for the understanding of spirit mediumship and shamanism as contemporary religious facts. In Vietnam, these studies have revealed, among others, the participation of "devotees-customers" in local festivals and the integration of commercial spirits in the pantheon of the Four Palaces (*len dong*), suggesting the growing commodification of spirit possession and the emergence of a new religious market. The sudden rise of one of the female deities present in southern Vietnam—known as the Lady of the Kingdom—has also been described, unveiling the hitherto unseen translocal quality of practices of Vietnamese spirit worship. Analyses have insisted on the modernity and the hybridity of the contemporary formation of spirit possession cults in Chiang Mai (northern Thailand), or on the prosperity cults that have multiplied in central Thailand around magic monks or spirit mediums. Throughout the whole region, the highly transactional nature of spirit possession made it possible for renewed forms of cult to flourish in modern and urban contexts.

Bénédicte Brac de la Perrière

See also: Ancestor Worship; Buddhism; Cambodia; Confucianism; Globalization; Goddess Traditions; Myanmar (Burma); Spirit Mediumship; Thailand; Uplanders; Vietnam; Women.

Further Reading

Brac de la Perrière, Bénédicte. "Un monde plus que jamais enchanté? Note de lecture sur la résurgence contemporaine des cultes aux esprits en Thaïlande et au Viêt-nam." *Aséanie* 20 (2007): 17–25.

Comaroff, Jean. "Defying Disenchantment: Reflections on Ritual, Power and History." In *Asian Visions of Authority: Religion and the Modern States of East and Southeast Asia*, edited by Charles F. Keyes, Laurel Kendall, and Helen Hardacre, 301–14. Honolulu: University of Hawaii Press, 1994.

Condominas, G. "Quelques aspects du chamanisme et des cultes de possession en Asie du Sud-est et dans le monde insulindien." In *L'autre et l'ailleurs: Mélanges offerts à Roger Bastide*, edited by J. Poirier and F. Raveau, 215–32. Paris, 1976.

Hamayon, R. "Chamanisme." *Dictionnaire des faits religieux*, edited by Règine Azria and Danièle Hervieu-Léger, 120–24. Paris: Quadrige, PUF, 2010.

Jackson, P. A. "The Political Economy of Twenty-first Century Thai Supernaturalism: Comparative Perspectives on Cross-Genderism and Limits to Hybridity in Resurgent Thai Spirit Mediumship." *Southeast Asia Research* 20, no. 4 (2012): 611–22.

SHARI'A

The word *shari'a* means "the way to the watering place," which indicates the clear and straight path to be followed. In Islamic literature, *shari'a* means the divine law, the totality of guidance that is contained in the revelation of God and the *Sunna*, the teachings of the Prophet Muhammad. *Shari'a* encompasses not only law, but also theology and ethical code. In terms of basic principles of Islam, moral values, and worship, *shari'a* provides clear injunctions. Likewise, *shari'a* sets definitive rulings on what is lawful (*halal*) and unlawful (*haram*). However, regarding civil transaction, economic and political matters, criminal law (with the exception of *hudud*, the prescribed punishment), *shari'a* is flexible and only provides general guidelines. *Shari'a* aims at safeguarding people's interests in this world, and this is achieved by educating the individual, administering justice, and considering public interests (*mashlaha*). Over the time, however, the meaning of *shari'a* is narrowed down to include the body of legal rules with all legal scholars' interpretations and opinions.

During the seventh century, the Muslim community became an independent political entity that needed Islamic rules in dealing with issues pertaining to devotion and civil transaction. This early generation referred legal issues to the Qur'an and the Prophet Muhammad for guidance. After the death of the Prophet, the first four Caliphs and senior companions continued this role. Notably, although there were numerous legal decisions given by the companions, the systematic Islam legal system was not yet established. Legal decisions were transferred between generations by means of oral transmission. It was at the end of the Umayyad period that the Caliphate established the office of the *qadi* (judge) in charge of overseeing the implementation of the government's decisions and settling disputes.

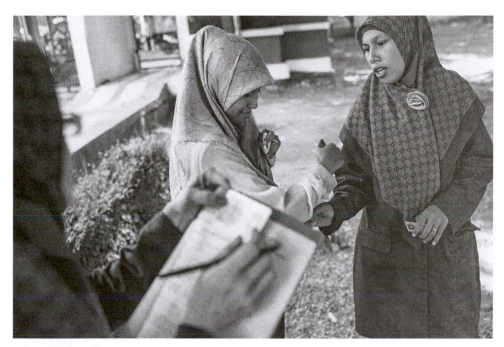

Members of the Shari'a Police stop two young women who are wearing tights, which goes against the prevailing Shari'a Law in Banda Aceh, on June 3, 2014. The Shari'a Police took down their personal details and gave them the first warning out of three. Anyone who receives three warnings is consequently sent to a religious rehabilitation center. (Jonas Gratzer/Getty Images)

The Abbasid caliphate played a significant role in the development of *shari'a* into a comprehensive legal system that took place in the eighth century. The caliphate was the patron for the study of Islamic sciences. In order to understand Islamic law in a comprehensive mode, the science of law or jurisprudence known as *fiqh* was developed. *Fiqh* focuses on the understanding of the practical rules of *shari'a*. Jurists and scholars in Islamic centers such as Medina, Kufah, Damascus, and Egypt developed a coherent Islamic law system. This period also showed the formulation of the sources of *shari'a* and methods to explain principles contained in these sources.

The Qur'an, the *Sunna* of the Prophet, *ijma'* (consensus of the community), and *ijtihad* (legal reasoning) are four sources of *shari'a*. The first two are revealed, and the rest are not revealed. All Muslims agree that the Qur'an is the revealed words of God to the Prophet Muhammad. It is the sourcebook of Islamic principles, values, and moral prescriptions. Although it contains legal codes, the Qur'an does not constitute a law book. Less than 3 percent of around 6,000 verses in the Qur'an deal with legal issues. In other words, the Qur'an gives Muslims general guidance of conduct rather than legislative rules. There are two rulings in the Qur'an: definitive (*qath'iy al-dalalah*) and speculative (*zhanniy al-dalalah*). The former consists of self-evident injunctions that require no interpretation. The latter are the ones conveyed in a language that needs further interpretation. However, Muslim scholars applied different approaches to the interpretation in the light of the Prophet's tradition and individual analysis. This, in turn, results in different legal decisions.

The *Sunna* of the Prophet is the second and complementary source of *shari'a*. The *Sunna* (*Hadith*) consists of the words and deeds of the Prophet and the actions he permitted. The Muslims have to obey the *Sunna* since it is divinely inspired and stands on the same footing as the Qur'an. The function of the *Sunna* encompasses strengthening the injunctions in the Qur'an, clarifying the ambiguous parts and specifying general rulings in the Qur'an. In addition, the *Sunna* stipulated certain rulings on which the Qur'an is silent. By the ninth century, the *Sunna* was compiled by scholars applying tough criteria to scrutinize the chains of narrators and the contents. This is to ensure the *hadith* authenticity. The scholars classify the *hadith* into two types: firstly, *hadith mutawatir*, in which the sources are numerous and the testimony is continuous and recurrent. The second classification is *hadith ahad*, solitary reports of the narrators. This type of *hadith* is divided into authentic (*shahih*), good (*hasan*), weak (*dha'if*), and refused (*mawdhu'*) based on the chains of narrators and the contents. The *Sunna* compilation culminated in the emergence of the six authoritative *Sunna* collections, namely, Ismail al-Bukhari (d. 870), Muslim ibn al-Hajjaj (d. 875), Abu Dawud (d. 888), Al-Nasa'i (d. 915), Al-Tirmidzi (d. 892), and Ibn Maja (d. 896). The first two compilations are considered as the most authoritative collections.

The authority of *ijma'* (consensus of the community) as the third source of *shari'a* is based on the Prophet's saying that his community would never agree on an error. *Ijma'* was conducted by the community of legal scholars who reached consensus in solving certain legal matters after the death of the Prophet. The Qur'anic interpretation and application on certain issues are considered valid as long as they are in accordance with *ijma'*. Hence, *ijma'* is considered as "a check on individual jurist opinions."

Ijtihad (legal reasoning) is the most important source of *shari'a* and the instrument to relate the Qur'an and the *Sunna* to the changing conditions of society. *Ijtihad*, with the meaning to struggle or to strive intellectually, constitutes the use of legal reasoning comprehensively by qualified individuals or groups (*mujtahid*, those who conduct *ijtihad*) to solve problems not found in the Qur'an and the *Sunna*. The use of *ijtihad* was legalized by the Prophet as one of the sources of *shari'a* as was shown in the *hadith* on Mu'adz ibn Jabal, who took a judicial post in Yemen. Jurists made use of *ijtihad* to maintain the continuity of the Islamic teachings and the reality of social changes. The jurists also employed some methods in *ijtihad*, such as *qiyas* (analogy), *istihsan* (juristic preference), *urf* (local custom) and, *istishhab* (presumption of continuity). Among the great jurists authoring influential works on Islamic law are Abu Hanifa (d. 767), Malik ibn Anas (d. 796), Muhammad al-Shafii (d. 819), and Ahmad ibn Hanbal (d. 855). Their followers systematized their thoughts and established *madzhab* (Islamic law school), the Hanafi, Maliki, Shafi'i and Hanbali, respectively. The Shafi'i school has many followers in Southeast Asia, such as in Indonesia, Malaysia, Brunei, the Philippines, and Singapore.

Bambang Budiwiranto

See also: Brunei Darussalam; Indonesia; Islam; Malaysia; Philippines; Reform Movements; Religion and Society; Religious Discrimination and Intolerance; Singapore; Women.

Further Reading

An-Na'im, Abdullahi Ahmad. *Dekonstruksi Syari'ah: Wacana kebebasan sipil, hak asasi manusia dan hubungan internasional dalam Islam.* Translated by Ahmad Suaedy and Amiruddin ar-Raniry. Yogyakarta: LKiS, 1990.

Ashmawi, Muhammad S. *Against Islamic Extremism.* Translated and edited by C. Fluehr-Lobban. Gainesville: University Press of Florida, 1998.

Esposito, John L. *Islam: The Straight Path.* Oxford: Oxford University Press, 2005.

Kamali, Mohammad Hasan. "The Shari'a: Law as the Way of God." In *Voices of Islam, Voices of Tradition,* edited by Vincent J. Cornell, Vol. 1, 149–82. Westport, CT: Praeger, 2007.

Roald, Anne Sofie. *Women in Islam: The Western Experience.* London: Routledge, 2001.

SIDDIQUE, MUHAMMAD ABDUL ALEEM

Muhammad Abdul Aleem Siddique contributed tremendously, in the first half of the twentieth century, to consolidating Islam in Singapore and in spreading the message of peace and unity around the world. Born into a pious and devout family in Meerut, India, in 1892, he is a descendant of Sayyidina Abu Bakar As-Siddique, the first caliph of Islam. As a child, Siddique took a keen interest in the study of Islam and, by the age of four, he had memorized the Quran. He soon became known as an orator and, at the age of 16, obtained a degree in Islamic theology. He also studied non-Islamic subjects such as modern science and law.

In 1930, Siddique traveled to Singapore as a missionary. He worked long and hard among the Muslims there, and many were drawn to his personality and message. He took the leadership in establishing the Malaya Muslim Missionary Society in 1932, an institute for the study and spread of Islam. The society is now known as Jamiyah and has branches in all the states of Malaysia.

Abdul Aleem Siddique also became an exponent of interreligious harmony. For 40 years, he traveled all over the world spreading the message of spiritual reform and enlightenment. For his ceaseless travel and message of goodwill, he became known as the "Roving Ambassador of Peace." In 1949, he took the initiative in establishing the Inter-Religious Organization (IRO) to build greater understanding between the various religions and to cultivate the spirit and message of peace.

The Abdul Aleem Siddique Mosque in Singapore remains as a lasting monument for Siddique's contributions for the growth of Islam in Singapore and for fostering interreligious harmony and world peace. He died in 1954 during the *hajj* (pilgrimage) in Saudi Arabia.

Jesudas M. Athyal

See also: Diaspora; Interreligious Relations and Dialogue; Islam; Missionary Movements; Pilgrimage; Singapore; Study of Religion.

Further Reading

"Maulana Abdul Aleem Siddique." http://www.aleemsiddique.org.sg/index.php?/Info/maulana-abdul-aleem-siddique.html (accessed October 25, 2014).

Maulana Muhammaad Abdul Aleem Siddique, Al Qadri. *The History of the Codification of Islamic Law: Being an Illuminating Exposition of the Conformist View-Point accepted by the Overwhelming Majority of the Islamic World.* Trinidad: Haji Mohammed Ibrahim, 1950.

Mutalib, Hussain. "Misperceptions of Islam and the Muslims: Making Sense of the Jaundiced Views of Westerners." In *The Past in Our Future: Challenges Facing Muslims in the 21st Century.* Singapore: Fount, National University of Singapore Muslim Society, 2001.

SIMATUPANG, T. B.

An Indonesian Christian leader, T. B. Simatupang had also served as a military leader of the Indonesia National Armed Forces. Born in Dairi in North Sumatra in 1920, he did his elementary studies at a Dutch colonial school and higher studies in Jakarta. After studies, he joined the army and steadily rose through the ranks to become, in 1950, the acting chief of staff in the Indonesian army (*Angkatan Perang*). However, Simatupang was accused of interfering in the political affairs of the country and, in 1953, was removed from his position as chief. During his public career, he had also served as an advisor to the nation's Ministry of Defence and a lecturer at the Army Staff College and the Military Legal Academy.

It was in his postmilitary life that Simatupang became known as a Christian leader and thinker. As an Asian voice critical of Western colonialism, he joined those Indonesian Christians who believed in shrugging off the colonial tag to their religion so as to build a truly indigenous church. While Simatupang acknowledged the services of the missionaries in the areas of education and health care, he preferred to associate the legacy of Indonesian Christianity with the "folk churches" in the country that were not part of either the Islamic or the Hindu movement, rather than with any mission board. He also believed that the pietism represented by the Western missionaries did great disservice to the indigenous growth of Christianity. While the missionary-inspired rediscovery of the evangelistic élan was welcomed as a much-needed reform, Simatupang affirmed that the stress of piety in personal salvation and charity left little room for a broad social concern to tackle the manifold problems in the country. He firmly believed that, especially in the Asian context

As a member of the Central Committee of the World Council of Churches (WCC), Simatupang was a key Asian presence in the ecumenical movement. He served as the chairperson of a subcommittee that drafted a statement leading to the establishment of a department to counter apartheid. The WCC Central Committee that met in Canterbury in 1969 adopted a resolution under which the Program to Combat Racism (PCR) and the fund for empowering groups fighting against racism were established. PCR played an important role in the overthrow of apartheid in several African countries in the 1970s.

Jesudas M. Athyal

marked by poverty and social injustice, religion need necessarily involve a faith response aimed at alleviating the suffering of people. As a leader of the Indonesian Council of Churches (DGI), he grappled with the question of how to bridge the gap between theological thought and social realities.

As an Indonesian Christian leader, Simatupang participated in several meetings of the World Council of Churches. He was especially concerned with the relationship between church and society, and he moderated a session at the historic World Conference on Church and Society that met in Geneva in 1966. Simatupang died in Jakarta in 1990. In recognition of his service to the nation, in 2013, he was declared a national hero of Indonesia (*Gelar Pahlawan Nasional Indonesia*).

Jesudas M. Athyal

See also: Christian Conference of Asia; Christianity; Colonialism; Contextualization; Education; Hinduism; Indonesia; Interreligious Relations and Dialogue; Islam; Missionary Movements; Popular Religion; Religion and Society.

Further Reading

Mujīburraḥmān. *Feeling Threatened: Muslim-Christian Relations in Indonesia's New Order.* Amsterdam: Amsterdam University Press, 2006.

Simatupang, T. B. *Indonesia Negeriku* [*Indonesia, My Country*]. Jakarta: Iman Kristen dan Pancasila, 1984.

Tobing, Richard Lumban. *Christian Social Ethics in the Thought of T. B. Simatupang: The Role of Indonesian Christians in Social Change.* Denver, CO: Iliff School of Theology and the University of Denver, 1996.

Yewangoe, Andreas A. *Theologia Crucis in Asia: Asian Christian Views on Suffering in the Face of Overwhelming Poverty and Multifaceted Religiosity in Asia.* Amsterdam: Rodopi, 1987.

SIN, CARDINAL JAIME LECHICA

Born on August 31, 1928, in New Washington, Philippines, Cardinal Jaime Lechica Sin was a Filipino Roman Catholic cleric widely regarded as the most iconic spiritual leader in the postauthoritarian Philippines. He is remembered for the crucial role he played in affecting political change in his country, particularly with respect to emphasizing the church's mandate as arbiters of social justice, morality and political integrity.

Born to paternal Chinese ancestry, he was ordained a priest at the age of 25, quickly rising the ranks in being appointed bishop of Obba (1967) and archbishop of Jaro (1972). In January 1974, he was elevated by Pope Paul VI to archbishop of Manila, where he served for just under three decades to 2003. Meanwhile, his elevation to cardinal in 1976, at the age of 48, made him the youngest member of the College of Cardinals at that time.

Cardinal Sin is remembered for the crucial role he played in denouncing political corruption. During the authoritarian regime of former president Ferdinand Marcos, he presided over a Philippine Roman Catholic Church that adopted a policy of "critical collaboration," in which clerics worked strategically with Marcos's social policies, even while Sin himself remained vocal against human rights abuses and political persecutions. This position became more pronounced as political volatility escalated in the early 1980s, following the assassination of Senator Benigno Aquino in 1983, and the highly contested presidential elections in 1986. Sin famously made a call for the Catholic faithful to take to the streets in support of rebel military defectors, who were protesting against the excesses of the Marcos regime. He is credited as galvanizing over a million Filipinos in peaceful demonstrations known as the "People Power" revolution, which led to Marcos's eventual overthrow.

Even throughout subsequent administrations, Sin continued to be outspoken about the role of the church as guardians of social morality, particularly relating to corrupt government officials, which drew criticism from politicians who thought that the church should stay out of politics. Clarifying his position on this matter, Sin reminded the Synod of Bishops in October 1987 that to shut oneself away from the demands of political transformation of Asia was, in a sense, a denial of Christian identity. The cardinal was a key figure once again in affecting major regime change, this time in 2001 during the second "People Power" revolution, which resulted in the removal of the then president Joseph Estrada from office.

In spite of his crucial role in Philippine politics, the cardinal was known for his engaging personality and sense of humor, famously referring to his official residence as "the House of Sin." He retired as archbishop of Manila in 2003, and died in Manila of illness on June 21, 2005, at the age of 76, a loss commemorated by a state funeral and a national day of mourning. On the day of his death, Pope Benedict XVI, in a telegram to the Archdiocese of Manila, recalled the cardinal's unfailing commitment to the spread of the Gospel and to the promotion of the dignity, common good, and national unity of the Philippine people.

Julius Bautista

See also: Christianity; Federation of Asian Bishops' Conferences; Liberation Theologies; Morality; Philippines; Religion and Society.

Further Reading

"Cardinal Sin, Leader of 'People Power' Movement, Dies at 76." *Catholic News Service*, June 21, 2005. http://www.catholicnews.com/data/stories/cns/0503641.htm (accessed May 13, 2014).

"Thousands Gather for Cardinal Sin's Funeral, Philippine's 'Champion of the Poor.'" *Catholic News Service*, June 28, 2005. http://m.catholicnewsagency.com/new.php?n=4245 (accessed May 13, 2014).

Yamsuan, Noli I. *Scenes of Sin: A Photographic Chronicle of Jaime L. Cardinal Sin*. Manila: Goodwill Trading Co., 1999.

SINGAPORE

Singapore is a city-state republic that lies to the south of the Malaya Peninsula. Its strategic geographical location and political stability make it a major economic and cultural hub for neighboring Southeast Asian countries, as well as a bridgehead of Western interests into the Asia Pacific. Similar to Hong Kong, the other leading financial center and competitor in the Asia Pacific, Singapore is a seaport, with a land area one-third less than Hong Kong. Both are predominantly ethnic Chinese and former British colonies. However, unlike Hong Kong, which is increasingly economically dependent on China's support, Singapore has needed to rely on its own resources for survival since its founding in 1965. It has no hinterland. It is surrounded by Muslim- and Malay-dominated, and sometimes anti-Chinese communities. It relies on the ingenuity and consensus of its local population to maintain an economically striving and politically stable country in a multireligious and multiethnic population.

According to the 2010 Singapore census, five million people live in Singapore, of which 74 percent are Singapore residents. The residents consist of 74 percent Chinese, 13 percent Malay, 9 percent Indian, and "others" (according to government classification) that are made up of Eurasians, Europeans, and other racial groups. Of those aged 15 years and over, about 44 percent profess Buddhism/Daoism, 18 percent Christianity, 15 percent Islam, 5 percent Hinduism, and 17 percent who see themselves with "no religion."

Singapore is a socially engineered state, with the active management of religion as a key concern. The rise of the Singaporean nation was punctuated by a series of political and ethnic crises in the 1950s and 1960s. Three riots stood out: the Maria Hertogh riots in 1950, the 1964 riot between Malays and Chinese on the Prophet Mohammed's birthday, and the 1969 racial riots that spilled over from Malaysia to the newly separated island-state. These traumatic events have become Singapore's institutional memory.

Devotees visit Kwan Im Thong Hood Cho Temple on Waterloo Street in Rochor, Singapore. The traditional Chinese temple has existed since 1884. (catchlights_sg /iStockphoto.com)

> Singapore is a socially engineered state, with the active management of religion as a key concern. Singapore's genius lies in its ability to build up a harmonious society amid the complex religious and ethnic interplays in the region and in the nation. Religious leaders can run the risk of exercising self-censorship, especially on justice issues, in order to serve national interests.
>
> *Michael Nai-Chiu Poon*

The government does not attempt to homogenize religious diversities: ethnic and religious distinctiveness are affirmed. Rather, it ensures that ethnic and religious communities would not live their own segregated lives. To do this, the government aims to build up a common Singaporean national identity through several measures: the National Pledge that is rehearsed in the annual National Day Parade, and the mandatory two years national service for all 18-year-old Singaporean males. The Housing Development Board sets up a quota to ensure that no particular racial group lives together in a concentrated way and thus prevent the growth of sectarianism.

Singapore's constitution, legislations, and policies reflect the proactive and directive role that the government assumes to safeguard the interests of religious communities and to ensure religious harmony. Articles 15 and 16 of the Singapore Constitution uphold the "Freedom of Religion" and the "Rights in Respect of Education." The constitution pays particular attention to safeguarding the interests of the racial and religious minority groups. It sets up a Presidential Council for Minority Rights. The Malays receive particular attention because of their sensitive geopolitical status in the region. The Administration of Muslim Act makes provision for regulating Muslim religious affairs and for constituting a council to advise the president in matters relating to the Muslim religion.

Legislative provisions are in place to regulate religious activities and preempt public disorder. There are Penal Code sanctions against offenses relating to religion or race. The Sedition Act proscribes against seditious tendency. Religious societies must be legally registered in Singapore under the Societies Act. Group Representation Constituency (GPC) was introduced in 1988 to ensure the representation of the minority groups in the Parliament. Accordingly, at least one of the members of Parliament in a GRC must be a member of the Malay, Indian, or another minority community of Singapore.

With the rise of religious fundamentalism from the 1980s, Singapore increasingly saw the need to wrestle with the impact of globalization on social harmony. Clearly, the government can harness the altruistic spirit that religion can inspire for nation-building purposes. At the same time, transnational networks of religious groups can become a potential source for ethno-religious antagonism. In the mid-1980s, the government was especially alarmed with the adverse social impact of religious revivalism and aggressive conversion practices. In 1987, the arrest of several Roman Catholic social activists and the expulsion from the country of the Christian Conference of Asia underscored the government's anxiety on the destabilizing impact of religious networks in a globalizing age. In response, the government enacted the Maintenance of Religious Harmony Act in 1992. A Presidential Council for Religious Harmony was also established under the provision of the Act. Following the 9/11 attacks and the arrest of members of the Jemaah Islamiyah terrorist network in Singapore in 2001, the government increasingly draws on the leaders of religious communities to regulate the conduct of their own adherents and to keep religious peace with one another. In 2003, the Declaration of Religious Harmony was issued by the national bodies of mainstream religious groups, with the affirmation that "religious harmony is vital for peace, progress and prosperity in our multi-racial and multi-religious Nation." The Inter-Religious Harmony Circle, Inter-racial and Religious Confidence Circles, and the Community Engagement Programme are set in place to foster unity and resilience among religious and ethnic communities at different levels of the society.

Singapore's genius lies in its ability to build up a harmonious society amid the complex religious and ethnic interplays in the region and in the nation. Singapore is a secular city-state: religion is strictly kept out of politics. However, Singapore has not enshrined "secularity" in its constitution. Local religious communities and peoples of diverse convictions are harnessed for nation-building. Religious leaders can run the risk of exercising self-censorship, especially on justice issues, in order to serve national interests. Singapore offers an interesting case study on how religious communities in decolonized states negotiate their social roles and find public expression of their beliefs in the present day.

Michael Nai-Chiu Poon

See also: Buddhism; Christianity; Colonialism; Daoism (Taoism); Education; Ethnicity; Freedom of Religion; Fundamentalism; Globalization; Hinduism; Interreligious Relations and Dialogue; Islam; Malaysia; Minorities; Nationalism; Religion and Society; Secularism.

Further Reading

Barr, Michael, and Carl A. Trocki. *Paths Not Taken: Political Pluralism in Post-War Singapore*. Singapore: NUS Press, 2008.

Hill, M. "The Rehabilitation and Regulation of Religion in Singapore." In *Regulating Religion: Case Studies from around the Globe*, edited by J. T. Richardson, 343–58. New York: Kluwer Academic, 2004.

Lai, Ah Eng. *Religious Diversity in Singapore*. Singapore: Institute of Southeast Asian Studies, jointly with Institute of Policy Studies, 2008.

Poon, M. *Religion and Governance for Social Harmony in Singapore*. Singapore: Trinity Theological College, 2012.

Poon, M., ed. *Engaging Society: The Christian in Tomorrow's Singapore*. Singapore: Trinity Theological College, 2013.

SISTERS IN ISLAM

Sisters in Islam (SIS) is an organization in Malaysia that campaigns for gender equality and women's rights. It was founded in 1987 and institutionalized in 1990. The group formally registered as "SIS Forum (Malaysia) Berhad" in 1993. The office is in Petaling Jaya, near Kuala Lumpur. Its members are mainly female Muslim professionals, many of them lawyers, academics, journalists, and activists. Zainah Anwar, a prominent Malaysian women's rights activist, is one of the founders and served as the long-term executive director before a committee took over. The organization campaigns for changes on the legal and policy levels, offers legal advice, and conducts research and trainings.

The group's original focus was to challenge laws and policies based on interpretations of Islamic traditions that the members considered discriminative against women. One of the group's foci has been the Islamic Family Law within the Malaysian quasi dual legal system in which matters regarding family are handled by so-called shari'a courts. SIS argues that the Malaysian Islamic Family Law used to be one of the most progressive in the Muslim world regarding the position of women, but that women's rights have been eroding since the late 1980s. A case in point are the polygamy laws: the fact that Islamic marriages are subject to state law rather than federal law makes it possible for men to travel to a neighboring state and marry a second wife without having to ask his first wife's consent. SIS also campaigns against a *shari'a* law that entitles men to support their polygamous marriage using the matrimonial assets of the first (or any other) wife. Later, the group's areas of work expanded to encompass larger issues of democracy, human rights, and constitutionalism. Their arguments are rooted in concepts of Islam as well as human rights and democracy. SIS members and supporters emphasize the need to reinterpret the Qur'an and Hadith. They interpret the Islamic sources within their respective historical contexts and work within traditions of liberal Muslims such as Abdullahi An-Na'im and Amina Wadud.

SIS has aimed campaigns at influencing amendments and claims some success in the field. Other areas of work are research, advocacy, legal counseling, public education, and publications. Between 2004 and 2010, SIS undertook a nationwide survey on impacts of polygamy on families, interviewing first and second wives as well as husbands of polygamous families. The organization also keeps an archive for local and foreign journalists and scholars. SIS has long used the media as one of the most significant parts of its advocacy work, issuing statements for the media, writing letters to the editors, and contributing regular columns. The group is domestically and globally well connected. In several of its campaigns, SIS has cooperated with a Malaysian coalition of NGOs known as the Joint Action Group for Gender Equality. It comprises six NGOs: SIS, Women's Aid Organization, All Women's Action Society, the Malaysian Trade Union Congress Women's Committee, Women's Development Collective, and Women's Centre for Change, Penang. SIS also has strong transnational ties to Muslim women's rights organizations in neighboring Indonesia. The similarity of the languages facilitates the exchange of material and expertise. SIS and their Indonesian counterparts such as the organization "Rahima," occasionally organize educational trainings across national borders. SIS has also hosted the Secretariat of the Musawah-network, a network "For Equality in the Muslim Family," connecting groups and individuals with similar interests from approximately 50 countries.

SIS has drawn criticism from religious scholars, from the Malaysian Islamic Development Department, other state religious bodies, and the Islamic opposition party Parti Islam Se-Malaysia. Many emphasize the members' lack of formal Islamic credentials and argue against their right to speak for Muslims and on Islamic issues. There have also been attempts to ban the association. In 2008, a prohibition order of a SIS publication was gazetted on the basis that the book was prejudicial to public order. The ban was lifted two years later.

SIS is regularly criticized for elitism and for its closed, invitation-only membership. They are also criticized for accepting foreign funding from Western agencies and for being better known internationally than in Malaysia itself. They counter the criticism of foreign funding with attempts to increase their domestic financial ties. Other criticism has been aimed at the focus on the Muslim family, rather than on Muslim women per se, especially those deviating from gender norms. Members of the group argue that the focus and membership cannot be overly expanded without losing its potency.

Saskia Louise Schäfer

See also: Education; Indonesia; Islam; Malaysia; Reform Movements; Sexuality; *Shari'a*; Women.

Further Reading

Anwar, Zainah. *Wanted: Equality and Justice in the Muslim Family*. Kuala Lumpur: Musawah, 2009.

International Congress of Islamic Feminism. http://feminismeislamic.org (accessed May 13, 2014).

Othman, Norani. *Muslim Women and the Challenge of Islamic Extremism*. Petaling Jaya: Sisters in Islam, 2005.

Sisters in Islam. http://www.sistersinislam.org.my (accessed May 13, 2014).

SIVARAKSA, SULAK

Sulak Sivaraksa is a Thai academic, scholar, Buddhist layperson, author, social critic, and outspoken activist. Sivaraksa is best known for his outspoken advocacy for the poor (both rural and urban) in resistance to those in power. Sivaraksa has also competently joined Buddhist morals and ethics into a powerful message for empowerment and temperament within the context of political equality and social justice in Thailand.

Sulak Sivaraksa was born on March 27, 1933, in what was then Siam. He attended elementary and secondary school in a Buddhist monastery before attending university at St. David's University College in Wales, where he received a Bachelor of Arts in 1958. Later in 1961, Sivaraksa earned a Barrister at Law from the Middle Temple, London. Sivaraksa was awarded a postgraduate grant from the Social Science Research Council in New York.

Upon returning to Thailand after finishing his formal academic training, he became involved in academics by teaching at prestigious universities in Thailand, such as the Mahidol and Chulalongkorn universities. He began his publishing career by founding one of Thailand's most respected academic journals, *Social Science*

Review (*SSR*), which gave voice to critics and academics of the time. Academic criticism via the *SSR* eventually led Sivaraksa to be persecuted, leading to his self-imposed exile after the violent military crackdown on student democracy protesters in 1976 (Sivaraksa n.d.). During his period of exile, Sivaraksa lectured at the University of California at Berkeley, Cornell University and University of Hawaii, among others. During this period of exile, Sivaraksa formulated extensive links with American advocacy groups, academics, and NGOs. Upon his return to Thailand in 1979, Sivaraksa began his engagement with Thailand's rural population by forming various NGOs such as the Asian Cultural Forum on Development as well as Buddhist sanctuaries such as Wongsanit Ashram where people could become engaged with Buddhist teachings as well as educated towards ethical and moral activism.

In 1989, Sivaraksa founded the International Network of Engaged Buddhists (INEB), an umbrella organization that links Buddhist communities and centers in 23 countries around the world. Sivaraksa has twice been arrested, in 1984 and 1991, both times being acquitted (Amnesty International 1991). He has been nominated for the Nobel Peace Prize on two occasions and, in 1995, was awarded the Right Livelihood Award (considered the alternative Nobel Prize) by the Swedish Parliament. Sivaraksa is a practitioner and advocate of Engaged Buddhism, which seeks an alternative reading of Buddhist scriptures and strives to empower individuals with moral and ethical foundations to engage the world in which we live and make changes for the better. Engaged Buddhism advocates human rights, environmental sustainability, social justice, rights for the poor and dispossessed, nonviolence, and fighting racism and discrimination, among many other worthy social causes (Dhammahaso 2009). Sivaraksa advocates a strong approach to solving social ills and social injustice by maintaining the Buddhist ethics of mindfulness, compassion, duty to oneself as well as others, self-realization, and empowerment to fight those that seek to take advantage of those which are vulnerable or lack power and the ability to fight against being taken advantage of (Sivaraksa 2001).

William J. Jones

See also: Buddhism; Education; Engaged Buddhism; Hanh, Thich Nhat; Morality; Reform movements; Religion and Society; Religious Discrimination and Intolerance; Study of Religion; Thailand.

Further Reading

Amnesty International. "Thailand: Prisoner of Conscience: Sulak Sivaraksa." Amnesty International, ASA 39/017/1991. September 1991. https://www.amnesty.org/es/library/asset/ASA39/017/1991/es/1068644d-ee3f-11dd-99b6-630c5239b672/asa390171991en.pdf (accessed May 13, 2014).

Dhammahaso, Phramaha Hansa. "Engage Buddhism in Thailand: A Case Study of Monks of New Movement in Interpretation and Dissemination of Buddhadhamma." Second Bi-Annual International Conference of the Association of Theravada Buddhist Universities, Sagaing, Myanmar, March 4–8, 2009.

Sivaraksa, Sulak. "Religion and World Order from a Buddhist Perspective." In *Toward a Global Civilization? The Contribution of Religions*, edited by Patricia M. Mische and Melissa Merkling. New York: Peter Lang. 2001.

SOUTHEAST ASIAN RELIGIONS IN THE USA

For the first two centuries of U.S. history, almost all its people came from Europe. That has changed in the past generation. The Immigration Act of 1965, which was initiated by John F. Kennedy, dropped the quotas that formerly favored Europeans. This paved the way for an increase in migration from Asia, including Southeast Asia, and by the 1970s, there were as many Asians as Europeans coming to the United States to live and work on a permanent basis. By the 1990s, U.S. population growth was more than one-third driven by immigration, as opposed to one-tenth before the act. Ethnic and racial minorities, as defined by the Census Bureau, rose from 25 percent in 1990 to 30 percent in 2000. According to the 2000 census, roughly 11 percent of U.S. residents were foreign-born, a major increase from the low of 4.7 percent in 1970. Subsequent data indicates the number of Asian immigrants increasing from 19 percent of all new immigrants in 2000 to 36 percent in 2010.

Islam is the most widely practiced religion in Southeast Asia. Muslims number approximately 240 million, which translates to about 40 percent of the entire population, with majorities in Brunei, Indonesia, and Malaysia. Significant minorities are located in the other Southeast Asian states. Most Muslims in Southeast Asia, as also their counterparts in the United States, follow the path of Sunni Islam, with its accent on the *Ummah*, the community of believers, its external success and its hermeneutical rigor. Within this tradition, the Shafi'i school of religious law stipulates four sources of authoritative jurisprudence: the Qur'an, the *Sunnah*, or the way taught and practically instituted by the Prophet Muhammad as a teacher and best exemplar, *ijma* ("consensus"), and *qiyas* ("analogy").

A generation ago, *Islam in Southeast Asia* had a greater reputation for pluralism flexibility, and tolerance than that is found in the Middle East, especially the literalist, strict, puritanical approaches of Wahhabist Islam. Even today, the picture of a fanatical, rigid, and militant Islam does not characterize the vast majority of Muslims in the region. Indeed, Southeast Asian Muslims are not only aware of, but identify with the global Islamic community. While sensing that Islam is a target of outside forces that want to weaken its place in the world, they practice their religion faithfully.

The terrorist attacks of September 11, 2001, significantly complicated relations between Muslims and the rest of North American society. When Southeast Asia was

---

The Philippines has produced the most immigrants to the United States among Southeast Asian countries. The majority of them are Roman Catholics. Between 1981 and 1995, the totals by country were: Vietnam, 676,000; Laos, 180,000; Cambodia, 116,000; and Thailand, 95,000. Vietnamese immigrants came from South Vietnam, which the United States supported in the Vietnam War. Many were military or civilian officials of the defeated South, some of them were Roman Catholics whose families had fled North Vietnam when it had fallen to the Communists in the mid-1950s, and some others were of Chinese descent.

David C. Scott

designated as a "second front" in the U.S. war against terrorism in late 2001, Muslims, including those of Southeast Asia, became the subject of much negative attention. The result was a plummeting of approval of the United States among Southeast Asian Muslims.

However, subsequent surveys found the number of U.S. mosques increasing dramatically in the decade since the September 11, 2001 attacks, despite protests against their construction and allegations that they have promoted radicalism. Current data from the Council on American-Islamic Relations and the Islamic Society of North America and other groups that track membership and various aspects of religious life in the United States indicate 2,106 mosques, a 74 percent increase since the year 2000, when 1,209 mosques were counted. Of these, 32 mosques are of Southeast Asian origin. A trend among Muslim congregations toward suburbanization and integration into American life was also noted.

The *Philippines* has produced the most immigrants to the United States among Southeast Asian countries. There are 1.6 million, 4 percent of all immigrants, foreign-born Filipinos residing in the United States.

Christians are in the majority in the Philippines, 80 percent Roman Catholic, and 10 percent other denominations. Initially, the vast majority of Filipino migrant workers in the United States were male and between 18 and 34 years old. Since they were young, single men and predominantly Catholic, U.S. church officials became concerned about the "moral rectitude" of these early migrants. A number of Filipino Catholic clubs were established to encourage Filipinos in the practice of their faith, as well as assist in making appropriate burial arrangements, finding jobs and suitable schools.

In the early 1950s, the Maryknoll and Columban orders, which had been involved in missionary activities in the Philippines, established parishes that catered primarily to Filipino Catholics. In general, the Roman Catholic Church in the United States was not actively involved in helping Filipino immigrants in those early years. There were Catholic churches that refused marriages between Filipinos and Caucasians, as also burials, particularly of poor Filipinos, education for the children of poor Filipino migrants, and even confessions involving non-English speakers. In spite of these forms of rejection, however, Filipinos remained Catholics and identified themselves as such even if they were not actively practicing the faith. Religious events like christening, *novenas*, and funeral wakes, became not just religious but cultural and social activities as well.

Other large numbers of immigrants from Southeast Asia can be traced from the Vietnam War. Between 1981 and 1995, the totals by country were (in thousands): Vietnam, 676,000; Laos, 180,000; Cambodia, 116,000; and Thailand, 95,000. According to the 2010 census, the Vietnamese American population had grown to 1,737,433 and remains the second-largest Southeast Asian American subgroup following the Filipino American community.

Vietnamese immigrants came from South Vietnam, which the United States supported in the Vietnam War. Many were military or civilian officials of the defeated South, some of them Roman Catholics whose families had fled North Vietnam when it fell to the communists in the mid-1950s, and some others of Chinese descent.

The majority of Vietnamese Americans are Buddhist, but more accurately practice a fusion of Buddhism, Daoism, Confucianism, and native animist practices, including ancestor veneration, that have been influenced by Chinese folk religion. There are approximately 160 Vietnamese Buddhist temples in the United States, with most adopting a mix of Pure Land (*Tịnh Do Tong*) doctrines and Zen (*Thien*) practices. Usually temples are small, consisting of a converted house with one or two resident monks or nuns.

Arguably the most prominent figure in Vietnamese American Buddhism is the Zen teacher Thich Nhat Hanh, a practitioner of Engaged Buddhism in the West. However, it is widely held that his fame as a proponent of Engaged Buddhism and a new Zen style has little if any affinity with or foundation in traditional Vietnamese Buddhist practices. This, even though Thich Nhat Hanh often speaks of his early Zen practices in Vietnam during his Dharma talks, asserting that he continued and developed this practice in the West which has a distinctive Vietnamese Thien flavor. Thich Nhat Hanh's Buddhist teachings have started to return to a Vietnam where the Buddhist landscape is now being shaped by a combined Vietnamese and Westernized Buddhism that is focused more on meditative practices.

Approximately 25 percent of Vietnamese Americans are Roman Catholic, while a smaller but increasing percentage are Protestant. Monsignor Luong, well known in Catholic circles for his work among Vietnamese immigrants, in 1983 founded a parish in New Orleans. This began a decade-long boom in the area's Vietnamese

Boston residents participate in a guided meditation led by international peace activist, author, and Zen master Thich Nhat Hanh in front of Trinity Church in Copley Square on September 15, 2013. (Boston Globe/Getty Images)

population, as immigrants who had been settled in other parts of the nation began to move here. The Archdiocese of New Orleans claims 20,000 Catholics of Asian background, primarily Vietnamese. Other big centers for Vietnamese Catholics are Houston; San Jose, California; and Orange County, California.

Immigrants from *Laos* were mostly animistic tribal people from the mountains of Laos, who were isolated from modern technology. These *Hmong* people sided with the Americans against the leaders of their country, who in turn had been installed by their more powerful Vietnamese neighbors. Lacking the affinities that were helpful to immigrants from the Philippines and Vietnam in adjusting to life in America, Laotian refugees as a group have needed considerable support.

Laotian American populations, largely urban, have constructed numerous Buddhist temples, called *vat* or *wat*. Usually devotees adapt local domestic houses for religious practices. Over time, with congregational support, the structure is enlarged and customized, adding ethnic artwork and craftsmanship. The result is a Laotian Buddhist temple that has some traditional features. Much of the chanting and ritual in these temples is conducted in Pali, the scriptural language of Theravada Buddhism. Though most laypeople do not understand Pali, the language sounds familiar enough that if they attend a temple where the vernacular language is used, the chanting and ceremony remind them of home.

Immigrants from *Cambodia* are primarily survivors of the infamous genocidal Khmer Rouge regime, the radical ideologues of the Communist Party of Kampuchea who were responsible for the death of untold millions. Coming from the better-educated parts of the Cambodian population, these refugees have adapted well to life in America.

In 1978, the Cambodian monk Venerable Maha Ghosananda began to establish Buddhist temples in refugee camps in Thailand and in 1981 came to the United States to head the Cambodian Buddhist community in Rhode Island. This became the center for establishing Buddhist temples in the Cambodian refugee community.

The number of Cambodian temples in the United States increased during the 1980s as the number of Cambodians in the country increased dramatically. Between 1983 and 1986, more than 80 monks came to Providence, Rhode Island, from Cambodia and were sent to the 41 temples that had opened in North America. Some of these monks came through centers that had been established in Thailand.

Theravada Buddhism, the predominant religious tradition in Cambodia, is strong among Cambodian groups in the United States. In the 1980s, Wat Khmer DC, home of the Cambodian Buddhist Society, was constructed near Washington, D.C., financed by a massive outpouring of donations from Cambodian Buddhists throughout North America. This *wat* is one of the few outside Southeast Asia that has the consecrated boundary within which ordinations may be performed.

Thai immigration to the United States began in earnest during and after the Vietnam War, in which Thailand was an ally of the United States and South Vietnam. In the decade between 1960 and 1970, some 5,000 Thais immigrated to the United States. In the following decade, the number increased to 44,000. From 1981 to 1990, approximately 64,400 Thai citizens moved to the United States. According to the 2000 census, there were 150,093 Thais in the United States.

Between 1970 and 1974, Thai immigrants began to organize temples in Los Angeles and Washington, D.C. In 1970, a Thai monk was invited to Los Angeles to teach and perform Buddhist ceremonies. The Los Angeles Thai community formed the Thai-American Buddhist Association that year, and three additional monks visited the United States to plan the founding of a temple. In June 1971, a mission of Thai monks arrived in Los Angeles, and laypeople began to raise funds to purchase land on which to build a Thai-style temple, which was completed and dedicated in 1979. Buddha images for the shrine hall and two sets of scriptures were carried to the United States by monks and laypeople from Thailand. Wat Thai L.A. has grown dramatically since 1971 and is currently the largest Thai temple in the United States, serving thousands of people per year. Not long afterward, a group of Thai lay people in Washington, D.C., began to raise funds for a temple of their own, and two Thai monks took up residence at Wat Thai Washington, D.C., in 1974. *Vajiradhammapadip* Temple in New York, *Wat Buddhawararam* and *Wat Dhammaram* in Chicago also were started before 1979.

Immigration continued apace in the 1980s resulting in the establishment of more than 40 Thai temples at the end of the decade, including temples associated with the *Mahanikaya* or Council of Thai Bhikkhus and the *Dhammayut* Order. Typically, a group of laypeople first formed a committee to consider the issues involved in building a temple. They often sought advice from the monks at Wat Thai L.A. or Wat Thai Washington, D.C., or from monks they knew in Thailand. Prior to committee collecting donations, often a monk came to visit and consult with local people. Typically, a single-family house or a former church building would be rented or purchased, and monks, ideally from Thailand rather than from another temple in the United States, would take up residence. Many temples remain in these original buildings now, while others, particularly those that continue to accumulate financial resources, purchase new buildings or land to build Thai-style buildings.

There is overwhelming evidence that Southeast Asians and their religious traditions have, over the years, been acculturated and played a significant role in the life of the United States.

David C. Scott

See also: Brunei Darussalam; Buddhism; Cambodia; Christianity; Communism; Engaged Buddhism; Ethnicity; Diaspora; Fundamentalism; Globalization; Hanh, Thich Nhat; Indonesia; Islam; Khmer Buddhism; Laos; Maha Ghosananda; Malaysia; Philippines; Thailand; Thien Buddhism; Vietnam.

Further Reading

Association of Southeast Asian Nations. http://www.asean.org (accessed May 13, 2014)

Eliade, Mircea, ed. *Encyclopedia of Religion*. New York: Macmillan Publishing Co., 1987.

Migration Policy Institute. http://www.migrationinformation.org/usfocus (accessed May 13, 2014).

Numrich, Paul D. *The Faith Next Door: American Christians and Their New Religious Neighbors*. Oxford: Oxford University Press, 2009.

Phan, Peter C. *Vietnamese-American Catholics*. New York: Paulist Press, 2005.

Seager, Richard H. *Buddhism in America*. New York: Columbia University Press, 1999.

Smith, Jane I. *Islam in America*. New York: Columbia University Press, 1999.

SPIRIT MEDIUMSHIP

Spirit mediumship, often subsumed in the larger category of shamanism, pertains to an area of practice and representations involving particular forms of contact with the spiritual world. The specific feature of spirit mediumship is the way that its spiritual agents, whatever their origin and however the agency attributed to them becomes manifest, act in this world through the body of their human mediums. The relationship between medium and spirit may imply that the latter takes physical possession of the former, or that the former incorporates the latter. They may be linked to one another by sexual attraction, or the medium may simply be the vehicle through which the spirit communicates with humans. The spirit may be thought to exert a negative influence over the medium, who may fight against it ritually by means of an exorcism. Or it may be thought to have potentially beneficial effects, which the cult solicits and institutionalizes. Spirits may be summoned for therapeutic purposes or as part of a process of enhancing a polity's legitimacy. Or the practice may, on the contrary, reflect subversive leanings. More generally, the practice may be said to seek life-giving effects at the societal level.

The theatrical dimensions of spirit mediumship have also received much attention. Such an emphasis justifies analyzing the rituals as a performing arts genre. Yet we must be careful to note how the array of roles the practice entails may allow for more complex identifications and may require more extensive negotiation than straightforward theatrical events usually imply. In other words, among groups where it is found, spirit mediumship constitutes a complex practice, one taking on diverse forms and revealing specific aspects of these groups' socioreligious life.

Although spirit mediumship, as a cultic institution in which spiritual beings make themselves manifest in this world, is to be found almost everywhere in mainland Southeast Asia, it received little attention in the region's area studies literature until the 1990s. As George Condominas emphasized in a seminal paper (1976),

A spirit medium walks in a street procession through Phuket Town as part of the Phuket Vegetarian Festival in Phuket Town, Thailand. The event is held over a nine-day period in October, celebrating the Chinese community's belief that abstinence from meat and various stimulants during the ninth lunar month of the Chinese calendar will help them obtain good health and peace of mind. (Stephen J. Boitano/Getty Images)

Spirit mediumship is observed in mainland Southeast Asia as a cultic institution in which spiritual beings make themselves manifest in this world through the body of their human mediums. Since the end of the Cold War and following the development of a market economy as well as increasing globalization, spirit possession séances have been reported in urban communities as sophisticated urban performances of danced theater.

Bénédicte Brac de la Perrière

the reason for this neglect may have been a then-prevalent Orientalist bias in favor of the study of "great traditions," namely Buddhism and Confucianism. In his paper, the French anthropologist drew the first general picture, mainly grounded in rural ethnography, of the practice of mediumship in the region. But it was only after the end of the Cold War that the study of spirit mediumship in mainland Southeast Asia really took off. Countries that were closed for two or three decades (Vietnam, Laos, and Cambodia), during which time authoritarian regimes kept cults under tight control, were suddenly reopened to field research just as religious practices started to blossom once again. Other countries that had not been subject to such repressive regimes (Thailand and Malaysia) nevertheless shared in novel developments whereby spirit possession became inscribed in contemporary dynamics of urbanization, the market economy, and globalization. Today, Western and Asian academics address a full range of topics reflecting the modernity of contemporary spirit mediumship in mainland Southeast Asia.

Monique Sélim's study of spirit cults in a liberalizing Laos (2003) is particularly revealing of this new turn in the nature of spirit mediumship. While the Communist Party had completely banned the old autochthonous spirits and the royal cult they were associated with, the move toward a market economy has encouraged the appearance of new spiritual agents. These, along with their mediums, show greater conformity with Buddhist values while helping to effect complex transactions in the contemporary world of commerce.

However, it is probably in Vietnamese studies that these recent developments have generated the greatest wealth of new academic work, research inspired by the profusion of renewed practices of spirit mediumship responding to the novel sociopolitical situation as well as to the specific demand for rituals concerning the war dead. Since the implementation of the "Renovation" policy in 1986, the Cult of the Four Palaces, once reported upon by Maurice Durand (*Techniques et pantheon des mediums vietnamiens* [1959]), has come back into the light of day. This has given rise to paradoxical developments. Spirit mediums have revived their practice of venerating such spirits in private temples, but they are excluded from joining in public ceremonies honoring them. Gorgeous private possession séances have been described taking place, mainly in Hanoi (see Chauvet [2012] and Endres [2011] for instances). These are organized by enterprising spirit mediums reviving an old form of the Cult of the Four Palaces, which developed among the merchant classes during the nineteenth century. This development reflects both ambiguities surrounding practices whose efficacy deals with and depends on personal enrichment, and a more general commodification of religious traditions.

Furthermore, the long-standing tradition of venerating local deities links up with the contemporary dynamics of pilgrimage, resulting in such phenomena as the recent growth of the cult dedicated to the Lady of the Realm, a goddess who has a sanctuary at the boundary of South Vietnam, as shown by Philip Taylor (2004). In the complex cultural context of state margins, this single figure, free of lineage affiliation, had already been harnessed by imperial agents in charge of the boundaries. In the context of the state's policy of "Renovation," the Lady is now granted the role of a spiritual banker. A considerable number of women engaged in the informal sector of the economy come to her sanctuary; they do so along with spirit mediums who are drawn there both by their contractual relation with the spirit and by the entertainment the pilgrimage provides.

Paralleling these developments, other innovations have been observed in the Vietnamese religious landscape, especially by Heonik Kwon and Paul Sorrentino, giving rise to new spaces for mediumship, particularly the emergence of new forms of possession by the dead aimed at dealing with the ritually unsolved death toll of the war. A wealth of new studies helps show that, far from vanishing with the advent of modernity, spirit mediumship enjoys an important place in Vietnam's many social worlds.

The same could be said of Thailand today where, far from having diminished, spirit mediumship has moved to urban centers, where it has flourished particularly in the marketplace. However, there are still very few comprehensive studies of Thai spirit mediumship. One of the first was Rosalind Morris's description of a new type of spirit possession in Chiengmai formed out of diverse Northern Thai practices and arising as part of the process of modernization and centralization (2000). New urban spirit mediums are legitimated in their practice through appearances made by figures belonging to the corpus of historical Northern Buddhist stories, stories that relate resistance against the imposition of a normative Buddhism by the Thai state apparatus. In making these images of the past show up in today's Chiengmai, spirit mediums also represent the city's ability to attract wealth while they share in modern practices of representation.

A study of popular Buddhism (2012) by the late Thai scholar Pattana Kitiarsa pertains to a different kind of approach, one seeking to renew the study of Thai religion by tracing how its historical components get hybridized in the midst of new markets and mass media. In the process, two contrasting figures emerge: the magician monk and the spirit medium. However, Kitiarsa writes, both of them operate at the same confluence of millenarian Buddhism, astrology, therapeutic cults, and amulet cults. In this way, spirit mediumship in his analysis becomes encompassed in the study of new Thai religious movements that have been dubbed "prosperity cults."

Spirit mediumship in Chinese communities in Southeast Asia is a distinct tradition. In Penang (DeBernardi 2006) and other sites of the Chinese diaspora, Chinese spirit mediums have been reported providing frequent therapeutic consultations, and practicing divination and exorcism, since the end of the nineteenth century. In their practice today, Buddhist notions of karma are adapted to a Daoist ethos linking together prosperity, social status, and longevity. While spirit mediums describe their actions as intended to help people by means of various kinds of advice and religious teaching they provide, their actual practice consists mainly of dance performances through which they make Chinese gods and goddesses visible to their public.

In today's Southeast Asia, spirit medium séances tend to be organized as sophisticated urban performances of danced theater. Spirit possession is occasioned by a wide range of entities who descend into their mediums. They do this in a culturally determined, hierarchical series. Spirit mediumship is an important vehicle for reaffirming past and particular identities, while at the same time constituting a performing arts genre. Spirit mediums act as individual entrepreneurs (Endres 2011), developing their own clientele in a highly competitive market and reproducing their practice among their own networks. Although in the past most Southeast Asian traditions of spirit mediumship, with the exception of Chinese spirit mediums, were predominantly women's domain, more and more transvestites and homosexuals (both male and female) have been attracted to these practices in their recent urban developments. This form of urban spirit mediumship emerged first in Burma (Brac de la Perrière 1989) and North Vietnam, probably due to a historically earlier enlargement of social space. It is only recently, since the end of the Cold War and following the development of a market economy, as well as increasing globalization, that it has been reported more generally in urban communities of Southeast Asia.

Bénédicte Brac de la Perrière

See also: Ancestor Worship; Buddhism; Cambodia; Confucianism; Dance and Drama (Theater); Daoism (Taoism); Goddess Traditions; Laos; Malaysia; Orientalism; Popular Religion; Sexuality; Shamanism; Thailand; Vietnam.

Further Reading

Brac de la Perrière, Bénédicte. *Les rituels de possession en Birmanie. Du culte d'Etat aux cérémonies privées.* Paris: ERC, 1989.

Chauvet, Claire. *Sous le voile rouge. Rituels de possession et réseaux cultuels à Hanoi (Vietnam).* Paris: Les Indes Savantes, 2012.

Condominas, G. "Quelques aspects du chamanisme et des cultes de possession en Asie du Sud-est dans le monde insulindien." *L'autre et l'ailleurs. Mélanges offerts à Roger Bastide,* edited by J. Poirier and F. Raveau, 215–32. Paris, 1976.

DeBernardi, Jean. *The Way That Lives in the Heart: Chinese Popular Religion and Spirit Mediums in Penang, Malaysia.* Stanford, CA: Stanford University Press, 2006.

Endres, Kirsten. *Performing the Divine: Mediums, Markets and Modernity in Urban Vietnam.* Copenhagen: Nordic Institute for Asian Studies Press, 2011.

Kitiarsa, Pattana. *Mediums, Monks and Amulets: Thai Popular Buddhism Today.* Bangkok: Silkworm, 2012.

Morris, Rosalind. *In the Place of the Origins: Modernity and Its Mediums in Northern Thailand.* Durham, NC: Duke University Press, 2000.

Sélim, Monique. *Pouvoirs et marché au Vietnam. Les morts et l'Etat.* Paris: L'Harmattan, 2003.

Taylor, Philip. *Goddess on the Rise: Pilgrimage and Popular Religion in Vietnam.* Honolulu: University of Hawaii Press, 2004.

STUDY OF RELIGION

The study of religion is surrounded by many conditions and limitations. First, there is the individual scholar's motive for entering the field. Second, there is the availability of material and the extent to which the investigator is personally equipped to understand and analyze it. But given adequate motivation and access to relevant material, there remain several questions. How is the material to be organized and classified? What procedures for understanding are appropriate in a given instance? And can these procedures be elevated into general principles applicable in all studies? Further questions suggest themselves. To what extent do the personal presuppositions of the investigator affect the manner in which a given body of material is approached and analyzed? Ought the study of religion remain aloof from matters involving personal commitment, or may the student be permitted, even expected, to affirm the value of one religious tradition over against others? These questions, and many more of a similar kind, have been hotly debated in recent years. Taken together, they have virtually made of "methodology" an independent subdiscipline within the study of religion.

Religion is, itself, of course, notoriously difficult to define and circumscribe. This being so, it is only to be expected that there should be corresponding difficulties in respect to the study of religion. That religion functions at several levels—individual and collective, emotional, intellectual, social, and ethical—is universally recognized in theory, while being difficult to apply in practice. Depending on the limits set by the individual investigator, the study of religion may concentrate on a single function or aspect of religion, such as myth or symbol, to the exclusion of others. A prior conviction on the observer's part that the "essential" component of religion is to be found in one of its functions rather than others has the effect of indicating that this function is primary among the range of observable phenomena. The sociologist examines one function, the psychologist another, simply as a matter of professional competence and personal choice. The philologist has been trained to interpret words and, if there is no textual material, may be completely disoriented. Specialization of this order is necessary, of course, but may become a danger when alternative methods and approaches are unrecognized and unappreciated, or when the range of religion's expressions is narrowed down to what the specialist is capable of mastering; in such cases, it is appropriate to speak of "reductionism." To the extent that the study of religion actually is a meeting point of disciplines, many of

> Specialization in the study of religion is necessary, but may become a danger when alternative methods and approaches go unrecognized and unappreciated, or when the range of religion's expressions is narrowed down to what the specialist is capable of mastering. In such cases it is appropriate to speak of "reductionism." To the extent that the study of religion actually is a meeting point of disciplines, it must accept a great diversity of possible approaches and methods. All of these are applicable to the study and classification of religious traditions in Southeast Asia.
>
> *David C. Scott*

which enjoy independent existence in the academic world, it must accept a great diversity of possible approaches and methods.

Method in the Study of Religion

The American scholar Morris Jastrow (1861–1921) is an example of one who insisted on the significant importance of method in the study of religion. He argued that method is the principal protection against the "personal equation," i.e., the assumptions and beliefs of the investigator that distorted the study of religion due to their own subjective biases, including "true believers" who study religions to laud the superiority of their own and belittle those of others and skeptics who start with the preconception that all religions are false. According to Jastrow, the cure for such naïveté and distortion was to adopt a historical approach, which consisted of gathering data from all times and places, arranging them systematically, interpreting them within a strictly natural and human framework, exploring their inner emotional aspects, and doing a comparative study to discover the essential laws of the development of religion. If one adds to this Jastrow's insistence on a methodological reservation, i.e., holding back on one's own views on ultimate truth and value as well as on a sympathetic understanding of other faiths and ways, one has a thumbnail sketch of the problems and concerns of the study of religion up to the last quarter of the twentieth century.

Evolutionary Theories of Religious Development

Scientific and intellectual developments of the seventeenth and eighteenth centuries provided the model for new approaches to the study of religion. The French philosopher Auguste Comte (1798–1857) discerned a progressive historical development of the sciences (from the simplest and most abstract to the most complex and concrete) and a corresponding development in society (from a theological-mythical stage to a positive-scientific stage). Although he may seem to have relegated religion to an infantile social stage, he saw it as a progressive force in previous ages and even proposed a "religion for humanity" for the modern scientific era.

The English philosopher Herbert Spencer (1820–1903) was another thinker proposing the theory of evolution from the simple to the complex in all fields of knowledge. Evolution was for him an "organic law," operating uniformly in all types of phenomena. He saw the origin of religion in the belief in spirits or ghosts, which was derived from dreams. This led to belief in an unchangeable human soul and, later, in gods as eternal, divine personalities. From the belief in ghosts came ancestor worship, the original religious cult. Spencer considered religion to be a valuable social force, binding human beings together and conserving traditional values. Together with Comte, Spencer made an evolutionary approach to the study of religion possible.

Comparative Study of Religion

It is customary to set the beginning of the comparative study of religion somewhere in the third quarter of the nineteenth century with the work of the German-British specialist in languages F. Max Muller (1823–1900). Muller's wide knowledge of

Indo-European languages, his comparative approach to the study of languages, and by extension of that method to the study of religion, resulted in his proposing a predictable dependence of thought on language and a search for the origin of god-names, religious beliefs, and myths.

Anthropological Approaches

E. B. Tylor (1832–1917), an English cultural anthropologist, is generally regarded as the founder of the anthropological study of religion. Assuming that the customs and beliefs of contemporary primitive cultures, such as those found in Southeast Asia, described by Western travelers, missionaries, colonial administrators, and so on, were survivals of a prehistoric era, he concluded that they provide evidence of the original stage of religion. He also assumed that the stage of spiritual culture corresponded to the crude stage of material culture in archaic or primitive societies. Tylor is most noted for his theory of animism: the earliest stage of religion consisted in the belief in souls/spirits present not only in human beings, but in all natural organisms and objects. There is still an active practice of animism in Malaysia and other parts of Southeast Asia.

The French sociologist Emile Durkheim (1858–1917) emphasized the social character of religion and totemism as the most elementary form of religious life. Totemism is a system of belief in which each human is thought to have a spiritual connection or a kinship with another physical being, such as an animal or plant, often called a "spirit-being" or "totem." The totem is thought to interact with a given kin group or an individual and to serve as their emblem or symbol. Durkheim further associated totemism with the distinction between the realms of the sacred and the profane. The totem is concrete symbol of the sacrality of the group and its god, and hence the focus of the group's cult. He proceeded from a definition of religion as a system of beliefs and practices regarding the sacred that unites human beings into a moral community. For him, religion is inherently a social reality.

An eminent proponent of firsthand observation was the Polish-British anthropologist Bronislaw Malinowski (1884–1942). He is best known for his practice of living with the people he was studying, learning their language, participating in their activities, getting to know the way they thought, and absorbing the intimate tone and color of their customs and ceremonies, as well as making a statistically documented analysis of their social organization and culture and recoding verbatim in the original language the statements, stories, folklore, and magical formulae of his informants. He is rightly noted for his heralding of "participant observation" as a key method in anthropological research.

Historical-Phenomenological Approaches

In contrast to the leading scholars in modern anthropology, many of the seminal scholars in the development of this new discipline were also theologians and deeply pious Christians. Rudolf Otto (1869–1937), a German theologian and specialist in the Hindu religious tradition, found throughout Southeast Asia, worked out a systematic relation between Christian theology and the world of religious experience, which he insisted possessed a unique quality irreducible to nonreligious categories, such as anthropological, sociological, economic, and so on. He found clues to this religious category in the idea of "the Holy," a fundamental category of meaning and value, and in the sense of "the numinous," i.e., awesome, extraordinary, mysterious, "wholly other" presence that evokes feelings of both fascination and fear. This is elaborated in his signal work *The Idea of the Holy* (1917) that has come to be recognized as a great founding work in twentieth-century phenomenology of religion.

Mircea Eliade (1907–1986), a Romanian-born historian of religions, produced a richly creative corpus of works on concrete subjects in the history of religions such as yoga and shamanism, and on the general patterns of religious experience, which culminated in an ambitious multivolume history of religious beliefs and ideas from the Stone Age to the Death-of-God era. Eliade sought the *arche*, or essential structure, of religion in its prehistoric and primitive forms. He saw these archaic expressions of religious experience as archetypal responses to the presence of the sacred in this-worldly objects and in events that are regularly repeated within a time frame that is cyclical rather than sequential. In contrast to isolated historical phenomena, Eliade's emphasis was on the general patterns he observed. He examined, for example, whole systems of plant, or water, or moon symbols, claiming that only within the context of such systems can the meanings of individual symbols be understood.

Psychological Approaches

Psychological approaches to the origin and nature of religion go back as far as the ancient Greeks. The Roman poet Lucretius put into immortal Latin verse the idea of religion's birth in fear. There is an obvious psychological component in Otto's "sense of the numinous." Moreover, the above survey of anthropological theories of religion should have made it evident that they comprise psychological as well as sociological viewpoints.

A great name in the psychology of religion is the American philosopher and psychologist William James (1842–1910). James approached religion from a basically pragmatic point of view. To find this, he focused on a descriptive survey and typology of personal religious experience, in keeping with his general view of the primacy of experience over thought and of the personal over the institutional. He viewed religious experience as involving intense human emotions and feelings directed toward some unseen order, reality, or power "out there," to which the human beings adjust and surrender.

C. G. Jung (1875–1961), a Swiss psychiatrist, developed a psychological view of religion through his studies of images in classical mythology, gnosticism, which teaches that salvation comes through secret spiritual truths, and his observation of similar images in his patients' dreams. This led him to the perception of a "collective unconscious" underlying individual consciousness. He concluded that the similar (or identical) themes and symbols expressed in ancient myths and in twentieth-century dreams were to be attributed to archetypes in the collective unconscious of the human race.

Sociological Approaches

As with psychological approaches to religion, thoughtful considerations of the relation between religion and society go back to the ancient Greeks. Eminent Christian thinkers, concerned both with the shaping role of religion on society and with religion's response to growing secular power and influence, continued these reflections. Modern secular philosophers carried on the study of the relation from a strictly secular viewpoint, as evident in the thought of Comte and Spencer, noted above. We have also observed the marked societal focus of anthropologists of religion, such as Durkheim.

Rich and significant contributions to the sociological approach to the study of religion were made by German scholars, of whom the most influential was Max Weber (1864–1920). Weber emphasized the mutual influence of the economic and social spheres on one another, discerning a three-part typology of authority (traditional, charismatic, and legal-rational) in both areas. Weber's specialty was sociological studies of specific historical religions, e.g., Chinese and Indian religion and ancient Judaism, focusing on the values, especially religious values, which are the dominant norms of social structures.

Joachim Wach (1898–1955) the German American historian of religions and sociologist of religion, won early fame for presenting the structure and agenda for a discipline of religious studies that would do justice to the task of describing the entire religious experience of humankind. He is also well known for his work on the sociology of religion, a discipline he regarded essential in the study of religion. The social for him is one of three basic expressions of religious experience, the theoretical and the practical being the others, and focuses on the relation of religious community to "ultimate reality." He insisted on the distinctive character of religious groups as distinct from other social forms because of their essential focus on reality that is awesome, extraordinary, mysterious reality or "the numinous."

The Current Situation

By the last quarter of the twentieth century, various new approaches in the social sciences and humanities had become the center of attention and inevitably influenced the study of religion. The new approaches may be summed up by the terms *structure*, *symbol* (or sign), and *system*. These had played a role in previous generations in human studies, but they assumed a different tone and direction in a new age. The notions of structure and system, for example, had previously been modeled on the biological concept of organism, but now they arose from linguistics, the study of language, with a corresponding shift from the generally biological to the specifically human and so to the operations of the human mind.

The central figure in this development has been the French anthropologist Claude Levi-Strauss (1908–2009). He sees human culture, myth, and religion as basically sign-systems whose deep structures or underlying patterns, embedded in the human unconscious, can be discerned through systematic analysis. He breaks down his argument into three main parts: (1) meaning is not isolated within specific fundamental parts of the myth, but rather is to be found within the entire myth;

(2) although myth and language are of similar categories, language functions differently in myth; and (3) language in myth exhibits more complex functions than in any other linguistic expression.

He finds order in the great variety of myths, rites, and kinship systems, which leads him to assert the fundamental rationality of primitive thought. Unlike Durkheim, who derived primitive classification from the primitive social order, Levi-Strauss finds the basis of social patterns in the structures of the human mind.

The American anthropologist Clifford Geertz (1926–2006), who is highly acclaimed for his research in Indonesia, sounds a distinctly new tone, epitomized by his stress on the term *meaning*, both in its referential sense and in the sense of meaningfulness. He likens the cultures and religions he has investigated to works of art. This inevitably involves a semiotic approach to culture, an approach that studies the way in which people communicate through signs and symbols, since the anthropologist is confronted with strange cultural contexts that he can understand only by unpacking the meanings of their signs (or symbols). He defines symbol as "any object, act, event, quality, or relation which serves as a vehicle for a conception—the conception is the symbol's meaning." Geertz sees sacred symbols as possessing a unique double quality. On the one hand, they provide a representation of the way things are, and on the other, a guide or program for human action—an ethics or aesthetics. Sacred symbols express both an "is" and an "ought to be."

David C. Scott

See also: Alatas, Syed Hussein; Christianity; Colonialism; Hinduism; Humanism; Ileto, Raymond C.; Missionary Movements; Myth/Mythology; Orientalism; Postcolonial Theory; Secularism; Shamanism; Spirit Mediumship.

Further Reading

Eliade, Mircea, and Joseph Kitagawa, eds. *The History of Religions: Essays in Methodology*. Chicago: University of Chicago Press, 1959.

Glock, Charles Y., and Phillip E. Hammond, eds. *Beyond the Classics? Essays in the Scientific Study of Religion*. New York: Harper Torchbooks, 1973.

Segal, Robert, ed. *The Blackwell Companion to the Study of Religion*. Oxford: Blackwell Publishing, 2006.

Sharpe, Eric J. *Understanding Religion*. New York: St. Martin's Press, 1983.

Waardenburg, Jacques. *Classical Approaches to the Study of Religion: Aims, Methods, Theories of Research*. 2 vols. The Hague: Mouton de Gruyter, 1973–1974.

SUFISM

Sufism (*tashawwuf* in Arabic) is the interiorization of Islamic teachings and practices that focus on the spiritual dimension. It is often contrasted to *shari'a* that puts the importance on the external dimension of Islam. Sufism uses the language of love, beauty, and mercy of God more than majesty, severity, and the wrath of God, commonly used in Sharia. From the Sufism perspective, Islam is perceived as the religion of love aiming at the unity of human and God and the actualization of God characters in the human's life. The term *sufi* derives from *suf* (wool) as the coarse

A whirling dervish performs in a Sufi tradition involving music and dance. (logosstock/iStockphoto.com)

material that the *sufi* used for clothing, symbolizing ascetics and renunciation. Other etymology suggests that *sufi* comes from the word *safa*—"to be pure"—or from *suffa*—the raised platform in the Prophet's mosque in Medina where poor people used to sit and exercise devotion.

The rise of Sufism was stimulated by a reaction to the secular life and attitude of the new ruling dynasty of the Umayyad at their court, the majority of whom behaved in contrast to the simple piety of the four early caliphs. Moreover, reaction to *kharijism* (a radical sect in Islam) and its political controversies encouraged people to desist not only from politics, but also from public affairs. This trend was in the eighth century in which people like Hasan of Bashra (d. 728 CE), who influenced the spiritual history of Islam, deepened the inwardness of people's ethical lives. Nevertheless, Sufism can be traced to the life of the Prophet and his companions who showed signs of the interiorization of the moral motive. One of the theological foundations of Sufism is the Prophet's *hadith* (Sayings) on three elements of Islamic religion consisting of *Iman* (belief), *Islam* (submission), and *Ihsan* (doing the beautiful). *Ihsan* is the worshipping of God as if you see Him. For Sufi, the keynote for Muslim obedience is responsibility to the moral ideal. To be a Muslim, people have to "do the beautiful" by purifying their spiritual dimension in addition to having belief and submission.

Rituals in Sufism are centered on *dhikr* and *sama'*. *Dhikr* means the remembrance and mentioning of God's names and emptying the heart from anything but God and

---

Often, *karama* (divine distinction) and *baraka* (blessing) are part of the charismatic authority of Muslim leaders who are associated with Sufism. *Karama* is the quality of a saint on whom Allah has bestowed the ability to understand divine things hidden from human sight. The power such a person receives from God enables that person to transcend the normal human situation and transfer God's blessing to the people. *Baraka* is the spiritual quality reflected through the saint who is gifted with *karama*. *Baraka* can be transferred to ordinary people through the saint's prayers and by building a good relationship with him.

Bambang Budiwiranto

establishing the divine qualities in the human being. Sufis, under a master's guidance, recite certain *dhikr* suitable to their condition. The second ritual is *sama'*, or listening to poetry and music. Poetry is an important means of Sufis' expression of their love and longing to God and is written in different languages: Arabic, Persian, Turkish, and Urdu. In *sama'*, the spiritual role of the listeners to the words of the poem that may be accompanied by the music is more important than that of the performers. Continuous *dhikr* and *sama'* will transform God's names in the Sufi's mind and consciousness and leave no room for remembrance of others. This eventually leads to the "seeing of God" and actualization of the divine image in human behavior.

In the ninth century, Sufism formulated the methodology of its "inner way," "spiritual itinerary" to God to standardize and objectify its practice. Dhu al-Nun of Egypt (d. 859) systematized the practice into stages (*maqamat*), that is stations the Sufi has to acquire to reach the peak of mystical path, and states (*ahwal*), psychological and spiritual transformation that Sufi undergoes in attempts to pass through the stations. This spiritual itinerary became definite and led to the doctrine of absorption and annihilation (*fana*) attributed to Abu Yazid al-Bisthami (d. 874) and al-Husayn ibn Mansur al-Hallaj (d. 922) who spoke ecstatic utterance (*shathahat*) in a state of intoxication such as, "I am your Lord" and "I am the Truth" (*Ana al-Haq*). These people are categorized as drunken Sufis that focused on experiencing God in this life (Gnostic, *Irfan*, unveiling God). Islamic orthodoxy considers intoxication as heresy and it was paid by al-Hallaj's execution for the charges of having identified himself with God and of deceiving people with sorcery. In the period of ninth and tenth centuries, the effort to bridge orthodoxy and Sufism was led by Junayd of Baghdad (d. 911), al-Sarraj (d. 987), and Kalabadhi (d. 995), who proposed a moderate Sufism with a structure of ideas consistent with and even lending support to orthodoxy (sober Sufism). This effort was followed by Qushayri (d. 1073) and Abu Hamid al-Ghazali (d. 1111) that synthesized Sufism and orthodox theology.

The interaction among fellow wayfarers through advice and counsel is essential for spiritual life's progression. This evolved in more structured interaction between master and disciples who then reside together in a hospice called *zawiyah* (*ribath*, *khanqah*, *tekke*) that consists of the center of spiritual activities. This center was first established by the Karramiyya movement in Iran. Such social organizations then developed and became Sufi orders or *thariqa* (a method of spiritual practice). *Thariqa* reached its golden age in the twelfth century when Sufi masters attached their names to groups that signified certain spiritual methods such as Qadiriya (Abd Qadir al-Jilani; d. 1166) in North Africa and Southeast Asia, Shadziliyya (Abu Hasan al-Shadhili; d. 1258) in North Africa, Christiyya (Mu'in al-Din Christi; d. 1236) in South Asia, and Mevleviyya in Turkey, known as "whirling dervishes" using music and dance. Common to *thariqa* is a "chain" (*silsilah*) connecting disciples and masters with upward lineage to the Prophet as the first source of Sufi practices. *Silsilah* also functions as a means for the transmission of spiritual power and blessings and signifies the master's authorization to disciples to practice the *dhikr* formula prescribed in his order.

Sufism entered Southeast Asia in the late sixteenth century, especially in Aceh Sultanate of North Sumatra. The two exponents of Sufism were Hamzah Fansuri (d. 1590) and Shamsuddin al-Sumatrani (d. 1630), who taught the Ibn Arabi doctrine of *wahdat al-wujud* (union of human with God) and of the seven stages of existence. Both of them belonged to the Qadiriyya and the Naqshabandiyya order, respectively, and served as religious advisors in Aceh Sultanate. From the seventeenth century, *thariqa* developed in Indonesia under the influence of more sober Sufi teachers in Arabia such as Ahmad Qushashi (d. 1071/1660) and Ibrahim Kurani (d. 1102/1691) through an intellectual network with Indonesian Archipelago students in Arabia. In 1957, Nahdlatul Ulama, the largest religious organization in Indonesia, established association with *Jam'iyyah Ahli Tarekat Mu'tabarah,* an association that united all Sufi orders in Indonesia whose work was suitable with Islamic orthodoxy. In the present time, Sufi orders in Indonesia serve not only spiritual purposes but also help in overcoming drug addiction and in focusing on mental health cure.

Bambang Budiwiranto

See also: Attas, Syed Muhammad Naquib al-; Indonesia; Islam; Malaysia; Music; Nahdlatul Ulama; Popular Religion; Ritual Dynamics; Secularism; *Shari'a.*

Further Reading

Azra, Azyumardi. *The Origins of Islamic Reforms in Southeast Asia: Networks of Malay-Indonesian and Middle Eastern Ulama in the Seventeenth and Eighteenth Centuries.* Crownest, NSW, Australia: Allen and Unwin, 2004.
Chittick, William C. *Sufism: A Short Introduction.* Oxford: Oneworld Publication, 2000.
Ernst, Carl W. *The Shambala Guide to Sufism.* Boston and London: Shambala, 1997.
Knysh, Alexander. *Islamic Mysticism: A Short History.* Leiden; Boston; Koln: Brill, 1999.
Rahman, Fazlur. *Islam.* Chicago: Chicago University Press, 1979.

SYNCRETISM

Syncretism can be defined as the combining or bringing together of different, often seemingly contradictory beliefs and practices, to create something new, which includes key elements of the streams that had come together. Syncretism happens in many areas such as art, architecture, literature, philosophy, and religion and has different connotations depending on how it is viewed. To some, syncretism represents openness and inclusivity; it is seen as a natural and even a necessary process in human development. Some others, particularly in the religious field, look upon syncretism as a problem and fear that it leads to compromises and watering down of the essentials of one's religious beliefs. However, in the course of history, borrowing, combining and integrating happens, either naturally or intentionally; as a result, there are no "pure" cultures, philosophies, art, or religions.

This is particularly true of religion in Southeast Asia, which is predominantly Buddhist with the exception of Indonesia, with the largest Islamic population in the world, and the Philippines, which is predominantly Roman Catholic. In addition to Buddhism, Southeast Asia also has the other major Asian religions like

Syncretism is one of those words in the English language that has undergone many changes over the centuries in what it connotes. What is syncretism to some is enrichment for others. It is also of interest that a religion such as Christianity, which is the result of extensive syncretism with the Jewish, Greco-Roman, Middle Eastern, and European religions and cultures, is the one that most feared syncretism when it moved into Asia and Africa. It shows that there are many underlying currents to the fear of syncretism.

S. Wesley Ariarajah

Hinduism and Confucianism. They affirm plurality and multiplicity as the nature of reality and, therefore, have not been averse to syncretism. In fact, in Asian thinking, the influence, infusion, and even transformation of religious beliefs as a result of new insights or contact with another tradition is not seen as syncretism.

In the Southeast Asian context, Buddhism is a good example of openness to syncretism. When Buddhism moved from its moorings in North India into Tibet, China, Myanmar, Thailand, Indochina, and beyond into Northeast Asia, it continually concretized into the religion of each of these lands by absorbing and integrating the cultures and religious practices of these countries. As a result, Buddhism in Asia manifests itself in many forms—into Tibetan, Chinese, Thai, Cambodian, Vietnamese, Korean, and Japanese Buddhisms, each shaped by the language, culture, and local religious practices syncretized into the original teachings of the Buddha. The openness goes to the point of allowing for different canons of scriptures in the languages of the country where it struck roots. Buddhism in Thailand, Myanmar, and Indochina has many elements of Hinduism, which had a large influence in the region before the advent of Buddhism. More importantly, all expressions of Buddhism in Southeast Asia borrow and integrate heavily from the pre-Buddhist and existing traditional and tribal religions and their cultural practices.

Syncretism, however, has negative connotations, particularly to Islam and Christianity. As a religion based on the revelation given to the Prophet Mohammed, recorded as the Holy Qur'an, Islam has been keen to preserve the purity of the original teachings and the original practices developed for the observance of the Islamic faith in worship and life in community. The Indonesian Muslims, for instance, have significant cultural traits that they have inherited from the pre-Islamic period, which are different from the Arabic-speaking Muslims; but the religious beliefs and religious practices remain essentially the same in all Muslim countries. Any deviations in these areas are considered heretical and rejected.

Christianity is perhaps the religion that has struggled most with the question of syncretism as it moved into Southeast Asia. Again, as a religion founded at a particular period of time around the significance of the meaning of a particular person, Jesus, it had to struggle to preserve the "purity" of its faith as it moved into the world of other religions. However, since the New Testament is not understood as a direct revelation, as the Qur'an is believed to be, various interpretations of the significance of Jesus arose in the early church. After a prolonged struggle, the church put down some basic beliefs as the Creed of the church, marking the boundaries for interpretations of the meaning of Jesus. Anything that strayed too far from it was considered heretical.

There is no doubt that the Creeds are themselves the result of considerable syncretism of the original teachings of Jesus and beliefs about him in the Jewish context with the religions and philosophies of the Greco-Roman world into which Christianity had moved. Yet the Creedal affirmations constituted the orthodoxy of the Christian faith. When Christianity, with this background, came into Southeast Asia, which had long-standing religious beliefs that predated Christianity and had a strong grip on people's religious, cultural, and social lives, the missionaries saw syncretism as the strongest threat to Christianity. This was aggravated by the sharply different analyses of the human predicament and the way out of it in Christianity and Buddhism. The inextricably close relationship between religion, culture, and the way of life in Southeast Asia led the Christian missions to create alternate communities that separated the converts to Christianity from their religious and cultural heritage. This had also often meant breaking away from their immediate family ties. As a result of the fear of syncretism, Christianity and Islam failed to integrate with the cultures of Southeast Asia and, in the view of others, remain "foreign" religions.

The Christian fear of syncretism, however, was somewhat mitigated in Asia by movements toward inculturation, indigenization, and contextualization. These involved the use and integration of Southeast Asian music, symbols, architecture, art, etc., for new forms of Christian expression. There were also attempts to use Asian religious and philosophical concepts to interpret Christianity in Southeast Asia. From one perspective, these constituted a form of syncretism, described in new terms, but they were seen to be important for the relevance of Christianity in Southeast Asia. Gradually, and in order to accommodate this development, in Christian thinking, syncretism was redefined as "uncritical" assimilation of elements from other religions or attempts to create a new religion by bringing elements from a number of different religious traditions. This development, however, did not completely resolve the Christian nervousness about syncretism. Christianity in Southeast Asia still remains isolated from the identity and culture of the masses of its peoples.

It should be noted that even though Christianity as a religious tradition did not make much headway into most of Southeast Asia, its educational services, the Dutch, Portuguese, French, Spanish, British, and Japanese colonization of different parts of Southeast Asia and the continuing impact of neocolonial and global forces have transformed and syncretized the religions and cultures of Southeast Asia. For instance, the contemporary movement within Buddhism, "Engaged Buddhism," spearheaded from Thailand, is an instance of attempts to bring significant impulses from Christianity into Buddhist teachings and practice. Such movements are not understood in the Buddhist context as syncretistic.

In the postmodern context, many would see the fear of syncretism as outdated. All religions and cultures are considered hybrids shaped and constituted by a variety of different and even alien concepts and practices, resulting in overlapping of cultures and religious impulses. This certainly would be an appropriate description of the religious reality of Southeast Asia.

S. Wesley Ariarajah

See also: Buddhism; Cao Dai; Christianity; Confucianism; Contextualization; Education; Engaged Buddhism; Ethnicity; Hinduism; Interreligious Relations and Dialogue; Indonesia; Islam; Judaism; Melanesian Religion; Minorities; Missionary Movements; Music; Myanmar (Burma); Philippines; Religious Conversions; Thailand.

Further Reading

Cook, Alistair D. B. *Culture, Identity and Religion in Southeast Asia*. Newcastle upon Tyne, UK: Cambridge Scholars Publishing, 2007.

Dubois, Thomas David. *Casting Faiths: Imperialism and Transformation of Religion in East and Southeast Asia*. Hampshire, UK: Palgrave Macmillan, 2009.

Gahral, Donny, and Adrian Gahral, ed. *Relations between Religions and Cultures in Southeast Asia*. Washington, DC: Council for Research in Values and Philosophy, 2009.

Lindenfeld, David, and Miles Richardson, eds. *Beyond Conversion and Syncretism: Indigenous Encounters with Missionary Christianity*. Oxford: Berghahn Books, 2011.

Picard, Michel, and Remy Madinier, eds. *The Politics of Religion in Indonesia: Syncretism, Orthodoxy and Religious Contention in Java and Bali*. Oxford: Taylor and Francis, 2011.

THAILAND

With a land area of approximately 513,000 square kilometers, Thailand is the largest country in mainland Southeast Asia. It is home to some 65 million people, roughly 20 percent of whom live within the confines of Greater Metropolitan Bangkok, the country's capital city and principal urban center. Until 1939, it was known to the world as Siam, a traditional kingdom with a rich and diverse cultural heritage. Well into the twentieth century, the subjects of the realm were divisible into more than 70 ethno-linguistic groupings. Top-down nation-building policies sought to fuse this aggregation into a composite, a "Thai race" (*chat thai*) that shared a single overarching national culture. The name change from Siam to Thailand was a reflection of this process.

Religion figured prominently in the Thai nation-building effort. In the late nineteenth and early twentieth centuries, the kingdom's rulers undertook to reform and reorganize the Buddhist monastic order or *sangha*, establishing in 1902 a centralized administrative apparatus that subsequently worked to standardize local religious practices and buttress the authority of the throne. From the 1920s onward, monastic education was expanded and utilized for secular ends. Temple schools staffed by monk-instructors were an early vector for public education, which from the outset stressed the importance of (Theravada) Buddhism in Thai national life. This agenda, aggressively pursued through compulsory schooling and state-run media over the better part of a century, played a critical role in shaping contemporary Thai self-perception: at present, some 94 percent of all people in the kingdom identify themselves as Buddhist.

The near-establishment of Buddhism as *the* national religion of Thailand, an idea openly touted as recently as 2007 when the country's constitution was undergoing one of its periodic revisions, has effectively marginalized the country's other religious groupings, Muslims being the most notable among them. Constituting around 5 percent of the total population, Muslims can be found living throughout the kingdom, the result of centuries of trade-related migration. Most, but not all, are Sunni. Their numbers are particularly concentrated in the southern region, an area that was once a part of the Malay sultanate of Patani. A center of Islamic learning in its prime, Patani fell under the sway of adjacent powers and its former territories were eventually parsed in two by an expanding imperial Great Britain and a contracting imperial Siam. As a result of this history and the region's proximity to a broader Malay world, it was not readily subsumed into an evolving Buddhist "Thai-land" and the resistance of Malay-speaking Muslims to the Buddhist-backed nationalism of the center continues to constitute one of the more obvious rifts in the modern Thai polity.

Representations and Realities

It would be wrong to conclude from the above that religion in Thailand can best be understood in terms of two discrete communities of belief, one Theravada Buddhist and the other Sunni Muslim. Syncretism is a word often used in the literature on Thai religious practice, and for good reason. Irrespective of their formal religious affiliations, the Thai people inhabit a remarkably complex and convoluted spiritual terrain, a landscape reworked over the centuries through the intermingling of migrants from South, East, and Central Asia together with the more recent émigrés of Europe and North America. The resulting accretion of disparate beliefs is everywhere manifest in the layered religious practices of daily life. Animism is widespread: offerings are regularly made to the protective spirits (*jao thi*) of trees, rivers, and local municipalities. Spirit houses (*san phra phoom*) can also be found in most homes and workplaces, often appearing alongside ancestor shrines that make use of Confucian and Daoist iconography. They frequently incorporate Hindu icons as well, however. Indeed, the spirit houses of public markets are usually dedicated to Shiva, and it is not uncommon to find *linga* worshipped at the stalls of individual merchants. In recent years, the mercantile classes have also turned to Ganesh worship, transforming the deity into a patron of commercial endeavor in general and restaurants in particular. At the same time, they have cultivated a number of other spiritual patrons, worshipping the portraits and statues of various political figures, living and dead. King Chulalongkorn, who reigned from 1868 to 1910, now sits at the center of a civic religious cult: a protector of taxi drivers and small-scale entrepreneurs, his picture draws votive offerings, his statue in downtown Bangkok is the site of weekly religious ceremonies, and he is one of several former rulers to be periodically channeled by local spirit mediums.

Religious eclecticism is everywhere part of Thai public life. Brahmans officiate at state ceremonies presided over by members of the royal family. Major Thai national holidays, such as *songkhran* and *loi kratong*, are based upon and patterned after South Asian religious festivals. Construction firms propitiate local spirits and consult with Chinese geomancers before starting work. Important endeavors are seldom entered into without first consulting a fortune teller to determine an auspicious date. Fate is a perennial concern that also dictates the choice of names, colors, and numbers. It lies at the heart of the country's flourishing amulet trade as well. While images of the Buddha and likenesses of well-known local monks are some of its staple components, Hindu gods and Daoist deities figure prominently in the mix. The more valuable are produced under the auspices of individual holy men, whose merit and spiritual power are thought to be conveyed to the amulet, affording its possessor with special protection. Once conducted in flea markets and on temple grounds, the trade in talismans and sacred merchandise is now the stuff of exhibition halls in up-end shopping centers.

The Limits of Buddhist Orthodoxy

Syncretism and religious eclecticism also extend to local Buddhist practices. Buddhism is not an exclusive belief system, and after more than a century of state intervention and reform, the religion provides an umbrella for an exceptionally wide range of texts, authorities, organizational groupings, and activities. In the past, fault lines within the *sangha* ran between diverging regional orders. There was also a broad cleavage between town-dwelling (*gamavasi*) and forest-dwelling (*arannavasi*) monks. The former tended to rely upon text-based traditions, and the latter placed greater emphasis upon meditation. Ironically, a further division arose as a result of the efforts of Crown Prince Mongkut to purify local Buddhist practices through the establishment of a royally backed reform sect in the 1830s. His *dhammayuttika nikaya* or *thammayut* sect quickly evolved into a prestigious and comparatively influential organization. *Thammayut*-ordained monks played a central role in the crown's efforts to construct a kingdom-wide *sangha* organization in the early twentieth century, and they subsequently dominated both monastic administration and education. They nonetheless remained a statistical minority, and as a result, monks ordained outside of *thammayut* came to be collectively known as the *maha nikaya* or Greater Order—something of a misnomer in that the "order" was all along (and has remained) a collection of "orders" with diverging teachings and practices.

The relative number of monks in the *thammayut* and *maha nikaya* camps serves to indicate the limits of state-imposed orthodoxy: the former constitute less than 10 percent of the total. They command a dominant position in the Supreme Sangha Council, which in theory oversees and delimits the boundaries of acceptable Buddhist practice in Thailand, but the Council has traditionally taken an exceptionally non-confrontational approach to *sangha* management, leaving most of the kingdom's 280,000 or so monks to follow their own practices. Oversight comes instead from the country's 37,000 temple abbots (*jao awat*) acting in conjunction with locally constituted temple lay committees.

Decentralized administration and localized funding arrangements have seemingly combined to further undermine Thai Buddhist orthodoxy. Although a number of temples derive revenue from extensive land holdings and temple market facilities, many others have far less in the way of resources. Each year, the country's temples receive an estimated 100–120 billion baht in donations, but here again the money is exceptionally unevenly distributed. The lion's share goes to the bigger, better-known temple facilities, which are usually overseen by equally well-known abbot-monks, individuals with regional or national standing. Acting in conjunction with temple lay committees, abbots are free to utilize donation income in any way they see fit and often enhance the standing of their respective institutions through both constant improvement of temple infrastructure and overt promotional efforts. This usually involves the promotion of both the temple and its leading monks. The better-known monks of the realm are famous for many things besides religious insight. Some are prolific writers, and some television personalities appreciated for their wit and wisdom. Others are reputed masters of the supernatural, individuals believed capable of healing sickness, absolving sin, removing curses, and breaking spells. Monks from the forest tradition have on occasion emerged as ecological champions. They have also become meditation retreat organizers bent on improving the concentration and academic records of middle-class schoolchildren. In short, for some number of years now, the discourse of social engagement has pulled the *sangha* in many directions, creating a street value for the public personas of monks whose celebrity standing and income potential is increasingly determined by market forces.

Phra Phothirak, a songwriter and media figure turned religious reformer, is a case in point. Ordained as a *thammayut* monk, he left the order in the mid-1970s to establish his own fundamentalist movement, Santi Asoke. The reform agenda it pursued was sufficiently radical that the Supreme Sangha Council eventually commanded Phothirak and his followers to leave *maha nikaya* as well. The movement flourished nonetheless, pulling a growing number of middle-class followers into a networked religious community. In addition to expanding economic interests run by Santi Asoke followers, the community has its own educational facilities, and in recent decades, it has emerged as a conservative force in politics, picking up influential patrons and followers in the process.

Another example is afforded by the Dhammakaya Movement, one of the fastest-growing Buddhist sects in Thailand. Founded as a meditation school by Phra Mongkolthepmuni in the early twentieth century, the Dhammakaya Movement became increasingly popular in the early 1970s under the charismatic leadership of Phra Thepyanmahamuni (Luang Po Thammachaijo, formerly Chaiyabun Sitthitphon). Working through university Buddhist clubs, the movement became increasingly adept at publicity management, organizing periodic "mental discipline" training sessions, publicizing student testimonials, and orchestrating mass ordinations. Donations and membership have continued to grow up to the present, and

A Thai woman offers water to a devotee near the Bang Neow Shrine in Phuket. (AP Images/ David Longstreath)

the movement reputedly now has millions of followers in Thailand and branch organizations in some 18 countries overseas.

Matthew Copeland

See also: Buddhism; Confucianism; Daoism (Taoism); Dhammakaya; Ethnicity; Fundamentalism; Hinduism; Islam; Koyama, Kosuke; Nationalism; Santi Asoke; Secularism; Sivaraksa, Sulak; Spirit Mediumship; Study of Religion; Syncretism; Uplanders.

Further Reading

Heikkilä-Horn, M.-L. *Santi Asoke Buddhism and Thai State Response.* Turku, Finland: Åbo Akademi University Press, 1996.

Kitiarsa, Pattana. *Mediums, Monks, and Amulets: Thai Popular Buddhism Today.* Seattle: University of Washington Press, 2013.

Mackenzie, Rory. *New Buddhist Movements in Thailand: Towards an Understanding of Wat Phra Dhammakāya and Santi Asoke.* Oxon: Routledge, 2007.

Tambiah, Stanley. *Buddhism and the Spirit Cults in North-East Thailand.* New York: Cambridge University Press, 1970.

Taylor, J. L. "Buddhist Revitalization, Modernization, and Social Change in Contemporary Thailand." *Sojourn* 8, no. 1 (1993): 62–91.

THAIPUSAM

Thaipusam is the annual celebration of the Hindu deity Lord Murugan, second son of the great deities Lord Siva and Parvati. It is celebrated in southern India at Palani, and in other parts of the world where there is a significant Tamil community. In Southeast Asia, Thaipusam is celebrated in Thailand, Myanmar (Burma), Indonesia, and Singapore; however, the most spectacular and grandest celebrations can be witnessed in Malaysia. Here, it is famously celebrated at Batu Caves in Kuala Lumpur and is also growing rapidly in other cities, particularly Penang and Ipoh. It draws hundreds of thousands of Indians from all over the country and even from overseas. In Penang it has also been attracting growing numbers of Malaysian Chinese participants.

The population of Malaysia today is around 30 million, of whom some 67 percent are Malays, some 25 percent Chinese, 7 percent Indian, and the remainder aboriginals. The independence declaration of 1957 included certain privileges, later enhanced in the New Economic Policy, for the original inhabitants of the peninsula, who came to be known as *bumiputras*—literally, "sons of the soil." One of the prerequisites for claiming *bumiputra* identity is profession of the Islamic faith, whereas no stipulations are made regarding religion for claiming Chinese or Indian ethnicity. Malays are forbidden by law from participating in non-Islamic religious activities. Broadly, Malays control political power, while the Chinese are popularly identified with economic dominance. A fervent Islamization program in Malaysia in recent decades has made the Muslim/Malay community boundary increasingly impermeable to non-Malays.

Today, the population of the island of Penang consists of some 41 percent Malays, 43 percent Chinese, and 10 percent Indian. Despite the small size of the Indian community in Penang and the many religious alternatives in Malaysia for the Chinese, Thaipusam is a major event in Penang's main city of George-town, and it has become increasingly popular among the Chinese. Many Chinese also attend Hindu temples throughout the year, and although the Chinese do not tend to become "Hinduized," they are welcomed by the Indians, who incorporate them while making no effort to convert them. This attitude mitigates against the politicization of religion and the etching of religious boundaries onto the sociocultural landscape.

Thaipusam originates from Palani, in Tamil Nadu. There are several legends about the origins of Thaipusam. One holds that Palani is the site at which the great deities Siva and Parvati promised the fruit of Siva's approval to the one of their two sons, Ganapati and Murugan, who could travel around the cosmos first. The plump, elephant-headed Ganapati simply walked around his parents, declaring them to be the cosmos and thus won the fruit. Murugan, who rode around the globe on a pea-cock, returned to find that he had lost and was so angry that he retreated to a hill in Palani to become an ascetic. Thaipusam celebrates his ability to destroy the demons of misfortune and malevolence with the lance of wisdom that he received from his mother. The celebrations take place in the Tamil harvest month of Thai, for three days around the full moon.

The Murugan cult follows the Hindu devotional tradition (*bhakti*), which stresses emotion rather than knowledge or status. *Bhakti* also opens a path to salvation for Hindus that does not require them to renounce the world—renunciation becomes internalized and transformed into disinterestedness. *Bhakti* also dissolves the Hindu religious/caste hierarchy, which elevates Brahmins, and it makes salvation accessible to anyone. The self-mastery required to worship Murugan is temporary, life-affirming, and often ecstatic.

The most characteristic event associated with Thaipusam is *kavadi* (burden) carrying, in which devotees carry a burden to the temple in fulfilment of a vow. The classic *kavadi* consists of an arch-shaped frame, often decorated with peacock feathers to represent Murugan. *Kavadi* bearers are often glitteringly decorated, many have their cheeks or tongue pierced with a lance, or hooks inserted on their backs and chests, and they may dance in a kind of frenetic intoxication as they approach the deity.

The issue of coconut smashing regularly stirs debate in Penang. The Consumers' Association of Penang has published various warnings about coconut prices rising at festival time and of some unscrupulous traders mixing low-quality coconuts into sacks sold as high quality. The low-quality coconuts are evidently harder to smash. The association has also stated that devotees who believe that the more coconuts they smash, the better luck they will enjoy are misguided, and that God would surely not want to see so many coconuts being dumped and burned, causing pollution.

Alexandra Kent

The festival lasts for three days, beginning in the early hours of the first day with a street procession in which an image of Murugan is transported from his normal housing in the city center out to a peripheral temple. In Kuala Lumpur, this is the spectacular cave temple at Batu Caves, but in Penang it is the Waterfall Junction temple, which is owned by a Chettiar subcaste, the Nattukottai Chettiars.

In Penang, on the first day, the procession image of Lord Murugan is dressed and removed from his housing at the Nattukottai Chettiar storeroom in the city center. It is mounted on a tall, silver chariot pulled by two decorated bullocks. A group of Chettiar men carrying wooden *kavadis* dance before it on its long, hot journey. All along the procession route, the streets are lined with piles of coconuts that people smash before the chariot arrives. The smashing of one or two coconuts is standard in Hindu worship; but in Penang, under Chinese influence, coconut smashing has taken on unique proportions. Many Chinese claim that offering many coconuts will bring prosperity. The Indian organizers make no attempt to limit them, and some Indians have begun copying the Chinese. The streets end up clogged with smashed coconuts that require dumper trucks to clear them so that the chariot can progress.

A priest and several assistants ride with the chariot, blessing the offerings of fruit, flowers, and incense from the crowds. Hundreds of devotees follow on foot the eight kilometers (five miles) to the Chettiar temple at Waterfall Junction, where the image remains for the duration of the festival before returning on the final night. For Chettiars, events then focus on this temple, but the stream of devotees who make their offerings and fulfill their vows the day after continues beyond this temple up to the hilltop Bala Thandayuthapani (another name for Murugan) temple. The hilltop temple was founded by Tamil laborers and is managed by the Hindu Endowment Board, comprising Hindus from various Indian communities. At the hilltop temple, devotees pour milk over the deity and have any spears and hooks removed.

Most devotees make vows to Murugan in a contractual arrangement, promising to make an offering at Thaipusam if the god grants their wish. The boons sought may be health, prosperity, or progeny, or less tangible benefits such as help to abstain from crime or strength to face raising a handicapped child. This harmonizes well with Chinese understandings of their own deities as providing humans with access to divine powers (*shen*).

Devotees are supposed to prepare for anything from one week to 48 days before fulfilling a vow at Thaipusam. They should eat no meat, abstain from sexual inter-course, limit social interaction, keep their thoughts pure, sleep on the floor, and abstain from cutting their hair or shaving. On the day of vow fulfilment, the devotee should fast and, before approaching the deity, take a ritual bath and dress in saffron clothing. A troupe of musicians may be employed to support the devotee, particu-larly if they are carrying out a great deal of body piercing and an experienced ritual officiant, usually a male Indian veteran *kavadi* bearer, will insert the skewers and hooks.

The atmosphere is charged as devotees prepare themselves for their *kavadis*. Particularly when piercing is involved, Indian as well as Chinese supporters and

A pierced devotee with Vel Kavadi, a wearable, portable alter, prepares to perform during Thaipusam on the street in Kuala Lumpur. Other locals also help devotees along the way while enjoying the Indian festival. (lim_jessica/iStockphoto.com)

Indian officiants gather around the devotee and prepare prayer items such as limes, coconuts, and incense. The devotee prays, and when they are ready, the officiant begins chanting mantras close to their face and blowing incense into their nostrils while others stand close by ready to support them as the skewers are put in place.

This is the one time of the year at which Hindu women may take to the streets in all their finery, and when Indians of all castes, classes, and genders gather alongside Chinese in the carnivalesque atmosphere to enjoy picnics or just watch the spectacle. Some groups of young men take their own drums and dance through the temple area alongside the *kavadi* bearers, exploiting the permissive atmosphere for an all-night party. People come for innumerable reasons, including not only the personal and salvific but also for communion with others and simply to have fun. It is a regular manifestation and celebration of a growing non-Malay, interethnic social body.

Indians express pride in the fact their religion offers anyone, regardless of ethnic background, a channel to the divine without requiring them to forego their own culture. Many Penang Chinese welcome the offer, patronizing the festival not only with their participation but also with substantial contributions of money and food to the organizing committees. The political significance of this non-Malay solidarity is acknowledged by the annual attendance of the chief minister of Penang. Chief Minister Lim Guan Eng, a Chinese member of the Democratic Action Party (DAP) and an outspoken critic of the Malay-dominated government, regularly attends Thaipusam. In his 2012 Thaipusam speech, he pointed out that many non-Hindus carry the *kavadi* in fulfilment of their vows and that this is in the spirit of harmony and mutual respect essential in any peaceful multicultural and multireligious society. He then added that the DAP wanted to wish everyone a happy Thaipusam and to remind them that the festival's message of wisdom and of good conquering evil would reinforce their commitment to fight endemic corruption and crony capitalism.

Instead of focusing on the institutional or ideological features of religion, which reify groups for political and socioeconomic interests, Thaipusam emphasizes the heterodox and operationally plural qualities of faith. The faith of the individual and their access to nonrational sources of power signal resistance to the world order propagated by Malaysia's bureaucracy. In the Malaysian media, Thaipusam is presented simply as a colorful tourist attraction that illustrates Malaysia's ethnic plurality. This tends to gloss over the political resonance of its liberalism and insistence on humankind's spiritual unity. It is a momentary rebuttal of the government's essentialization of difference and thus provides a subtle yet critical commentary on the way modernity has evolved in Malaysia and beyond.

Alexandra Kent

See also: Contextualization: Dharma/Dhamma; Ethnicity; Hinduism; Interreligious Relations and Dialogue; Localization of Hinduism in Indonesia; Malaysia; Oka, Gedong Bagus; Pilgrimage; Popular Religion; Religion and Society; Ritual Dynamics; Sathya Sai Baba Movement; Tourism; Water Festivals.

Further Reading

Clothey, Fred W. *The Many Faces of Murugan: The History and Meaning of a South Indian God.* The Hague: Mouton, 1978.

Kent, Alexandra. "Transcendence and Tolerance: Cultural Diversity in the Tamil Celebration of Taipūcam in Penang, Malaysia." *International Journal of Hindu Studies* 8, no. 1–3 (2004): 81–105.

Lee, Raymond L.M. "Taipūcam in Malaysia: Ecstasy and Identity in a Tamil Hindu Festival." *Contributions to Indian Sociology*, n.s., 23, no. 2 (1989): 317–37.

Ward, Colleen. "Thaipusam in Malaysia: Psychoanthropological Analysis of Ritual Trance, Ceremonial Possession and Self-mortification Practices." *Ethos* 12, no. 4 (1984): 307–34.

Wilford, Andrew. "Weapons of the Meek: Ecstatic Ritualism and Strategic Ecumenism among Tamil Hindus in Malaysia." *Identities: Global Studies in Culture and Power* 9 (2002): 247–80.

THIEN BUDDHISM

Thien is the Vietnamese name for the most well-known Zen school of Buddhism, the Chinese *Ch'an-zong*, popularly known as *Chan*. The Chinese character *Ch'an* derives from the Sanskrit *dhyāna*. The traditional account is that in 580 CE, an Indian monk named Vinitaruci (Vietnamese: Tì-ni-đa-lư-chi) traveled to Vietnam after completing his studies with Jianzhi Sengcan, the third patriarch of Chinese Zen. This is the first appearance of Thien Buddhism. After an initial period of obscurity, the Vinitaruci School became one of the most influential Buddhist groups in Vietnam by the tenth century, particularly under the patriarch Vạn-Hạnh. Other early Vietnamese Zen schools included Vô Ngôn Thông, which was associated with the teaching of Mǎzǔ Dàoyī, an influential abbot of the Chinese Ch'an School, and the Thảo Đường, which incorporated *Nianfo,* a chanting technique that involves the repetition of the name of Amitabha Buddha, or the "Buddha of Infinite Wisdom" in order to achieve "mindfulness of the Buddha" (Snkt. *buddhanusmriti*). Following a number of permutations, which evinced a deep influence from Confucian and Daoist philosophy, a more domesticated school, named *Liễu Quán*, was founded in the eighteenth century and has since been the predominant branch of Vietnamese Zen.

As there is considerable interaction between Zen Buddhism and Pure Land Buddhism in Vietnam, it may be useful before proceeding any further to attempt all-too-brief characterizations of each of these traditions. Zen is the focus of meditation to attain enlightenment. This is a practice of sitting in stillness, focusing on single-mindedness, and investigating Zen, which can be approximately translated as "absorption" or "meditative state."

Pure Land Buddhism is the focus of reciting Amitabha Buddha's name. The recitation of Buddha's—actually *bodhisattva's*—name can cause one to enter *Samadhi*, a Sanskrit term referring to a state of mindfulness and clear comprehension achieved through concentrative awareness of the rise and fall of feelings, perceptions, and thoughts.

Because it employs the single-minded focus that is aimed for in Zen meditation, the Pure Land school's main desired goal from recitation of Amitabha Buddha is liberation from the *saha* (Sanskrit: to endure) world. This endurance refers to a life filled with suffering that stems from greed, anger, foolishness, and other earthly desires. The "Land of Eternally Tranquil Light" connotes the Buddha's land. The Buddha's enlightened wisdom is often compared to light. Together, the phrases imply that the mundane world in which we live is, itself, the Buddha land.

Buddhists in Vietnam practice differing traditions without any problem or sense of contradiction. Few Vietnamese Buddhists would identify themselves with a particular kind of Buddhism, as a Christian might identify him or herself by a denomination, for example. Although Vietnamese Buddhism does not have a strong centralized structure, the practice is similar throughout the country at almost any temple.

Gaining merit is the most common and essential practice in Vietnamese Buddhism with a belief that liberation takes place with the help of Buddhas and *bodhisattvas*. Buddhist monks commonly chant sutras, reciting Buddhas' names. The Lotus Sutra and Amitabha Sutra are the most commonly used sutras. Most sutras and texts have come to Vietnam from China and have been translated into Sino-Vietnamese (Han-Viet) rather than the vernacular, making them largely incomprehensible to most practitioners.

Thien is the Vietnamese name for the most well-known Zen school of Buddhism, the Chinese *Ch'an-zong*, popularly known as *Chan*. The traditional account is that in 580 CE, an Indian monk named Vinitaruci (Vietnamese: Tì-ni-đa-lưu-chi) traveled to Vietnam after completing his studies with Jianzhi Sengcan, the third patriarch of Chinese Zen. This is the first appearance of Thien Buddhism. After an initial period of obscurity, the Vinitaruci School became one of the most influential Buddhist groups in Vietnam by the tenth century. In the process, there was a good deal of interface with the less meditative Pure Land Buddhism.

David C. Scott

A woman lights incense at the Thien Hau Pagoda in Ho Chi Minh City in Vietnam. (Stuart Freedman/Corbis News/Corbis)

Three services are regularly engaged in—at dawn, noon, and dusk. They include sutras, mainly devotional; reciting *dharanis*, generally understood as a mnemonic device which encapsulates the meaning of a section or chapter of a *sutra*. *Dharaṇis* are also considered to protect the one who chants them from malign influences and calamities. Recitation of the Buddha's name and circumambulation (walking meditation) are also part of these services. Laypeople at times join the services at the temple and some devout Buddhists practice the services at home. Special services, such as Sam Nguyen/Sam Hoi (confession/repentance) take place on the full moon and new moon each month. Chanting the name of the Buddha is one way of repenting and purifying bad karma.

The overall doctrinal position of Vietnamese Buddhism is the inclusive system of Tiantai, with the higher metaphysics informed by the Huayan tradition, that makes extensive use of paradox in argument and literary imagery. Paradox originates in the tension between conventional truth and absolute truth. However, the orientation of Vietnamese Buddhism is syncretic without making such distinctions. Therefore, the modern practice of Vietnamese Buddhism can be very eclectic, including elements from Zen, Pure Land, and Tiantai traditions as well as popular practices from Esoteric Buddhism.

We will not consider here the misconceptions presented in most English-language materials regarding the variety of doctrines and practices in traditional Vietnamese Buddhism, the distinctness of these schools, and the strong inclination for syncretism found in Chinese and Vietnamese Buddhism. While much has been said about the incompatibility of different schools and their difficulty in successfully communicating with each other and combining their doctrines, none of these theories reflects the realities in Vietnam (or China), past or present. The followers have little problem adopting diverse teachings and practices at the same time.

The methods of Pure Land Buddhism are perhaps the most widespread within Vietnam. It is common for practitioners to recite sutras, chants, and *dharanis* looking to gain protection through a Dharma-Protector, an emanation of a Buddha or a *bodhisattva* whose main functions are to avert the inner and outer obstacles that prevent practitioners from gaining spiritual realization, and to arrange all the necessary conditions for their practice. It is a devotional practice where those practicing put their faith in Amitabha Buddha, the Buddha of Infinite Wisdom (Đà Phật). Followers believe they will gain rebirth in the Pure Land by chanting Amitabha's name. The Pure Land is where one can more easily gain enlightenment, since suffering does not exist.

Some scholars argue that the importance and prevalence of Thien in Vietnam has been overstated and that Thien has played more of an elite rhetorical role than a role of common practice. The *Thiền Uyển Tập Anh*, or "Outstanding Figures in the Vietnamese Zen Community," has been the dominant text used to legitimize the Zen Buddhist lineage and history within Vietnam. However, there is credible critical opinion that the text has, in fact, been used to create a history of Zen Buddhism that is "fraught with discontinuity." Current-day Thien Buddhist practices are not reflective of a Zen past in that modern-day Vietnamese common practices are more focused on ritual and devotion characteristic of the Pure Land School (Chinese, *Ching T'u*)—probably the oldest and least philosophical of Mahayana Buddhism—than the Zen focus on meditation and the direct experience of Reality through a maturation of an inner experience. Nonetheless, we are seeing an increased attention being paid to Zen today. Two figures who have been responsible for this increased interest in Thien are Thich Nhat Hanh, who resides in France, and Thich Thanh Tu, who lives in Da Lat, a Vietnamese provincial capital.

David C. Scott

See also: Buddhism; Confucianism; Daoism (Taoism); Dharma/Dhamma; Hanh, Thich Nhat; Shamanism: Syncretism; Vietnam.

Further Reading

Jones, Charles B. "Transitions in the Practice and Defense of Pure Land Buddhism." In *Buddhism in the Modern World: Adaptions of an Ancient Tradition*, edited by Steven Heine and Charles S. Prebish. New York: Oxford University Press, 2003.

Karuna Dharma. "The Reconciliation of Zen and Pure Land Buddhism." http://www.urbandharma.org/ibmc (accessed May 14, 2014).

Nguyen, Cuong Tu. *Zen in Medieval Vietnam*. Honolulu: University of Hawaii Press, 1997.

Suzuki, D. T. *An Introduction to Zen Buddhism*. New York: Grove Press, 1964.

Swearer, Donald K. "Buddhism in Southeast Asia." In *Encyclopedia of Religion*, vol. 2: 385–99.

TIMOR LESTE (EAST TIMOR)

Timor Leste lies in the Lesser Sunda islands. It occupies the eastern half of Timor Island, along with the Oecussi (Ambeno) region on the northwest portion of the island, and the islands of Pulau Atauro and Pulau Jaco. It has a total land area of

14,874 square kilometers. It is surrounded in the west, north, and east by the Indonesian archipelago. To the southeast lies Australia. Dili is the country's biggest city and its capital. A July 2012 estimate places the population of the country at 1,143,667. The land is predominantly mountainous, with a tropical climate; hot and humid, with distinct rainy and dry seasons. Only 8.2 percent of the land is arable. The inhabitants of Timor Leste are comprised mostly of Malayo-Polynesian and Papuan ancestry, with a small Chinese minority. Tetum is the official language, along with Portuguese. Bahasa Indonesian and English are also used. There are also an estimated 16 indigenous languages. An overwhelming majority of the population is Roman Catholic—98 percent; Protestants comprise 1 percent, while Muslims account for less than 1 percent (Central Intelligence Agency).

Residents carrying a statue of Virgin Mary during a religious procession commemorating her grief over the death of Jesus Christ in Dili, East Timor, on April 10, 2007. Roman Catholicism is the dominant religion in Timor Leste. (AP Images/Binsar Bakkara)

Portuguese and Dutch traders made contact with inhabitants of Timor Leste in the sixteenth century. There was occasional contact with Roman Catholic missionaries until Portugal colonized it in 1672 and controlled the island until 1974, with a brief Japanese occupation during World War II. Portugal relinquished control of its colony in 1975, resulting in a civil war. Independence was declared on November 28, 1975. However, Indonesia invaded a month later. During the Indonesian occupation, Indonesian migrants increased the number of the Muslim population. At the same time, a significant number of the Indonesian security forces are Protestant and facilitated the establishment of Protestant churches in the country (Hefner 2000; U.S. Department of State 2007).

The resignation of Indonesian president Suharto resulted in the United Nations sponsoring an agreement between Indonesia and Portugal that allowed for a UN-supervised popular referendum in August 1999, the results of which showed an overwhelming vote for independence. Indonesian-backed East Timor militia started a violent campaign, however, necessitating the intervention of an Australian-led peacekeeping force. The force assumed administrative control of Timor Leste until independence was formalized on May 20, 2002, with Xanana Gusmao as the country's first president.

The new country's constitution promulgated in 2002 guarantees freedom of religion and worship. Although there is no state religion, Roman Catholicism remains the dominant group. According to a report by the U.S. State Deparrent, the pervasive influence of the Catholic Church can sometimes affect the decisions of government officials. Prime Minister Jose Ramos Horta was repeatedly quoted as saying that it is important for the government to consult with the Roman Catholic Church on important national issues. Despite this, Protestants and Muslims have also held high positions in the executive and legislative branches of government and also in the military. Though some Muslims and non-Catholics report harassment, there are no religious prisoners or detainees in Timor Leste, nor are there incidents of forced religious conversion, according to the International Religious Freedom Report.

George Amurao

See also: Belo, Carlos Filipe Ximenes; Christianity; Colonialism; Ethnicity; Freedom of Religion; Indonesia; Interreligious Relations and Dialogue; Islam; Melanesian Religion; Minorities; Missionary Movements; Religious Conversions; Religious Discrimination and Intolerance.

Further Reading

Central Intelligence Agency. *The World Factbook.* https://www.cia.gov/library/publications/the-world-factbook/fields/2122.html (accessed October 25, 2014).

"East Timor Profile." BBC News Asia Pacific, June 26, 2012. http://www.bbc.co.uk/news/world-asia-pacific-14919009 (accessed May 14, 2014)

Hefner, Robert W. "Religious Ironies in East Timor." *Religion in the News* 3, no. 1 (Spring 2000). http://www.trincoll.edu/depts/csrpl/rinvol3no1/east_timor.htm (accessed May 14, 2014).

U.S. Department of State. "Timor Leste: International Religious Freedom Report 2007," http://www.state.gov/j/drl/rls/irf/2007/90135.htm (accessed May 14, 2014)

TOURISM

Tourism in recent years has developed into one of Southeast Asia's largest industries and a major engine for economic growth. Globally, tourism is a $3 billion a day business that all countries at all levels can potentially benefit from. The Asian region will soon be the fastest-growing market in terms of inbound and outbound tourism, with arrivals projected to increase significantly by 330 million in two decades—from 204 million arrivals in 2010 to 535 million arrivals in 2030. The region is home to the highest and the second-highest mountain peaks of the world, with Mount Everest and K2. Most of the world's quality water resources are in the region, with river systems originating from the Himalayas. Some of the world's best ocean resources, beaches, and mangrove areas are located in the region. Its biodiversity is unmatched by any other region of the earth. This region is home to historical marvels. The heritage and culture of the region dates back thousands of years.

The region is home to almost all of the world's religions. The cuisine of the region is exquisite. People are friendly and warm. Southeast Asia has all the ingredients to delight their visitor. All these factors combined make the region a viable and attractive tourism region.

The Questions

While the growth of tourism as an industry has been phenomenal, from a religious and social perspective, several questions linger. Can a tourist sector unconditioned by social checks bring benefit to host communities? Who benefits from tourism? What are the negative impacts? Can these be reversed? Is tourism smokeless, or is the pollution camouflaged in all the fun and distraction that tourism provides? Must not the spaces of the original inhabitants of lands where tourism remains "sacred" to the extent that they have been under their safe stewardship for all times? How can human, social, and cultural rights be protected? In short, the question is, is a renewed tourism possible?

Modern-day tourism in Southeast Asia is the story of distorted lifestyles. Dispassionately viewed, tourism is often about abused hospitality by travelers and about unscrupulous people/profiteers whose only goal is to make profits. It has too often been about disregard and exploitation of vulnerable women, young girls, and boys forced into prostitution because the alternative may simply be poverty or hunger. It is the unconscionable invasion and plunder of nature reserves, protected areas, wildlife habitats, rain forests, and bird sanctuaries.

Tourism in Southeast Asia is also much too frequently the story of people deceived by drugs, gambling, consumerism, unrestrained and ruthless competition, and the eventual sense of powerlessness of the victims. It is the venal displacement of farmers, fisher folk, and indigenous persons only to make way for the arrival of a tourist enterprise, which could take the form of a five-star hotel, a golf course, or a new amusement park. And unnoticed, it is the arena where the overworked, underpaid worker creates packages of bliss for the affluent holiday maker.

The Case of Southeast Asia

The development of Southeast Asian tourism clearly illustrates how all-pervasive the commodification of tourism can be. It is not uncommon for countries to advertise their destinations with slogans such as "paradise," "God's own country," and such. When, for example, Thailand advertised the "Visit Thailand Year" in the 1980s, just when tourism was going into economic liberalization mode, it was a shameless extravaganza of commercialism that depicted everything up for sale—from spotless white beaches to luscious jungles, from colorful cultural events to beautiful Thai women. In the past, most people would spend their free hours playing with their children, going on family picnics, or visiting their relatives and friends. Most people would enjoy some hobbies that would deeply satisfy them. Some would go for walks in the countryside, climb hills, swim in rivers and seas, and go fishing. Leisure would thus bring people close to nature, build healthy bonds within the

> In Rangoon of Burma, girls who appear to be 13 and 14 years old are frequently paraded in front of customers at nightclubs where a beauty contest thinly veils child prostitution. The girls participate in a nightly "modeling," but the show is not so much modeling as marketing. Prostitution, particularly involving children, is a serious crime in military-ruled Burma, but girls taken from the club usually have no problem with the authorities.
>
> *Ranjan Solomon*

family and with the community, deepen one's knowledge of humanity and the world, and manifest one's human creativity and feelings.

Child Trafficking

The trafficking of children in Southeast Asia is linked to a range of factors and vulnerabilities. A child's vulnerability to trafficking is influenced by individual, familial, and socioeconomic factors. Importantly, trafficked children are children who are already vulnerable. Demand for cheap labor, young brides, sex with children, and adoption drives the trafficking of children. The demand for sex with children and/or young brides is largely attributed to the value placed on virginity among East Asian cultures, demand from child sex offenders who often come from outside the region—usually from Western nations—the undersupply of girls and women available for marriage, and the myth that sex with young children or virgins can cure HIV.

Reported forms of child trafficking in the region include child prostitution or the production of child pornography, forced marriage, and adoption. The growing use of social networking sites, chat rooms, e-mail, and voiceover Internet protocols has had an impact on trafficking in the region, with cases of Thai women and girls trafficked to Japan from initial contact over the Internet and reports in Vietnam of students and other adolescents being trafficked after Internet chatting.

Water is a critical resource for human survival and dignity. Yet, in popular holiday destinations, local inhabitants have had to compete with the tourism sector over the access, allocation and use of water for their personal and domestic daily needs as the tourism industry exerts an enormous strain on water supplies. The local people also have had to fight against the tourism industry, which pollutes much of the water on which the industry is dependent.

Continuing contamination, depletion, and unequal distribution of water not only poses a direct threat to people's right to health and life, but it also exacerbates existing poverty and has been a source of conflict and societal instability. Priority in the allocation of water must be given to the right to water for personal and domestic use and for preventing starvation and disease.

As every tourist, especially in Southeast Asia, consumes between 300 and 850 liters of water per day, tourism development has become virtually synonymous with water depletion, scarcity, and shortages. In all tourism areas, tourism has contributed to a severe lack of drinking water. Due to the water shortage caused by tourism, the coastal communities are forced to produce drinking water out of sea-water or to import expensive drinking water from elsewhere. Consequently, traditional economic activities, such as agriculture, are marginalized by the lack of water"

Moreover, extensive landscaping, water parks, swimming pools, and golf courses are typical tourist facilities that require water during the dry season. On average, a golf course needs between 10,000 and 15,000 cubic meters of water per hectare a year. The surface of a golf course lies between 50 and 150 hectares, which means that the annual consumption of a golf course is around 1 million cubic meters per year, or the equivalent of the water consumption of a city of 12,000 inhabitants.

Displacement and Pilgrimage

Tourism has been a major source of the displacement of people in Southeast Asia. People are evicted from their homes either by governments or developers. In other cases, they are forced to move due to environmental disasters or economic reasons. Frequently tourism causes dramatic price rises, and local people can no longer afford rents and are forced to migrate. In the worst cases, eviction includes people having a gun put to their heads to force them to surrender their lands.

Pilgrimage is an important form of tourism in the region. A traveler is on a pilgrimage of sorts. A pilgrimage, by definition, is a journey or search of moral or spiritual significance. This is a traditional notion that confines travel or pilgrimage to religious sites or destination. But the distinction between the secular and sacred is often an artificial one. For, after all, everything in our world is integral to God's creation, be it culture, nature, seas, hills and mountains, rivers, water bodies, and culture. How then, can tourism begin to acquire the traits of a pilgrimage?

A pilgrim goes off in search of God and in the pursuit of truth.

The Kyaiktiyo Pagoda, also known as "Golden Rock," is a popular Buddhist pilgrimage site and tourist attraction in Mon State, Myanmar. (Marc Dozier/Latitude/Corbis)

God's truth cannot be found outside the ambit of justice and true community. In a world torn asunder by economic divisions, a traveler can choose to search for people-to-people encounters, as part of which is that each discovers the other, understands each other, shares with each other what they can and have. This pilgrim pathway can lead to mutuality, solidarity, and to the real discovery of human community.

A relationship would evolve in such an encounter. That relationship could then set in motion a trail—one that leads to the cessation of abuses of the previous ways of exploitation rooted in greed. It could symbolize the abandonment of the search for profit alone and, instead, instil stewardship values of God's world of people, the mountains, seas, islands, the air, the birds, and the trees—indeed, all of God's precious creation. For a pilgrim is not a mere tourist.

Three distinguishing features between a hedonistic tourist and pilgrim are pertinent:

- The pilgrim treads sensitively on the Holy Ground and spaces they enter—the tourist tends to trample over this sacred space.
- The pilgrim respects the host, accepts their ways, and even tries to learn from them while offering to share her or his own ways. The tourist often sees the ways of the host as a good commodity best reserved for display at the "evening show."
- The pilgrim is humble and patient, waiting for it to be time to do things, for the host to be ready, too. The tourist can be in a hurry, hasty, even arrogant.

Toward Responsible Tourism

Tourism in the Southeast Asian context has the potential to stimulate and facilitate dialogue among civilizations, cultures, and faiths. The complex relationship between the development of tourism and the dialogue between faiths and cultures finds its basis in the fact that tourism shares with religions and civilizations values such as tolerance and respect of diversity as well as rediscovery of oneself and of the others. In this sense, Asian tourism can create a niche market where the role of religious tourism can be an effective development tool and a facilitator of peace. There is the need to develop a dynamic relationship between religious and cultural heritage values in order to serve the interests of residents, tourists, and the religious community. For this, it is vital to maintain the authenticity and the core feature of religious sites and cultural routes and the assertion of heritage and ancient traditions aimed at bringing visitors closer to the values and spirituality of the host community.

At the Second Vatican Council, the following pertinent observation was made: "Shorter working hours are becoming the general rule everywhere and provide greater prospects for [a] large number of people. This leisure time must be properly employed to refresh the spirit and improve the health of mind and body by means of travel to broaden and enrich people's minds by learning from others."

Rest constitutes one important reason why people try to have free time, and it is also the most common reason for engaging in tourism. Rest can be easily construed as a time for doing nothing. In fact, rest consists principally in regaining the full personal equilibrium that normal living conditions tend to destroy. Therefore, just stopping all activity is not enough; certain conditions must also be created in order to regain one's equilibrium. Tourism can facilitate these conditions because it offers avenues that makes new experiences possible.

The tourism we must seek out is different. If this were the ideal world, we would seek to match tourism and societal forces in a way that they serve the common good rather than serve the directives of the market. To take this argument one step further, one would argue that tourism must cease to be viewed as a mere industry. We should, rather, begin to view it as a social force.

Ranjan Solomon

See also: Globalization; Indonesia; Interreligious Relations and Dialogue; Pilgrimage; Popular Religion; Religion and Society; Secularism; Sexuality; Thailand; Thaipusam; Vietnam; Women.

Further Reading

D'Mello, Caesar, ed. *Transforming Re-Forming Tourism: Perspectives on Justice and Humanity in Tourism*. Chiang Mai, Thailand: Ecumenical Coalition on Tourism (ECOT), 2008.

Jones, Andrew, and Michael Phillips, eds. *Disappearing Destinations: Climate Change and Future Challenges for Coastal Tourism*. Oxfordshire, UK: CABI, 2011

Picard, Michel. *Bali: Cultural Tourism and Touristic Culture*. Singapore: Archipelago Press, 1996.

Snodgrass, Adrian. *The Symbolism of the Stupa*. Ithaca, NY: Cornell University, Southeast Asia Program Publications, 1985.

Suresh K. T., Liyakath Syed, and Roy Saroop, eds. *Indigenous Peoples, Wildlife, and Ecotourism*. Bangalore: Equations, 2002.

U

UPLANDERS

The uplands in Southeast Asia, as elsewhere, are often markedly different from low-land areas, and this distinction has been an important analytical dimension of research in the region. While historical states have spread in lowland and coastal areas of Southeast Asia, the uplands are commonly characterized by non-centralized, village-based societies. The difference between uplands and lowlands is framed in somewhat different terms in insular Southeast Asia and on the mainland. In insular Southeast Asia, powerful polities based on trade historically emerged on coasts, while the hinterland provided trade goods, but was less integrated into state structures. Thus, the distinction is known as one between coastal, down-river regions and those up river. On the mainland, the genesis of states was based on permanent wet rice fields, but their influence ceased where the terrain is more rugged and only allows for temporary dry rice fields, called shifting cultivation or swidden. For the upland areas of the mainland, scholars have used the terms "Southeast Asian Massif" and "Zomia" in recent years. While world religions like Buddhism on the mainland and Islam in Indonesia spread in the lowlands, often as the state religions of newly emerging polities, uplanders commonly practiced local religions, conventionally termed animist.

In the course of history, states and the religions associated with them slowly encroached on the highlands. However, more or less efficient administrative structures were often only established during the second half of the twentieth century, especially on the mainland. In terms of religion, animist uplanders responded in four different ways to lowland influence: subtly including some lowland religious practices into their local systems; full conversion to the lowland religion; conversion to a foreign and markedly different religion, in particular Christianity; and millenarianism.

Conversion to lowland religion was often accompanied by slow acculturation, and presumably the ancestors of numerous current lowlanders originated in the uplands. However, sometimes lowland religion was adopted in the uplands while keeping upland cultural identities intact, as is the case with the Buddhist Phunoy in Laos. However, uplanders' ethnic and religious identities can be constantly shifting. Thus, anthropologist Edmund Leach reported on persons who passed as non-Buddhist Kachin in the uplands and as Buddhist Shan in the lowlands of Myanmar.

The second option is to convert to a different world religion, but one that is marked off from those of the lowlands. For example, many uplanders of Myanmar have converted to Christianity since the late nineteenth century. Conversion is often reasoned on the base of local socio-cosmic concepts. As animism is based on careful and laborious negotiations with spirit forces, Allah or Christ appear as superior spirit protectors, or Buddhist ritual as an improved technique to control spirits. Thus, Buddhism or Christianity were not perceived as alternative cosmologies but as more efficient means to engage with the established cosmology. Also, conversion promised a new way of engaging with new types of relationships, including global trade and the expansion of the modern nation-state. Christianity in Myanmar or Eastern Indonesia often proved to be an important means to articulate local identities in the face of aggressively expanding nation-states. Being Christian meant to be different from the state.

A third option, even more explicit in its engagement with the increasing power of state centers, consisted in millenarian uprisings. These characterized the mainland of Southeast Asia much more than the archipelago. Millenarianism denotes the idea that a catastrophic upturning of the established order is near, often leading to a more just leadership, a golden age or the predominance of a previously oppressed group. These movements were not restricted to uplanders, but often attracted any marginalized group.

Millenarian movements like the Phi Bun uprising in Thailand and Laos in the early twentieth century were as political as they were religious. They often focus on charismatic leaders and spread among people who experience themselves as disempowered. Millenarianism thus necessarily emerges in a context of strongly felt social inequality. Characteristically, millenarian movements create their own cosmologies, but often make strong use of religious imagery borrowed from the outside, often from dominant and state religions. Thus, Kommadam, the leader of a revolt in southern Laos in the first half of the twentieth century, was celebrated as the Maitreya Buddha, the Buddha of the coming age, even though most of his followers were probably not Buddhist. Uprisings of the Hmong, an ethnic group originating from China, sometimes centered on the idea of regaining their mythical lost script, a cultural feature that would put them on equal terms with the Chinese empire or the lowland Southeast Asian states. Some of these millenarian cults still survive today in a politically less volatile form, e.g. among Hmong in northern Thailand.

All these types of responses to lowland states share a particular quality. Uplanders often combine elements from their own local rituals with external elements, in order to create constantly changing ritual systems. Sometimes, these systems serve to stress local identity and the difference to lowlands. Sometimes, elements from lowland societies and religions were integrated into quite different societies in the uplands. The process is highly selective and creative, but historically served to maintain upland identities. In many cases, only a limited number of elements from a lowland religion were integrated into upland ritual systems, as for example in the form of Buddhist ritual verses endowed with healing powers.

Today, the state administration of the uplands has intensified. Therefore, the forms that uplanders use to express their identities have changed. While some people try to escape from lowland prejudices about superstitious and unrefined uplanders by embracing lowland lifestyles, others find new ways of showing their distinctiveness to the world. This often takes the form of ritual. Typically, local rituals like New Year festivals or harvest rituals are transformed and become platforms for performing folkloric versions of local culture. Shows of costumes and dances, some newly invented, are less addressed to benevolent spirits but to national and global media, state majorities, and tourists. These local culture festivals can be called neither authentic nor inauthentic. Although they have little to do with the rituals uplanders performed 50 years ago, they still serve the same purpose: to relate them to an outside world of spirits and states, foreign religions, and peoples, by selectively combining local usages with external ideas.

Guido Sprenger

See also: Ancestor Worship; Animism; Buddhism; Christianity; Contextualization; Dance and Drama (Theater); Ethnicity; Indonesia; Islam; Laos; Messianic Movements; Myanmar (Burma); Myth/Mythology; Religious Conversions; Ritual Dynamics; Spirit Mediumship; Thailand; Tourism.

Further Reading

Kirsch, A. Thomas. *Feasting and Social Oscillation: Religion and Society in Upland Southeast Asia*. Ithaca, NY: Cornell University Press, 1973.

Leach, Edmund. *Political Systems of Highland Burma: A Study of Kachin Social Structure*. London and New York: Continuum, 2001 [1954].

Michaud, Jean. *Historical Dictionary of the Peoples of the Southeast Asian Massif*. Lanham, MD; Toronto; and Oxford: Scarecrow Press, Historical Dictionaries of Peoples and Cultures no. 4, 2006.

Scott, James C. *The Art of Not Being Governed: An Anarchist History of Upland Southeast Asia*. New Haven, CT: Yale University Press, 2009.

V

VIETNAM

Vietnam, officially known as the Socialist Republic of Vietnam, stretches along the eastern coast of mainland Southeast Asia and extends about 1,650 kilometers from north to south. The country covers a total area of 331,212 square kilometers and is bordered by the Gulf of Tonkin and the South China Sea to the east, China to the north, Laos and Cambodia to the west, and the Gulf of Thailand to the south. The capital, Hanoi, is located in the northern region on the banks of the Red River. Ho Chi Minh City (formerly Saigon) is Vietnam's economic and financial hub in the south of the country near the eastern edge of the Mekong Delta. Vietnam's topography varies from the low-lying delta regions in the north and south to hilly, mountainous terrain in the far north, northwest, and central provinces. Due to its wide range of latitude and topographical relief, Vietnam's climate and weather patterns vary greatly from one region to another. Whereas the northern part of the country features a subtropical climate, the southern region is tropical with more consistent year-round temperatures.

Vietnam is an ethnically and culturally diverse country with a population estimated at 87.84 million in 2011. The Vietnamese government recognizes 54 ethnic groups, with the Viet (or Kinh) majority comprising more than 80 percent of the total population. Whereas the latter mainly inhabit lowland delta and coastal regions, most ethnic minority groups reside in the highland and mountainous areas. The official language is Vietnamese, a tonal and monosyllabic language commonly classified as belonging to the Mon-Khmer branch of the Austroasiatic language family. Besides the latter, four other language families are represented by Vietnam's ethnic minority groups: Austronesian, Thai-Kadai, Hmong-Mien (Miao-Yao), and Sino-Tibetan.

Vietnam's ethnic and cultural diversity also encompasses a plurality of local religious traditions that have historically been shaped in dynamic interaction with various imported philosophies and religions. One of the most commonly held beliefs in Vietnam is the notion that spiritual beings coexist with humans and wield influence over their affairs. The unseen world is hence viewed as inhabited by an extensive array of powerful male and female divinities, mythical and human ancestors, and guardian spirits and wandering ghosts that need to be revered and propitiated in order to ensure their goodwill. Over the centuries, particularly during the centuries of Chinese domination (111 BCE–938 CE), Vietnam's spirit-based religion has fused with elements from Mahayana Buddhism, Confucianism, and Daoism. Other major world religions appeared in later stages of Vietnam's history. The most widespread Christian denomination, Catholicism, was first introduced by Western missionaries in the late fifteenth century and gained a firm foothold in Vietnamese society during the French colonial period. In the first three decades of the twentieth century, the south of Vietnam saw the emergence of several indigenous religious movements, the best known of which are the Cao Dai (a syncretistic blend of Vietnamese and Western spiritualism, Buddhism, Confucianism, Daoism and Christianity, founded in the 1920s) and Hòa Hảo Buddhism (a reformist millenarian Buddhist movement founded in 1939).

Vietnam's recent history is marked by the struggle against French colonial rule, the 1954 division of the country into the Democratic Republic of Vietnam (North Vietnam) and the Republic of South Vietnam, and the protracted "Vietnam War" that ended with Vietnam's reunification under communist rule in 1975. Despite constitutional guarantees of religious freedom since the declaration of independence in 1945, the Vietnamese state placed religious beliefs, practices, and organizations under firm control in order to advance its goal of building a socialist society. Whereas complex religious organizations were deemed as potential hotbeds of political dissent, certain components of traditional religious beliefs and practices were discredited as superstitious, wasteful, and backward remnants of a past that needed to be overcome in order to advance scientific progress and socialist construction.

In 1986, the Vietnamese government committed itself to a series of policy measures (known as Đổi Mới) that entailed the shift from a centrally planned to a market-oriented economy. Alongside economic restructuring, popular beliefs and ritual practices experienced a tremendous resurgence. Temples and shrines that had been neglected due to the government's restrictive measures were reclaimed by local communities as places of worship and ritual practice. Funds were raised for the renovation, restoration, or new construction of village communal houses, pagodas, and family ancestral halls. Life-cycle rituals, such as weddings and funerals, and village ritual festivals were again celebrated with much grandeur. Spirit mediumship reemerged from the secrecy to which it had resorted and subsequently flourished into a vibrant religious movement known as the Four Palace Religion (Dao Tu Phu) or Mother Goddess Religion (Dao Mau). Alongside this religious revivification, a careful reassessment of Vietnamese "traditional culture" took place as part of the state's project of preserving and promoting a strong national cultural identity in the process of global integration. While this view has come a long way from perceiving religion, in the Marxian sense, as a mystifying tool of power, official discourse now tends to essentialize certain aspects of Vietnamese religious belief as timeless cultural heritage imbued with national ideals. Recent scholarship has challenged this view by emphasizing that religion in present-day Vietnam constitutes a multifaceted arena of dynamic and creative interaction with the challenges of the contemporary globalized world.

Census data on religious affiliation do not necessarily reflect the deep embeddedness of spirit-based religious beliefs and practices in Vietnamese daily life. Moreover, the latter are subsumed under the category of "folk belief" (tin nguong dan gian), defined as an aspect of traditional culture and customs, and therefore not subject to the state's religious politics. In contrast, the term "religion" (ton giao) refers only

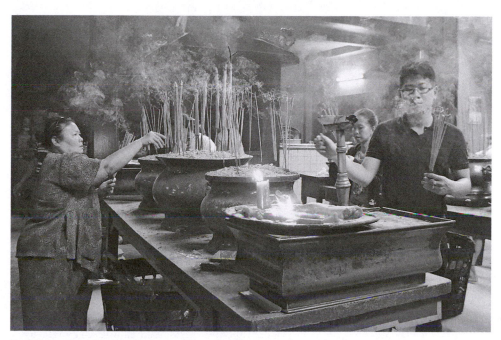

Buddhists burning incense at ancient temple in Ho Chi Minh city, Vietnam. (xuanhuongho/iStockphoto.com)

to institutionalized religious denominations. The government currently recognizes 12 religions, of which the following 6 are the most prominent: Buddhism, Catholicism, Protestantism, Islam, Cao Dai, and Hòa Hảo Buddhism. Estimates of the number of adherents vary to some extent, depending on the data source, survey methods, and the ways in which adherence is defined. Buddhists are estimated to make up 10–50 percent of the population; Roman Catholics, 8–10 percent; Cao Dai, 2.5–4 percent; Hòa Hảo, 1.5–3 percent; Protestants, 1–2 percent (of which two-thirds are members of ethnic minorities); and Muslims, less than 0.1 percent of the population.

Since the early 2000s, a number of locally founded (Buddhist/syncretistic) as well as international (mainly Protestant) denominations have received legal status. Yet despite the general relaxation of restrictions on religious expression in the past decades, Vietnam's record on religious freedom has remained a matter of concern to various international human rights groups and governmental agencies. A major point of criticism is that the Vietnamese government keeps holding significant control over the institutional lives and activities of organized religions. The legal framework governing religious activities stipulates that all religious organizations must be officially recognized and registered with appropriate state agencies at various levels. Unrecognized and unregistered religious groups risk coercive and punitive action by the authorities, particularly if their activities are perceived as a potential threat to state authority and national unity. One prominent example is the Unified Buddhist Church of Vietnam (UBCV). Established in South Vietnam in 1964 with clear political aims, the UBCV refused to integrate into the government-affiliated

Vietnam Buddhist Sangha (VBS) and has thus been effectively banned since 1981. Like his predecessor and other reputed UBCV leaders, the UBCV's current supreme patriarch and human rights defender, Venerable Thich Quang Do, has reportedly been subjected to various forms of detentions and house arrests in the last three decades. Members of officially recognized religious groups have likewise been faced with varying levels of government interference and pressure.

In recent years, a number of clashes between security forces and Roman Catholic communities were sparked by government claims to church land. Land usage rights remain a contentious issue in Vietnam, where "the people own and the state manages the land," which is why the government does not conceive of church land confiscations as a violation of religious freedom. Other contentious issues are the inconsistencies and uncertainties with regard to registration procedures of religious groups. This pertains especially to the many and varied Protestant denominations that had been attracting fast-growing followings among ethnic minority groups in the northwest and central highlands. Although the government continues to grant legal recognition to smaller, recently arrived Protestant denominations, many local congregations had their registration applications rejected, and members of unregistered "house churches"' reportedly face consistent, often violent harassment from the authorities. Such restrictions regarding religious activities and organizations are hardly surprising, given that Vietnam as a single-party state is wary of the powerful political potential of religious groups. Yet it is also vital to stress that the proliferation and diversification of religious life in present-day Vietnam must be viewed as part of an ongoing dialogic process of negotiation between state and society actors that involves continuous changes and adaptations on both sides.

Kirsten W. Endres

See also: Buddhism; Cambodia; Cao Dai; Christianity; Colonialism; Confucianism; Daoism (Taoism); Duc, Thich Quang; Engaged Buddhism; Ethnicity; Goddess Traditions; Hanh, Thich Nhat; Hòa Hảo Buddhism; Interreligious Relations and Dialogue; Islam; Laos; Minorities; Missionary Movements; Myth/Mythology; Popular Religion; Reform Movements; Ritual Dynamics; Shamanism, Spirit Mediumship; Syncretism; Thailand.

Further Reading

Fjelstad, Karen, and Nguyen Thi Hien, eds. *Possessed by the Spirits: Mediumship in Contemporary Vietnamese Communities*. Ithaca, NY: Cornell Southeast Asia Program Publications, 2006.

Malarney, Shaun K. "Return to the past? The dynamics of contemporary religious and ritual transformation." In *Postwar Vietnam: Dynamics of a Transforming Society*, edited by Hy Van Luong, 225–56. Lanham, MD: Rowman & Littlefield Publishers, 2003.

Soucy, Alexander. *The Buddha Side: Gender, Power, and Buddhist Practice in Vietnam*. Honolulu: University of Hawaii Press, 2012.

Taylor, Philip, ed. *Modernity and Re-Enchantment: Religion in Post-Revolutionary Vietnam*. Singapore: ISEAS, 2007.

W

WAHID, ABDURRAHMAN

Abdurrahman Wahid (1940–2009), popularly known as Gus Dur, was one of the most influential Southeast Asian Muslim scholars and an Indonesian statesman. As the great *Ulema* (Muslim scholar) and the leader of Indonesia's largest Muslim organization, Nahdlatul Ulama (NU) and the first democratically elected president of the Republic of Indonesia (1999–2001), his role in promoting religious tolerance and establishing the spirit of peace was internationally acknowledged. He also became the symbol of peace and the antidiscrimination movement in the country.

Gus Dur was born in Jombang, East Java on September 7, 1940. He grew up in a traditional Islamic scholar family, which was pluralist, nationalist, and religiously open-minded. The name Abdurrahman Wahid was taken from his original full name, Abdul-Rahman al-Dākhil bin Abdul Wahid bin Hashim bin Ashari. Wahid is a family name adopted from his grandfather's and father's names. Gus Dur has also been acknowledged as the great Ulema, the national hero, the founder of the modern Indonesian nation and also the founder of the Nahdlatul Ulama (NU) organization. His family background had significantly influenced his roles and achievements in the social and political arenas.

Gus Dur was sent to several *pesantren*, or Islamic boarding schools, to enrich his knowledge in Islamic literature. He had the opportunity to follow a part-time educational method to complement with his study in the state primary school in Jakarta and, subsequently, in the junior high school in Yogyakarta. His father's broad network as one of the top figures in the revolution era, great Islamic scholar, and the first minister of religious affairs in the country was an advantage and brought Gus Dur into an open, multicultural, and intellectual community at both the national and international levels. The supportive environment encouraged him to widen his horizon of knowledge not only in religious issues, but also in social, political, humanities, and literature studies. Since the time he was a teenager, Gus Dur had explored a wide range of philosophical thoughts developed by Karl Marx, Plato, Thales, Ibn Khaldun, and others. He also enjoyed reading outstanding novels written by William Bochner and a few others. He was fluent in foreign languages such as English, Arabic, Dutch, and Mandarin, which made him special and distinctive among other teenagers. Even though he failed to graduate from Al-Azhar University in Cairo, he successfully accomplished his study in the College of Arts, Baghdad University, Iraq, in 1970.

Gus Dur's breadth of reading and knowledge had significantly influenced his worldview in making Islamic discourses more compatible with modernity, democracy, human rights, and other modern principles. He became an inclusive, progressive, and also controversial Muslim scholar in the country. He was confidently willing to take risks for upholding his principles, idealism, and values, although he had to directly confront with the authoritarian and discriminatory ruling power. He obliged the majority of Indonesian Muslims by protecting the non-Muslim minorities in the country. He consistently became a fearless defender of tolerance, pluralism, equality, and constitutionalism. All his material resources, power, and influence as the Muslim leader of the Nahdlatul Ulama (NU) organization were used to protect the various disadvantaged and minority groups—no matter what their religion, race, and social backgrounds were—who had systematically been suppressed by the rulers. Gus Dur was convinced that Islam must protect humanity and the values of justice, tolerance, and decency, including the spirit of freedom and democracy.

After the authoritarian Suharto's administration had been toppled by the 1998 reform movement, Indonesia entered a phase of political transition toward democracy—an uneasy path that seriously threatened the country's future, including its national integration. Gus Dur and the elites of NU initiated and established the National Awakening Party (PKB) to become the political vehicle for the *Nahdliyyin*, or the NU followers; and the party, in the 1999 general election, successfully became the fourth-largest party. Since the split of power between the Islamist and nationalist political wings were very strong, a long-standing debate and complex negotiation had been conducted in the struggle for power, especially in electing the president in the transitional era. To bridge the communication impasse between the two groups, in the end, Gus Dur was democratically elected as the fourth president of the Republic of Indonesia.

With minimal political support in parliament, Gus Dur remained consistent with his leadership style, which was assertive, straightforward, and also sometimes overconfident, at least in a few cases. He was also consistent in promoting peace, tolerance, and justice by optimizing the state's resources and alignments to protect the minorities, even though it forced him at odds with the mainstream groups that did not agree with his ideas. For instance, Gus Dur advocated and tried to restore the dignity of the Chinese minority to seek their rights by removing the prohibition of Chinese cultural activities, publications, and other formal discrimination policies imposed by the Suharto administration. After three decades of discrimination, the Chinese-Indonesian citizens finally enjoyed an air of freedom. In 2000, as the president and the leader of the NU organization, Gus Dur also publicly offered an apology and admitted to the role of Ansor, the youth wing of NU, in the mass killings of 1966 and the victimizing of Indonesian Communist Party (PKI) members, their families, and innocent people. As president, Gus Dur also ordered a stop to the harassment and imprisonment of the political prisoners from the Suharto regime and then released them to freedom and restored their good name to obtain civil rights that had been lost before. Although his eyes were blind, his humanist spirit and "controversial approaches' had proven him as a special and highly distinguished leader and statesman—a rare category among national leaders and Islamic scholars, many of whom are often inconsistent, especially when facing challenges and threats from the majority and mainstream groups of society.

His role as a president with an overconfident leadership style was finally ended by his rivals and pro–status quo political actors, who, through impeachment in 2001, removed him.

Gus Dur's sacrifice and struggle has become a role model for how a good Muslim can promote a friendly and tolerant Islam in a developing country. His concept of Islamic spirituality had been interpreted and implemented into the daily life behavior that is compatible with democracy and constitutionalism principles. Gus Dur also taught us that simplicity can be a virtue so as to gain enlightenment and consciousness to free human beings from ego, greed, and hatred, which are the main sources of conflict, violence, and the destruction of the political and economic system in Muslim-majority countries. He passed away in Jakarta, on December 30, 2009. Many interfaith and inter-race communities have proposed his name to the government for awarding the national honor, as an Indonesian hero who served his country with rare distinction, honor, and dedication. Many civil society groups and the media have already dubbed him as the "Hero of Pluralism in Indonesia."

Ahmad Khoirul Umam

See also: Indonesia; Interreligious Relations and Dialogue; Islam; Nahdlatul Ulama; *Pesantren.*

Further Reading

Barton, Greg, and Greg Fealy. *Nahdlatul Ulama, Traditional Islam and Modernity in Indonesia.* Clayton, Australia: Monash Asia Institute, Monash University, 1996.

Barton, Greg. *Gus Dur: The Authorized Biography of Abdurrahman Wahid.* Yogyakarta, Indonesia: LKiS, 2003.

Bush, Robin. *Nahdlatul Ulama and the Struggle for Power within Islam and Politics in Indonesia.* Singapore: ISEAS, 2009.

Fealy, Greg. "Abdurrahman Wahid and the al-Khidr Question." In *The Presidency of Abdurrahman Wahid: An Assessment of the First Year*, edited by D. Kingsbury, 1–13. Clayton, Australia: Monash University Publishing, 2001.

Fielard, Andree. *NU vis a vis Negara: Pencarian Isi, Bentuk, dan Makna.* Yogyakarta, Indonesia: LKiS, 1999.

Wahid, Abdurrahman. *Islamku, Islam anda, Islam kita: Agama, Masyarakat, Negara, Demokrasi (My Islam, the Author's Islam, Our Islam: Religion, Society, and the Democratic State).* Jakarta, Indonesia: The Wahid Institute, 2006.

WALI SANGA (WALI SONGO)

The Wali Sanga (also called Wali Songo) are the nine Javanese Islamic saints who, during a period stretching from the early fifteenth century to the mid-sixteenth century CE, played a key role in the consolidation of Islam in Indonesia. All of them, who lived on the north coast of Java, were related to each other biologically or by teacher-student relationship. Apart from being religious leaders, many of them were also social reformers and made distinct contributions in the areas of health care, education, farming, commerce, and community governance. While Islam had arrived in Java before the Wali Songo period, the credit for the spread and consolidation of the faith there is primarily attributed to them.

Malik Ibrahim, who lived in the fourteenth century CE, is considered to be the first Wali. While credible information on his life is not easily available, it is believed that he set in motion the process of the Islamization of Indonesia. He also traveled to present-day Vietnam for missionary work and converted many to Islam. Malik Ibrahim was a social reformer who worked among the farmers and peasants. He is also believed to be the grand master of the *pesantren*, the popular Islamic boarding schools of Indonesia. Both his son Sunan Ampel and his nephew Sunan Giri were later considered Wali Songo.

Several of the Wali Songo made illustrious contributions to the larger religious and social life of the region. Sunan Giri was known for his vast knowledge in Islamic jurisprudence. Sunan Gunungjati, another one of the nine Apostles of Islam, was not only a religious leader but also a political ruler as he founded the sultanates of Banten and Cirebon. With political power, he succeeded in spreading Islam all along the northern coast of Java.

Of particular significance are the interreligious and intercultural relations of the Wali Songo. Sunan Bogan, the son of Sunan Ampel, in his preaching, utilized the symbols of Hinduism and Buddhism and incorporated Islamic thought into traditional Javanese songs, which had been heavily influenced by Hindu philosophy. Sunan Kalijaga, another Wali Songo, was tolerant toward local cultures, and he adapted a syncretic approach in the preaching of Islam. He believed that indigenous cultural media such as puppets, sculpture, and gamelan music could be employed in preaching and contextualizing Islam. Sunan Kudus, yet another one of the nine apostles, utilized the symbols of Hinduism and Buddhism in the architecture of the mosques and minarets that was built during his time.

Despite the benevolent approach of some of the Wali Songo toward other religions and cultures, their period is considered to mark the end of the Hindu-Buddhist dominance in Indonesia, and under their leadership, the existing cultures were replaced with Islamic culture. While several sociopolitical and religious factors too were at play, the role of the nine saints in transforming the culture of a region and in consolidating Islam there is almost unparalleled. The Wali Songo's sense of patriotism and religious fervor laid the foundations of Indonesian nationalism that helped the people, centuries later, to prevail over the colonial forces.

Jesudas M. Athyal

See also: Buddhism; Colonialism; Contextualization; Education; Hinduism; Indonesia; Interreligious Relations and Dialogue; Islam; Missionary Movements; Music; Nationalism; *Pesantren*; Puppetry; Religion and Society; Religious Conversions; Syncretism.

Further Reading

Geertz, Clifford. *Islam Observed: Religious Development in Morocco and Indonesia*, 25–28. Chicago: University of Chicago Press, 1968.

Ricklefs, Merle Calvin. *A History of Modern Indonesia since c.1300*. 2nd ed. London: MacMillan, 1991.

Ricklefs, Merle Calvin. *Islam in the Indonesian Social Context*. Victoria: Centre of Southeast Asian Studies, Monash University, 1991.

WATER FESTIVALS

The Southeast Asian region has deep roots in Hinduism as a result of its long history of being part of the Indianized states. The most common feature of all the Indianized states was the religious influence of Hinduism and Buddhism, which were brought in by the Indian traders. Soon after, the Brahmins followed these traders and played an important role in the region. They were warmly welcomed by the local kings and their religious practices, including the festivals, were widely adopted.

An important Hindu festival is Holi, which marks the beginning of the New Year and is commonly seen as the festival of water and colors. Originally known as Holika in India, the festival is detailed in the Vedas, Puranas, Jaimini's Purvamimamsa Sutras, and Kathaka-Grhya-Sutras. In India, the day is celebrated on the last day of the year, Phalgun Purnima, and the beginning of the year, Vasant Ritu, thus commencing the spring season and is also known as the Vasanta-Mahotsava. Several myths are associated with the festival, and it is associated with the great king of demons, Hiranyakashyap, who was granted a boon by Brahma not to be killed. The boon made him arrogant, and he demanded to be worshipped instead of the gods. His own son, Prahlad, however, was a great devotee of Visnu and rejected worshipping his own father. Hiranyakashyap failed several times

Indian men participating in the Hindu Holi Water Festival by pouring colored water on each other in Delhi, India, on March 20, 2011. (SoumenNath/iStockphoto.com)

to kill his son and at last ordered Prahlad to enter a blazing fire with his aunt Holika. The aunt had received a boon preventing her from being burned by fire. To everyone's surprise, Holika was burnt to death for her sinful desires, while Prahlad survived unharmed because of his devotion to Visnu. The festival thus celebrates the victory of good and the triumph of devotion.

In Southeast Asia, the New Year festival adopted the element of water splashing and colors from Holi and is a widely celebrated occasion in most countries in the region. As a religious ceremony in ancient India, the festival was first carried out to pray for good rainfall and harvests. The ritual was then adopted by the Buddhists, and as Buddhism spread to different parts of Asia, the water-splashing elements evolved into a folk festival. The celebration in most Southeast Asian countries falls in March or mid-April every year, marking the end of one solar year. In agrarian societies, the festival also marks the beginning of the harvest season.

In Southeast Asia, there is intense tropical heat in March and April, and many countries here celebrate the water festival to ease the burden of the heat and also to bring a festive mood to the communities with strong agricultural roots. It is the time when farmers gather their harvest and perform rituals, praying for a good monsoon for the next harvest season. The water festival thus plays a significant role in agricultural societies where ample rainfall is vital to the well-being of the population. This three-to-five-day festival, also marking the New Year, is celebrated in many countries in Southeast Asia under different names: Songkran (Thailand), Feast of Thingyan (Myanmar), Pi Mai (Laos), Chaul Chnam Thmey (Cambodia), Tet (Vietnam), and Water splashing festival (Yunnan, China).

Buddhism became closely associated with the water festival and today plays an important role in the festivity. The origin of the festival can be traced back to the time of Buddha and is described in the chapter of "Sermon on Maha Songkran." The celebration of Songkran was brought to Thailand through the Burmese influence in the eleventh century. Since then, the traditional New Year is observed in the ancient Lanna Kingdom with the northern city of Chiang Mai being the main place of attraction. From there it spread to the other parts of Thailand. Songkran is a three-day festival celebrated on April 13–15, when days are longer and it is the hottest time of the year. Thais express their gratitude to Buddha, clean their houses, and pay respect to the elderly by splashing water. Traditional food is cooked and colorful costumes are worn. The festival is a traditional time to visit and pay respect to the elders in the family, friends, neighbors, and monks. This Buddhist festival is the time to visit monasteries and to pray and offer food to monks. Water mixed with fragrance is poured over Buddha images, and this blessed water is believed to bring good fortune to the elders.

In Cambodia, Chaul Chnam Thmey (Entering the New Year) lasts three days based on the lunar calendar. Representing the end of the harvest, the time is for the farmers to enjoy the harvest and relax before the rainy season begins. The first day is Maha Sahgkrant, which starts with the beat of drum or bell at the Buddhist temple symbolizing the arrival of the New Angel (Guardian of the New Year). The second day, Vana Bat, involves offerings made to monks as an expression of respect to the monks. The third and last day, Loenung Sack, is the bathing ceremony for

Buddha, where people clean their statues with perfumed water. Doing so is believed to bring good luck, happiness, and long life in addition to the hope of sufficient rainfall for the rice harvest. Colored water is splashed over each other to symbolize a colorful future.

In Myanmar, the festival is known as the Feast of Thingyan (Feast of New Year). This three-day festival marks the annual visit of Thagyamin (King of Gods) on earth. The first day is the Day of Descent (his arrival), the second day is the Day of Sojourn, and the last day is the Day of Ascent (his departure). The day celebrates the return of Thagyamin annually and is observed with a special feast prepared and shared with neighbors. New Year pots filled with flowers and leaves is prepared, and the head of the family lifts the pots to pay homage to Thagyamin. On the Day of his Ascent, the pot is poured slowly along with prayers for good fortune, rainfall, and good harvest in the coming years. On all these three days, water is splashed on each other outside the houses.

Unlike the traditional Vietnamese and the Chinese New Year that focus more on family reunions and ancestral worship, the water-splashing festival is more community-oriented and open to the participation of all, even visitors. People of all ages, genders, classes, and languages join the festivities of dance, singing, drinking, and splashing water over one another.

Ruchi Agarwal

See also: Ancestor Worship; Buddhism; Cambodia; Dance and Drama (Theater); Hinduism; Laos; Myanmar (Burma); Myth/Mythology; Popular Religion; Ritual Dynamics; Thailand; Thaipusam; Vietnam.

Further Reading

Agarwal, Ruchi. "Water Festival of Thailand: The Indian Connection." *Silpakorn University International Journal* 9–10 (2010): 7–18.

Aung, Maung Htin. *Folk Elements in Burmese Buddhism*. London: Oxford University Press, 1962.

Murphey, Rhoads. *A History of Asia*. 2nd ed. New York: HarperCollins College Publishers, 1996.

Rinehart, Robin. *Contemporary Hinduism: Ritual, Culture, and Practice*. Santa Barbara, CA: ABC-CLIO, 2004.

Wyatt, David K. *Thailand: A Short History*, Chiang Mai: Silkworm Books, 1984.

WOMEN

Southeast Asia, like Asia as a whole, has long embodied a complex intertwining of mass poverty and religious plurality. Recent years, however, have witnessed multiple new manifestations of these two characteristics, as they have become embedded in the rapid development of technology and information as well as the economic boom brought forward by the changing contours of the global economic landscape. Describing women in religion in such a context implies that gender is a determining factor in the interplay between Asian multiple religiosity and widespread poverty. However, the vast diversity of the religious landscape in each Southeast Asian context makes it impossible to generalize about either its religions or the region, or even to depict a single image of the so-called "Southeast Asian women."

This article is not an exhaustive discussion of the theme. It cannot fairly cover each country. Given the wide variety of loci and the diverse approaches of the current literature on the theme of "women, religion, and Southeast Asia," this article focuses on the issue at hand by looking at it through the lens of this two-part guiding question: What are the common features and the significant contributions of women in the context of religion in Southeast Asia?

The response to this question is organized around two thematic foci, namely, "women in dialogue" and "women in public space." The purpose is to depict the ways in which women have played transformative roles in shaping religious discourse and practice in the context of Southeast Asian religious and cultural diversity and, by implication, society itself.

Women in Dialogue

"Women in dialogue" is the predominant feature of the discourse and practice of women in the context of religion in Southeast Asia. For many years, interreligious dialogue was perceived as both a male and an academic-elite exercise. The concept of "women in dialogue" has emerged as a response to the multiple layers that women's long involvement in interreligious cooperation and in interreligious daily activities brings to the dialogue. The multiple intersections of gender, religion, and justice are the dominant focus of women in dialogue. Gender analysis and critique shape fresh interpretations of sacred texts and the lives of religious communities. Any discussion of religion thus requires a gender perspective.

Women in dialogue is the intersectional space of not only various religious traditions, but, even more, of the geographies of women. Discussion of religion in Southeast Asia requires an acknowledgment of the different sociopolitical, economic, and cultural realities that shape women's religious experiences. The status of Islam as the state religion in Malaysia and as the religion of Brunei Darussalam Sultanate creates a different religious landscape for Muslim women and women of other faiths in those two contexts in comparison with Muslim women in Indonesia. Although Indonesia has the largest Muslim population in the world, Islam is not the religion of the state—Indonesia recognizes six official religions, i.e., Islam, Protestantism, Roman Catholicism, Daoism, Buddhism, and Confucianism. The diverse geography and political history of religion thus determine the relevancy and the importance of women in dialogue on the topic of religion. In a country like Indonesia, interfaith cooperation and dialogue of women is necessary in defining the pluralistic character of the nation. It is, therefore, imperative that the voices of Indonesian women are heard at every level of society.

Women in dialogue has become a commonly shared space for women from various faith traditions across Southeast Asia. Any discussion about women in religion is characterized by the particularities of women's religions in their respective contexts. Muslim women from Indonesia, Malaysia, and Brunei Darussalam can share similar experiences of being women in Islam. Their respective social locations and histories

shape the unique manifestations of their contributions to the life and future of religion. Women's interpretations of religious texts and traditions are common features
of the involvement of women in dialogue, in addition to their perspectives on issues
of justice. The history of Indonesian Muslim women's organizations, which can be
dated back to the early twentieth century, reveals the interrelatedness of the reinterpretation of religious texts and traditions and social concerns and efforts to achieve
basic rights for Muslim women. Similarly, in countries like the Philippines, women
in dialogue appear in the ways women work together across faith traditions in dealing with theological questions and challenges of empire and globalization.

Southeast Asian women played an important role in developing Asian Christian
feminist theologies in the late 1970s, from the publication of Indonesian
Protestant feminist theologian Marianne Katoppo's *Compassionate and Free* (1981),
and the pioneering work of Filipina feminist theologian Sister Virginia Fabella and
Korean feminist poet and minister Sun Ai Lee Park, to the first publication of the
journal *In God's Image* in 1982. The pioneering publication of *In God's Image* is
one of the earliest Asian (Christian) feminist theological journals. Five years later,
in 1987, their work continued at the Asian Women Theologian's Conference in
Singapore that founded the Asian Women's Resource Centre for Culture and
Theology (AWRC).

The establishment of AWRC in this location was significant, as Singapore is
scarcely identified with religious discourse; Singapore is most well known in
Southeast Asia for its economic prosperity and stability. In reference to the history
of AWRC, it is reasonable to argue that women's role in public life in Singapore is
not disconnected from their belief. The role of women in religion in public space
in Singapore is a simple yet effective example of how religion can play a transformative role in public life. The current Speaker of Parliament in Singapore, Madam
Halimah Yacob, is a hijab-wearing Muslim. She comes across as fair and impartial,
with a particular concern for those on the margins. She proposes no Islamic teaching in her public role. Yet, her hijab sends an effective message of how religion can
transform public life.

Although the emphasis of the pioneering Asian feminist theologians' early work
was on Christian traditions, the awareness of the challenges and the opportunities
presented by the Asian multireligious character and poverty shaped their work from
the beginning. In fact, one of AWRC's objectives is to create spaces for dialogue
among Asian women of diverse cultures and faiths. This objective was realized
through two interfaith conferences in Kuala Lumpur (1989) and in Colombo, Sri
Lanka (1991), which were significant events in the early years of AWRC. Women
across religious boundaries—Muslim, Buddhist, Christian, Hindus, Jews, and
adherents of Asian indigenous religions—participated in both conferences
(Bouma, Ling, and Pratt 2010, 250).

Issues such as women's leadership, religion and gender, gender and justice,
women and nonviolence efforts, women and poverty, religious fundamentalism,
and women and globalization have become shared themes across religious traditions. These themes have played a major role in shaping women's contributions
to interreligious dialogue. Moreover, the ethnic and cultural backgrounds of

Muslim women reading the Koran and praying in a mosque in Kuala Lumpur. (Viviane Moos/ Corbis News/Corbis)

Southeast Asian women contribute to the intercultural character of women in dialogue. Women in dialogue unveil a common feature in the phenomenon of women in religion, which is women reclaiming their authority in interpreting their religious sources and histories by going back to their roots while extending their conversational dialogue to women of other faiths.

Women in Public Space

Unlike many other places in the world, Southeast Asia reflects the explicit presence and significance of religion in its public space. Many have identified public space in Southeast Asia as being shaped by the intertwinement of modernity, globalization, democracy, and religious diversity. The Southeast Asian religious landscape displays a unique interconnectedness among various religious worship places because they often share spaces in public areas. It is not unusual to see a Hindu temple, a Christian church, and a mosque near each other in one public area. Religious symbols, texts, and rituals are present and are a visible part of the public landscape. This reality demonstrates that religious life in Southeast Asia is vibrant and very public. These dimensions create a unique sense of the role of women in the public life of religion. Therefore, descriptions of women in religion should address the dimensions of women's contributions to the public dimension of religion.

In places such as Myanmar, the role of women in religion is shaped by a long history of civil war and militarism. The symbolic presence and role of Aung San Suu Kyi in public space—although she was denied political power for a certain period of time—symbolizes the complex dimension of women's lives in the country. Women in Myanmar hold a respected position in the cultural context, but under the military regime, they must contest the public extension of the regime's power. Religion is a source of inspiration for Myanmar women's active participation in public life through women's organizations until the time when the symbolic presence of Aung San Suu Kyi unveils the power that had marginalized women from political power and public life.

The role of women in public space in Thailand is shaped by the predominance of Theravada Buddhism. Since Buddhist teaching provides a hierarchical structure based on age rather than gender, the role of women in Thailand in the public space has to be positioned within the complex structure of generations rather than simply located within the gender demarcation. The public role of women mirrors the intertwinement of their familial role and domestic responsibilities, their culturally high position, and their participation in worship that provides an open avenue for women's equity in public life (see Limanonda 2000).

The predominant influence of patriarchy embedded in Confucianism in Vietnam has a significant effect on the role of women in that country. Women's location and duties in domestic space is seen as natural. However, the domestic sphere is not necessarily seen as a subordinate space for women. In fact, women are highly regarded as playing an authoritative role in family life. They are referred to as *noi tuong* (internal generals) (Phan 2003, 106–7). Contemporary Vietnam has also experienced the emerging role of educated, middle-class women who are shaping a shift in the character of the public space in their country. Worth mentioning is the fact that interreligious dialogue, through the symbols of women in various religious traditions, is providing an important starting point for shaping the role of women in the public sphere. The symbols of Mary and Kwan-Yin have "common traits" (Phan 2003, 107–8) that can provide a starting point for interreligious dialogue between the minority Vietnamese Catholics and the Vietnamese Buddhist, Confucian, Daoist, and indigenous religious groups.

Catholicism, as the predominant religion in the Philippines, influences the religious symbols and texts and the emphasis on women's spirituality in Filipino women's work and roles in public space. Filipino women are well known for their creative and strategic role in shaping the democratic dimensions of postmodern public life through women's empowerment. Their extensive work in politics, educational systems, and the sociocultural and economic aspects of society are embedded in their religious narratives. Interfaith women's organizations that bring together Catholic, Protestant, and Muslim women and women of indigenous religions play an important role in defining the voice and presence of Filipino women in public space, especially in regard to gender and justice issues in the lives of migrant workers and issues related to efforts to overcoming violence against women.

Participation in religious organizations for women is significant in the role of women in the public sphere in Southeast Asia. In Malaysia, the National Council of Women's Organisations Malaysia (NCWO), established in 1963, is a manifestation of the voice of women in religion in public space. Its concern for supporting the leadership of women in the public sphere has opened many avenues for the rise of solidarity among women in Malaysia in regard to domestic violence, Sharia law, and policies that have direct effects on the life of women.

In Indonesia, Muslim women leaders are typically members of one of two influential Muslim organizations—Nahdlatul Ulama (NU) and Muhammadiyah. The two organizations are well known for their influence in the political discourse of Indonesia. The women of these two organizations illustrate the face of tolerant and moderate Islam. The work of NU Muslim women scholars and theologians, such as Musdah Mulia, in reinterpreting Islamic sources to reclaim the place and transformative role of Muslim women illustrates the ways in which women's role in public space is embedded in their highly respected expertise in religious teaching and tradition. Mulia's research and publications on reinterpretation of Islamic text and tradition also reflect the intentional efforts of Muslim women scholars and theologians to use media and publication as a means of introducing and discussing their ideas and, by implication, to insert religious transformative teaching into the public discourse.

A relatively new Christian women's organization in Indonesia, the Association of Theologically Trained Women in Indonesia (PERUATI), established in 1995, has since its founding gathered as members more than 3,000 ordained and theologically trained Protestant women across Christian denominations from all over Indonesia. Similar to many women's religious organizations, PERUATI focuses its work on the roles and public lives of Christian women while embedding its vision in reclaiming and reinterpreting of the roles of women in Christian texts, symbols, and rituals in dialogue with women of other faiths. In 2000, PERUATI published *Sophia*, the first Christian feminist theological journal in Indonesia. PERUATI's vision of developing feminist-interfaith discourse is realized through *Sophia*, which invites Christian, Catholic, Muslim, and Buddhist writers to share their visions about religion and justice for all.

In the context of theological education, women theologians provide space for dialogue through courses such as feminist theologies. At Sekolah Tinggi Teologi Jakarta (Jakarta Theological Seminary)—the oldest ecumenical seminary in Indonesia—professors of the feminist theologies course invited Muslim feminist scholars to speak on the theme of Islam, feminist theology, and Indonesia. At the University of Indonesia, gender studies for graduate studies are offered by inviting feminist theologians as well as feminist-male theologians to teach courses on religion that emphasize the roles of women in religion.

At regional levels, women of faiths have their own religious organizations or are affiliated to their religious organizations that address concerns specific to women in their contexts. The contemporary situation of women in the context of religion in Southeast Asia is also shaped by various conflicts and violence, the spread of HIV-AIDS, the reality of human trafficking and migrant work, the lack of education for many women and children, and the limited access to health systems for the poor. Women in the context of religion provide a different approach to reading the reality of Southeast Asia, which is shaped by the diversity of religions, by the continuing reality of the poverty of women and children, and by the continuing works and expertise of women of faiths at various sociopolitical, economic, and religious levels.

The two dimensions of women in the context of religion in Southeast Asia addressed here demonstrate the complexity of the roles that women play as they embody their religious beliefs in every aspect of their lives. Women in dialogue provide a wide range of contributions to religion as they shape and are shaped by their religious teachings and traditions. Women in public space ground their concern and work for justice in their religious sources. No discussion about women in Southeast Asia can be held without identifying women's roles in and contributions to religion.

Septemmy E. Lakawa

See also: Aisyiyah and Nasyiatul Aisyiyah; Brunei Darussalam; Buddhism; Christianity; Confucianism; Daoism (Taoism); Diaspora; Education; Ethnicity; Feminism and Islamic Traditions; Fundamentalism; Globalization; Hinduism; Indonesia; Interreligious Relations and Dialogue; Islam; Judaism; Malaysia; Muhammadiyah; Muslimat NU; Myanmar (Burma); Nahdlatul Ulama; Oka, Gedong Bagus; Philippines; Popular Religion; Religion and Society; Ritual Dynamics; Sexuality; *Shari'a*; Study of Religion; Thailand; Tourism; Vietnam; Women's Monastic Communities.

Further Reading

Bouma, Gary D., Rod Ling, and Douglas Pratt. *Religious Diversity in Southeast Asia and the Pacific: National Case Studies.* Dordrecht: Springer, 2010.

Edwards, Louise, and Mina Roces, eds. *Women in Asia: Tradition, Modernity, and Globalisation.* Ann Arbor: University of Michigan Press, 2000.

Katoppo, Marianne. *Compassionate and Free: An Asian Woman's Theology.* Maryknoll, NY: Orbis Books, 1981.

King, Ursula, and Tina Beattie, eds. *Gender, Religion, and Diversity: Cross-Cultural Perspectives.* London: Continuum, 2005.

Limanonda, Bhassorn. "Exploring Women's Status in Contemporary Thailand." In *Women in Asia: Tradition, Modernity, and Globalisation*, edited by Louise Edwards and Mina Roces, 247–61. Ann Arbor: University of Michigan Press, 2000.

Phan, Peter C. *In Our Own Tongues: Perspectives from Asia on Mission and Inculturation.* Maryknoll, NY: Orbis Books, 2003.

Van Doorn–Harder, Pieternella. *Women Shaping Islam: Indonesian Women Reading the Qur'an in Indonesia.* Urbana: University of Illinois Press, 2006.

WOMEN'S MONASTIC COMMUNITIES

The canonical tradition classifies people in Theravada Buddhist societies into four categories. Men are ordained as monks (*bhikkhus*), followed by women ordained as monks (*bhikkhunis*). Both bhikkhus and bhikkhunis rank high in the hierarchy of persons in the ideal Theravada Buddhist society. This signifies that others can make karmic merits by giving to them. Devoted lay men (ubaasok) and women (ubaasi-kaa) rank lower in this hierarchy but can make merit by giving to monks and ordained nuns. For a long time, the Theravada Buddhist societies comprised of Myanmar, Cambodia, Laos, Sri Lanka, and Thailand had no one eligible to fill the category of ordained nuns. By 1998, the Theravada Order of Nuns had not been active for almost 700 years. The reason for this is still contested.

Cambodia's Buddhist temples often house greater numbers of ascetic women (*don chees*) than monks. Women may enter religious life in Cambodia by taking the prescribed vows and wearing white or black and white. *Don chees* are often elderly women who are free from family responsibilities, though there are also temples that attract younger women, many of whom become respected for their knowledge of the scriptures. The *don chees* tend to depend upon their relatives or the monks for food since they are not considered a strong field of merit to which to make donations, and they are forbidden from practicing alms rounds.

Alexandra Kent

According to oral tradition, Buddha established the order of the nuns years after he founded the order of monks. As a result of the patriarchal society of his time, Buddha required female monks to follow eight main precepts. These precepts affix additional ascetic practices, and those who commit to follow them refrain from all sexual activities, do not eat solid food after noon, and avoid entertainments, makeup, jewelry and colorful cloths. Additionally, female monks were required to observe 94 more percepts.

Female monastic orders spread from India to Sri Lanka and, as a part of the Mahayana tradition, also spread into China, Vietnam, Korea, and Japan. The Bhikkhuni order disappeared in India after the ninth century but flourished in Sri Lanka until the eleventh century when both male and female monastic orders broke down. With the help of Thai and Burmese monks, the male order was later restored. In Burma, the bhikkhuni *sangha* was introduced in the eleventh century and was active until the thirteenth century.

The re-establishment of the bhikkhuni order in Sri Lanka has been an issue for several decades, as the bhikkhuni ordination requires a person to be ordained by both the bhikkhu and the bhikkhuni orders. This was no longer possible with the disappearance of the Theravada bhikkhuni order during the eleventh century. However, the bhiksuni order, which originated from Theravada tradition, remained in the Mahayana tradition in East Asian countries. In the fifth century, bhikkhuni from Sri Lanka had traveled to China to establish the bhikkhuni order. The Sri Lankan female ascetics trying to revive the Theravada bhikkhuni order asked Mahayana bhiksuni to help them with dual ordination. In 1996, 10 Sri Lankan females were ordained in Sarnath, followed by another 20 in 1998 in Bodh Gaya along with 111 women from different countries. Later in 1998, the bhikkhuni ordination was held in Sri Lanka for the first time since the order disappeared in the eleventh century.

Mae chii and bhikkhuni are the two categories of Buddhist ascetic women. As noted above, bhikkhuni date from the time of Buddha himself. Mae chii is a Thai term used for female Thai Buddhist ascetics. In Thailand, females are considered to have a lower karmic standing than males. Therefore, living a monastic life is considered the best way to gain merits. As women cannot be fully ordained as bhikkhuni, mae chii emerged as an alternative. They fall between the lay and the religious realms; they are not part of the *sangha* but stand apart from the lay world as well. They keep a low profile and are less visible in the society when compared to the monks.

Bhikkhunis are very new to Thai Buddhism, and Ajarn Chatsumarn is the first Thai women to be ordained as a *samaneri bhikkhuni* (novice female monk) in the Theravada tradition. She was ordained in Sri Lanka in 2001 and thereafter adopted the name Dhammananda. Her full bhikkhuni ordination happened in 2003 in Sri Lanka, but as of this writing, the Thai *sangha* had not yet recognized her ordination status.

Ruchi Agarwal

See also: Bhikkhuni; Buddhism; Cambodia; Dhammananda; Dharma/Dhamma; Engaged Buddhism; Goddess Traditions; Laos; Liberation Theologies; Myanmar (Burma); Study of Religion; Thailand; Women.

Further Reading

Harvey, P., ed. *Buddhism*. London, New York: Continuum, 2001.

Harvey, P. *An Introduction to Buddhism: Teachings, History, and Practices*. Cambridge: Cambridge University Press, 1990.

Falk, L. M. *Making Fields of Merit: Buddhist Female Ascetics and Gendered Orders in Thailand*. Denmark: NIAS Press, 2007.

Muecke, M. "Female Sexuality in Thai Discourses about Maechii." *Culture, Health, and Sexuality*, Taylor & Francis Health Sciences, 6, no. 3 (May–June 2004): 221–38.

Z

ZOROASTRIANISM

With a history of some 3,000 years, the Zoroastrian religious tradition is one of the most ancient religious traditions. It is the most important and best-known religious tradition of ancient, or pre-Islamic Iran, also known as Persia. It takes its name from that of its founder, Zarathustra (Zoroaster), who probably lived around the beginning of the first millennium BCE. Another name for it, Mazdaism, is derived from the tradition's supreme deity, Mazda ("wise") or Ahura Mazda ("wise lord").

The roots of the religious tradition can be located in an eastern Iranian tribal and basically pastoral society. The tradition originated approximately 1000 BCE. But its clear conservatism and strong traditionalism appear to be manifestations of a cultural attitude that emerged during the Sasanid period (third to seventh century CE). The Sasanids consciously sought to resuscitate Iranian traditions and to obliterate Greek cultural influence.

Central to the Zoroastrian tradition is a monotheistic belief in God, known by the Avestan name Ahura Mazda. He is the supreme lord of creation, and for practical and devotional purposes, the only one. Indeed, the primary innovation of Zoroastrian religious tradition, which sets it apart from other Indo-European peoples in the Near East and Central Asia, is its emphasis on monotheism. At the same time, its outstanding feature, in the context of the entire Indo-Mediterranean world, is its radical dualism. Monotheism and dualism are closely linked in the Zoroastrian religious tradition. They are not in conflict with each other, for monotheism is in opposition to polytheism, not to dualism. In fact, dualism, far from being a protest against monotheism, is a necessary and logical consequence of monotheism; its purpose is to explain the origins of evil. The basis of dualism is essentially ethical. The nature of the two opposing Zoroastrian spirits, Spenta Mainyu ("beneficent spirit") and Angra Mainyu ("hostile spirit"), who are twin children of Ahura Mazda, results from the choices they made between "truth" and "falsehood," between good thoughts, good words, and good deeds and evil thoughts, evil words, and evil deeds. The choices made by the two spirits lie at the root of Zoroastrian dualism and act as a prototype of the choices faced by each individual as he or she decides whether to follow the path of truth or that of untruth. It is incumbent on the faithful to choose the truth, not only so that individually they may achieve the reward of the righteous beyond death, but so that the truth may triumph in the world. Upon death, according to Zoroastrian belief, the soul of the deceased crosses the Bridge of the Separator (Chinvat), that widens to permit easy passage of the righteous and narrows to a knife-edge for the wicked so they fall into the abyss of torment below.

A representation of Ahura Mazda, a divinity exalted by Zoroaster as the one true God. (Vladimir Melnik/Dreamstime.com)

The tradition also associates with Ahura Mazda, in a subordinate way, and to a number of other divine figures, such as Mithra. In addition to the good entities and spirits, the tradition supposes corresponding evil spirits. From the creation through the present age to the final judgment and reordering of the universe, the events of this world are seen as a contest between the powers of good and evil. Zoroastrian ethical teachings place great stress on personal honesty and on striving for the harmony of all creatures, both in the world of nature and in human society. The world, as such, is seen as good and to be enjoyed. At the same time, there is the danger of pollution in the world; so elaborate steps are taken in Zoroastrian ritual and practice to maintain purity.

Ceremonial obligations are carried out in large measure by the priests, who are always male. Eligibility for the priesthood is hereditary, as priests may marry and raise families. To become a priest, a boy learns the Avestan prayers and services, usually by rote. Prayers are said on behalf of the individual by the priest, whether or not the individual is present in the temple. Prayers are always said in Avestan—the language of Zoroastrian scripture, Avesta, from which its name derives—rather than

With a history of some 3,000 years, Zoroastrianism is one of the most ancient religious traditions. It is preserved by the Parsis, a community in western India. During the nineteenth century CE, Parsi traders, along with their Zoroastrian tradition, followed the sea routes of the British Empire around the Indian Ocean, settling in such major Southeast Asian ports as Rangoon and Singapore. From these centers they expanded their trade throughout the region, until today Parsi communities are to be found in Singapore, by far the largest, with smaller communities in Malaysia, Indonesia, Thailand, and Brunei.

David C. Scott

modern vernaculars. Zoroastrians have traditionally held that the proper pronunciation of the specific Avestan sounds has a *mantra*-like power to make the prayer efficacious. Prayers are said by the priest on behalf of the individual.

Central to Zoroastrian worship is the maintenance of a fire as the sign of divine power, presence, and purity. In Fire Temples (*Agiari*), such a fire will burn perpetually, while in other prayer halls and private homes, the fire may be kindled for observances outside the temple.

Every Zoroastrian child is initiated into the duties of the religious tradition before puberty in a ceremony called *Navjote* ("new birth"). Boys and girls receive a white undershirt, *sudreh*, and a woven wool cord, *kusti*, to be wrapped three times around the waist. Both are to be worn constantly, except when bathing.

Zoroastrians' funeral practices include washing the corpse, putting the *sudreh* and *kusti* on and covering it with a white sheet. After relatives and friends respectfully file past, the body is consigned to the Tower of Silence (*Dakhma*) for final disposal by carnivorous birds and the natural elements, so as not to pollute the earth or fire. On the third and fourth days after death, prayers are offered for safe passage of the soul across the Chinvat Bridge, to face judgment of the actions done during life on earth.

The Zoroastrian religious tradition is preserved by the Parsis, a community in western India. As their name, meaning "Persians," indicates, they trace their ancestry to pre-Islamic Iran where, as noted above, the tradition had been the established religion of the Sasanid Empire. During the nineteenth century, the Parsi traders, along with their Zoroastrian tradition, followed the sea routes of the British Empire around the Indian Ocean, settling in such major Southeast Asian ports as Rangoon and Singapore. From these centers, they expanded their trade throughout the region. Today, Parsi communities are to be found in Singapore, by far the largest, followed by Malaysia, Indonesia, Thailand, and Brunei.

The prominent Parsi Association in Singapore was established and registered in 1954. Membership in the association is open to all Parsi-Zoroastrians residing in Singapore, Malaysia, Indonesia, Thailand, and Brunei. The object of the association is to promote the welfare of Parsis resident in these countries. Some of the incidental objects of the association are the promotion of the knowledge and understanding of the Zoroastrian religion, the proper care of the Parsi Funeral Ground, and assisting the Public Trustee in the management of the Parsi Lodge Charity.

Today, Zoroastrians number scarcely more than 130,000 worldwide, chiefly in India and Iran. Nevertheless, many of the current Zoroastrians are highly educated and enjoy an influence out of all proportion to their numbers. Modern-era influences have a significant impact on individual/local beliefs, practices, values, and vocabulary, often complementing and enriching tradition but sometimes displacing tradition entirely. A sense of a need for maintenance of tradition through adaptive change, including the possible admission of non-Zoroastrian spouses to membership and certainly a sophisticated presentation of Zoroastrian belief and practice, is one of the recent contributions of overseas Parsis. With them may lie the chapters of Zoroastrian history still to be written.

David C. Scott

See also: Brunei Darussalam; Colonialism; Diaspora; Indonesia; Islam; Malaysia; Morality; Myanmar (Burma); Ritual Dynamics; Singapore; Spirit Mediumship; Thailand.

Further Reading

Eduljee, K. E. *Zoroastrian Heritage*. http://heritageinstitute.com/zoroastrianism/ (accessed May 14, 2014).

Eliade, Mircea. "New Iranian Syntheses." In *A History of Religious Ideas*, vol. 2, 306 –29. Chicago: University of Chicago Press, 1982.

Eliade, Mircea. "Zarathustra and the Iranian Religion." In *A History of Religious Ideas*, vol. 1, 302 –33. Chicago: University of Chicago Press, 1978.

Encyclopedia Britannica, 2002 ed., S.v. "Zoroastrianism."

Nanavutty, Piloo. *The Parsis*. New Delhi: National Book Trust, 1977.

Selected Bibliography

Ackerman, Susan E., and Raymond L. M. Lee. *Heaven in Transition: Non-Muslim Religious Innovation and Ethnic Identity in Malaysia.* Honolulu: University of Hawaii Press, 1988.

"Ahmad Syafii Maarif: Magsaysay Award Citation." Ramon Magsaysay Award Foundation http://www.rmaf.org.ph/newrmaf/main/awardees/awardee/profile/154 (accessed May 16, 2014).

Ahmed, Ishtiaq, ed. *The Politics of Religion in South and Southeast Asia.* New York: Routledge, 2011.

Alatas, Syed Hussein. *The Myth of the Lazy Native: A Study of the Image of the Malays, Filipinos and Javanese from the 16th to the 20th Century and Its Function in the Ideology of Colonial Capitalism.* London: Frank Cass & Co., 1977.

Ali, Muhamad. "The Rise of the Liberal Islam Network (JIL) in Contemporary Indonesia." *American Journal of Islamic Social Sciences* (22:1). http://i-epistemology.net/attachments/877_ajiss22-1-stripped%20-%20Ali%20-%20The%20Rise%20of%20the%20Liberal%20Islam%20Network.pdf (accessed May 16, 2014).

Ananta, A., and E. N. Arifin. International Migration in Southeast Asia. *Singapore: ISEAS Publications, 2004.*

Appleby, R. Scott. *The Ambivalence of the Sacred: Religion, Violence and Reconciliation.* Lanham, MD: Rowman & Littlefield Publishers, 2000.

Ariarajah, S. Wesley. *Not Without My Neighbour: Issues in Inter-Faith Relations.* Geneva: WCC, 1999.

Aritonang, Jan Sihar, and Karel Steenbrink, eds. *A History of Christianity in Indonesia.* Leiden, Boston: Brill, 2008.

Ashmawi, Muhammad S. *Against Islamic Extremism.* Translated and edited by C. Fluehr-Lobban. Gainesville: University Press of Florida, 1998.

Attas, Syed Muhammad Naquib al-. *Islam and Secularism.* Kuala Lumpur: Muslim Youth Movement of Malaysia (ABIM); reprint, Kuala Lumpur: ISTAC, 1993.

Aung, Maung Htin. *Folk Elements in Burmese Buddhism.* Rangoon: Buddha Sasana Council, 1959.

Aung, Maung Htin. *Folk Elements in Burmese Buddhism.* London: Oxford University Press, 1962.

Azyumardi, Azra. *The Origins of Islamic Reformism in Southeast Asia: Networks of Malay-Indonesian and Middle Eastern Ulama in the Seventeenth and Eighteenth Centuries.* Honolulu: Allen & Unwin and University of Hawaii Press, 2004.

Bakker, F. L. *The Struggle of the Hindu Balinese Intellectuals, Developments in Modern Hindu Thinking in Independent Indonesia.* Amsterdam: VY University Press, 1993.

Barr, Michael, and Carl A. Trocki. *Paths Not Taken: Political Pluralism in Post-War Singapore.* Singapore: NUS Press, 2008.

Beatty, A. *Varieties of Javanese Religion: An Anthropological Account.* Cambridge: Cambridge University Press, 1999.

Berger, Mark T. *The Battle for Asia, from Decolonization to Globalization*. Oxford: RoutledgeCurzon, 2004.

Bouma, Gary D., Douglas Pratt, and Rod Ling, eds. *Religious Diversity in Southeast Asia and the Pacific: National Case Studies*. New York: Springer, 2010.

Boyd, Jeff. "The Role of the Church in the Philippines' Nonviolent People Power Revolution." Nonviolence and Christian Faith in the 20th Century, June 29, 2010. http://pacificador99.files.wordpress.com/2012/01/philippines-jeff-boyd.pdf (accessed May 16, 2014).

Brenner, Suzanne. *The Domestication of Desire: Women, Wealth, and Modernity in Java*. Princeton, NJ: Princeton University Press, 1998.

Brock, Colin, and Lorrane Pe Symaco. *Education in South-East Asia*. Oxford Studies in Comparative Education. Oxford: Symposium Books, 2011.

Buehler, Michael. "Islam and Democracy in Indonesia." *Insight Turkey* 11:4 (2009): 51–63. http://www.columbia.edu/cu/weai/pdf/Insight_Turkey_2009_4_Michael_Buehler.pdf (accessed May 16, 2014).

Bullock, Katherine. *Rethinking Muslim Women and the Veil: Challenging Historical and Modern Stereotypes*. London: The International Institute of Islamic Thought, 2002.

Burke, Farkhunda. "Muslim Minorities and Majorities of Southeast Asia: Focus on Realities." *Pakistan Horizon* 57:2 (April 2004): 37–49. http://www.jstor.org/discover/10.2307/41394045?uid=3739696&uid=2&uid=4&uid=3739256&sid=21102247449271 (accessed May 16, 2014).

Bush, Robin. *Nahdlatul Ulama and the Struggle for Power within Islam and Politics in Indonesia*. Singapore: ISEAS, 2009.

Camilleri, Joseph, and Sven Schottmann. *Culture, Religion and Conflict in Muslim Southeast Asia: Negotiating Tense Pluralisms*. New York: Routledge, 2012.

Chittick, William C. *Sufism: A Short Introduction*. Oxford: Oneworld Publications, 2000.

Cook, Alistair D. B. *Culture, Identity and Religion in Southeast Asia*. Newcastle upon Tyne, UK: Cambridge Scholars Publishing, 2007.

Cornell, Vincent J., ed. *Voices of Islam: Voices of Tradition*. Vol. 1. Westport, CT: Praeger, 2007

Cravath, Paul. "The Ritual Origins of the Classical Dance Drama of Cambodia." *Asian Theatre Journal* 3, no. 2 (1986): 179–203.

Creese, Helen. *Women of the Kakawin World: Marriage and Sexuality in the Indic Courts of Java and Bali*. Armonk, NY: M. E. Sharpe, 2004.

DeBernardi, Jean. *The Way That Lives in the Heart: Chinese Popular Religion and Spirit Mediums in Penang, Malaysia*. Stanford, CA: Stanford University Press, 2006.

De La Torre, Miguel A., ed. *The Hope of Liberation in World Religions*. Waco, TX: Baylor University Press, 2008.

Desai, Santosh N., *Hinduism in Thai Life*. Mumbai: Popular Prakashan, 1980.

DharmaNet: Resources for "Engaged Buddhism." http://www.dharmanet.org/lcengaged.htm (accessed May 16, 2014).

Doorn-Harder, P. V. *Women Shaping Islam: Indonesian Women Reading the Qur'an*. Urbana: University of Illinois Press, 2006.

Dubois, Thomas David. *Casting Faiths: Imperialism and Transformation of Religion in East and Southeast Asia*. Hampshire, UK: Palgrave Macmillan, 2009.

Eduljee, K. E. "Zoroastrian Heritage." http://heritageinstitute.com/zoroastrianism/ (accessed May 16, 2014).

Edwards, Louise, and Mina Roces, eds. *Women in Asia: Tradition, Modernity, and Globalisation*. Ann Arbor: University of Michigan Press, 2000.

Eliade, Mircea, ed. *Encyclopedia of Religion*. New York: Macmillan Publishing Co., 1987.

Eliade, Mircea. "Zarathustra and the Iranian Religion." In *A History of Religious Ideas*, vol. 1, 302–33. Chicago: University of Chicago Press, 1978.

Eliade, Mircea. "New Iranian Syntheses." In *A History of Religious Ideas*, vol. 2, 306–29. Chicago: University of Chicago Press, 1982.

Eliade, Mircea, and Willard R. Trask. *The Sacred and the Profane: The Nature of Religion*. New York: Harcourt, 1961.

Emerson, Michael O., and Hartman, David. "The Rise of Religious Fundamentalism." *Annual Review of Sociology* 32 (August 2006): 127–44.

Endres, Kirsten. *Performing the Divine: Mediums, Markets and Modernity in Urban Vietnam*. Copenhagen: Nordic Institute for Asian Studies Press, 2011.

Esack, Farid. *Qur'an, Liberation, and Pluralism*. Oxford: Oneworld, 1997.

Esposito, John L. *Islam and Politics*. 4th ed. Syracuse, NY: Syracuse University Press, 1998.

Esposito, John L. *Islam: The Straight Path*. New York and Oxford: Oxford University Press, 2005.

Falk, L. M. *Making Fields of Merit: Buddhist Female Ascetics and Gendered Orders in Thailand*. Denmark: NIAS Press, 2007.

Finucane, Juliana, and R. Michael Feener, eds. *Proselytizing and the Limits of Religious Pluralism in Contemporary Asia*. Singapore: Springer, 2014.

Fishchel, Walter. "New Sources for the History of the Jewish Diaspora in Asia in the 16th Century." *Jewish Quarterly Review* 40, no. 4 (April 1950): 380.

Fisher, Mary Pat. *Living Religions: An Encyclopaedia of the World's Faiths*. London and New York: I. B. Tauris Publishers, 1997.

Fjelstad, Karen, and Nguyen Thi Hien, eds. *Possessed by the Spirits: Mediumship in Contemporary Vietnamese Communities*. Ithaca, NY: Cornell Southeast Asia Program Publications, 2006.

Friend, Theodore, ed. *Religion and Religiosity in the Philippines and Indonesia: Essays on State, Society, and Public Creeds*. Baltimore: Johns Hopkins University Press, 2006.

Gahral, Donny, and Adrian Gahral, ed. *Relations between Religions and Cultures in Southeast Asia*. Washington, DC: Council for Research in Values and Philosophy, 2009.

Geertz, Clifford. *Islam Observed: Religious Development in Morocco and Indonesia*, 25–28. Chicago: University of Chicago Press, 1968.

Ghosananda, Maha. *Step by Step: Meditations on Wisdom and Compassion*. Berkeley, CA: Parallax Press, 1991.

Gomes, Gabriel J. *Discovering World Religions: A Guide for the Inquiring Reader*. Bloomington, IN: iUniverse, 2012.

Hanh, Thich Nhat. *Being Peace*. Berkeley, CA: Parallax Press, 1987.

Hanh, Thich Nhat. *Vietnam: Lotus in a Sea of Fire*. New York: Farrar, Straus & Giroux, 1967.

Harnish, David, and Anne Rasmussen, eds. *Divine Inspirations: Music and Islam in Indonesia*. Oxford: Oxford University Press, 2011.

Harris, Ian. *Buddhism in a Dark Age: Cambodian Monks under Pol Pot*. Honolulu: University of Hawaii Press, 2013.

Harris, Ian. *Cambodian Buddhism: History and Practice*. Chiang Mai, Thailand: Silkworm Books, 2005.

Harrison, Rachel V., and Peter A. Jackson, eds. *The Ambiguous Allure of the West: Traces of the Colonial in Thailand*. Hong Kong: Hong Kong University Press, 2010.

Hassan, R. "The Issue of Woman-Man Equality in the Islamic Tradition." In *Eve and Adam; Jewish, Christian, and Muslim Readings on Genesis and Gender*, edited by Kristen E.

Kvam, Linda S. Schearing, and Valarie H. Ziegler, 464–76. Bloomington: Indiana University Press, 1999.

Hefner, Robert W. *Civil Islam, Muslim and Democratization in Indonesia*. Princeton, NJ: Princeton University Press, 2000.

Hefner, Robert W. *Politics of Multiculturalism: Pluralism and Citizenship in Malaysia, Singapore, and Indonesia*. Honolulu: University of Hawaii Press, 2001.

Hefner, Robert W., and Muhammad Qasim Zaman. *Schooling Islam: The Culture and Politics of Modern Muslim Education*. Princeton, NJ: Princeton University Press, 2007.

Hefner, R. W. "South-East Asia from 1910." In *The New Cambridge History of Islam*, edited by F. Robinson, vol. 5, *The Islamic World in the Age of Western Dominance*, 591–622. Cambridge: Cambridge University Press, 2010.

Heikkilä-Horn, Marja-Leena. *Santi Asoke Buddhism and Thai State Response*. Turku, Finland: Åbo Akademi University Press, 1996.

Heine-Geldern. Robert, "Conceptions of State and Kingship in Southeast Asia." *Journal of Asia Studies* 2. Cambridge: Cambridge University Press, 1942.

Hill, M. "The Rehabilitation and Regulation of Religion in Singapore." In *Regulating Religion: Case Studies from Around the Globe*, edited by J. T. Richardson, 343–58. New York: Kluwer Academic, 2004.

Holt, John Clifford. *Spirits of the Place. Buddhism and Lao religious culture*. Honolulu: University of Hawai'i Press, 2009.

Hooker, M. B. "Muhammadan Law and Islamic Law." In *Islam in South-East Asia*, edited by M. B. Hooker, 160–82. Leiden and New York: E. J. Brill, 1988.

Horstmann, Alexander. Performing Multi-Religious Ritual in Southern Thailand." MMG Working Paper 11-05. Max Planck Institute for the Study of Religious and Ethnic Diversity, 2011. http://www.mmg.mpg.de/workingpapers.

Hue-Tâm Ho Tai. *Millenarianism and Peasant Politics in Viêtnam*. Cambridge, MA: Harvard University Press, 1983.

Hui, Yew Foong. "The Ten Most Influential Books on Southeast Asia." *SOJOURN: Journal of Social Issues in Southeast Asia* 24, no. 1 (2009).

Ileto, Reynaldo C. "Orientalism and the Study of Philippine Politics," in *Knowing America's Colony: A Hundred Years from the Philippine War*, Philippine Studies Occasional Paper Series No. 13, 41–65. Honolulu: University of Hawaii at Manoa, 1999. See also the essays on the "Forum on Orientalism and Philippine Politics," *Philippine Political Science Journal* 23, no. 46 (2002): 119–74.

Ileto, Reynaldo C. *Pasyon and Revolution: Popular Movements in the Philippines, 1840–1910*. Quezon City, Philippines: Ateneo University Press, 1979.

Jackson, Peter. 1993. "Thai Buddhist Identity: Debates on the *Traiphuum Phra Ruang*." In *National Identity and its Defenders: Thailand 1939–1989*, edited by Craig Reynolds. Chiang Mai, Thailand: Silkworm Books.

Jackson, Peter A. *Buddhism, Legitimation, and Conflict: The Political Functions of Urban Thai Buddhism*. Singapore: ISEAS, 1989.

Jessup, Helen Ibbitson, and Barry Brukoff. *Temples of Cambodia: The Heart of Angkor*. Bangkok: River Books, 2011.

Jewish Center of Cambodia. http://www.jewishcambodia.com/ (accessed May 16, 2014).

Jones, Charles B. "Transitions in the Practice and Defense of Pure Land Buddhism." In *Buddhism in the Modern World: Adaptions of an Ancient Tradition*, edited by Steven Heine and Charles S. Prebish. New York: Oxford University Press, 2003.

Jordt, Ingrid. *Burma's Mass Lay Meditation Movement: Buddhism and the Cultural Construction of Power*. Athens: Ohio University Research in International Studies, Southeast Asia Series, No. 115, 2007.

Juergensmeyer, Mark. *Global Rebellion, Religious Challenge to the Secular State*. Berkeley: University of California Press, 2007.

Kabilsingh, Chatsumarn. *Thai Women in Buddhism*. Berkeley, CA: Parallax Press, 1991.

Kahin, George McTurnan. *Nationalism and Revolution in Indonesia*. Ithaca, NY: Cornell University Press, 1952.

Kamarulnizam, Abdullah. *The Politics of Islam in Contemporary Malaysia*. Bangi: Penerbit Universiti Kebangsaan Malaysia, 2003.

Karuna Dharma. "The Reconciliation of Zen and Pure Land Buddhism." http://www.urbandharma.org/ibmc (accessed May 16, 2014).

Kasiarz, Katarzyna, and Edmund Chia. "Forty Years of Liberation Theology: Revisiting Praxis." East Asia Pastoral Institute.http://eapi.admu.edu.ph/content/forty-years-liberation-theology-revisiting-praxis (accessed May 16, 2014).

Katoppo, Marianne. *Compassionate and Free: An Asian Woman's Theology*. Maryknoll, NY: Orbis Books, 1981.

Kent, Alexandra. "Transcendence and Tolerance: Cultural Diversity in the Tamil Celebration of Taipūcam in Penang, Malaysia." *International Journal of Hindu Studies* 8, no. 1–3 (2004): 81–105.

"Key Issues for Religious Minority Rights in Asia." Minority Rights Group International. http://www.refworld.org/cgi-bin/texis/vtx/rwmain?docid=469cbfa90 (accessed May 16, 2014).

Keyes, Charles F., Laurel Kendall and Helen Hardacre, eds. *Asian Visions of Authority: Religion and the Modern States of East and Southeast Asia*. Honolulu: University of Hawaii Press, 1994.

Kirsch, A. Thomas. *Feasting and Social Oscillation: Religion and Society in Upland Southeast Asia*. Ithaca, NY: Cornell University Press, 1973.

Kitiarsa, Pattana. *Mediums, Monks, and Amulets: Thai Popular Buddhism Today*. Chiang Mai, Thailand: Silkworm Press, 2012.

Knysh, Alexander. *Islamic Mysticism: A Short History*. Leiden: Brill, 1999.

Kohen, Arnold. *From the Place of the Dead: The Epic Struggles of Bishop Belo of East Timor*. New York: St. Martin's Press, 1999.

Kornfield, Jack. *Living Dharma: Teachings and Meditation Instructions from Theravada Masters*. Boston and London: Shambhala Publications, 2010.

Kosmin, Barry A., and Ariela Keysar. *Secularism and Secularity: Contemporary International Perspectives*. Hartford, CT: Institute for the Study of Secularism in Society and Culture, 2007.

Koyama, Kosuke. *Waterbuffalo Theology: A Thailand Theological Notebook*. Singapore: SPCK, 1970.

Lai, Ah Eng. *Religious Diversity in Singapore*. Singapore: Institute of Southeast Asian Studies jointly with Institute of Policy Studies, 2008.

"Lao Tzu Biography." *Encyclopedia of World Biography*. http://www.notablebiographies.com/Ki-Lo/Lao-Tzu.html (accessed May 16, 2014).

Lee, Julian C. H. *Islamization and Activism in Malaysia*. Singapore: ISEAS, 2010.

Leibo, Steven A. *The World Today Series 2012: East and Southeast Asia*. 45th ed. Lanham, MD: Styker-Post Publications, 2012.

Levi-Strauss, Claude. *Myth and Meaning.* Toronto: University of Toronto Press, 1978.

Lim, S. H. *Giving Voice to Asian Christians: An Appraisal of the Pioneering Work of I-To Loh in the Area of Congregational Song.* Saarbrucken: VDM Verlag, 2008.

Lindenfeld, David, and Miles Richardson, eds. *Beyond Conversion and Syncretism: Indigenous Encounters with Missionary Christianity.* Oxford: Berghahn Books, 2011.

Liow, Joseph Chinyong. *Piety and Politics: Islamism in Contemporary Malaysia.* New York: Oxford University Press, 2009.

Loh, I-to. *In Search for Asian Sounds and Symbols in Worship.* Edited by Michael Poon. Singapore: Trinity Theological College, 2012.

Lowenstein, Tom. *The Glories of Sacred Asia: Treasures of the Buddha.* New York: Metro Books, 2006.

Mackenzie. Rory. *New Buddhist Movements in Thailand: Towards an Understanding of Wat Phra Dhammakaya and Santi Asoke.* New York: Routledge. 2007.

Manisegaran, A. *Jewel among Nations: An Account of the Early Days of the Baha'i Faith in West Malaysia.* Ampang, Selangor: Splendour Publications, 2003.

Marr, David G. *Vietnamese Anti-Colonialism 1885–1925.* Berkeley: University of California Press, 1971.

Marston, John, and Elizabeth Guthrie. *History, Buddhism, and New Religious Movements in Cambodia.* Honolulu: University of Hawaii Press, 2004.

Mazumdar, Vina. *Gender Issues and Educational Development: An Overview from Asia.* http://www.cwds.ac.in/OCPaper/GenderIssuesVM.pdf (accessed May 16, 2014).

McCargo, Duncan. "The Changing Politics of Thailand's Buddhist Order." *Critical Asian Studies* 44, no. 4 (2012): 627–42.

McDaniel, Justin. *Gathering Leaves and Lifting Words: Histories of Buddhist Monastic Education in Laos and Thailand.* Seattle: University of Washington Press, 2008.

McLeod, Melvin, ed. *The Pocket Thich Nhat Hanh.* Boston: Shambhala Publications, 2012.

Michaud, Jean. *Historical Dictionary of the Peoples of the Southeast Asian Massif.* Lanham, MD; Toronto; and Oxford: The Scarecrow Press, Historical Dictionaries of Peoples and Cultures no 4. (2006).

Miettinen, Jukka O. *Classical Dance and Theatre in South-East Asia.* Singapore: Oxford University Press, 1992.

Miller, Terry, and Sean Williams. "Waves of Cultural Influences." In *Southeast Asia, The Garland Encyclopedia of World Music.* New York and London: Garland, 1998.

Morris, Rosalind. *In the Place of the Origins: Modernity and Its Mediums in Northern Thailand.* Durham, NC: Duke University Press, 2000.

Morse, M. *Kosuke Koyama: A Model for Intercultural Theology.* Frankfurt: Peter Lang, 1991.

Muecke, M. "Female Sexuality in Thai Discourses about Maechii." *Culture, Health, and Sexuality*, Taylor & Francis Health Sciences, 6, no. 3 (May–June 2004): 221–38.

Mujīburraḥmān. *Feeling Threatened: Muslim-Christian Relations in Indonesia's New Order.* Amsterdam: Amsterdam University Press, 2006.

Narakobi, B. *The Melanesian Way.* Port Moresby: Institute of PNG Studies, 1983.

Nguyen, Cuong Tu. *Zen in Medieval Vietnam.* Honolulu: University of Hawaii Press, 1997

Numrich, Paul D. *The Faith Next Door: American Christians and Their New Religious Neighbors.* Oxford: Oxford University Press, 2009.

Nyi, U Nyi. "Venerable Mahasi Sayadaw: A Biographical Sketch." Insight Meditation Online. http://www.buddhanet.net/mahabio.htm (accessed May 16, 2014).

Ong, Aiwah. "The Politics of Multiculturalism: Pluralism and Citizenship in Malaysia, Singapore and Indonesia." *Journal of Social Issues in Southeast Asia*, July 30, 2005).

Ooi, Keat Gin, ed. *Southeast Asia: A Historical Encyclopedia from Angkor Wat to Timor*. Santa Barbara, CA: ABC CLIO, 2004.

Osnes, Beth. *The Shadow Puppet Theatre of Malaysia*. Jefferson, NC: McFarland & Co., 2010.

Othman, Norani. *Muslim Women and the Challenge of Islamic Extremism*. Petaling Jaya: Sisters in Islam, 2005.

Pangalangan, Raul. "Religion and the Secular State: National Report for the Philippines." In *Religion and the Secular State: Interim National Reports Issued for the Occasion of the XVIIIth International Congress of Comparative Law*, edited by Javier Martínez-Torrón, W. Cole Durham, and Brigham Young University, International Center for Law and Religion Studies, 559–71. Provo, UT: International Center for Law and Religion Studies, Brigham Young University, 2010.

Parrinder, Geoffrey. *Introduction to Asian Religions*. New York: Oxford University Press, 1976.

Peacock, James L. *Purifying the Faith: The Muhammadijah Movement in Indonesian Islam*. Arizona: Arizona State University, 1992.

Paul, Diana. "Kuan-Yin: Savior and Savioress in Pure Land Buddhism." In *The Book of the Goddess Past and Present*, edited by Carl Olson, 161–75. New York: Crossroad Publishing Company, 1983.

Pereira, Shane N. "A New Religious Movement in Singapore: Syncretism and Variation in the Sathya Sai Baba Movement." *Asian Journal of Social Science* 36 (2008): 250–70. http://www.academia.edu/232635/A_New_Religious_Movement_in_Singapore_Syncretism_and_Variation_in_the_Sathya_Sai_Baba_Movement (accessed May 16, 2014).

Phan, Peter C. *Mission and Catechesis: Alexandre de Rhodes and Inculturation in Seventeenth-Century Vietnam,* Maryknoll, NY: Orbis Books, 1998.

Phan, Peter C. *Vietnamese-American Catholics*. New York: Paulist Press, 2005.

Pholsena, Vatthana. *Post-War Laos. The Politics of Culture, History and Identity*. Singapore: Institute of Southeast Asian Studies, 2006.

Picard, Michel. *Bali: Cultural Tourism and Touristic Culture*. Singapore: Archipelago Press, 1996.

Picard, Michel, and Remy Madinier, eds. *The Politics of Religion in Indonesia: Syncretism, Orthodoxy and Religious Contention in Java and Bali*. Oxford: Taylor and Francis, 2011.

Pohl, F. "Islamic Education and Civil Society: Reflection on the Pesantren Tradition in Contemporary Indonesia." *Comparative Education Review* 50, no. 3 (2006).

Poplawska, Marzanna. "Christianity and Inculturated Music in Indonesia." *Southeast Review of Asian Studies* 33 (2011): 186–98.

Prager, Michael. "Structure, Process, and Performance in Eastern Indonesia Rituals: A Review Article." *Anthropos* 87 (1992): 548–55.

Preston, James J., ed. *Mother Worship, Theme and Variations*. Chapel Hill: University of North Carolina Press, 1982.

Pringle, R. *Understanding Islam in Indonesia: Politics and Diversity*. Honolulu: University of Hawaii Press, 2010.

Prothero, Stephen. *God Is Not One: The Eight Rival Religions that Run the World, and Why their Differences Matter*. New York: HarperOne Publishers, 2010.

Queen, Christopher S., and Sallie B. King, eds. *Engaged Buddhism: Buddhist Liberation Movements in Asia*. Albany: State University of New York Press, 1996.

Rafael, Vicente. *Contracting Colonialism: Translation and Christian Conversion in Tagalog Society under Early Spanish Rule*. Manila: Ateneo de Manila Univ. Press, 1988.

Raid, Hasan. "The Struggles of a Muslim Communist." http://mrzine.monthlyreview.org/2011/raid090311.html (accessed May 16, 2014).

Rambo, Lewis R. *Understanding Religious Conversion*. New Haven, CT: Yale University Press, 1993.

Ramstedt, Martin. *Hinduism in Modern Indonesia: A Minority Religion between Local, National, and Global Interests*. London and New York: RoutledgeCurzon, 2004.

Ramstedt, Martin. "Two Balinese Hindu Intellectuals—Ibu Gedong Bagoes Oka and Prof. I Gusti Nguarah Bagun." *IIAS Newsletter* 23 (October 2000): 12–13.

Ricklefs, Merle Calvin. *Islam in the Indonesian Social Context*. Victoria: Centre of Southeast Asian Studies, Monash University, 1991.

Rinehart, Robin. *Contemporary Hinduism: Ritual, Culture, and Practice*. Santa Barbara, CA: ABC-CLIO, 2004.

Roald, Anne Sofie. *Women in Islam: The Western Experience*. London: Routledge, 2001

Robinson, Kathryn, and Sharon Bessell. *Women in Indonesia: Gender, Equity and Development*. Singapore: Institute of Southeast Asian Studies, 2002.

Saeed, Abdullah. *Approaches to the Qur'an in Contemporary Indonesia*, 107–34. London: Oxford University Press, 2005.

Saeed, Abdullah and Hassan Saeed: *Freedom of Religion, Apostasy and Islam*. Farnham, Surrey: Ashgate Publishing, 2004.

Safi, O. *Progressive Muslims: On Justice, Gender and Pluralism*. Oxford: Oneworld, 2003.

SarDesai, D. R. *Southeast Asia: Past and Present*. Boulder, CO: Westview Press, 2012.

Scott, James C. *The Art of Not Being Governed: An Anarchist History of Upland Southeast Asia*. New Haven, CT: Yale University Press, 2009.

Seager, Richard H. *Buddhism in America*. New York: Columbia University Press, 1999.

Segal, Robert, ed. *The Blackwell Companion to the Study of Religion*. Oxford: Blackwell Publishing, 2006.

Sidel, John T. "The Fate of Nationalism in the New States: Southeast Asia in Comparative Historical Perspective." *Comparative Studies in Society and History* 54, no. 1 (2012): 114–44.

Silverman, H. J., ed. *Talk about Sexuality in Thailand: Notion, Identity, Gender Bias, Women, Gay, Sex Education, and Lust*. Yogyakarta: Southeast Asia Consortium on Gender, Sexuality and Health, 2004.

Singapore Jain Religious Society. http://www.sjrs.org.sg/ (accessed May 16, 2014).

Sirikanchana, Pataraporn. *In Search of Thai Buddhism*. Bangkok: Office of National Buddhism, 2010.

Sisters in Islam. http://www.sistersinislam.org.my (accessed May 16, 2014).

Sivaraksa, Sulak. "Religion and World Order from a Buddhist Perspective." In *Toward a Global Civilization? The Contribution of Religions*, edited by Patricia M. Mische and Melissa Merkling. New York: Peter Lang. 2001.

Smith, D. *Dharma Mind Worldly Mind: A Buddhist Handbook on Complete Meditation*. Thailand: Aloka Publications, 2002.

Smith, Jane I. *Islam in America*. New York: Columbia University Press, 1999.

Snodgrass, Adrian. *The Symbolism of the Stupa*. Ithaca, NY: Cornell University, Southeast Asia Program Publications, 1985.

Soucy, Alexander. *The Buddha Side: Gender, Power, and Buddhist Practice in Vietnam*. Honolulu: University of Hawaii Press, 2012.

Spiro, Melford E. *Buddhism and Society: A Great Tradition and Its Burmese Vicissitudes*. 2nd expanded ed. Berkeley: University of California Press, 1982.

Sprenger, Guido. "The End of Rituals. A Dialogue between Theory and Ethnography in Laos." *Paideuma* 52 (2006): 51–72.

Sprenger, Guido. "Political Periphery, Cosmological Center: The Reproduction of Rmeet Sociocosmic Order and the Laos-Thailand Border." In *Centering the Margin: Agency and Narrative in Southwest Asia Borderlands*, edited by Alexander Horstmann and Reed L. Wadley, 67–84. New York and Oxford: Berghahn Books, 2006.

Srimulyani, E. *Women from Traditional Islamic Educational Institutions in Indonesia: Negotiating Public Spaces*. Amsterdam: Amsterdam University, 2012.

Steinberg, David I. *Burma: The State of Myanmar*. Washington, DC: Georgetown University Press, 2001.

Steinberg, David I. *Burma/Myanmar: What Everyone Needs to Know*. Oxford: Oxford University Press, 2010.

Stiglitz, Joseph E. *Globalization and Its Discontents*. New York: W. W. Norton & Company, 2003.

Stuart-Fox, Martin. *Buddhist Kingdom, Marxist State: The Making of Modern Laos*. Bangkok: White Lotus Press, 2002.

Swearer, Donald K. "Buddhism in Southeast Asia." In *Encyclopedia of Religion*, vol. 2: 385–99.

Swearer, Donald K. *The Buddhist World of Southeast Asia*. Albany: State University of New York Press, 1995.

Swearer, Donald K. *The Buddhist World of Southeast Asia*. 2nd ed. Chiang Mai, Thailand: Silkworm Books, 2009.

Syamsiyatun, Siti. "A Daughter in the Indonesian Muhammadiyah: Nasyiatul Aisyiyah Negotiates a New Status and Image." *Journal of Islamic Studies* 18, no. 1 (2007): 69–94. http://jis.oxfordjournals.org/content/18/1/69.abstract (accessed May 16, 2014).

"Taoism." *Patheos Library*. http://www.patheos.com/Library/Taoism.html (accessed May 16, 2014).

Tarling, Nicholas. *Nationalism in Southeast Asia: "If the People Are with Us."* New York: Routledge, 2004.

Taylor, J. L. "Buddhist Revitalization, Modernization, and Social Change in Contemporary Thailand." *Sojourn* 8, no. 1 (1993): 62–91.

Taylor, Philip. *Goddess on the Rise: Pilgrimage and Popular Religion in Vietnam*. Honolulu: University of Hawaii Press, 2004.

Taylor, Philip, ed. *Modernity and Re-enchantment: Religion in Post-Revolutionary Vietnam*. Singapore: ISEAS, 2007.

Thio, Li-ann. "Constitutional Accommodation of the Rights of Ethnic and Religious Minorities in Plural Democracies: Lessons and Cautionary Tales from South-East Asia." *Pace International Law Review* 22, no. 1 (Winter 2010). http://digitalcommons.pace.edu/cgi/viewcontent.cgi?article=1025&context=pilr (accessed May 16, 2014).

Thomas, Scott M. *The Global Resurgence of Religion and the Transformation of International Relations: The Struggle for the Soul of the Twenty-First Century*. New York: Palgrave Macmillan, 2005.

Tibi, Bassam. *The Challenge of Fundamentalism, Political Islam and the New World Order*. Berkeley: University of California Press, 1998.

Tobing, Richard Lumban. *Christian Social Ethics in the Thought of T. B. Simatupang: The Role of Indonesian Christians in Social Change*. Denver: Iliff School of Theology and the University of Denver, 1996.

Torre, Miguel A. de la, ed. *The Hope of Liberation in World Religions*. Waco, TX: Baylor University Press, 2008.

Trompf, G., and C. Loeliger. *New Religious Movements in Melanesia*. Port Moresby: University of Papua New Guinea Press, 1985.

Suu Kyi, Aung San. *Freedom from Fear and Other Writings*. London: Penguin Books, 1991.

United Nations Human Rights, Office of the High Commissioner for Human Rights. "Freedom of Religion: UN Rights Expert Reports on the Plight of Religious Minorities in the World." http://www.ohchr.org/en/NewsEvents/Pages/DisplayNews.aspx ?NewsID=13083&LangID=E (accessed May 16, 2014).

Valentine, Simon Ross. *Islam and the Ahmadiyya Jama'at: History, Belief, Practice*. New York: Columbia University Press, 2008.

van der Kroef, Justus M. "The Hinduization of Indonesia Reconsidered." *Far Eastern Quarterly* 11 (1951): 17–30.

Van Doorn-Harder, Pieternella. *Women Shaping Islam: Indonesian Women Reading the Qur'an in Indonesia*. Urbana: University of Illinois Press, 2006.

Van Ness, Edward C., and Prawirohardjo. *Javanese Wayang Kulit: An Introduction*. London: Oxford University Press, 1984.

Vasquez, M. More Than Belief: A Materialist Theory of Religion. Oxford: Oxford University Press, 2011.

Wadud, M. A. *Qur'an and Woman: Rereading the Sacred Text from a Woman's Perspective*. New York: Oxford University Press, 1999.

Wertheim, W. F. "Religious Reform Movements in South and Southeast Asia." http://www .jstor.org/discover/10.2307/30123249?uid=3739696&uid=377567133&uid=2&uid=3 &uid=3739256&uid=60&sid=21102043006493 (accessed May 16, 2014).

Wiley, Kristi L. *The A to Z of Jainism*. New York: Scarecrow Press, 2009.

Williams, Paul. *Buddhism: Buddhist Origins and the Early History of Buddhism in South and Southeast Asia*. Oxford: Taylor & Francis, 2005.

Willis, Jennifer Schwamm, ed. *A Lifetime of Peace: Essential Writings by and about Thich Nhat Hanh*. New York: Marlowe & Co., 2003.

Winzeler, L. Robert. *The Peoples of Southeast Asia Today: Ethnography, Ethnology, and Change in a Complex Region*, chap. 8, 143–71. New York: AltaMira Press, 2011.

Wolters, O. W. *History, Culture, and Region in Southeast Asian Perspectives*. Rev. ed. Ithaca, NY: Cornell Southeast Asia Program in collaboration with the Institute of Southeast Asian Studies, Singapore, 1999.

Woodward, M. "Indonesia, Islam and the Prospect of Democracy." *SAIS Review* 21, no. 2 (2001): 29–37.

Wright, Nadia H. *Respected Citizens: The History of Armenians in Singapore and Malaysia*. Melbourne: Amassia Publishing, 2003.

Yewangoe, Andreas A. *Theologia Crucis in Asia: Asian Christian Views on Suffering in the Face of Overwhelming Poverty and Multifaceted Religiosity in Asia*. Amsterdam: Rodopi, 1987.

About the Editor and Contributors

Editor's Profile

Jesudas M. Athyal is visiting researcher at the Boston University School of Theology, Boston, Massachusetts. He is also the president of the New England and Maritimes Region, American Academy of Religion (NEMAAR). He was previously associate professor of Dalit theology and social analysis at the Gurukul Lutheran Theological College, Chennai, India. His edited and published works include OUP's *Oxford Encyclopedia of South Asian Christianity*, Volumes 1 and 2 (2011); CSS's *The Community We Seek: Perspectives on Mission* (2003); and CCA's *Religion, State and Communalism: A Post-Ayodhya Reflection* (1995). Athyal holds a doctorate in philosophy from the University of Poona.

Contributors' Profiles

Ruchi Agarwal is a senior lecturer of South Asian Studies at Mahidol University International College, where she teaches courses in Economics and Religious Experiences and Traditions. Her articles have appeared in journals such as *Silpakorn University Journal of Social Sciences, Humanities and Arts*, and *Interdisciplinary Journal of Social Sciences*, Mahidol University.

George Amurao works as an editor for the official publication of Mahidol University International College in Thailand. A former journalist in the Philippines, he is doing graduate work on ASEAN studies in a public university in Bangkok. His research interests include mass media and Southeast Asian studies.

Raja Antoni is a PhD candidate in the School of Political Science and International Studies, the University of Queensland, Australia. He is doing research on religious peacebuilders in Southeast Asia with particular reference to the conflict in Maluku, Indonesia, and Mindanao, the Philippines. He is the former executive director of MAARIF Institute for Culture and Humanity, Jakarta.

S. Wesley Ariarajah is professor of ecumenical theology at the Drew University School of Theology, Madison, New Jersey. Before joining Drew, he served as the director of the Interfaith Dialogue program of the World Council of Churches for 12 years. He has published widely on ecumenism, interfaith relations and the theology of religions. His latest volume is *Your God, My God, Our God—Rethinking Christian Theology for Religious Plurality* (WCC Publications).

Achmad Zainal Arifin is a lecturer in the Sociology Department, Islamic State University of Sunan Kalijaga, where he teaches Sociology of Pesantren, Introduction to Sociology, and

Classical Theory of Sociology. He also teaches the history of Islam at Pesantren al-Munawwir of Krapyak, Yogyakarta.

Julius Bautista is senior lecturer in the Department of Southeast Asian Studies, the National University of Singapore (NUS). He received his PhD in Southeast Asian studies (anthropology) from the Australian National University. He is a specialist in the religion of Asia, and is author of *Figuring Catholicism: An Ethnohistory of the Santo Niño de Cebu* (Ateneo, 2010), editor of *The Spirit of Things: Materiality and Religious Diversity in Southeast Asia* (Cornell SEP, 2012), and coeditor of *Christianity in the State in Asia: Complicity and Conflict* (Routledge, 2009).

Adrian Bird is affiliate professor of church history at Union Presbyterian Seminary, Charlotte, where he teaches courses in Christian Encounters with World Religions, Missiology, and Christian History. His articles have appeared in such journals as *Religion and Society*, *Bangalore Theological Journal*, and the online resource *Justice Unbound*. Several of his articles have appeared in books, including *Duncan Forrester on Christian Ethics and Practical Theology* and *Contextualization: A Re-reading of M. M. Thomas*, and he is the author of *M. M. Thomas and Dalit Theology* (2008).

Ben Bohane is an Australian writer and photojournalist who has covered Asian and Pacific island religion and conflict for 25 years. He is the author of *The Black Islands—Spirit and War in Melanesia*, and *Song of the Islands* about cult and *kastom* movements in the region.

Pascal Bourdeaux is assistant professor at the École pratique des hautes études (EPHE, Paris) and a statuary member of the research laboratory "Groupe Sociétés, Religions, Laïcités." His research concerns the history of religious sciences in Southeast Asia, contemporary religiosities in southern Vietnam, and the riverine civilization of the Mekong Delta. He has edited the book *Pluralisme religieux: une comparaison franco-vietnamienne* (Brepols-EPHE, 2013). From 2012 to 2014, He was posted to Vietnam, where he was representative of the École française d'Extrême-Orient in Ho Chi Minh City.

Bénédicte Brac de la Perrière is the acting director of Centre Asie du Sud-est, CNRS-EHESS, Paris. An anthropologist specialist on Burma, she is the author of *Les rituels de possession en Birmanie: du culte d'Etat aux cérémonies privées*: Editions Recherche sur les Civilisations, ADPF, Paris, 1989. "An Overview on the Field of Religion in Burmese Studies," in *Power, Authority and Contested Hegemony in Burmese-Myanmar Religion*, edited by Kawanami and Brac de la Perrière, eds. *Asian Ethnology* 68, no. 2 (2009): 185–210, Nanzan Institute for Religion and Culture.

Peter J. Braeunlein is senior researcher in the DORISEA network at the Department of Social and Cultural Anthropology of the University of Goettingen (Germany). His articles have appeared in *Asian Journal of Social Science*, *Journal of Religion in Europe*, and *Studies in History and Philosophy of Biological and Biomedical Sciences*. He is the author of *Passion/Pasyon: Rituale des Schmerzes im europaeischen und philippinischen Christentum* (2010), and *Zur Aktualitaet von Victor W. Turner: Einleitung in sein Werk* (2012).

Bambang Budiwiranto holds a PhD in communication from the University of Queensland, Australia and Master of Arts (Asian Studies) from the Australian National University. He is a lecturer at Raden Intan State Institute for Islamic Studies of Lampung, Indonesia, where he teaches media, communication, and Islamic studies.

Matthew Copeland is chair of the Social Science Division at Mahidol University International College in Salaya, Thailand, where he teaches courses on East and Southeast Asian history.

Kirsten W. Endres is head of Research Group at the Department "Resilience and Transformation in Eurasia," Max Planck Institute for Social Anthropology, Halle/Saale. She has conducted research in northern Vietnam since 1996, focusing on social-cultural transformation processes that arise from the dynamic interplay between state, society, and market. She is author of *Performing the Divine. Mediums, Markets, and Modernity in Urban Vietnam* (2011).

Ahmad Fuad Fanani is research director at MAARIF Institute for Culture and Humanity and Lecturer at Faculty of Social and Political Sciences (FISIP) at State Islamic University (UIN) Syarif Hidayatullah Jakarta, Indonesia. He graduated from the School of International Studies, Flinders University, Australia, and completed his undergraduate studies at the State Islamic University (UIN), Jakarta. His articles about Islam, politics, and global issues have been published widely in academic journals and the national mass media in Indonesia.

Marja-Leena Heikkilä-Horn is assistant professor at Mahidol University International College (MUIC) in Thailand, teaching Southeast Asian history and religions. She graduated with a PhD from Åbo Akademi University in Turku Finland in religious studies. She has published several books on Southeast Asian history in Finnish, and her dissertation, "Santi Asoke Buddhism and Thai State Response" was published by Åbo Akademi University Press. She has further published articles in English on religion, politics, and ethnicity in Thailand and Myanmar.

Jeremy Jammes serves as associate professor of social anthropology in the Institute of Asian Studies, Universiti Brunei Darussalam. He is the author of the book, *Les oracles du Cao Dai. Etude d'un mouvement religieux vietnamien et de ses réseaux* (Les Indes savantes, 2014) and has coedited a special issue on "Evangelical Protestantism and South-East Asian Societies" (*Social Compass* 60 [2013]), along other book chapters and articles (*Aséanie, Moussons, Péninsule, Social Compass*). Between 2010 and 2014, he served in Bangkok as Deputy Director of the Research Institute on Contemporary Southeast Asia (IRASEC), (co-)editing three regional outlooks on Southeast Asia geopolitics.

William J. Jones is a lecturer in International Relations at Mahidol University International College and a PhD candidate. His articles have been published in *Semiotica*, *ASIEN*, and *Journal of Southeast Asian Affairs*, among other journals. His research interests include comparative regionalism and politics of Southeast Asia.

Alexandra Kent is an associate professor of social anthropology at the Nordic Institute of Asian Studies in Copenhagen. Since 2002, she has been focusing on religion, security, and justice in Cambodia. Her articles have appeared in journals such as the *Journal of Southeast Asia Studies*, the *Journal of Contemporary Religion*, and numerous other journals.

She is also the author of the book, *Divinity and Diversity: A Hindu Revitalization Movement in Malaysia* (NIAS Press Copenhagen, 2004), and coeditor of the anthology, *People of Virtue: Reconfiguring Religion, Power and Moral Order in Cambodia Today* (NIAS Press Copenhagen, 2008).

Stéphanie Khoury is a cultural anthropologist with a specialty in ethnomusicology. Her area of expertise is Southeast Asia, with a focus on Cambodia. She obtained her PhD at the University of Paris X-Nanterre and is now a researcher affiliated with both the Research Center for Ethnomusicology (CREM, CNRS) and the Southeast Asian Center (CASE, CNRS), located in Paris, as well as the secretary of the Société Française d'Ethnomusicologie (SFE, French Society for Ethnomusicology). In the past, she had served as lecturer in ethnomusicology at Boston College and Emmanuel College, Boston.

Sallie B. King is professor of philosophy and religion at James Madison University. She is the author of *Buddha Nature* (SUNY Press, 1991), *Journey in Search of the Way: The Spiritual Autobiography of Satomi Myodo* (SUNY Press, 1993), *Being Benevolence: The Social Ethics of Engaged Buddhism* (Hawaii, 2005), and *Socially Engaged Buddhism* (Hawaii, 2009). She is coeditor (with Christopher S. Queen) of *Engaged Buddhism: Buddhist Liberation Movements in Asia* (SUNY Press, 1996) and, with Paul O. Ingram, of *The Sound of Liberating Truth: Buddhist-Christian Dialogues in Honor of Frederick J. Streng* (Curzon Press, 1999).

Michael Kleinod is a PhD candidate at the Department of Southeast Asian Studies/Global Transformation, Institute for Asian and African Studies, Humboldt-Universität zu Berlin (Germany) and researcher in the research network Dynamics of Religion in Southeast Asia (DORISEA), funded by the German Ministry of Education and Research. His PhD thesis focuses on transformations of symbolic and material nature relations in Laos in the context of nature conservation and ecotourism.

Ninan Koshy is former director of the Commission of the Churches on International Affairs of the World Council of Churches, Geneva (1981–1991). He was a visiting fellow in the Human Rights Program of the Harvard Law School (1991–1992). He is the author of several books including *Religious Freedom in a Changing World* (WCC, Geneva 1992), *Churches in a World of Nations* (WCC, Geneva, 1994), and *War on Terror Reordering the World* (LeftWord, New Delhi, 2003). He is a specialist on foreign affairs, and his articles have appeared in *Economic and Political Weekly*, *Foreign Policy in Focus*, and *Asia Times Online*.

Septemmy E. Lakawa is the director of Graduate Studies of Jakarta Theological Seminary, where she teaches missiology and contextual theology. Her articles have appeared in *International Review of Mission*, *Reformed World*, and in various journals and book compilations in Indonesia.

Albertus Bagus Laksana, S.J., is on the faculty at Sanata Dharma University, Yogyakarta, Indonesia; he is also a visiting lecturer at Loyola Marymount University, Los Angeles, California. He is the author of *Muslim and Catholic Pilgrimage Practices: Explorations through Java* (Ashgate, 2014). His previous publications (both in English and Indonesian) and research interests include various areas such as Christian-Muslim comparative theology, Asian theology, history of mission, religious pluralism, and encounters between religion and culture.

Julian CH Lee is a lecturer in Global Studies, School of Global, Urban and Social Studies, RMIT University. His research has focused on civil society, gender, sexuality, and multiculturalism, with an area focus on Malaysia. He was an Economic and Social Research Council postdoctoral fellow at the University of Kent. He is the author of *Islamization and Activism in Malaysia*, and *Policing Sexuality: Sex, Society, and the State*. He is also the editor of *The Malaysian Way of Life*, and coeditor with Yeoh Seng Guan of *Fringe Benefits* and with Julian Hopkins of *Thinking through Malaysia*.

Caryn Lim is a PhD candidate at Monash University Malaysia in the School of Arts and Social Sciences. Her research interests include the study of ethnicity, identity politics, and urban anthropology. Her research is focused on studying the development of the funeral industry and its effects on the understanding and practice of death in urban Malaysia. She is also a contributor in the edited volume *Thinking through Malaysia*, in which she examines the experiences of "mixed-race" Malaysians in a racialized context.

Samuel Ngun Ling is professor of systematic theology and president of the Myanmar Institute of Theology since 2010. An ordained Baptist pastor, he is serving as the president of the Association for Theological Education in Myanmar (ATEM). He authored three books in English, including *Communicating Christ in Myanmar: Issues, Interactions and Perspectives* (2005) and *Christianity through our Neighbors' Eyes* (2014), and contributed about 70 articles in English. He also wrote about 100 articles in the Chin dialect, which is spoken by one of the eight major ethnic groups in Myanmar.

Christian Oesterheld is a lecturer in Southeast Asian Studies and Anthropology at Mahidol University International College (MUIC), Thailand. He has done research on ethnic conflicts in Kalimantan (Indonesian Borneo), the Catholic Church and inculturation in Borneo and Bali, Cambodian anti-Vietnamism, and the Khmer Rouge Tribunal. He is a contributor to the volume, *Ancestors in Borneo Religions* (NIAS Press 2012). He is finishing his PhD dissertation, "Genealogies of Just(ified) Violence in Borneo."

Analiza Perez-Amurao is working on her PhD in multicultural studies at the Research Institute for Languages and Cultures of Asia (RILCA) of Mahidol University in Thailand, where she is specializing in migration studies. She also holds a Postgraduate Diploma-TESOL from RELC-Singapore, an MA-ELLT from the Ateneo de Manila University, and an AB-BSE from the Philippine Normal University. She teaches in Mahidol University International College where she also serves as English Studies program coordinator.

Michael Nai-Chiu Poon is canon of Saint Andrew's Cathedral, Singapore. Since 2005, he has chaired the documentation study group (DABOH) of the International Association for Mission Studies. He is a member of the Inter-Anglican Standing Commission on Unity, Faith and Order, and an Anglican member of the Anglican Roman-Catholic International Commission. He was director and Asian Christianity research coordinator of the Centre for the Study of Christianity in Asia, Trinity Theological College, Singapore, from 2005 to 2014. He was MacKay Professor of World Christianity at Princeton Theological Seminary in 2011.

Alimatul Qibtiyah is a director of Center for Women's Studies (since 2013) and lecturer at Dakwah and Communication Faculty (since 1997) in Islamic State University (UIN Sunan

Kalijaga Yogyakarta, Indonesia). She finished her PhD at the University of Western Sydney. She is a speaker at various national and international seminars on women's issues. She regularly writes in *ESEAS* (*Austrian Journal of South-East Asian Studies*, Sweden), *Intersection* (ANU-Australia), *JIIs-Journal of Indonesian Islam* (LSAS-PPs-Indonesia) and the *Women's Studies Journal* in Pakistan.

Dana Rappoport obtained her PhD. in ethnomusicology at Paris X-Nanterre University and is a fellow ethnomusicologist at the Southeast Asian Center in Paris (CASE, CNRS-EHESS), Paris. Her research deals with Austronesian music of the Indonesian archipelago, studied by way of formal musicology, anthropology of religion, and social organization. She is the author of *Songs from the Thrice-Blooded Land: Ritual Music of the Toraja (Sulawesi, Indonesia)*.

Saskia Louise Schäfer is a postdoctoral fellow in Modern Southeast Asian Studies at the Weatherhead East Asian Institute and at the Institute for Religion, Culture, and Public Life at Columbia University. She completed her doctorate at the Graduate School of Muslim Cultures and Societies at Freie Universität Berlin and has taught at the Institute of Asian and African Studies at Humboldt Universität Berlin and at Columbia's School of International and Public Affairs. Her research interests include Islam and politics in Indonesia and Malaysia, discourse and media analysis, religious and political authority, secularism, public morality, and Islamic feminism.

David C. Scott is Professor Emeritus, Religion and Culture, United Theological College, Bangalore, India, where he taught courses on the religions and cultures of South and Southeast Asia. His articles have appeared in professional journals such as *Religion and Society*, *Journal of Religious Studies*, and *Journal of Dharma*. He has authored *The Bhagavadgita and the Bible* (1973) and *Re-Visioning India's Religious Traditions* (1996), and edited *Religious Traditions of India* (1988). On the occasion of his *Shashti Poorthi* (an Indian celebration of one's 60th birthday), Scott was felicitated by Indian Council of Philosophical Research for "Significant Contribution to the Study of Indian Religion."

Eva Sevenig is a PhD student enrolled at the University of Heidelberg, Germany. Her PhD thesis deals with ritual dynamics and transcultural communication in Laos. She holds a seminar on the Ethnology of Laos at the Institute of Anthropology, University of Heidelberg. Some reflections on her fieldwork in northwestern Laos can be found at the home page of the network, Dynamics of Religion in Southeast Asia (DORISEA). A paper for the DORISEA Working Paper Series under the topic "Spatial Dynamics of Religion between Modulation and Conversion" is in process.

Peter Smith teaches courses in the History of Social Thought, the History of Psychology and Modern World History at Mahidol University International College (MUIC), a component part of Mahidol University, Thailand, where he is an associate professor. He has been a university administrator (the equivalent of academic dean) and for many years served as the chair of the Social Science Division. His PhD is in the sociology of religion and was completed at the University of Lancaster, England.

Ranjan Solomon served the YMCA in India from 1971 and then went on to serve in the Asia regional office and the global headquarters. He served the Ecumenical Coalition on Third World Tourism as Executive Director. He now serves as consultant of the Palestine-Israel

Ecumenical Forum of the World Council of Churches. He consults for justice tourism networks in Palestine and India and has contributed articles to a variety of secular and ecumenical journals on tourism and Palestine. His book *Challenge and Prospects of Tourism in Goa* is a popular reading on issues of tourism in Goa.

Guido Sprenger is Professor of Social Anthropology at the Institute of Ethnology, University of Heidelberg. His research interests include exchange, kinship and social morphology, human-environment relations, animism, cultural identity, and gender and sexuality. His work has been published in his book, *Die Männer, die den Geldbaum fällten* (*The Men Who Cut the Money Tree: Concepts of Exchange and Society among Rmeet of Takheung*; Laos, 2006) and in numerous articles in edited volumes and journals, including the *Journal of Asian Studies*, *Ethnology*, and *Anthropology Today*. He is coeditor, with Kaj Arhem, of *Animism in Southeast Asia*.

Ahmad Khoirul Umam is a PhD candidate at the School of Political Science & International Studies, the University of Queensland, Australia. He is also a senior researcher at Paramadina Public Policy Institute (PPPI), Jakarta. His articles have appeared in journals such as *International Journal of Indonesian Studies* (2014), Faculty of Arts Monash University; *Global & Strategis* (2012), Airlangga University; and other Indonesian journals. He is also the author of *Kiai and Corruption Culture in Indonesia* (2006).

Index

Note: Page numbers for main entries are presented in **boldfaced** type.